Paris

timeout.com/paris

Time Out Guides Ltd
Universal House
251 Tottenham Court Road
London W1T 7AB
United Kingdom
Tel: +44 (0)20 7813 3000
Fax: +44 (0)20 7813 6001
Email: guides@timeout.com
www.timeout.com

Published by Time Out Guides Ltd, a wholly owned subsidiary of Time Out Group Ltd.
Time Out and the Time Out logo are trademarks of Time Out Group Ltd.

10 9 8 7 6 5 4 3 2 1

This edition first published in Great Britain in 2013 by Ebury Publishing.
A Random House Group Company
20 Vauxhall Bridge Road, London SW1V 2SA

Random House Australia Pty Ltd 20 Alfred Street, Milsons Point, Sydney, New South Wales 2061, Australia

Random House New Zealand Ltd 18 Poland Road, Glenfield, Auckland 10, New Zealand

Random House South Africa (Pty) Ltd Isle of Houghton, Corner Boundary Road & Carse O'Gowrie, Houghton 2198, South Africa

Random House UK Limited Reg. No. 954009

Distributed in the US and Latin America by Publishers Group West (1-510-809-3700)

For further distribution details, see www.timeout.com.

ISBN: 978-1-84670-372-0

A CIP catalogue record for this book is available from the British Library.

Printed and bound in Great Britain by Butler Tanner & Dennis, Frome, Somerset.

The Random House Group Limited supports The Forest Stewardship Council (FSC®), the leading international forest certification organisation. Our books carrying the FSC label are printed on FSC® certified paper. FSC is the only forest certification scheme endorsed by the leading environmental organisations, including Greenpeace. Our paper procurement policy can be found at www.randomhouse.co.uk/environment

Time Out carbon-offsets its flights with Trees for Cities (www.treesforcities.org).

Contents

Introduction

The City of Light may have spent much of the last 12 months in the global shadows as cross-channel rival London lapped up the Olympic limelight, but there has been plenty of homegrown political drama for Parisians to tune into as bookies' favourite Mr Flanby (François Hollande) trounced President Bling Bling (Nicolas Sarkozy) down the back straight to take Socialist gold, along with the 24th Presidency of France. Sadly, though, in politics as in sport, you're only as good as your last race and the new incumbent's 'popularity' has already sunk to new lows – clearly, being nicknamed after a wobbly caramel pudding with a soft centre has done Mr Hollande no great favours.

There have been no such popularity wobbles for Paris, though, which continues to reign culturally supreme, with three of the world's top ten most visited art museums within its clutch – the Musée du Louvre holds an unassailable lead with 8.8 million visitors in 2011, nearly three million ahead of its closest rival the British Museum, while the Centre Pompidou and Musée d'Orsay squeeze in at at no.8 and no.10 respectively. *Plus ça change*? To a certain degree, yes, but this continued success is also partly due to Paris's innnate talent for reinvention.

A decade ago, a weekend for many in the French capital would have meant a quick dash round the Louvre and Musée d'Orsay, a hike up the Eiffel Tower and a twilight cruise on the Seine, followed by *steak-frites* and a carafe of Bordeaux in a cramped, smoky St-Germain bistro. Fast-forward to 2013 and the Louvre is now home to a dramatic subterranean Islamic Arts gallery, the Musée d'Orsay has had a dynamic revamp, and the Dame de Fer is putting the finishing touches to its new glass floor. *Sacré bleu*, even the old *steak-frites* joints are being edged out in favour of a raft of *néo-bistros* sweeping Paris and turning out some of the city's best food for years. Thanks to Mayor Delanoë's courageous Rives de Seine urban planning project, the murky Seine is having a makeover too, with a stretch of the gloomy Left Bank expressway between Musée d'Orsay and Pont de l'Alma pedestrianised for 'culture, sport and walks'. Who said you can't teach an old dog new tricks?

Dominic Earle, Editor

About the Guide

GETTING AROUND

The back of the book contains street maps of Paris, as well as an overview map of the city and its surroundings. The maps start on page 396; on them are marked the locations of hotels (**❶**), restaurants (**❶**), and cafés and bars (**❶**). The majority of businesses listed in this guide are located in the areas we've mapped; the grid-square references in the listings refer to these maps.

THE ESSENTIALS

For practical information, including visas, disabled access, emergency numbers, lost property, websites and local transport, see Essential Information. It begins on page 364.

THE LISTINGS

Addresses, phone numbers, websites, transport information, hours and prices are all included in our listings, as are selected other facilities. All were checked and correct at press time. However, business owners can alter their arrangements at any time, and fluctuating economic conditions can cause prices to change rapidly.

The very best venues in the city, the must-sees and must-dos in every category, have been marked with a red star (★). In the Sights chapters, we've also marked venues with free admission with a FREE symbol.

THE LANGUAGE

Many Parisians speak a little English, but a few basic French phrases go a long way. You'll find a primer on page 383, along with some help with restaurants on page 168.

PHONE NUMBERS

The area code for Paris is 01. Even if you're calling from within Paris, you'll always need to use the code. From outside France, dial your country's international access code (00 from the UK, 011 from the US) or a plus symbol, followed by the French country code (33), 1 for Paris (dropping the initial zero) and the eight-digit number. So, to reach the Louvre, dial +33.1.40.20.50.50. For more on phones, *see p380*.

FEEDBACK

We welcome feedback on this guide, both on the venues we've included and on any other locations that you'd like to see featured in future editions. Please email us at guides@timeout.com.

Time Out Guides

Founded in 1968, Time Out has grown from humble beginnings into the leading resource for anyone wanting to know what's happening in the world's greatest cities. Alongside our influential weeklies in London, New York, Chicago and Dubai, we publish more than 20 magazines in cities as varied as Beijing and Beirut; a range of travel books, with City Guides now joined by the pocket-sized Shortlist series; and an information-packed website. The company remains proudly independent, still owned by Tony Elliott four decades after he launched *Time Out London*.

Written by local experts and illustrated with original photography, our books also retain their independence. No business has been featured because it has advertised, and all restaurants and bars are visited and reviewed anonymously.

ABOUT THE EDITOR

Dominic Earle is a freelance editor and travel writer. In addition to editing Time Out Guides to Paris, Copenhagen, Stockholm, France and Skiing in Europe, he has also written travel features and reviews for publications including *The Guardian, The Observer, The Independent and Condé Nast Traveller*.

A full list of the book's contributors can be found on page 13.

GO
LENS
GO

THE
LOUVRE
OPENING
IN LENS

LOUVRE

Lens

mmunauté d'Agglomération
de Lens-Liévin

Pas-de-Calais
Le Département

PROJET INITIÉ PAR LA RÉGION

Nord-Pas de Calais
La culture au cœur

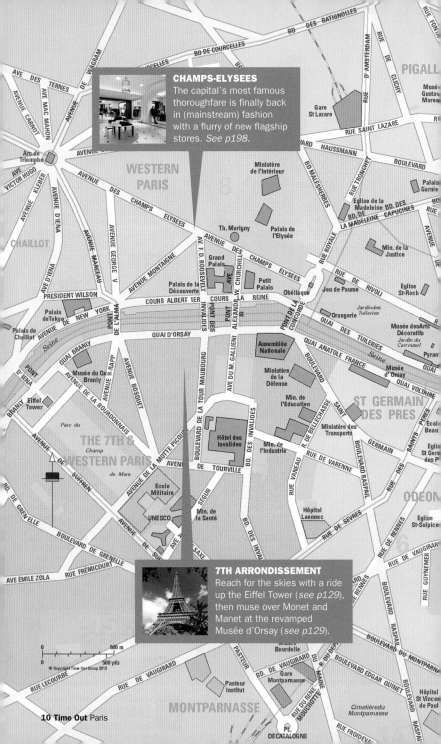

CHAMPS-ELYSEES
The capital's most famous thoroughfare is finally back in (mainstream) fashion with a flurry of new flagship stores. *See p198.*

7TH ARRONDISSEMENT
Reach for the skies with a ride up the Eiffel Tower (*see p129*), then muse over Monet and Manet at the revamped Musée d'Orsay (*see p129*).

© Copyright Time Out Group 2013

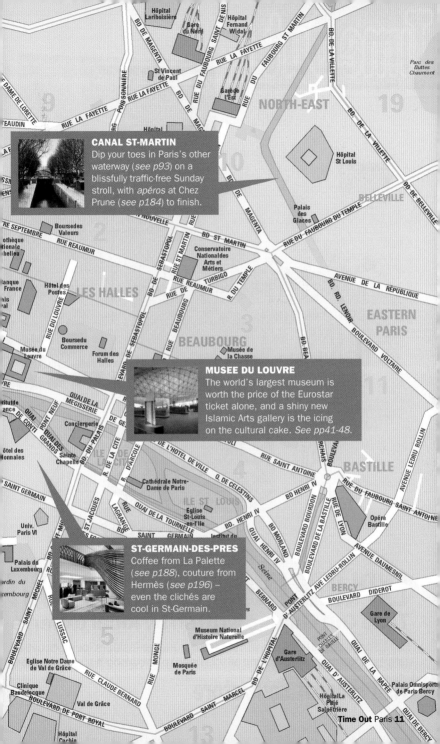

CANAL ST-MARTIN
Dip your toes in Paris's other waterway (*see p93*) on a blissfully traffic-free Sunday stroll, with *apéros* at Chez Prune (*see p184*) to finish.

MUSEE DU LOUVRE
The world's largest museum is worth the price of the Eurostar ticket alone, and a shiny new Islamic Arts gallery is the icing on the cultural cake. *See pp41-48.*

ST-GERMAIN-DES-PRES
Coffee from La Palette (*see p188*), couture from Hermès (*see p196*) – even the clichés are cool in St-Germain.

Time Out Paris

Editorial
Editor Dominic Earle
Listings Editor Barbara Chossis
Proofreader Marion Moisy
Indexer Holly Pick

Editorial Director Sarah Guy
Management Accountant Margaret Wright

Design
Senior Designer Kei Ishimaru
Designer Darryl Bell
Group Commercial Senior Designer Jason Tansley

Picture Desk
Picture Editor Jael Marschner
Picture Researcher Ben Rowe
Freelance Picture Researcher Isidora O'Neill

Advertising
Sales Director St John Betteridge
Head of French Advertising Sales Charlie Sokol

Marketing
Senior Publishing Brand Manager Luthfa Begum
Head of Circulation Dan Collins

Production
Group Production Manager Brendan McKeown
Production Controller Katie Mulhern-Bhudia

Time Out Group
Chairman & Founder Tony Elliott
Chief Executive Officer Aksel Van der Wal
Editor-in-Chief Tim Arthur
UK Chief Commercial Officer David Pepper
Time Out International Ltd MD Cathy Runciman
Group IT Director Simon Chappell
Group Marketing Director Carolyn Sims

Contributors
Introduction Dominic Earle. **Paris Today** Alison Culliford. **Class of 2013** Alison Culliford. **Diary** Dominic Earle. **Explore** Anna Brooke, Alison Culliford, Dominic Earle, Rich Woodruff. **Restaurants** Rosa Jackson, Ellen Hardy. **Cafés & Bars** Anna Brooke, Ellen Hardy. **Shops & Services** Alison Culliford; **Fashion** Katie Walker; **Galleries** Natasha Edwards. **Hotels** Alison Culliford, Dominic Earle, Katie Walker. **Children** Anna Brooke. **Film** Anna Brooke. **Gay & Lesbian** Robert Vallier. **Nightlife** Anna Brooke, Julien Sauvalle. **Performing Arts** Anna Brooke, Stephen Mudge, Estelle Ricoux. **Sport & Fitness** Rich Woodruff. **Escapes & Excursions** Anna Brooke, Dominic Earle, Julien Sauvalle. **History** Simon Cropper. **Architecture** Natasha Edwards. **Essential Information** Barbara Chossis.

Maps john@jsgraphics.co.uk, except page 416.

Cover photograph The Seine and Notre-Dame Cathedral by Renaud Visage.
Back cover photography Olivia Rutherford, Oliver Knight, Shutterstock.

Photography pages 3, 79, 214 Elan Fleisher; 4 (top left), 299 (bottom), 337 (bottom) Roland Halbe; 4 (top right), 14/15, 21, 35, 36, 37, 41, 42, 43, 44, 47 (right), 62, 77, 95, 110 (top), 138, 194, 200, 216, 237, 262, 264, 273, 304, 314, 325 Heloise Bergman; 4 (bottom left), 5 (top right), 10 (bottom), 11 (top), 32/33, 58, 71, 120, 121, 127, 179, 320/321, 324, 330, 334, 338/339, 340, 347, 348, 364/365, 396/397 Shutterstock; 4 (bottom right), 5 (bottom right), 38, 39, 51, 56, 57, 61, 64, 66, 81, 91, 98, 111, 118, 150, 151, 158, 161, 165, 167, 172, 178, 189, 192, 205, 241, 269, 279, 280, 286, 292, 302 (top), 313, 327, 362, 363 Olivia Rutherford; 5 (bottom left) Jean Baptiste Soulliat; 6, 47 (left), 101, 106, 108, 109, 110 (bottom), 113, 131, 134, 141, 146, 156, 168, 181, 204 (left), 274, 278, 284, 288, 299 (top), 303, 311, 312, 317, 322, 326, 328, 331 Karl Blackwell; 16, 353 Getty Images; 17 Keith Levit; 20 Alison Culliford; 22, 40, 50, 54, 55, 69, 72, 75, 85, 94, 102, 105 (left and bottom), 117, 122, 124, 152, 157, 170, 173, 182, 185, 188, 190, 191, 193, 202, 204 (right), 206, 207, 209, 210, 212, 217, 220, 223, 232, 242, 243, 251, 255, 263, 268, 272, 276, 277, 281, 285, 289, 302 (bottom), 305, 310 Oliver Knight; 26 Zdenek Krchak/Shutterstock.com; 27 Eric Emo/Parisienne de Photo/Roger-Viollet; 28 ilolab/Shutterstock.com; 31 Nicolas Brunet; 46 Mikhail Zahranichny/Shutterstock.com; 52 Robin Cambianica; 63 Patrick Berger et Jacques Anziutti Architectes/L'autre Image; 70 Goussset Fabrice Paris; 84 Manuelle Gautrand Architecture © Philippe Ruault; 90, 105 (top), 132, 133, 155, 174, 275, 307 Jean-Christophe Godet; 125 Thierry Ardouin/Tendance Floue; 128 Agence Moatti-Rivière; 140 Love Editions; 153, 154, 195 Jessica Orchard; 19, 159 Food Snob – www.foodsnobblog.wordpress.com; 162 Fanny B – www.playlikeagirl.fr; 169 Ming Tang Evans; 199 (bottom) Oliver Dixon/Imagewise; 219 Marc Dantan; 236 Jacques Lebar; 240 Christophe Bielsa; 245 Serge Ramelli; 260 Ritz Hotel Paris; 287 Jean Picon; 293 Stéphane Monier; 309 P.Tourneboeuf/Tendance Floue; 318 Cheryl Ann Quigley/Shutterstock.com; 333 Charlie Pinder; 337 (top) Olivier H Dancy; 355 Roger Viollet/Getty Images; 356 AFP/Getty Images; 361 Apur – J.C. Choblet.

The following images were supplied by the featured establishments: pages 5 (top left), 10 (top), 11 (middle and bottom), 45, 67, 82, 119, 135, 136/137, 139, 144, 145, 147, 160, 163, 171, 176, 177, 187, 197, 198, 199 (top), 213, 227, 228, 229, 239, 248, 258/259, 265, 267, 271, 290, 295, 296, 298, 329, 358.

Illustrations pages 23, 24, 25 by Calyn Pickens.

The Editor would like to thank all contributors to the Time Out Paris website (www.timeout.fr) and previous editions of Time Out Paris, whose work forms the basis for parts of this book.

In Focus

Paris Today

The honeymoon's over for Hollande.

TEXT: ALISON CULLIFORD

The French capital has been busy rejigging and renovating itself over the past few years to create a contemporary city of culture *par excellence*. The belle époque Théâtre de la Gaîté Lyrique has been turned into Paris's first digital cultural centre; the expanded Institut du Monde Arabe has reopened after a three-year, €5 million extension; and the Musée d'Orsay revamp is also now complete – the museum reopened its gleaming doors in autumn 2011 to gasps of admiration. And to top it all, the world's largest museum also expanded its artistic girth in 2012, with the opening of the dramatic new two-storey Islamic Arts department below the Cour Visconti following a nine-year, €100 million makeover. Still not satisfied? Come 2013, there will be even more new or good-as-new cultural treats awaiting arts lovers, including a renovated Musée Picasso, the new Fondation Jérôme Seydoux-Pathé showcase of film memorabilia and the launch of the high-profile Louvre-Lens museum just an hour's TGV ride from the capital.

CRIME AND GRIME

Despite all this urban regeneration, though, don't expect a grand entrance when you pull into the Gare du Nord. While Parisians arriving at London's St Pancras are treated to a clean and serene station complete with bookshops, beauty stores, organic food stalls, taxis on tap and no hassle from beggars and pickpockets, head in the other direction and things are very different, with Gare du Nord and the surrounding area plagued by escalating crime and grime. The only redeeming feature is the civilised art deco Terminus Nord brasserie just opposite the station, but even there it's wise to steer clear of the terrace – one prevalent city-wide scam involves child thieves thrusting printed matter in your face while stealing your phone off the table. Instead, buy a *carnet* of métro tickets and head out to explore the wonders of Paris.

HOLLANDE'S DECLINE

On 6 May 2012, François Hollande was elected 24th President of the French Republic and the first Socialist president in almost two decades, ousting Nicolas Sarkozy from the Elysée Palace after just five years in power. But Hollande's post-election elation was short-lived and after his first six months in charge, a flagging economy, sliding opinion polls and close media scrutiny of his love life – his current partner is Valérie Trierweiler, but his former partner was Ségolène Royal, the mother of his four children and herself a former Socialist party presidential candidate – mean the honeymoon period is most definitely over for France's '*président normal*'. At the time of writing, his popularity was plummeting faster than any Fifth Republic predecessor – to 54 per cent negative, with 44 per cent of people saying that Sarkozy would tackle the economic crisis better. The right-wing press is capitalising, crowing that the irrascible ex-president will return. Meanwhile Sarko is still jogging, sporting Gainsbourg-style stubble and perfecting his public speaking skills in order to emulate Tony Blair on the lucrative after-dinner speech circuit.

Hollande is particularly unpopular in regard to his austerity plans. Although he's careful not to mention the 'A' word, after promising a new approach based on growth not cuts, in September 2012 he launched a raft of measures that are perceived as hitting the middle and working classes just as hard as Sarkozy's, while his tax on the rich has caused a selling panic on millionaires' homes and a rush of applications to banking jobs in London. The fact that Hollande doesn't flaunt his own wealth

IN FOCUS

Gare du Nord.

Le Chateaubriand. *See p21.*

IN FOCUS

(at €1.1 million, half that of Sarkozy's) hasn't done him any favours either. Deep in their psyche, the French love to have a monarch figure on whom to pin either aspirational dreams or revolutionary disgust. Either way, the Sarkozy presidential soap opera at least gave them the illusion that things could perhaps get better.

PETANQUE AND PICNICS
On the bright side, anyone who has read George Orwell's *Down and Out in Paris and London* will appreciate that Paris does austerity rather well. While the staple solace for England's Depression-era poor was a cup of sugary tea, Orwell's stint in Paris involved pawning his coat to pay for endless red wine in the local *troquet*, where singalongs and debauchery softened the awfulness of working in hell's kitchen deep in the bowels of what is reputed to have been the Hôtel Crillon.

Today, the red wine is still flowing and it seems the grungier the location the more attractive it is to night-time revellers. In the hip 10th arrondissement, around bars Chez Jeannette, Le Tribal and L'Inconnu, hobos and bobos share pavement space, the former clutching their tinnies and the latter their mojitos.

On summer nights, the Canal St-Martin is so crowded with picnickers that the Mairie has had to bring in Amsterdam-style portable *pissoirs*.

Budget-conscious young Parisians have also rediscovered the joy of *pétanque*, previously the preserve of old age pensioners. All along the Canal de l'Ourcq, beside the Buttes-Chaumont or in even prettier locations such as the Palais-Royal, *boules* parties with bring-your-own champagne are all the rage. The Mairie, always quick to cotton on to city-wide trends, has now decided to go ahead with plans to replace part of the Left Bank expressway with a 'Spanish-style Ramblas by the Seine'.

BISTRO CHIC
In 2009, American wine writer Michael Steinberger published *Au Revoir to All That*, a stinging critique of the Gallic food scene that claimed France's economic, political, social and spiritual crisis had caused the country to go from being the beacon of the culinary arts to the world's second largest outlet for McDonald's. But, under the surface, new green shoots were already pushing through in the shape of 'bistronomy' – a food movement that was perfect for a scaled-down economy and

Alternative Art

A new tour explores Paris's street art stars.

A couple of years ago visitors to the French capital might not have looked much further than a quick dash round the Louvre and a twilight cruise on the Seine to tick the boxes for their perfect weekend, but now there's a thoroughly 21st-century attraction to add to the list – street art. 'Though Berlin would like to claim it, Paris was the originator of street art,' says Demian Smith, a former *taggeur* and founder of Underground Paris (www.underground paris.org) street art tours.

Posting up political art on Paris walls began as early as the 19th century, was a form of resistance as people defaced German propaganda during the Occupation, and re-emerged in 1968 with the '*atelier populaire*' at the Ecole des Beaux-Arts that produced iconic posters exhorting Parisians to strike and protest against the government. Now the work of artists such as Space Invader, Jérôme Mesnager and Nemo have become city landmarks and the Mairie has even established a massive billboard, Le M.U.R. (Modulable Urbain Réactif), on rue Oberkampf for a new

street artist to daub every few weeks. 'Street art is less political today,' says renowned street artist Fred Le Chevalier. 'It's more about wanting to speak to a wider audience than through a gallery or book. It's also immediate; you don't have to jump through hoops.'

The excitement of going on one of Alternative Paris's street art tours is that the canvas is changing all the time. One work might appear on a wall and before long there's a cluster, all mixed in with half-torn Communist Party posters and blue street signs. On place Maurice-Chevalier in the 20th, a makeshift homeless shelter is watched over by various artworks, including the upper half of a Zoo Project and a Le Chevalier figure holding a heart.

'London's the commercial capital of street art, with works going for tens of thousands of pounds,' says Smith. 'But there is more of an underground scene in Paris. Street art is always being gone over, but people push to keep things going.' Look up from this guide for a minute and you'll see exactly what he means.

the word-of-mouth food culture spread by blogs and Twitter. Fast-forward a few years and now you can enjoy a sublime three-course lunch from a no-choice market menu for the price of a mediocre *steak-frites* and *crème brulée* in many old-school brasseries. Frenchie, La Gazzetta and Le Chateaubriand are all stars of this positive new trend. A closer look reveals that many of these neo-bistro chefs are not French but American, British, Australian, Italian or Swedish, and those who are native have often travelled abroad to learn their craft – Frenchie's Gregory Marchand trained with Jamie Oliver and his tiny restaurant remains the most prized booking in Paris. Fortunately he has now opened Frenchie Bar à Vins, encapsulating another *nouvelle vague* on the Paris food scene: the no-reservations wine bar serving tapas-style plates.

While Anglophone blogs have helped make foodies salivate over Paris once again, the evolution began with the Fooding movement, founded in the early noughties by former *Nova* journalist Alexandre Cammas. By breaking down the traditional snobbery of French food via its guide, mega-picnics and gastronomic events, Fooding spawned a sea change in how Parisians approached dining out.

Cammas says it's a worldwide trend, with 'dollar-hungry neighbourhoods' such as eastern Paris and Brooklyn engendering 'a new race of chefs, better read but less well shaven, some with tattoos, all young (for now) and totally radical'.

TOUR DE FARCE

While Paris may have spent 2012 in the sporting shadow of its cross-Channel rival, London, the eyes of the sporting world will be firmly trained on the French capital in July 2013 as the world's most famous bike race rolls into town for its centennial grand finale after a three-week slog around the provinces. For the first time, the sprint finish down the Champs-Elysées will take place in the evening twilight, but some fans might claim the race is already shrouded in enough dark controversy. In stark contrast to the blissfully scandal-free success of the London Olympics, the *maillot jaune* has been forever tainted by the doping revelations surrounding Lance Armstrong. He has now been stripped of his seven Tour titles and International Cycling Union President Pat McQuaid had this to say: 'Lance Armstrong has no place in cycling and he deserves to be forgotten.' Forgotten, yes, but almost certainly never forgiven.

IN FOCUS

Lance Armstrong winning the Tour de France.

Class of 2013

Alison Culliford charts the rise of the capital's new social tribes, from JCD to néo-bobo.

Once upon a time, Parisians were either BCBG (*bon chic bon genre* – the French equivalent of Sloane Rangers) – or cool. Belonging to either one of these groups – or appearing to – was as easy as buying the right accessory. A Lacoste V-neck slung casually around the shoulders for the BCBG; a Palestinian *keffiyeh* worn as a scarf for the hipster. But then everything changed. While Britain's chavs were appropriating the crocodile logo, Paris was undergoing a very different social metamorphosis: boboisation.

A diminutive for bourgeois-bohemian, the term 'bobo' was actually invented by American David Brooks in his sociological study *Bobos in Paradise*, but Parisians embraced it as their own creation: after all, they could lay claim to both *bourgeois* and *bohème* as distinctly Parisian social denominations. Bringing them together meant you no longer had to be ashamed of being *bourgeois*. Living in a 'loft' (which just involved knocking out a few walls in your Haussmannian apartment), buying organic, espousing a freelance lifestyle – it was the natural successor to the *gauche caviar* of the 1970s. But then, as escalating rents gentrified virtually all of inner Paris, sealing it off from the *banlieue*, suddenly no one wanted to be bobo any more. Classic bobos can still be spotted, but Paris now has a whole new fauna that is desperately trying to be different while still remaining the same.

BECEBRANCHE

Jean-Philippe is 'Versaillais and proud', as his Facebook group proclaims. BCBG version 2.0, he is a sleeker, more connected version of his father, and uses his iPhone to organise the perpetual round of *apéros*, *soirées en boîte* and *pique-niques*. Jean-Phil has never been so happy to be pigeonholed, seeing Jean Sarkozy and Kate Middleton as the media-hyped role models of his tribe; after all, blue blood doesn't count for everything these days. Raised in Versailles, like most of his pals he now has a small pad with a good postcode (the 16th or, at a push, the 17th) with which his parents indulged him so he could sow his wild oats before the inevitable big Catholic marriage. The style he and his chums sport is a more relaxed version of the BCBG look, incorporating Converse, figure-skimming jackets, shirts and jeans for the boys, Repetto *ballerines* and Gérard Darel handbags for the girls. But the main difference between Jean-Phil and the BCBG of the past is that his girlfriend Marie-Christine wears a thong under her jeans, and his mobile contains not only the number of his priest but also that of his dealer.

Natural habitat L'Arc (12 rue de Presbourg, 16th) and Hippodrome de Longchamp (*see p313*) for the Prix de l'Arc de Triomphe.
Career Banking (BNP) or, if female, in an art gallery.
Reads *Paris Match*, *Le Figaro*.
Politics Sarkozy forever.

DANDY-DECADENT

An example of Paris's most colourful fauna, Ayméric spends a great deal of time preening his facial hair. Handlebar moustache, Victorian sideburns and floppy coiffure are the current look of this more virile version of the belle époque dandy. He flies in the face of traditional Paris uniformity, and his extensive wardrobe runs from vintage Paco Rabanne to 1970s gold lamé shirts. Ayméric is on everyone's party list and his life is a constant round of private views, magazine launches, artistic happenings and record label parties. Despite appearances, Ayméric is heterosexual, rampantly so, and is constantly surrounded by an adoring female fan club who dress in vintage fur and Isabel Marant.

Natural habitat Le Pompon (39 rue des Petites Ecuries, 10th), Hôtel du Nord (102 Quai de Jemmapes, 10th), Le Baron (*see p283*).
Career Art publishing, multimedia and DJs at private parties.
Reads Frédéric Beigbeder, *The Sartorialist*.
Politics May the best-dressed win.

INTELLO-PRECAIRE These days it just isn't easy being an intellectual in Paris. Since leaving the Sorbonne, Noémie has done a succession of internships with book publishers but it never seems to lead to a job. She tries to keep her spirits up by teaching French to foreigners, attending *café-philo* meetings, book signings and Nouvelle Vague director's cut screenings, and enjoys earnest debate over Lebanese food at her friends' supper parties, where she never seems to meet the right man (could her brains be scaring them off?). She dreams of playing De Beauvoir to a better-looking Sartre, and thinks she should look for an older man – maybe becoming a mistress would be liberating. Daddy rents a flat for her in the 5th, and she keeps saying she must get rid of the old Doisneau posters but they remind her of her halcyon student days.

Natural habitat Bar Basile (34 rue de Grenelle, 7th) opposite Sciences-Po or the literary café Les Editeurs (*see p188*), where she hopes to run into an editor looking for an assistant while whiling away a *crème* for several hours.

Career Hopefully publishing, one day.

Reads Anything published by Gallimard, *Le Monde*.

Politics Parti Socialiste, after a brief flirtation with Jean-Luc Mélenchon led nowhere.

IN FOCUS

> *'She keeps saying she must get rid of her old Doisneau posters, but they remind her of her halcyon student days.'*

JCD (JEUNE CADRE DYNAMIQUE)
After his prestigious Grande Ecole d'Ingénieurs where he didn't meet any girls until the final year ball, André rapidly rose through the ranks of a prominent telecoms company to his present position, where he manages an aggressive programme deploying phone masts across Africa. He lives in a Quai de Grenelle condominium with a view of the Eiffel Tower, which is ideal as it has secure parking for his BMW, ensuring he need never be late for work on strike days. His apartment is bare except for his Bang & Olufsen stereo and his iMac, though his fridge is always stocked with champagne and beers, for when his *potes* come round to watch the rugby. These days, André finds his powers of seduction much enhanced by his Paul Smith suits and his car, but he's not into settling down until he's got his MBA and moved to London, where he dreams of living in 'Nottinge 'ill' and dating a sexually liberated British girl like Kelly Reilly, his pin-up since Klapisch's *Russian Dolls*.

Natural habitat Bar of the Plaza Athénée (*see p237*), shopping for late-night foie gras and champagne at Monop' (www.monoprix.fr) or picking up fresh pasta at Fuxia (www.fuxia.fr).

Career Telecoms exec.

Reads *Le Figaro*, *L'Express*.

Politics Ultra-capitalist.

JEMENFOUTISTE

It's official: a Gallup poll has revealed that the French are the most pessimistic nation on earth, but Lionel *s'en fout de tout ça. Il s'en fout du gouvernement, il s'en fout de la crise économique, il s'en fout du foot, putain!* In other words, he doesn't give a flying f*** for anything at all. The only thing that gets him worked up is when people use Jemenfoutiste as an insult – for him it is a badge of honour (incidentally, Jemenfoutisme began as a genuine philosophy towards the end of the 19th century, but Lionel *s'en fout de ça aussi*).

Natural habitat The Jemenfoutiste prefers bars where you can still get a *demi* for €2.50, preferably with free couscous. Le Chope du Château Rouge (40 rue de Clignancourt, 18th) suits him fine, though *il s'en fout des bobos de merde* who have invaded his favourite café.

Career Nothing, he's a professional *chômeur*.

Reads *Canard Enchaîné*, comic books.

Politics *Il s'en fout*.

NEO-BOBO

Florence is committed – to organic food, natural childbirth, the preservation of the rainforests and independent journalism. This baby bobo is a product of the noughties, where she saw her elder siblings only pretend to care about what matters. Not for her the titanium kitchen, the iPad and the 4x4. Our *néo-bobo* still ekes out an existence in a rented flat (albeit now €800 a month) on the Canal St-Martin and takes part in a community vegetable purveying scheme, whereby she mans a stall once a month to sell Ile-de-France-produced broccoli only to those who've ordered it in advance. But let's not be too harsh: the *néo-bobo* is our future. Paris might not have a working class any more, but it has held out, in its own way, against globalisation.

Natural habitat Nanashi (31 rue de Paradis, 10th), a bobo organic canteen, or picking up her veg box from outside Epicerie de la Cour (cour des Petites Ecuries, 10th).

Career Works for an NGO.

Reads *Le Monde Diplomatique*, *Courrier International*, www.mediapart.fr.

Politics Green.

'Lionel s'en fout de tout ça. Il s'en fout du gouvernement, il s'en fout de la crise économique, il s'en fout du foot, putain!'

IN FOCUS

Diary

Plan your perfect weekend with our guide to the year ahead.

Paris is bursting with culture, and a spate of new festivals has added to the already crowded calendar. Eco music festival We Love Green and culinary champion Fête de la Gastronomie both started up in 2011, while 2012 saw the launch of Nuit Blanche-style Paris Face Cachée. During summer, many of the capital's parks turn into alfresco classical concert venues and theatrical stages. Among them is the lovely Parc Floral de Paris, which holds weekend concerts throughout the warmer months. Elsewhere, Solidays, Rock en Seine, Festival des Inrockuptibles and the Techno Parade all attract top rock acts. And if sports fans don't manage to get tickets for the Six Nations, there's always the finale of the Tour de France, which celebrates its centennial climax in 2013 after a gruelling ride north from Corsica.

SPRING

Paris Face Cachée
Various venues (01.43.48.08.02, www.parisface cachee.fr). **Tickets** varies. **Date** early Feb.
See p27 **Open Doors**.

Six Nations
Stade de France, 93210 St-Denis (www.rbs 6nations.com). RER B La Plaine Stade de France or RER D Stade de France St-Denis.
Admission varies. **Date** Feb-Mar.
Paris hosts two massive rugby weekends during the spring. Log on to the website at least three months in advance to be in with any chance of getting tickets. France finished a lowly fourth in 2012. A date for rugby fans' diaries: France play their final home match of the 2013 tournament against Scotland on 16 March.

Fashion Week
Various venues (www.modeaparis.com).
Date Mar, July, Oct & Jan.
Paris presents its haute couture and prêt-à-porter collections at a variety of venues across town, but to invited guests only. See the website for accreditation details. Dates for the Spring/Summer 2013 Haute Couture shows are 21-24 January.

Le Printemps des Poètes
Various venues (01.53.80.08.00, www.printemps despoetes.com). **Date** 9-24 Mar 2013.

The 15th edition of this national poetry festival will have 'Les Voix du Poème' as its theme in 2013, and will include a major celebration of the work of Pablo Neruda on the 40th anniversary of his death.

Printemps du Cinéma
Various venues (www.printempsducinema.com).
Date 17-19 Mar 2013.
Film tickets at a variety of cinemas all across the city are cut to a bargain €3.50 for this hugely popular three-day film bonanza, now in its 14th year.

★ Banlieues Bleues
Various venues in Seine-St-Denis (01.49.22.10.10, www.banlieuesbleues.org). **Admission** varies.
Date Mid Mar-mid Apr 2013.
A five-week festival of French and international jazz, blues, R&B, soul, funk, flamenco and world music.
▶ *For more on music festivals in and around Paris, see p292.*

Le Chemin de la Croix
Square Willette, 18th. M° Abbesses or Anvers.
Date Good Friday.
A crowd of pilgrims follows the Archbishop of Paris from the bottom of Montmartre up to Sacré-Coeur as he performs the Stations of the Cross.

Foire du Trône
Pelouse de Reuilly, 12th (www.foiredutrone.com).
M° Porte Dorée. **Admission** free; rides €2-€5.
Date Apr-June.

France's biggest funfair runs for two months, with a mix of stomach-churning rides, bungee jumping and candyfloss. It's well worth buying a pass (around €30) in advance. At the weekends the Mairie runs a free shuttle bus service from Bercy and Nation.

★ **Marathon de Paris**
Av des Champs-Elysées, 8th, to av Foch, 16th (01.41.33.15.68, www.parismarathon.com).
Date 7 Apr 2013.
One of the world's most picturesque marathons, with up to 40,000 runners heading off from the Champs-Elysées along the Right Bank to the Bois de Vincennes, and back along the Left Bank to the Bois de Boulogne. Registration begins in the previous September. If you're looking for something to aim at, the 2012 men's winner was Kenyan Stanley Biwott in 2hrs 5mins 11secs.

Foire de Paris
Paris-Expo, pl de la Porte de Versailles (01.49.09.60.00, www.foiredeparis.fr). M° Porte de Versailles. **Admission** €12; €7 reductions; free under-7s. **Date** 30 Apr-12 May 2013.
This enormous lifestyle fair includes world crafts and foods, the latest health gizmos, plus everything you need to know about buying a swimming pool or doing up your home.

Open Doors

Experience Paris at work with a trip behind the scenes for Paris Face Cachée.

If Mayor Delanoë goes down in history, it won't be for a grand architectural project but for his talent in event organising. Last year, a new date was added to the calendar that already includes Nuit Blanche and Paris-Plages. Brightening the dark days of early February, it has been named **Paris Face Cachée** (*see p26*) – 'Paris's Hidden Face' – and is a chance to 'penetrate forbidden places, experience what you've never done before and meet the unknown'.

Both quirky and educational, avant-garde and communal, Paris Face Cachée is in the same vein as the popular Nuit Blanche, where the public is invited into unusual or industrial spaces for art happenings. But this new festival is not exclusively an art event. During the inaugural festival, in February 2012, a huge variety of places and activities lifted the lid on places you might never have known existed, and gave participants a chance to experience Paris at work behind the scenes. The Forbidden Places category allowed people to snoop about a masonic lodge, 'infiltrate' the control room for traffic signalling, hide in a World War II bunker, or spend the night in the printworks of a daily newspaper. There were ghoulish tours of cemeteries, of the medical history museum (Musée d'Histoire de la Médecine), the sewers, and a mysterious tunnel under the Seine. On the more arty side, there were tours of squats and artists' studios, and a graffiti walk led by a *graffeur*.

Parisians' hunger for this type of discovery is phenomenal, and all tickets were sold out days in advance (with rates from €2 for a visit of a pump factory to €40 for a four-hour tour on electric bikes).

Cryptic names meant that festival-goers had to use their insider knowledge to guess where some of the venues were – or take pot luck. One of the most popular events, entitled 'Roulez jeunesse' (literally, 'youth roll'), was snapped up by those nostalgic for the 1980s *boum*-era roller-disco, La Main Jaune. This was off-beat Paris at its very best – an old but beloved relic revived in surreal fashion, with circus performers, hip hop dancers and ghostly fairies. If it's anything like Nuit Blanche, which gave birth to a permanent arts venue in the old funeral parlours of 104, perhaps La Main Jaune will be the next building to be rehabilitated as a creative space. In the meantime, don't miss the next edition of Paris Face Cachée for a chance to really get under Paris's skin.

IN FOCUS

IN FOCUS

Fête du Travail
Date 1 May.
May Day is strictly observed. Key sights (the Eiffel
Tower aside) close, and unions march in eastern
Paris via Bastille. Sweet-smelling posies of lily of the
valley (*muguet*) are sold on every street corner.

Le Printemps des Rues
*Various venues (01.47.97.36.06, www.leprintemps-
desrues.com).* **Admission** free. **Date** early May.
This annual two-day street-theatre festival takes
place along the Canal St-Martin and has a distinctly
experimental vibe.

★ La Nuit des Musées
All over France (www.nuitdesmusees.culture.fr).
Admission free. **Date** mid May.
During this pan-European one-night culture fest,
museums open their doors late for special events and
entertainment, including concerts, dance, lectures,
unique access and special exhibitions.

Quinzaine des Réalisateurs
*Forum des Images, Porte St-Eustache, Forum
des Halles, 1st (01.44.76.63.00, www.quinzaine-
realisateurs.com). Mº Les Halles.* **Admission**
€5.50. **Date** mid May.
The Cannes Directors' Fortnight sidebar comes to
Paris; 2012 was the 33rd anniversary of this festival
of screenings and events.

Festival Jazz à Saint-Germain-des-Prés
*Various venues, St-Germain-des-Prés
(www.espritjazz.com).* **Date** mid May-early June.
This two-week celebration of jazz and blues celebrated its 12th anniversary in 2012 with everything
from piano cruises on the Seine to gigs in the Eglise
St-Germain-des-Prés. Many of the concerts are free.

Art St-Germain-des-Prés
Various venues (www.artsaintgermaindespres.com).
Admission free. **Date** end May.
Timing your trip to Paris to coincide with a night of
vernissages (private views) gives a taste not only of
the art on offer but also of the personalities who frequent the art scene. The big rendezvous of the year
is Art St-Germain-des-Prés. Nicknamed the 'block
party', it sees more than 50 galleries get together to
showcase their top artists. The galleries involved are
mostly concentrated on rue de Seine, rue des Beaux-
Arts, rue Visconti, rue Guénégaud and rue Mazarine.

French Tennis Open
*Stade Roland-Garros, 2 av Gordon-Bennett,
16th (01.47.43.48.00, www.frenchopen.org).
Mº Porte d'Auteuil.* **Admission** €21-€75.
Date 26 May-9 June 2013.
Paris plays host to the second event in the Grand
Slam calendar and the most prestigious clay court
competition in the world. Rafael Nadal and Maria
Sharapova took the spoils in 2012.

SUMMER

Festival de St-Denis
*Various venues in St-Denis (01.48.13.06.07,
www.festival-saint-denis.com). Mº St-Denis
Basilique.* **Admission** €17-€60. **Date** June.
The Gothic St-Denis basilica and other historic
buildings in the neighbourhood host four weeks
of top-quality classical concerts.

Fête du Vélo
Across Paris (www.feteduvelo.fr). **Date** Early June.
The Fête du Vélo is a celebration of urban riding with
thousands of cyclists invited to meet up at various
points in the suburbs and pedal to Paris en masse.
The result is what the organisation calls '*la conver-
gence*', with a procession of two-wheelers meeting up
for a huge picnic in the city centre. During the two-
day festival visitors can also try in-line skating, as
well as bicycles specially designed for children and
people of reduced mobility.

Prix de Diane
*Hippodrome de Chantilly, 16 av du Général-
Leclerc, 90209 Chantilly (03.44.62.41.00,
www.prix-de-diane.com).* **Admission** €8;
€4 reductions; free under-18s. **Date** mid June.

Marche des Fiertés.

The French Derby draws the crème de la crème of high society to Chantilly, sporting silly hats and keen to have a flutter at this handsome racecourse next to the famous château and stables.

★ Fête de la Musique

All over France (01.40.03.94.70, www.fetedela musique.culture.fr). **Admission** free. **Date** 21 June.
Free gigs take place across the country as part of this festival on the summer solstice. Highlights for 2012 included sets from acoustic folk outfit Moriarty and rising star Mina Tindle.

★ Marche des Fiertés (Gay Pride)

Information: Centre Gai et Lesbien (01.43.57.21.47, www.centrelgbtparis.org). **Date** June 2013.
Outrageous floats and flamboyant costumes parade towards Bastille; then there's an official fête and various club and nightlife events.

Festival Chopin à Paris

Orangerie de Bagatelle, Parc de Bagatelle, Bois de Boulogne, 16th (01.45.00.22.19, www.frederic-chopin.com). M° Porte Maillot, then bus 244. **Admission** €17-€34 (plus €5 park entry). **Date** mid June-mid July.
Organised by the Chopin Society, candlelit evening recitals of the composer's works are performed in the idyllic Parc de la Bagatelle.

★ Paris Jazz Festival

Parc Floral de Paris, Bois de Vincennes, 12th (www.parisjazzfestival.fr). M° Château de Vincennes. **Admission** *Park* €5.50; €2.75 reductions; free under-7s. **Date** June, July.
Two months of free jazz weekends take place in the Parc Floral. Highlights for 2012 included Daniel Humair and Stéphane Belmondo.

Solidays

Longchamp Hippodrome (01.53.10.22.22, www.solidays.org). M° Porte Maillot. **Admission** *Day* €32. *Weekend* €49. **Date** end June.
A three-day music festival, for the benefit of AIDS charities. The 2012 event welcomed more than 160,000 festivalgoers and saw performances from the likes of Garbage and Metronomy.

Paris Cinéma

Various venues (01.55.25.55.25, www.paris cinema.org). **Admission** varies. **Date** early July.
Premieres, tributes and restored films make up the diverse programme at the city's excellent summer filmgoing initiative, which celebrated its tenth anniversary in 2012.

Le Quatorze Juillet (Bastille Day)

All over France. **Date** 14 July.
France's national holiday commemorates the storming of the Bastille in 1789. The evening before the holiday, Parisians dance at place de la Bastille.

At 10am on the 14th, crowds line up along the Champs-Elysées as the President reviews a full military parade. By night, the Champ de Mars fills for the fireworks display.

★ Le Tour de France

Av des Champs-Elysées, 8th (01.41.33.14.00, www.letour.fr). **Date** July.
The ultimate spectacle in cycling is reserved for the end of July, when the world's biggest bike race arrives in Paris. And it doesn't get much bigger than 2013, when the Tour celebrates its centenary with a start in Corsica. After three weeks of racing, the battle for the leader's famed yellow jersey is all but over, and the final stage usually climaxes in a mass sprint with everyone finishing together. It's an incredible spectacle as the riders propel themselves at speeds of up to 65 km/h (40mph) around nine laps of a four-mile finishing circuit that takes in the Champs-Elysées and Tuileries area. Turn up early for a front-row spot.

Etés de la Danse

Théâtre du Châtelet, 1st (01.40.28.28.40, www.lesetesdeladanse.com). M° Châtelet. **Tickets** €13-€100. **Date** 4-27 July 2013.
A three-week festival featuring an impressive line-up of both classical and contemporary dance. The 2012 edition saw performances from the Alvin Ailey American Dance Theater, while the 2013 edition will welcome the Vienna State Ballet.

Paris, Quartier d'Eté

Various venues (01.44.94.98.00, www.quartier dete.com). **Admission** free-€20. **Date** mid July-mid Aug.
This multidisciplinary outdoor festival features a lively mix of classical and jazz concerts, dance and theatre performances, plus open-air cinema in the Parc André-Citroën.

★ Paris-Plages

Various venues (08.20.00.75.75, www.paris.fr). **Admission** free. **Date** mid July-mid Aug.
Palm trees, huts, hammocks and around 2,000 tonnes of fine sand bring a seaside vibe to the city. The project began in 2002 and there are now three venues – two on opposite banks of the Seine and one around the Bassin de la Villette in the 19th. As well as urban sunbathing, there's a floating pool, concerts, boules, art classes and a lending library too.
▶ *A stretch of the Left Bank from the Musée d'Orsay to just before the Eiffel Tower is now set to become a permanent park, footpath and cycle track. See p35.*

Le Cinéma en Plein Air

Parc de la Villette, 19th (01.40.03.75.75, www.villette.com). M° Porte de Pantin. **Admission** free. **Date** mid July-end Aug.
A themed season of films screened under the stars on Europe's largest inflatable screen.

IN FOCUS

Festival Classique au Vert

*Parc Floral de Paris, Bois de Vincennes, 12th
(01.45.43.81.18, www.classiqueauvert.fr).
M° Château de Vincennes.* **Admission**
Park €5.50; €2.75 reductions; free under-7s.
Date Aug-Sept.
Free classical music recitals in a park setting every
weekend throughout August and September.

Fête de l'Assomption

*Cathédrale Notre-Dame de Paris, pl du Parvis
Notre-Dame, 4th (01.42.34.56.10, www.
cathedraledeparis.com). M° Cité/RER St-Michel
Notre-Dame.* **Admission** free. **Date** 15 Aug.
A national holiday. Notre-Dame becomes a place
of religious pilgrimage for Assumption Day.

★ Rock en Seine

*Domaine National de St-Cloud (www.rockenseine.
com). M° Porte de St-Cloud.* **Admission** *Day*
€45. *3 days* €99. **Date** end Aug.
Three days, four stages, and one world-class line-
up of rock and indie groups. Big names such as
Green Day, Placebo and Ed Sheeran all made an
appearance in 2012.

AUTUMN

Jazz à la Villette

*Cité de la Musique & various venues
(01.44.84.44.84, www.jazzalavillette.com).*
Admission €6-€30. **Date** early Sept.
The first fortnight in September brings one of Paris's
best jazz festivals with big-name stars such as
Archie Shepp and Macy Gray taking to the stage.
There's also a series of Jazz for Kids concerts run-
ning alongside the main festival.

We Love Green Festival

*Parc de Bagatelle, Bois de Boulogne, 16th (www.
welovegreen.fr).* **Tickets** varies. **Date** mid Sept.
This three-day eco festival, which had its first outing
in 2011, is held in the verdant surroundings of the
Parc de Bagatelle. Highlights for 2012 included
Norah Jones and Django Django.

Festival Paris Ile-de-France

*Various venues (01.58.71.01.10, www.festival-
ile-de-france.com).* **Tickets** varies. **Date** early
Sept-mid Oct.
Each year, the Ile-de-France Festival offers a brilliantly varied programme of music from classical to
contemporary, traditional and folk to cutting-edge
electronic, at venues ranging from central Paris to
Vincennes via Fontainebleau.

Techno Parade

www.technoparade.fr. **Date** 14 Sept 2013.
The Saturday parade (which finishes up at Bastille)
is followed by several late, late club nights around
the capital.

Journées du Patrimoine

*All over France (www.journeesdupatrimoine.
culture.fr).* **Date** mid Sept.
Embassies, ministries, scientific establishments
and corporate headquarters open their doors to the
public, allowing for some fascinating glimpses of
their interiors. The festive Soirée du Patrimoine
takes place on the first Journée. Get *Le Monde* or
Le Parisien for a full programme.

★ Festival d'Automne

*Various venues. Information: 156 rue de Rivoli,
1st (01.53.45.17.00, www.festival-automne.com).*
Admission €7-€45. **Date** mid Sept-late Dec.
This major annual arts festival focuses on bringing
challenging contemporary theatre, dance and modern opera to Paris. It is also intent on bringing non-
Western culture into the French consciousness.

Fête de la Gastronomie

Various venues (www.fete-gastronomie.fr).
Admission varies. **Date** late Sept.
This recently launched nationwide festival is aimed
at celebrating the wonders of French cuisine. The
inaugural theme was 'terroir', with more than 3,000
events across the country: Michelin-starred chef Guy
Martin set up market stalls in his cooking workshop
L'Atelier Guy Martin, so that visitors could choose
ingredients before being shown how to cook a gourmet dish with them. He also offered diners free
kitchen tours around his temple of gastronomy,
Le Grand Véfour, in Palais Royal.

Mondial de l'Automobile

*Paris-Expo, pl de la Porte de Versailles
(01.56.88.22.40, www.mondial-automobile.com).
M° Porte de Versailles.* **Admission** €13;
€7 reductions; free under-10s. **Date** early Oct.
Started in 1898, the biennial Paris Motor Show features cutting-edge design from all over the world.

★ Nuit Blanche

Various venues (http://nuitblanche.paris.fr).
Admission free. **Date** early Oct.
The decade-old Nuit Blanche is a free dusk-
to-dawn carnival of arts and culture inspired by
St Petersburg's 'White Nights'. The premise is simple: an ever-changing roster of artistic directors
takes over different portions of the city every year,
commissioning hundreds of works that are all about
finding new ways for citizens to interact with the
urban space. From clouds of paper butterflies settling on neoclassical columns to church naves
sprouting enormous bejewelled skulls, Nuit Blanche
is a riotously popular way to engage with cutting-
edge artistry.

Prix de l'Arc de Triomphe

*Hippodrome de Longchamp, Bois de Boulogne,
16th (01.44.30.75.00, www.prixarcdetriomphe.
com). M° Porte d'Auteuil, then free shuttle bus.*

Rock en Seine.

hop acts. Bill-toppers in 2012 included the likes of Hot Chip and Alabama Shakes.

Armistice Day
Arc de Triomphe, 8th. M° Charles de Gaulle Etoile. **Date** 11 Nov.
To commemorate French combatants who served in the World Wars, the President lays wreaths at the Tomb of the Unknown Soldier under the Arc de Triomphe. The *bleuet* (a cornflower) is worn.

Fête du Beaujolais Nouveau
Various venues (www.beaujolaisgourmand.com). **Date** late Nov.
The third Thursday in November sees cafés and wine bars buzzing in the capital as patrons assess the new vintage.

Admission €8; €4 reductions; free under-18s. **Date** early Oct.
France's richest flat race meeting attracts the elite of horse racing for a weekend of pomp and ceremony. The big race gallops off on Sunday afternoon.

Fête des Vendanges de Montmartre
Rue des Saules, 18th (www.fetedesvendanges demontmartre.com). M° Lamarck Caulaincourt. **Date** early Oct.
This is perhaps the most quintessentially Gallic of the capital's annual festivals. The event takes place in Montmartre in the vicinity of the Clos Montmartre vineyard, which sits on the northern side of the Butte. Although the vines cover a mere 1,560sq m and produce an average of just 1,000 bottles a year, the modest harvest is the pretext for a long weekend of Bacchanalian street parties.

FIAC
Various venues (01.47.56.64.20, www.fiac paris.com). **Admission** €35; €20 reductions; free under-12s. **Date** mid Oct.
The Grand Palais is the main venue for this week-long international contemporary art fair featuring more than 180 galleries, along with a series of outdoor installations in the Jardins des Tuileries.

Les Puces du Design
Bercy Village, 12th (01.53.40.78.77, www. pucesdudesign.com). M° Jaurès. **Admission** free. **Date** Oct & May.
Having moved to a new location in Bercy Village for 2011, this biannual weekend-long fair continues to specialise in modern and vintage furniture, and design classics.

★ Festival des Inrockuptibles
Various venues (01.42.44.16.16, www.lesinrocks. com). **Admission** varies. **Date** early Nov.
This festival, which is curated by popular music magazine *Les Inrockuptibles*, boasts a decent selection of top international indie, rock, techno and trip

WINTER

Africolor
Various venues in suburbs, including Montreuil, St-Denis & St-Ouen (01.47.97.69.99, www. africolor.com). **Admission** €5-€15. **Date** late Nov-late Dec.
This month-long music and dance festival has been running for more than 20 years, featuring artists from all across Africa.

Noël (Christmas)
Date 24, 25 Dec.
Christmas is a family affair in France, with a dinner on Christmas Eve (*le Réveillon*), normally after mass. Usually the only bars and restaurants open are the ones in the city's main hotels.

★ New Year's Eve/New Year's Day
Date 31 Dec, 1 Jan.
Jubilant crowds swarm along the Champs-Elysées. Nightclubs and restaurants hold expensive New Year's Eve soirées, and on New Year's Day the Grande Parade de Paris brings floats, bands and dancers.

Fête des Rois (Epiphany)
Date 6 Jan.
Pâtisseries sell *galettes des rois*, cakes with a frangipane filling in which a *fève*, or tiny charm, is hidden.

Mass for Louis XVI
Chapelle Expiatoire, 29 rue Pasquier, 8th (01.42.65.35.80). M° St-Augustin. **Date** Jan.
On the Sunday closest to 21 January – the anniversary of the beheading of Louis XVI in 1793 – right-wing crackpots mourn the end of the monarchy.

Nouvel An Chinois
Around av d'Ivry & av de Choisy, 13th. M° Porte de Choisy or Porte d'Ivry. Also av des Champs Elysées, 8th. **Date** 10 Feb 2013.
Lion and dragon dances, and lively martial arts demonstrations to celebrate the Chinese New Year.

IN FOCUS

Explore

challenge your senses

after the rain spa
St James & Albany hotel
202 rue de Rivoli • Paris 1er
T. +33 (0)1 44 58 43 77
reception@aftertherain.fr
www.aftertherain.ch

after the rain
switzerland

The Seine & Islands

Where it all began.

Paris owes its very existence to the Seine, and dutifully acknowledges the importance of its river with waves and a sailboat on the city's coat of arms. The Seine was the transport route that brought settlers here in the first place, many millennia ago, and it also gave them the economic wherewithal to stay put. As the city grew, so did the river's cultural importance, until it became what it still is today – the symbolic boundary between intellectual Left Bank Paris and the mercantile activities of the Right Bank. In between the two sides, like a double bullseye, are the

islands: the western Ile de la Cité, with its heavy payload of history, state machinery and religious grandeur; and the adjacent Ile St-Louis, once a mess of marshland and islets, and now one of the most exclusive residential districts in the city. In 2013, Mayor Delanoë's ambitious redesign plans for the Left Bank will see a stretch of road between the Musée d'Orsay and Pont de l'Alma converted into a promenade dotted with gardens, cafés and possibly even a floating cinema. Forget the Côte d'Azur next August – and head for the banks of the Seine instead.

ALONG THE SEINE

It's perhaps surprising that it took quite so long for the Seine to become a tourist magnet. For much of the 19th and 20th centuries, it was barely given a second thought by anyone who wasn't working on it or driving along its quayside roads. But in 1994, UNESCO added 12 kilometres of Paris riverbank to its World Heritage register. Floating venues such as **Batofar** (*see p287*) became super-trendy; and in the last 15 years, it's been one new Seine-side attraction after another.

It's at its best in summer. The Port de Javel and Jardin Tino-Rossi become open-air dancehalls; party boats bob up and down on the Left Bank; and there's the summer jamboree of Paris-Plages, Mayor Delanoë's inspired city beaches that bring sand, palm trees, loungers and free entertainment to both sides of the Seine. The **Piscine Joséphine-Baker** (*see p319*) has revived the floating swimming pool concept that was so popular in the 19th and early 20th centuries. Come on Sundays, and stretches of riverside roads will be closed for the benefit of cyclists and rollerskaters. And, of course, there's a wealth of boat tours (*see p369*).

The bridges

From the honeyed arches of the oldest, the **Pont Neuf**, to the handsome, swooping lines of the newest, the **Passerelle Simone-de-Beauvoir**, the 37 bridges spanning the Seine are among the best-known landmarks in the city, and enjoy some of its finest views.

There was already a bridge on the site of the **Petit Pont** in the first century BC, when the Parisii Celts ran their river trade and toll-bridge operations. The Romans put up a cross-island thoroughfare in the form of a reinforced bridge to the south of Ile de la Cité, and another one

INSIDE TRACK RING CYCLE

Notre-Dame (*see p39*) is currently undergoing a facelift in advance of its 850th anniversary in 2013. Updates include new lighting, an organ overhaul and the sweet sound of nine new bells to replace the dreadfully discordant 19th-century incarnations. The bells will be inaugurated in February 2013.

Rising Damp

It's a century since Paris's worst flooding – and it could happen again.

When the original, 19th-century Pont de l'Alma was replaced in the early 1970s by the wider, stronger version that you see today, one feature of the old bridge was retained: the Zouave statue that stands at the foot of the supporting pillar in midstream. Initially a straightforward emblem of French military success in the Crimean War, the Zouave became better known as a yardstick during the Seine's periodic floods. The fact that it was reinstated on the new bridge, alone of four statues that adorned the old one, is a measure of its stature in Paris folklore.

January 2010 was the centenary of the Zouave's dampest hour, when heavy rainfall and a badly timed thaw swelled the Seine to its highest level in recorded history, and the waters lapped around the stone soldier's neck. Hundreds of streets in central Paris were several feet deep in water, and inhabitants were obliged to get around by boat: the vast photographic record of the disaster (a boon for photographers and postcard publishers) contains scenes more reminiscent of Venice than Paris. Many residents had to get into and out of buildings via a ladder and first-storey window.

As it turns out, the Zouave's new base is higher above the average water level than previously, so if the Seine does rise to its neck, the city will be in even more trouble than it was a century ago. The deluge of 1910 was a so-called 'hundred-year flood', which means, statistically speaking, that the next one is already overdue; and since the new bridge was installed, the waters have risen as far as his belt (in 1985). Today, flooding of the riverside expressways is a nearly annual event.

But worryingly, despite years of discussion by the city council and the government, Paris has no equivalent of London's Thames Barrier – although smaller barrages and reservoirs much further upstream have gone some way to alleviating the effects of high water runoff. So that just leaves the rather ominous 'in case of flooding' advice on the Mairie de Paris website and smart street maps shaded to show likely zones of flooded streets and electricity outage. In the meantime, the Zouave watches and waits.

north of it (where the **Pont Notre-Dame** now stands), thus creating a straight route all the way from Orléans through to Belgium. Since then, the city's *ponts* have been bombed, bashed by buses and boats, weather-beaten and even trampled to destruction: in 1634, the Pont St-Louis collapsed under the weight of a religious procession. In the Middle Ages, the handful of bridges linking the islands to the riverbanks were lined with shops and houses, but the flimsy wooden constructions regularly caught fire or got washed away. The Petit Pont sank 11 times before councillors decided to ban building on top of bridges.

The Pont Neuf was inaugurated in 1607 and has been standing sturdy ever since. This was the first bridge to be built with no houses to obstruct the view of the river. It had a raised stretch of road at the edge to protect walkers from traffic and horse dung (the new-fangled 'pavement' soon caught on); the alcoves that now make pit stops for lovers were once filled with tooth-pullers, peddlers and *bouquinistes*.

The 19th century was boom time for bridge-building: 21 were built in all, including the city's first steel, iron and suspension bridges. The **Pont de la Concorde** used up what was left of the Bastille after the storming of 1789; the romantic **Pont des Arts** was the capital's first solely pedestrian crossing (built in 1803 and rebuilt in the 1980s). The most glitteringly exuberant bridge is the **Pont Alexandre III**, with its bronze and glass, garlanding and gilded embellishments. More practical is the **Pont de l'Alma**, with its Zouave statue that has long been a flood monitor: when the statue's toes get wet, the state raises the flood alert and starts to close the quayside roads; when he's up to his ankles in Seine, it's no longer possible to navigate the river by boat. This offers some indication of how devastating the great 1910 flood was, when the plucky Zouave disappeared up to his neck (*see p36* **Rising Damp**).

The 20th century brought some spectacular additions. **Pont Charles-de-Gaulle**, for example, stretches resplendently like the wing of a huge aeroplane, and iron **Viaduc d'Austerlitz** (1905) is striking yet elegant as it cradles métro line 5. The city's newest crossing, the Passerelle Simone-de-Beauvoir, is a walkway linking up the Bibliothèque Nationale to the Parc de Bercy.

ILE DE LA CITE

In the 1st & 4th arrondissements.

The Ile de la Cité is where Paris was born around 250 BC, when the Parisii, a tribe of Celtic Gauls, founded a settlement on this convenient bridging point of the Seine. Romans,

Pont Neuf.

Merovingians and Capetians followed, in what became a centre of political and religious power right into the Middle Ages: royal authority at one end, around the Capetian palace; the Church at the other, by Notre-Dame.

When Victor Hugo wrote *Notre-Dame de Paris* in 1831, the Ile de la Cité was still a bustling quarter of narrow medieval streets and tall houses. Despite its name, it is in fact the oldest bridge in Paris, begun under the reign of Henri III and Catherine de Médicis in 1578 and taking 30 years to complete. In 1991, the bridge (or, rather, a full-size facsimile of it) played a starring role in Leos Carax's budget-busting film *Les Amants du Pont Neuf*.

Down the steps is a leafy triangular garden, square du Vert-Galant. You can take to the water here on the Vedettes du Pont Neuf. In the centre of the bridge is an equestrian statue of Henri IV; the original went up in 1635, was

tall houses: 'the head, heart and very marrow of Paris'. Baron Haussmann performed a marrow extraction when he supervised the expulsion of around 25,000 people from the island, razing tenements and some 20 churches, and leaving behind large, official buildings – the law courts, the **Conciergerie**, Hôtel-Dieu hospital, the police headquarters and the cathedral. The lines of the old streets are traced into the parvis in front of **Notre-Dame**.

Perhaps the most charming spot on the island is the western tip, where Pont Neuf spans the Seine.

EXPLORE

Cathédrale Notre-Dame de Paris.

melted down to make cannon during the Revolution, and replaced in 1818. On the bridge's eastern side, place Dauphine, home to restaurants, wine bars and the ramshackle Hôtel Henri IV, was built in 1607, on what was then a sandy bar that flooded every winter. It was commissioned by Henri IV, who named it in honour of his son, the future King Louis XIII. The brick and stone houses, similar to those in place des Vosges (though subsequently much altered to accommodate sun terraces), look out over the quays and square. The eastern side was demolished during the 1860s, when the new Préfecture de Police was built. Known by its address, quai des Orfèvres, it was immortalised by Clouzot's film and Simenon's Maigret novels.

The towers of the Conciergerie dominate the island's north bank. Along with the Palais de Justice, it was originally part of the Palais de la Cité, residential and administration complex of the Capetian kings. It occupies the site of an earlier Merovingian fortress and, before that, the Roman governor's house. Etienne Marcel's uprising prompted Charles V to move the royal retinue to the Louvre in 1358, and the Conciergerie was assigned a more sinister role as a prison for people awaiting execution. The interior is worth a visit for its prison cells and the vaulted Gothic halls. On the corner of

boulevard du Palais, the Tour de l'Horloge, built in 1370, was the first public clock in Paris.

Sainte-Chapelle, Pierre de Montreuil's masterpiece of stained glass and slender Gothic columns, stands among the nearby law courts. Enveloping the chapel, the Palais de Justice was built alongside the Conciergerie. Behind elaborate wrought-iron railings, most of the present buildings around the fine neoclassical entrance courtyard date from the 1780s reconstruction by Desmaisons and Antoine. After passing through security, you can visit the **Salle des Pas Perdus**, busy with plaintiffs and barristers, and sit in on cases in the civil and criminal courts. The Palais is still the centre of the French legal system.

Across boulevard du Palais, behind the Tribunal du Commerce, place Louis-Lépine is occupied by the Marché aux Fleurs, where horticultural suppliers sell flowers, cacti and exotic trees. On Sundays, they are joined by caged birds and small animals in the Marché aux Oiseaux. The Hôtel-Dieu, east of the market place, was founded in the seventh century. During the Middle Ages, your chances of survival here were, at best, slim; today, the odds are much improved. The hospital originally stood on the other side of the island facing the Latin Quarter, but after a series of fires in the 18th century it was rebuilt here in the 1860s.

Notre-Dame cathedral dominates the eastern half of the island. On the parvis in front of the cathedral is the bronze 'Kilomètre Zéro' marker, the point from which distances between Paris and the rest of France are measured. The **Crypte Archéologique** hidden under the parvis gives a sense of the island's multi-layered past, when it was a tangle of alleys, houses, churches and cabarets. Notre-Dame is still a place of worship, and holds its Assumption Day procession, Christmas Mass and Nativity scene on the parvis.

INSIDE TRACK BOOK CLUB

Baudelaire wrote part of *Les Fleurs du Mal* while living at 17 quai d'Anjou; he and fellow poet Théophile Gautier also organised meetings of their dope-smokers' club here. A couple of centuries earlier, Racine, Molière and La Fontaine resided at the same address as guests of La Grande Mademoiselle, cousin of Louis XIV.

Walk through the garden by the cathedral to appreciate its flying buttresses. To the north-east, a medieval feel persists in the few streets untouched by Haussmann, such as rue Chanoinesse, rue de la Colombe and rue des Ursins, though the crenellated medieval remnant on the corner of rue des Ursins and rue des Chantres was redone in the 1950s for the Aga Khan. The capital's oldest love story unfolded in the 12th century at 9 quai aux Fleurs, where Héloïse lived with her uncle Canon Fulbert, who had her tutor and lover, the scholar Abélard, castrated. Héloïse was sent to a nunnery. Behind the cathedral, at the eastern end of the island, is the **Mémorial des Martyrs de la Déportation**, remembering people sent to Nazi concentration camps.

★ FREE Cathédrale Notre-Dame de Paris

Pl du Parvis-Notre-Dame, 4th (01.42.34.56.10, www.cathedraledeparis.com). M° Cité/RER St-Michel. **Open** 8am-6.45pm Mon-Fri; 8am-7.15pm Sat, Sun. *Towers* Apr-Sept 10am-6.30pm daily *(June-Aug* until 11pm Sat, Sun). Oct-Mar 10am-5.30pm daily. **Admission** free. *Towers* €8.50; €5.50 reductions; free under-18s, under-26s (EU citizens). PMP. **Credit** MC, V. **Map** p406 J7.
Notre-Dame was constructed between 1163 and 1334, and the amount of time and money spent on it reflected the city's growing prestige. The west front remains a high point of Gothic art for the balanced proportions of its twin towers and rose window, and the three doorways with their rows of saints and sculpted tympanums: the *Last Judgement* (centre), *Life of the Virgin* (left) and *Life of St Anne* (right). Inside, take a moment to admire the long nave with its solid foliate capitals and high altar with a marble Pietà by Coustou. To truly appreciate the masonry, climb up the towers. The route runs up the north tower and down the south. Between the two you get a close-up view of the gallery of chimeras – the fantastic birds and hybrid beasts designed by Viollet-le-Duc along the balustrade.

★ La Conciergerie

2 bd du Palais, 1st (01.53.40.60.80). M° Cité/ RER St-Michel Notre-Dame. **Open** 9.30am-6pm daily. **Admission** €8.50; €5.50 reductions; free under-18s (accompanied by an adult), under-26s (EU citizens). *With Sainte-Chapelle* €12.50; €8.50 reductions. PMP. **Credit** MC, V. **Map** p408 J6.
The Conciergerie looks every inch the forbidding medieval fortress. However, much of the façade was added in the 1850s, long after Marie-Antoinette, Danton and Robespierre had been imprisoned here. The 13th-century Bonbec tower, built during the reign of St Louis, the 14th-century twin towers, César and Argent, and the Tour de l'Horloge all survive from the Capetian palace. The visit takes you through the Salle des Gardes, the medieval kitchens with their four huge chimneys, and the Salle des Gens d'Armes, a vaulted Gothic hall built between 1301 and 1315 for Philippe 'le Bel'. After the royals moved to the Louvre, the fortress became a prison under the watch of the Concierge. The wealthy had private cells with their own furniture, which they paid for; others crowded on beds of straw. A list of Revolutionary prisoners, including a hairdresser, shows that not all victims were nobles. In Marie-Antoinette's cell, the Chapelle des Girondins, are her crucifix, some portraits and a guillotine blade.

La Crypte Archéologique

Pl Jean-Paul II, 4th (01.55.42.50.10, www.crypte. paris.fr). M° Cité/RER St-Michel Notre-Dame. **Open** 10am-6pm Tue-Sun. **Admission** €4; €2-€3 reductions; free under-14s. PMP. **Credit** (€15 minimum) MC, V. **Map** p406 J7.

EXPLORE

La Conciergerie.

Sainte-Chapelle

Hidden under the forecourt in front of the cathedral is a large void that contains bits and pieces of Roman quaysides, ramparts and hypocausts, medieval cellars, shops and pavements, the foundations of the Eglise Ste-Geneviève-des-Ardens (the church where Geneviève's remains were stored during the Norman invasions), an 18th-century foundling hospital and a 19th-century sewer, all excavated since the 1960s. It's not always easy to work out exactly which wall, column or staircase is which – but you do get a vivid sense of the layers of history piled one atop another during 16 centuries.

FREE Mémorial des Martyrs de la Déportation

Sq de l'Ile de France, 4th (01.46.33.87.56).
M° Cité/RER St-Michel Notre-Dame. **Open** *Oct-Mar* 10am-noon, 2-5pm daily. *Apr-Sept* 10am-noon, 2-7pm daily. **Admission** free. **Map** p406 J7.
This sober tribute to the 200,000 Jews, Communists, homosexuals and *résistants* deported to concentration camps from France in World War II stands on the eastern tip of the island. A blind staircase descends to river level, where simple chambers are lined with tiny lights and the walls are inscribed with verse. A barred window looks out at the Seine.

Sainte-Chapelle

6 bd du Palais, 1st (01.53.40.60.80). M° Cité/RER St-Michel Notre-Dame. **Open** *Mar-Oct* 9.30am-6pm daily. *Nov-Feb* 9am-5pm daily. **Admission** €8.50; €5.50 reductions; free under-18s (with an adult), under-26s (EU citizens). *With Conciergerie* €12.50; €8.50 reductions. **Credit** MC, V. **Map** p408 J6.
Devout King Louis IX (St Louis, 1226-70) had a hobby of accumulating holy relics. In the 1240s, he bought what was advertised as the Crown of Thorns, and ordered Pierre de Montreuil to design a shrine. The result was Sainte-Chapelle. With 15m (49ft) windows, the upper level appears to consist almost entirely of

stained glass. The windows depict hundreds of scenes from the Old and New Testaments, culminating with the Apocalypse in the rose window.

ILE ST-LOUIS

In the 4th arrondissement.

The Ile St-Louis is one of the most exclusive addresses in the city. Delightfully unspoiled, it has fine architecture, narrow streets and pretty views from the tree-lined quays.

For hundreds of years, the island was a swampy pasture belonging to Notre-Dame, known as Ile Notre-Dame and used as a retreat for fishermen, swimmers and courting couples. In the 14th century, Charles V built a fortified canal through the middle, thus creating the Ile aux Vaches ('Island of Cows'). Its real-estate potential wasn't realised until 1614, though, when speculator Christophe Marie persuaded Louis XIII to fill in the canal (present-day rue Poulletier) and plan streets, bridges and houses. The island was renamed in honour of the king's pious predecessor, and the venture proved a huge success, thanks to architect Louis Le Vau, who from the 1630s built fashionable residences along the quai d'Anjou, quai de Bourbon and quai de Béthune, as well as the **Eglise St-Louis-en-l'Ile**. By the 1660s the island was full; its smart reception rooms were set at the front of courtyards to give residents riverside views.

Rue St-Louis-en-l'Ile runs the length of the island. The grandiose **Hôtel Lambert** at no.2 was built by Le Vau in 1641 for Louis XIII's secretary, and has sumptuous interiors by Le Sueur, Perrier and Le Brun. At no.51 – **Hôtel Chenizot** – look out for the bearded faun adorning the rocaille doorway, flanked by stern dragons. Across the street, the **Hôtel du Jeu de Paume** at no.54 was once a tennis court; at no.31, famous ice-cream maker **Berthillon** (www.berthillon.fr) still draws a crowd. At the western end there are great views of the flying buttresses of Notre-Dame from the terraces of the **Brasserie de l'Ile St-Louis** and the **Flore en l'Ile** café. At 6 quai d'Orléans, the **Adam Mickiewicz library-museum** (01.55.42.83.83) is dedicated to the poet, journalist and campaigner for Polish freedom.

FREE Eglise St-Louis-en-l'Ile

19bis rue St-Louis-en-l'Ile, 4th (01.46.34.11.60, www.saintlouisenlile.catholique.fr). M° Pont Marie. **Open** 9.30am-1pm, 2-7.30pm Mon-Sat; 9am-1pm, 2-7pm Sun. **Admission** free. **Map** p409 L7.
The island's church was built between 1664 and 1765, following plans by Louis Le Vau and later completed by Gabriel Le Duc. The Baroque interior boasts Corinthian columns and a sunburst over the altar, and sometimes hosts classical music concerts.

The Louvre

Extravagant architecture and extraordinary art.

The world's largest museum is also its most visited, with a remarkable 8.5 million visitors in 2011. It is a city within the city, a vast, multi-level maze of galleries, passageways, staircases and escalators. It's famous for the artistic glories within, but the very fabric of the museum is a masterpiece in itself – or rather, a collection of masterpieces modified and added to from one century to another. And the additions and modifications continue into the present day, with the opening of a wonderful new two-storey Islamic Arts department beneath the Cour Visconti

in late 2012, and the franchising of the Louvre 'brand' via new outposts in Lens in northern France (www.louvrelens.fr) and Abu Dhabi. If any place demonstrates the central importance of culture in French life, this is it.

ABOUT THE LOUVRE

Much like the building itself, the Louvre's collections were built up over the centuries. They encompass a rich visual history of the western world, from Ancient Egypt and Mesopotamia to the 19th century. Indeed, one of the most impressive things about the Louvre is the way it juxtaposes architecture and content. Look up from a case of Greek or Roman antiquities and you might see an 18th-century painted ceiling, or two doves by Braque. In the Egyptian section you'll find Louis XIV's bedchamber, complete with gilded bed, while Renaissance art is housed in the Grande Galerie, where the Sun King performed the 'scrofula ceremony', blessing the sick. In between exhibits, the Louvre's long windows afford stunning views of the building's façades, gardens and lovely interior courtyards.

Some 35,000 works of art and artefacts are on show, split into eight departments and housed in three wings: **Denon**, **Sully** and **Richelieu**. Under the atrium of the glass pyramid, each wing has its own entrance, though you can pass from one to another. Treasures from the Egyptians, Etruscans, Greeks and Romans each have their own galleries in the Denon and Sully wings, as do Middle Eastern and Islamic art, now accommodated in a brand new space in the Cour Visconti. The first floor of Richelieu is taken up with European decorative arts from the Middle Ages up to the 19th century, including room after room of Napoleon III's lavish apartments.

The main draw, though, is the painting and sculpture. Two glass-roofed sculpture courts contain the famous Marly horses on the ground floor of Richelieu, with French sculpture below and Italian Renaissance pieces in the Denon wing. The Grande Galerie and Salle de la Joconde (home to the *Mona Lisa*), like a mini Uffizi, run the length of Denon's first floor with French Romantic painting alongside. Dutch and French painting occupies the second floor of Richelieu and Sully. Jean-Pierre Wilmotte's minimalist galleries in the Denon wing were designed as a taster for the Musée du Quai Branly, with art from Africa, the Americas and Oceania.

Mitterrand's Grand Louvre project expanded the museum two-fold. But the organisation and restoration of the Louvre are still a work in progress: check the website or lists in the Carrousel du Louvre to see which galleries are closed on certain days to avoid missing out on what you want to see.

The museum is also trying to strike a balance between highbrow culture and accessibility. Photography was banned a few years ago at the request of mainly French visitors; meanwhile, laminated panels found throughout provide a surprisingly lively commentary, and the superb website is a technological feat unsurpassed by any of the world's major museums.

ADVANCE TICKETS AND ENTRY

IM Pei's glass pyramid is a wonderful piece of architecture, but it's not the only entrance to the museum – there are three others. Buying a ticket in advance means you can go in directly via the passage Richelieu off rue de Rivoli, or via the Carrousel du Louvre shopping mall (there are steps down either side of the Arc de Triomphe du Carrousel, at 99 rue de Rivoli or from the métro).

Advance tickets are valid for any day, and are available from the Louvre website or branches of **Fnac** and **Virgin Megastore** (for both, *see p225*). You can buy one from the Virgin in the Carrousel du Louvre and use it immediately. Another option is to buy a ticket at the Cour des Lions entrance (closed Fridays) in the south-west corner of the complex, convenient for the Italian collections. The Louvre is also accessible with the all-in **Paris Museum Pass**. Finally, don't forget that the Louvre is closed on Tuesdays.

OTHER TIPS

● The Louvre's website, much of which is in English, is an unbeatable resource. Every work on display is photographed, and you can search the Atlas database by room, artist or theme.

● Laminated cards in each room provide useful background information. Audioguides (€6, €2-€4 reductions; ID must be left) are available.
● Don't try to see more than two collections in one day. Your ticket is valid all day and you can leave and re-enter the museum as you wish.
● On Fridays after 6pm entry is free for the under-26s, but if you plan to make several visits, the Carte Louvre Jeunes (€15 per year under-26s, €30 per year under-30s) is worth getting.
● Some rooms are closed on a weekly basis – check on 01.40.20.53.17 or at www.louvre.fr.

LISTINGS INFORMATION

Louvre, Rue de Rivoli, 1st (01.40.20.50.50, recorded information 01.40.20.53.17, disabled access 01.40.20.59.90, www.louvre.fr). Mº Palais Royal Musée du Louvre. **Open** 9am-6pm Mon, Thur, Sat, Sun; 9am-9.45pm Wed, Fri. **Admission** *Permanent collections* €11 (incl entry to the Musée Delacroix but not shows at the Salle Napoléon); free under-18s, under-26s (EU citizens), all under-26s 6-9.45pm Fri, all 1st Sun of mth. PMP. *Exhibitions* €12. *Combined ticket* €15. **Credit** AmEx, MC, V. **Map** p403 G5.

REFRESHMENTS

Take your pick from **Richelieu**, **Denon** or **Mollien** cafés; the last of these is just off the Mollien staircase and has a terrace. Under the

Ancient Egypt.

pyramid, there's a sandwich bar and the smart, sophisticated **Grand Louvre** restaurant. The **Restorama**, in the Carrousel du Louvre, has self-service outlets. The terrace of **Café Marly** serves pricey brasserie fare and cocktails.

The collections

History of the Louvre

Sully: lower ground floor. Shown as dark brown on Louvre maps.
Here you can explore the medieval foundations of the Louvre, dating back to Philippe-Auguste's reign. Uncovered in 1985 during excavations for the Grand Louvre project, they include the remains of the moat that once surrounded the fort and the pillars of two drawbridges; the La Taillerie tower, with heart symbols cut into the stone by masons; and the outside of the dungeons. A well and a portion of ground have been left undisturbed, showing artefacts just as they were found, and a scale model shows the fortress at the time of Charles V. An exhibition in the Saint-Louis room recounts the history of the Louvre through rare archaeological finds, as well as an unfinished staircase and carved pillars.

Ancient Egypt

Denon: lower ground floor; Sully: lower ground, ground & 1st floors. Green on Louvre maps.

INSIDE TRACK
PLAN YOUR ROUTE

Pick up a map at the information desk. The collections are colour-coded on it, and signs point the way to the most popular exhibits. Leaflets suggesting various thematic trails are also available. *Destination Louvre*, which is on sale at the Réunion des Musées Nationaux shop in the Carrousel du Louvre, is a good English-language guide.

Announced by the pink granite Giant Sphinx (1898-1866 BC), the Egyptian department divides into two routes. The Thematic Circuit on the ground floor presents Nile culture (fishing, agriculture, hunting, daily and cultural life, religion and death). One of the big draws is the Mastaba of Akhethetep, a decorated burial chamber from Sakkara dating back to 2400 BC. Six small sphinxes, apes from Luxor and the lion-headed goddess Sekhmet recreate elements of temple complexes, while stone sarcophagi, mummies, amulets, jewellery and entrails form a vivid display on funeral rites. A display of Egyptian furniture (room 8, ground floor) dating from 1550 to 1069 BC contains pieces that look almost contemporary in design.

On the first floor the Pharoah Circuit is laid out chronologically, from the Seated Scribe and other stone figures of the Ancient Empire, via painted figures of the Middle Empire, to the New Empire, with animal-headed statues of gods and goddesses, hieroglyphic tablets and papyrus scrolls. Look for the statue of the god Amun protecting Tutankhamun, and the black diorite 'cube statues' of priests and attendants. The collection, one of the largest hoards of Egyptian antiquities in the world, has its origins in Napoleon's Egyptian campaign of 1798 and 1799, and the work of Egyptologist Jean-François Champollion, who deciphered hieroglyphics in 1824. The Coptic gallery, on the lower ground floor, houses textiles and manuscripts.

Oriental antiquities

Richelieu: lower ground & ground floors; Sully: ground floor. Yellow on Louvre maps.
This section deals with Mesopotamia, Persia and the Levant from the fifth millennium BC to the first century AD. The huge Mesopotamian rooms contain glistening diorite sculptures from the Akkad dynasty and Gudea from the third millennium BC. Make sure you don't miss the serene alabaster sculpture of Ebih-II, the superintendant of Mari (room 1b), and the earliest evidence of writing, in the form of fourth-century BC Sumerian tablets (room 1a).

EXPLORE

Oriental antiquities.

The Hammurabi Code, an essential document of Babylonian civilisation, is a black basalt stele recording 282 laws beneath reliefs of the king and the sun god; it's one of the oldest collections of laws in the history of mankind (room 3).

Next come two breathtaking palace reconstructions: the great court, c713 BC, from the palace of Sargon II at Khorsabad (in present-day Iraq), with its giant bearded and winged bulls and friezes of warriors and servants (room 4); and the palace of Darius I at Susa (now Iran), c510 BC, with its glazed-brick reliefs of archers, lions and griffins (room 12). The double-bull-headed column was one of 36 such gigantic supports at the palace. Entering the Iranian section, you find 5,000-year-old statues from Susa housed in the circular room 8, and a fine view of the Cour Napoléon. The Levantine section includes Cypriot animalistic vases and carved reliefs from Byblos.

Islamic arts
Denon: lower ground & ground floors of Cour Visconti. Turquoise on Louvre maps.
See p45 **Unseen Treasures***.

Greek, Roman & Etruscan antiquities
Denon: lower ground & ground floors; Sully: ground & 1st floors. Blue on Louvre maps.
The *Winged Victory of Samothrace*, a headless Greek statue dating from the second century BC, stands sentinel at the top of the grand staircase, giving an idea of its original dramatic impact on a promontory overlooking the Aegean

sea. This huge department is made up of pieces amassed by François I and Cardinal Richelieu, plus the Borghese collection (acquired in 1808), and the Campana collection of thousands of painted Greek vases and small terracottas. Endless dark rooms on the first floor harbour small bronze, silver and terracotta objects, but the really exciting stuff is on the ground floor. The grandiose, vaulted marble rooms are a fitting location for such masterpieces as the 2.3m (7.5ft) *Athena Peacemaker* and the *Venus de Milo* (room 12), and overflow with gods and goddesses, swords and monsters.

Also on the ground floor are artefacts from the Etruscan civilisation of south-central Italy, spanning the seventh century BC until submission to the Romans in the first century AD. The highlight is the painted terracotta Sarcophagus of the Cenestien Couple (c530-510 BC), which illustrates a smiling couple reclining at a banquet. Key Roman antiquities include a vivid relief of sacrificial animals, intricately carved sarcophagi, mosaic floors and the Boscoreale Treasure: magnificent silverwork excavated at a villa near Pompeii. Pre-classical Greek art on the lower ground floor includes a large Cycladic head and Mycenean triad.

French painting
Denon: 1st floor; Richelieu: 2nd floor; Sully: 2nd floor. Red on Louvre maps.
There are around 6,000 of the most famous paintings in the world on show here, the most impressive being the huge 18th- to 19th-century

Unseen Treasures

Take a stroll through 1,200 years of Islamic art.

What do you picture when you think of the Musée du Louvre? The *Mona Lisa*? IM Pei's dramatic glass pyramid? Egyptian mummies? Or perhaps the *Winged Victory of Samothrace* or Géricault's haunting *Radeau de la Méduse*?

What almost certainly doesn't spring to mind is Islamic art, despite the fact that this former royal palace has been amassing the largest collection of its kind in the western world since the 19th century, with a cache of more than 18,000 objects gathered from three continents and covering 1,200 years of history.

The reason the collection has never made the headlines before has been because the Louvre, despite its illustrious proportions, has simply lacked the space in which to display it properly. But now, after a nine-year, €100 million makeover (instigated by ex-president Jacques Chirac in 2003 and executed by architects Rudy Ricciotti and Mario Bellini), the stunning Département des Arts de l'Islam

has finally opened its doors. Set in the Visconti wing, the two-storey, 3,000sq m gallery actually lies underneath the courtyard (Ricciotti and Bellini couldn't change the Louvre's structure, so they had to dig down), beneath a floating golden roof of 2,350 triangles designed to look like a dragonfly wing but reportedly nicknamed the flying carpet. The two floors are linked together by a remarkable staircase cast from a single, monumental block of black concrete.

As for the collection within, you can feast your eyes on some 3,000 works, including gold treasures from Syria, ivories, miniatures, Ottoman ceramics and textiles, all displayed in chronological order. Aside from finally giving a home to some of its most fabulous and hitherto hidden artefacts, the Louvre's message is plain to see: despite today's political and religious tensions, the history and culture of the Arab and Western worlds are forever intertwined.

EXPLORE

canvases hanging in the Daru and Mollien rooms in the Denon wing, serving Classicism and Romanticism respectively. Here, art meets politics with David's enormous *Sacre de Napoléon*, Gros' propagandising *Napoléon Visitant le Champ de Bataille d'Eylau* and Delacroix's flag-flying *La Liberté Guidant le Peuple*. Géricault's beautiful but disturbing *Le Radeau de la Méduse* illustrates the grisly true story of the abandoned men who resorted to cannibalism and murder after a famous shipwreck in 1816, while his generals on flame-eyed horses fuel the myth of the dashing French officer. Biblical and historical scenes rub shoulders with aristocracy and grand depictions of great moments in mythology. Ingres' *Grande Odalisque* is also found here, along with a new Ingres acquisition, a portrait of the Duc d'Orléans.

In the Richelieu wing you can find the earliest known non-religious French portrait, an anonymous depiction of French king Jean Le Bon (c1350); the *Pietà de Villeneuve-lès-Avignon*, later attributed to Enguerrand Quarton; Jean Clouet's *Portrait of François I* (marking the influence of the Italian Renaissance on portraiture); and various works from the Ecole de Fontainebleau, including the anonymous *Diana the Huntress*, an elegant nude who strangely resembles Diane de Poitiers, the mistress of Henri II. Poussin's religious and mythological subjects epitomise 17th-century French classicism, and are full of erudite references for an audience of cognoscenti.

His works spill over into the Sully wing, where you'll also find Charles Le Brun's wonderfully pompous *Chancellier Séguier* and his four grandiose battle scenes, in which Alexander the Great is a suitable stand-in for Louis XIV.

The 18th century begins with Watteau's *Gilles* and the *Embarkation for Cythera*. Works by Chardin include sober still lifes, but also fine figure paintings. If you're used to the sugary images of Fragonard, don't miss the *Fantaisies*, which forgo sentimentality for fluent, broadly painted fantasy portraits, intended to capture moods rather than likenesses. Also in the Sully wing are sublime neoclassical portraits by David, Ingres' *La Baigneuse* and *Le Bain Turc*, portraits and Orientalist scenes by Chassériau, and landscapes by Corot.

French sculpture

Richelieu: lower ground & ground floors.
Light brown on Louvre maps.

French sculpture is displayed in and around two covered courts. A tour of the medieval regional schools takes in the *Virgins* from Alsace, 14th-century figures of Charles V and Jeanne de Bourbon that once adorned the exterior of the Louvre, and the 15th-century tomb of Philippe Pot, an effigy of a Burgundian knight carried by eight mourners. Fine Renaissance memorials, fountains and portals include Jean Goujon's friezes from the Fontaine des Innocents.

In the Cour Marly, pride of place goes to Coustou's *Chevaux de Marly*, rearing horses being restrained by their grooms, plus two

earlier equestrian pieces by Coysevox. Hewn from single blocks of marble, they were sculpted for the royal château at Marly-le-Roi before being moved to the Tuileries gardens, where copies now stand. In Cour Puget are the four bronze captives by Martin Desjardins, Clodion's rococo frieze and Pierre Puget's twisting, Baroque *Milo of Croton*. Amid the 18th-century heroes and allegorical subjects, look out for Pigalle's *Mercury* and *Voltaire*.

Italian & Spanish painting

Denon: 1st floor. Red on Louvre maps.
Starting from the Sully end of the Denon wing, three rooms of fragile frescoes by Botticelli, Fra Angelico and Luini, and 13th- to 15th-century Florentine paintings on wood by Cimabue, Giotto, Fra Angelico and Lippi, open the Italian department, before you move into the long, skylit Grande Galerie. To the right, the Salle des Sept Mètres has highlights of the Sienese school, including Simone Martini's *Christ Carrying the Cross* and Piero della Francesca's *Portrait of Sigismondo Malatesta*. Now that the *Mona Lisa* has moved, there is no need to bowl along the Grande Galerie at speed in your haste to see her, missing the wonders on either side.

Most notably, about a quarter of the way along on the left are Leonardo's *Virgin of the Rocks*, *Virgin and Child with Saint Anne* and *Saint-Jean Baptiste*, which form part of the Northern Italian section, along with Bellini's *Calvary* and *Portrait of a Man* and Raphael's *Portrait of Dona Isabel de Requesens*. The first

turning on the right after the da Vincis leads into the Salle de La Joconde, whose toffee-coloured brushed concrete walls provide a suitably golden setting for Veronese's lavish *Wedding at Cana*, his *Crucifixion* and *Sainte Famille* and other Venetian masterpieces such as Lotto's *Adulterous Woman* and red-robed *Christ Carrying the Cross*, Tintoretto's *Suzanne Bathing* and Bassano's earthy canvases. Don't miss the exquisite Titians hidden behind the *Mona Lisa* on her stand-alone wall.

A trip back down the Passage de Mollien, containing 16th-century cartoons, frames Giorgio Vasari's *Annunciation*, revealing how much better it is to stand back and look at these paintings. In between the two in the Grande Galerie are Arcimboldo's famous *Four Seasons*, various Bronzinos and Caravaggios, plus works by Albani, Carracci and Reni. A small Spanish section takes in *Christ on the Cross Adored by Two Donors* by El Greco and his contemporary Jusepe de Ribera's *Club Foot*.

Graphic arts

Denon: 1st floor; Sully: 2nd floor. Pink on Louvre maps.
The Louvre's huge collection of drawings includes works by Raphael, Michelangelo, Dürer, Holbein and Rembrandt. However, owing to their fragility, drawings are not shown as permanent exhibits. Four galleries (French and Northern schools on the 2nd floor; Italian and the latest acquisitions on the 1st) feature changing exhibitions. Other works can be

viewed in the Salle de Consultation only upon written application to the management (01.40.20.52.51, cabinet-des-dessins@louvre.fr).

Italian, Spanish & Northern sculpture
Denon: lower ground & ground floors.
Light brown on Louvre maps.
Michelangelo's *Dying Slave* and *Captive Slave* are the real showstoppers here, but other Renaissance treasures include a painted marble relief by Donatello, Adrien de Vriesse's bronze *Mercury and Psyche*, Giambologna's *Mercury* and the ethereal *Psyche Revived by Cupid's Kiss* by Antonio Canova. Benvenuto Cellini's *Nymph of Fontainebleau* relief is on the Mollien staircase.

Napoleon III's former stables were reopened in 2004 to house princely collections of statuary acquired by Richelieu and the Borghese and Albani families in the 17th and 18th centuries. The statues, either copies of classical works or restored originals, demonstrate the relationship between antique and modern sculpture. The height of the room also allows oversized works such as *Jupiter* and *Albani Alexander* to be displayed. Northern sculpture, on the lower ground floor, ranges from Erhart's Gothic *Mary Magdalene* to the neoclassical work of Thorvaldsen; pre-Renaissance Italian pieces include Donatello's clay relief *Virgin and Child*.

Northern schools
Richelieu: 2nd floor; Sully: 1st floor.
Red on Louvre maps.
Northern Renaissance works include Flemish altarpieces by Memling and van der Weyden, Bosch's fantastical, proto-surrealist *Ship of Fools*, Metsys' *The Moneylender and his Wife*, and the northern mannerism of Cornelius van Haarlem. The Galerie Médicis houses Rubens' Médicis cycle; Marie de Médicis, the widow of Henri IV, commissioned the 24 canvases for the Palais de Luxembourg in the 1620s. They blend historic events and classical mythology for the glorification of the queen, never afraid to put her best features on public display. Look out for Rubens' more personal portrait of his second wife, *Hélène Fourment and her Children*, plus van Dyck's *Charles I and his Groom* and David Teniers the Younger's peasant-filled townscapes.

Dutch paintings in this wing include early and late self-portraits by Rembrandt, his *Flayed Ox* and the warmly glowing nude *Bathsheba at her Bath*. There are Vermeer's *Astronomer* and *Lacemaker* amid interiors by De Hooch and Metsu, and the meticulously finished portraits and framing devices of Dou, plus works from the Haarlem school. German paintings in side galleries include portraits by Cranach, Dürer's *Self-Portrait* and Holbein's *Anne of Cleves*.

The rooms of Northern European and Scandinavian paintings include Caspar David Friedrich's *Trees with Crows*, the sober, classical portraits of Christian Købke, and pared-back views by Peder Balke. A fairly modest but high-quality British collection located on the first floor of the Sully includes landscapes by Wright of Derby, Constable and Turner, and portraits by Gainsborough, Reynolds and Lawrence.

Decorative arts
Richelieu: 1st floor; Sully: 1st floor.
Magenta on Louvre maps.
The decorative arts collection runs from the Middle Ages to the mid 19th century, and includes entire rooms decorated in the fashion of the day. Many of the finest medieval items came from the treasury of St-Denis, amassed by the powerful Abbot Suger, counsellor to Louis VI and VII, among them Suger's 'Eagle' (a porphyry vase), a serpentine plate surrounded by precious stones, and the sacred sword of the kings of France, dubbed 'Charlemagne's Sword' by the Capetian monarchs.

The Renaissance galleries display the *Hunts of Maximilien*, a dozen 16th-century tapestries depicting the months, zodiac and hunting scenes. Seventeenth- and 18th-century French decorative arts are shown in superb panelled rooms, and include characteristic brass and tortoiseshell pieces by Boulle. Displays then move on to French porcelain, silverware, watches and scientific instruments. Napoleon III's opulent apartments, used until the 1980s by the Ministry of Finance, have been preserved, with chandeliers and upholstery intact.

Next to the Denon wing is the Galerie d'Apollon. It was built for Louis XIV and is a showcase of talents from this golden age: architecture by Louis Le Vau, painted ceilings by Charles Le Brun and sculpture by François Girardon, the Marsy brothers and Thomas Regnaudin. Napoleon III then commissioned Delacroix to paint the central medallion, *Apollo Vanquishing the Python*, and now it houses the crown jewels and Louis XIV vases. Merry-Joseph Blondel's *Chute d'Icare* graces the ceiling of an anteroom of the adjacent Rotonde d'Apollon.

African, Asian, Oceanic & American arts
Denon: ground floor. White on Louvre maps.
A new approach to '*arts premiers*' is seen in these eight rooms in the Pavillon des Sessions. The spare, modern design allows each of the 100 key works to stand alone. The pure aesthetics of such objects as a svelte Zulu spoon with the breasts and buttocks of a woman, a sixth-century BC Sokoto terracotta head, and a recycled iron sculpture of the god Gou that anticipates Picasso can be appreciated in their own right. Computer terminals with mahogany benches offer visitors multimedia resources.

Opéra to Les Halles

Money makes this world go round.

In centuries gone by, these two adjoining central districts – bounded by the Grands Boulevards to the north and the river to the south – were the city's commercial and provisioning powerhouses, home to most of the newspapers, banks and major mercantile institutions. Nowadays, although there is still a strong financial slant thanks to the presence of the two stock exchanges and the Banque de France, the focus is firmly on shopping: mass-market stuff in and around Les Halles, shading progressively into more exclusive and expensive brands the further one moves west, in particular on and just off rue St-Honoré. Les Halles itself was, famously, the city's wholesale food market until 1969, when the Second Empire iron-framed buildings that housed it were ripped out, and a thousand commentators gnashed their teeth in print. The soulless shopping centre that filled the gap in the 1970s has been one of the city's least liked features, and is itself doomed to destruction during the next few years, to be replaced by what promises to be a 21st-century glory of gardens, glass, and brighter, more open spaces.

Map pp401-402   **Restaurants** p141
Hotels p232   **Cafés & bars** p172

EXPLORE

TUILERIES & PALAIS-ROYAL

In the 1st arrondissement.

Once the monarchs had moved from the Ile de la Cité to spacious new quarters on the Right Bank, the Louvre and, later, the palaces of the **Tuileries** and **Palais-Royal** became the centres of royal power. **The Louvre** (*see pp41-48*) still exerts considerable influence today: first as a grandiose architectural ensemble; and, second, as a symbol of the capital's cultural pre-eminence. What had been simply a fortress along Philippe-Auguste's city wall in 1190 was transformed by Charles V into a royal residence with all the latest Gothic comforts; François I turned it into a sumptuous palace. For centuries, it was a work in progress: everyone wanted to make their mark – including the most monarchical of presidents, François Mitterrand, who added IM Pei's glass pyramid, doubled the exhibition space and added the Carrousel du Louvre shopping mall, auditorium and food halls.

The palace has always attracted crowds: first courtiers and ministers; then artists; and, since 1793, when it was first turned into a museum, art-lovers – though the last department of the Finance Ministry moved out as late as 1991. Around the Louvre, other subsidiary palaces grew up: Catherine de Médicis commissioned Philibert Delorme to begin work on one in the Tuileries; and Richelieu built the Palais Cardinal, which later became the Palais-Royal.

On place du Louvre, opposite Claude Perrault's grandiose eastern façade of the Louvre, is **Eglise St-Germain-l'Auxerrois**, once the French kings' parish church and home

INSIDE TRACK GET CONNECTED

If you're looking to get online during your stay, Paris's parks and gardens are littered with free Wi-Fi access points, including two in the Jardin des Halles. For a full list of locations, visit www.paris.fr/wifi.

Comédie Française.

to the only original Flamboyant Gothic porch in Paris, built in 1435. Mirroring it to the left of the belfry is the 19th-century first arrondissement *mairie*, with its fanciful rose window and classical porch. Next door is the stylish **Le Fumoir** (*see p172*), with a Mona Lisa of its own: amaretto, orange juice and champagne.

Across rue de Rivoli from the Louvre, past the **Louvre des Antiquaires** antiques emporium (*see p222*), stands the understatedly elegant **Palais-Royal**, once Cardinal Richelieu's private mansion and now the Conseil d'Etat and ministry of culture. After a stroll in its quiet gardens, it's hard to believe that this was once the most debauched corner of Paris.

In the 1780s, the Palais was a boisterous centre of Paris life, where aristocrats and the financially challenged inhabitants of the *faubourgs* rubbed shoulders. The coffee houses in its arcades generated radical debate: here Camille Desmoulins called the city to arms on the eve of the storming of the Bastille; and after the Napoleonic Wars, Wellington and Field Marshal von Blücher lost so much money in the gambling dens that Parisians claimed they had won back their entire dues for war reparations. Only haute cuisine restaurant **Le Grand Véfour** (*see p140*), founded as Café de Chartres in the 1780s, survives from this era, albeit with decoration dating from a little later.

The **Comédie Française** theatre ('La Maison de Molière'; *see p308*) stands on the south-west corner. The company, created by Louis XIV in 1680, moved here in 1799. Molière himself is honoured with a fountain on the corner of rue Molière and rue de Richelieu. Brass-fronted Café Nemours on place Colette – Colette used to buy cigars from old-fashioned **A la Civette** nearby (157 rue St-Honoré, 1st, 01.42.96.04.99) – is another thespian favourite. In front of it, the métro entrance by artist Jean-Michel Othoniel, all glass baubles and aluminium struts, is a kitsch take on Guimard's celebrated art nouveau métro entrances.

Today, the stately arcades of the Palais-Royal house an eclectic succession of antiques dealers, philatelists, specialists in tin soldiers and musical boxes – and fashion showcases. Here you'll find the European flagship of renowned New York designer **Marc Jacobs** (*see p200*), chic vintage clothes specialist **Didier Ludot** (*see p207*), and the elegant perfumery **Salons du Palais-Royal Shiseido** (*see p221*). Passing through the arcades to rue de Montpensier, the neo-rococo Théâtre du Palais-Royal and the centuries-old café **L'Entr'acte** (*see p172*), you'll find narrow, stepped passages that run between here and rue de Richelieu. On the other side of the palace towards Les Halles is galerie Véro-Dodat. Built by rich *charcutiers* during the Restoration period, it features wonderfully preserved neoclassical wooden shopfronts.

At the western end of the Louvre, by rue de Rivoli, are the **Musée des Arts Décoratifs**, the **Musée de la Mode et du Textile** and

EXPLORE

the **Musée de la Publicité**. All of these are administered independently of the Musée du Louvre, but were refreshed as part of the Grand Louvre scheme. Across place du Carrousel from the Louvre pyramid, the **Arc du Carrousel**, a mini-Arc de Triomphe, was built in polychrome marble for Napoleon Bonaparte from 1806 to 1809. The chariot on the top was originally drawn by the antique horses from San Marco in Venice, snapped up by Napoleon but returned in 1815. From the arch, the extraordinary axis along the **Jardin des Tuileries**, the Champs-Elysées up to the Arc de Triomphe and on to the Grande Arche de la Défense is plain to see.

The Jardin des Tuileries stretched as far as the Tuileries palace, until that was destroyed in the 1871 Paris Commune. The garden was laid out in the 17th century by André Le Nôtre and remains a pleasure area, with a funfair in summer; it also serves as an open-air gallery for modern art sculptures. Overlooking focal **place de la Concorde** is the **Musée de l'Orangerie** and the **Jeu de Paume**, built as a court for real tennis and now a centre for photographic exhibitions.

The stretch of rue de Rivoli running beside the Louvre towards Concorde was laid out by Napoleon's architects Percier and Fontaine from 1802 to 1811, and is notable for its arcaded façades. It runs in a straight line between place de la Concorde and rue St-Antoine, in the Marais; at the western end it's filled with tacky souvenir shops – though old-fashioned hotels remain, and there are also gentlemen's outfitters, bookshop **WH Smith** (*see p194*)

and tearoom **Angelina** (*see p171*). The area was inhabited by English aristocrats, writers and artists in the 1830s and '40s after the Napoleonic Wars, sleeping at **Le Meurice** (*see p231*) and dining in the fancy restaurants of the Palais-Royal.

Place des Pyramides, at the junction of rue de Rivoli and rue des Pyramides, contains a gleaming gilt equestrian statue of Joan of Arc. One of four statues of her in the city, it's fêted as a proud symbol of French nationalism every May Day by supporters of the Front National.

Ancient rue St-Honoré, running parallel to rue de Rivoli, is one of those streets that changes style as it goes along: smart shops line it near place Vendôme, small cafés and inexpensive bistros predominate towards Les Halles. The Baroque **Eglise St-Roch** is still pitted with bullet holes made by Napoleon's troops when they crushed a royalist revolt in 1795. With its old houses, adjoining rue St-Roch still feels wonderfully authentic; a couple of shops are built into the side of the church. Further up stands **Chapelle Notre-Dame de l'Assomption** (1670-76), now used by the city's Polish community, its dome so disproportionately large that locals have dubbed it *sot dôme* ('stupid dome'; a pun on 'Sodom').

Concept store **Colette** (*see p202*) brought some glamour to a once-staid shopping area, drawing a swarm of similar stores along in its wake. All are ideally placed for the fashionistas and film stars who touch down at **Hôtel Costes** (*see p231*). Opposite Colette is rue du Marché-St-Honoré, which once led to the covered Marché

EXPLORE

Jardin des Tuileries. *See p53.*

Living History

The ancient streets are brought to life by Visites-Spectacles.

A gaggle of tourists waiting at the entrance to the Passage des Princes in Paris's theatre district are hailed from afar by a man running in a bowler hat. Jean-Jacques de la Tour, as he introduces himself, is a 19th-century historian investigating the mystery of Nathaniel de Cantaussel, who was murdered in Passage Jouffroy in 1870 but whose body was never found. Thus begins a thoroughly original tour by **Visites-Spectacles** (01.48.59.92.97, www.visites-spectacles.com) of Paris's covered passages that plunges you into a world of *élégantes*, courtesans, pickpockets and greedy industrialists – the Second Empire brought to life.

As he leads us through the Passage des Panoramas, Passage des Variétés, Passage Verdeau and Passage Jouffroy, where the mystery is delightfully solved, Jean-Jacques packs his narrative with delicious trivia about the life of the *boulevardiers*: a dish of small birds that was eaten with a napkin over your head, Masonic symbolism in the Eiffel Tower,

the construction of unforgeable visiting cards and silk umbrellas, and a popular romantic walk that involved looking at the cadavers in a morgue. He teases people, poses enigmas and drops in a few modern references for laughs. But there's more: surprises pop out from doorways in the form of other actors in character – a dandy court reporter, a courtesan who knew Cantaussel's lover, a prostitute who makes people's black thoughts disappear in flames, and the vivacious Fée Verte (absinthe personified) who dances down a boulevard then disappears behind a newspaper stand. And clues materialise too in the windows of some of the historic shops that line the passages.

A huge amount of information is packed into 90 minutes, knitted into an engaging theatrical performance with convincing actors and great costumes. As a historical tour and interactive theatre performance rolled into one, it's great value for money and a brilliant way to discover things even the history books don't tell you.

St-Honoré, since replaced by offices, in a square lined with trendy restaurants; to the north, rue Danielle-Casanova boasts 18th-century houses.

Further west along rue St-Honoré lies the wonderful, eight-sided **place Vendôme** and a perspective stretching from rue de Rivoli up to Opéra. At the end of the Tuileries, place de la Concorde, originally laid out for the glorification of Louis XV, is a masterclass in the use of open space, and spectacular when lit up at night. The winged Marly horses (only reproductions, the originals are in the Louvre) frame the entrance to the Champs-Elysées.

Smart rue Royale has tearoom **Ladurée** (*see p176*) and famed restaurant **Maxim's** (3 rue Royale, 8th, 01.42.65.27.94), with a fabulous museum of art nouveau, **La Collection 1900**, attached. Rue Boissy d'Anglas proffers stylish shops and the trendy **Buddha Bar** (no.8, 8th, 01.53.05.90.00); and high-end designs at **Yves Saint Laurent** (*see p202*) and others set the plush tone.

La Collection 1900

Maxim's, 3 rue Royale, 8th (01.42.65.30.47, www.maxims-musee-artnouveau.com). M° Madeleine. **Open** *Guided tours (reservations essential)* 2pm Wed-Sun (English); 3.15pm, 4.30pm (French). **Admission** €15. **No credit cards. Map** p401 F4.
Couturier Pierre Cardin has owned belle époque restaurant Maxim's since 1981, and now he has added a museum of art nouveau, which he has been collecting since the age of 18. There are rooms and rooms of exhibits, arranged so as to evoke a 19th-century courtesan's boudoir. Read Zola's *Nana* before your visit to grasp the full effect of the dreamy lake maidens sculpted in glistening faience, pewter vanity sets in the shape of reclining nudes, and beds inlaid with opium flowers to promote sleep. Dinner settings on display include Gustav Eiffel's own chunky tureens, just crying out for turtle soup.

FREE Eglise St-Germain-l'Auxerrois

2 pl du Louvre, 1st (01.42.60.13.96, www.saint germainauxerrois.cef.fr). M° Louvre Rivoli or Pont Neuf. **Open** 8am-7pm Mon-Sat; 9am-8pm Sun. **Admission** free. **Map** p406 H6.
The architecture of this former royal church spans several eras: the elaborate Flamboyant Gothic porch is the most striking feature. The interior is home to the 13th-century Lady Chapel and a canopied, carved bench by Le Brun, which was made for the royal family in 1682. The church achieved notoriety on 24 August 1572, when its bell signalled the St Bartholomew's Day massacre.

★ FREE Eglise St-Roch

296 rue St-Honoré, 1st (01.42.44.13.20, www.saintrochparis.cef.fr). M° Pyramides or Tuileries. **Open** 8am-7pm daily. **Admission** free. **Map** p401 G5.

Begun in the 1650s in what was then the heart of Paris, this long church was designed chiefly by Jacques Lemercier; work took so long, the church was consecrated only in 1740. Famed parishioners and patrons are remembered in funerary monuments: Le Nôtre, Mignard, Corneille and Diderot are all here, as are busts by Coysevox and Coustou, Falconet's statue *Christ on the Mount of Olives* and Anguier's superb *Nativity*. Bullet marks from a 1795 shoot-out between royalists and conventionists still pit the façade.

★ FREE Jardin des Tuileries

Rue de Rivoli, 1st. M° Concorde or Tuileries. **Open** *Apr, May* 7am-9pm daily; *June-Aug* 7am-11pm daily; *Sept-Mar* 7.30am-7.30pm daily. **Admission** free. **Map** p401 G5.
Between the Louvre and place de la Concorde, the gravelled alleyways of these gardens have been a chic promenade ever since they opened to the public in the 16th century; and the popular mood persists with the funfair that sets up along the rue de Rivoli side in summer. André Le Nôtre created the prototypical French garden with terraces and central vista running down the *Grand Axe* through circular and hexagonal ponds. When the Tuileries palace was burned down during the Paris Commune in 1871, the park was expanded. As part of Mitterrand's Grand Louvre project, fragile sculptures such as Coysevox's winged horses were transferred to the Louvre and replaced by reproductions, and the Maillol sculptures were returned to the Jardins du Carrousel; a handful of modern sculptures has been added, including bronzes by Laurens, Moore, Ernst, Giacometti, and Dubuffet's *Le Bel Costumé*. Replanting has restored parts of Le Nôtre's design and replaced damaged trees, and there's a gardeners' bookshop by place de la Concorde. *Photo p51.*

Jeu de Paume

1 pl de la Concorde, 8th (01.47.03.12.50, www.jeudepaume.org). M° Concorde. **Open** 11am-9pm Tue; 11am-7pm Wed-Sun (last entry 30mins before closing). **Admission** €8.50; €5.50 reductions; free under-26s 5-9pm last Tue of mth. **Credit** MC, V. **Map** p401 F5.
The Centre National de la Photographie moved into this site in 2005. The building, which once served as a tennis court, has been divided into two white, almost hangar-like galleries. It is not an intimate space, but it works well for showcase retrospectives. A video art and cinema suite in the basement shows new digital installation work, as well as feature-length films made by artists. There's also a sleek café and a decent bookshop.

★ Musée des Arts Décoratifs

107 rue de Rivoli, 1st (01.44.55.57.50, www.lesarts decoratifs.fr). M° Palais Royal Musée du Louvre or Pyramides. **Open** 11am-6pm Tue, Wed, Fri-Sun; 11am-9pm Thur (late opening during exhibitions only). **Admission** (with Musée de la Mode &

Musée de la Publicité) €9.50; €8 reductions;
free under-18s, under-26s (EU citizens). PMP.
Credit MC, V. **Map** p402 H5.

Taken as a whole along with the Musée de la Mode et du Textile (*see below*) and Musée de la Publicité (*see p55*), this is one of the world's major collections of design and the decorative arts. Located in the west wing of the Louvre since its opening a century ago, the venue reopened a few years ago after a decade-long, €35-million restoration of the building and of 6,000 of the 150,000 items donated mainly by private collectors.

The major focus here is French furniture and tableware. From extravagant carpets to delicate crystal and porcelain, there is much to admire. Clever spotlighting and black settings show the exquisite treasures – including *châtelaines* made for medieval royalty and Maison Falize enamel work – to their best advantage. Other galleries are categorised by theme: glass, wallpaper, drawings and toys. There are cases devoted to Chinese head jewellery and the Japanese art of seduction with combs. Of most immediate attraction to the layperson are the reconstructed period rooms, ten in all, showing how the other (French) half lived from the late 1400s to the early 20th century.

Musée de la Mode et du Textile

107 rue de Rivoli, 1st (01.44.55.57.50, www. lesartsdecoratifs.fr). Mº Palais Royal Musée du Louvre or Pyramides. **Open** 11am-6pm Tue, Wed, Fri-Sun; 11am-9pm Thur (late opening during exhibitions only). **Admission** (with Musée des

Arts Décoratifs & Musée de la Publicité) €9.50; €8 reductions; free under-18s, under-26s (EU citizens). PMP. **Credit** MC, V. **Map** p402 H5.

This municipal fashion museum holds Elsa Schiaparelli's entire archive and hosts exciting themed exhibitions. Dramatic black-walled rooms make a fine background to the clothes, and video screens and a small cinema space show how the clothes move, as well as interviews with the creators.

★ Musée de l'Orangerie

Jardin des Tuileries, 1st (01.44.77.80.07, www.musee-orangerie.fr). Mº Concorde. **Open** 9am-6pm Mon, Wed-Sun. **Admission** €7.50; €5 reductions; free under-18s, under-26s (EU citizens), all 1st Sun of mth. PMP. **Credit** MC, V. **Map** p401 F5.

This Monet showcase is a firm fixture on the tourist radar: expect long queues. The look is utilitarian and fuss-free, with the museum's eight, tapestry-sized *Nymphéas* (water lilies) paintings housed in two plain oval rooms. They provide a simple backdrop for the astonishing, ethereal romanticism of Monet's works, painted late in his life. Depicting Monet's 'jardin d'eau' at his house in Giverny, the *tableaux* have an intense, dreamy quality – partly reflecting the artist's absorption in the private world of his garden. Downstairs, the Jean Walter and Paul Guillaume collection of Impressionism and the Ecole de Paris is a mixed bag of sweet-toothed Cézanne and Renoir portraits, along with works by Modigliani, Rousseau, Matisse, Picasso and Derain.

Musée de l'Orangerie.

Musée de la Publicité

107 rue de Rivoli, 1st (01.44.55.57.50, www.lesarts decoratifs.fr). M° Palais Royal Musée du Louvre or Pyramides. **Open** 11am-6pm Tue, Wed, Fri-Sun; 11am-9pm Thur (late opening during exhibitions only). **Admission** (with Musée des Arts Décoratifs & Musée de la Mode) €9.50; €8 reductions; free under-18s, under-26s (EU citizens). PMP. **Credit** MC, V. **Map** p402 H5.

The upstairs element of the trio of museums in the Louvre west wing, the advertising museum has a distressed interior by Jean Nouvel. Only a fraction of the vast collection of posters, promotional objects and packaging can be seen at one time; vintage posters are accessed in the multimedia space.

★ FREE Palais-Royal

Pl du Palais-Royal, 1st. M° Palais Royal Musée du Louvre. **Open** Gardens 7.30am-8.30pm daily. **Admission** free. **Map** p402 H5.

Built for Cardinal Richelieu by Jacques Lemercier, this building was once known as the Palais Cardinal. Richelieu left it to Louis XIII, whose widow Anne d'Autriche preferred it to the chilly Louvre and rechristened it when she moved in with her son, the young Louis XIV. In the 1780s, the Duc d'Orléans, Louis XVI's fun-loving brother, enclosed the gardens in a three-storey peristyle and filled it with cafés, shops, theatres, sideshows and accommodation to raise money for rebuilding the burned-down opera. In stark contrast to Versailles, the Palais-Royal was a place where people of all classes could mingle,

and its arcades became a trysting venue. Today, Daniel Buren's installation of black-and-white columns graces the main courtyard. *Photos p56.*

FREE Place de la Concorde

1st, 8th. M° Concorde. **Map** p401 F5.

This is the city's largest square, its grand east–west perspectives stretching from the Louvre to the Arc de Triomphe, and north–south from the Madeleine to the Assemblée Nationale across the Seine. Royal architect Gabriel designed it in the 1750s, along with the two colonnaded mansions astride rue Royale; the west one houses the chic Hôtel de Crillon (currently closed for renovations) and the Automobile Club de France, the other is the Naval Ministry. In 1792, the centre statue of Louis XV was replaced with the guillotine that would be used on Louis XVI, Marie-Antoinette and many more. The square was embellished in the 19th century with sturdy lamp-posts, the Luxor obelisk (from the Viceroy of Egypt), and ornate tiered fountains. *Photo p57.*

FREE Place Vendôme

1st. M° Opéra or Tuileries. **Map** p401 G4.

Elegant place Vendôme got its name from a *hôtel particulier* built by the Duc de Vendôme that stood on the site. Opened in 1699, the eight-sided square was conceived by Hardouin-Mansart to show off an equestrian statue of the Sun King, torn down in 1792 and replaced in 1806 by the Colonne de la Grande Armée. Modelled on Trajan's Column in Rome and featuring a spiral comic strip illustrating

EXPLORE

Palais-Royal. See p55.

Napoleon's military exploits, it was cast from 1,250 Russian and Austrian cannon captured at the Battle of Austerlitz. During the 1871 Commune this symbol of 'brute force and false glory' was pulled down; the present column is a replica. Hardouin-Mansart designed only the façades, with their ground-floor arcade and giant Corinthian pilasters; the buildings behind were put up by nobles and speculators. Today, the square houses sparkling jewellers, top fashion houses and the justice ministry. At no.12, you can visit the Grand Salon where Chopin died in 1849; its fabulous allegorical decoration dates from 1777 and has been restored as part of the new museum above the jewellers Chaumet (01.44.77.26.26).

THE BOURSE

In the 1st & 2nd arrondissements.

Far less frenzied than Wall Street, the city's traditional business district is squeezed between the elegant calm of the Palais-Royal and shopping hub the Grands Boulevards. Along rue du Quatre-Septembre, **La Bourse** (the stock exchange) is where financiers and stockbrokers beaver away in grandiose buildings. The Banque de France, France's national central bank, has occupied the 17th-century Hôtel de Toulouse since 1811, its long gallery still hung with Old Masters. Nearby, fashion and finance meet at stylish **place des Victoires**, designed by Hardouin-Mansart, forming an intimate circle of buildings.

West of the square is shop-lined galerie Vivienne, the smartest of the covered passages in Paris, adjoining galerie Colbert. Also look out for temporary exhibitions at the **Bibliothèque Nationale de France – Richelieu**. You can linger at the luxury food and wine merchant **Legrand** (*see p215*), or head along passage des Petits-Pères to admire the 17th- to 18th-century **Eglise Notre-Dame-des-Victoires**, the remains of an Augustine convent with a cycle of paintings around the choir by Carle van Loo.

Rue de la Banque leads to the Bourse, behind a commanding neoclassical colonnade. The area has a relaxed feel – it's dead at weekends – but animated pockets exist at such places as **Le Vaudeville** (29 rue Vivienne, 2nd, 01.40.20.04.62, www.vaudevilleparis.com) and **Gallopin** (40 rue Notre-Dame-des-Victoires, 2nd, 01.42.36.45.38, www.brasseriegallopin.com), busy brasseries frequented by stockbrokers and journalists. Rue des Colonnes is a quiet street lined with porticoes and acanthus motifs dating from the 1790s; its design nemesis, the 1970s concrete-and-glass HQ of Agence France-Presse, the nation's biggest news agency, stands on the other side of busy rue du Quatre-Septembre.

EXPLORE

FREE Bibliothèque Nationale de France – Richelieu & Musée du Cabinet des Médailles

58 rue de Richelieu, 2nd (01.53.79.59.59, www.bnf.fr). Mº Bourse. **Open** *times vary.* **Admission** varies. **Credit** AmEx, MC, V. **Map** p402 H4.

The history of the French National Library began in the 1660s, when Louis XIV moved manuscripts that couldn't be housed in the Louvre to this lavish Louis XIII townhouse. The library was first opened to the public in 1692, and by 1724 it had received so many new acquisitions that the adjoining Hôtel de Nevers had to be added.

Some of the original painted decoration by Romanelli and Grimaldi can still be seen in Galeries Mansart and Mazarine. The highlights, however, are the two circular reading rooms: the Salle Ovale, which is full of researchers, note-takers and readers, and the magnificent Salle de Travail, a temple to learning, with its arrangement of nine domes supported on slender columns. On the first floor is the Musée du Cabinet des Médailles, a modest two-room collection of coins and medals, including Greek, Roman and medieval examples. There is also a miscellany of other items, including Merovingian king Dagobert's throne, Charlemagne's chess set and small artefacts from the Classical world and ancient Egypt. The whole site is undergoing major renovation until at least 2017, and while much of the library's stock will remain on site, some of the collection has been transferred to the Bibliothèque Nationale de France François Mitterrand (*see p107*). During the first phase of works, entry to the site is via 5 rue Vivienne.

La Bourse

Palais Brongniart, pl de la Bourse, 2nd (http://palaisbourse.euronext.com). Mº Bourse. **Open** Guided tours only; see website for details. **Admission** €8.50; €5.50 reductions. **No credit cards. Map** p402 H4.

After a century at the Louvre, the Palais-Royal and rue Vivienne, in 1826 the stock exchange was transferred to the Bourse, a dignified testament to First Empire classicism designed at Napoleon's behest by Alexandre Brongniart. It was enlarged in 1906 to create a cruciform interior, where brokers buzzed around a central enclosure known as the *corbeille* ('basket' or trading floor). Computers have now made the place obsolete, but it carries on as a conference centre.

FREE Place des Victoires

1st, 2nd. Mº Bourse. **Map** p402 H5.

This circular square, the first of its kind, was designed by Hardouin-Mansart in 1685 to show off a statue of Louis XIV that marked victories against Holland. The original statue was destroyed after the Revolution (although the massive slaves from its base are now in the Louvre), and replaced in 1822 with an equestrian statue by Bosio. Among the

Place de la Concorde. *See p55.*

Palais Garnier

occupants of the grand buildings that encircle the 'square' are the fashion boutiques Kenzo (no.3) and Victoire (no.10).

OPERA & GRANDS BOULEVARDS

In the 2nd, 8th, 9th & 10th arrondissements.

Opéra & Madeleine

Charles Garnier's wedding-cake **Palais Garnier** is all gilt and grandeur, as an opera house should be. Garnier was also responsible for the ritzy **Café de la Paix** (*see p173*) and the **InterContinental Paris Le Grand** (*see p232*) overlooking place de l'Opéra. Behind, in the basement of what is now the Hôtel Scribe, the Lumière brothers held the world's first public cinema screening in 1895. Outfitter **Old England** (no.12, 9th, 01.47.42.81.99), just opposite on boulevard des Capucines, with its wooden counters, Jacobean-style ceilings and old-style goods and service, could have served as their costume consultants. The **Olympia** concert hall (*see p293*), the celebrated host of the Beatles, Piaf and anyone in *chanson*, was knocked down, but rose again nearby. Over the road at no.35, pioneering portrait photographer Nadar opened a studio in the 1860s, frequented by the likes of Dumas père, Offenbach and Doré. In 1874, it hosted the first Impressionists' exhibition. Pedestrianised rue Edouard VII, laid out in 1911, leads to the octagonal square of the same name with Landowski's equestrian statue of the English monarch. Through an arch, another square contains the belle époque **Théâtre de l'Athénée-Louis Jouvet**.

The **Eglise de la Madeleine**, a monument to Napoleon's army, stands guard at the end of the boulevard. At the head of rue Royale, its classical portico mirrors the Assemblée Nationale on the other side of place de la Concorde and over the river, and the interior is a riot of marble and altars. Well worth a browse is wonderfully extravagant delicatessen **Fauchon** (*see p218*) and other luxury food shops; here, too, is haute cuisine restaurant **Senderens** (*see p149*).

Landmark department stores **Printemps** and the **Galeries Lafayette** (for both, *see p191*), which opened just behind the Palais Garnier in the late 19th century, also merit investigation. Behind the latter stands the Lycée Caumartin, designed as a convent in the 1780s by Bourse architect Brongniart, and later one of the city's most prestigious schools. West along boulevard Haussmann is a small square containing the **Chapelle Expiatoire** dedicated to Louis XVI and Marie-Antoinette.

★ Chapelle Expiatoire

29 rue Pasquier, 8th (01.44.32.18.00). M° St-Augustin. **Open** 1-5pm Thur-Sat. **Admission** €5.50; €4 reductions; free under-18s, under-26s (EU citizens). PMP. **Map** p401 F3.

The chapel was commissioned by Louis XVIII in memory of his executed predecessors, his brother Louis XVI and Marie-Antoinette. Their remains, along with those of 3,000 victims of the Revolution, including Camille Desmoulins, Danton, Malesherbes and Lavoisier, were found in 1814 on the spot where the altar stands. The bodies of Louis XVI and Marie-Antoinette were transferred the following year to the Basilique St-Denis; the pair are now represented by marble statues, kneeling at the feet of Religion. Every January, ardent (albeit unfulfilled) royalists gather here for a memorial service.

FREE Eglise de la Madeleine

Pl de la Madeleine, 8th (01.44.51.69.00, www.eglise-lamadeleine.com). M° Concorde or Madeleine. **Open** 9.30am-7pm daily. **Admission** free. **Map** p401 G4.

The building of a church on this site began in 1764, and in 1806 Napoleon sent instructions from Poland for Barthélémy Vignon to design a 'Temple of Glory' dedicated to his Grand Army. After the emperor's fall, construction slowed and the building, by now a church again, was finally consecrated in 1845. The exterior is ringed by huge, fluted Corinthian columns, with a double row at the front, and a frieze of the Last Judgement just above the portico. Inside are giant domes, an organ and pseudo-Grecian side altars in a sea of multicoloured marble. It's a favourite venue for society weddings.

FREE Eglise St-Augustin

46 bd Malesherbes, 8th (01.45.22.23.12, www.saintaugustin.net). M° St-Augustin. **Open** 8.30am-7pm Mon-Fri; 8.30am-noon, 2.30-7.30pm Sat; 8.30am-12.30pm, 4-7.30pm Sun. **Admission** free. **Map** p401 F3.

St-Augustin, designed between 1860 and 1871 by Victor Baltard, architect of the defunct Les Halles pavilions, is not what it seems. The domed, neo-Renaissance stone exterior is merely a shell: inside is an iron vault structure; even the decorative angels are cast in metal. Impressive paintings by Adolphe William Bouguereau hang in the transept.

Musée de la Franc-Maçonnerie

16 rue Cadet, 9th (01.45.23.74.09, www.museefm.org). M° Cadet. **Open** 10am-12.30pm, 2-6pm Tue-Fri; 10am-1pm, 2-7pm Sat. **Admission** €6; €4 reductions; free under-18s. **No credit cards. Map** p402 H3.

Tucked away at the back of the French Masonic Great Lodge, the Musée de la Franc-Maçonnerie first opened in 1973. It traces the history of French freemasonry, ranging from detailed information on stonemasons' guilds to prints of masons General

Lafayette and the 1848 revolutionary leaders Blanc and Barbès. The museum reopened in 2010 after a hefty makeover.

Musée de l'Opéra

Palais Garnier, 1 pl de l'Opéra, 9th (01.53.79.37.47, www.bnf.fr). M° Opéra. **Open** 10am-5pm daily. **Admission** €7; €5 reductions; free under-18s. **No credit cards. Map** p401 G4.

The Palais Garnier houses temporary exhibitions relating to current opera or ballet productions, along with a permanent collection of paintings, scores and bijou opera sets housed in period cases. The entrance fee includes a visit to the auditorium, if rehearsals permit.

FREE Musées des Parfumeries-Fragonard

9 rue Scribe, 9th (01.47.42.04.56, www.fragonard.com) & 39 bd des Capucines, 2nd (01.42.60.37.14, www.fragonard.com). M° Opéra. **Open** 9am-6pm Mon-Sat; 9am-5pm Sun (rue Scribe only). **Admission** free. **Map** p401 G4.

The rue Scribe museum showcases the collection of perfume house Fragonard: five rooms range from Ancient Egyptian ointment flasks to Meissen scent bottles; the boulevard des Capucines museum has bottles by Lalique and Schiaparelli.

★ Palais Garnier

1 pl de l'Opéra, 9th (08.92.89.90.90, www.operadeparis.fr). M° Opéra. **Open** *16 July-2 Sept* 10am-6pm daily. *3 Sept-15 July* 10am-5pm daily. *Guided tours in English* (08.25.05.44.05) July, Aug 11.30am, 2.30pm daily. Sept-June 11.30am, 2.30pm Wed, Sat & Sun. **Admission** €9; €6 reductions; free under-10s. Guided tours €13.50; €6.50-€9.50 reductions. **Credit** AmEx, MC, V. **Map** p401 G4.

See p299 **Night at the Opera**.

Quartier de l'Europe

Its streets named after European cities, the area from Gare St-Lazare towards place de Clichy was the Impressionists' quarter. In those days, it epitomised modernity, with the station, which opened in 1837, serving the line from Paris to

EXPLORE

St-Germain-en-Laye (it was rebuilt in the 1880s). The long shabby commuter hub has had a revamp; a glass dome now disgorges travellers from the métro interchange. The adjoining **Hôtel Concorde Opéra Paris** (*see p233*) was the city's first great station hotel, with a grandiose hallway built by Eiffel in 1889 for visitors to the Exposition Universelle as he was putting up his Tower. Monet, who lived nearby in rue d'Edimbourg, depicted the steam age in *La Gare St-Lazare* and *Pont de l'Europe*; Pissarro and Caillebotte painted views of the new boulevards, and Manet had a studio on rue de St-Petersbourg. Rue de Budapest remains a red-light district; rue de Rome has long been home to stringed-instrument makers. East of St-Lazare stands the **Eglise de la Trinité**.

FREE Eglise de la Trinité

Pl Estienne-d'Orves, 9th (01.48.74.12.77, www.latriniteparis.com). M° Trinité. **Open** 7.15am-8pm Mon-Fri; 11am-8pm Sat; 8.30am-8.30pm Sun. **Admission** free. **Map** p401 G3. Noted for its tiered bell tower, this neo-Renaissance church was constructed between 1861 and 1867.
▶ *Composer Olivier Messiaen (1908-92) was organist at the church for over 30 years.*

The Grands Boulevards

Contrary to popular belief, the string of Grands Boulevards between Madeleine and République (des Italiens, Montmartre, Poissonnière, Bonne-Nouvelle, St-Denis, St-Martin) was not built by Baron Haussmann, but by Louis XIV in 1670, replacing the fortifications of King Philippe-Auguste's city wall. Their ramparts have left their traces in the strange changes of levels, with stairways climbing up to side streets at the eastern end. The boulevards burgeoned after the French Revolution, as residences, theatres and covered passages were put up on land taken from aristocrats and monasteries. To this day, they offer a glimpse of the city's divergent personalities – a stroll from Opéra to République runs from luxury shops via St-Denis prostitutes – and the phrase *théâtre des boulevards* is still used for lowbrow theatre. Between boulevard des Italiens and rue de Richelieu is place Boïeldieu, where Bizet's *Carmen* had its première in 1875.

The 18th-century Hôtel d'Angny, now the town hall of the ninth arrondissement, was once home to the infamous *bals des victimes*, where every guest had to have a relative who had lost his or her head to the guillotine. The **Hôtel Drouot** auction house is ringed by antiques shops, coin- and stamp-dealers and wine bar Les Caves Drouot. There are several grand *hôtels particuliers* on rue de la Grange-Batelière, which leads on one side down the

curious passage Verdeau, occupied by a range of antiques dealers, and on the other back to the boulevards via passage Jouffroy. With its grand, barrel-vaulted glass-and-iron roof, this is home to the lovely **Hôtel Chopin** (*see p235*), shop windows of doll's houses, antique walking sticks, art books and film posters, and the colourful entrance of the **Grévin** waxworks (*see p262*).

Over the boulevard, passage des Panoramas is the oldest remaining covered arcade in Paris. When it opened in 1800, panoramas – vast illuminated circular paintings – of Rome, Jerusalem, London and other cities drew large crowds. Today, it contains coin- and stamp-sellers, furniture-makers and old-fashioned printers. The passage leads into a tangle of other little passages and the stage door of the **Théâtre des Variétés** (7 bd Montmartre, 2nd, 01.42.33.09.92, www.theatre-des-varietes.fr), a pretty neoclassical theatre where Offenbach premièred *La Belle Hélène*.

Rue du Fbg-Montmartre is home to celebrated belle époque *bouillon* Chartier, which serves up hundreds of meals a day to the budget-minded. The street is also part of a significant Jewish quarter, less well known than the Marais, that grew up in the 19th century. There are several kosher bakers and restaurants, and France's largest synagogue at 44 rue de la Victoire, an opulent Second Empire affair completed in 1876. Cobbled Cité Bergère, constructed in 1825 with desirable residences, now houses budget hotels, though the pretty iron-and-glass *portes-cochères* remain. On rue Richer stands the art deco **Folies-Bergère** (no.32, 9th, 08.92.68.16.50), nowadays only sporadically used for cabaret revues. To the south of boulevard Bonne-Nouvelle lies the **Sentier** district, and to the north rue du Fbg-Poissonnière is a mixture of rag-trade outlets and *hôtels particuliers*.

Back on the boulevard is evidence of a move north of the Marais by trendsetting hubs, including **Rex** (*see p285*) and chic **De la Ville Café** (*see p173*). East of here are Louis XIV's twin triumphal arches, the **Porte St-Denis** and **Porte St-Martin**, which were erected to commemorate his military victories.

★ Grand Rex

1 bd Poissonnière, 2nd (www.legrandrex.com). M° Bonne Nouvelle. **Tour** *Les Etoiles du Rex* every 5mins 10am-7pm Wed-Sun; daily during school hols. **Admission** €10; €8.50 reductions. **Credit** AmEx, MC, V. **Map** p402 J4. Opened in 1932, this huge art deco cinema (*see also p268*) was designed by Auguste Bluysen with fantasy Hispanic interiors by US designer John Eberson. Go behind the scenes in the crazy 50-minute Etoiles du Rex guided tour, which includes

Grand Rex.

a presentation about the construction of the auditorium and a visit to the projection room, complete with nerve-jolting Sensurround effects.

Hôtel Drouot

9 rue Drouot, 9th (01.48.00.20.20, www.drouot.fr). Mº Richelieu Drouot. **Open** 11am-6pm Mon-Sat. **Auctions** 2pm Mon-Sat. **Map** p402 H3.
A spiky aluminium-and-marble concoction is the unlikely location for France's second largest art market. Inside, escalators take you up to a number of small salerooms, where everything from medieval manuscripts and antique furniture to oriental arts, modern paintings, posters, jewellery and fine wines might be up for sale. Details of forthcoming auctions are published in the weekly *Gazette de l'Hôtel Drouot*, sold at various newsstands around the city. Not as daunting as it might seem, an afternoon at Drouot can be great fun, even if you don't fancy spending. On the day before the auction (and on the morning itself), drool over the objects for sale, then come back for the show (usually 2pm). Anyone can take part; and you don't have to sign up beforehand. Neither do you have to worry about sneezing or scratching your head – it's the role of Drouot's *commissaires des ventes* (auctioneers) to distinguish a real bid from nose twitching. **Other location** Drouot-Montmartre, 64 rue Doudeauville, 18th (01.48.00.20.99).

FREE Porte St-Denis & Porte St-Martin

Rue St-Denis/bd St-Denis, 2nd/10th; 33 bd St-Martin, 3rd/10th. Mº Strasbourg St-Denis. **Map** p402 K4.
These twin triumphal gates were erected in 1672 and 1674 at important entry points to the city as part of Colbert's strategy to glorify Paris and celebrate Louis XIV's victories on the Rhine. They are modelled on the triumphal arches of Ancient Rome. The Porte St-Denis is based on a perfect square with a single arch, bearing Latin inscriptions and decorated with military trophies and battle scenes. Porte St-Martin bears allegorical reliefs of Louis XIV's campaigns.

LES HALLES & SENTIER

In the 1st & 2nd arrondissements.

Les Halles is an ugly nexus of commerce and entertainment, with a massive RER-métro interchange as its centrepiece. The area is undergoing a vast makeover during the next few years, however.

For centuries, Les Halles was the city's wholesale food market. Covered markets were set up here in 1181 by King Philippe-Auguste; in the 1850s Baltard's spectacular cast-iron and glass pavilions were erected. In 1969, the market was relocated to the southern suburb of Rungis. Baltard's ten pavilions were knocked down (one was saved and now stands at Nogent-sur-Marne), leaving a giant hole. After a long political dispute, it was filled in the early 1980s by the miserably designed **Forum des Halles** underground shopping and transport hub, and the unloved Jardin des Halles.

East of the Forum, in the middle of place Joachim-du-Bellay, stands the Renaissance **Fontaine des Innocents**. The canopied fountain has swirling stone reliefs of water nymphs and titans by Jean Goujon (the ones you see today are replicas; the originals are in

Eglise St-Eustache. See p64.

the Louvre). It was inaugurated for Henri II's arrival in Paris in 1549 on the traditional royal route along rue St-Denis. It was moved and reconstructed here when the nearby Cimetière des Innocents, the city's main burial ground, was demolished in 1786, after flesh-eating rats started gnawing into people's living rooms; the bones were transferred to the catacombs.

Pedestrianised rue des Lombards is a beacon of live jazz, with **Sunset/Sunside** (*see p297*), **Baiser Salé** (*see p296*) and **Au Duc des Lombards** (*see p296*). In 1610, King Henri IV was assassinated by a Catholic fanatic named François Ravaillac on nearby rue de la Ferronnerie. Today, the street has become an extension of the Marais gay circuit.

The ancient, easternmost stretch of rue St-Honoré runs into the southern edge of Les Halles. The Fontaine du Trahoir stands at the corner with rue de l'Arbre-Sec. Opposite, the **Hôtel de Truden** (52 rue de l'Arbre-Sec) was built in 1717 for a rich wine merchant; in the courtyard on rue des Prouvaires, the market-traders' favourite **La Tour de Montlhéry** (*see p145*) serves up meaty fare through the night. Fashion chains line the commercial stretch of the rue de Rivoli south of Les Halles. Running towards the Seine, ancient little streets such as rue des Lavandiers-Ste-Opportune and rue Jean-Lantier show a different side of Les Halles. Between rue de Rivoli and the Pont Neuf is former department store La Samaritaine, which is due to reopen in 2015 as luxury hotel Le Cheval Blanc. Next door, a former section of it contains the chic **Kenzo** flagship store. From here, quai de la Mégisserie leads towards Châtelet.

Looming over the northern edge of the Jardin des Halles is the massive **Eglise St-Eustache**, with Renaissance motifs inside and chunky flying buttresses outside. At the western end of the gardens is the circular, domed **Bourse de Commerce**. In front of it, an astrological column is all that remains from a grand palace belonging to Marie de Médicis that stood here.

The empire of French designer **Agnès b** (*see p204*) stretches along most of rue du Jour, with outlets such as **Kiliwatch** (*see p207*) clustered along rue Tiquetonne. On rue Etienne-Marcel, the restored **Tour Jean Sans Peur** is a weird Gothic relic of the fortified medieval townhouse of Jean Sans Peur, duke of Burgundy.

Busy, pedestrianised rue Montorgueil is lined with grocers, delicatessens and cafés. Some historic façades remain from when this was an area in which the well-heeled and the working class mingled: **Pâtisserie Stohrer** (no.51, 2nd, 01.42.33.38.20, www.stohrer.fr), founded in 1730 and credited with the invention of the sugary *puits d'amour*; and the golden snail sign in front of **L'Escargot Montorgueil** (no.38, 01.42.36.83.51), a restaurant established in 1832.

All Change at Les Halles

Paris's biggest architectural nightmare is getting a much-needed makeover.

On the night of 4 March 1969, Les Halles' wholesale food market transplanted to the suburb of Rungis, turning the 'belly' of Paris into its 'trou'. Left with a giant hole in the middle of the city, Paris's then mayor, Jacques Chirac, could have done something great with it. But instead he created an urban nightmare – a sprawling underground shopping mall covered with a park that quickly became the haunt of drug dealers and addicts. Now it's Mayor Bertrand Delanoë's turn to put it right.

Eight years of public consultations dragged out the affair, but in 2010 work tentatively began with the laying out of a children's playground. The horrendous, mirror-fronted Willerval pavilions, a pastiche of the old Baltard pavilions housing a variety of public services (music school, library, nurseries), were destroyed the following year and work started on revamping the underground traffic tunnels that alienate pedestrians and cyclists. But the new Les Halles will really start to take shape in 2013, with a revamp of the park

and the building of a canopy over the shopping mall that will allow in natural light and air. The project is due to be completed in 2016.

Despite the hype, though, Parisians seems oddly unexcited by the prospect. Rebuilding something approximating to the old Baltard market pavilions that once covered the site could have restored the heart now lacking in the neighbourhood, as exemplified by the transformation of the iron-framed pavilions at the old La Villette meat market into a space for arts and culture events. As it is, the canopy designed by Patrick Berger and Jacques Anziutti already looks outmoded, with echoes of the Millennium Dome. A larger park is great, but how will it be policed at night? And notwithstanding the addition of a hip hop studio, the five subterranean floors of shopping will remain the preserve of *banlieusards* shooting in on the RER to buy a new pair of trainers and eat fast food. If anti-capitalist looting was ever to start in Paris, Les Halles would be ripe for it.

EXPLORE

Stretching north, bordered by boulevard de Bonne-Nouvelle to the north and boulevard Sébastopol to the east, lies Sentier, the historic garment district, and cocky rue St-Denis, which has long relied on strumpets and strip joints. The grime is unremitting along its northern continuation, rue du Fbg-St-Denis.

Rue Réaumur is lined with striking art nouveau buildings. Between rue des Petits-Carreaux and rue St-Denis is the site of the medieval Cour des Miracles – a refuge where paupers would 'miraculously' regain use of their eyes or limbs. A disused aristocratic estate, it was a sanctuary for the underworld until it was cleared out in 1667.

Sentier's streets buzz with porters shouldering linen bundles, as sweatshops churn out copies of catwalk creations. Streets such as rue du Caire, rue d'Aboukir and rue du Nil reflect the craze that followed Napoleon's Egyptian campaign in 1798 and 1799 – look out too for sphinx heads and mock hieroglyphics at 2 place du Caire.

FREE Bourse de Commerce
2 rue de Viarmes, 1st (01.55.65.55.65). M° Louvre Rivoli. **Open** *tour groups* 9am-6pm Mon-Fri. **Admission** free. **Map** p402 J5.
Housing the Paris chamber of commerce, this trade centre for coffee and sugar was built as a grain market in 1767. The circular building was then covered by a wooden dome, replaced by an avant-garde iron structure in 1809. In his 1831 novel *Notre-Dame de Paris*, Victor Hugo summed up the building thus: '*Le dôme de la Halle-au-Blé est une casquette de jockey anglais sur une grande échelle.*'

FREE Eglise St-Eustache
Rue du Jour, 1st (01.42.36.31.05, www.saint-eustache.org). M° Les Halles. **Open** 9.30am-7pm Mon-Fri; 10am-7pm Sat; 9am-7pm Sun. **Admission** free. **Map** p402 J5.
This barn-like church, built between 1532 and 1640, has a Gothic structure but Renaissance decoration in its façade and Corinthian capitals. Among the paintings in the side chapels are a *Descent from the Cross* by Luca Giordano. *Photos p62.*

FREE Forum des Halles
1st. M° Les Halles/RER Châtelet Les Halles. **Admission** free. **Map** p402 J5.
The labyrinthine mall and transport interchange extends three levels underground and includes the Ciné Cité multiplex cinema and the Forum des Images. Despite an open central courtyard, a sense of gloom prevails. All should change over the next few years, with a new landscaping of the area now underway. *See also p63* **All Change at Les Halles**.

★ Tour Jean Sans Peur
20 rue Etienne-Marcel, 2nd (01.40.26.20.28, www.tourjeansanspeur.com). M° Etienne Marcel. **Open** *Mid Nov-Mar* 1.30-6pm Wed, Sat, Sun. *Apr-mid Nov* 1.30-6pm Wed-Sun. Tour 3pm. **Admission** €5; €3 reductions; free under-7s. *Tour* €8. **No credit cards**. **Map** p402 J5.
This Gothic turret (1409-11) is the remnant of the townhouse of Jean Sans Peur, duke of Burgundy. He was responsible for the assassination of his rival Louis d'Orléans, which sparked the Hundred Years' War and saw Burgundy become allied to the English crown. You can climb the tower.

Tour Jean Sans Peur.

EXPLORE

Champs-Elysées & Western Paris

Culture and consumerism combine in the city's golden triangle.

There seems to be an unwritten law in France that no mention of the capital's most famous thoroughfare can be made without immediately calling it *'la plus belle avenue du monde'*. In truth, it's not especially beautiful and it heaves with cars, crowds and overpriced restaurants at pretty much any time of the day. The hordes aren't here for beauty, though. They're here for the shops, which the avenue, after years in the retail doldrums, now supplies in abundance thanks to an international influx of megabrands such as Banana Republic, Abercrombie & Fitch, and Levi's. Fortunately, in the midst of all

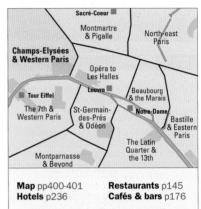

| Map pp400-401 | Restaurants p145 |
| Hotels p236 | Cafés & bars p176 |

Map pp400-401 · Hotels p236 · Restaurants p145 · Cafés & bars p176

this rampant consumerism are a good number of museums covering such cerebral topics as architecture, human evolution and life on the ocean waves, plus a greatly extended Palais de Tokyo that now lays claim to the title of Europe's largest contemporary art centre.

CHAMPS-ELYSEES

In the 8th & 16th arrondissements.

The Champs-Elysées is, and has long been, a symbolic gathering place. Sports victories, New Year's Eve, displays of military might on 14 July – all are celebrated here. Over the past decade, the avenue has undergone a renaissance, thanks initially to a facelift instigated by Jacques Chirac.

Chi-chi shops and chic hotels have set up in the 'golden triangle' (avenues George V, Montaigne and the Champs): **Louis Vuitton** (*see p200*), **Chanel** (*see p196*) and **Jean-Paul Gaultier** (*see p197*), the **Marriott** (70 av des Champs-Elysées, 8th, 01.53.93.55.00) and **Pershing Hall** (*see p239*). The **Four Seasons George V** (*see p236*) has undergone a revamp, and fashionable restaurants such as **Spoon, Food & Wine** (12 rue de Marignan,

8th, 01.40.76.34.44) draw affluent and screamingly fashionable diners. Crowds line up for the glitzy **Le Lido** cabaret (*see p289*), the now commercialised **Queen** nightclub (*see p285*) and numerous cinemas, or stroll down the avenue to floodlit place de la Concorde. The famous **Drugstore Publicis** (*see p192*) is where locals head to stock up on late-night wines and groceries.

This great spine of western Paris started life as an extension to the Tuileries, laid out by Le Nôtre in the 17th century. By the Revolution, the avenue had reached its full extent, but it was during the Second Empire that it became a focus for fashionable society, military parades and royal processions. Bismarck was so impressed when he arrived with the conquering Prussian army in 1871 that he had a replica, the Ku'damm, built in Berlin, and Hitler's troops made a point of marching down it in 1940, as did their Allied counterparts four years later.

Arc de Triomphe.

The lower, landscaped reach of the avenue hides two theatres and elegant restaurants **Laurent** (41 av Gabriel, 8th, 01.42.25.00.39, www.le-laurent.com) and **Ledoyen** (1 av Dutuit, 8th, 01.53.05.10.01, www.ledoyen.com), housed in fancy Napoleon III pavilions. At the Rond-Point des Champs-Elysées, no.7 (now the Artcurial gallery bookshop and auction house) and no.9 give visitors some idea of the magnificent mansions that once lined the avenue. From here on, it's platinum cards and lanky women aplenty, as avenue Montaigne rolls out a full deck of fashion houses.

Models and magnates nibble on the terrace at fashionable restaurant **L'Avenue** (no.41, 8th, 01.40.70.14.91, www.avenue-restaurant.com). You can admire the lavish **Hôtel Plaza Athénée** (*see p237*) and Auguste Perret's innovative 1911-13 **Théâtre des Champs-Elysées** concert hall (*see p304*), with an auditorium painted by Maurice Denis.

South of the avenue, the glass-domed **Grand Palais** and Petit Palais, both built for the 1900 Exposition Universelle and still used for major art exhibitions, create a magnificent vista across the Pont Alexandre III to Les Invalides. The rear wing of the Grand Palais, opening on to avenue Franklin-D-Roosevelt, contains **Palais de la Découverte** science museum.

To the north lie more smart shops, antiques dealers and bastions of officialdom; on circular place Beauvau, wrought-iron gates herald the Ministry of the Interior. The 18th-century Palais de l'Elysée, the official presidential residence, is at 55-57 rue du Fbg-St-Honoré. Nearby, with gardens extending to avenue Gabriel, are the palatial **British Embassy** and ambassadorial residence, which was once the Hôtel Borghèse.

The western end of the Champs-Elysées is dominated by the **Arc de Triomphe**

towering above place Charles-de-Gaulle, also known as L'Etoile. Built by Napoleon, the arch was modified to celebrate the Revolutionary armies. From the top, visitors can gaze over the square (commissioned later by Haussmann), with 12 avenues radiating out in all directions.

South of the arch, avenue Kléber leads to the monumental buildings and terraced gardens of the panoramic Trocadéro, now housing the aquarium and cinema, **Cinéaqua**. The vast 1930s **Palais de Chaillot** dominates the hill and houses four museums, plus the **Théâtre National de Chaillot** (*see p310*).

To the west of Chaillot, on avenue du Président-Wilson, are two major museums: the **Musée d'Art Moderne de la Ville de Paris** and the **Palais de Tokyo: Site de Création Contemporaine** are both inside the **Palais de Tokyo** building. Up the hill at place d'Iéna are the Asian and oriental art collections of the **Musée National des Arts Asiatiques – Guimet**.

Towards the Champs-Elysées, the former townhouse of avant-garde patron Marie-Laure de Noailles has been given a cheeky revamp. It now houses the **Galerie-Musée Baccarat**.

★ Arc de Triomphe

Pl Charles-de-Gaulle (access via underpass), 8th (01.55.37.73.77). M° Charles de Gaulle Etoile. **Open** *Oct-Mar* 10am-10.30pm daily. *Apr-Sept* 10am-11pm daily. **Admission** €9.50; €6 reductions; free under-18s, under-26s (EU citizens). PMP. **Credit** AmEx, MC, V. **Map** p400 C3. The Arc de Triomphe is the city's second most iconic monument after the Eiffel Tower – older, shorter, but far more symbolically important: indeed, the island on which it stands, in the centre of the vast traffic junction of l'Etoile, is the nearest thing to sacred ground in all of secular France, indelibly associated as it is with two of French history's greatest men – Napoleon and Charles de Gaulle. Despite such grand associations, until recently the interior of the Arc was far less impressive, having changed little since the 1930s. But now, after a revamp by architect Christophe Girault and artist Maurice Benayouna, there is an impressive museum with interactive screens allowing visitors to look at other famous arches throughout Europe and the world, as well as displays exploring the Arc's tumultuous 200-year history. But the main reason to head up here is the rooftop view, one of the finest in the city.

🆓 Cimetière de Passy

2 rue du Commandant-Schloesing, 16th (01.53.70.40.80). M° Trocadéro. **Open** *16 Mar-5 Nov* 8am-5.30pm Mon-Fri; 8.30am-5.30pm Sat; 9am-5.30pm Sun. *6 Nov-15 Mar* 8am-6pm Mon-Fri; 8.30am-6pm Sat; 9am-6pm Sun. **Admission** free. **Map** p400 B5.

Since 1874, this cemetery has been one of the most desirable Paris locations in which to be laid to rest. Here you'll find Debussy and Fauré, Manet and his sister-in-law Berthe Morisot, writer Giraudoux, along with various generals and politicians.

★ Cinéaqua

2 av des Nations Unies, 16th (01.40.69.23.23, www.cineaqua.com). M° Trocadéro. **Open** 10am-7pm daily. **Admission** €19.50; €12.90-€15.50 reductions; free under-3s. **Credit** MC, V. **Map** p400 B5.

This aquarium and three-screen cinema is a wonderful attraction and a key element in the renaissance of the once moribund Trocadéro. Children in particular love the shark tunnel and the petting pool (*bassin de caresses*) where you can stroke friendly sturgeon. Also interesting (though less theatrical) is the section on the River Seine, showing the sorts of

Tokyo Rebirth

The expanded Palais de Tokyo art space is still pushing the boundaries.

Paris's most happening art space since it opened in 2002, the **Palais de Tokyo** (*see p70*) has now virtually tripled in size to become the largest contemporary art centre in Europe. The organisation is known for its highly international approach, and for blurring boundaries between art, music, science and politics – as well as for its artist-designed Tokyo Eat restaurant and Black Block shop. Architects Lacaton & Vassal, who transformed the 1937 building in 2002, employing a deliberately raw, distressed style (as much for budget reasons as aesthetics), have now tackled the vast remaining spaces, many of them unused for over 30 years. And it's symbolic that the Triennale, previously held in the Grand Palais, has moved here, under art director Okwui Enwezor.

Some people fear that the extension heralds the museification of the Palais de Tokyo – that it will lose its contemporaneity and spirit of independence as it becomes part of the big state machine, with shows by established and 'mid-generation' artists and an express mission to promote French art. However, new president Jean de Loisy argues: 'True to its genetic code, the Palais de Tokyo above all supports the most experimental, the newest and the most intense artists, whatever their age.'

Last autumn saw a group show, 'Imaginary Detours', and a solo show by Fabrice Hyber, in a rhythm where large exhibitions are punctuated by *modules*

(small exhibitions by emerging artists) and *alertes*, where artists react to current events at short notice. 'This is not an institution preoccupied by art history but a laboratory experimenting with the best of our time, when art is impregnated by and sometimes revises the boundaries of other disciplines,' says de Loisy. Perhaps not so much the organised shelves of a laboratory as the hubble bubble of an artistic cauldron.

EXPLORE

fish that still survive in Paris's river despite the pollution. Many people baulk at the admission fee, but you can easily spend a long afternoon here, watching cartoons in the cinemas and observing the sealife. On Wednesdays and weekends, there are special children's shows too.

★ Cité de l'Architecture et du Patrimoine
Palais de Chaillot, 1 pl du Trocadéro, 16th (01.58.51.52.00, www.citechaillot.fr). M° Trocadéro. **Open** 11am-7pm Mon, Wed, Fri-Sun; 11am-9pm Thur. **Admission** €8; €5 reductions; free under-18s, under-26s (EU citizens). **Credit** MC, V. **Map** p400 B5.

Opened in 2007, this architecture and heritage museum impresses principally by its scale. The expansive ground floor is filled with life-size mock-ups of cathedral façades and heritage buildings, and interactive screens place the models in context. Upstairs, darkened rooms house full-scale copies of medieval and Renaissance murals and stained-glass windows. The highlight of the modern architecture section is the walk-in replica of an apartment from Le Corbusier's Cité Radieuse in Marseille. Temporary exhibitions are housed in the large basement area.

FREE Fondation d'Enterprise Paul Ricard
12 rue Boissy d'Anglas, 8th (01.53.30.88.00, www.fondation-entreprise-ricard.com). M° Concorde. **Open** 11am-7pm Tue-Sat. **Admission** free. **Map** p401 F4.

The Pastis firm promotes modern art with the Prix Paul Ricard – young French artists are shortlisted by an independent curator for an annual prize.
▶ *The Prix Paul Ricard coincides with FIAC (see p31) each autumn.*

Fondation Pierre Bergé Yves Saint Laurent
3 rue Léonce-Reynaud, 16th (01.44.31.64.31, www.fondation-pb-ysl.net). M° Alma Marceau. **Open** 11am-6pm Tue-Sun (only during exhibitions). Closed Aug. **Admission** €7; €5 reductions; free under-10s. **Credit** AmEx, MC, V. **Map** p400 D5.

When the late Yves Saint Laurent bowed out of designing in 2002, he reopened his fashion house as this foundation, exhibiting Picasso and Warhol paintings with the dresses they closely inspired. Every sketch and every *toile* has been carefully catalogued, and many of Saint Laurent's friends and clients presented the designer with the dresses he created for them. The foundation stages two or three exhibitions every year.

★ Galerie-Musée Baccarat
11 pl des Etats-Unis, 16th (01.40.22.11.00, www.baccarat.fr). M° Boissière or Iéna. **Open** 10am-6pm Mon, Wed-Sat. **Admission** €5; €3.50 reductions; free under-18s. **Credit** *Shop* AmEx, DC, MC, V. **Map** p400 C4.

Philippe Starck has created a neo-rococo wonderland in the former mansion of the Vicomtesse de Noailles. From the red-carpet entrance with a chandelier in a fish tank to the Alchemy room, decorated by Gérard Garouste, there's a play of light and movement that makes Baccarat's work sing. See items by designers Georges Chevalier and Ettore Sottsass, services made for princes and maharajahs, and monumental items made for the great exhibitions of the 1800s.
▶ *If you want to eat at the opulent Le Cristal Room restaurant (01.40.22.11.10), be sure to book.*

Galeries Nationales du Grand Palais
3 av du Général-Eisenhower, 8th (01.44.13.17.17, www.grandpalais.fr). M° Champs-Elysées Clemenceau. **Open** times vary. **Admission** €11-€12; €8 reductions; free under-13s. **Credit** MC, V. **Map** p401 E5.

Built for the 1900 Exposition Universelle, the Grand Palais was the work of three different architects, each of whom designed a façade. During World War II it accommodated Nazi tanks. In 1994, the magnificent glass-roofed central hall was closed when bits of metal started falling off. After major restoration, the Palais reopened in 2005. The space hosts blockbuster exhibitions, from Monet to Hopper.

Mona Bismarck American Center for Art & Culture
34 av de New-York, 16th (01.47.23.38.88, www.monabismarck.org). M° Alma Marceau. **Open** 10.30am-6.30pm Tue-Sat. Closed Aug. **Admission** €7; €5 reductions; free under-12s. **Map** p400 C5.

The Mona Bismarck Foundation supports this Paris cultural centre set in Countess Bismarck's former townhouse across the Seine from the Eiffel Tower. The Foundation puts on an eclectic programme of exhibitions, from Etruscan antiquities to folk art.

FREE Musée d'Art Moderne de la Ville de Paris
11 av du Président-Wilson, 16th (01.53.67.40.00, www.mam.paris.fr). M° Alma Marceau or Iéna. **Open** 10am-6pm Tue-Sun. **Admission** free.

INSIDE TRACK M&S IS BACK

If you're hankering after a thick slice of shortbread or a decent cup of tea, the big news for 2012 was the long-awaited return of **Marks & Spencer** (*see p191*) to the Champs-Elysées after a ten-year absence. And there's more to come, with two much bigger stores set to open in the Paris suburbs in the next few months.

EXPLORE

Temporary exhibitions €5-€11; €2.50-€5.50 reductions; free under-13s. **No credit cards**. **Map** p406 H7.

This monumental 1930s building, housing the city's modern art collection, is strong on the Cubists, Fauves, the Delaunays, Rouault and Ecole de Paris artists Soutine and van Dongen. The museum was briefly closed in May 2010 after the theft of five masterpieces. The €100-million haul netted paintings by Picasso, Matisse, Braque, Modigliani and Léger.

Musée de la Contrefaçon

16 rue de la Faisanderie, 16th (01.56.26.14.03, www.unifab.com). M° Porte Dauphine. **Open** 2-5.30pm Tue-Sun. **Admission** €4; €3 reductions; free under-12s. **No credit cards. Map** p400 A4.

This museum was set up by the French anti-counterfeiting association with the aim of deterring forgers – but playing spot-the-fake with such brands as Reebok, Lacoste and Vuitton is fun for visitors.

Musée Dapper

35bis rue Paul-Valéry, 16th (01.45.00.91.75, www.dapper.com.fr). M° Victor Hugo. **Open** 11am-7pm Mon, Wed, Fri-Sun. **Admission** €6; €4 reductions; free under-26s, all last Wed of mth. **Credit** MC, V. **Map** p400 B4.

Named after the 17th-century Dutch humanist Olfert Dapper, the Fondation Dapper began as an organisation dedicated to preserving sub-Saharan art. Reopened in 2000, the venue created by Alain Moatti houses a performance space, bookshop and café.

★ Musée National des Arts Asiatiques – Guimet

6 pl d'Iéna, 16th (01.56.52.53.00, www.guimet.fr). M° Iéna. **Open** 10am-6pm Mon, Wed-Sun. **Admission** €7.50; €5.50 reductions; free under-18s, under-26s (EU citizens). PMP. **Credit** *Shop* AmEx, DC, MC, V. **Map** p400 C5.

Founded by industrialist Emile Guimet in 1889 to house his collection of Chinese and Japanese religious art, and later incorporating oriental collections from the Louvre, the museum has 45,000 objects from neolithic times onwards. Lower galleries focus on India and South-east Asia, centred on stunning Hindu and Buddhist Khmer sculpture from Cambodia. Don't miss the Giant's Way, part of the entrance to a temple complex at Angkor Wat. Upstairs, Chinese antiquities include mysterious jade discs. Afghan glassware and Moghul jewellery also feature.

Musée National de la Marine

Palais de Chaillot, 17 pl du Trocadéro, 16th (01.53.65.69.69, www.musee-marine.fr). M° Trocadéro. **Open** 11am-6pm Mon, Wed, Thur, Fri; 11am-7pm Sat, Sun. **Admission** *Main collection & temporary exhibitions* €9; €3-€7 reductions. *Main collection* €7; €5 reductions; free under-18s, under-26s (EU citizens). PMP. **Credit** *Shop* MC, V. **Map** p400 B5.

Four centuries of French naval history are outlined in detailed models of battleships and Vernet's series of paintings of French ports (1754-65). There's also an imperial barge, built when Napoleon's delusions of grandeur were reaching their zenith in 1810.

FREE Palais de Chaillot

Pl du Trocadéro, 16th. M° Trocadéro. **Admission** free. **Map** p400 C5.

This immense pseudo-classical building was constructed by Azéma, Boileau and Carlu for the 1937 international exhibition, with giant sculptures of Apollo by Henri Bouchard, and inscriptions by Paul Valéry. The Palais houses the Musée National de la Marine and the Musée de l'Homme (closed for renovation until 2014). In the east wing are the Théâtre National de Chaillot (*see p306*) and the Cité de l'Architecture et du Patrimoine (*see p68*).

EXPLORE

Galerie-Musée Baccarat.

★ Palais de la Découverte

Av Franklin-D.-Roosevelt, 8th (01.56.43.20.21, www.palais-decouverte.fr). M° Champs-Elysées Clemenceau or Franklin D. Roosevelt. **Open** 9.30am-6pm Tue-Sat; 10am-7pm Sun (last entry 30mins before closing). **Admission** €8; €6 reductions; free under-6s. *Planetarium* €3 supplement. **Credit** AmEx, MC, V. **Map** p401 E5. This science museum houses designs dating from Leonardo da Vinci's time to the present. Models, real apparatus and audio-visual material bring displays to life, and permanent exhibits cover astrophysics, astronomy, biology, chemistry, physics and earth sciences. The Planète Terre section highlights meteorology, and one room is dedicated to the sun.

Palais de Tokyo: Site de Création Contemporaine

13 av du Président-Wilson, 16th (01.81.97.35.88, www.palaisdetokyo.com). M° Alma Marceau or Iéna. **Open** noon-midnight Mon, Wed-Sun. **Admission** €8; €6 reductions; free under-18s. **Map** p400 B5.

See p67 **Tokyo Rebirth**.

Picture Perfect

World-class artworks on display at the Pinacothèque.

At place de la Madeleine, renowned for its luxury food boutiques and designer shops, every square metre of real estate is so sought after that you'd never think there'd be room for a large museum. So imagine Paris's surprise when, a few years ago, the Crédit Agricole bank decided to turn its office block at 28 place de la Madeleine into the **Pinacothèque** (*see p71*) – an art museum dedicated to expression through the ages, displaying everything from archaeological finds to contemporary art.

It was a risky move, but one that has ultimately paid off: since opening, the museum has reeled in more than two million visitors by offering a wide variety of artworks rarely shown in France. Artists Roy Lichtenstein, Chaïm Soutine and Jackson Pollock have all had retrospectives, and treasures such as China's Xi'an Dynasty warrior statues and gold from the Incas have been displayed. In short, the Pinacothèque has fast become an appealing option if you can't face the crowds at the Louvre or Musée d'Orsay.

Aside from its world-class exhibitions, the museum (its name derives from *pinacothēkē* in Greek – meaning 'box of paintings') has also recently acquired a building just opposite (at 8 rue Vignon) and an impressive permanent collection of a hundred or so paintings on loan from private collectors. Here you'll find works by artists such as Van Dyck, Monet, Modigliani, Delacroix and Pollock, some of which have never before been hung in a museum space.

It's not just the joy of seeing rare artworks all together that makes the display interesting, it's also the way they are presented: museum director Marc Restellini pays tribute to art collectors (who rarely stick to just one style or era) by abandoning traditional conventions, displaying his collection according to colour, theme or subject, so creating a dialogue between the artworks regardless of when they were painted. You might see, for example, Bouguereau's 'academic' *Beauté Romaine* (1904) alongside Duchamp's 'futurist' *Course de Chevaux* (1910); or 15th-century rabbits by Miquel Barcelo next to 17th-century chickens painted by Carstian Luyckx.

Pinacothèque
28 place de la Madeleine, 8th (01.42.68.02.01, www.pinacotheque.com). M° Madeleine. **Open** 10.30am-6.30pm Mon, Tue, Thur, Sat, Sun; 10.30am-9pm Wed, Fri. **Admission** €10-€22; €8-€18 reductions; free under-12s. **Map** p401 F4. *See p70* **Picture Perfect**.

MONCEAU & BATIGNOLLES

In the 8th & 17th arrondissements.

Parc Monceau, with its wonderful neo-antique follies and large lily pond, lies at the far end of avenue Hoche (the main entrance is on boulevard de Courcelles, the circular pavilion by Ledoux). Three museums capture the extravagance of the area when it was newly fashionable in the 19th century: the **Musée Jacquemart-André**, with its Old Masters, the **Musée Nissim de Camondo** (superb 18th-century decorative arts), and the **Musée Cernuschi** (Chinese art). There are some nice exotic touches too, such as the unlikely red lacquer **Galerie Ching Tsai Too** (48 rue de Courcelles, 8th), built in 1926 for a dealer in oriental art near the wrought-iron gates of Parc Monceau, and the onion domes of the Russian Orthodox **Alexander Nevsky Cathedral** on rue Daru. Built in the mid 19th century, when a stay in Paris was essential to the education of every Russian aristocrat, it is still very much at the heart of an émigré little Russia.

Famed for its stand during the 1871 Paris Commune, the Quartier des Batignolles to the north-east towards place de Clichy is more working class, housing the rue de Lévis market, tenements lining the deep railway canyon and square des Batignolles park, with the pretty **Eglise Ste-Marie-de-Batignolles** looking on to a semicircular square. It's fast becoming trendy, with a restaurant scene to match.

★ FREE Alexander Nevsky Cathedral
12 rue Daru, 17th (01.42.27.37.34, www.cathedrale-orthodoxe.com). M° Courcelles. **Open** times vary. **Admission** free. **Map** p400 D3.
All onion domes, icons and incense, this Russian Orthodox church was completed in 1861 in the neo-Byzantine Novgorod-style of the 1600s, by the tsar's architect Kouzmin, responsible for the Fine Arts Academy in St Petersburg.

FREE Cimetière des Batignolles
8 rue St-Just, 17th (01.53.06.38.68). M° Porte de Clichy. **Open** *16 Mar-6 Nov* 8am-5.45pm Mon-Fri; 8.30am-5.45pm Sat; 9am-5.45pm Sun & public hols. *7 Nov-15 Mar* 8am-5.15pm Mon-Fri; 8.30am-5.15pm Sat; 9am-5.15pm Sun & public hols. **Admission** free.

Parc Monceau. *See p72.*

Squeezed inside the Périphérique are the graves of poet Paul Verlaine, Surrealist André Breton, and Léon Bakst, costume designer of the Ballets Russes.

★ FREE Musée Cernuschi
7 av Velasquez, 8th (01.53.96.21.50, www.cernuschi.paris.fr). M° Monceau or Villiers. **Open** 10am-6pm Tue-Sun. **Admission** free. *Temporary exhibitions* €7; €3.50-€5 reductions; free under-14s. **Map** p401 E2.
Since the banker Henri Cernuschi built a *hôtel particulier* by the Parc Monceau for the treasures he found in the Far East in 1871, this collection of Chinese art has grown steadily. The fabulous displays range from legions of Han and Wei dynasty funeral statues to refined Tang celadon wares and Sung porcelain.

★ Musée Jacquemart-André
158 bd Haussmann, 8th (01.45.62.11.59, www.musee-jacquemart-andre.com). M° Miromesnil or St-Philippe-du-Roule. **Open** 10am-6pm daily (late opening Mon & Sat until 9pm during exhibitions). **Admission** €11; €9.50 reductions; free under-7s. **Credit** AmEx, MC, V. **Map** p401 E3.
Long terrace steps and a pair of handsome stone lions usher visitors into this grand 19th-century mansion, home to a collection of *objets d'art* and fine paintings. The collection was assembled by Edouard André and his artist wife Nélie Jacquemart, using money inherited from his rich banking family. The mansion was built to order to house their art hoard, which includes Rembrandts, Tiepolo frescoes and various paintings by Italian masters Uccello, Mantegna and Carpaccio.
► *The adjacent tearoom (open 11.45am-5.30pm daily), with its fabulous tottering cakes, is a favourite with the smart lunch set.*

EXPLORE

Bois de Boulogne.

★ Musée National Jean-Jacques Henner

43 av de Villiers, 17th (01.47.63.42.73,
www.musee-henner.fr). M° Malesherbes. **Open**
11am-6pm Mon, Wed-Sun (11am-9pm 1st Thur
of mth). **Admission** €5; €3 reductions; free
under-18s, under-26s (EU citizens), all 1st Sun
of mth. **Credit** AmEx, MC, V. **Map** p401 E2.
The Musée National Jean-Jacques Henner traces the
life of one of France's most respected artists, from
his humble beginnings in Alsace in 1829 to his rise
as one of the most sought-after painters in Paris. On
the first floor, Alsatian landscapes and family portraits are a reminder of the artist's lifelong attach-
ment to his native region. What brought the artist
most acclaim (and criticism), however, was his trademark nymph paintings. The museum is set to close
in summer 2013 for renovations.

Musée Nissim de Camondo

63 rue de Monceau, 8th (01.53.89.06.50,
www.lesartsdecoratifs.fr). M° Monceau or Villiers.
Open 10am-5.30pm Wed-Sun. **Admission**
€7.50; €5.50 reductions; free under-18s, under-
26s (EU citizens). PMP. **Credit** AmEx, MC, V.
Map p401 E3.
Put together by Count Moïse de Camondo, this collection is named after his son Nissim, who was
killed in World War I. Moïse replaced the family's
two houses near Parc Monceau with this palatial
residence and lived here in a style in keeping with
his love of the 18th century. Grand first-floor reception rooms are filled with furniture by craftsmen of
the Louis XV and XVI eras, silver services, Sèvres
and Meissen porcelain, Savonnerie carpets and
Aubusson tapestries.

FREE Parc Monceau

Bd de Courcelles, av Hoche, rue Monceau, 8th.
M° Monceau. **Open** *Nov-Mar* 7am-8pm daily.
Apr-Oct 7am-10pm daily. **Admission** free.
Map p401 E2.
Surrounded by grand *hôtels particuliers* and elegant
Haussmannian apartments, Monceau is a favourite
with well-dressed children and their nannies. It was
laid out in the 18th century for the Duc de Chartres
in the English style, with a lake, lawns and a variety
of follies: an Egyptian pyramid, a Corinthian colonnade, a Venetian bridge and sarcophagi. *Photo p71.*

PASSY & AUTEUIL

In the 16th arrondissement.

West of l'Etoile, the extensive 16th
arrondissement is the epitome of bourgeois
respectability, with grandiose apartments and
exclusive residences lining the private roads.
It's also home to some seminal examples of
modernist architecture, plus several of the
city's most important museums. When Balzac
lived at no.47 rue Raynouard in the 1840s,

Passy was a country village (it was absorbed
into the city in 1860) where the rich came to
take cures at its mineral springs – a history
alluded to by rue des Eaux. The novelist's
former abode, **Maison de Balzac**, is open to
the public. The **Musée du Vin** is of interest
if only for its setting in the cellars of the wine-
producing Abbaye de Minimes, destroyed in the
Revolution. Rue de Passy, formerly the village
high street, and parallel rue de l'Assomption,
are the focus of local life, with fashion shops
and *traiteurs*, the department store **Franck
et Fils** (80 rue de Passy, 16th, 01.44.14.38.00,
www.francketfils.fr) and a covered market.

West of the former high-society pleasure
gardens of the Jardin du Ranelagh you'll find
the **Musée Marmottan**, with its superb
collection of Monet's late water-lily canvases,
other Impressionists and Empire furniture.

Next to the Pont de Grenelle stands the circular
Maison de Radio France, the giant home of
state broadcasting, which is currently undergoing
a massive six-year renovation. From here, in
more upmarket Auteuil, you can head up rue
La Fontaine, the best place to find art nouveau
architecture by Hector Guimard, of *métro*
entrance fame. He also designed the less
ambitious nos.19 and 21. At no.96 pay homage
to Marcel Proust, who was born here.

Nearby, the **Fondation Le Corbusier**
occupies two of the architect's avant-garde
houses in square du Dr-Blanche. A little further
up rue du Dr-Blanche sculptor Henri Bouchard
himself commissioned the studio and house that
is now the dusty Atelier-Musée Henri Bouchard.
Much of the rest of Auteuil is private territory,
with exclusive streets of residences off rue

EXPLORE

Chardon-Lagache; the studio of 19th-century sculptor Jean-Baptiste Carpeaux remains, looking rather lost, at no.39 boulevard Exelmans. The top storey was later added by Guimard.

West of the 16th, across the Périphérique, sprawls the parkland of **Bois de Boulogne**. At porte d'Auteuil is the romantic **Jardin des Serres d'Auteuil** and sports venues the **Parc des Princes**, home of football club Paris St-Germain, and **Roland Garros** (for both, *see p312*), host of the French Tennis Open. Another attraction will open in 2013: the **Fondation Louis-Vuitton** (www.fondationlouisvuitton.fr), to be housed in a new Frank Gehry glass construction.

★ FREE Bois de Boulogne
16th. M° Les Sablons or Porte Dauphine.
Admission free.
Covering 865 hectares, the Bois was once the Forêt de Rouvray hunting grounds. It was landscaped in the 1860s, when artificial grottoes and waterfalls were created around the Lac Inférieur. The Jardin de Bagatelle (route de Sèvres à Neuilly, 16th, 01.40.67.97.00) is famous for its roses, daffodils and water lilies, and contains an orangery that rings to the sound of Chopin in summer. The Jardin d'Acclimatation (*see p266*) is a children's amusement park, with a miniature train, farm, rollercoaster and boat rides. The Bois also boasts two racecourses (Longchamp and Auteuil), sports clubs and stables, and restaurants, including the seriously smart Le Pré Catelan (route de Suresnes, 16th, 01.44.14.41.00).

Castel Béranger
14 rue La Fontaine, 16th. M° Jasmin.
Guimard's masterpiece of 1895-98 epitomises art nouveau in Paris. From outside you can see his love of brick, wrought iron and asymmetry, and his renunciation of harsh angles not found in nature. Green seahorses climb the façade; the faces on the balconies are thought to be self-portraits, inspired by Japanese figures, to ward off evil spirits.

Fondation Le Corbusier
Maison La Roche, 8-10 square du Dr-Blanche, 16th (01.42.88.75.72, www.fondationlecorbusier.fr). M° Jasmin. **Open** 1.30-6pm Mon; 10am-6pm Tue-Sat. Closed Aug. **Admission** €5; €3 reductions; free under-14s. **No credit cards.**
Designed by Le Corbusier in 1923 for a Swiss art collector, this house shows the architect's ideas in practice, with its stilts, strip windows, roof terraces and balconies, built-in furniture and an unsuspected use of colour inside: sludge green, blue and pinky beige. A sculptural cylindrical staircase and split volumes create a variety of geometrical vistas; inside, Le Corbusier's own neo-Cubist paintings and furniture sit alongside pieces by Perriand. The adjoining Maison Jeanneret houses the foundation's extensive library.

FREE Le Jardin des Serres d'Auteuil
3 av de la Porte d'Auteuil, 16th. M° Porte d'Auteuil. **Open** *Winter* 10am-5pm daily. *Summer* 10am-6pm daily. **Admission** free.
These romantic glasshouses were opened in 1895 to cultivate plants for Paris parks and public spaces. Today, there are seasonal displays of orchids and begonias. Look out for the tropical pavilion, which is home to palms, birds and Japanese ornamental carp.

FREE Maison de Balzac
47 rue Raynouard, 16th (01.55.74.41.80). M° Passy. **Open** 10am-6pm Tue-Sun. **Admission** free. *Exhibitions* €4; €2-€3 reductions; free under-13s. **Credit** MC, V. **Map** p404 B6.
Honoré de Balzac rented this apartment in 1840 to escape his creditors. Mementos include first editions and letters, plus portraits of friends and the novelist's mistress Mme Hanska. Along with a 'family tree' of his characters that extends across several walls, you can see Balzac's desk and the monogrammed coffee pot that fuelled all-night work on *La Comédie Humaine.*

★ Musée Marmottan – Claude Monet
2 rue Louis-Boilly, 16th (01.44.96.50.33, www.marmottan.com). M° La Muette. **Open** 10am-6pm Tue, Wed, Fri-Sun; 10am-8pm Thur. **Admission** €10; €5 reductions; free under-7s. **Credit** MC, V.
Originally a museum of the Empire period left to the state by collector Paul Marmottan, this old hunting pavilion has become a famed holder of Impressionist art thanks to two bequests: the first by the daughter of the doctor of Manet, Monet, Pissarro, Sisley and Renoir; the second by Monet's son Michel. Its Monet collection, the largest in the world, numbers 165 works, plus sketchbooks, palette and photos. A special circular room was created for the breathtaking late water lily canvases; upstairs are works by Renoir, Manet, Gauguin, Caillebotte and Berthe Morisot, 15th-century primitives, a Sèvres clock and a collection of First Empire furniture.

Musée du Vin
5 square Charles Dickens, Rue des Eaux, 16th (01.45.25.63.26, www.museeduvinparis.com). M° Passy. **Open** 10am-6pm Tue-Sun. **Admission** (with guidebook and glass of wine) €11.90; €9.90 reductions; free under-14s, diners in the restaurant. **Credit** *Shop, restaurant* AmEx, DC, MC, V. **Map** p404 B6.
Here the Confrères Bacchiques defend French wines from imports and advertising laws. In the cellars of an old wine-producing monastery are displays on the history of viticulture, with waxwork peasants, old tools, bottles and corkscrews. Visits finish with a wine tasting and, a paid extra, a meal. The museum is a reminder that, for centuries, Passy was a wine-growing area. Louis XIII used to stop off for a drink here after hunting in the Bois de Boulogne.

EXPLORE

Montmartre & Pigalle

Uphill for romance, downhill for sleaze.

Alas, long gone are the days when Montmartre was a tranquil village packed with windmills and vineyards, although two *moulins* and a small patch of vines do still survive. Today, perched high on the 'Butte' (Paris's highest hill), the area is tightly packed with houses spiralling round the mound below the sugary-white dome of the Sacré-Coeur. Despite the thronging tourists (chiefly around place du Tertre), it remains the most unabashedly romantic district in Paris – a place in which to climb quiet stairways, peer down narrow alleys on to ivy-clad houses, and watch the world go by in atmospheric cafés. At the foot of Montmartre, Pigalle has a reputation as Paris's centre for sleaze. But while peep shows and sex shops do still tout for business on the boulevard de Clichy, a younger, hipper and more wholesome crew also line the pavements nowadays, queuing to get into cool music clubs.

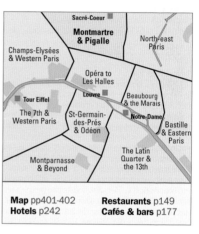

Map pp401-402	**Restaurants** p149
Hotels p242	**Cafés & bars** p177

MONTMARTRE

In the 18th arrondissement.

For centuries, Montmartre was a tranquil village. When Haussmann sliced through the capital during the mid 19th century, working-class families started to move out, and migrants poured into an industrialising Paris from across France. The population of Montmartre swelled. The *butte* was absorbed into the city of Paris in 1860, but remained proudly independent. Its key role in the Commune in 1871, fending off government troops, is marked by a plaque on rue du Chevalier-de-la-Barre.

Artists started to move into the area from the 1880s. Renoir found plenty of subject matter in the cafés and *guinguettes*, while Toulouse-Lautrec patronised the local bars and immortalised its cabarets in his famous posters. Later, it was frequented by Picasso and artists of the Ecole de Paris.

You can start a wander from Abbesses métro station, one of only two in Paris (along with Porte Dauphine) to retain its original art nouveau metal-and-glass awning designed by Hector Guimard. Across place des Abbesses is art nouveau **St-Jean-de-Montmartre** church, a pioneering reinforced concrete structure with turquoise mosaics around the door. Along rue des Abbesses and adjoining rue Lepic, which winds its way up the hill, are food shops, boutiques, wine merchants and cafés, including the ever-popular **Le Sancerre** (*see p178*).

In the other direction from Abbesses, at 11 rue Yvonne-Le-Tac, is the Chapelle du Martyr. According to legend, St Denis picked up his head here after his execution during the third century. Rue Orsel, with a cluster of retro design, ethnic and second-hand clothes shops, leads to place Charles-Dullin, where a few cafés overlook the respected Théâtre de l'Atelier (1 pl Charles-Dullin, 18th, 01.46.06.49.24, www.theatre-atelier.com).

Cimetière de Montmartre. *See p77.*

Up the hill, the cafés of rue des Trois-Frères are popular spots for evening drinks. The street leads into sloping place Emile-Goudeau, whose staircases, wrought-iron streetlights and old houses are particularly evocative of days gone by. The Bâteau Lavoir, a piano factory that stood at no.13, witnessed the birth of Cubism. Divided in the 1890s into a warren of studios for impoverished artists of the day, it was here that Picasso painted *Les Demoiselles d'Avignon* in 1906 and 1907, when he, Braque and Juan Gris were all residents. The building burned down in 1970, but has since been reconstructed.

On rue Lepic, which winds up the hill from rue des Abbesses, are the village's two remaining windmills: the **Moulin Radet**, which was moved here in the 17th century from its hillock in rue des Moulins near the Palais-Royal; and the **Moulin de la Galette**, site of the celebrated dancehall depicted by Renoir (now in the Musée d'Orsay) and today a smart restaurant (www.lemoulindelagalette.eu). Vincent van Gogh and his beloved brother Theo lived at no.54 from 1886 to 1888.

On tourist-swamped place du Tertre at the top of the hill, painters flog lurid sunset views of Paris or offer (sometimes aggressively) to draw your portrait; nearby **Espace Dalí** (11 rue Poulbot, 18th, 01.42.64.40.10, www. daliparis.com) has rather more illustrious art. Round here, so legend has it, the bistro concept was born in the early 1800s, when Russian soldiers shouted '*Bistro!*' ('Quickly!') to be served. Just off the square is **St-Pierre-de-Montmartre**, the oldest church in the district, with columns that have bent with age. Founded by Louis VI in 1133, it's an example of early Gothic, in contrast to its extravagant mock Romano-Byzantine neighbour, the Sacré-Coeur.

For all its kitsch and swarms of tourists, **Sacré-Coeur** is well worth the visit for its 19th-century excess. Rather than the main steps, take the staircase down rue Maurice-Utrillo to pause on a café terrace on the small square at the top of rue Muller, or wander down through the adjoining park to the Halle St-Pierre. The old covered market is now used for shows of naïve art, but the surrounding square and streets, known as the **Marché St-Pierre**, are packed with fabric shops.

On the north side of place du Tertre in rue Cortot is the quiet 17th-century manor that houses the **Musée de Montmartre**, dedicated to the neighbourhood and its famous former inhabitants. Dufy, Renoir and Utrillo all used

INSIDE TRACK
DALIDA'S MONTMARTRE

During her 30-year career, Egyptian-born icon Dalida recorded more than 1,000 songs, scoring 45 gold records and two platinum albums, before committing suicide in the late 1980s. Much of the Dalida myth is rooted in Montmartre: she lived in the 'Castle of Sleeping Beauty', a four-storey house on rue d'Orchampt; place Dalida is graced by a bronze bust of the idol; and her grave in the Montmartre cemetery is a place of pilgrimage.

My museum in Paris...

to have studios in the entrance pavilion. Nearby in rue des Saules is the Montmartre vineyard, planted by local artist Poulbot in 1933 in commemoration of the vines that once covered the area. The grape harvest here every autumn is a local highlight, celebrated with great pomp. Further down the hill, among rustic, shuttered houses, is the cabaret **Au Lapin Agile** (*see p290*). This old artists' meeting point got its name from André Gill, who painted the inn sign of a rabbit (the 'lapin à Gill').

A series of squares leads to rue Caulaincourt, crossing the **Cimetière de Montmartre** (enter on avenue Rachel, reached by stairs from rue Caulaincourt or place de Clichy). A stone's throw south of here is the pocket-sized *chanson* venue **Les Trois Baudets** (*see p294*), which saw the Paris debuts of Brel, Brassens, Vian, Gainsbourg, Gréco and others. Winding down the back of the hill, avenue Junot is lined with exclusive residences, such as the avant-garde house built by Adolf Loos for poet Tristan Tzara at no.15, exemplifying his Modernist maxim: 'Ornament is crime.'

★ FREE Cimetière de Montmartre

20 av Rachel, access by staircase from rue Caulaincourt, 18th (01.53.42.36.30). Mº Blanche or Place de Clichy. **Open** *6 Nov-15 Mar* 8am-5.30pm Mon-Fri; 8.30am-5.30pm Sat; 9am-5.30pm Sun & public holidays. *16 Mar-5 Nov* 8am-6pm Mon-Fri; 8.30am-6pm Sat; 9am-6pm Sun & public holidays. **Admission** free. **Map** p401 G1.
Truffaut, Nijinsky, Berlioz, Degas, Offenbach and German poet Heine are all buried here. So, too, are La Goulue, the first great cancan star and model for Toulouse-Lautrec, celebrated local beauty Mme Récamier, and the consumptive heroine Alphonsine Plessis, inspiration for Dumas's *La Dame aux Camélias* and Verdi's *La Traviata*. Flowers are still left on the grave of pop diva and gay icon Dalida, who lived on nearby rue d'Orchampt. *Photo p75.*
▶ *For a review of celebrity-filled Père-Lachaise cemetery, see p88.*

Musée d'Art Halle St-Pierre

2 rue Ronsard, 18th (01.42.58.72.89, www.halle saintpierre.org). Mº Anvers. **Open** *Jan-July, Sept-Dec* 10am-6pm Mon-Fri; 10am-7pm Sat; 11am-6pm Sun; *Aug* noon-6pm Mon-Fri. **Admission** prices vary. **Credit** *Shop* MC, V. **Map** p402 J2.
The former covered market in the shadow of Sacré-Coeur specialises in *art brut*, *art outsider* and *art singulier* from its own and other collections.

Musée de Montmartre

12 rue Cortot, 18th (01.49.25.89.37, www. museedemontmartre.fr). Mº Anvers or Lamarck-Caulaincourt. **Open** 10am-6pm daily. **Admission** €8; €4-€6 reductions; free under-10s. **Credit** *Shop* MC, V. **Map** p402 H1.

Sacré-Coeur.

At the back of a garden, this 17th-century manor displays the history of the hilltop, with rooms devoted to composer Gustave Charpentier and a tribute to the Lapin Agile cabaret, with original Toulouse-Lautrec posters. There are paintings by Suzanne Valadon, who had a studio above the entrance pavilion, as did Renoir, Raoul Dufy and Valadon's son Maurice Utrillo. The museum's three gardens have just been renovated and make a delightful place for a contemplative stroll away from the tourist bustle of Montmartre.

★ FREE Sacré-Coeur

35 rue du Chevalier-de-la-Barre, 18th (01.53.41.89.00, www.sacre-coeur-montmartre.com). Mº Abbesses or Anvers. **Open** *Basilica* 6am-11pm daily. *Crypt & dome Winter* 10am-5.45pm daily. *Summer* 9am-6.45pm daily. **Admission** free. *Crypt & dome* €5. **Credit** MC, V. **Map** p402 J1.
Work on this enormous mock Romano-Byzantine edifice began in 1877. It was commissioned after the nation's defeat by Prussia in 1870, voted for by the Assemblée Nationale and built from public subscrip-tion. Finally completed in 1914, it was consecrated in 1919 – by which time a jumble of architects had suc-ceeded Paul Abadie, winner of the original competi-tion. The interior boasts lavish mosaics, including 'Christ in Majesty' in the apse – one of the world's largest. It sits atop Paris's highest point, and the views are as heavenly as the surroundings.

La Goutte d'Or

The area north of Barbès Rochechouart métro station was the backdrop for Zola's *L'Assommoir*, his novel set among the district's laundries and absinthe cafés. Today, heroin has replaced absinthe as the means of escape.

La Goutte d'Or is primarily an African and Arab neighbourhood, and can seem like a slice of the Middle East or a state under perpetual siege owing to the frequent police raids. Down rue Doudeauville, you'll find lively ethnic music shops; rue Polonceau contains African grocers and Senegalese restaurants. Mayor Delanöe has tried to attract young designers to the area by designating rue des Gardes 'rue de la mode', and square Léon is the focus for La Goutte d'Or en Fête in June, which brings together local musicians. Some of them, such as Africando and the Orchestre National de Barbès, have become well known across the capital. A market sets up under the métro tracks along boulevard de la Chapelle on Monday, Wednesday and Saturday mornings, with stalls selling exotic vegetables and rolls of African fabrics.

Further north, at porte de Clignancourt, is the city's largest flea market, the Marché aux Puces de St-Ouen (*see p222*), which teems with 3,000 traders and up to 180,000 bargain-hunters each weekend.

PIGALLE

In the 9th arrondissement.

In the 1890s, Toulouse-Lautrec's posters of Jane Avril at the Divan Japonais, Chat Noir and Moulin Rouge, and of *chanson* star Aristide Bruant, were landmarks of art and advertising and immortalised Pigalle's cabarets. It's still a happening area: Le Divan Japonais is now **Le Divan du Monde** (*see p283*), a club and music venue; a hip young crowd packs into **La Fourmi** (*see p177*) opposite; and up the hill, there's a cluster of *atelier*-boutiques where designers have set up their sewing machines at the back of the shop.

Along the boulevard, behind its bright red windmill, the **Moulin Rouge** (*see p289*), once the image of naughty 1890s Paris, is now a

cheesy tourist draw. Its befeathered dancers still cancan and cavort across the stage, but are no substitute for La Goulue and Joseph Pujol – *le pétomane* who could pass wind melodically. In stark contrast is the **Cité Véron** next door, a cobbled alley with a small theatre and cottagey buildings.

Musée de l'Erotisme

72 bd de Clichy, 18th (01.42.58.28.73, www. musee-erotisme.com). M° Blanche. **Open** 10am-2am daily. **Admission** €10; €8 reductions. **Credit** MC, V. **Map** p401 H2.

Seven floors of erotic art and artefacts amassed by collectors Alain Plumey and Joseph Khalif. The first three run from first-century Peruvian phallic pottery through Etruscan fertility symbols to Yoni sculptures from Nepal; the fourth gives a history of Paris brothels; and the refurbished top floors host exhibitions of modern erotic art.

La Nouvelle Athènes

Just south of Pigalle and east of rue Blanche lies this often overlooked quarter, dubbed the New Athens when it was colonised by a wave of artists, writers and composers in the early 19th century. Long-forgotten actresses and *demi-mondaines* had mansions built here; some are set in tiny rue de la Tour-des-Dames, which refers to one of the many windmills owned by Couvent des Abbesses. To glimpse more of these miniature palaces, wander through the adjoining streets and passageways.

Just off rue Taitbout is square d'Orléans, a remarkable housing estate that was built in 1829 by the English architect Edward Cresy. These flats and studios attracted the glitterati of the day, including George Sand and her lover Chopin. In the house built for Dutch painter Ary Scheffer in nearby rue Chaptal, the **Musée de la Vie Romantique** displays many of Sand's mementos.

The **Musée National Gustave Moreau** on rue de La Rochefoucauld is reason alone to visit, featuring the artist's apartment and magnificent studio. Fragments of bohemia can still be gleaned in the area, although the Café La Roche, where Moreau met Degas for drinks and rows, has been downsized to **Café Matisse** (57 rue Notre-Dame-de-Lorette, 9th, 01.53.16.44.58). Degas painted most of his memorable ballet scenes in rue Frochot, and Renoir hired his first proper studio at 35 rue St-Georges. A few streets away in Cité Pigalle, a collection of studios, is van Gogh's last Paris house (no.5), from where he moved out to Auvers-sur-Oise. There is a plaque here, but nothing marks the building in rue Pigalle where Toulouse-Lautrec slowly drank himself to an early grave.

EXPLORE

The area around the neoclassical **Eglise Notre-Dame-de-Lorette** was built up in Louis-Philippe's reign and was famous for its courtesans or *lorettes*, elegant ladies named after their haunt of rue Notre-Dame-de-Lorette. In 1848, Gauguin was born at no.56; from 1844 to 1857, Delacroix had a studio at no.58.

The lower stretch of rue des Martyrs is packed with tempting food shops, and a little further up the hill you should look out for the prosperous residences of the Cité Malesherbes and avenue Trudaine. The circular place St-Georges was home to the true Empress of Napoleon III's Paris: the Russian-born Madame Païva. She lived in the neo-Renaissance no.28, thought to be outrageous at the time of its construction. La Païva shot herself after a passionate affair with the millionaire cousin of Chancellor Bismarck.

★ Musée National Gustave Moreau

14 rue de La Rochefoucauld, 9th (01.48.74.38.50, www.musee-moreau.fr). M° Trinité. **Open** 10am-12.45pm, 2-5.15pm Mon, Wed, Thur; 10am-5.15pm Fri-Sun. **Admission** €5; €3 reductions; free under-18s, under-26s (EU citizens), all 1st Sun of mth. PMP. **Credit** MC, V. **Map** p401 G3.

This wonderful museum combines the small private apartment of Symbolist painter Gustave Moreau (1825-98) with the vast gallery he built to display his work – set out as a museum by the painter himself, and opened in 1903. Downstairs shows his obsessive collector's nature with family portraits, Grand Tour souvenirs and a boudoir devoted to the object of his unrequited love, Alexandrine Durem. Upstairs is Moreau's fantasy realm, which plunders Greek mythology and biblical scenes for canvases filled with writhing maidens, trance-like visages, mystical beasts and strange plants.

▶ *Printed on boards that you can carry around the museum are the artist's lengthy, rhetorical and mad commentaries.*

FREE Musée de la Vie Romantique

Hôtel Scheffer-Renan, 16 rue Chaptal, 9th (01.55.31.95.67, www.vie-romantique.paris.fr). M° Blanche or St-Georges. **Open** 10am-6pm Tue-Sun. *Tearoom* mid Apr-mid Oct 11.30am-5.30pm Tue-Sun. **Admission** free. *Exhibitions* prices vary. **Credit** AmEx, DC, MC, V. **Map** p401 G2.

When Dutch artist Ary Scheffer lived in this small villa, the area teemed with composers, writers and artists. Aurore Dupin, Baronne Dudevant (George Sand) was a guest at Scheffer's soirées, along with great names such as Chopin and Liszt. The museum is devoted to Sand, although the watercolours, lockets, jewels and plastercast of her right arm that she left behind reveal little of her ideas or affairs.

Musée de l'Erotisme.

EXPLORE

Beaubourg & the Marais

Modern art, medieval architecture and modish magasins.

For the last two decades the Marais (sandwiched between St-Paul and République) has been one of the hippest parts of the city, packed with modish hotels, vintage boutiques, restaurants and bars – in no small part due to its popularity with the gay crowd (this is the only part of Paris where the blokes get winked at more than the ladies). But it's also prime territory for art-lovers, with a vast concentration of art galleries and museums, more often than not set in aristocratic 18th-century mansions spared by Haussmann. The Marais has also long been the focus of the Jewish community: amble along rue des Rosiers, rue des Ecouffes and rue Pavée (where there's a synagogue designed by Guimard, the brains behind Paris's iconic métro stations) and the air fills with the scent of falafels and sizzling shawarmas, sold in their hundreds from stalwarts Chez Hannah and L'As du Falafel. The Marais' neighbour to the west is Beaubourg, the focal point of which is the iconic Centre Pompidou, with the city's all-important Hôtel de Ville a stone's throw to the south.

Map p406	**Restaurants** p151
Hotels p244	**Cafés & bars** p178

BEAUBOURG & HOTEL DE VILLE

In the 4th arrondissement.

Modern architecture in Paris took off with the **Centre Pompidou**, a benchmark of inside-out high tech designed by Richard Rogers and Renzo Piano that's as much an attraction as the **Musée National d'Art Moderne** within. The piazza outside attracts all manner of street performers and artists; the reconstructed **Atelier Brancusi**, left by the sculptor to the state, was moved here from the 15th arrondissement.

On the other side of the piazza, rue Quincampoix houses galleries, bars and cobbled passage Molière. Beside the Centre Pompidou is place Igor-Stravinsky and the Fontaine Stravinsky – full of spraying kinetic fountains,

and a colourful snake by the late artists Niki de Saint Phalle and Jean Tinguely – as well as the red-brick **IRCAM** music institute (*see p302*), also designed by Renzo Piano.

South of here stands the spiky Gothic **Tour St-Jacques**. Towards the river, on the site of the Grand Châtelet (a fortress put up in the 12th century to defend Pont au Change), place du Châtelet's Egyptian-themed fountain is framed by twin theatres designed by Davioud as part of Haussmann's urban improvements in the 1860s. They're now two of the city's main arts venues: the **Théâtre de la Ville** (*see p304*) and the **Théâtre du Châtelet** (*see p306*).

Beyond Châtelet, the **Hôtel de Ville** (city hall) has been the symbol of municipal power since 1260. The equestrian statue out front is of 14th-century merchant leader and rebel Etienne Marcel. Revolutionaries made the Hôtel de Ville

Centre Pompidou.

their base in the 1871 Commune, but it was set on fire by the Communards themselves and wrecked during savage fighting. It was rebuilt according to the original model, on a larger scale, in fanciful neo-Renaissance style, with knights in armour along the roof and statues of French luminaries dotted all over the walls. The square outside was formerly called place de Grève, after the nearby riverside wharf where goods were unloaded for market. During the 16th-century Wars of Religion, Protestant heretics were burned in the square, and the guillotine stood here during the Terror, when Danton, Marat and Robespierre made the Hôtel de Ville their own seat of government. Today, the square hosts an ice rink every December, and screenings of major sports events. Across the road stands the Bazar de l'Hôtel de Ville department store, or **BHV** (*see p190*).

FREE Atelier Brancusi

Piazza Beaubourg, 4th (01.44.78.12.33, www.centrepompidou.fr). Mº Hôtel de Ville or Rambuteau. **Open** 2-6pm Mon, Wed-Sun. **Admission** free. **Credit** AmEx, V. **Map** p406 K6.
When Constantin Brancusi died in 1957, he left his studio and its contents to the state, and it was later moved and rebuilt by the Centre Pompidou. His fragile works in wood and plaster, the endless columns and streamlined bird forms show how Brancusi revolutionised sculpture.

★ Centre Pompidou (Musée National d'Art Moderne)

Rue St-Martin, 4th (01.44.78.12.33, www.centrepompidou.fr). Mº Hôtel de Ville or Rambuteau. **Open** 11am-9pm (last entry 8pm) Mon, Wed-Sun (until 11pm some exhibitions). **Admission** *Museum & exhibitions* €11-€13; €9-€10 reductions; free under-18s, under-26s (EU citizens), all 1st Sun of mth (museum only). PMP. **Credit** AmEx, DC, MC, V. **Map** p406 K6.
The primary colours, exposed pipes and air ducts make this one of the best-known sights in Paris. The then-unknown Italo-British architectural duo of Renzo Piano and Richard Rogers won the competition with their 'inside-out' boilerhouse approach, which put air-conditioning, pipes, lifts and the escalators on the outside, leaving an adaptable space within. The multidisciplinary concept of modern art museum (the most important in Europe), library, exhibition and performance spaces, and repertory cinema was also revolutionary. When the centre opened in 1977, its success exceeded all expectations. After a two-year revamp, the centre reopened in 2000 with an enlarged museum, renewed performance spaces, vista-rich Georges restaurant and a mission to get back to the stimulating interdisciplinary mix of old. Entrance to the forum is free (as is the library, which has a separate entrance), but you now have to pay to go up the escalators (€3).

The Centre Pompidou (or 'Beaubourg') holds the largest collection of modern art in Europe, rivalled only in its breadth and quality by MoMA in New York. Sample the contents of its vaults (50,000 works of art by 5,000 artists) on the website, as only a fraction – about 600 works – can be seen for real at any one time. There is a partial rehang each year. For the main collection, buy tickets on the ground floor and take the escalators to level four for post-1960s art. Level five spans 1905 to 1960. There are four temporary exhibition spaces on each of these two levels (included in the ticket). Main temporary exhibitions take place on the ground floor, in gallery two on level six, in the south gallery, level one and in the new Espace 315, which is devoted to artists aged under 40.

On level five, the historic section takes a chronological sweep through the history of modern art, via Primitivism, Fauvism, Cubism, Dadaism and Surrealism up to American Color-Field painting and Abstract Expressionism. Masterful ensembles let you see the span of Matisse's career on canvas and in bronze, the variety of Picasso's invention, and the development of cubic orphism by Sonia and Robert Delaunay. Others on the hits list include Braque, Duchamp, Mondrian, Malevich, Kandinsky, Dali, Giacometti, Ernst, Miró, Calder, Magritte, Rothko and Pollock. Don't miss the reconstruction of a wall of André Breton's studio, combining the tribal art, folk art, flea-market finds and drawings by fellow artists that the Surrealist artist and theorist had amassed. The photography collection also has an impressive roll call, including Brassaï, Kertész, Man Ray, Cartier-Bresson and Doisneau.

Level four houses post-'60s art. Its thematic rooms concentrate on the career of one artist or focus on movements such as Anti-form or *arte povera*. Recent acquisitions line the central corridor, and at the far end you can find architecture and design. Video art and installations by the likes of Mathieu Mercier and

EXPLORE

Superior Sandals

Slip into open-toed style at K Jacques.

Those who love clothes and understand style appreciate that if you're up close to Mother Nature, you have to ditch the follies of the fashion spread for something more fit for purpose. But what they also realise is that such restraint doesn't have to mean dowdy clothes. The fashionable in a field rely on 'elemental chic' brands, whose collections usually have some high-tech or artisanal origin and strike the right balance between form and function, but in terms of price point, heritage and celebrity endorsement, bear a reassuring resemblance to the designer brands they wear back in town. So, for example, you might catch the fash pack in Moncler in the mountains, Barbour in the countryside, and if paparazzi shots of Kate Moss on holiday are anything to go by, **K Jacques** (*see p212*) sandals at the beach.

Set up in Saint-Tropez in 1933 by Jacques Keklikian and his wife, the workshop started life stitching basic leather sandals for visitors to the Med resort. The Homère (or Homer), a Greco Roman-style sandal with five horizontal straps across the foot, was, and still is, the signature piece –

Picasso loved them, and over the years they've counted the likes of Colette and Brigitte Bardot among their fans.

Now the company, run by grandson Bernard, offers a range of around 60 styles that subtly reflect the trends of the last 80 years, but remain, in essence, simple, hard-wearing sandals. Examples of each and every style are squeezed into the Marais outpost, where makeshift seating, wooden floors and cramped dimensions make the attempt to find the perfect pair about as comfortable as getting changed in a beach hut.

Dominique Gonzalez-Foerster are in a room devoted to *nouvelle création*. Just an 80-minute TGV ride from Paris, the Centre Pompidou Metz (*see p328* **Moving Masterpieces**) opened in 2010.

FREE Hôtel de Ville
29 rue de Rivoli, 4th (01.42.76.40.40, www. paris.fr). M° Hôtel de Ville. **Open** 10am-7pm Mon-Sat. **Map** p406 K6.
Rebuilt by Ballu after the Commune, the palatial, multi-purpose Hôtel de Ville is the very heart of the city administration, and a place in which to entertain visiting dignitaries. Free exhibitions are held in the Salon d'Accueil (open 10am-6pm Mon-Fri). The rest of the building, which is accessible by weekly guided tours (you need to book in advance), has parquet floors, marble statues, crystal chandeliers and painted ceilings.

Tour St-Jacques
Square de La-Tour-St-Jacques, 4th. M° Châtelet. **Map** p406 J6.
Loved by the Surrealists, this solitary Flamboyant Gothic belltower with its leering gargoyles is all that remains of St-Jacques-La-Boucherie church, which was built for the powerful Butchers' Guild in 1508-22. The statue of Blaise Pascal at the base

commemorates his experiments on atmospheric pressure, carried out in the 17th century. A weather station now crowns the 52m (171ft) tower.

THE MARAIS

In the 3rd & 4th arrondissements.

The narrow streets of the Marais contain aristocratic *hôtels particuliers*, art galleries, boutiques and stylish cafés, with beautiful carved doorways and early street signs carved into the stone. The Marais, or 'marsh', started life as a piece of swampy ground inhabited by a few monasteries, sheep and market gardens. This was one of the last parts of central Paris to be built up. In the 16th century, the elegant Hôtel Carnavalet and Hôtel Lamoignon sparked the area's phenomenal rise as an aristocratic residential district; Henri IV began building **place des Vosges** in 1605. Nobles and royal officials followed, building smart townhouses where literary ladies such as Mme de Sévigné held court. The area fell from fashion a century later; many of the narrow streets remained unchanged as mansions were transformed into workshops, studios, schools and tenements.

Rue des Francs-Bourgeois, crammed with impressive mansions and original boutiques, runs like a backbone right through the Marais, becoming more aristocratic as it leaves the food shops of rue Rambuteau behind. Two of the most refined early 18th-century residences are **Hôtel d'Albret** (no.31), a venue for jazz concerts during the Paris, Quartier d'Eté festival (*see p29*), and the palatial **Hôtel de Soubise** (no.60), the national archives. Begun in 1704 for the Prince and Princesse de Soubise, it has interiors by Boucher and Lemoine and currently hosts the **Musée de l'Histoire de France**, along with the neighbouring Hôtel de Rohan. There's also a surprising series of rose gardens.

Facing the Archives Nationales, the **Crédit Municipal** (no.55) acts as a sort of municipal pawnshop: people exchange goods for cash, and items never reclaimed are sold at auction. On the corner of rue Pavée is the Renaissance Hôtel Lamoignon. Built in 1585, it now contains the **Bibliothèque Historique de la Ville de Paris** (no.24, 01.44.59.29.40). Further up, the **Musée Carnavalet** runs across the Hôtel Carnavalet and Hôtel le Peletier de St-Fargeau.

At its eastern end, rue des Francs-Bourgeois leads into the beautiful brick-and-stone place des Vosges. At one corner is the **Maison de Victor Hugo**, where the writer lived from 1833 to 1848. An archway in the south-west corner leads to the **Hôtel de Sully**, which houses the headquarters of the Centre des Monuments Nationaux. Designed in 1624, the building belonged to Henri IV's minister, the Duc de Sully.

Several other important museums are also found in sumptuous *hôtels*. The Hôtel Salé on rue de Thorigny, built in 1656, was nicknamed ('salty') after its owner, Fontenay, who collected the salt tax. Home to the **Musée National Picasso**, it is currently under restoration until summer 2013. Nearby, the pretty Hôtel Donon, built in 1598, contains the **Musée Cognacq-Jay** and has remarkable 18th-century panelled interiors, and the Hôtel Guénégaud contains the **Musée de la Chasse et de la Nature**.

The Marais has also long been a focus for the Jewish community. Today, Jewish businesses are clustered along rue des Rosiers, rue des Ecouffes and rue Pavée, where there's a synagogue designed by Guimard. Originally made up mainly of Ashkenazi Jews, who fled the pogroms in eastern Europe at the end of the 19th century (many were later deported during World War II), the community expanded in the 1950s and '60s with a wave of Sephardic Jewish immigration after French withdrawal from North Africa.

The lower ends of rue des Archives and rue Vieille-du-Temple are the centre of café life and the hub of the gay scene. Bars such as the **Open Café** (*see p275*) draw gay crowds in the early evening. In their midst, the 15th-century **Cloître des Billettes** at 22-26 rue des Archives is the only surviving Gothic cloister in Paris.

Workaday rue du Temple is full of surprises. Near rue de Rivoli, **Le Noveau Latina** (*see p270*) specialises in Latin American films and holds tango balls in the room above. At no.41, an archway leads into the former Aigle d'Or coaching inn, now the **Café de la Gare** *café-théâtre* (*see p290*). Further north, at no.71, the grandiose Hôtel de St-Aignan, built in 1650, contains the **Musée d'Art et d'Histoire du Judaïsme**. The top end of rue du Temple and adjoining streets, such as rue des Gravilliers, are packed with costume jewellery, handbag and rag-trade wholesalers in what is the city's oldest Chinatown.

The north-west corner of the Marais hinges on the **Musée des Arts et Métiers**, a science museum with early flying machines displayed in the 12th-century chapel of the former priory of St-Martin-des-Champs, and the adjoining Conservatoire des Arts et Métiers. Across rue St-Martin on square Emile-Chautemps, the **Théâtre de la Gaîté Lyrique** reopened in 2011 as a centre for contemporary music and the 'digital arts'.

Despite the Marais' rise to fashion, the less gentrified streets around the northern stretch of rue Vieille-du-Temple towards place de la République are awash with designers on the rise and old craft workshops. Rue Charlot, housing an occasional contemporary art gallery at the passage de Retz at no.9, is typical of the trend. At the top, the **Marché des Enfants-Rouges** (once an orphanage whose inhabitants were attired in red uniforms) is one of the city's oldest markets, founded in 1615.

★ Gaîté Lyrique

3bis rue Papin, 3rd (01.53.01.51.51, www.gaite-lyrique.net). M° Réaumur Sébastapol. **Open** *Box office* 2-8pm Tue-Sat; 2-6pm Sun. **Map** p402 K5.
After a ten-year revamp, the belle époque Gaîté Lyrique theatre, built in 1862, has been turned into Paris's first digital cultural centre; a seven-floor, multi-disciplinary concert hall-cum-gallery that thrusts visitors deep into the realms of digital art, music, graphics, film, fashion, design and video games. After being an haut-lieu of operetta and Russian ballet, it was pillaged by the Nazis, only to become a circus school in the 1970s and a mini-theme park in the 1980s. But this time its multi-million euro interior, which combines the original belle époque foyer with starkly modern spaces by architect Manuelle Gautrand, is set to become a permanent fixture on the cultural scene. There are no fewer than three electronic music concerts each week and around 120 live multimedia performances a year, along with guest appearances by artists, musicians and DJs and film projections. *Photo p84.*

EXPLORE

Gaîté Lyrique. *See p83.*

FREE Maison de Victor Hugo

Hôtel de Rohan-Guéménée, 6 pl des Vosges, 4th (01.42.72.10.16, www.musee-hugo.paris.fr). M° *Bastille or St-Paul.* **Open** 10am-6pm Tue-Sun. **Admission** free. *Exhibitions* prices vary. **Credit** MC, V. **Map** p409 L6.

Victor Hugo lived here from 1833 to 1848, and today the house is a museum devoted to the life and work of the great man. On display are his first editions, nearly 500 drawings and, more bizarrely, Hugo's home-made furniture.

★ Musée d'Art et d'Histoire du Judaïsme

Hôtel de St-Aignan, 71 rue du Temple, 3rd (01.53.01.86.60, www.mahj.org). M° *Rambuteau.* **Open** 11am-6pm Mon-Fri, Sun. Closed Jewish hols. **Admission** €6.80; €4.50 reductions; free under-26s. **Credit** *Shop* MC, V. **Map** p409 K6.

It's fitting that a museum of Judaism should be lodged in one of the grandest mansions of the Marais, for centuries the epicentre of local Jewish life. It sprang from the collection of a private association formed in 1948 to safeguard Jewish heritage after the Holocaust. Pick up a free audio-guide in English to help you navigate through displays illustrating ceremonies, rites and learning, and showing how styles were adapted across the globe through examples of Jewish decorative arts. Photographic portraits of modern French Jews, each of whom tells his or her own story on the audio soundtrack, bring a contemporary edge. There are documents and paintings relating to the emancipation of French Jewry after the Revolution and the infamous Dreyfus case, from Zola's *J'Accuse!* to anti-Semitic cartoons. Paintings by the early 20th-century avant-garde include works by El Lissitsky and Chagall. The Holocaust is marked by Boris Taslitzky's stark sketches from Buchenwald and Christian Boltanski's courtyard memorial to the Jews who lived in the building in 1939, 13 of whom died in the camps.

Musée des Arts et Métiers

60 rue Réaumur, 3rd (01.53.01.82.00, www. arts-et-metiers.net). M° *Arts et Métiers.* **Open** 10am-6pm Tue, Wed, Fri-Sun; 10am-9.30pm Thur. **Admission** €6.50; €4.50 reductions; free under-26s, all 6-9.30pm Thur & 1st Sun of mth. PMP. **Credit** V. **Map** p402 K5.

The 'arts and trades' museum is, in fact, Europe's oldest science museum, founded in 1794 by the constitutional bishop Henri Grégoire, initially as a way to educate France's manufacturing industry in useful scientific techniques. Housed in the former Benedictine priory of St-Martin-des-Champs, it became a museum proper in 1819; it's a fascinating, attractively laid out and vast collection of treasures. Here are beautiful astrolabes, celestial spheres, barometers, clocks, weighing devices, some of Pascal's calculating devices, amazing scale models of buildings and machines that must have demanded at least as much engineering skill as the originals, the Lumière brothers' cinematograph, an enormous 1938 TV set, and still larger exhibits like Cugnot's 1770 'Fardier' (the first ever powered vehicle) and Clément Ader's bat-like, steam-powered Avion 3. The visit concludes in the chapel, which now contains old cars, a scale model of the Statue of Liberty, the monoplane in which Blériot crossed the Channel in 1909, and a Foucault pendulum.
► *Try to time your visit to coincide with one of the spellbinding demonstrations of the museum's old music boxes in the Théâtre des Automates.*

★ FREE Musée Carnavalet

23 rue de Sévigné, 3rd (01.44.59.58.58, www. carnavalet.paris.fr). M° *St-Paul.* **Open** 10am-6pm Tue-Sun. **Admission** free. *Exhibitions* prices vary. **Credit** *Shop* AmEx, MC, V. **Map** p409 L6.

Here, 140 chronological rooms depict the history of Paris, from pre-Roman Gaul to the 20th century. Built in 1548 and transformed by Mansart in 1660, this fine house became a museum in 1866, when

Haussmann persuaded the city to preserve its beautiful interiors. Original 16th-century rooms house Renaissance collections, with portraits by Clouet and furniture and pictures relating to the Wars of Religion. The first floor covers the period up to 1789, with furniture and paintings displayed in restored, period interiors; neighbouring Hôtel Le Peletier de St-Fargeau covers the period from 1789 onwards. Displays relating to 1789 detail that year's convoluted politics and bloodshed, with prints and memorabilia, including a chunk of the Bastille. There are items belonging to Napoleon, a cradle given by the city to Napoleon III, and a reconstruction of Proust's cork-lined bedroom.

★ Musée de la Chasse et de la Nature

Hôtel Guénégaud, 62 rue des Archives, 3rd (01.53.01.92.40, www.chassenature.org). M° Rambuteau. **Open** 11am-6pm Tue, Thur-Sun; 11am-9.30pm Wed. **Admission** €6; €4.50 reductions; free under-18s, all 1st Sun of mth. **Map** p409 K5.

A two-year overhaul turned the three-floor hunting museum from a musty old-timer into something really rather special. The history of hunting and man's larger relationship with the natural world are examined in such things as a quirky series of wooden cabinets devoted to the owl, wolf, boar and stag, each equipped with a bleached skull, small drawers you can open to reveal droppings and footprint casts, and a binocular eyepiece you can peer into for footage of the animal in the wild. A cleverly simple mirrored box contains a stuffed hen that is

Musée Carnavalet

replicated into infinity on every side; and a stuffed fox is set curled up on a Louis XVI chair as though it were a domestic pet. Thought-provoking stuff.

FREE Musée Cognacq-Jay

Hôtel Donon, 8 rue Elzévir, 3rd (01.40.27.07.21, www.paris.fr/musees). M° St-Paul. **Open** 10am-6pm Tue-Sun. **Admission** free. **Map** p409 L6.

This cosy museum houses a collection put together in the early 1900s by La Samaritaine founder Ernest Cognacq and his wife Marie-Louise Jay. They stuck mainly to 18th-century French works, focusing on rococo artists such as Watteau, Fragonard, Boucher, Greuze and pastellist Quentin de la Tour, though some English artists (Reynolds, Romney, Lawrence) and Dutch and Flemish names (an early Rembrandt, Ruysdael, Rubens), plus Canalettos and Guardis, have managed to slip in. Pictures are displayed in panelled rooms with furniture, porcelain, tapestries and sculpture of the same period.

Musée de l'Histoire de France (Musée des Archives Nationales)

Hôtel de Soubise, 60 rue des Francs-Bourgeois, 3rd (01.40.27.60.96, www.archivesnationales.culture. gouv.fr/chan/chan/musee). M° Hôtel de Ville or Rambuteau. **Open** 10am-5.30pm Mon, Wed-Fri; 2-5.30pm Sat, Sun. **Admission** €4-€6; €2-€4 reductions; free under-26s. **Credit** V. **Map** p409 K6.

Documents and artefacts covering everything from the founding of the Sorbonne to an ordinance about umbrellas are displayed in the recently renovated Hôtel de Soubise. Its rococo interiors feature paintings by François Boucher and Carle van Loo.

FREE Place des Vosges

4th. M° St-Paul. **Map** p409 L6.

Paris's first planned square was commissioned in 1605 by Henri IV and inaugurated by his son Louis XIII in 1612. With harmonious red-brick and stone arcaded façades and steeply pitched slate roofs, it differs from the later pomp of the Bourbons. It was called place Royale prior to the Napoleonic Wars, when the Vosges was the first region to pay its war taxes. Mme de Sévigné, salon hostess and letter-writer, was born at no.1bis in 1626. At that time the garden hosted duels and trysts; now it attracts children from the nearby nursery school.

EXPLORE

The St-Paul district

In 1559, Henri II was fatally wounded jousting on today's rue St-Antoine, marked by Pilon's marble *La Vierge de Douleur* in the **Eglise St-Paul-St-Louis**. South of rue St-Antoine is the sedate residential area of St-Paul, lined with dignified 17th- and 18th-century façades. The linked courtyards of Village St-Paul house antiques sellers. On rue des Jardins-St-Paul is the largest surviving section of the fortified wall of Philippe-Auguste (www.philippe-auguste.com), complete with towers.

By St-Paul métro station on the corner of rue François-Miron and rue de Fourcy is the Hôtel Hénault de Cantorbe, renovated and given a minimalist modern extension as the **Maison Européenne de la Photographie**. Down rue de Fourcy towards the river, across a medieval formal garden, you can see the rear of the Hôtel de Sens, a rare medieval mansion built as the Paris residence of the Archbishops of Sens in the 15th century, with an array of turrets. It is home to the **Bibliothèque Forney** (1 rue du Figuier, 01.42.78.14.60, closed Mon & Sun), which holds exhibitions of applied arts and design.

Near Pont Sully are square Henri-Galli, with a rebuilt piece of the Bastille, and the **Pavillon de l'Arsenal**, built by a rich timber merchant to put on art shows, and home to displays relating to Paris architecture.

Winding rue François-Miron leads you back towards the Hôtel de Ville. At 17 rue Geoffroy-l'Asnier, the Mémorial du Martyr Juif Inconnu is being extended as part of the **Mémorial de la Shoah**, a museum, memorial and study centre devoted to the Holocaust that opened in 2005. As you pass no.26, note the Cité des Arts complex of artists' studios, and the ornate lion's head and giant shell motif on the doorway of the 17th-century Hôtel de Châlon-Luxembourg. Rue du Pont-Louis-Philippe contains jewellers, designer furniture and gift shops.

████ Eglise St-Gervais-St-Protais

Pl St-Gervais, 4th (01.48.87.32.02). M° Hôtel de Ville. **Open** times vary. **Admission** free. **Map** p409 K6.

Gothic at the rear and classical at the front, this church also has an impressive Flamboyant Gothic interior, most of which dates from the 16th century. The nave gives an impression of enormous height, with tall columns that soar up to the vault. There are plenty of fine funerary monuments, especially the Baroque statue of Chancellor Le Tellier.

████ Eglise St-Paul-St-Louis

99 rue St-Antoine, 4th (01.42.72.30.32, www.saintpaulsaintlouis.com). M° St-Paul. **Open** 8am-8pm Mon-Fri; 8am-7.30pm Sat; 9am-8pm Sun. **Admission** free. **Map** p409 L7.

This domed Baroque Counter-Reformation church is modelled, like all Jesuit churches, on the Chiesa del Gesù in Rome. Completed in 1641, it features a single nave, side chapels and a three-storey façade featuring statues of Saints Louis, Anne and Catherine – all replacements. The provider of confessors to the kings of France, the Eglise St-Paul-St-Louis was richly endowed until Revolutionary iconoclasts pinched its treasures, including the hearts of Louis XIII and XIV. Afterwards, in 1802, it was converted back into a church, and today it houses Delacroix's *Christ in the Garden of Olives*.

Maison Européenne de la Photographie

5-7 rue de Fourcy, 4th (01.44.78.75.00, www.mep-fr.org). M° St-Paul. **Open** 11am-8pm Wed-Sun. **Admission** €7; €4 reductions; free under-8s, all 5-8pm Wed. **Credit** MC, V. **Map** p409 L6.

Probably the capital's best photography exhibition space, hosting major retrospectives alongside work by emerging photographers. The building, an airy mansion with a modern extension, contains a huge permanent collection.

★ ████ Le Mémorial de la Shoah

17 rue Geoffroy-l'Asnier, 4th (01.42.77.44.72, www.memorialdelashoah.org). M° Pont Marie or St-Paul. **Open** 10am-6pm Mon-Wed, Fri, Sun; 10am-10pm Thur. *Research centre* 10am-5.30pm Mon-Wed, Fri, Sun; 10am-7.30pm Thur. **Admission** free. **Map** p409 K6.

Airport-style security checks mean queues, but don't let that put you off: the Mémorial du Martyr Juif Inconnu is an impressively presented and moving memorial to the Holocaust. Enter via the Wall of Names, where limestone slabs are engraved with the first and last names of each of the 76,000 Jews deported from France from 1942 to 1944 with, as an inscription reminds the visitor, the say-so of the Vichy government. The basement-level permanent exhibition documents the plight of French and European Jews through photographs, texts, films and individual stories: 'The French,' reads one label (captioning is also given in English), 'were not particularly interested in the fate of French Jews at this point.'

████ Pavillon de l'Arsenal

21 bd Morland, 4th (01.42.76.33.97, www.pavillon-arsenal.com). M° Sully Morland. **Open** 10.30am-6.30pm Tue-Sat; 11am-7pm Sun. **Admission** free. **Credit** *Shop* MC, V. **Map** p409 L7.

The setting is a fantastic 1880s gallery with an iron frame and glass roof; the subject is the built history of Paris. Exhibits were previously limited to a few storyboards, maps and photos, and three city models set into the floor (done far more impressively at the Musée d'Orsay), but a brand new permanent exhibition, Paris, a City in the Making, has just opened complete with a 37sq m Google Earth model of the city with four touchscreens to explore the different *quartiers* in delicious digital detail.

EXPLORE

Bastille & Eastern Paris

Revolutionary roundabout.

Place de la Bastille has remained a potent symbol of popular revolt ever since the storming of the grim fortress-prison that kicked off the Revolution in 1789. The square is still a gathering point for demonstrations and Bastille Day festivities, but the only remnants of the prison are found in the métro station underneath. In fact, with its modern opera house, lively market along boulevard Richard-Lenoir, and bobo bars and restaurants, Bastille is positively hip – especially at night when three streets (rue Amelot, rue de la Roquette and rue de Charonne) serve party-crazed Parisians enough drinks to sink the canal boats in the nearby Port de l'Arsenal.

| **Map** pp406-407 | **Restaurants** p153 |
| **Hotels** p247 | **Cafés & bars** p180 |

BASTILLE & FURTHER EAST

In the 11th, 12th & 20th arrondissements.

The area around place de la Bastille was transformed in the 1980s with the arrival of the **Opéra Bastille** (*see p302*), along with a slew of fashionable cafés, restaurants and bars. The present-day square occupies the site of the long-vanished prison ramparts, and is dominated by the Opéra's curved façade. Opened in 1989 on the bicentenary of Bastille Day, the venue remains controversial, criticised for its poor acoustics and design. South of the square is the Port de l'Arsenal marina, where the Canal St-Martin meets the Seine. The canal continues underground north of the square, running beneath boulevard Richard-Lenoir.

Rue du Fbg-St-Antoine has been the heart of the furniture-makers' district for centuries. Showrooms still line the street, though they've been joined by clothes shops and bars. Cobbled rue de Lappe typifies the shift, as the last remaining furniture workshops hold out against theme bars overrun at weekends by suburban youths. Pockets of bohemian resistance remain on rue de Charonne, however, with the **Pause Café** (*see p183*) and its busy terrace, bistro **Chez Paul** (no.13, 11th, 01.47.00.34.57, www.chezpaul.com) and dealers in colourful 1960s furniture. Rue des Taillandiers and rue Keller are a focus for record stores, streetwear shops and fashion designers.

Narrow street frontages hide cobbled alleys, lined with craftsmen's workshops or quirky bistros dating from the 18th century. Note the cours de l'Ours, du Cheval Blanc, du Bel Air (and hidden garden) and de la Maison Brûlée, the passage du Chantier on rue du Fbg-St-Antoine, the rustic-looking passage de l'Etoile d'Or and the passage de l'Homme, with wooden shopfronts on rue de Charonne. This area was originally located outside the city walls on the lands of the Convent of St-Antoine (parts of which survive as the Hôpital St-Antoine). In the Middle Ages, skilled furniture-makers not belonging to the city's restrictive guilds earned the neighbourhood a reputation for free thinking that was cemented a few hundred years later during the Revolution.

Walk Dead Famous

Take a stroll round Père-Lachaise, home to some of France's most creative corpses.

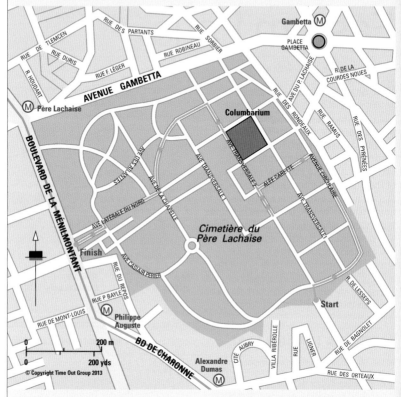

The Cimetière du Père-Lachaise, Paris's largest cemetery, is probably still best known to foreign visitors as the final resting place of one **James Douglas Morrison**, lead singer of the Doors. But ask a local what this 48-hectare site in the 20th arrondissement means to them, and they're more likely to mention the Mur des Fédérés or **Molière** than the Lizard King. On this walk, therefore, you'll pay tribute to the heroes and victims of French political history, and visit the tombs of some of France's greatest writers.

Rather than entering Père-Lachaise by the main entrance on boulevard Ménilmontant, start at the much more discreet gate set into the southern wall of the cemetery on rue de la Réunion,

just off rue de Bagnolet. You join avenue Circulaire, which hugs the cemetery wall. Turn right and then follow the path round until you reach the **Mur des Fédérés** in the south-east corner.

It was here, during the last week of May 1871, that the few remaining partisans of the **Paris Commune** (known as *fédérés* or communards) were lined up against a wall and summarily executed by troops loyal to the National Assembly at Versailles. A memorial procession to the wall, the Montée au Mur des Fédérés, takes place every year in May.

Across the path, in plot or '*division*' No.97, stand a number of memorials to the victims of Nazism and Fascism. Next to an urn containing ashes from the crematorium

EXPLORE

at the Flossenburg concentration camp is a striking ziggurat commemorating people who were 'tortured, gassed, shot or hanged' at Mauthausen. And just behind this loom two enormous manacled hands hewn from stone, a deeply unsettling monument to the women who died at Ravensbrück. A little further along avenue Circulaire, on the same side, is the tomb of people who perished in 1962 at the hands of the police at Charonne métro station, after a demonstration in favour of Algerian independence.

Follow avenue Circulaire along the northern wall until you reach the Jardin du Souvenir. Turn left up avenue Carette, keeping an eye out on your right for the monumental sarcophagus housing the remains of **Oscar Wilde**, who died in Paris in 1900 aged just 46.

When you reach avenue Transversale no.2, turn left and walk down the hill until you reach a bronze effigy of **Victor Noir**, a journalist who was shot by a cousin of Napoleon III in 1870. You'll notice that the effigy depicts Noir with a distinct enlargement in the region of the groin, and also that the area in question appears to have been rubbed down rather energetically: many *parisiennes* have believed that a little *frottage* with Victor would make them fertile.

Now retrace your steps in the direction of the crematorium and columbarium. On your left, in division 86, is the rough-hewn headstone of **Guillaume Appolinaire**. Across the path, **Marcel Proust** lies in an austere tomb with other family members.

Continue along avenue Transversale No.2, until you reach avenue des Thuryas. Turn left and walk down the hill into gently curving chemin Casimir Delavigne. About halfway down on the right is a bronze bust of **Honoré de Balzac**. The bust is accompanied by a bronze book and quill, upon which, on a recent visit, an admirer had left an apple with a heart carved in it.

Walk straight on, down chemin Mont-Louis. Through the trees you'll catch a few tantalising glimpses of the Paris skyline as you head towards avenue Principale, and beyond that the main gate of the cemetery, and the din and traffic of boulevard Ménilmontant.

Further down rue du Fbg-St-Antoine is place d'Aligre, home to a rowdy, cheap produce market, a more sedate covered food hall and the only flea market within the city walls. The road ends in the major intersection of place de la Nation, another grand square. It was originally called place du Trône, after a throne that was positioned here when Louis XIV and his bride Marie-Thérèse entered the city in 1660. After the Revolution, between 13 June and 28 July 1794, thousands were guillotined on the site, their bodies carted to the nearby Cimetière de Picpus. The square still has two of Ledoux's toll houses and tall Doric columns from the 1787 Mur des Fermiers-Généraux. In the centre stands Jules Dalou's sculpture *Le Triomphe de la République*, erected for the centenary of the Revolution in 1889. East of place de la Nation, broad cours de Vincennes has a market on Wednesday and Saturday mornings.

North of place de la Bastille, boulevard Beaumarchais divides Bastille from the Marais. East of place Voltaire, on rue de la Roquette, which heads east towards the Ménilmontant area and **Père-Lachaise** cemetery, a small park and playground marks the site of the prison of La Roquette, where a plaque remembers the 4,000 Resistance members imprisoned here in World War II.

★ FREE Cimetière du Père-Lachaise

Bd de Ménilmontant, 20th (01.55.25.82.10). M° Père-Lachaise. **Open** *6 Nov-15 Mar* 8am-5.30pm Mon-Fri; 8.30am-5.30pm Sat; 9am-5.30pm Sun. *16 Mar-5 Nov* 8am-6pm Mon-Fri; 8.30am-6pm Sat; 9am-6pm Sun. **Admission** free. **Map** p407 P5. *See left* **Walk**.

La Maison Rouge – Fondation Antoine de Galbert

10 bd de la Bastille, 12th (01.40.01.08.81, www.lamaisonrouge.org). M° Quai de la Rapée. **Open** 11am-7pm Wed, Fri-Sun; 11am-9pm Thur. **Admission** €7; €5 reductions; free under-13s. **Credit** MC, V. **Map** p406 M7.
Created by art collector Antoine de Galbert and set in a former printworks, the Red House is an independently run space focusing on contemporary works. Solo shows alternate with themed exhibitions featuring pieces from international collections. The bright on-site café is run by the Rose Bakery team.

BERCY & DAUMESNIL

The **Viaduc des Arts** is a former railway viaduct along avenue Daumesnil; its row of glass-fronted arches enclose craft boutiques and workshops. Above sprout the blooms and bamboo of the **Promenade Plantée**. In 1969, the steam engines on avenue Daumesnil's viaduct whistled their last and the train line

Bois de Vincennes.

between Bastille and Vincennes closed forever. While the Bastille station was replaced by today's opera house, the old lines became a 5km-long trail (the Promenade Plantée), made up of elevated gardens, the Jardin de Reuilly and tree-lined cycling paths.

Start at the Bastille end and climb up one of the staircases from avenue Daumesnil to the elevated gardens for a new perspective of the city. Nosy parkers will be in their element as you can glimpse into people's apartments along the way. You'll also notice architectural features not obvious from ground level, such as the gigantic 1930s-style muses decorating the police station. To make a day of it, pack a picnic and stop in the Jardin de Reuilly or carry on to the Bois de Vincennes with its lakes and parkland.

Eglise du Saint-Esprit is a copy of Istanbul's Hagia Sofia; the nearby **Cimetière de Picpus** contains the graves of many of the victims of the Terror, as well as American War of Independence hero General La Fayette.

Just before the Périphérique, the **Palais de la Porte Dorée** was built in 1931 for the Exposition Coloniale. It features striking, albeit politically incorrect, reliefs on the façade and two beautiful art deco offices. Originally the Musée des Colonies, then the Musée des Arts d'Afrique et d'Océanie (its collections now absorbed by the **Musée du Quai Branly**; *see p130*), it's home to the **Cité Nationale de l'Histoire de l'Immigration**. There's also an aquarium in the basement.

As recently as the 1980s, wine was unloaded from barges at Bercy, but this stretch of the Seine is now home to the vast Ministère de l'Economie et du Budget and, to the west, the **Palais Omnisports de Paris-Bercy** (*see p312*). To the east is the Bercy Expo exhibition and trade centre. In between lie the modern **Parc de Bercy** and the former American

Center, built in the 1990s by Frank Gehry. It now houses the Cinémathèque Française. At the eastern edge of the park is **Bercy Village**, where warehouses have been sympathetically restored and opened as shops and cafés.

★ FREE Bois de Vincennes

12th. M° Château de Vincennes or Porte Dorée.
This is Paris's biggest park, created when the former royal hunting forest was landscaped by Alphand for Baron Haussmann. There are boating lakes, a Buddhist temple, a racecourse, restaurants, a baseball field (*see p314*) and a small farm. The park also contains the Cartoucherie theatre complex (*see p307*). The Parc Floral is a cross between a botanical garden and an amusement park, including Paris-themed crazy golf and an adventure playground. Next to the park stands the imposing Château de Vincennes, where England's Henry V died in 1422.

Cimetière de Picpus

35 rue de Picpus, 12th (01.43.44.18.54). M° Daumesnil, Nation or Picpus. **Open** *15 Apr-14 Oct* 2-6pm Tue-Sun. *15 Oct-14 Apr* 2-4pm Tue-Sun. **Admission** €3. **No credit cards. Map** p407 Q8.
Redolent with revolutionary associations, both French and American, this cemetery in a working convent is the resting place for the thousands of victims of the Revolution's aftermath, guillotined at place du Trône (now place de la Nation) between 13 June and 28 July 1794. At the end of a walled garden is a graveyard of aristocratic French families. In one corner is the tomb of General La Fayette, who fought in the American War of Independence and was married to the aristocratic Marie Adrienne Françoise de Noailles. Clearly marked are the sites of two communal graves, and you can see the doorway where the carts arrived. It was thanks to a maid who had seen the carts that the site was rediscovered, including the cemetery and adjoining convent, founded by descendants of the Noailles family. In the chapel,

two tablets list the names and occupations of the executed: 'domestic servant' and 'farmer' figure alongside 'lawyer' and 'prince and priest'.

★ Cité Nationale de l'Histoire de l'Immigration

293 av Daumesnil, 12th (01.53.59.58.60, www.histoire-immigration.fr). M° Porte Dorée. **Open** 10am-5.30pm Tue-Fri; 10am-7pm Sat, Sun. **Admission** €3-€5; €2-€3.50 reductions; free under-26s. *Aquarium* €4.50-€6.50; €3-€5 reductions. PMP. **No credit cards.**

Set in the stunning, colonial-themed Palais de la Porte Dorée, the collections trace over 200 years of immigration history. There are thought-provoking images (film and photography), everyday objects (suitcases, accordions, sewing machines and so on) and artworks that symbolise the struggles immigrants had to face when integrating into French society. Don't miss the permanent Repères (bearings) exhibition that looks at why many immigrants chose France, the problems they faced upon arrival, and the way sport, work, language, religion and culture can ease integration. One of the most moving areas is the Galerie des Dons – a collection of personal memorabilia donated by individuals whose families came from foreign countries.

FREE Eglise du Saint-Esprit

186 av Daumesnil, 12th (01.44.75.77.50, www.st-esprit.org). M° Daumesnil. **Open** 9.30am-noon, 3-7pm Mon-Fri; 9.30am-noon, 4-6pm Sat; from 9am Sun. **Admission** free. **Map** p407 P9.

Cité Nationale de l'Histoire de l'Immigration.

Behind a red-brick exterior cladding, this unusual 1920s concrete church follows a square plan around a central dome, lit by a scalloped ring of windows. Architect Paul Tournon was directly inspired by the Hagia Sofia cathedral in Istanbul, though the inside is decorated with frescoes rather than mosaics.

Musée des Arts Forains

53 av des Terroirs-de-France, 12th (01.43.40.16.22, www.pavillons-de-bercy.com). M° Cour St-Emilion. **Open** groups only, min 15 people, by appointment. **Admission** €14; €5 reductions. **No credit cards. Map** p407 P10.

Housed in a collection of Eiffel-era wine warehouses is a fantastical collection of 19th- and early 20th-century fairground attractions. The venue is hired out for functions on most evenings, and staff may well be setting the tables when you visit. Of the three halls, the most wonderful is the Salon de la Musique, where a musical sculpture by Jacques Rémus chimes and flashes in time with the 1934 Mortier organ and a modern-day digital grand piano playing *Murder on the Orient Express*. In the Salon de Venise you are twirled round on a gondola carousel; in the Salon des Arts Forains you can play a ball-throwing game that sets off a race of moustached waiters. The venue is open only to groups of 15 or more, but individuals can visit on the occasional guided tours. Call ahead.

FREE Parc de Bercy

Rue de Bercy, 12th. M° Bercy or Cour St-Emilion. **Open** *Winter* 8am-5.30pm Mon-Fri; 9am-5.30pm Sat, Sun. *Summer* 8am-9pm Mon-Fri; 9am-9pm Sat, Sun. **Map** p407 N9/10.

Created in the 1990s, the Bercy park features a large lawn, a grid with square rose, herb and vegetable plots, an orchard, and gardens laid out to represent the four seasons.

FREE Le Viaduc des Arts

15-121 av Daumesnil, 12th (www.viaducdesarts.fr). M° Gare de Lyon or Ledru-Rollin. **Map** p407 M8/N8. Glass-fronted workshops in the arches beneath the Promenade Plantée provide showrooms for furniture and fashion designers, picture-frame gilders, tapestry restorers, porcelain decorators, and chandelier, violin and flute makers.

EXPLORE

North-east Paris

Keeping it real on the streets of Belleville.

In the city's folklore, north-east Paris is working-class Paris – and although patches of it are gentrifying and little actual industry remains, the area still has a distinctive rough and ready vibe. Many of the streets here are somewhat on the tatty side, but others are artsy and fashionable, especially those close to the Canal St-Martin; and large swaths of the north-east – for example rue du Fbg-St-Denis and the thoroughfares leading off it – are excitingly multi-ethnic, with thriving North African, Turkish and Caribbean enclaves. In the top right corner is La Villette (through which the German occupiers entered the city in 1940), with its science museums, wacky gardens and arts space in a building that once housed the city's undertakers.

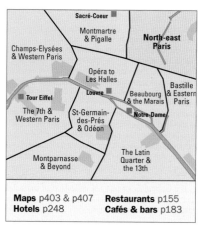

Maps p403 & p407	**Restaurants** p155
Hotels p248	**Cafés & bars** p183

FBG-ST-DENIS TO GARE DU NORD

In the 10th arrondissement.

North of Porte St-Denis and Porte St-Martin, two of the oldest thoroughfares leading out of the city, rue du Fbg-St-Denis and rue du Fbg-St-Martin, traverse an area that was transformed in the 19th century by the railways, when it became the site of the Gare du Nord and Gare de l'Est. The grubby rue du Fbg-St-Denis is almost souk-like with its food shops, narrow passages and sinister courtyards. Garishly lit passage Brady is a surprising piece of India in Paris, full of restaurants, hairdressers and costume shops, whereas the art deco passage du Prado is more a continuation of the Sentier rag trade. Rue du Fbg-St-Martin follows the trace of the Roman road out of the city, and is home to clothes wholesalers, atmospheric courtyards and the ornate Mairie for the tenth. Rue des Petites-Ecuries was once known for saddlers, but now has shops, cafés and jazz venue **New Morning** (*see p297*), and is home to Turkish and Afro-Caribbean communities.

Rue de Paradis is known for its porcelain and glass outlets, and rue d'Hauteville shows traces of the area's grander days (notably the **Petit**

Hôtel Bourrienne, at no.58, a Consulaire-style apartment open to the public). Opposite, the Cité Paradis is an alley of early industrial buildings. At the top of the street are the twin towers and terraced gardens of the **Eglise St-Vincent-de-Paul**. On boulevard Magenta, **Marché St-Quentin**, built in the 1860s, is one of the city's last remaining cast-iron, covered market halls.

Boulevard de Strasbourg was cut through in the 19th century to create a vista up to the Gare de l'Est. At no.2, a neo-Renaissance creation houses the last fan-maker in Paris and the **Musée de l'Eventail**. Towards the station, Eglise St-Laurent (69 bd de Magenta, 119 rue du Fbg-St-Martin, 10th) is one of the city's oldest churches, an eclectic composition with a 12th-century tower, Gothic nave, Baroque lady chapel, 19th-century façade and 1930s stained glass. Between the Gare de l'Est and **Canal St-Martin** are the restored **Couvent des Récollets** and Square Villemin park.

FREE Couvent des Récollets
148 rue du Fbg-St-Martin, 10th. Mº Gare de l'Est. **Admission** free. **Map** p402 L3.
Founded as a monastery in the 17th century when still outside the city walls, this barracks, spinning factory and hospice was a military hospital from 1860 to 1968. Left empty, the convent was squatted

by artists, Les Anges des Récollets, in the early 1990s. The buildings were renovated and reopened in 2004. One half, the Maison de l'Architecture (www.maisonarchitecture-idf.org, open 2-6pm Mon-Fri), hosts a garden café and architectural debates. The other is the Centre International d'Accueil et d'Echanges des Récollets: 85 studios and duplexes for foreign 'creators' – artists and researchers (from painters to neurobiologists) – invited to stay for extended periods. In rehabilitating the building, architect Frédéric Vincendon left traces of its history: the ghostly 17th-century stonework, 20th-century reinforced concrete columns and squatters' graffiti.

★ FREE Eglise St-Vincent-de-Paul

5 rue Belzunce, 10th (01.48.78.47.47, www. paroissesvp.fr). M° Gare du Nord. **Open** 2-7pm Mon; 8am-noon, 2-7pm Tue-Fri; 8am-noon, 2-7.30pm Sat; 9.30am-noon, 4.30-7.30pm Sun. **Admission** free. **Map** p402 K2.
Set at the top of terraced gardens, this church was begun in 1824 by Lepère and completed in 1844 by Hittorff. The twin towers, pedimented Greek temple portico and sculptures of the four evangelists along the parapet are in high classical mode. The interior has a splendid double-storey arcade of columns, murals by Flandrin and church furniture by Rude.

Gare du Nord

Rue de Dunkerque, 10th (08.91.36.20.20). M° Gare du Nord. **Map** p402 K2.
The grandest of the great 19th-century train stations (and Eurostar terminal since 1994) was designed by Hittorff between 1861 and 1864. A conventional stone façade, with Ionic capitals and statues representing towns served by the station, hides a vast iron-and-glass vault. The Gare du Nord is the busiest station in Europe, with more than 550,000 passengers passing through every day.

Musée de l'Eventail

2 bd de Strasbourg, 10th (01.42.08.90.20, www.annehoguet.fr). M° Strasbourg St-Denis. **Open** 2-6pm Mon-Wed (Mon-Fri during school hols). *Children's activities* Wed afternoons. Closed Aug. **Admission** €6; €3-€4 reductions; free under-8s. **No credit cards. Map** p402 K4.
Anne Hoguet keeps the tradition of her ancestors alive in this arcane museum, which has been a fanmaker's *atelier* since 1805. One room houses the tools of the trade; beside it is Hoguet's studio, where she works on fans for fashion and the stage. The former *salle d'exposition*, lined in blue silk, is where the collection of almost 1,000 historic fans is shown.

Petit Hôtel Bourrienne

58 rue d'Hauteville, 10th (01.47.70.51.14). M° Bonne Nouvelle or Poissonnière. **Open** *Guided visits* 1-15 July, Sept noon-6pm daily. Rest of year by appointment Sat. **Admission** €7. **No credit cards. Map** p402 K3.

A rare example of the Consulaire style, this small *hôtel particulier* was built between 1789 and 1798. It was occupied by Fortunée Hamelin, born (like her friend the Empress Josephine) on the French Caribbean island of Martinique, and notorious for parading topless down the Champs-Elysées. A bedroom boudoir painted with tropical birds was her only decoration before the site was taken over by Louis Fauvelet de Bourrienne, Napoleon's private secretary. He had it decorated according to the latest fashion, making sure to keep his political options open (the dining room ceiling is painted with motifs favourable to monarchy and empire).

CANAL ST-MARTIN TO LA VILLETTE

In the 10th & 19th arrondissements.

Canal St-Martin, built between 1805 and 1825, begins at the Seine at Pont Morland, disappears underground at Bastille, hides under boulevard Richard-Lenoir, then emerges after crossing rue du Fbg-du-Temple, east of place de la République. Rue du Fbg-du-Temple itself is scruffy and cosmopolitan, lined with cheap grocers and discount stores, hidden courtyards and stalwarts of Paris nightlife: **Le Gibus**, bar-restaurant **Favela Chic** and vintage dancehall **La Java** (for all, *see p283*), as well as the **Palais des Glaces** (no.37, 10th, 01.42.02.27.17, www.palaisdesglaces.com), which programmes seasons of French comics.

The first stretch of the canal, lined with shady trees and crossed by iron footbridges and locks, has the most appeal. The quays are traffic-free on Sundays. Many canalside warehouses have been snapped up by artists and designers or turned into loft apartments.

East of here, the Hôpital St-Louis was commissioned in 1607 by Henri IV to house plague victims, and was built as a series of isolated pavilions in the same brick-and-stone

---

INSIDE TRACK
THE ART OF EATING

Every month, **104** (*see p94*) opens its doors to Omnivore, a dynamic culinary movement that supports and promotes France's most exciting young chefs. Omnivore selects two chefs each month to concoct themed food nights for around 100 hungry punters. It's a fabulous way to sample contemporary French cooking and it won't break the bank either: four courses and an *apéro* cost just €39. Dates are announced online so check the website (www.omnivore.com).

EXPLORE

104.

the city's main abattoir district (still reflected in the Grande Halle de la Villette and in some of the old meaty brasseries along boulevard de la Villette), the area has been revitalised since the late 1980s by the postmodern **Parc de la Villette** complex, with the **Cité des Sciences et de l'Industrie** science museum and the **Cité de la Musique** concert hall.

★ FREE 104

104 rue d'Aubervilliers, 19th (01.53.35.50.00, www.104.fr). M° Riquet. **Open** noon-7pm Tue-Fri; 11am-7pm Sat, Sun. **Admission** free. *Exhibitions* prices vary. **Credit** AmEx, MC, V.

It's more than a century since Montmartre was the centre of artistic activity in Paris. But now the north of Paris is again where the action is – albeit a couple of kilometres east of place du Tertre, in a previously neglected area of bleak railway goods yards and dilapidated social housing. 104, described as a 'space for artistic creation', occupies a vast 19th-century building on the rue d'Aubervilliers that used to house Paris's municipal undertakers. The site was saved from developers by Roger Madec, the mayor of the 19th, who made its renovation the centrepiece of a massive project of cultural and urban renewal. There aren't any constraints on the kind of work the resident artists do – 104 is open to 'all the arts' – but they're expected to show finished pieces in one of four annual 'festivals'. And they're also required to get involved in projects with the public, the fruits of which are shown in a space next door. The community vibe continues via the onsite café, bookshop and kids' play area. *See also p93* **Inside Track**.

★ La Cité des Sciences et de l'Industrie

La Villette, 30 av Corentin-Cariou, 19th (01.40.05.70.00, www.cite-sciences.fr). M° Porte de la Villette. **Open** 10am-6pm Tue-Sat; 10am-7pm Sun. **Admission** €8; €6 reductions; free under-6s. PMP. **Credit** MC, V. **Map** p403 inset.

This ultra-modern science museum, which first opened in 1986 as Halley's Comet passed overhead, pulls in nearly three million visitors a year. Explora, the permanent show, occupies the upper two floors, whisking visitors through 30,000sq m (320,000sq ft) of space, life, matter and communication: scale models of satellites including the Ariane space shuttle, planes and robots, plus the chance to experience weightlessness, make for an exciting journey. In the Espace Images, try the delayed camera and other optical illusions, draw 3D images on a computer or lend your voice to the *Mona Lisa*. The hothouse garden investigates developments in agriculture and biotechnology.

▶ *The brilliant Cité des Enfants, which spreads across several themed zones and is aimed at under-12s, runs loads of workshops for younger children. See the website for details.*

style as place des Vosges, far enough from the town to prevent risk of infection. Behind the hospital, the rue de la Grange-aux-Belles housed the Montfaucon gibbet, put up in 1233, where victims were hanged and left to the elements. East of the hospital, the lovely cobbled rue Ste-Marthe and place Ste-Marthe have a provincial air, busy at night with multi-ethnic eateries.

North, on place du Colonel-Fabien, is the headquarters of the **Parti Communiste Français**, a modernist masterpiece built between 1968 and 1971 by Brazilian architect Oscar Niemeyer with Paul Chemetov and Jean Deroche. The canal disappears briefly again under place de Stalingrad, a locale best avoided after dark. The square was landscaped in 1989 to showcase the Rotonde de la Villette, one of Ledoux's grandiose 1780s toll houses that once marked the boundary of Paris; it now displays exhibitions and archaeological finds.

Here the canal widens into the Bassin de la Villette, and the new developments along the quai de Loire and further quai de la Marne, as well as some of the worst 1960s and '70s housing in the colossal blocks that stretch along rue de Flandres. At 104 rue d'Aubervilliers, the old municipal undertaker's has been turned into a multimedia art space, **104**.

At the eastern end of the basin is an unusual 1885 hydraulic lifting bridge, Pont de Crimée. Thursday and Sunday mornings add vitality with a market at place de Joinville. East of here, the Canal de l'Ourcq (created in 1813 to provide drinking water, as well as for freight haulage) divides: Canal St-Denis runs north towards the Seine, and Canal de l'Ourcq continues east through La Villette and the suburbs. Long

EXPLORE

Musée de la Musique

Cité de la Musique, 221 av Jean-Jaurès, 19th (01.44.84.44.84, www.cite-musique.fr). M° Porte de Pantin. **Open** noon-6pm Tue-Sat; 10am-6pm Sun. **Admission** €8; €6.40 reductions; free under-26s. PMP. **Credit** AmEx, MC, V. **Map** p403 inset.

Alongside the concert hall, this innovative music museum houses a gleamingly restored collection of instruments from the old Conservatoire, interactive computers and scale models of opera houses and concert halls. Visitors are supplied with an audio-guide in a choice of languages, and the musical commentary is a joy, playing the appropriate instrument as you approach each exhibit. Alongside the trumpeting brass, curly woodwind instruments and precious strings (highlights include a Stradivarius violin and Django Reinhardt's guitar) are more unusual items, such as the Indonesian gamelan orchestra, whose sounds influenced the work of Debussy and Ravel. Concerts in the amphitheatre use instruments from the collection.

★ FREE Parc de la Villette

Av Corentin-Cariou, 19th (01.40.03.75.75, www.villette.com). M° Porte de la Villette. Av Jean-Jaurès, 19th. M° Porte de Pantin. **Map** p403 inset.

Dotted with red pavilions, or *folies*, the park was designed by Bernard Tschumi and is a postmodern feast. The *folies* serve as glorious giant climbing frames, as well as a first-aid post, burger bar, children's art centre and gig venue. As well as the lawns, which are used for an open-air film festival in summer, there are ten themed gardens bearing evocative names, such as the Garden of Mirrors, of Mists, of Acrobatics and of Childhood Frights. South of the canal are the Zénith concert venue (*see p294*), and the Grande Halle de la Villette – now used for trade fairs, exhibitions and September's jazz festival (*see p30*). It is flanked by the Conservatoire de la Musique and the Cité de la Musique, with rehearsal rooms, concert halls and the Musée de la Musique, but come 2015 the whole will be overshadowed by Jean Nouvel's sparkling 2,400-seat Philharmonie.

Party in the Park

Skip the Tuileries and head for the 19th instead.

There are plenty of handsomely ordered opportunities to indulge in a bit of park life in Paris, from the pathways of the Jardin des Tuileries to the ponds of the Jardin du Luxembourg. But if you're looking for something a little less formal, one patch of greenery worth a visit is the **Parc des Buttes-Chaumont** (*see p96*). Set up in Belleville and often missed by weekenders keen not to stray too far from the tourist loop, this 19th-arrondissement gem is one of the city's most magical spots.

When the city's boundaries were expanded in 1860, Belleville – once a village that provided Paris with fruit, wine and weekend escapes – was absorbed and the Buttes-Chaumont was created on the site of a former gypsum and limestone quarry. The park, with its meandering paths, waterfalls, temples and vertical cliffs, was designed by Adolphe Alphand for Haussmann, and was opened as part of the Universal Exhibition in 1867.

After lounging with the locals for a few hours, head for an *apéro* at the Rosa Bonheur *guinguette* (www.rosabonheur.fr, noon-midnight Wed-Sun). Its name refers to 19th-century French painter and sculptor Rosa Bonheur, famous for her depictions of animals and for her role in the early feminist movement (alongside George Sand and Sarah Bernhardt). Managed by Michelle Cassaro (aka Mimi, who used to run lesbian

club Pulp), the bar is a popular hangout with the lesbian crowd, especially on Sunday evenings. But the Bonheur is nothing if not relaxed in every sense, and for Parisians of all persuasions its terrace is the place to see and be seen in the summer – with just the birds, bees and bobos for company.

EXPLORE

EXPLORE

BELLEVILLE, MENILMONTANT & CHARONNE

In the 11th, 19th & 20th arrondissements.

When the city boundaries were expanded in 1860, Ménilmontant, Belleville and Charonne, once villages that provided Paris with fruit, wine and weekend escapes, were all absorbed. They were built up with housing for migrants, first from rural France and later from former colonies in North Africa and South-east Asia. The area encompasses one of the city's most beautiful parks, the romantic **Buttes-Chaumont**. Despite attempts to dissipate workers' agitation by splitting the village between the 11th, 19th and 20th administrative districts, Belleville became the centre of opposition to the Second Empire. Cabarets, artisans and workers typified 1890s Belleville; colonised by artists in the 1990s, today Belleville is a trendy hangout.

On boulevard de Belleville, Chinese and Vietnamese shops rub shoulders with Muslim and kosher groceries, and couscous and falafel eateries; a street market takes place here on Tuesday and Friday mornings.

North of here, along avenue Simon-Bolivar, is the Parc des Buttes-Chaumont. This is the most desirable part of north-east Paris, with Haussmannian apartments overlooking the park: to the east, near place de Rhin-et-Danube, is a small area of tiny, hilly streets lined with small houses and gardens, known by locals as the Quartier Mouzaïa.

Up on the slopes of the Hauts de Belleville, there are views over the city from rue Piat and rue des Envierges, which lead to the modern but charming **Parc de Belleville** with its Maison des Vents devoted to birds and kites. Below the park, rue Ramponneau mixes new housing and relics of old Belleville. At no.23 an old smithy has been turned into La Forge, an artists' squat.

'Mesnil-Montant' used to be a few houses on a hill with vines and fruit trees – then came the bistros, bordellos and workers' housing. It became part of Paris in 1860 along with Belleville, and has a similar history. These days it's a thriving centre of alternative Paris, as artists and young professionals have moved in. Although side streets still have male-only North African cafés, rue Oberkampf is home to some of the city's most humming bars.

The area mixes 1960s and '70s housing projects with older dwellings, some gentrified, some derelict. Just below rue des Pyrénées, which cuts through the 20th, you can rummage around the rustic Cité Leroy or Villa l'Ermitage, cobbled cul-de-sacs of little houses and gardens, and old craft workshops. Rue de l'Ermitage has a curious neo-Gothic house at no.19 – and a bird's-eye view from the junction with rue de Ménilmontant, right down the hill to the Centre Pompidou. On rue Boyer, **La Maroquinerie** (*see p293*) puts on an eclectic mix of literary events, political debate and live music, and at 88 rue de Ménilmontant, graffiti-covered art squat **La Miroiterie** opens house for art shows and the *magasin gratuit*, a free swap shop.

East of Père-Lachaise on rue de Bagnolet, **La Flèche d'Or** (*see p292*), a converted station on the defunct Petite Ceinture railway line, is a landmark music venue. Beyond, the medieval Eglise St-Germain-de-Charonne (currently closed for renovations) is at the heart of what is left of the village of Charonne. Set at the top of steps next to its presbytery, below a hill once covered with vines, it is one of only two churches in Paris still to have its own graveyard. Below here, centred on the old high street of rue St-Blaise, is a prettified backwater of quiet tearooms and bistros, where old shops have been taken over by art classes.

Towards porte de Bagnolet, where rue de Bagnolet and rue des Balkans meet on the edge of a small park, the **Pavillon de l'Hermitage** is a small aristocratic relic built in the 1720s for Françoise-Marie de Bourbon, the daughter of Louis XIV, when it was in the grounds of the Château de Bagnolet. A little further south at porte de Montreuil, cross the Périphérique for the Puces de Montreuil market (7am-7pm Mon, Sat, Sun). Less famous (and less charming) than its older brother up north in St-Ouen, Montreuil's flea market is where real folk rifle for antiques nowadays; mostly because it's off the beaten tourist track so you can still get a bargain and find the occasional treasure. You'll find pretty much everything, from vintage clothes and toys to old cutlery, 1940s light fittings, furniture and antique glassware.

FREE Musée Edith Piaf

5 rue Crespin-du-Gast, 11th (01.43.55.52.72). M° Ménilmontant. **Open** *By appointment only* 1-6pm Mon-Wed. **Admission** free (donations welcome).
Set in an apartment where Piaf lived at the age of 18, when she sang on the streets of Ménilmontant, this tiny museum consists of two red-painted rooms crammed with letters, pictures, framed discs and objects belonging to the singer. The museum's real treasures are two letters, one a chatty number written on her 28th birthday, and another more passionate pen to actor Robert Dalban. These – and the well-worn, human-sized teddy bear cuddling a tiny monkey soft toy – are the only clues to the real Piaf, the greatest singer the nation has ever known.

★ FREE Parc des Buttes-Chaumont

Rue Botzaris, rue Manin, rue de Crimée, 19th. M° Buttes Chaumont. **Open** *Oct-Apr* 7am-8pm daily. *May-Sept* 7am-10pm daily. **Map** p407 N2. *See p95* **Party in the Park**.

The Latin Quarter & the 13th

From the scholarly old to the screamingly new.

The Latin Quarter holds a considerable mystique for many foreign visitors, thanks to the historical presence of Hemingway, Orwell and Miller and to it being the seedbed of the 1968 revolt. Granted, many of the narrow, crooked streets (like the Marais, the Latin Quarter was a part of Paris largely untouched by Haussmann) are charming, and there are some real architectural glories, especially ecclesiastical ones; but the crowds can make the experience rather dispiriting. The 'Latin' in the area's name probably derives from the fact that it has been the university quarter since medieval times, when Latin was the language of instruction. To the east of the Latin Quarter, the part of the 13th arrondissement known as the ZAC Rive Gauche, anchored by the four book-like towers of the Bibliothèque Nationale, is one of the city's fastest rising quarters, and the Cité de la Mode, which finally, belatedly opened its doors in 2012, is set to further transform the area into an essential Left Bank hangout.

Sacré-Coeur
Montmartre & Pigalle
Champs-Elysées & Western Paris
North-east Paris
Opéra to Les Halles
Tour Eiffel
Louvre
Beaubourg & the Marais
The 7th & Western Paris
St-Germain-des-Prés & Odéon
Notre-Dame
Bastille & Eastern Paris
Montparnasse & Beyond
The Latin Quarter & the 13th

Map p406	**Restaurants** p158
Hotels p249	**Cafés & bars** p186

EXPLORE

ST-SEVERIN & ST-JULIEN-LE-PAUVRE

In the 5th arrondissement.

Boulevard St-Michel used to be synonymous with student rebellion; now it's a largely unprepossessing ribbon of fast-food joints and clothing shops, though **Gibert Joseph** (*see p192*) continues to furnish books and stationery to students. East of here, the semi-pedestrianised patch by the Seine has retained much of its medieval street plan. Rue de la Huchette and rue de la Harpe are now best known for their kebabs and pizzas, though there are 18th-century wrought-iron balconies and carved masks in the latter street. At the tiny **Théâtre de la Huchette** (*see p310*), Ionesco's absurdist drama *La Cantatrice*

Chauve (*The Bald Soprano*) has been playing continuously since 1957. Also of interest are rue du Chat-qui-Pêche, supposedly the city's narrowest street, and rue de la Parcheminerie, named after the parchment sellers and copyists who once lived here. Among the tourist shops stands the city's most charming medieval church, the **Eglise St-Séverin**, with leering gargoyles, spiky gabled side chapels and an exuberantly vaulted Flamboyant Gothic interior.

Across ancient rue St-Jacques is the **Eglise St-Julien-le-Pauvre**, built as a resting place for 12th-century pilgrims. Nearby rue Galande has old houses and the Trois Mailletz cabaret (5th, 01.43.54.42.94, www.lestroismailletz.fr). The medieval cellars of the **Caveau des Oubliettes** jazz club (*see p297*) were used as a prison after the French Revolution (*oubliette* is the French word for a pit into which prisoners

Musée National du Moyen Age.

were thrown, then forgotten). At no.42 is arts cinema **Studio Galande** (*see p272*). Nearby, in place Viviani, stands what is perhaps the city's oldest tree, a false acacia that was planted in 1602; it's now half-swamped by ivy and propped up by concrete buttresses.

The little streets between here and the eastern stretch of boulevard St-Germain are among the city's oldest: streets such as rue de Bièvre, which follows the course of the Bièvre river that flowed into the Seine in the Middle Ages, rue du Maître-Albert, and rue des Grands-Degrès, with traces of old shop signs painted on its buildings' façades. Remnants of the Collège des Bernardins, built for the Cistercian order, can be seen in rue de Poissy, where the 13th- to 14th-century Gothic monks' refectory has been restored after service as firemen's barracks. Nearby are the **Eglise St-Nicolas du Chardonnet** (23 rue Bernardins, 5th, 01.44.27.07.90), associated with the schismatic Society of St Pius X and one of a small number of churches where you can hear the Tridentine Mass in Paris, and the art deco **Maison de la Mutualité** (24 rue St-Victor, 5th, 01.83.92.24.00), home to everything from trade unions meetings to rock concerts.

You'll find food for all budgets along quai de la Tournelle, starting with Michelin-starred **La Tour d'Argent** (*see p160*), said to have been founded as an inn in 1582. After 60 years at the helm, owner Claude Terrail died in 2006, passing the restaurant to his son André. Place Maubert, which is now a breezy morning marketplace (Tue, Thur, Sat), witnessed the hanging of Protestants during the 16th-century Wars of Religion. Just behind the square, the modern police station is home to an array of grisly criminal evidence in the **Musée de la Préfecture de Police**.

On the corner of boulevard St-Germain and boulevard St-Michel stand the striking ruins of the late second-century **Thermes de Cluny**, the Romans' main baths complex; the adjoining Gothic Hôtel de Cluny provides a suitable setting for the **Musée National du Moyen Age**, the national collection of medieval art. Adjoining boulevard St-Germain, its garden has been replanted with species portrayed in medieval tapestries, paintings and treatises.

🆓 Eglise St-Julien-le-Pauvre

Rue St-Julien-le-Pauvre, 5th (01.43.54.52.16, www.sjlpmelkites.fr). Mᵒ Cluny La Sorbonne. **Open** 9.30am-1pm, 3-6.30pm daily. **Admission** free. **Map** p408 J7.

A former sanctuary for pilgrims en route to Compostela, this much-mauled church dates from the late 12th century, on the cusp of Romanesque and Gothic, and has capitals richly decorated with vines, acanthus leaves and winged harpies. Once part of a priory, it became the university church when colleges migrated to the Left Bank. Since 1889, it has been used by the Greek Orthodox Church.

★ 🆓 Eglise St-Séverin

3 rue des Prêtres-St-Séverin, 5th (01.42.34.93.50, www.saint-severin.com). Mᵒ Cluny La Sorbonne or St-Michel. **Open** 11am-7.30pm Mon-Sat; 9am-8.30pm Sun. **Admission** free. **Map** p408 J7.

Built on the site of the chapel of the hermit Séverin, itself set on a much earlier Merovingian burial ground, this lovely Flamboyant Gothic edifice was long the parish church of the Left Bank. It was rebuilt on various occasions to repair damage after ransacking by Normans and to meet the needs of the growing population. The church dates from the 15th century, though the doorway, carved with foliage, was added in 1837 from the demolished Eglise St-Pierre-aux-Boeufs on Ile de la Cité. The double ambulatory is famed for its forest of 'palm tree' vaulting, which meets at the end in a unique spiral column that inspired a series of paintings by Robert Delaunay. The bell tower, a survivor from one of the earlier churches on the site, has the oldest bell in Paris (1412). Around the nave are stained-glass windows dating from the 14th and 15th centuries (most of those in the side chapels are by 19th-century Chartres master Emile Hersh), and the choir apse has striking stained glass designed by artist Jean René Bazaine in the 1960s. Next door, around the former cemetery, is the only remaining charnel house in Paris.

★ Musée National du Moyen Age – Thermes de Cluny

6 pl Paul-Painlevé, 5th (01.53.73.78.00, www.musee-moyenage.fr). M° Cluny La Sorbonne. **Open** 9.15am-5.45pm Mon, Wed-Sun. **Admission** €8; €6 reductions; free under-18s, under-26s (EU citizens), all 1st Sun of mth. PMP. **Credit** *Shop* MC, V. **Map** p408 J7.

The national museum of medieval art is best known for the beautiful, allegorical *Lady and the Unicorn* tapestry cycle, but it also has important collections of medieval sculpture and enamels. The building itself, commonly known as Cluny, is also a rare example of 15th-century secular Gothic architecture, with its foliate Gothic doorways, hexagonal staircase jutting out of the façade and vaulted chapel. It was built from 1485 to 1498 – on top of a Gallo-Roman baths complex. The baths, built in characteristic Roman bands of stone and brick masonry, are the finest Roman remains in Paris. The vaulted *frigidarium* (cold bath), *tepidarium* (warm bath), *caldarium* (hot bath) and part of the hypocaust heating system are all still visible. A themed garden fronts the whole complex. Recent acquisitions include the illuminated manuscript *L'Ascension du Christ* from the Abbey of Cluny, dating back to the 12th century, and the 16th-century triptych *Assomption de la Vierge* by Adrien Isenbrant of Bruges.

FREE Musée de la Préfecture de Police

4 rue de la Montagne-Ste-Geneviève, 5th (01.44.41.52.50, www.prefecturedepolice.interieur. gouv.fr). M° Maubert Mutualité. **Open** 9am-5pm Mon-Fri; 10.30am-5.30pm Sat. **Admission** free. **Map** p406 J7.

The police museum is housed in a working *commissariat*, which makes for a slightly intimidating entry procedure. You need to walk boldly past the police officer standing guard outside and up the steps to the lobby, where you have to ask at the reception booth to be let in – queuing, if necessary, with locals there on other, but usually police-related, errands. The museum is on the second floor; start from the *Accueil* and work your way clockwise.

None of the displays is labelled in English (though there is a bilingual booklet), and a handful are not labelled at all; but if you have basic French and any sort of interest in criminology, this extensive collection is well worth seeing. It starts in the early 17th century and runs to the Occupation, via the founding of the Préfecture de Police by Napoleon in 1800. Exhibits include a prison register open at the entry for Ravaillac, assassin of Henri IV; a section on the Anarchist bombings of the 1890s; the automatic pistol used to assassinate President Doumer in 1932; a blood-chilling collection of murder weapons – hammers, ice picks and knives; sections on serial killers Landru and Petiot; and less dangerous items, such as a gadget used to snag banknotes from the apron pockets of market sellers.

THE SORBONNE, MONTAGNE STE-GENEVIEVE & MOUFFETARD

In the 5th arrondissement.

An influx of well-heeled residents in the 1980s put paid to the days of horn-rims, pipes and turtlenecks: accommodation here is now well beyond the reach of most students. The intellectual tradition persists, however, in the concentration of academic institutions around Montagne Ste-Geneviève, and students throng the specialist bookstores and art cinemas on rue Champollion and rue des Ecoles.

The district's long-running association with learning began in about 1100, when a number of renowned scholars, including Pierre Abélard, began to live and teach on the Montagne, independent of the established cathedral chool of Notre-Dame. This loose association of scholars came to be referred to as a 'university'. The Paris schools attracted students from all over Europe, and the 'colleges' – in reality student residences dotted round the area (some still survive) – multiplied, until the University of Paris was given official recognition with a charter from Pope Innocent III in 1215.

By the 16th century, the university – named the **Sorbonne**, after the most famous of its colleges – had been co-opted by the Catholic Church. A century later, Cardinal Richelieu rebuilt it. Following the Revolution, when it was forced to close, Napoleon revived the Sorbonne as the cornerstone of his new, centralised education system. The university participated enthusiastically in the uprisings of the 19th century; it was also a seedbed of the

1968 revolt, when it was occupied by protesting students. These days, it's far less turbulent. Also on rue des Ecoles, the independent **Collège de France** was founded in 1530 by a group of humanists led by Guillaume Budé under the patronage of François I. The neighbouring **Brasserie Balzar** (no.49, 5th, 01.43.54.13.67) has been fuelling amateur philosophy for years.

From here, climb rue St-Jacques to rue Soufflot for the most impressive introduction to place du Panthéon. Otherwise, follow rue des Carmes – with its Baroque chapel, now used by the Syrian Church – and continue on rue Valette past the brick and stone entrance of the **Collège Ste-Barbe**, where Ignatius Loyola, Montgolfier and Eiffel studied. Alternatively, follow the serpentine rue de la Montagne-Ste-Geneviève; at the junction of rue Descartes, cafés and eccentric wine bistros overlook the sculpted 19th-century entrance to what was once the elite Ecole Polytechnique (since moved to the suburbs) and is now the research ministry. There's a small park here, and popular bistro **L'Ecurie** (2 rue Laplace, 5th, 01.46.33.68.49) – an old stable burrowed into medieval cellars.

Louis XV commissioned the huge, domed **Panthéon** to honour Geneviève, the city's patron saint, but it was converted during the Revolution into a secular temple for France's *grands hommes*. The surrounding place du Panthéon, also conceived by Panthéon architect Jacques-Germain Soufflot, is one of the city's great set pieces: looking on to it are the elegant fifth arrondissement town hall and, opposite, the law faculty. On the north side, the Ste-Geneviève university library, built by Labrouste with an iron-framed reading room, contains medieval manuscripts. On the other side you'll find the historic **Hôtel des Grands Hommes** (no.17, 5th, 01.46.34.19.60, www.hoteldesgrands hommes.com), where Surrealist mandarin André Breton invented 'automatic writing' in the 1920s.

Pascal, Racine and the remains of Sainte Geneviève are all interred within **Eglise St-Etienne-du-Mont**, on the north-east corner of

the square. Just behind it, within the illustrious and elitist Lycée Henri IV, is the Gothic-Romanesque **Tour de Clovis**, part of the former Abbaye Ste-Geneviève. Take a look through the entrance (open during termtime) and you'll also catch glimpses of the cloister and other monastic structures.

Further from place du Panthéon, along rue Clovis, is a chunk of Philippe-Auguste's 12th-century city wall. The exiled monarch James II once resided at 65 rue du Cardinal-Lemoine, in the severe buildings of the former Collège des Ecossais (now a school), founded in 1372 to house Scottish students; the king's brain was preserved here until carried off and lost during the French Revolution. Other well known ex-residents include Ernest Hemingway, who lived at 79 rue du Cardinal-Lemoine (note the plaque) and 39 rue Descartes in the 1920s, and James Joyce; the latter completed *Ulysses* while staying at 71 rue du Cardinal-Lemoine. Rimbaud lived in rue Descartes, and Descartes himself lived on nearby rue Rollin.

This area is still a mix of tourist picturesque and gentle village, where some of the buildings hide surprising courtyards and gardens. Pretty place de la Contrescarpe has been a famous rendezvous since the 1530s, when writers as renowned as Rabelais, Ronsard and Du Bellay frequented the Cabaret de la Pomme de Pin at no.1; it still has some lively cafés. When George Orwell stayed at 6 rue du Pot-de-Fer in 1928 and 1929 (he described his time here and his work as a dishwasher in *Down and Out in Paris and London*), it was a place of astounding poverty; today, the street is lined with bargain bars and restaurants, and the restored houses along rue Tournefort bear little relation to the garrets of Balzac's *Le Père Goriot*.

Rue Mouffetard, originally the road to Rome and one of the oldest streets in the city, winds south as a spate of cheap bistros, Greek and Lebanese tavernas and knick-knack shops thronged with tourists; the vibe described by Hemingway – 'that wonderful narrow crowded market street, beloved of bohemians' – has faded. The street market (Tue-Sat, Sun morn) on the lower half seethes on weekends, when it spills on to the square and around the cafés in front of the **Eglise St-Médard**. There's another busy market, more frequented by locals, at place Monge (Wed, Fri, Sun morning).

Back to the west of the Panthéon, head south beyond rue Soufflot and you'll notice that rue St-Jacques becomes prettier. Here you'll find several ancient buildings, including the elegant *hôtel* at no.151, good food shops and vintage bistro **Perraudin** (no.157, 5th, 01.46.33.15.75, www.restaurant-perraudin.com). Rue d'Ulm contains the elite **Ecole Normale Supérieure** (no.45, 5th, 01.44.32.30.00, www.ens.fr),

Le Panthéon. *See p102.*

occupied in protest by the unemployed in January 1998; in an echo of 1968, students also joined in.

Turn off up hilly rue des Fossés-St-Jacques to discover place de l'Estrapade; in the 17th century the *estrapade* was a tall wooden tower from which deserters were dropped repeatedly until they died. Nearby, in rue des Irlandais, the Centre Culturel Irlandais hosts concerts, exhibitions, films, plays and spoken-word events promoting Irish culture. Back to the west of rue St-Jacques, rue Soufflot and broad rue Gay-Lussac (a hotspot of the May 1968 revolt), with their Haussmannian apartment buildings, lead to boulevard St-Michel and the Jardin du Luxembourg.

Further south along rue St-Jacques, in the potters' quarter of Roman Lutetia, is the most ornate of the city's Baroque churches, the **Eglise du Val-de-Grâce**. Round the corner, at 6 rue du Val-de-Grâce, is the former home of Alfons Maria Mucha, the influential Moravian art nouveau artist, who was best known for his posters of Sarah Bernhardt.

FREE **Collège de France**
11 pl Marcelin-Berthelot, 5th (01.44.27.12.11, 01.44.27.11.47, www.college-de-france.fr). M° Cluny La Sorbonne or Maubert Mutualité/RER Luxembourg. **Open** 9am-5pm Mon-Fri. **Admission** free. **Map** p408 J7.
Founded in 1530 with the patronage of François I, the college is a place of learning and a research institute. The present building dates from the 16th and 17th centuries; there's also a later annexe. All lectures are free and open to the public; some have been given by such eminent figures as anthropologist Claude Lévi-Strauss, philosopher Maurice Merleau-Ponty and mathematician Jacques Tits.

★ FREE **Eglise St-Etienne-du-Mont**
Pl Ste-Geneviève, 5th (01.43.54.11.79, www.saint etiennedumont.fr). M° Cardinal Lemoine/RER Luxembourg. **Open** 8.45am-7.45pm Tue-Fri; 8.45am-noon, 2-7.45pm Sat; 8.45am-12.15pm, 2-7.45pm Sun (*July, Aug* 10am-noon, 4-7.45pm Tue-Sun). **Admission** free. **Map** p408 J8.
Geneviève, patron saint of Paris, is credited with having miraculously saved the city from the ravages of Attila the Hun in 451, and her shrine has been a site of pilgrimage ever since. The present church was built in an amalgam of Gothic and Renaissance styles between 1492 and 1626, and once adjoined the abbey church of Ste-Geneviève. The façade mixes Gothic rose windows with rusticated roman columns and reliefs of classically draped figures. The interior is wonderfully tall and light, with soaring columns and a classical balustrade. The stunning Renaissance rood screen, with its double spiral staircase and ornate stone strapwork, is the only surviving one in Paris, and was possibly designed by Philibert Delorme. The decorative canopied wooden pulpit by Germaine Pillon dates from 1651, and is adorned with figures of the Graces and supported by a muscular Samson sitting on the defeated lion. Sainte Geneviève's elaborate neo-Gothic brass-and-glass shrine (shielding the ancient tombstone) is located to the right of the choir, surrounded by an assortment of reliquaries and dozens of marble plaques bearing messages of thanks. At the back of the church (reached through the sacristy), the catechism chapel constructed by Baltard in the 1860s has a cycle of paintings relating the saint's life story.

FREE **Eglise St-Médard**
141 rue Mouffetard, 5th (01.44.08.87.00, www.saintmedard.org). M° Censier Daubenton. **Open** 8am-12.30pm, 2.30-7.30pm Tue-Sat; 8.30am-12.30pm, 4-8.30pm Sun. **Admission** free. **Map** p406 J9.

The original chapel here was a dependency of the Abbaye Ste-Geneviève. The rebuilding towards the end of the 15th century created a somewhat larger, late Gothic structure best known for its elaborate vaulted ambulatory.

Eglise du Val-de-Grâce

Pl Alphonse-Laveran, 5th (01.40.51.51.92). RER Luxembourg or Port-Royal. **Open** noon-6pm Tue, Wed, Sat, Sun. **Admission** €5; €2.50 reductions; free under-6s. **No credit cards**. **Map** p406 H9.

Anne of Austria, the wife of Louis XIII, vowed to erect 'a magnificent temple' if God blessed her with a son. She got two. The resulting church and surrounding Benedictine monastery – these days a military hospital and the Musée du Service de Santé des Armées (*see below*) – were built by François Mansart and Jacques Lemercier. This is the most luxuriously Baroque of the city's 17th-century domed churches, its ornate altar decorated with twisted barley-sugar columns. The swirling colours of the dome frescoes painted by Pierre Mignard in 1669 (which Molière himself once eulogised) are designed to give a foretaste of heaven. In contrast, the surrounding monastery offers the perfect example of François Mansart's classical restraint. Phone in advance if you're after a guided visit.

Musée du Service de Santé des Armées

Val de Grâce, pl Alphonse-Laveran, 5th (01.40.51.51.92). RER Luxembourg or Port Royal. **Open** noon-6pm Tue, Wed, Sat, Sun. Closed Aug. **Admission** €5; €2.50 reductions; free under-6s. **No credit cards**. **Map** p406 J9.

Housed in the royal convent designed by Mansart, next door to a military hospital, this museum traces the history of military medicine via replicas of field hospitals and ambulance trains, as well as displays of antique medical instruments. The section on World War I demonstrates how much the conflict propelled medical progress.

★ Le Panthéon

Pl du Panthéon, 5th (01.44.32.18.00). M° Cardinal Lemoine/RER Luxembourg. **Open** 10am-6pm (until 6.30pm summer) daily. **Admission** €8.50; €5.50 reductions; free under-18s, under-26s (EU citizens). PMP. **Credit** MC, V. **Map** p408 J8.

Soufflot's neoclassical megastructure was the architectural *grand projet* of its day, commissioned by a grateful Louis XV to thank Sainte Geneviève for his recovery from illness. But by the time it was ready in 1790, a lot had changed; during the Revolution, the Panthéon was rededicated as a 'temple of reason' and the resting place of the nation's great men. The austere barrel-vaulted crypt now houses Voltaire, Rousseau, Hugo and Zola. New heroes are installed but rarely: Pierre and Marie Curie's remains were transferred here in 1995; Alexandre Dumas in 2002. Inside are Greek columns and domes, along with

Grande Galerie de l'Evolution.

EXPLORE

19th-century murals of Geneviève's life by Symbolist painter Puvis de Chavannes, a formative influence on Picasso during the latter's blue period.

Mount the steep spiral stairs to the colonnade encircling the dome for superb views. A replica of Foucault's Pendulum hangs here; the original proved that the earth does indeed spin on its axis, via a universal joint that lets the direction of the pendulum's swing rotate as the earth revolves. *Photo p101.*

La Sorbonne

17 rue de la Sorbonne, 5th (01.40.46.22.11, www.sorbonne.fr). M° Cluny La Sorbonne. **Open** 9am-5pm Mon-Fri. *Tours* by appointment. Closed July & Aug. **Map** p408 J7.

Founded in 1253, the University of the Sorbonne was at the centre of the Latin Quarter's intellectual activity from the Middle Ages until 1968, when it was occupied by students and stormed by the riot police. The authorities then split the University of Paris into safer outposts, but the Sorbonne still houses the Faculté des Lettres. Rebuilt by Richelieu and reorganised by Napoleon, the present buildings date from the late 1800s, and have a labyrinth of classrooms and lecture theatres, as well as an observatory tower. The elegant dome of the 17th-century chapel dominates place de la Sorbonne; Cardinal Richelieu is buried inside. It's open to the public only for exhibitions or concerts.

AROUND THE JARDIN DES PLANTES

In the 5th arrondissement.

The quiet, easternmost part of the fifth arrondissement is home to yet more academic institutions, the Paris mosque and another Roman relic. Old-fashioned bistros on rue des Fossés-St-Bernard contrast with the forbidding 1960s architecture of the massive university campus of Paris VI and VII, the science faculty (known as Jussieu) built on what had been the site of the important Abbaye St-Victor. Between the Seine and Jussieu is the newly revamped glass-faced **Institut du Monde Arabe**, which has a programme of concerts and exhibitions and a restaurant with a great view. The **Jardin Tino Rossi**, by the river, contains the slightly dilapidated **Musée de la Sculpture en Plein Air**; in summer this is a spot for dancing and picnicking.

Hidden among the hotels of rue Monge is the entrance to the **Arènes de Lutèce**, a Roman amphitheatre. The remains of a circular arena and its tiers of stone seating were discovered in 1869. Excavation started in 1883, thanks to lobbying by Victor Hugo. Nearby rise the white minaret and green pantiled roof of the **Mosquée de Paris**, built in 1922. Its beautiful Moorish tearoom is a student haunt.

INSIDE TRACK MOVIE MAGIC

As if film buffs weren't already spoilt for choice in Paris, they'll have more reason to get excited come 2013. The **Fondation Jérôme Seydoux-Pathé** (www.fondation-jeromeseydoux-pathe.com) is opening a showcase centre for its collection of film memorabilia and artefacts, including a space for temporary exhibitions, on the site of a former cinema near place d'Italie.

The mosque looks over the **Jardin des Plantes** botanical garden. Opened in 1626 as a garden for medicinal plants, it features an 18th-century maze and a winter garden bristling with rare species. It also houses the Muséum National d'Histoire Naturelle, with its brilliantly renovated **Grande Galerie de l'Evolution**, and a zoo, La Ménagerie, unlikely by-product of the Revolution, when royal and noble collections of wild animals were impounded. Street names and the lovely animal-themed fountain on the corner of rue Cuvier pay homage to the many naturalists and other scientists who worked here. A short way away, at 11-13bis rue Geoffroy-St-Hilaire, the words 'Chevaux', 'Poneys' and 'Anes' are still visible on the façade of the old horse market.

FREE Arènes de Lutèce

Rue Monge, rue de Navarre or rue des Arènes, 5th. M° Cardinal Lemoine or Place Monge. **Open** *Summer* 9am-9.30pm daily. *Winter* 8am-5.30pm daily. **Admission** free. **Map** p406 K8.

This Roman arena, where wild beasts and gladiators once fought, could seat 10,000 people. It was still visible during the reign of Philippe-Auguste in the 12th century, then disappeared under rubble. The site was only rediscovered in 1869 and now incorporates a romantically planted garden. These days, it attracts skateboarders, footballers and boules players.

★ Grande Galerie de l'Evolution

36 rue Geoffroy-St-Hilaire, 2 rue Bouffon or pl Valhubert, 5th (01.40.79.56.01, www.mnhn.fr). M° Gare d'Austerlitz or Jussieu. **Open** *Grande Galerie* 10am-6pm Mon, Wed-Sun. *Galerie d'Anatomie Comparée et de Paléontologie* 10am-5pm Mon, Wed-Fri; 10am-6pm Sat, Sun. **Admission** *Grande Galerie* €7; €5 reductions. *Galerie d'Anatomie Comparée et de Paléontologie* €7; €5 reductions; free under-26s. **No credit cards. Map** p406 K9.

One of the city's most child-friendly attractions (*see also p263*), this is guaranteed to bowl adults over too. Located within the Jardin des Plantes (*see p104*), this beauty of a 19th-century iron-framed, glass-roofed

EXPLORE

structure has been modernised with lifts, galleries and false floors, and filled with life-size models of tentacle-waving squids, open-mawed sharks, tigers hanging off elephants and monkeys swarming down from the ceiling. The centrepiece is a procession of African wildlife across the first floor that resembles the procession into Noah's Ark. Glass-sided lifts take you up through suspended birds to the second floor, which deals with man's impact on nature (crocodile into handbag). The third floor focuses on endangered and extinct species. The separate Galerie d'Anatomie Comparée et de Paléontologie contains more than a million skeletons, as well as a world-class fossil collection.

Institut du Monde Arabe

1 rue des Fossés-St-Bernard, 5th (01.40.51.38.38, www.imarabe.org). M° Jussieu. **Open** *Museum* 10am-6pm Tue-Thur; 10am-9.30pm Fri; 10am-7pm Sat, Sun. *Library* 1-8pm Tue-Sat (July, Aug 1-6pm). *Tours* 3pm Tue-Fri; 3pm & 4.30pm Sat, Sun.* **Admission** *Museum* €8; €6 reductions; free under-18s, under-26s (EU citizens). *Library* free. PMP. *Exhibitions* varies. **Credit** MC, V. **Map** p406 K7.
See p105 **Brave New World**.
▶ *Jean Nouvel's other landmark Paris buildings include the Musée du Quai Branly (see p130) and the Fondation Cartier (see p118).*

★ FREE Jardin des Plantes

36 rue Geoffroy-St-Hilaire, 2 rue Buffon, pl Valhubert or 57 rue Cuvier, 5th. M° Gare d'Austerlitz or Place Monge (01.40.79.56.01, www.jardindesplantes.net). **Open** *Main garden* Winter 8am-5.30pm daily. Summer 7.30am-7.45pm daily. *Alpine garden* Apr-Oct 8am-4.40pm Mon-Fri; 1.30-6pm Sat; 1.30-6.30pm Sun. Closed Nov-Mar. *Ménagerie* 9am-6pm Mon-Sat; 9am-6.30pm Sun. **Admission** *Alpine Garden* free Mon-Fri; €2 Sat, Sun. *Jardin des Plantes* free. *Ménagerie* €10; €8 reductions; free under-4s. **Credit** AmEx, MC, V. **Map** p406 L8.
The Paris botanical garden – which contains more than 10,000 species and includes tropical greenhouses and rose, winter and Alpine gardens – is an enchanting place. Begun by Louis XIII's doctor as the royal medicinal plant garden in 1626, it opened to the public in 1640. The formal garden, which runs between two dead-straight avenues of trees parallel to rue Buffon, is like something out of *Alice in Wonderland*. There's also the Ménagerie (a small zoo) and the terrific Grande Galerie de l'Evolution (*see p103*). Ancient trees on view include a false acacia planted in 1636 and a cedar from 1734. *Photos p106.*

FREE Jardin Tino Rossi (Musée de la Sculpture en Plein Air)

Quai St-Bernard, 5th. M° Gare d'Austerlitz. **Open** 8am-dusk Mon-Fri; 9am-dusk Sat, Sun. **Admission** free. **Map** p406 L8.

This open-air sculpture museum by the Seine fights a constant battle against graffiti. Still, it's a pleasant place for a stroll. Most of the works are second-rate, aside from Etienne Martin's bronze *Demeure I* and the Carrara marble *Fenêtre* by Cuban artist Careras.
▶ *From May to September, the gardens turn into an open-air dance studio.*

La Mosquée de Paris

2 pl du Puits-de-l'Ermite, 5th (01.45.35.97.33, 01.43.31.18.14, www.mosquee-de-paris.net). M° Monge. **Open** *Tours* 9am-noon, 2-6pm Mon-Thur, Sat, Sun (closed Muslim hols). *Tearoom* 10am-11.30pm daily. *Restaurant* noon-2.30pm, 7.30-10.30pm daily. *Baths* (women) 10am-9pm Mon, Wed, Sat; 2-9pm Fri; (men) 2-9pm Tue, Sun. **Admission** €3; €2 reductions; free under-7s. *Tearoom* free. *Baths* €15-€35. **Credit** MC, V. **Map** p406 K9.
Some distance removed from the Arabic-speaking inner-city enclaves of Barbès and Belleville, this vast Hispano-Moorish construct is nevertheless the spiritual heart of France's Algerian-dominated Muslim population. Built from 1922 to 1926 with elements inspired by the Alhambra and the Bou Inania Medersa in Fès, the Paris mosque is dominated by a stunning green-and-white tiled square minaret. In plan and function it divides into three sections: religious (grand patio, prayer room and minaret, all for worshippers and not curious tourists); scholarly (Islamic school and library); and, via rue Geoffroy-St-Hilaire, commercial (café and domed hammam). La Mosquée café is delightful – a modest courtyard with blue-and-white mosaic-topped tables shaded beneath green foliage and scented with the sweet smell of sheesha smoke (€6).

LES GOBELINS & LA SALPETRIERE

In the 13th arrondissement.

Its defining features might be 1960s tower blocks, but the 13th arrondissement is also historic, especially in the area bordering the fifth. The **Manufacture Nationale des Gobelins**, home to the state weaving companies, continues a tradition founded in the 15th century, when tanneries, dyers and weaving workshops lined the Bièvre river. This putrid waterway became notorious, and the slums that grew up around it were depicted in Victor Hugo's *Les Misérables*.
   The area was tidied up in the 1930s, when a small park, square René-Le-Gall, was laid out on the allotments used by tapestry workers. The river was built over, but local enthusiasts have since opened up a small stretch in the park. Nearby, through a gateway at 17 rue des Gobelins, you can spot the turret and first floor of a medieval house, recently renovated as

Brave New World

The Institut du Monde Arabe's fabulous museum has reopened after a revamp.

One of Paris's most innovative museums reopened to the public in 2012 after a three-year, €5 million revamp. The beautiful museum of the **Institut du Monde Arabe** (*see p104*), dedicated to the development of Islamic art and the history and culture of the Arab world, has been transformed, just in time to mark its 25th anniversary. Collections from the 22 Arab countries that co-founded the museum can now be enjoyed once again, in an exciting and dynamic new interior.

A clever blend of high-tech and Arab influences, this Seine-side *grand projet* was constructed between 1980 and 1987 to a design by Jean Nouvel, who sought to build a modern interpretation of a Moorish palace. Some 600 items are on display, from places as diverse as Damascus, Aleppo, Latakia, Amman, Kairouan and Manama, as well as the Louvre, Musée du Quai Branly and the Bibliothèque Nationale de France. And whereas before the collection was limited to Islamic art, the new museum has widened its scope (as well as its physical space), showcasing the Arab world in thematic ways, covering its ethno-linguistic, cultural, historical, anthropological and geographical diversity. Museographer Roberto Ostinelli's subtle but dynamic staging – conceived as a pathway dotted with bridges between past and present – manages to work on both an emotional and intellectual level.

What's more, there's a lively programme of cultural events (exhibitions, film screenings, music and dance events) and an excellent Middle East bookshop on the ground floor, and the views from the roof terrace are fabulous.

And if your thirst for Arab culture is still unquenched after a visit here, head to the Louvre (*see p41*) to check out its dynamic new Département des Arts d'Islam.

EXPLORE

apartments. The so-called Château de la Reine Blanche on rue Gustave-Geffroy is named after Queen Blanche of Provence, who had a château here; it was probably rebuilt in the 1520s for the Gobelin family. Blanche was also associated with a nearby Franciscan monastery, of which a fragmentary couple of arches survive on the corner of rue Pascal and rue de Julienne.

In the northern corner of the 13th, next to Gare d'Austerlitz, sprawls the huge Hôpital de la Pitié-Salpêtrière founded in 1656, with its striking **Chapelle St-Louis**.

The busy intersection of place d'Italie has seen a number of developments in recent years. Opposite the 19th-century town hall stands the Centre Commercial Italie 2, a bizarre high-tech confection. It houses a shopping centre but, sadly, no longer the Gaumont Grand Ecran Italie cinema. You'll also find a food market on boulevard Auguste-Blanqui (Tue, Fri, Sun).

FREE Chapelle St-Louis-de-la-Salpêtrière

47 bd de l'Hôpital, 13th (01.42.16.04.24). M° Gare d'Austerlitz. **Open** 8.30am-6pm Mon-Fri, Sun; 11am-6pm Sat. **Admission** free. **Map** p406 L9.
This austerely beautiful chapel, designed by Libéral Bruand and completed in 1677, features an octagonal dome in the centre and eight naves in which the sick were separated from the insane, the destitute from the debauched. Around the chapel sprawls the vast

Hôpital de la Pitié-Salpêtrière, founded on the site of a gunpowder factory (hence the name, derived from saltpetre) by Louis XIV to house rounded-up vagrant women. It became a centre for research into insanity in the 1790s, when renowned doctor Philippe Pinel began to treat some of the inmates as sick rather than criminal; Jean-Martin Charcot later pioneered neuropsychology here, famously receiving a visit from Freud. Salpêtrière is today one of the city's main teaching hospitals, but the chapel is also used for contemporary art installations, notably during the Festival d'Automne (*see p30*), when its striking architecture provides a backdrop for artists such as Bill Viola, Anish Kapoor and Nan Goldin.

Manufacture Nationale des Gobelins

42 av des Gobelins, 13th (01.44.08.53.59). M° Les Gobelins. **Open** 11am-6pm Tue-Sun. **Admission** €6; €4 reductions; free last Sun of mth. *Tours* call for details. **No credit cards**. **Map** p406 K10.
The royal tapestry factory was founded by Colbert when he set up the Manufacture Royale des Meubles de la Couronne in 1662; it's named after Jean Gobelin, a dyer who owned the site. It reached the summit of its renown during the *ancien régime*, when Gobelins tapestries were produced for royal residences under artists such as Le Brun. Tapestries are still made here and visitors can watch weavers at work. Tours (in French; €7.50-€10) through the 1912 factory take in the 18th-century chapel and the Beauvais workshops.

Jardin des Plantes. *See p104.*

EXPLORE

CHINATOWN & THE BUTTE-AUX-CAILLES

South of rue de Tolbiac, the shop signs turn Chinese or Vietnamese, and even McDonald's is decked out *à la chinoise*. The city's main Chinatown runs along avenue d'Ivry, avenue de Choisy and the 1960s tower blocks between. Whereas much of the public housing in and around Paris is pretty bleak, here a distinctly eastern vibe reigns, with restaurants, Vietnamese *pho* noodle bars and Chinese pâtisseries, hairdressers and purveyors of exotic groceries; not to mention the expansive **Tang Frères** supermarket (48 av d'Ivry, 13th, 01.45.70.80.00). There's even a Buddhist temple hidden in a car park beneath the tallest tower (av d'Ivry, opposite rue Frères d'Astier-de-la-Vigerie, 13th). Lion and dragon dances, and martial arts demonstrations, take place on the streets at **Chinese New Year** (*see p31*).

In contrast to Chinatown, the villagey Butte-aux-Cailles, occupying the wedge between boulevard Auguste-Blanqui and rue Bobillot, is a neighbourhood of old houses, winding streets, funky bars and restaurants. This area, which was home in the 19th century to many small factories, was one of the first to fight during the 1848 Revolution and the Paris Commune.

The Butte has preserved its rebellious character, with residents standing up to commercial developers. This predominantly *soixante-huitard* resistance is concentrated in the cobbled rue de la Butte-aux-Cailles and rue des Cinq-Diamants. Here you'll find inexpensive bistros such as **Le Temps des Cerises** (18 rue Butte-aux-Cailles, 13th, 01.45.89.69.48), run as a co-operative, and **Chez Gladines** (30 rue des Cinq-Diamants, 13th, 01.45.80.70.10). The cottages built in 1912 in a mock-Alsatian style around a central green at 10 rue Daviel were among the earliest public-housing schemes in Paris. Just across rue Bobillot, the **Piscine Butte-aux-Cailles** (*see p319*) is a charming Arts and Crafts-style swimming pool.

Further south, you can explore passage Vandrezanne, the little houses and gardens of square des Peupliers, rue des Peupliers and rue Dieulafoy, and the flower-named streets of the Cité Florale. By the Périphérique, the **Stade Charléty** (17 av Pierre-de-Coubertin, 13th, 01.44.16.60.60) is that unlikely thing, a superb piece of stadium architecture.

Further east

The construction in the mid-1990s of the **Bibliothèque Nationale de France** breathed new life into the desolate area, now known as the **ZAC Rive Gauche**, between Gare d'Austerlitz and the Périphérique. The ambitious, long-term ZAC project includes a new university quarter, new housing projects and a tramway providing links to the suburbs. The pedestrian-only **Passerelle Simone-de-Beauvoir** spans the Seine between the BNF and the Cinémathèque Française; the floating Piscine Josephine-Baker (*see p319*) is now a focus for the Paris-Plages entertainments; and the much-delayed **Cité de la Mode et du Design** (**Docks en Seine**), originally due to open in early 2009, is finally up and running.

Further south-east, rue Watt is the lowest street in Paris (it runs below river level). At 12 rue Cantagrel is Le Corbusier's Cité de Réfuge de l'Armée de Salut hostel, a reinforced concrete structure built to house 1,500 homeless men.

Bibliothèque Nationale de France François Mitterrand

10 quai François-Mauriac, 13th (01.53.79.59.59, www.bnf.fr). M° Bibliothèque François Mitterrand. **Open** 2-7pm Mon; 9am-7pm Tue-Sat; 1-7pm Sun. **Admission** *1 day* €3.50. *1 year* €38; €20 reductions. **Credit** MC, V. **Map** p407 M10.
Opened in 1996, the new national library was the last and costliest of Mitterrand's *grands projets*. Its architect, Dominique Perrault, was criticised for his dated design, which hides readers underground and stores the books in four L-shaped glass towers. He also forgot to specify blinds to protect books from sunlight; they had to be added afterwards. In the central void is a garden (filled with 140 trees, which were transported from Fontainebleau at enormous expense). The library houses over ten million volumes and can accommodate 3,000 readers. The research section, just below the public reading rooms, opened in 1998. Much of the library is open to the public: books, newspapers and periodicals are accessible to anyone over 18, and you can browse through photographic, film and sound archives in the audio-visual section.

Docks en Seine

28-36 quai d'Austerlitz, 13th (www.paris-docks-en-seine.fr). M° Chevaleret or Gare d'Austerlitz.
Since 2005, the apple-green caterpillar of Docks en Seine has been pupating on the banks of the river between the Gare d'Austerlitz and the BnF. It finally, belatedly opened its doors in 2012, transforming an industrial wasteland into a futuristic vision of culture and entertainment as imagined by architects Dominique Jakob and Brendan MacFarlane. From now on, its future is assured. A grassy terrace runs down to the water, there's a spanking new restaurant on the roof (the Moon Roof) and a bar/club (Wanderlust, by the team behind Silencio) on the first floor, and there are open-air screenings and exhibitions at the Cité de la Mode et du Design. The resurrection was completed with the opening of another club from the team behind Le Baron (another supremely cool nightspot) in late 2012. *See also p287* **River Dance**.

St-Germain-des-Prés & Odéon

Lounge with the literati and glitterati on the Left Bank.

St-Germain may be more Louis Vuitton than Boris Vian these days, but there are still enough small galleries and bookshops to ensure that it retains a whiff of its bohemian past. In the middle third of the 20th century, the area was prime arts and *intello* territory, a place known as much for its high jinks as its lofty thinking: the haunt of Picasso, Giacometti, Camus, Prévert and, *bien sûr*, the Bonnie and Clyde of French philosophy, Jean-Paul Sartre and Simone de Beauvoir; the hotspot of the Paris jazz boom after World War II; and the heart of the Paris book trade. This is where the cliché of café terrace intellectualising was coined, but nowadays most of the local patrons of the Flore and the Deux Magots are in the fashion business, and couturiers have largely replaced publishers. Never mind: it's a smart and attractive part of the city to wander around in, and also has some very good restaurants.

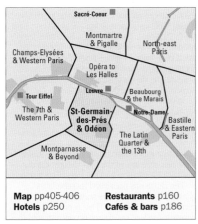

Map pp405-406	**Restaurants** p160
Hotels p250	**Cafés & bars** p186

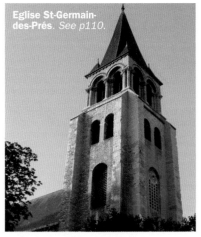

Eglise St-Germain-des-Prés. *See p110.*

FROM THE BOULEVARD TO THE SEINE

In the 6th arrondissement.

Hit by shortages of coal during World War II, Sartre shunned his cold apartment on rue Bonaparte. 'The principal interest of the Café de Flore,' he noted at the time, 'was that it had a stove, a nearby métro and no Germans.' Although you can spend more on a few coffees here than on a week's heating these days, the **Café de Flore** (*see p187*) remains an arty favourite, and hosts *café-philo* evenings in English. Its rival, **Les Deux Magots** (*see p187*), facing historic **Eglise St-Germain-des-Prés**, is frequented largely by tourists. Nearby is the celebrity favourite **Brasserie Lipp** (151 bd St-Germain, 6th, 01.45.48.53.91); art nouveau fans tend to prefer **Brasserie Vagenende** (142 bd St-Germain, 6th, 01.43.26.68.18, www.vagenende.com).

EXPLORE

Institut de France. *See p110.*

Swish bookshop **La Hune** (*see p192*) provides sustenance of a more intellectual kind.

St-Germain-des-Prés grew up around the medieval abbey, the oldest church in Paris. There are traces of its cloister and part of the abbot's palace behind the church on rue de l'Abbaye. Constructed in 1586 in red brick with stone facing, the palace prefigured the architecture of **place des Vosges**. Charming place de Furstemberg (once the palace stables) is home to the house and studio where the elderly Delacroix lived when painting the murals in St-Sulpice; it now houses the **Musée National Delacroix**. Wagner, Ingres and Colette lived on nearby rue Jacob; its elegant 17th-century *hôtels particuliers* now contain specialist book, design and antiques shops and a few pleasant hotels.

Further east, rue de Buci hosts a street market and upmarket food shops, and is home to legendary local **Bar du Marché** (no.16, 6th, 01.43.26.55.15). **Hôtel La Louisiane** (60 rue de Seine, 6th, 01.44.32.17.17, www.hotel-lalouisiane. com) has hosted jazz stars Chet Baker and Miles Davis, and Existentialist lovers Sartre and de Beauvoir. Rue de Seine, rue des Beaux-Arts and rue Bonaparte (Manet was born in the latter, at no.5, in 1832) are still packed with art galleries. It was in rue des Beaux-Arts, at the Hôtel d'Alsace, that Oscar Wilde complained about the wallpaper and then checked out for good. Now fashionably renovated, it houses the hip **L'Hôtel** (*see p251*). **La Palette** (*see p188*)

is a great pit stop with an enviable terrace; rue Mazarine, with shops selling lighting, vintage toys and jewellery, is also home to Terence Conran's bright, buzzing and wonderfully stylish **L'Alcazar** brasserie (no.62, 6th, 01.53.10.19.99, www.alcazar.fr). Set in the confines of a 17th-century real tennis court, and once a notorious transvestite bar, the space has been transformed with a glass roof, cool lighting and a changing series of photographic exhibits.

On quai de Conti stands the neoclassical Hôtel des Monnaies, built for Louis XV by architect Jacques-Denis Antoine; formerly the mint (1777-1973), it's now the **Musée de la Monnaie** (www.monnaiedeparis.fr) and traces the history of French coinage. Next door stands the domed **Institut de France**, cleaned to within an inch of its classical life. Opposite, the iron Pont des Arts footbridge leads directly to the Louvre. Further along, the city's main fine arts school, the **Ecole Nationale Supérieure des Beaux-Arts**, occupies an old monastery.

Ecole Nationale Supérieure des Beaux-Arts (Ensb-a)

14 rue Bonaparte, 6th (01.47.03.50.00, www. ensba.fr). M° St-Germain-des-Prés. **Open** 1-7pm Tue-Sun. **Admission** €4; €2 reductions. *Exhibitions* prices vary. **Credit** V. **Map** p408 H6. The city's most prestigious fine arts school resides in what remains of the 17th-century Couvent des Petits-Augustins, the 18th-century Hôtel de Chimay,

Eglise St-Sulpice. *See p113.*

some 19th-century additions and some chunks of assorted French châteaux that were moved here after the Revolution (when the buildings briefly served as a museum of French monuments, before becoming the art school in 1816).

★ FREE Eglise St-Germain-des-Prés
3 pl St-Germain-des-Prés, 6th (01.55.42.81.33, www.eglise-sgp.org). M° St-Germain-des-Prés.
Open 8am-7.45pm Mon-Sat; 9am-8pm Sun.
Admission free. **Map** p408 H7.
This is the oldest church in Paris. On the advice of Germain (later Bishop of Paris), Childebert, son of Clovis, had a basilica and monastery built here around 543. It was first dedicated to St Vincent, and came to be known as St-Germain-le-Doré ('the gilded') because of its copper roof, then later as St-Germain-des-Prés ('of the fields'). During the Revolution the abbey was burned and a saltpetre refinery installed; the spire was added in a clumsy 19th-century restoration. Still, most of the present structure is 12th century, and ornate carved capitals and the tower remain from the 11th. Tombs include those of Jean-Casimir, the deposed King of Poland who became Abbot of St-Germain in 1669, and of Scots nobleman William Douglas. Under the window in the second chapel is the funeral stone of philosopher-mathematician Descartes. *Photo p108.*

Institut de France
23 quai de Conti, 6th (01.44.41.44.41, www. institut-de-france.fr). M° Louvre Rivoli or Pont Neuf. **Open** *Guided tours only* (call 01.44.41.43.32 for times). **Admission** prices vary. **No credit cards. Map** p408 H6.
This elegant domed building with two sweeping curved wings was designed as a school by Louis Le Vau and opened in 1684. The five academies of the Institut (Académie Française, Académie des Inscriptions et Belles-Lettres, Académie des Beaux-Arts, Académie des Sciences, Académie des Sciences Morales et Politiques) moved here in 1805. Inside is Mazarin's ornate tomb by Hardouin-Mansart, and the Bibliothèque Mazarine (open to over-18s with ID and two photos; €15/year). The Académie Française was founded by Cardinal Richelieu in 1635 with the aim of preserving the purity of French from corrupting outside influences (such as English). *Photo p109.*

Musée National Delacroix
6 rue de Furstenberg, 6th (01.44.41.86.50, www.musee-delacroix.fr). M° St-Germain-des-Prés. **Open** 9.30am-5pm Mon, Wed-Sun.
Admission €5; free under-18s, under-26s (EU citizens), all 1st Sun of mth. PMP.
Credit MC, V. **Map** p408 H7.
Eugène Delacroix moved to this apartment and studio in 1857 in order to be near the Eglise St-Sulpice, where he was painting murals. This collection includes small oil paintings, free pastel studies of skies, sketches and lithographs, as well as his palette.

ST-SULPICE & THE LUXEMBOURG

In the 6th arrondissement.

Crammed with historic buildings and inviting shops, the quarter south of boulevard St-Germain between Odéon and Luxembourg epitomises civilised Paris. Just off the boulevard lies the covered market of St-Germain, now the site of a shopping arcade, auditorium, food hall and underground swimming pool. There are bars and bistros along rue Guisarde, nicknamed rue de la Soif ('thirst street') thanks to its carousers; it contains the late-night **Birdland** bar (no.8, 6th, 01.43.26.97.59) and a couple of notable bistros, including **Mâchon d'Henri** (no.8, 6th, 01.43.29.08.70). Rue Princesse and rue des Canettes are a mix of budget restaurants and nocturnal haunts.

Pass the fashion boutiques, pâtisseries and antiquarian book and print shops and you come to **Eglise St-Sulpice**, a surprising 18th-century exercise in classical form with two unmatching turrets and a colonnaded façade. The square in front was designed in the 19th century by Visconti; it contains his lion-flanked Fontaine des Quatre Points Cardinaux (a pun on

INSIDE TRACK
PICTURE WINDOW

Squashed in between bistro tables, galleries and a wing of the art school on a side street, **Pièce Unique** (4 rue Jacques Callot, 6th, 01.43.26.54.58, www.galeriepieceunique.com) is indeed unique: a shopfront space where a specially created artwork is displayed in the window to catch the attention not just of the art world cognoscenti but also of casual passers-by – the *vitrine* remains illuminated until 2am.

cardinal points and the statues of Bishops Bossuet, Fénelon, Massilon and Flechier, none of whom was actually a cardinal).

Among shops of religious artefacts, the chic boutiques on place and rue St-Sulpice include **Yves Saint Laurent** (*see p202*), **Vanessa Bruno** (*see p205*) and milliner **Marie Mercié** (*see p208*). Prime shopping continues further west: clothes on rue Bonaparte and rue du Four, and accessory and fashion shops on rue du Dragon, rue de Grenelle and rue du

Jardin du Luxembourg. *See p115.*

EXPLORE

BATOBUS PARIS

RIVER-BOAT SHUTTLE SERVICE

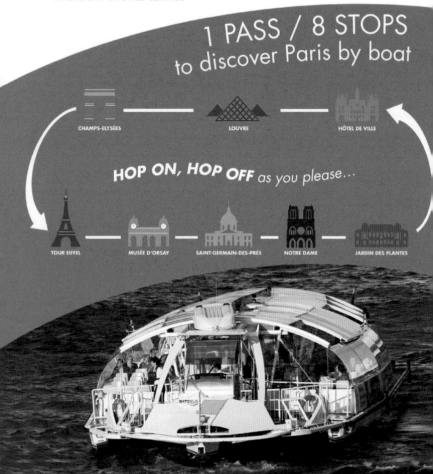

1 PASS / 8 STOPS
to discover Paris by boat

CHAMPS-ELYSÉES · LOUVRE · HÔTEL DE VILLE

HOP ON, HOP OFF as you please...

TOUR EIFFEL · MUSÉE D'ORSAY · SAINT-GERMAIN-DES-PRÉS · NOTRE DAME · JARDIN DES PLANTES

Batobus shows you a different view of Paris...
Your ticket is a pass: you can get on and off the boat where you like,
when you like for 1 day , 2 days, 5 days or a year.

Information and booking:
0 825 05 01 01 (0.15€/min) www.batobus.com

a **sodexo** company

Odéon, Théâtre de L'Europe.

EXPLORE

Cherche-Midi. If you spot a queue in the latter, it's most likely for bread at **Poilâne** (*see p214*). Across the street, at the junction of rue de Sèvres and rue du Cherche-Midi, César's bronze *Centaur* is the sculptor's tribute to Picasso.

The early 17th-century chapel of St-Joseph-des-Carmes – once a Carmelite convent, now hidden within the **Institut Catholique** (21 rue d'Assas, 6th, 01.44.39.52.00, www.icp.fr) – was the scene of the murder of 115 priests during the Terror in 1792. To the east lies wide rue de Tournon, lined by such grand 18th-century residences as the elegant Hôtel de Brancas (no.6), with figures of Justice and Prudence over the door. This street opens up to the **Palais du Luxembourg**, which now serves as the Senate, and the adjoining **Jardin du Luxembourg**.

Towards boulevard St-Germain is the neoclassical **Odéon, Théâtre de l'Europe** (*see p310*), built in 1779. A house in the square in front was home to Revolutionary hero Camille Desmoulins, who incited the mob to attack the Bastille in 1789. It's now occupied by **La Méditerranée** (2 pl de l'Odéon, 6th, 01.43.26.02.30, www.la-mediterranee.com); the restaurant's menus and plates were designed by Jean Cocteau. Joyce's *Ulysses* was first published in 1922 by Sylvia Beach at the celebrated **Shakespeare & Company** (*see p193*) at 12 rue de l'Odéon.

Further along the street, at 12 rue de l'Ecole-de-Médecine, is the neoclassical Université René Descartes (Paris V) medical school, and the Musée d'Histoire de la Médecine. The Club des Cordeliers, set up by Danton in 1790, devised revolutionary plots across the street at the **Couvent des Cordeliers** (no.15); the 14th-century refectory, all that remains of the monastery founded by St Louis, houses modern art exhibitions. Marat, one of the club's leading lights, was stabbed to death in the bathtub at his home in the same street; David depicted the moment after the crime in his iconic painting, the *Death of Marat*. This was the surgeons' district: observe the building at no.5, once the barbers' and surgeons' guild. Climb rue André-Dubois to rue Monsieur-le-Prince to budget restaurant **Polidor** (no.41, 6th, 01.43.26.95.34, www.polidor.com), open since 1845.

FREE Eglise St-Sulpice

Pl St-Sulpice, 6th (01.42.34.59.98, www.paroisse-saint-sulpice-paris.org). M° St-Sulpice. **Open** 7.30am-7.30pm daily. **Admission** free. **Map** p408 H7.

It took 120 years and six architects to finish St-Sulpice. The grandiose façade, with its two-tier colonnade, was designed by Jean-Baptiste Servandoni. He died in 1766 before the second tower was finished, leaving one tower a good five metres shorter than the other. The trio of murals by Delacroix in the first

EXPLORE

Cycle Left Bank Lunch

Pedal your way to a perfect picnic.

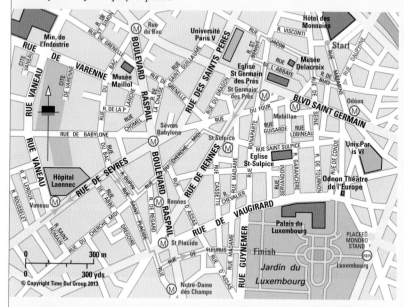

Aside from art and books, the sixth arrondissement (and its neighbour the seventh) is also a great place to shop for food, since it has some of the finest artisanal bakeries and *traiteurs* in Paris.

And thanks to Vélib (www.velib.paris.fr), it's easier than ever to get around the *quartier* in order to stock up. What's more, the standard-issue bike is equipped with a basket that should carry all you'll need for a sumptuous picnic. This itinerary will probably take you the best part of two hours. Don't bother searching for a station each time you need to stop; just use the chain provided to lock your bike.

Detach your bike from the *borne* at 1 rue Jacques-Callot, 6th (Mº Mabillon) and cycle down rue Mazarine as far as the carrefour de Buci. Turn left into rue de Buci and carry on until the junction with rue de Seine. The stretch of rue de Seine between here and boulevard St-Germain is lined with butchers and greengrocers. Ignore the smell of roasting chickens (you'll be getting cooked meat elsewhere), and just buy salad leaves and fruit. Then head back down rue de Seine towards the river. About halfway

down, turn left into rue Jacob. Cross rue Bonaparte and take the next left into rue St-Benoît. Pause for a moment to look in the window of **Librairie St-Benoît-des-Prés** (2 rue St-Benoît, 6th, 01.40.20.43.42), which specialises in rare books, manuscripts and letters.

Continue down rue St-Benoît as far as place St-Germain-des-Prés, where you'll find three venerable institutions: **Café de Flore** (*see p187*), **Les Deux Magots** (*see p187*) and **La Hune** bookshop (*see p192*). The Flore and the Deux Magots buzz more with tourists than writers these days, though the former is still a favoured haunt of *enfant terrible* Bernard-Henri Lévy. If you spot a man with a mane of black hair and a white shirt open to the navel poring over a notebook, it's probably BHL. Next door, La Hune is a kind of holy shrine for that nearly extinct species, the Left Bank Intellectual.

But it's not books we're after, it's bread; so cross boulevard St-Germain and follow rue Gozlin round into rue de Rennes. This is a broad, busy main road lined with chain stores. There's not a great deal to distract as you bowl south for half a kilometre or so, until you reach rue du Vieux-Colombier on the right. You'll have to do battle with buses and taxis in this narrow cut-through, which leads to the far more charming rue du Cherche-Midi. On the left-hand side of the street, wedged among the boutiques, jewellers and galleries, stands **Poilâne** (*see p214*), the renowned family bakers. You can expect to have to queue here for the famous Poilâne loaf – but it's worth it: dark, firm and distinctively flavoured. The tarts and the biscuits are wonderful too.

Having loaded the bread into your basket, carry on down rue du Cherche-Midi. Go straight across boulevard Raspail, then take the first right into rue Dupin. You'll eventually reach rue de Sèvres. Lock your bike against the railings here and cross the road on foot to La Grande Epicérie, the food hall in Paris's oldest department store, **Le Bon Marché** (*see p190*). This is a gastronome's paradise. Make your way to the *traiteurs* in the centre of the hall and choose from a staggering array of cooked meats. While you're here, you can also pick up dressing for the salad and a bottle of wine (and a corkscrew if needed).

It just remains to buy some cheese, and for this you'll need to cycle a little further south down rue de Sèvres. You'll pass the wonderful art deco entrance to the Vaneau metro station on the right, with its green iron lattices and globe lanterns. A little further along on the same side of the street, on the corner of rue Pierre-Leroux, stands **Fromagerie Quatrehomme** (*see p214*). Run by Marie Quatrehomme, this place is famous across Paris for its comté fruité, beaufort and oozy st-marcellin.

Your basket will be near to overflowing. It's time to head for a picnic spot in the Jardin du Luxembourg. Turn round and cycle back up rue de Sèvres, then turn right into rue St-Placide. Shortly after you pass the St-Placide métro station, turn left into rue de Fleurus. The **Jardin du Luxembourg** (*see right*) is ahead of you, on the far side of rue Guynemer. There's a Vélib station at 26 rue Guynemer. As is usual in Paris, the grass here is not for sitting on. Instead, find a bench in the shade and tuck in.

chapel – *Jacob's Fight with the Angel, Heliodorus Chased from the Temple* and *St Michael Killing the Dragon* – create a sombre atmosphere. *Photo p110.*

★ FREE Jardin & Palais du Luxembourg

Pl André Honnorat, pl Edmond-Rostand or rue de Vaugirard, 6th (01.44.54.19.49, www. senat.fr/visite). M° Odéon/RER Luxembourg. **Open** *Jardin* summer 7.30am-dusk daily; winter 8am-dusk daily. **Map** p408 H8.

The palace itself was built in the 1620s for Marie de Médicis, widow of Henri IV, by Salomon de Brosse on the site of the former mansion of the Duke of Luxembourg. Its Italianate style was intended to remind her of the Pitti Palace in her native Florence. The palace now houses the French parliament's upper house, the Sénat (open only by guided visits).

The mansion next door (Le Petit Luxembourg) is the residence of the Sénat's president. The gardens, though, are the real draw: part formal (terraces and gravel paths), part 'English garden' (lawns and mature trees), they are the quintessential Paris park. The garden is crowded with sculptures: a looming Cyclops (on the 1624 Fontaine de Médicis), queens of France, a miniature Statue of Liberty, wild animals, busts of Flaubert and Baudelaire, and a monument to Delacroix. There are orchards and an apiary. The Musée du Luxembourg (*see below*) hosts prestigious exhibitions. Most interesting, though, are the people: a mixture of *flâneurs* and *dragueurs*, chess players and martial-arts practitioners, as well as children on ponies, in sandpits, on roundabouts and playing with the sailing boats on the pond. *Photo p111.*

★ Musée des Lettres et Manuscrits

222 Blvd St-Germain, 6th (01.42.22.48.48, www.museedeslettres.fr). M° Rue du Bac. **Open** 10am-7pm Tue, Wed, Fri-Sun; 10am-9.30pm Thur. **Admission** €7; €5 reductions; free under-12s. **Credit** (€16 minimum) MC, V. **Map** p408 H7.

More than 2,000 documents and letters give an insight into the lives of the great and the good, from Magritte to Mozart. Einstein arrives at the theory of relativity on notes scattered in authentic disorder, Baudelaire complains about his money problems in a letter to his mother, and HMS *Northumberland*'s logbook records the day Napoleon boarded the ship to be taken to St Helena.

Musée du Luxembourg

19 rue de Vaugirard, 6th (01.40.13.62.00, www.museeduluxembourg.fr). M° Cluny La Sorbonne or Odéon/RER Luxembourg. **Open** 10am-10pm Mon, Fri; 10am-7.30pm Tue-Thur, Sat, Sun. **Admission** €11; €7.50 reductions; free under-13s. **Credit** MC, V. **Map** p408 H7.

When it opened in 1750, this small museum was the first public gallery in France. After closing for more than a year, the museum reopened in early 2011 with a Cranach exhibition, followed by a major Cézanne retrospective. Book ahead to avoid queues.

EXPLORE

Montparnasse & Beyond

The rise and fall of 'Mount Parnassus'.

Montparnasse's heyday was short, but for a few years between the two world wars it was the emblematic 'gay Paree' district of after-dark merriment and fruitful artistic exchange. A great number of its most prominent figures were expats (including its finest chronicler, the Hungarian photographer Brassaï), and the late-night bars and artists' studios formed a bubble of cordial international relations that was irreparably popped in 1939. The local atmosphere soured further with the completion of the much-loathed Tour Montparnasse in the early 1970s, a dark monolith that cast an ominous spell on the whole quarter. The dismay with which its construction was greeted prompted a change in building regulations in the city. Granted, this is rich territory for art museums – and the Musée Zadkine should be sparkling in 2013 after a lengthy revamp – but with the exception of the Fondation Cartier, they're all about past glories.

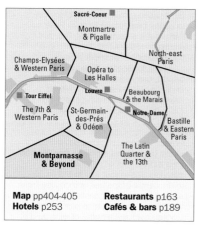

Sacré-Coeur
Montmartre & Pigalle
Champs-Elysées & Western Paris
North-east Paris
Opéra to Les Halles
Tour Eiffel
Louvre
Beaubourg & the Marais
The 7th & Western Paris
St-Germain-des-Prés & Odéon
Notre-Dame
Bastille & Eastern Paris
The Latin Quarter & the 13th
Montparnasse & Beyond

Map pp404-405 **Restaurants** p163
Hotels p253 **Cafés & bars** p189

MONTPARNASSE

In the 6th & 14th arrondissements.

Artists Picasso, Léger and Soutine fled to 'Mount Parnassus' in the early 1900s to escape the rising rents of Montmartre. They were soon joined by Chagall, Zadkine and other refugees from the Russian Revolution, along with Americans such as Man Ray, Henry Miller, Ezra Pound and Gertrude Stein. Between the wars the neighbourhood was the epitome of modernity: studios with large windows were built by avant-garde architects; artists, writers and intellectuals drank and debated in the quarter's showy bars; and naughty pastimes – including the then risqué tango – flourished.

Sadly, the Montparnasse of today has lost much of its former soul, dominated as it is by the lofty **Tour Montparnasse** – the first

skyscraper to be built in central Paris. At its foot are a shopping centre, the **Mix Club** (www.mixclub.fr), and in winter an open-air ice rink. There are fabulous panoramic views from the newly renovated terrace on the 56th floor, reaching up to 40km (25 miles) on a clear day.

The old Montparnasse station witnessed two events of historical significance. In 1898, a runaway train burst through its façade; and on 25 August 1944, the German forces surrendered Paris here. The station was rebuilt in the 1970s, a grey affair above which can be found the surprisingly oasis-like Jardin Atlantique, the **Mémorial du Maréchal Leclerc** and the **Musée Jean Moulin**.

Rue du Montparnasse, appropriately for a street near the station that sends trains to Brittany, is dotted with crêperies. Nearby, strip joints have replaced most of the theatres on ever-saucy rue de la Gaîté, but boulevard

Edgar-Quinet has pleasant cafés and a street market (Wed, Sat), plus the entrance to the Cimetière du Montparnasse. Boulevard du Montparnasse still buzzes at night, thanks to its many cinemas and dining spots: giant art deco brasserie **La Coupole** (*see p165*); opposite, classic café **Le Select** (*see p189*); **Le Dôme** (no.108, 14th, 01.43.35.25.81), now a top fish restaurant and bar; and restaurant **La Rotonde** (no.105, 6th, 01.43.26.48.26, www.rotondemontparnasse.com). All were popularised by the literati between the wars, and now use this heritage to their advantage; Le Select seems the most authentic. Nearby, on boulevard Raspail, stands Rodin's statue of Balzac, whose rugged rather than flattering appearance caused such a scandal that it was put in place only after the sculptor's death.

For a whiff of Montparnasse's artistic history, wander down rue de la Grande-Chaumière. Bourdelle and Friesz taught at the venerable **Académie de la Grande-Chaumière** (no.14, 01.43.26.13.72, www.grande-chaumiere.fr), frequented by Calder, Giacometti and Pompon among others (it still offers drawing lessons); Modigliani died at no.8 in 1920, ruined by tuberculosis, drugs and alcohol; nearby **Musée Zadkine** occupies the sculptor's old house and studio. Rue Vavin and rue Bréa, leading to the Jardin du Luxembourg, have become an enclave of children's shops. Look out for no.6, the 1912 white-tiled apartment building where art nouveau architect Henri Sauvage lived.

Cimetière du Montparnasse. See p118.

Serge Gainsbourg
1928 - 1991

Further east on boulevard du Montparnasse, literary café **La Closerie des Lilas** (no.171, 6th, 01.40.51.34.50, www.closeriedeslilas.fr) was a pre-war favourite with everyone from Lenin and Trotsky to Picasso and Hemingway; brass plaques on the tables indicate where each historic figure used to sit. Next to it is the lovely 19th-century **Fontaine de l'Observatoire**, featuring bronze turtles and thrashing sea horses by Frémiet, and figures of the four continents by Carpeaux.

From here, the Jardins de l'Observatoire form part of the green axis between the Palais du Luxembourg and the royal observatory, the **Observatoire de Paris**. A curiosity next door is the Maison des Fontainiers, built over an expansive (now dry-ish) underground reservoir originally commissioned by Marie de Médicis to supply water to fountains around the city.

A relatively recent addition to boulevard Raspail is the glass and steel **Fondation Cartier pour l'Art Contemporain**. Designed by architect Jean Nouvel, it houses the jewellers' head offices and an exhibition space dedicated to contemporary art and photography.

West of the train station, the redevelopment of Montparnasse is also evident in the circular place de Catalogne, a piece of 1980s postmodern neoclassicism by Mitterrand's favourite architect, Ricardo Bofill, and the housing estates of rue Vercingétorix.

There are still some traces of the old, arty Montparnasse for those willing to look for it: in impasse Lebouis, an avant-garde studio building houses the **Fondation Henri Cartier-Bresson**; at 21 avenue du Maine, an ivy-clad alleyway of old studios contains the artist-run exhibition space Immanence, as well as the **Musée du Montparnasse**, housed in the former academy and canteen of Russian painter Marie Vassilieff; on rue Antoine-Bourdelle, the **Musée Bourdelle** includes another old cluster of studios, where sculptor Antoine Bourdelle, Symbolist painter Eugène Carrière and, briefly, Marc Chagall all worked. Towards Les Invalides, on rue Mayet, craft and restoration workshops are still tucked away in the old courtyards.

EXPLORE

Fondation Cartier pour l'Art Contemporain.

You walk up a winding garden path to get to this museum, founded by Jean Dubuffet, wine merchant and master of *art brut*. The foundation ensures that a fair body of his works is accessible to the public. There's a changing display of Dubuffet's lively drawings, paintings and sculptures, as well as models of the architectural sculptures from the *Hourloupe* cycle.
► *The foundation also looks after the Closerie Falbala, the 3D masterpiece of the Hourloupe cycle, housed at Périgny-sur-Yerres, east of Paris.*

★ Fondation Henri Cartier-Bresson
2 impasse Lebouis, 14th (01.56.80.27.00, www.henricartierbresson.org). M° Gaîté. **Open** 1-6.30pm Tue, Thur, Fri, Sun; 1-8.30pm Wed; 11am-6.45pm Sat. Closed Aug & between exhibitions. **Admission** €6; €4 reductions; free 6.30-8.30pm Wed. **No credit cards. Map** p405 F10.
This two-floor gallery is dedicated to the work of acclaimed photographer Henri Cartier-Bresson. It consists of a tall, narrow *atelier* in a 1913 building, with a minutely catalogued archive, open to researchers, and a lounge on the fourth floor screening films. In the spirit of Cartier-Bresson, who assisted on three Jean Renoir films and drew and painted all his life, the Fondation opens its doors to other disciplines with three annual shows. The convivial feel of the Fondation – and its Le Corbusier armchairs – fosters relaxed discussion with staff and other visitors.

FREE Cimetière du Montparnasse
3 bd Edgar-Quinet, 14th (01.44.10.86.50). M° Edgar Quinet or Raspail. **Open** 16 Mar-5 Nov 8am-6pm Mon-Fri; 8.30am-6pm Sat; 9am-6pm Sun. 6 Nov-15 Mar 8am-5.30pm Mon-Fri; 8.30am-5.30pm Sat; 9am-5.30pm Sun. **Admission** free. **Map** p405 G9.
Formed by commandeering three farms (you can still see the ruins of a windmill by rue Froidevaux), the Montparnasse boneyard has plenty of literary clout: Beckett, Baudelaire, Sartre, de Beauvoir and Maupassant all rest here. There are also artists, including Brancusi, Frédéric Bartholdi (sculptor of the Statue of Liberty) and Man Ray. The celebrity roll-call continues with Serge Gainsbourg, André Citroën and actress Jean Seberg. *Photo p117.*

★ Fondation Cartier pour l'Art Contemporain
261 bd Raspail, 14th (01.42.18.56.50, www.fondation.cartier.fr). M° Denfert-Rochereau or Raspail. **Open** 11am-10pm Tue; 11am-8pm Wed-Sun. **Admission** €9.50; €6.50 reductions; free under-10s & under-18s 2-6pm Wed. **Credit** AmEx, MC, V. **Map** p405 G9.
Jean Nouvel's glass and steel building, an exhibition centre with Cartier's offices above, is as much a work of art as the installations inside. Shows by artists and photographers often have wide-ranging themes, such as 'Birds' or 'Desert'. Live events around the shows are called Nuits Nomades.

Fondation Dubuffet
137 rue de Sèvres, 6th (01.47.34.12.63, www.dubuffetfondation.com). M° Duroc. **Open** 2-6pm Mon-Fri. Closed Aug. **Admission** €6; €4 reductions; free under-10s. **No credit cards. Map** p405 E8.

FREE Mémorial du Maréchal Leclerc de Hauteclocque et de la Libération de Paris & Musée Jean Moulin
Jardin Atlantique, 23 allée de la 2e DB (above Gare Montparnasse), 15th (01.40.64.39.44, www.ml-leclerc-moulin.paris.fr). M° Montparnasse Bienvenüe. **Open** 10am-6pm Tue-Sun. **Admission** free. *Exhibitions* €4; €2-€3 reductions; free under-13s. **Credit** *Shop* MC, V. **Map** p405 F9.
This double museum retraces World War II and the Resistance through the Free French commander Maréchal Leclerc and left-wing hero Jean Moulin. Documentary material and film archives complement an impressive 270° slide show, complete with sound effects, which tells the story of the Liberation of Paris.

FREE Musée-Atelier Adzak
3 rue Jonquoy, 14th (01.45.43.06.98). M° Plaisance. **Open** usually 3-7pm Sat, Sun (call in advance). **Admission** free.
The eccentric house, studio and garden built by the late Roy Adzak, a British-born painter and sculptor who died in 1987, harbour traces of the conceptual artist's plaster body columns and dehydrations. Now a registered British-run charity, it gives mostly foreign artists a chance to exhibit in Paris.

FREE Musée Bourdelle
16-18 rue Antoine-Bourdelle, 15th (01.49.54.73.73, www.bourdelle.paris.fr). M° Falguière or Montparnasse Bienvenüe. **Open**

Back Stories

Every object tells a story at this magical new Montparnasse shop.

Once upon a time in Montparnasse, Brit Fiona Cameron saw a 'For rent' sign below her apartment... and that was the beginning of **Storie** (20 rue Delambre, 14th, 01.83.56.01.98, www.storieblog. com), the magical shop that's become a word-of-mouth success with its eclectic collection of objects from around the world, ranging from €2 to €1,000.

'My mum would pick things out of dustbins when we lived in Singapore,' Cameron laughs. 'I guess that's where it all began.' Today, her parents live in Sri Lanka, which is the source of some of the most striking finds in the shop, including the brightly painted wooden deer heads (€350) – like ecological hunting trophies – made by a village carpenter. Other objects are made from papier mâché, or come in humorous DIY flat-pack kits printed with patchwork patterns (€28-€100).

Cameron also stocks unusual, artisanal objects from closer to home, such as porcelain vases cast from throwaway plastic containers, or Béa Corteel's reworking of jumble-sale floral china plates overlaid with spiders or scorpions.

'I suppose you could call it anti-IKEA,' she says. 'If someone tells you where something comes from – the story behind it – you will treasure it more. I know lots of creative people and thought it would be great if it could be a platform for traditional artisans and young designers.'

A classic example is the beautiful hand-cut Korean coffee cups by Ji Hyan Chung (€24-€40). Petal-like, they use the same transparent rice technique as Chinese restaurant teacups, but are then hand-cut to reveal circles of colour and degrees of transparency. Tine De Ruysser's origami brooches, meanwhile, are made from bank notes (€28.50-€35) that cock a snook at the banking crisis.

If the nomadic treasure-trove atmosphere is a little like the French shop Caravane, the difference here is that spark of British humour. 'My husband is French and he sometimes looks at things in horror, like the plastic duck watering-cans we had – but they turned out to be bestsellers. Sometimes people come in and pull the most crazy things out of bags, like full-size Madame Tussaud-style models of Buddhist monks – the guy started putting them all around the shop, and I had to say a polite "no".'

Keen to pull in all strands of artistic activity, Fiona programmes exhibitions, storytelling, even a flash concert of a seven-piece band. Check the blog for details of the latest events.

EXPLORE

Tour Montparnasse.

10am-6pm Tue-Sun. **Admission** free. *Exhibitions*
€7; €3.50-€5.50 reductions; free under-14s.
Credit MC, V. **Map** p405 F8.
The sculptor Antoine Bourdelle (1861-1929), who
was a pupil of Rodin, produced a number of monumental works including the modernist relief friezes
at the Théâtre des Champs-Elysées, which were
inspired by Isadora Duncan and Nijinsky. The
museum includes the artist's apartment and studios, which were also used by Eugène Carrière,
Dalou and Chagall. A 1950s extension tracks the
evolution of Bourdelle's equestrian monument to
General Alvear in Buenos Aires, and his masterful
Hercules the Archer. A new wing by Christian de
Portzamparc houses bronzes, including various
studies of Beethoven in different guises.

Musée du Montparnasse

*21 av du Maine, 15th (01.42.22.91.96, www.
museedumontparnasse.net). M° Montparnasse
Bienvenüe.* **Open** 12.30-7pm Tue-Sun. **Admission**
€6; €5 reductions; free under-12s. **No credit
cards. Map** p403 F8.
Set in one of the last surviving alleys of studios,
this was home to Marie Vassilieff, whose academy
and cheap canteen – 'la Cantine des Artistes' – welcomed poor artists, including famous names such as
Picasso, Cocteau, Matisse, Braque and Modigliani.
Trotsky and Lenin were also guests. The museum's
shows focus on present-day artists and the area's
creative past.

Musée Pasteur

*Institut Pasteur, 25 rue du Dr-Roux, 15th
(01.45.68.82.83, www.pasteur.fr). M° Pasteur.*
Open 2-5.30pm Mon-Fri. Closed Aug.
Admission €7; €3 reductions. **Credit** MC, V.
Map p405 E9.

The flat where the famous chemist and his wife lived
at the end of his life (1888-95) has not been touched;
you can see their furniture and possessions, photos
and instruments. An extravagant mausoleum on the
ground floor houses Pasteur's tomb, decorated with
mosaics depicting his scientific achievements.

Musée de la Poste

*34 bd de Vaugirard, 15th (01.42.79.24.24, www.
ladressemuseedelaposte.com). M° Montparnasse
Bienvenüe.* **Open** 10am-6pm Mon-Sat. **Admission**
€5; €3.50 reductions; free under-26s. PMP.
Temporary exhibitions €6.50; €5 reductions; free
under-13s. **No credit cards. Map** p405 E9.
From among the uniforms, pistols, carriages, official
decrees and fumigation tongs emerge snippets of
history: during the 1871 Siege of Paris, hot-air bal-
loons and carrier pigeons were used to get post out
of the city, and *boules de Moulins*, balls crammed
with hundreds of letters, were floated down the Seine
in return, mostly never to arrive. The second section
covers French and international philately.

★ FREE Musée Zadkine

*100bis rue d'Assas, 6th (01.55.42.77.20,
www.zadkine.paris.fr). M° Notre-Dame-des-
Champs/RER Port-Royal.* **Open** 10am-6pm
Tue-Sun. **Admission** free. *Exhibitions* €4;
€2-€3 reductions; free under-13s. **Credit**
(€15 minimum) MC, V. **Map** p408 G8.
Works by the Russian-born Cubist sculptor Ossip
Zadkine are displayed around this tiny house and
garden near the Jardin du Luxembourg. Zadkine's
works cover musical, mythological and religious
subjects, and his style varies with his materials.
There are drawings and poems by Zadkine and
paintings by his wife, Valentine Prax. The museum
will have a new look in 2013 after a two-year revamp.

FREE Observatoire de Paris

61 av de l'Observatoire, 14th (01.40.51.23.97, www.obspm.fr). Entry for visitors at 77 av Denfert-Rochereau, 14th. M° St-Jacques/RER Port-Royal. **Tours** Email visite.paris@obspm or write to Observatoire de Paris, 61 av de l'Observatoire, 75014 Paris. **Map** p405 H10.

The Paris observatory was founded by Louis XIV's finance minister, Colbert, in 1667; it was designed by Claude Perrault (who also worked on the Louvre), with labs and an observation tower. The French meridian line drawn by François Arago in 1806 (which was used here before the Greenwich meridian was adopted as an international standard) runs north–south through the centre of the building. The dome on the observation tower was added in the 1840s.
► *You'll need to apply for an appointment at the Observatoire by letter or email, but it's also worth checking the website for openings linked to astronomical events – or visit on the Journées du Patrimoine (see p30).*

★ **Tour Montparnasse**

33 av du Maine, 15th (01.45.38.52.56, www. tourmontparnasse56.com). M° Montparnasse Bienvenüe. **Open** Oct-Mar 9.30am-10.30pm Mon-Thur, Sun; 9.30am-11pm Fri, Sat. Apr-Sept 9.30am-11.30pm daily. **Admission** €13; €6-€9.50 reductions; free under-7s. **Credit** MC, V. **Map** p405 F9.

Built in 1974 on the site of the old station, this 209m (686ft) steel-and-glass monolith is actually shorter than the Eiffel Tower, but better placed for fabulous views of the city – including, of course, the Eiffel Tower itself. A lift whisks you up in 38 seconds to the 56th floor, where you'll find a display of aerial scenes of Paris, an upgraded café-lounge, a souvenir shop – and lots and lots of sky. On a clear day you can see up to 40km (25 miles). Another lift takes you all the way up to the roof. Classical concerts are held on the terrace.

DENFERT-ROCHEREAU & MONTSOURIS

In the 14th & 15th arrondissements.

In the run-up to the 1789 Revolution, the bones of six million Parisians were taken from the handful of overcrowded city cemeteries and wheelbarrowed to the **Catacombes**, a vast network of tunnels that stretches under much of Paris. The sections under the 13th and 14th arrondissements are open to the public; the gloomy Denfert-Rochereau entrance is next to one of the toll gates of the Mur des Fermiers-Généraux, built by Ledoux in the 1780s.

The bronze *Lion de Belfort* dominates place Denfert-Rochereau, a favourite starting point for countless political demonstrations. The regal beast was sculpted by Bartholdi, of Statue of Liberty fame, and is a scaled-down replica of one in Belfort that commemorates the brave defence by Colonel Denfert-Rochereau of the town in 1870. Nearby, the southern half of rue Daguerre is a pedestrianised market street brimming with cafés and food stores.

One of the big draws of the area is the **Parc Montsouris**, with lovely lakes, dramatic cascades and an unusual history. Surrounding the western edge of the park are a number of modest, quiet streets – including rue du Parc Montsouris and rue Georges-Braque – that used to be lined during the 1920s and '30s with charming villas and artists' studios by avant-garde architects Le Corbusier and André Lurçat. On the southern edge of the park sprawls the **Cité Universitaire** complex.

★ **Les Catacombes**

1 av du Colonel-Henri-Rol-Tanguy, 14th (01.43.22.47.63, www.catacombes-de-paris.fr). M°/RER Denfert Rochereau. **Open** 10am-5pm

EXPLORE

Les Catacombes.

Tue-Sun (last entry 4pm). **Admission** €8; €4-€6 reductions; free under-14s. **Credit** (€15 minimum) MC, V. **Map** p407 H10.

This is the official entrance to the 3,000km (1,864-mile) tunnel network that runs under much of the city. With public burial pits overflowing in the late 18th century, the bones of six million people were transferred to the *catacombes*. The bones of Marat, Robespierre and their cronies are packed in with wall upon wall of their fellow citizens. A damp, cramped tunnel takes you through a series of galleries before you reach the ossuary, the entrance to which is announced by a sign engraved in the stone: 'Stop! This is the empire of death.' The tour lasts approximately 45 minutes.

FREE Cité Universitaire

17 bd Jourdan, 14th (01.44.16.64.00, www.ciup.fr). RER Cité Universitaire.

The Cité Universitaire is an odd mix. Created between the wars in a mood of internationalism and inspired by Oxbridge colleges, its 37 halls of residence across landscaped gardens were designed in a variety of supposedly authentic national styles. Some are by architects of the appropriate nationality (Dutchman Willem Dudok, for instance, designed the De Stijl-style Collège Néerlandais); others, such as the Khmer sculptures and bird-beak roof of the Asie du Sud-Est building, are merely pastiches. You can visit the sculptural white Pavillon Suisse (01.44.16.10.16, www.fondationsuisse.fr), which has a Le Corbusier mural on the ground floor. The spacious landscaped gardens are open to the public.

Parc Montsouris.

FREE Parc Montsouris

Bd Jourdan, 14th. RER Cité Universitaire.
Open 8am-dusk Mon-Fri; 9am-dusk Sat, Sun.

The most colourful of the capital's many parks, Montsouris was laid out for Baron Haussmann by Jean-Charles Adolphe Alphand. It includes a series of sweeping, gently sloping lawns, an artificial lake and cascades. On the opening day in 1878, the lake inexplicably emptied, and the engineer responsible committed suicide.

The 15th arrondissement

The expansive 15th arrondissement has little to offer tourists, though as a largely residential district it has plenty of good restaurants, street markets, and some good small shops, notably on rue du Commerce and rue Lecourbe. It's worth making a detour to visit **La Ruche** ('beehive'), designed by Eiffel as a wine pavilion for the 1900 Exposition Universelle and moved here to serve as artists' studios. Nearby is **Parc Georges Brassens**, opened in 1983, and at the porte de Versailles the sprawling **Paris-Expo** exhibition centre was created in 1923.

FREE Parc Georges Brassens

Rue des Morillons, 15th. Mº Porte de Vanves or Porte de Versailles. **Open** 8am-dusk Mon-Fri; 9am-dusk Sat, Sun. **Map** p404 D10.

Built on the site of the old Abattoirs de Vaugirard, Parc Georges Brassens prefigured the industrial regeneration of Parc André Citroën and La Villette. The gateways, crowned by bronze bulls, have been kept, as have a series of iron meat-market pavilions, which house a second-hand book market at weekends. The Jardin des Senteurs is planted with aromatic species, and a small vineyard yields 200 bottles of Clos des Morillons every year. The park is named in honour of the legendary French singer, who lived nearby at 42 rue Santos-Dumont.

Paris-Expo

1 pl de la Porte de Versailles, 15th (01.40.68.22.22, www.viparis.com). Mº Porte de Versailles. **Map** p404 B10.

This vast exhibition centre, spread over different halls, hosts trade and art fairs. Many, such as the Foire de Paris (*see p27*), are open to the public.

La Ruche

Passage de Dantzig, 15th (www.la-ruche.fr). Mº Convention or Porte de Versailles. **Map** p404 D10.

Have a peep through the fence to see the iron-framed former wine pavilion built by Gustave Eiffel for the 1900 Exposition Universelle, and later rebuilt by philanthropic sculptor Alfred Boucher to be let as studios for struggling artists. Chagall, Soutine, Brancusi, Modigliani, Lipchitz and Archipenko all spent periods here, and the 140 studios are still sought after by today's artists and designers.

The 7th & Western Paris

Old masters, new ministers and some of Paris's poshest quartiers.

The seventh arrondissement has long played host to the heavy machinery of state and diplomacy: this is the home of France's parliament, several ministries and a gaggle of foreign embassies, as well as the French army's training establishment and the headquarters of UNESCO. Unsurprisingly, much of the district is formal and aloof as a result. Thankfully, though, two of its greatest attractions – an A-shaped assembly of 19th-century iron lattice beside the river and a gallery in an old Beaux Arts train station – have decided to embrace the future with thoroughly modern makeovers. The Eiffel Tower is installing a dramatic glass floor for 2013 and the Musée d'Orsay has been nicknamed the 'Nouvel Orsay' after a stunning renovation.

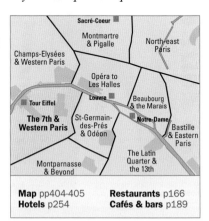

| Map pp404-405 | Restaurants p166 |
| Hotels p254 | Cafés & bars p189 |

EXPLORE

THE FAUBOURG ST-GERMAIN

In the 7th arrondissement.

In the early 18th century, when the Marais went out of fashion, aristocrats built palatial new residences on the Faubourg St-Germain, the district developing around the site of the former city wall. It is still a well-bred part of the city, government ministries and foreign embassies colouring the area with flags and diplomatic plates. Many fine *hôtels particuliers* survive; glimpse their elegant entrance courtyards on rue de Grenelle, rue St-Dominique, rue de l'Université and rue de Varenne.

Just west of St-Germain, the 'Carré Rive Gauche' – the quadrangle enclosed by quai Voltaire, rue des Sts-Pères, rue du Bac and rue de l'Université – is filled with antiques shops. On rue des Sts-Pères, *chocolatier* **Debauve & Gallais** (no.30, 7th, 01.45.48.54.67) has been making chocolates since 1800. Rue du Pré-aux-Clercs, named after a field where students used to duel, is now a favourite with fashion insiders.

There are still students to be found on rue St-Guillaume, home of the prestigious **Fondation Nationale des Sciences-Politiques** (no.27), more commonly known as 'Sciences-Po'.

Rue de Montalembert is home to two of the Left Bank's most fashionable hotels: the **Hôtel Montalembert** (*see p254*) and the Hôtel Pont Royal, a gastronomic magnet ever since the addition of the trendy **Atelier de Joël Robuchon** (www.joel-robuchon.com). By the

INSIDE TRACK
SPARKLING SIGHTS

For a river cruise with a difference, **Vedettes de Paris** (Port de Suffren, 7th, www.vedettesdeparis.com) runs one-hour evening champagne sightseeing trips (€45). A sommelier will guide you through three different champagnes as you cruise the Seine, all in the civilised comfort of the foredeck's private glass panorama room.

EXPLORE

Chapelle de la Médaille Miraculeuse. *See p127.*

river, a Beaux-Arts train station – the towns once served still listed on the façade – houses the unmissable art collections of the **Musée d'Orsay**; outside on the esplanade are 19th-century bronze animal sculptures.

Next door is the lovely 1780s Hôtel de Salm, once the Swedish embassy and now home to the **Musée National de la Légion d'Honneur et des Ordres de Chevalerie** (2 rue de la Légion d'Honneur, 7th, 01.40.62.84.25, www. musee-legiondhonneur.fr), devoted to France's honours system since Louis XI. The Legion of Honour was established by Napoleon in 1802. Across the street, a modern footbridge, the Passerelle Solférino, crosses the Seine to the Tuileries. The fancy Hôtel Bouchardon today houses the **Musée Maillol**. Right beside its curved entrance, the Fontaine des Quatre Saisons by Edmé Bouchardon features statues of the seasons surrounding allegorical figures of Paris above the rivers Seine and Marne.

You'll have to wait for the open-house **Journées du Patrimoine** (*see p30*) to see the decorative interiors and private gardens of other *hôtels*, such as the **Hôtel de Villeroy** (Ministry of Agriculture; 78 rue de Varenne, 7th), **Hôtel Boisgelin** (Italian Embassy; 51 rue de Varenne, 7th), **Hôtel d'Avaray** (Dutch ambassador's residence; 85 rue de Grenelle, 7th), **Hôtel d'Estrées** (Russian ambassador's residence; 79 rue de Grenelle, 7th) or **Hôtel de Monaco** (Polish Embassy; 57 rue St-Dominique, 7th). Among the most beautiful is the **Hôtel Matignon** (57 rue de Varenne, 7th), residence of the prime minister. Once used by French statesman Talleyrand for lavish receptions, it contains the biggest private garden in Paris. The Cité Varenne at no.51 is a lane of exclusive houses complete with private gardens.

Rue du Bac is home to the city's oldest and most elegant department store, **Le Bon Marché** ('the good bargain'), and to an unlikely pilgrimage spot, the **Chapelle de la Médaille Miraculeuse**. On nearby rue de Babylone, budget bistro **Au Babylone** (no.13, 7th, 01.45.48.72.13) has been serving up cheap lunches for decades, but the Théâtre de Babylone, where Beckett's *Waiting for Godot* was premiered in 1953, is long gone.

At the foot of boulevard St-Germain, facing place de la Concorde across the Seine, is the **Assemblée Nationale**, the lower house of the French parliament. Behind, elegant place du Palais-Bourbon leads into rue de Bourgogne, a rare commercial thoroughfare amid the official buildings, with some delectable pâtisseries and designer-furniture showrooms.

Beside the Assemblée is the Foreign Ministry, often referred to by its address, 'quai d'Orsay'. Beyond it, a long, grassy esplanade leads up to golden-domed Les Invalides. The vast military hospital complex, with its Eglise du Dôme and St-Louis-des-Invalides churches, all built by Louis XIV, epitomises the official grandeur of the Sun King as expression of royal and military power. It now houses the **Musée de l'Armée**, as well as Napoleon's tomb inside the Eglise du Dôme. Stand with your back to the dome to survey the cherubim-laden Pont Alexandre III and the **Grand** and **Petit Palais** over the river, all put up for the 1900 Exposition Universelle.

Just beside Les Invalides is the **Musée National Rodin**, occupying the charming 18th-century Hôtel Biron and its romantic gardens. Many of his great sculptures, including the *Thinker*, the *Burghers of Calais*

and the swarming *Gates of Hell*, are displayed in the building and around the gardens – as are those of his mistress, Camille Claudel.

FREE Assemblée Nationale

33 quai d'Orsay, 7th (www.assemblee-nationale.fr). M° Assemblée Nationale. **Map** p405 F5.

Like the Sénat, the Assemblée Nationale (also known as the Palais Bourbon) is a royal building adapted for republicanism. It was built between 1722 and 1728 for the Duchesse de Bourbon, daughter of Louis XIV and Madame de Montespan, who also put up the neighbouring Hôtel de Lassay for her lover, the Marquis de Lassay. The *palais* was modelled on the Grand Trianon at Versailles, with a colonnaded *cour d'honneur* opening on to rue de l'Université and gardens running down to the Seine. The Prince de Condé

Nouvel Orsay

The Musée d'Orsay is gleaming after a groundbreaking revamp.

The revamp of the **Musée d'Orsay** (*see p129*) hasn't changed the former railway station's exterior one iota – the wonder is all inside. On the museum's 25th anniversary, director Guy Cogeval has finally achieved a long-held dream to obliterate white walls, 'the enemy of painting', and give the Impressionist movement the brush-up it deserves.

After partially closing for 18 months, the 'Nouvel Orsay' opened its doors in October 2011 to gasps of admiration from the first visitors. On arriving at the fifth-floor Impressionist galleries one is confronted with a huge, wide space where the giant clockface window, previously hidden by corridors, floods the dark room with light. To the left, a giant mushroom pouffe invites visitors to sink into its comfortable folds.

The Impressionist galleries, previously a series of bland, skylit rooms that suffered from bottlenecks and overcrowding, have been utterly transformed with a sense of space and dark, moody colours such as anthracite, purple, vermillion and bottle-green. But it's not just the walls that make the paintings of Monet, Manet, Renoir and Cézanne sing out as if they had been painted yesterday. It is also the Solux lighting, which reveals every colour in the spectrum. The effect is extra-sensory: you can smell the surf of Monet's *Rough Sea at Etretat*, feel the heat of Renoir's surprising *Mosque in Algiers*, and taste the crispness of Pissarro's *White Freeze*, which hangs on a wall of winter paintings directly facing hot, southern scenes.

This is part of a dynamic approach to hanging that throws out the traditional chronological or artist-by-artist approach to juxtapose different visions of the same theme, even to the extent of bringing sculpture into the gallery. And the seating is a work of art in itself, with Tokujin Yoshioka's glass benches rippling in the centre of each room.

Cogeval had to fight to get his plans – which also involved building new galleries into the Pavillon Amont and ripping out the columns in the erstwhile Columns Room – approved. He brushes this off: 'People will always say change is impossible.' But here and there little rebel statements appear. In the Lille wing, a room devoted to 'Nocturnes' has a notice saying: 'This display aims to shake up the sacrosanct classifications of traditional art history.' Whatever Guy Cogeval does next, it's sure to be noticed.

EXPLORE

The Sightseeing Cruise
Get the best of Paris in 1 hour

Sightseeing cruise
Pleasure cruise
Snacking cruise
Snacking + cruise

The Parisian sightseeing cruise has to be at the top of your list of things to do when in the French Capital. Ideally located, it's charming boats enhance the pleasure of a guided cruise on the Seine.
The river banks offer you some of the most well-known monuments such as the Eiffel Tower, the Louvre, the Orsay Museum and Notre Dame Cathedral amongst others. Recorded multilingual commentary and a bar service on board.

Departures every day of the year from October to March from 11.15am to 21pm (every 45 min), from April to September from 10.30am to 22pm(every 30 min).

1hr Sightseeing or "By Night" Cruises: Adult: 12€;
Children 4-11 y.o: 5€; free under 4 y.o

Exclusive: The Champagne Cruise
1 hr Sightseeing Cruise + 1 glass of Champagne for **18€**

*On this guide's presentation, valid for adult ticket for 2013. Terms and conditions apply. Not Cumulative offer.

At the foot of the Eiffel Tower
Port de Suffren - 75007 Paris
M° Bir Hakeim RER C Champs de Mars
+33 (0) 1 44 48 19 50
www.vedettesdeparis.com

vedettes de paris

extended the palace, linked the two *hôtels* and laid out place du Palais-Bourbon. The Greek temple-style façade facing Pont de la Concorde (the rear of the building) was added in 1806.

Flanking this riverside façade are statues of four great statesmen: L'Hôpital, Sully, Colbert and Aguesseau. The Napoleonic frieze on the pediment was replaced by a monarchist one after the restoration: between 1838 and 1841, Cortot sculpted the figures of France, Power and Justice. After the Revolution, the palace became the meeting place for the Conseil des Cinq-Cents. It was the forerunner of the parliament's lower house, which set up here for good in 1827. Visits are by arrangement through a serving *député* (if you're French) – or, after long queuing, during the Journées du Patrimoine (*see p30*).

★ FREE Chapelle de la Médaille Miraculeuse

Couvent des Soeurs de St-Vincent-de-Paul, 140 rue du Bac, 7th (www.chapellenotredame delamedaillemiraculeuse.com). M° Sèvres Babylone. **Open** 7.45am-1pm, 2.30-7pm Mon, Wed-Sun; 7.45am-7pm Tue. **Admission** free. **Map** p405 F7.
In 1830, saintly Catherine Labouré was said to have seen a vision of the Virgin, who told her to cast a medal that copied her appearance – standing on a globe with rays of light appearing from her outstretched hands. This kitsch chapel – murals, mosaics, statues and the embalmed bodies of Catherine and her mother superior – attracts two million pilgrims every year. *Photos p124.*

FREE Espace Fondation EDF

6 rue Récamier, 7th (www.edf.fr). M° Sèvres Babylone. **Open** noon-7pm Tue-Sun. **Admission** free. **Map** p405 G7.
This former electricity substation, converted by Electricité de France for PR purposes, is now used for varied, well-presented exhibitions.

★ Les Invalides & Musée de l'Armée

Esplanade des Invalides, 7th (08.10.11.33.99, www.invalides.org). M° La Tour Maubourg or Les Invalides. **Open** *Apr-Sept* 10am-6pm Mon, Wed-Sun (Dôme until 7pm July, Aug); 10am-9pm Tue. *Oct-Mar* 10am-5pm daily. Closed 1st Mon of mth. **Admission** *Courtyard* free. *Musée de l'Armée & Eglise du Dôme* €9; €7 reductions; free under-18s, under-26s (EU citizens). PMP. **Credit** MC, V. **Map** p405 E6.
Topped by its gilded dome, the Hôtel des Invalides was (and in part still is) a hospital. Commissioned by Louis XIV for wounded soldiers, it once housed as many as 6,000 invalids. Designed by Libéral Bruand (the foundations were laid in 1671) and completed by Jules Hardouin-Mansart, it's a magnificent monument to Louis XIV and Napoleon. Behind lines of cannon and bullet-shaped yews, the main (northern) façade has a relief of Louis XIV (Ludovicus Magnus) and the Sun King's sunburst. Wander

Les Invalides.

through the main courtyard and you'll see grandiose arcades and a statue of Napoleon glaring down from the end; the dormer windows around the courtyards are sculpted to resemble suits of armour.

The complex contains two churches – or, rather, a sort of double church: the Eglise St-Louis was for the soldiers, the Eglise du Dôme for the king. An opening behind the altar connects the two. The long, barrel-vaulted nave of the church of St-Louis is hung with flags captured from enemy troops. Since 1840 the Baroque Eglise du Dôme has been dedicated to the worship of Napoleon, whose body was brought here from St Helena. On the ground floor, under a dome painted by de la Fosse, Jouvenet and Coypel, are chapels featuring monuments to Vauban, Foch and Joseph Napoleon (Napoleon's older brother and King of Naples, Sicily and Spain). Napoleon II (King of Rome) is buried in the crypt opposite his father the emperor. Two dramatic black figures holding up the entrance to the crypt, the red porphyry tomb, the ring of giant figures, and the friezes and texts eulogising the emperor's heroic deeds give the measure of the cult of Napoleon, cherished in France for ruling large swaths of Europe and for creating an administrative and educational system that endures to this day.

The Invalides complex also houses the enormous Musée de l'Armée, in effect several museums in one. Even if militaria are not your thing, the building is splendid, and there's some fine portraiture, such as Ingres' *Emperor Napoleon on his Throne*. The Antique Armour wing is packed full of armour and weapons that look as good as new, from the 16th-century suit made for François I to cabinets full of

EXPLORE

swords, maces, crossbows and muskets and arque-buses. The Plans-Reliefs section is a collection of gorgeous 18th- and 19th-century scale models of French cities, used for military strategy; also here is a 17th-century model of Mont St-Michel, made by a monk from playing cards.

The World War I rooms bring the conflict into focus with uniforms, paintings, a scale model of a trench and, most sobering of all, white plastercasts of the hideously mutilated faces of two soldiers. The World War II wing covers the Resistance, the Battle of Britain and the war in the Pacific (there's a replica of Little Boy, the bomb dropped on Hiroshima), alternating artefacts with film footage. Also included in the entry price is the Historial Charles de Gaulle (closed Mon).

Musée Maillol

59-61 rue de Grenelle, 7th (01.42.22.59.58, www.museemaillol.com). Mº Rue du Bac. **Open** 10.30am-7pm (last admission 6.15pm) Mon-Thur, Sat, Sun; 10.30am-9.30pm (last admission 8.45pm) Fri. **Admission** €11; €9 reductions; free under-11s. **Credit** *Shop* AmEx, MC, V. **Map** p405 G7.
Dina Vierny was 15 when she met Aristide Maillol and became his principal model for the next decade, idealised in such sculptures as *Spring, Air* and *Harmony.* In 1995 she opened this delightful museum, exhibiting Maillol's drawings, engravings, pastels, tapestry panels, ceramics and early Nabis-related paintings, as well as the sculptures and terracottas that epitomise his calm, modern classicism. Vierny also set up a Maillol Museum in the Pyrenean village

EXPLORE

Walking in the Air

The Iron Lady gets a glass floor.

No building better symbolises Paris than the **Eiffel Tower** (*see p129*). Maupassant claimed he left Paris because of it, William Morris visited daily to avoid having to see it from afar – and it was originally meant to be a temporary structure. The radical cast-iron tower was built for the 1889 World Fair and the centenary of the 1789 Revolution by engineer Gustave Eiffel, who made use of new technology that was already popular in iron-framed buildings. Construction took more than two years and used some 18,000 pieces of metal and 2,500,000 rivets. And not a great deal has changed since – until now. In an attempt to brighten up the rather dingy first floor and make it as much of an attraction as the summit

itself, the Eiffel Tower is undergoing its third facelift since opening more than 120 years ago – and what a facelift: the €25m revamp is radical, to say the least, with the central void being filled in with a solid glass floor surrounded by inclined safety barriers, so visitors with a head for heights will be able to peer over and eyeball the queues of tourists 57m below. The 18-month project will feature other future-proofing ideas too, including environmentally friendly lighting and power, new teaching areas and the introduction of full disabled access to the first floor. Having welcomed more than 200 million people during her illustrious history, the Dame de Fer is finally shedding a few rivets in favour of a more 21st-century style.

of Banyuls-sur-Mer. This Paris venue also has works by Picasso, Rodin, Gauguin, Degas and Cézanne, a whole room of Matisse drawings, rare Surrealist documents and works by naïve artists. Vierny has also championed Kandinsky and Ilya Kabakov, whose *Communal Kitchen* installation recreates the atmosphere of Soviet domesticity. Monographic exhibitions are devoted to modern and contemporary artists. In 2012, there was a fascinating exhibition devoted to Canaletto's Venice.

Musée National Rodin

Hôtel Biron, 79 rue de Varenne, 7th (01.44.18.61.10, www.musee-rodin.fr). M° Varenne. **Open** 10am-5.45pm Tue, Thur-Sun; 10am-8.45pm Wed. **Admission** €9; €5 reductions; free under-18s, under-26s (EU citizens), all 1st Sun of mth. PMP. *Gardens* €1; free under-18s, under-26s (EU citizens). **Credit** MC, V. **Map** p405 F6.
The Rodin museum occupies the *hôtel particulier* where the sculptor lived in the final years of his life. The *Kiss*, the *Cathedral*, the *Walking Man*, portrait busts and early terracottas are exhibited indoors, as are many of the individual figures or small groups that also appear on the *Gates of Hell*. Rodin's works are accompanied by several pieces by his mistress and pupil, Camille Claudel. The walls are hung with paintings by Van Gogh, Monet, Renoir, Carrière and Rodin himself. Most visitors have greatest affection for the gardens: look out for the *Burghers of Calais*, the *Gates of Hell* and the *Thinker*. The museum is undergoing renovations until 2013, but will remain open throughout with a series of rolling exhibitions.

★ Musée d'Orsay

1 rue de la Légion-d'Honneur, 7th (01.40.49.48.14, www.musee-orsay.fr). M° Solférino/RER Musée d'Orsay. **Open** 9.30am-6pm Tue, Wed, Fri-Sun; 9.30am-9.45pm Thur. **Admission** €9; €6.50 reductions; free under-18s, under-26s (EU citizens), all 1st Sun of mth. PMP. **Credit** *Shop* MC, V. **Map** p405 G6.
See p125 **Nouvel Orsay**.

WEST & SOUTH OF LES INVALIDES

The 7th & 15th arrondissements.

South-west of the Invalides is the enormous **Ecole Militaire** (av de La Motte-Picquet, 7th), the military academy built by Louis XV to educate the children of penniless officers; it would later train Napoleon. The serene neoclassical building, designed by Jacques Ange Gabriel, is still used by the army and closed to the public.

From the north-western side of the Ecole Militaire begins the vast Champ de Mars, a market garden converted into a military drilling ground in the 18th century. It has long been home to the most celebrated Paris monument of all, the **Eiffel Tower**. At the south-eastern end of the Champ de Mars stands the Mur pour la Paix ('wall for peace'), erected in 2000 to articulate hopes for peace. South-east of the Ecole are the Y-shaped **UNESCO** building, built in 1958, and the modernist Ministry of Labour. Fashionable apartments line broad avenue Bosquet and avenue Suffren, though there's much architectural eclecticism in the area: look at the pseudo-Gothic and pseudo-Renaissance houses on avenue de Villars; Lavirotte's fabulous art nouveau doorway at 27 avenue Rapp; and the striking, box-shaped **Notre Dame de l'Arche de l'Alliance** church (81 rue d'Alleray, 15th, 01.56.56.62.56, www.ndarche.org), which was completed in 1998. For signs of life, visit the Saxe-Breteuil street market. The upper reaches of rue Cler contain classy food shops.

★ Eiffel Tower

Champ de Mars, 7th (08.92.70.12.39, www.tour-eiffel.fr). M° Bir-Hakeim/RER Champ de Mars Tour Eiffel. **Open** *By lift* Mid June-Aug 9am-12.45am daily (last ascent 11pm). Sept-mid June 9.30am-11.45pm daily (last ascent 10.30pm). *By stairs* (1st & 2nd levels) Mid June-Aug 9am-12.45am (last ascent midnight). Sept-mid June 9.30am-6.30pm (last ascent 6pm). **Admission** *By stairs* €5; €3-€3.50 reductions; free under-4s. *By lift* (1st & 2nd level) €8.50; €4-€7 reductions; (3rd level) €14; €9.50-€12.50 reductions; free under-4s. **Credit** AmEx, MC, V. **Map** p404 C6.
The 300m (984ft) tower stands on four massive concrete piles; it was the tallest structure in the world until it was overtaken by New York's Empire State Building in the 1930s. Vintage double-decker lifts ply their way up and down; you can walk as far as the second level. There are souvenir shops, an exhibition space, a café and even a post office. The smart Alain Ducasse-run Jules Verne restaurant, on the second level, has its own lift in the north tower. At the top (third level), there's Eiffel's cosy salon and a viewing platform. Views can reach 65km (40 miles) on a good day, although the most fascinating perspectives are of the ironwork itself. At night, for ten minutes on the hour, 20,000 flashbulbs attached to the tower provide a beautiful effect. *See also p128* **Walking in the Air**.

Musée des Egouts

Entrance opposite 93 quai d'Orsay, by Pont de l'Alma, 7th (01.53.68.27.81). M° Alma Marceau/RER Pont de l'Alma. **Open** 11am-4pm Mon-Wed, Sat, Sun (until 5pm May-Sept). Closed 2wks Jan. **Admission** €4.30; €3.50 reductions; free under-6s. **No credit cards**. **Map** p400 D5.
For centuries, the main source of drinking water in Paris was the Seine, which was also the main sewer. Construction of an underground sewerage system

began at the time of Napoleon. Today, the Egouts de Paris constitutes a smelly museum; each sewer in the 2,100km (1,305-mile) system is marked with a replica of the street sign above.

FREE Musée Valentin Haüy

5 rue Duroc, 7th (01.44.49.27.27, www.avh.asso.fr). M° Duroc. **Open** 2.30-5pm Tue, Wed (closed July-mid Sept). **Admission** free. **Map** p405 E8.

This tiny museum is devoted to the history of braille. You can explore on your own with the aid of French, English or braille explanatory texts, or allow the curator, Noële Roy, to show you round. She will give a tour in English if preferred. The first exhibit is a shocking print, depicting the fairground freak show that inspried Valentin Haüy to devote his life to educating not only the blind, but also the backward public who came to laugh at the likes of this blind orchestra forced to perform in dunces' hats. Next begins the tactile tour, with a chance to touch books printed in embossed letters.

FREE UNESCO

7 pl de Fontenoy, 7th (01.45.68.10.00, tours (book in advance) 01.45.68.03.59, www.unesco.org). M° Ecole Militaire. **Open** *Tours* 3pm Wed (in English 3pm Mon). **Admission** free. **Map** p405 D7.

The Y-shaped UNESCO headquarters, built in 1958, is home to a swarm of international diplomats. It's worth visiting for the sculptures and paintings – by Picasso, Arp, Giacometti, Moore, Calder and Miró – and for the Japanese garden. Tours need to be reserved three months in advance.

FREE Village Suisse

78 av de Suffren or 54 av de La Motte-Picquet, 15th (www.villagesuisse.com). M° La Motte Picquet Grenelle. **Open** 10.30am-7pm Mon, Thur-Sun. **Map** p404 D7.

The mountains and waterfalls created for the Swiss Village at the 1900 Exposition Universelle are long gone, but the village lives on. The street level has been colonised by some 150 boutiques offering various high-quality, pricey, antiques and collectibles.

Along the Seine

Downstream from the Eiffel Tower is the **Musée du Quai Branly**, which opened in 2006. A short way further on, the high-tech **Maison de la Culture du Japon** stands near Pont Bir-Hakeim on quai Branly. Beyond, the 15th-arrondissement Fronts de Seine riverfront, with its tower-block developments, had some of the worst architecture of the 1970s inflicted upon it. This would-be brave new world of walkways, suspended gardens and tower blocks has no easily discoverable means of access. The adjacent Beaugrenelle shopping centre is more straightforward to get into but has always been rather dingy, although that is

set to change in 2013 when the mall reopens with a spectacular redesign – the winning scheme, from design team Agence Search, will feature vast oval wooden lattices suspended in the atriums *à la* Hèrmes store in St-Germain.

Further west, things look up: the sophisticated former headquarters of the Canal+ TV channel (2 rue des Cévennes, 15th), designed by American architect Richard Meier, is surrounded by fine modern housing; and the pleasant **Parc André Citroën**, created in the 1990s on the site of the former Citroën car works, runs down to the Seine quayside.

FREE Maison de la Culture du Japon

101bis quai Branly, 15th (01.44.37.95.01, www.mcjp.asso.fr). M° Bir-Hakeim/RER Champ de Mars Tour Eiffel. **Open** noon-7pm Tue, Wed, Fri, Sat; noon-8pm Thur. Closed Aug. **Admission** free. **Map** p404 C6.

Constructed in 1996 by the architectural partnership of Kenneth Armstrong and Masayuki Yamanaka, this glass-fronted Japanese cultural centre screens films and puts on exhibitions and plays. It also contains a library, an authentic Japanese tea pavilion on the roof and a well-stocked book and gift shop.

★ Musée du Quai Branly

37 quai Branly, 7th (01.56.61.70.00, www. quaibranly.fr). RER Pont de l'Alma. **Open** 11am-7pm Tue, Wed, Sun; 11am-9pm Thur-Sat. **Admission** €8.50; €6 reductions; free under-18s, under-26s (EU citizens), all 1st Sun of mth. *Temporary exhibitions* €7; €5 reductions; free under-18s, all 1st Sun of mth. **Credit** AmEx, DC, MC, V. **Map** p404 C6.

Surrounded by trees on the banks of the Seine, this museum, housed in an extraordinary building by Jean Nouvel, is a vast showcase for non-European cultures. Dedicated to the ethnic art of Africa, Oceania, Asia and the Americas, it joins together the collections of the Musée des Arts d'Afrique et d'Océanie and the Laboratoire d'Ethnologie du Musée de l'Homme, as well as contemporary indigenous art. Treasures include a tenth-century anthropomorphic Dogon statue from Mali, Vietnamese costumes, Gabonese masks, Aztec statues, Peruvian feather tunics and rare frescoes from Ethiopia.

FREE Parc André Citroën

Rue Balard, rue St-Charles or quai Citroën, 15th. M° Balard or Javel. **Open** 8am-dusk Mon-Fri; 9am-dusk Sat, Sun, public hols. **Map** p404 A9.

This park is a fun, postmodern version of a French formal garden, designed in the 1990s by Gilles Clément and Alain Prévost. It comprises glasshouses, computerised fountains, waterfalls, a wilderness and themed gardens, and is currently being extended. The tethered Eutelsat helium balloon takes visitors up for panoramic views. If the weather looks unreliable, call 01.44.26.20.00 to check the programme.

Beyond the Périphérique

Branch out into the banlieue.

Ten years ago, visitors might not have looked much further than a quick dash round the Louvre and a twilight cruise on the Seine to tick the boxes for their perfect Paris weekend. But now the capital's pleasures are spreading well beyond the cramped confines of the Grands Boulevards, even crossing the Périphérique and into the formerly forbidden lands of the *banlieue*. From art complexes to anatomy museums, Paris no longer stops at the 20th arrondissement, with big-hitters Thadaeus Ropac and Larry Gagosian both opening landmark galleries in the suburbs in

late 2012 – Ropac in Pantin (www.ropac.net) and Gagosian (www.gagosian.com) in Le Bourget. Big chunks of the Périphérique itself, long a symbolic frontier between 'inside' and 'outside', are set to be boxed over by gardens and other vote-winning urban amenities during the next decade, with a particular focus on beefed-up transport links across the greater Paris region, from the eastern extension of the tram network to the reopening of the Voguéo river shuttle between Suresnes and the Musée d'Orsay.

LA DEFENSE

The skyscrapers and walkways of La Défense – named after a stand against the Prussians in 1870 – create a whole new world. The area has been a showcase for French business since the mid 1950s, when the CNIT hall was built to host trade shows, but it was the arrival of the **Grande Arche** that gave the district its most dramatic monument. Today, more than 100,000 people work here, and another 35,000 live in the blocks of flats on the southern edge of the complex, served by the inevitable mall, a huge multiplex and leisure centre. On the central esplanade are fountains and sculptures by Miró and Serra.

Grande Arche de La Défense

92044 Paris La Défense (01.49.07.27.27, www.grandearche.com). M° La Défense. **Open** *Apr-Aug* 10am-8pm daily. *Oct-Mar* 10am-7pm daily. **Admission** €10 (€5 Tue); €8.50 reductions; free under-6s. **Credit** MC, V.

Completed for the bicentenary of the Revolution in 1989, the Grande Arche was designed by Danish architect Johan Otto von Spreckelsen. Though it lines up neatly on the Grand Axe – from the Louvre, up the Champs-Elysées to the Arc de Triomphe – the building itself is skewed. A vertigo-inducing glass lift soars up through canvas 'clouds' to the roof, for a fantastic view over Paris.

▶ *Also here is the Musée de l'Informatique (08.20.21.03.10, www.museeinformatique.fr), which traces the story of computing with old machines and multimedia displays.*

ST-DENIS & THE NORTH

North of Paris, the *département* of Seine St-Denis (and part of adjoining Val d'Oise) best fulfils the negative stereotype of the *banlieue*. It's a victim of its 19th-century industrial boom and the 20th-century housing shortage, when colossal estates went up in La Corneuve, Aulnay-sous-Bois and Sarcelles. It includes some of the poorest *communes* in all of France.

EXPLORE

Yet the *département* boasts a buzzing theatre scene, with the **MC93** in Bobigny (*see p311*), the **Théâtre Gérard-Philipe** (*see p311*) in St-Denis, and the Théâtre de la Commune in Aubervilliers, plus prestigious music festivals such as the **Festival de St-Denis** (*see p298*). Amid the sprawl stands one of the treasures of Gothic architecture: the **Basilique St-Denis**, final resting place for the majority of France's former monarchs.

Le Bourget, home to the city's first airport and still used for private jets and an air fair, contains the **Musée de l'Air et de l'Espace** in its original passenger terminals and hangars. The area also became home to a bold new Gagosian gallery (www.gagosian.com) in late 2012, located in a 1950s industrial building and designed by Jean Nouvel. North-east of Paris, Pantin arrived on the cultural scene with the opening in 2004 of the **Centre National de la Danse** (*see p305*) in a cleverly revamped office block, and 2012 saw the opening of Thaddaeus Ropac's new art gallery space (www.ropac.net) in a 19th-century ironware factory. North-west of St-Denis, Ecouen, noted for its beautiful Renaissance château, now the **Musée National de la Renaissance**, allows for a glimpse of a more rural past.

★ Basilique St-Denis

1 rue de la Légion-d'Honneur, 93200 St-Denis (01.48.09.83.54). M° St-Denis Basilique/tram 1. **Open** *Apr-Sept* 10am-6.15pm Mon-Sat; noon-6.15pm Sun. *Oct-Mar* 10am-5pm Mon-Sat; noon-5.15pm Sun. *Tours* 10.30am, 3pm Mon-Sat; 12.15pm, 3pm Sun. **Admission** €7.50; €4.50 reductions; free under-18s, under-26s (EU citizens). PMP. **Credit** MC, V.

Legend has it that when St Denis was beheaded, he picked up his noggin and walked with it to Vicus Catulliacus (now St-Denis) to be buried. The first church, parts of which can be seen in the crypt, was built over his tomb in around 475. The present edifice was begun in the 1130s by Abbot Suger, the powerful minister of Louis VI and Louis VII. It is considered to be the first example of Gothic architecture, uniting the elements of pointed arches, ogival vaulting and flying buttresses. In the 13th century, master mason Pierre de Montreuil erected the spire and rebuilt the choir nave and transept. St-Denis was the burial place for all but three French

Basilique St-Denis.

monarchs between 996 and the end of the *ancien régime*, so the ambulatory is a museum of French funerary sculpture. It includes a fanciful Gothic tomb for Dagobert, the austere effigy of Charles V, and the Renaissance tomb of Louis XII and his wife Anne de Bretagne. In 1792, these tombs were desecrated, and the royal remains thrown into a pit.

★ FREE Musée de l'Air et de l'Espace

Aéroport de Paris-Le Bourget, 93352 Le Bourget Cedex (01.49.92.70.00, www.mae.org). M° Gare du Nord, then bus 350/RER Le Bourget, then bus 152. **Open** *Apr-Sept* 10am-6pm Tue-Sun. *Oct-Mar* 10am-5pm Tue-Sun. **Admission** free. *With 1-3 animations* €8-€16; €6-€12 under-26s; free under-4s. PMP. **Credit** MC, V.

Set in the former passenger terminal at Le Bourget airport, the museum's collection begins with the pioneers, including fragile-looking biplanes and the command cabin of a Zeppelin airship. On the runway are Mirage fighters, a US Thunderchief, a Boeing 747 and Ariane launchers 1 and 5. Hangars house the prototype Concorde 001 and a Dakota. Entry to the main collection is free, but there's a charge for each *animation* (Forfait Avions, Planète Pilote, Planétarium, Simulateurs, Cockpits Secrets).

Musée National de la Renaissance

Château d'Ecouen, 95440 Ecouen (01.34.38.38.50, www.musee-renaissance.fr). Train Gare du Nord to Ecouen-Ezanville then bus 269 or walk. **Open** *16 Apr-Sept* 9.30am-12.45pm, 2-5.45pm Mon, Wed-Sun. *Oct-14 Apr* 9.30am-12.45pm, 2-5.15pm Mon, Wed-Sun. **Admission** €4.50; €3 reductions; free under-26s, all 1st Sun of mth. **Credit** MC, V.

The Renaissance château completed in 1555 for Royal Constable Anne de Montmorency and wife Margaret de Savoie is the setting for a collection of 16th-century decorative arts (some sections are open

INSIDE TRACK GOING UP

La Défense's most ambitious project to date will soon start to rise in the shape of **Hermitage Plaza**, a pair of 320m (1,050ft) skyscrapers courtesy of Norman Foster, topping London's Shard by a few metres.

only at certain times so it's a good idea to phone ahead). Best are the painted chimney pieces, decorated with biblical and mythological scenes.

VINCENNES & THE EAST

The more upmarket residential districts in the east surround the **Bois de Vincennes**, such as Vincennes, with its royal château, St-Mandé and Charenton-le-Pont. **Joinville-le-Pont** and **Champigny-sur-Marne** draw weekenders for the riverside *guinguette* dancehalls.

Château de Vincennes

Av de Paris, 94300 Vincennes (01.48.08.31.20, www.chateau-vincennes.fr). M° Château de Vincennes. **Open** *Mid May-mid Sept 10am-6pm daily. Mid Sept-mid May 10am-5pm daily.* **Admission** €8.50; €5.50 reductions; free under-18s, under-26s (EU citizens). **Credit** *Shop* MC, V.
An imposing curtain wall punctuated by towers encloses this 52m-high fortress, which is the tallest medieval fortified structure in Europe. Originally the site of a hunting lodge built for Louis VII in the 12th century, the square keep was begun by Philippe VI and completed in the 14th century by Charles V, who added the curtain wall. Henry V died here in 1422, and Louis XIII used the château for hunting expeditions and had the Pavillon du Roi and Pavillon de la Reine built by Louis Le Vau, although any decorative elements disappeared when they became barracks.

★ MAC/VAL

Pl de la Libération, 94404 Vitry-sur-Seine (01.43.91.64.20, www.macval.fr). M° Porte de Choisy then bus 183/RER C Gare de Vitry-sur-Seine then bus 180. **Open** 10am-6pm Tue-Fri; noon-7pm Sat, Sun. **Admission** €5; €2.50 reductions; free under-26s, students, all 1st Sun of mth. **Credit** AmEx, V.
This contemporary art museum's collection offers a stunning snapshot of French art from 1950 to the present, with installations by Gilles Barbier, Jesús Rafael Soto and Christian Boltanski. *Photo p134.*

Musée Fragonard

7 av du Général de Gaulle, 94704 Maisons-Alfort (01.43.96.71.72, http://musee.vet-alfort.fr). M° Ecole Vétérinaire de Maisons-Alfort. **Open** 2-6pm Wed, Thur; 1-6pm Sat, Sun. Closed Aug. **Admission** €7; free under-26s. **No credit cards**.
In 18th-century French medical schools, study aids were produced in one of two ways. They were either sculpted in coloured wax or made from the real things – organs, limbs, tangled vascular systems – dried or preserved in formaldehyde. Veterinary surgeon Honoré Fragonard was a master of the second method, and many of his most striking works are now on display here. *Homme à la mandibule* is a flayed, grimacing man holding a jawbone in his right hand. *Tête humaine injectée* is a rather more sober human head whose blood vessels were injected with coloured wax, red for arteries and blue for veins. And, most grandiose of all, *Cavalier de l'apocalypse* is a flayed man on the back of a flayed galloping horse, inspired by a painting by Dürer.

Pavillon Baltard

12 av Victor-Hugo, 94130 Nogent-sur-Marne (01.48.73.45.81, www.pavillonbaltard.fr). RER Nogent-sur-Marne. **Open** during exhibitions only.
When the market at Les Halles was demolished, someone had the nous to save one of its Baltard-designed iron-and-glass market pavilions (no.8, eggs and poultry) and relocate it here.

Musée de l'Air et de l'Espace.

EXPLORE

MAC/VAL. *See p133.*

BOULOGNE & THE WEST

The capital's most desirable suburbs lie to the west. La Défense, Neuilly-sur-Seine, Boulogne-Billancourt, Levallois-Perret and, over the river, Issy-les-Moulineaux have become accepted business addresses for Parisians. Neuilly-sur-Seine is where Nicolas Sarkozy cut his political teeth as mayor in the early 1990s.

Boulogne-Billancourt is the main town and a lively centre in its own right. In 1320, the Gothic Eglise Notre-Dame was begun in tribute to a miraculous statue of the Virgin that washed up at Boulogne-sur-Mer. By the 18th century, Boulogne was known for its wines and laundries, then, early in the 20th century, for its artist residents (Landowski, Lipchitz, Chagall, Gris), whereas Billancourt was known for car manufacturing, aviation and its film studios.

In the 1920s and '30s, Boulogne-Billancourt was proud of its modernity: Tony Garnier built the elegant new town hall on avenue André-Morizet; a new post office, apartments and schools all went up in the modern style; and private houses were built by the leading avant-garde architects of the day – Le Corbusier, Mallet-Stevens, Perret, Lurçat, Pingusson and Fischer – notably on rue Denfert-Rochereau and rue du Belvédère. The **Musée des Années 30** focuses on artists and architects who lived or worked in the town at the time. The innovative glass-fronted apartment block by Le Corbusier – including the flat where he lived from 1933 to 1965 – can be visited each Saturday at 24 rue Nungesser et Coli (reserve on 01.42.88.75.72, www.fondationlecorbusier.asso.fr).

In the 19th century, riverside towns such as **Chatou**, **Asnières** and **Argenteuil** became places of entertainment – for promenades, *guinguettes* and rowing on the Seine – as depicted in many Impressionist paintings.

At Rueil-Malmaison, the romantic **Château de Malmaison** was loved by Napoleon and Josephine. Josephine had a second château, **La Petite Malmaison** (229bis av Napoléon-Bonaparte), built nearby. The empress is buried in the Eglise St-Pierre St-Paul in the old centre, as is her daughter Hortense de Beauharnais, Queen of Holland and mother of Napoleon III.

Suresnes, across the Seine from the Bois de Boulogne, has been a wine-producing village since Roman times, and still celebrates the Fête des Vendanges every autumn. The 162m (532ft) Mont Valérien was a place of pilgrimage. In 1841, a huge fortress was built here to defend Paris. It was occupied by the German army in World War II; French *résistants* were brought here at night to be shot. The fortress still belongs to the French army, and is the centre of its eavesdropping network. On the surrounding hill is the **American Cemetery** (190 bd de Washington), which contains the graves of American soldiers from World Wars I and II.

St-Germain-en-Laye is a smart suburb with a historic centre and a château. Henri II lived here with his wife Catherine de Médicis and his mistress Diane de Poitiers; it was here also that Mary Queen of Scots grew up, Louis XIV was born and the deposed James II lived for 12 years. Napoléon III turned the château into the **Musée d'Archéologie Nationale**.

Château de Malmaison

Av du Château, 92500 Rueil-Malmaison (01.41.29.05.55, www.chateau-malmaison.fr). RER La Défense then bus 258. **Open** *Apr-Sept* 10am-12.30pm, 1.30-5.45pm Mon, Wed-Fri; 10am-12.30pm, 1.30-6.15pm Sat, Sun. *Oct-Mar* 10am-12.30pm, 1.30-5.15pm Mon, Wed-Fri; 10am-12.30pm, 1.30-5.45pm Sat, Sun. **Admission** €6-€8; €4.50-€6.50 reductions; free under-18s, under-26s (EU citizens), all 1st Sun of mth. PMP. **Credit** AmEx, MC, V.

Napoleon and Josephine's love nest, bought by Josephine in 1799, was the emperor's favourite retreat during the Consulate (1800-03). After their divorce, Napoleon gave the château to his ex, who died here in 1814. The couple redesigned the entrance as a military tent; you can see Napoleon's office, the billiard room and Josephine's tented bedroom.

★ FREE Mémorial de la France Combattante

Rue du Professeur-Léon-Bernard, 92150 Suresnes (01.47.28.46.35, www.mont-valerien.fr). Train to Suresnes-Mont-Valérien/RER La Défense then bus 160, 360 or tram 2. **Open** tour times vary (see website for details). **Admission** free.

Sixteen bronze sculptures by 16 artists represent France's struggle for liberation. Behind an eternal flame, the crypt contains tombs of 16 heroes from 16 French battles in World War II. The memorial was built on the site where Resistance members were brought from prisons in Paris. A staircase from within the crypt leads visitors inside the curtain wall, then up to the chapel where prisoners were locked before execution, and down to the Clairière des Fusillés, the clearing where they were shot. The chapel walls were covered in the prisoners' last graffiti; it also contains five of the wooden firing posts. More than 1,000 men were shot here (women were deported). A monument lists the names of victims.

Musée d'Archéologie Nationale

Château St-Germain, pl Charles-de-Gaulle, 78105 St-Germain-en-Laye (01.39.10.13.00, www.musee-archeologienationale.fr). RER St-Germain-en-Laye. **Open** 10am-5pm Mon, Wed-Sun. **Admission** €6; €4.50 reductions; free under-18s, all 1st Sun of mth. **Credit** *Shop* MC, V.
This awe-inspiring museum traces France's rich archaeological heritage. The redesigned Neolithic galleries feature statue-menhirs, female figures and an ornate tombstone from Cys-la-Commune.

Musée des Années 30

Espace Landowski, 28 av André-Morizet, 92100 Boulogne-Billancourt (01.55.18.53.00, www.annees30.com). Mº Marcel Sembat. **Open** 11am-6pm Tue-Sun. Closed 2wks Aug. **Admission** (incl Musée-Jardin Paul Landowski) €6; €4 reductions; free under-16s. **Credit** MC, V.
The Musée des Années 30 highlights just how much second-rate art was produced in the 1930s, though there are decent modernist sculptures by the Martel brothers, graphic designs, and Juan Gris still lifes and drawings. The star exhibits are the designs by avant-garde architects Auguste Perret, Le Corbusier and Louis-Raymond Fischer.

Musée Belmondo

14 rue de L'Abreuvoir, 92100 Boulogne-Billancourt (01.55.18.69.01, www.museepaul belmondo.fr). Mº Boulogne Jean Jaurès. **Open** 2-6pm Tue-Fri; 11am-6pm Sat, Sun. **Admission** €5; €3.70 reductions; free under-16s. **Credit** MC, V.
See below **Father Figure**.

Father Figure

Jean-Paul Belmondo's dad was also one of France's finest sculptors.

For most people in France, the name Belmondo has always been associated with *nouvelle vague* actor Jean-Paul – that sexy, thick-lipped heart-throb, with a distinguished boxer's nose, who shot to stardom in such 1960s films as Jean-Luc Godard's *A Bout de Souffle* (*Breathless*). What most of us don't know is that the actor's father, Paul (1898-1982), was one of France's most important 20th-century sculptors, and one of the last to use neoclassical, academic techniques.

Many of his works (characterised by harmonious forms, unfussy lines and smooth surfaces) epitomise the 1930s style, particularly the gracious proportions of *La Danse*, in the Théâtre de Chaillot, which was commissioned for Paris's Universal Exposition in 1937; and two statues in the Jardin de Tuileries (a well

hung *Apollo* and an elegant *Jeannette*). Since World War II, Belmondo's talents have mysteriously remained unknown to most, but the recently opened **Musée Belmondo** (*see above*), set inside the 18th-century, neoclassical Château Buchillot in Boulogne-Billancourt, has thrust his works firmly back into the limelight. The space, which was entirely revamped by architects Chartier-Corbasson, is an interior designer's dream – the mix of stark white, black and timber materials creates a different mood in each section.

Several rooms harbour niches and alcoves in which Belmondo's sculptures sit enticingly, as if in a workshop; and numerous artificial backdrops, along with raised floors and frames, create multiple sightlines. Clever use of natural and artificial lighting highlights the details on each sculpture, and a special 'replica' room on the first floor encourages visitors to feel the works' grooves and textures.

The visit ends in the château gardens, where works created by Belmondo's contemporaries – Raoul Lamourdedieu, Pierre Traverse, Léon Séverac, Karl-Jean Longuet, Henri Le Pecq, Marcel Chauvenet-Delclos and Marguerite Cossaceanu-Lavrillier – pepper the lawns in 1930s glory. A real treat for lovers of art deco and a godsend on a sunny day.

EXPLORE

Consume

Restaurants

Updated for a new generation, the bistro continues to reign supreme.

Thankfully, the French continue to love classic bistro style. Many are old favourites, but the last few years have also seen the rise of the neo-bistro scene, updated for a new generation. At the very centre are places such as Frenchie, Abri and Le Chateaubriand, the *coeur d'artichaut* of this dining trend, which the compulsive categorisers call 'bistronomy'. So, what are the magic ingredients of the bistronomy boom? First, take the same flair long associated with Parisian gastronomy but use a little less finesse and significantly more innovation; next, add world-

beating raw ingredients of thoroughly researched provenance and chefs who are generally young autodidacts enjoying success with their first business (Inaki Aizpitarte, Le Chateaubriand's Basque chef-owner, was previously a *paysagiste*, his sommelier an actor, his olive oil supplier a tight-rope walker). Finally, sprinkle liberally with reasonable prices and an atmosphere that is informal, relaxed and intentionally unbourgeois.

EATING IN PARIS

Except for the very simplest restaurants, it's wise to book ahead. This can usually be done on the same day as your intended visit, although really top-notch establishments require bookings weeks or months in advance and confirmation the day before. All listings have been checked at the time of going to press but are liable to change. Many venues close for their annual break in August, and some also close at Christmas. Restaurants are presented by area. For more restaurant reviews, refer to www.timeout.fr.

With our reviews, we give the average price for a standard main course chosen from the à la carte menu. If 'Main courses' is not listed, only prix fixe options are available. 'Prix fixe' indicates the price of the venue's set menu at lunch and/or dinner. All bills include a service charge, but an additional tip of a few euros (for the whole table) is polite unless you're unhappy with the service. Budget eateries are marked €.

> ❶ Blue numbers given in this chapter correspond to the location of each restaurant on the street maps.
> *See pp400-409.*

THE ISLANDS

Brasserie de l'Ile St-Louis
55 quai de Bourbon, 4th (01.43.54.02.59).
Mº Pont Marie. **Open** noon-11pm Mon, Tue, Thur-Sun. Closed Aug. **Main courses** €20.
Credit MC, V. **Map** p409 K7 ❶ **Brasserie**
Happily, this old-fashioned brasserie soldiers on while a stream of exotic juice bars on the Ile St-Louis come and go. The terrace has one of the best summer views in Paris and is invariably packed; the dining room exudes shabby chic. Nicotined walls make for an authentic Paris mood, though nothing here is gastronomically gripping: a well-dressed *frisée aux lardons* perhaps, or a more successful pan of warming tripes.

Mon Vieil Ami
69 rue St-Louis-en-l'Ile, 4th (01.40.46.01.35,
www.mon-vieil-ami.com). Mº Pont Marie. **Open** noon-2.30pm, 6.30-11pm Wed-Sun. Closed 3wks Jan & 1st 3wks Aug. **Main courses** €13-€23.
Prix fixe €46. **Credit** AmEx, DC, MC, V.
Map p409 K7 ❷ **Bistro**
Antoine Westermann from the Buerehiesel in Strasbourg has created a true foodie destination here. Starters such as tartare of finely diced raw vegetables with sautéed baby squid on top impress with their deft seasoning. Typical of the mains is a

cast-iron casserole of roast duck with caramelised turnips and couscous. Even the classic room has been successfully refreshed with black beams, white Perspex panels and a long *table d'hôte*.

THE LOUVRE & PALAIS-ROYAL

★ L'Ardoise

28 rue du Mont-Thabor, 1st (01.42.96.28.18, www.lardoise-paris.com). Mᵒ Concorde or Tuileries. **Open** noon-3pm, 6.30-11pm Mon-Sat; 6.30-11pm Sun. Closed mid July-mid Aug. **Main courses** €25. **Prix fixe** €36. **Credit** MC, V. **Map** p401 G5 ❸ **Bistro**

This plain-looking bistro attracts a fair number of foreigners given its location near place Vendôme and early opening hours, but the food proves their judgement to be spot-on. Chef Pierre Jay doesn't skimp on quality ingredients in dishes such as shellfish papillote or chicken in parmesan cream sauce, making his €36 set menu a bargain. A lightly chilled Chinon is a perfect complement. Unusually for Paris, the restaurant is open on Sundays.

Chez La Vieille

37 rue de l'Arbre-Sec, 1st (01.42.60.15.78). Mᵒ Louvre Rivoli. **Open** noon-1.45pm, 7.30-9.45pm Mon-Sat. Closed Aug. **Prix fixe** *Lunch* €28. *Dinner* €38. **Credit** AmEx, MC, V. **Map** p406 J5 ❹ **Bistro**

The rustic ground floor of this bistro bursts with well-rounded regulars, whereas upstairs is plain and bright. A wondrous ad-lib selection of starters might include hot *chou farci* and home-made *terrine de foie gras*. Equally impressive is *foie de veau*, coated in a pungent reduction of shallots and vinegar and served with potato purée. Puddings follow the same cornucopian principle as the starters. Opening hours are limited and booking ahead is essential, but the lunchtime prix fixe is a bargain.

Chez Vong

10 rue de la Grande-Truanderie, 1st (01.40.26.09.36, www.chez-vong.com). Mᵒ Etienne Marcel or Les Halles. **Open** noon-2.20pm, 7-11.20pm Mon-Sat. Closed 3wks Aug. **Main courses** €21. **Prix fixe** *Lunch* €24.50. **Credit** AmEx, DC, MC, V. **Map** p402 J5 ❺ **Chinese**

The staff at this cosy Chinese restaurant take pride in its excellent cooking. From the greeting at the door to the knowledgeable, trilingual service (Cantonese, Mandarin and French), each part of the experience is thoughtfully orchestrated. Any doubts about authenticity are extinguished with the arrival of the beautifully presented dishes. Expertly cooked spicy shrimp glistens in a smooth, characterful sauce of onions and ginger, and *ma po* tofu melts in the mouth, its spicy and peppery flavours melding with those of the fine pork mince.

Les Fines Gueules

43 rue Croix-des-Petits-Champs, 1st (01.42.61.35.41, www.lesfinesgueules.fr). Mᵒ Bourse or Sentier. **Open** noon-2.30pm, 7.30-10.30pm Mon-Fri; noon-3pm, 7.30-11pm Sat, Sun. **Main courses** €18-€26. **Credit** MC, V. **Map** p402 H5 ❻ **Bistro/wine bar**

CONSUME

Mon Vieil Ami.

Le Grand Véfour.

At first glance, Les Fines Gueules might seem like an ordinary corner café, but a closer look at the menu reveals unusual attention to ingredients at this mini wine bar/bistro. Even if you've never heard of Hugo (Desnoyer, star butcher and supplier to some of the city's finest restaurants) or Jean-Luc (Poujauran, a celebrity Paris baker), you can taste the difference when the pedigree steak tartare arrives with a salad of baby leaves dressed in truffle oil. There are just a few seats around the bar, but upstairs is a buzzy dining room. A good selection of 'natural' and organic wines comes by the glass and the bottle.

★ Frenchie

5 rue du Nil, 2nd (01.40.39.96.19, www.frenchie-restaurant.com). M° Sentier. **Open** 7-10.30pm Mon-Fri. **Prix fixe** €45. **Credit** MC, V. **Map** p402 J4 **❼ Bistro**

Grégory Lemarchand honed his craft with Jamie Oliver in London before opening this loft-style bistro next to the market street rue Montorgueil. It has been a hit thanks to the bold flavours of dishes such as gazpacho with calamari, squash blossoms and plenty of herbs; braised lamb with roasted aubergine and spinach; and coconut tapioca with strawberry sorbet. Book several days ahead for a table.

Le Grand Véfour

17 rue de Beaujolais, 1st (01.42.96.56.27, www.grand-vefour.com). M° Palais Royal Musée du Louvre. **Open** 12.30-1.30pm, 8-9.30pm Mon-Fri. Closed Aug. **Main courses** €80. **Prix fixe** *Lunch* €96. *Dinner* €298. **Credit** AmEx, DC, MC, V. **Map** p402 H5 **❽ Haute cuisine**

Opened in 1784 (as the Café de Chartres), this is one of the oldest and most historic restaurants in Paris. An à la carte meal begins with a fantasia suite of

delicacies: tiny frogs' legs, for example, arranged within a circle of sage sauce; a first course of creamed Breton sea urchins served in their spiny shells with a quail's egg and topped with caviar. Fish dishes may be a touch overcooked, and the adventurous desserts are not always successful, but you'll forgive all after a glass of vintage armagnac.

Kaï

18 rue du Louvre, 1st (01.40.15.01.99). M° Louvre Rivoli. **Open** 12.30-2.15pm, 7.30-10.30pm Tue-Sat. Closed 1wk Apr & 3wks Aug. **Main courses** €27. **Prix fixe** *Lunch* €25-€42. *Dinner* €69, €110. **Credit** AmEx, MC, V. **Map** p402 H5 **❾ Japanese**

This restaurant has developed a following among fashionable diners. The 'Kaï-style' sushi is a zesty take on a classic: marinated and lightly grilled yellowtail is pressed on to a roll of *shiso*-scented rice. Not to be outdone, the grilled aubergine with miso, seemingly simple, turns out to be a smoky, luscious experience. A generous main of breaded pork lacks the finesse and refinement of the starters, but is still satisfying. Thoroughly French desserts come courtesy of celebrity pastry chef Pierre Hermé.

★ Le Meurice

Hôtel Meurice, 228 rue de Rivoli, 1st (01.44.58.10.55, www.lemeurice.com). M° Tuileries. **Open** 7-10.30am, 12.30-2pm, 7.30-10pm Mon-Fri; 7-11am Sat, Sun. Closed 2wks Mar & Aug. **Main courses** €95-€140. **Prix fixe** *Breakfast* €40-€72. *Lunch* €105. *Dinner* €260. **Credit** AmEx, DC, MC, V. **Map** p401 G5 **❿ Haute cuisine**

Yannick Alléno produces some glorious, if rather understated, contemporary cooking here. Alléno has a light touch, teasing the flavour out of every leaf, frond, fin or fillet. Turbot is sealed in clay before cooking and then sauced with celery cream and a coulis of flat parsley. Bresse chicken stuffed with foie gras and served with truffled *sarladais* potatoes is breathtakingly good. A fine cheese tray comes from Quatrehomme; the pastry chef amazes with his millefeuille. Jacket required for men.

★ Restaurant du Palais-Royal

110 galerie Valois, 1st (01.40.20.00.27, www. restaurantdupalaisroyal.com). Mº Bourse or Palais Royal Musée du Louvre. **Open** noon-2pm, 7-10pm daily. **Main courses** €23-€40. **Credit** AmEx, DC, MC, V. **Map** p402 H5 ⓫ **Bistro**
There can be few more magical places to dine on a summer evening than the terrace of the Restaurant du Palais-Royal. Inside is memorable too: you sit in a red dining room alongside the commissars of arts and letters who work at the ministry of culture a few doors down. Risotto is a speciality and the Black, Black and Lobster is tremendous; rice simmered in rich squid ink is served al dente, topped with tender but fleshy pink lobster, sun-dried tomato and spring vegetables. Don't miss out on the *baba au rhum*.

Restaurant du Palais-Royal.

★ Thaïm

46 rue de Richelieu, 1st (01.42.96.54.67). Mº Bourse or Palais Royal Musée du Louvre. **Open** noon-3pm, 7-11.30pm Mon-Fri; 7-11pm Sat. **Prix fixe** *Lunch* €16.50. *Dinner* €26.50. **Credit** MC, V. **Map** p402 H5 ⓬ **Thai**
Steering well away from Thai clichés, Thaïm has an elegant decor of dark wood and plum fabrics, and a brief menu that changes often, keeping the regulars coming back. Particularly good value is the three-course lunch menu, which might bring crisp fried parcels filled with spiced vegetables, an aromatic green fish curry (there is a choice of fish, meat or poultry every day), and sweet coconut-pumpkin soup. There is an extensive choice of teas, including a delicious iced ginger-coconut version.

Zen

8 rue de l'Echelle, 1st (01.42.61.93.99). Mº Louvre Rivoli. **Open** noon-2.30pm, 7-10.30pm Mon-Fri; noon-3pm, 7-10.30pm Sun. Closed Aug. **Prix fixe** *Lunch* €12-€20. *Dinner* €20-€65. **Credit** MC, V. **Map** p401 H5 ⓭ **Japanese**
There's no shortage of Japanese restaurants in this neighbourhood, but the recently opened Zen is refreshing in a couple of ways. First, there is no pale wood in sight; the colour scheme here is sharp white, green and yellow for a cheerful effect. Second, the menu has a lot to choose from – bowls of ramen, sushi and *chirashi*, hearty dishes such as chicken with egg on rice or *tonkatsu* – yet no detail is neglected. A perfect choice if you're spending a day at the Louvre – you can be in and out in 30 minutes.

OPERA TO LES HALLES

L'Autobus Impérial

14 rue Mondétour, 1st (01.42.36.00.18, www. autobus-imperial.fr). Mº Les Halles. **Open** 10am-2am Mon-Sat. **Main courses** €18. **Prix fixe** *Lunch* €13.50, €15.50. *Dinner* €24.50, €29.50. **Credit** MC, V. **Map** p402 J5 ⓮ **Brasserie**
Tucked away in a corner of Les Halles, L'Autobus Impérial is a hidden gem. The rather unattractive entrance does little justice to the superb art nouveau dining room, built in 1910 and boasting a listed glass ceiling. Food is traditional but inventive, and remains very reasonably priced. The bar has the longest zinc counter in Paris.

★ € Bistrot Victoires

6 rue de la Vrillière, 1st (01.42.61.43.78). Mº Bourse. **Open** noon-3pm, 7-11pm daily. **Main courses** €11. **Credit** MC, V. **Map** p402 H5 ⓯ **Bistro**
Bistros with vintage decor serving no-nonsense food at generous prices are growing thin on the ground in Paris, so it's no surprise that this gem is packed to the gills with bargain-loving office workers and locals every day. The *steak-frites* are exemplary, featuring a slab of entrecôte topped with a smoking

CONSUME

sprig of thyme, but *plats du jour* such as *blanquette de veau* (veal in cream sauce) are equally comforting. The wines by the glass can be rough, but the authentic buzz should make up for any flaws.

Blend
44 rue d'Argout, 2nd (01.40.26.84.57, www. blendhamburger.com). M° Bourse or Sentier. **Open** noon-3pm, 7.30-11pm Mon-Sat; noon-4pm Sun. **Main courses** €10. **Credit** MC, V. **Map** p402 J5 ⑯ Burgers
See p162 **Brilliance in a Bun**.

La Bourse ou la Vie
12 rue Vivienne, 2nd (01.42.60.08.83). M° Bourse. **Open** noon-10pm Mon-Fri; 6-10pm Sat. Closed 1wk Aug & 1wk Dec. **Main courses** €10-€20. **Credit** MC, V. **Map** p402 H4 ⑰ Bistro
After a career as an architect, the round-spectacled owner of La Bourse ou la Vie has a new mission in life: to revive the dying art of the perfect *steak-frites*. The only decision you'll need to make is which cut of beef to order with your chips, unless you pick the cod. Choose between ultra-tender *coeur de filet* or a huge, surprisingly tender *bavette*. Rich, creamy pepper sauce is the speciality here, but the real surprise is the chips, which gain a distinctly animal flavour from the suet in which they are cooked.

★ Chez Miki
5 rue de Louvois, 2nd (01.42.96.04.88). M° Bourse. **Open** noon-10.30pm Tue-Sat; 7-10.30pm Sun. **Main courses** €15-€20. **Prix fixe** €15. **Credit** MC, V. **Map** p402 H4 ⑱ Japanese
There are plenty of Japanese restaurants to choose from along nearby rue Ste-Anne, but none is as original – nor as friendly – as this tiny restaurant run entirely by women, next to the square Louvois. The speciality here is bento boxes, which you compose yourself from a scribbled blackboard list (in Japanese and French). For €15 you can choose two small dishes – marinated sardines and fried chicken wings are especially popular – and a larger dish, such as grilled pork with ginger. Don't miss the inventive desserts, which might include lime jelly spiked with alcohol.

Drouant
18 pl Gaillon, 2nd (01.42.65.15.16, www.drouant. com). M° Pyramides or Quatre Septembre. **Open** noon-2.30pm, 7pm-midnight daily. **Main courses** €18-€30. **Prix fixe** *Lunch* €44-€60. *Dinner* (10.30pm-midnight) €42-€54. **Credit** AmEx, DC, MC, V. **Map** p401 H4 ⑲ Brasserie
Star chef Antoine Westermann has whisked this landmark 1880 brasserie into the 21st century with bronze-coloured banquettes and butter-yellow fabrics. Westermann has dedicated this restaurant to the art of the hors d'oeuvre: they're served in themed sets of four ranging from global (Thai beef salad with brightly coloured vegetables, coriander,

THE BEST ALFRESCO TABLES

For terrace chic
Restaurant du Palais-Royal. *See p141.*

For an eyeful of the Eiffel
Au Bon Accueil. *See p166.*

For courtyard crudivores
Cru. *See p152.*

and a sweet and spicy sauce) to nostalgic (silky leeks in vinaigrette). The bite-sized surprises continue with the main course accompaniments – four for each dish – and the multiple mini-desserts.

Au Gourmand
17 rue Molière, 1st (01.42.96.22.19, www.augourmand.fr). M° Palais Royal Musée du Louvre or Pyramides. **Open** 7.30-10pm Mon, Sat; 12.30-2pm, 7.30-10pm Tue-Fri. **Main courses** €29-€37. **Prix fixe** €26-€83. **Credit** MC, V. **Map** p401 H5 ⑳ Bistro
Au Gourmand specialises in exemplary classic and contemporary French dishes, accompanied by exceptional wines. Only the season's best makes it to the award-winning kitchen. Vegetables come from celebrity market gardener Joël Thiébault; the suckling lamb comes from Biarritz; the foie gras is from the Gers; and wild green asparagus is grown in Provence. The fresh interior revamp seems to be a hit with the celebrity patrons, of which there are a fair few.

€ Higuma
32bis rue Ste-Anne, 1st (01.47.03.38.59, www.higuma.fr). M° Pyramides. **Open** 11.30am-10pm daily. **Main courses** €6.50-€8. **Prix fixe** €10-€12. **Credit** MC, V. **Map** p401 H4 ㉑ Japanese
Higuma's no-nonsense food and service make it one of the area's most popular destinations. On entering, customers are greeted by plumes of aromatic steam emanating from the open kitchen-cum-bar, where a small team of chefs ladle out giant bowls of noodle soup piled with meat, vegetables or seafood. You can slurp at the counter or sit at a plastic-topped table.
Other location 163 rue St-Honoré, 1st (01.58.62.49.22).

★ Liza
14 rue de la Banque, 2nd (01.55.35.00.66, www.restaurant-liza.com). M° Bourse. **Open** noon-2.15pm, 8-10pm Mon-Thur; noon-2.15pm, 8-11pm Fri; 8-11pm Sat; noon-3.30pm Sun. **Main courses** €25. **Prix fixe** *Lunch* €16, €21. *Dinner* €42, €49. **Credit** AmEx, MC, V. **Map** p402 H4 ㉒ Lebanese

CONSUME

Liza. See p143.

Liza Soughayar's restaurant showcases the style and superb food of contemporary Beirut. Lentil, fried onion and orange salad is delicious, as are the *kebbe* (minced seasoned raw lamb) and grilled halloumi cheese with home-made apricot preserve. Main courses, such as minced lamb with coriander-spiced spinach and rice, are light, flavoursome and well presented. Try one of the excellent Lebanese wines to accompany your meal, and finish with the halva ice-cream with carob molasses.

Le Pharamond
24 rue de la Grande Truanderie, 1st (01.40.28.45.18, www.pharamond.fr). M° Etienne Marcel. **Open** noon-2.30pm, 7.30-11pm Tue-Sat. **Main courses** €15-€25. **Prix fixe** *Lunch* €14.90 (Tue-Fri), €29.50, €39.50. *Dinner* €29.50, €39.50. **Credit** AmEx, DC, MC, V. **Map** p406 J5 ㉓ **Brasserie**
There has been a restaurant on this site for well over a century and the interior is a joy to behold, with its carved wood panelling, elaborate tiling and stunning painted mirrors. Guests over the years have included Fitzgerald, Hemingway and Mitterrand, and the building is listed as a *monument historique*. The menu runs the gamut from *terrine de lapin* and *escargots* to *tripes à la mode de Caen* and *baba Normand au Calvados*. One thing's for sure – you won't be going home hungry.

Racines
8 passage des Panoramas, 2nd (01.40.13.06.41). M° Bourse or Bonne Nouvelle. **Open** noon-2.30pm, 8-10.30pm Mon-Fri. **Main courses** €19-€32. **Credit** MC, V. **Map** p402 J4 ㉔ **Wine bar**
The 19th-century passage des Panoramas contains an eclectic collection of shops and restaurants – among them this wildly popular wine bar opened by the former owners of La Crèmerie in St-Germain-des-Prés. The menu is limited to superb-quality cheese and charcuterie plates, plus a couple of hot dishes, perhaps pork cheeks stewed in red wine or braised lamb, and a few comforting desserts. Many of the intense-tasting wines are biodynamic and, despite the rather hectic atmosphere, lingering over an extra glass or two is cheerfully tolerated.

Racines 2
39 rue de l'Arbre Sec, 1st (01.42.60.77.34). M° Louvre Rivoli. **Open** noon-2.30pm, 7.45-10.30pm Mon-Fri. **Main courses** €25-€30. **Credit** MC, V. **Map** p402 J5 ㉕ **Bistro**
Racines' little brother is the rebellious one, with its tattooed young chef and Scandinavian-influenced decor from bad-boy designer Philippe Starck (we particularly like the antler lamps). The feel is modern bistro with attitude: starters might include puff pastry *feuilleté* with snails, cream of shallots and fresh herbs or *vitello tonnato*, followed by pork belly with crisp vegetables or beef with herby potato purée and mesclun salad. Prices are on the steep

side, but the area's upmarket clientele are unlikely to be too fazed by the bill.

★ La Tour de Montlhéry (Chez Denise)

5 rue des Prouvaires, 1st (01.42.36.21.82).
Mº Les Halles/RER Châtelet Les Halles. **Open**
noon-3pm, 7.30pm-5am Mon-Fri. Closed 15 July-
15 Aug. **Main courses** €25. **Credit** MC, V.
Map p402 J5  **Bistro**
At the stroke of midnight, this place is packed, jovial and hungry. Savoury traditional dishes, washed down by litres of the house Brouilly, are the order of the day. Les Halles was the city's wholesale food market, and game, beef and offal still rule here. Diners devour towering rib steaks served with marrow and a heaped platter of chips,

among the best in town. Brave souls can also try *tripes au calvados*, grilled *andouillette*, or perhaps go for a stewed venison, served with celery root and home-made jam.

CHAMPS-ELYSEES & WESTERN PARIS

Alain Ducasse au Plaza Athénée

Hôtel Plaza Athénée, 25 av Montaigne, 8th
(01.53.67.65.00, www.alain-ducasse.com). Mº
Alma Marceau. **Open** 7.45-10.15pm Mon-Wed;
12.45-2.15pm, 7.45-10.15pm Thur, Fri. Closed late
July-late Aug & 1wk Dec. **Main courses** €80-
€135. **Prix fixe** €260-€380. **Credit** AmEx, DC,
MC, V. **Map** p400 D5 ⓦ **Haute cuisine**

Market Menu

Starck has started serving in the Puces de St-Ouen.

It's official: Philippe Starck has finally got over 'baroque modern' with not a single Perspex Louis XVI chair in sight at his new 250-seat restaurant, **Ma Cocotte** (106 rue des Rosiers, St-Ouen, 01.49.51.70.00, www.macocotte-lespuces.com), in the Marché aux Puces de St-Ouen. Housed in a red-brick loft building at the entrance to the gorgeous Serpette antiques market, it has more in common with Terence Conran's taste for steel open kitchens and tiles, although perhaps that's no accident. Surfing on the current vogue for 1960s and '70s furniture, Habitat is planning to open a 'vintage space' (77-81 rue des Rosiers, St-Ouen, www.habitat.fr/vintage) just down the road for owners of old Habitat classics to re-sell their vintage pieces.

On a wet Sunday afternoon soon after its launch, Ma Cocotte was bustling with families and young couples queuing for a seat at the high communal tables or regular Formica ones, umbrellas dripping on the decorative encaustic floor tiles. On the menu conviviality is the order of the day, with litre cocktail pitchers (€39) of Starck (champagne, passionfruit, cucumber, ginger and mint); sharing plates of radish, foie gras or caviar; and mains such as rôtisserie farm chicken for four (€72) or côte de boeuf for two or three (€85), prepared by head chef Yannick Papin and a vast army of kitchen staff decked out in Chairman Mao-style blue cap and overalls.

After several years in the doldrums, the Puces is starting to show signs of life again, and the weekend crowds are sure to fancy a post-browse brunch at Ma Cocotte.

CONSUME

Granterroirs.

The sheer glamour factor would be enough to recommend this restaurant, Alain Ducasse's most lofty Paris undertaking. The dining room ceiling drips with 10,000 crystals. An *amuse-bouche* of a single langoustine in a lemon cream with a touch of Iranian caviar starts the meal off beautifully, but other dishes can be inconsistent: a part-raw/part-cooked salad of autumn fruit and veg in a red, Chinese-style sweet-and-sour dressing, or Breton lobster in an overwhelming sauce of apple, quince and spiced wine. Cheese is predictably delicious, as is the *rum baba comme à Monte-Carlo*.

Astrance

4 rue Beethoven, 16th (01.40.50.84.40). M° Passy.
Open 12.15-1.30pm, 8.15-9pm Tue-Fri. Closed 1wk
Nov, 1wk Dec, 1wk May & Aug. **Prix fixe** *Lunch*
€70. *Dinner* €210. **Credit** AmEx, DC, MC, V.
Map p404 B6 ㉘ **Haute cuisine**
When Pascal Barbot opened Astrance, he was praised for creating a new style of Paris restaurant – refined, yet casual and affordable. A few years later, this small, slate-grey dining room feels just like an haute cuisine restaurant. Most customers, having reserved at least a month ahead, give free rein to the chef with the 'Menu Astrance'. Barbot has an original touch, combining foie gras with slices of white mushrooms and a lemon condiment, or sweet lobster with candied grapefruit peel, a grapefruit and rosemary sorbet, and raw baby spinach. Wines, which are available by the glass, are reasonably priced.

Le Bistrot Napolitain

18 av Franklin D. Roosevelt, 8th (01.45.62.08.37).
M° St-Philippe-du-Roule. **Open** noon-2.30pm,
7-10.30pm Mon-Fri. Closed 1wk July, Aug & 1wk
Dec. **Main courses** €18-€25. **Credit** MC, V.
Map p401 E4 ㉙ **Italian**
This chic Italian bistro is as far from a tourist joint as it is possible to be. At lunchtimes, it is full of suave Italianate businessmen. Generosity defines the food – not just big plates, but lashings of the ingredients that others skimp on, such as the slices of tangy parmesan piled high over rocket on the tender beef carpaccio. The pizzas are very good: the Enzo comes with milky, almost raw *mozzarella di bufala* and tasty tomatoes. For pasta you can choose between dried and fresh, with variations such as fresh saffron tagliatelle.

★ Granterroirs

30 rue de Miromesnil, 8th (01.47.42.18.18,
www.granterroirs.com). M° Miromesnil. **Open**
9am-4pm Mon, Fri; 9am-8pm Tue; 9am-7pm Wed;
9am-10pm Thur. *Food served* noon-3pm Mon-Fri
& 7-9.30pm Thur (reserve in advance). Closed
2wks Aug. **Main courses** €16-€25. **Credit**
MC, V. **Map** p401 F3 ㉚ **Bistro**
This *épicerie* with a difference is the perfect remedy for anyone for whom the word '*terroir*' conjures up visions of grease-soaked peasant food. Here, the walls heave with more than 600 enticing specialities from southern France, including Périgord foie gras, charcuterie from Aubrac and a fine selection of wines. All make excellent gift ideas – but why not sample some of the goodies by enjoying the midday *table d'hôte* feast? Come in early to ensure that you can choose from the five *plats du jour* on offer (such as marinated salmon with dill on a bed of warm potatoes).

€ Le Hide

10 rue du Général-Lanrezac, 17th (01.45.74.15.81,
www.lehide.fr). M° Charles de Gaulle Etoile.
Open noon-2pm, 7-10pm Mon-Fri; 7-10pm Sat.
Main courses €14-€18. **Prix fixe** *Lunch*
€19.80, €27. *Dinner* €24, €31. **Credit** MC, V.
Map p400 C3 ㉛ **Bistro**
Ever since it opened, this snug bistro has been packed with a happy crowd of bistro-lovers who appreciate Japanese-born chef Hide Kobayashi's superb cooking and good-value prices. Expect such dishes as duck foie gras terrine with pear-and-thyme compôte to start, followed by tender *faux-filet* steak in a light foie gras sauce or skate wing with a lemon-accented *beurre noisette*. Desserts are excellent: perfect tarte tatin comes with crème fraîche from Normandy. Good, affordable wines explain the merriment, including a glass of the day for €2.

Lasserre

17 av Franklin-Roosevelt, 8th (01.43.59.02.13,
www.restaurant-lasserre.com). M° Franklin
D Roosevelt. **Open** 7-10pm Tue, Wed, Sat;

CONSUME

noon-2pm, 7-10pm Thur, Fri. **Main courses** €70-€120. **Prix fixe** *Lunch* €80, €195. *Dinner* €195. **Credit** AmEx, DC, MC, V. **Map** p401 E5 ⓷ **Haute cuisine**

Lasserre's rich history is definitely a part of the dining experience: Audrey Hepburn, André Malraux and Salvador Dali were regulars. But its illustrious past is nothing next to the food: chef Christophe Moret (ex-Plaza Athénée) and his pastry chef Claire Heitzler (ex-Ritz) create lip-smacking delicacies to die for. The upstairs dining room, accessed by a bellboy-operated lift, is a sumptuous affair in taupe and white, with solid silver table decorations and a retractable roof that opens just enough for you to see the stars at night.

Pierre Gagnaire

6 rue Balzac, 8th (01.58.36.12.50, www.pierre-gagnaire.com). M° Charles de Gaulle Etoile or George V. **Open** noon-1.30pm, 7.30-9.30pm Mon-Fri. Closed Aug. **Prix fixe** *Lunch* €115, €280. *Dinner* €280. **Credit** AmEx, MC, V. **Map** p400 D3 ⓸ **Haute cuisine**

At Pierre Gagnaire the prix fixe starts at a staggering €115, which seems to be the price of culinary experimentation these days. This cheaper lunch menu is far from the full-blown experience of the *carte*: the former is presented in three courses, whereas the latter involves four or five plates for each course. Even the *amuse-bouches* fill the table: an egg 'raviole', ricotta with apple, fish in a cauliflower jelly, and glazed monkfish. The best thing about the lunch menu is that it includes four very indulgent desserts: clementine, raspberry and vanilla, chocolate, and passion fruit.

Rech

62 av des Ternes, 17th (01.45.72.29.47, www.restaurant-rech.fr). M° Ternes. **Open** noon-2pm, 7.30-10pm Tue-Sat. Closed Aug & 1wk Dec. **Main courses** €38. **Prix fixe** *Lunch* €32. *Dinner* €54. **Credit** AmEx, MC, V. **Map** p400 C2 ⓸ **Bistro**

Alain Ducasse's personal touches are everywhere in this art deco seafood restaurant, from the Japanese fish prints on the walls of the upstairs dining room to the blown glass candleholders on the main-floor tables. The kitchen turns out the kind of precise, Mediterranean-inspired cooking you would expect from Ducasse: glistening sardine fillets marinated with preserved lemon, silky lobster ravioli, and octopus carpaccio painted with pesto. As the fish dishes are light, you can justify indulging in a perfectly aged camembert and the XL éclair, an event in itself.

★ Restaurant L'Entredgeu

83 rue Laugier, 17th (01.40.54.97.24). M° Porte de Champerret. **Open** noon-2pm, 7.30-11pm Tue-Sat. Closed 1wk Apr, 1st 3wks Aug & 1wk Dec. **Prix fixe** *Lunch* €23, €33. *Dinner* €33. **Credit** DC, MC, V. **Map** p400 C2 ⓸ **Bistro**

Reading the menu here will make you seriously doubt your capacity for pudding. But have no fear. The heartiness of the dishes belies refined, perfectly gauged cooking, served in civilised portions. The table turnover is fast, but this is not a place to linger smoochily in any case – you'll be too busy marvelling at the sharp *gribiche* sauce cutting through the milky crisp-battered oysters, the depth and aroma of the saffron-infused fish soup, the

Lasserre.

CONSUME

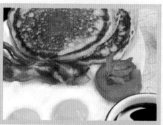

perfect layered execution of the caramelised pork belly, and the delicate desserts. The wine list is creative and assured.

Senderens

9 pl de la Madeleine, 8th (01.42.65.22.90, www.senderens.fr). M° Madeleine. **Open** noon-2.45pm, 7.30-11pm daily. Closed 1st 3wks Aug. **Main courses** €40-€51. **Prix fixe** €116, €160 (with wine). **Credit** AmEx, DC, MC, V. **Map** p401 G4 ㊴ **Haute cuisine**

Alain Senderens reinvented his art nouveau institution (formerly Lucas Carton) a few years ago with a *Star Trek* interior and a mind-boggling fusion menu. Now, you might find dishes such as roast duck foie gras with a warm salad of black figs and liquorice powder, or monkfish steak with Spanish mussels and green curry sauce. Each dish comes with a suggested wine, whisky, sherry or punch (to match a rum-doused *savarin* with slivers of ten-flavour pear), and although these are perfectly chosen, the mix of flavours and alcohols can prove overwhelming at times.

★ Stella Maris

4 rue Arsène-Houssaye, 8th (01.42.89.16.22, www.stellamaris-paris.com). M° Charles de Gaulle Etoile. **Open** 12.30-2.30pm, 7.30-10pm Mon-Fri; 7.30-10pm Sat. Closed 2wks Aug. **Main courses** €41-€75. **Prix fixe** *Lunch* €52. *Dinner* €75, €130. **Credit** AmEx, DC, MC, V. **Map** p400 D3 ㊲ **Haute cuisine**

Tateru Yoshino has divided his life between Paris and Tokyo for many years. Trained by Robuchon and Troisgros, he turns out food that is resolutely French. The service is at times faltering, but charmingly so, and the space is beautiful. You might float your way through foie gras with carrots, truffles and pistachio oil, pan-fried sea bass with saffron risotto, and a perfectly lopsided Grand Marnier soufflé. The exquisite, powdery blandness of the tasting menu going-home present, *cake aux marrons glacés*, brings it all softly, dreamily, back next morning at breakfast. Expensive but wonderful.

La Table Lauriston

129 rue de Lauriston, 16th (01.47.27.00.07, www.restaurantlatablelauriston.com). M° Trocadéro. **Open** noon-2.30pm, 7-10.30pm Mon-Fri; 7-10.30pm Sat. Closed 3wks Aug & 1wk Dec. **Main courses** €25-€30. **Prix fixe** *Lunch* €26. *Dinner* €40, €61. **Credit** AmEx, MC, V. **Map** p400 B5 ㊳ **Bistro**

Serge Barbey's dining room has a refreshingly feminine touch. The emphasis here is firmly on good-quality ingredients, skilfully prepared to show off their freshness. In spring, stalks of asparagus from the Landes are carefully trimmed to avoid any trace of stringiness and delightfully served with the simplest *vinaigrette d'herbes*. More extravagant is the *foie gras cuit au torchon*, in which the duck liver is

wrapped in a cloth and poached in a bouillon. Skip the crème brûlée, which you could have anywhere, and order a dessert with attitude instead: the giant *baba au rhum*.

Taillevent

15 rue Lamennais, 8th (01.44.95.15.01, www.taillevent.com). M° George V. **Open** 12.15-1.30pm, 7.15-9.30pm Mon-Fri. Closed Aug. **Main courses** €48-€188. **Prix fixe** *Lunch* €82, €98, €198. *Dinner* €198. **Credit** AmEx, DC, MC, V. **Map** p400 D3 ㊵ **Haute cuisine**

Prices here are not quite as shocking as in some restaurants at this level; for instance, there's an €82 lunch menu. *Rémoulade de coquilles St-Jacques* is a technical feat, with slices of raw, marinated scallop wrapped in a tube shape around a finely diced apple filling, encircled by a mayonnaise-like *rémoulade* sauce. An earthier and lip-smacking dish is the signature *épeautre* – an ancient wheat – which is cooked 'like a risotto' with bone marrow, black truffle, whipped cream and parmesan, and topped with sautéed frogs' legs. *Ravioli au chocolat araguani* is a surprising and wonderful dessert. Men must wear a jacket.

MONTMARTRE & PIGALLE

Big Fernand

55 rue du Faubourg Poissonnière, 9th (01.47.70.54.72, www.bigfernand.com). M° Cadet or Poissonnière. **Open** noon-2.30pm, 7.30-10.30pm Mon-Sat. **Main courses** €10-€20. **Credit** AmEx, MC, V. **Map** p402 J3 ㊴ **Burgers**

See p162 **Brilliance in a Bun.**

Le Coq Rico

98 rue Lepic, 18th (01.42.59.82.89, www.lecoq rico.com). M° Abbesses, Blanche or Lamarck-Caulincourt. **Open** noon-2.30pm, 7.30-11pm daily. **Main courses** €20-€38. **Credit** AmEx, MC, V. **Map** p401 H1 ㊶ **Bistro**

Antoine Westermann's new culinary venture, Coq Rico, is a classy '*bistrotisserie*' hybrid nestled in the heights of Montmartre, a place where comfort food standards are transformed into gourmet treats – gooey boiled egg comes with crunchy soldiers and truffle-infused butter, and the *planchette de béatilles* features nibble-sized pieces of chicken heart, gizzards and sticky chicken wings, all perfectly seasoned. There's a list of poultry suppliers at the bottom of the menu, a transparency that will appeal to health-conscious locals – even if prices are high (€95 for a whole chicken serving two to four). Wine choice is excellent, including a seriously quaffable Faugères for €29.

Les Fils à Maman

7 bis Rue Geoffroy-Marie, 9th (01.48.24.59.39, www.lesfilsamaman.com). M° Grands Boulevards. **Open** 11.30am-2.30pm, 7-11pm Mon-Fri; 7-11pm

CONSUME

Sat. **Main courses** €17. **Prix fixe** *Lunch* €11, €15, €19. **Credit** DC, MC, V. **Map** p402 J3 ⑫ **Bistro**

In the up-and-coming neighbourhood near the Folies Bergère a band of five 'mothers' boys' has created a restaurant evoking their mums' home cooking. Even the mums themselves get into the kitchen on the first Tuesday of the month to turn out *blanquette de veau*, chicken cordon bleu with beaufort cheese and Nutella-flavoured puddings. Whether or not you think Babybel has a place in Gallic cuisine, it's a chance to relive the school French exchange or 1980s après-ski in the company of an ebullient crowd.

La Maison Mère
4 rue de Navarin, 9th (01.42.81.11.00, www. lamaisonmere.fr). M° Saint-Georges or Pigalle. **Open** noon-3pm, 7pm-2am Tue-Sat; noon-3pm Sun. **Main courses** €15-€20. **Credit** AmEx, MC, V. **Map** p402 H2 ⑬ **Bistro**

Forget any ideas of a traditional French kitchen: this place is more Mom than Mère. Embrace, instead, the New York-style decor, with white tiles, vintage furniture, enamelled mirrors, lamps disguised as bowler hats and a sign declaring: 'In food we trust'. The menu is much what you'd expect given the setting, with a few dashing bourgeois touches. Leek vinaigrette, eggs 'mimosa', bone marrow sandwiches, grilled cockerel and chocolate mousse all appear alongside crab cake, Brooklyn platters, Long Island platters and so on. The five burgers will delight enthusiasts, be it a breaded cod burger or the Black Label with its thick-cut Black Angus steak. The house fries could be better and the whole doesn't come cheap, but nobody's perfect. Friendly service, a good wine selection and top cheesecake all go a long way towards sweetening the bill.

Le Miroir
94 rue des Martyrs, 18th (01.46.06.50.73). M° Abbesses. **Open** noon-2pm, 7.30-10pm Tue-Sat. **Main courses** €20. **Prix fixe** *Lunch* €19, €26, €33, €42. *Dinner* €26, €33, €42. **Credit** AmEx, MC, V. **Map** p402 H2 ⑭ **Bistro**

This friendly modern bistro is a welcome addition to a neighbourhood where good-value restaurants are scarce. Big mirrors, red banquettes and a glass ceiling at the back give it character, while the very professional food and service reflect the owners' haute cuisine training. Expect such dishes as a salad of whelks with white beans, crisp-skinned duck and chanterelle mushrooms, and a *petit pot de crème vanille* with little chocolate cakes.

Le Moulin de la Galette
83 rue Lepic, 18th (01.46.06.84.77, www. lemoulindelagalette.eu). M° Notre-Dame-de-Lorette. **Open** noon-11pm daily. **Main courses** €25. **Prix fixe** *Lunch* €23, €29 (Mon-Sat). *Dinner* €59. **Credit** AmEx, MC, V. **Map** p402 H1 ⑮ **Bistro**

La Maison Mère.

The Butte Montmartre was once dotted with windmills, and this survivor houses a chic modern restaurant with a few tables in the cobbled courtyard. It's hard to imagine a lovelier setting in Montmartre, but the kitchen makes an effort nonetheless, coming up with dishes such as foie gras with melting beetroot cooked in lemon balm and juniper, and suckling pig alongside potato purée. Desserts look like a painter's tableau. If you're on a budget, stick to the set menus and order carefully from the wine list.

★ € Pétrelle
34 rue Pétrelle, 9th (01.42.82.11.02, www. petrelle.fr). M° Anvers. **Open** 8-10pm Tue-Sat. Closed 1st wk May, 4wks July/Aug & 1wk Dec. **Main courses** €25. **Prix fixe** €38. **Credit** AmEx, MC, V. **Map** p402 J2 ⑯ **Bistro**

Jean-Luc André is as inspired a decorator as he is a cook, and the quirky charm of his dining room has made it popular with fashion designers and film stars. But behind the style there's some serious substance. André seeks out the best ingredients from local producers, and the quality shines through. The no-choice menu is very good value for money (marinated sardines with tomato relish, rosemary-scented rabbit with roasted vegetables, deep-purple poached figs) – or you can splash out with luxurious à la carte dishes such as tournedos Rossini.

€ Rose Bakery
46 rue des Martyrs, 9th (01.42.82.12.80). M° Notre-Dame-de-Lorette. **Open** 9am-6pm

CONSUME

Tue-Sun. Closed 2wks Aug & 1wk Dec. **Main courses** €14.50-€17. **Credit** AmEx, MC, V. **Map** p402 H2 ⑰ **British**

This English-themed café run by a Franco-British couple stands out for the quality of its ingredients – organic or from small producers – as well as the too-good-to-be-true puddings: carrot cake, sticky toffee pudding and, in winter, a chocolate-chestnut tart. The DIY salad plate is crunchily satisfying, but the thin-crusted *pizzettes*, daily soups and occasional risottos are equally good choices. Don't expect much beyond scones in the morning except at weekends, when brunch is served to a packed-out house. **Other location** 30 rue Debelleyme, 3rd (01.49.96.54.01).

BEAUBOURG & THE MARAIS

★ L'Ambassade d'Auvergne

22 rue du Grenier-St-Lazare, 3rd (01.42.72.31.22, www.ambassade-auvergne.com). M° Arts et Métiers. **Open** noon-2pm, 7.30-10pm daily. **Main courses** €18. **Prix fixe** *Lunch* €20, €31. **Credit** AmEx, MC, V. **Map** p409 K5 ⑱ **Bistro**

This rustic-style *auberge* is a fitting embassy for the hearty fare of central France. An order of cured ham comes as two hefty, plate-filling slices, and the salad bowl is chock-full of green lentils cooked in goose fat, studded with bacon and shallots. The *rôti d'agneau* arrives as a pot of melting chunks of lamb in a rich, meaty sauce with a helping of tender white beans. Dishes arrive with the flagship *aligot*,

the creamy, elastic mash-and-cheese concoction. Among the regional wines (Chanturgue, Boudes, Madargues), the fruity AOC Marcillac makes a worthy partner.

€ Breizh Café

109 rue Vieille-du-Temple, 3rd (01.42.72.13.77, www.breizhcafe.com). M° Filles du Calvaire. **Open** 11.30am-11pm Wed-Sun. Closed 3wks Aug. **Main courses** €7-€15. **Credit** AmEx, MC, V. **Map** p409 L5 ⑲ **Crêperie**

With its modern interior of pale wood and its choice of 15 artisanal ciders, this outpost of a restaurant in Cancale, Brittany, is a world away from the average crêperie. For the complete faux-seaside experience, you might start with a plate of creuse oysters from Cancale before indulging in an inventive buckwheat *galette* such as the Cancalaise, made with potato, smoked herring from Brittany and herring roe. The choice of fillings is fairly limited, but the ingredients are of high quality – including the use of Valrhona chocolate with 70% cocoa solids in the dessert crêpes. *Photo p152.*

★ € Cantine Merci

111 bd Beaumarchais, 3rd (01.42.77.78.92). M° St-Sébastien Froissart. **Open** noon-3.30pm Mon-Sat (until 6pm for tea). **Main courses** €8-€18. **Credit** AmEx, MC, V. **Map** p409 L5 ⑳ **Café**

The new fairtrade concept store Merci is all about feeling virtuous even as you indulge, and its basement canteen is a perfect example. Fresh and colourful salads, soup and risotto of the day, an organic salmon plate, and the *assiette merci* (perhaps chicken kefta with two salads) make up the brief, Rose Bakery-esque menu, complete with invigorating teas and juices. Rustic desserts add just the right handmade touch.

★ € Chez Hanna
54 rue des Rosiers, 4th (01.42.74.74.99).
Mº St-Paul. **Open** noon-midnight Tue-Sun.
Main courses €12-€16. **Credit** MC, V.
Map p409 K6 ③ **Jewish**
By noon on a Sunday, there is a queue outside almost every falafel shop along rue des Rosiers. The long-established L'As du Fallafel, a little further up the street, still reigns supreme, whereas Chez Hanna remains something of a locals' secret, quietly serving up falafel and shawarma sandwiches to rival any in the world. A pitta sandwich bursting with crunchy chickpea-and-herb balls, tahini sauce and vegetables costs just €4 if you order from the takeaway window, €8 if you sit at one of the tables in the buzzy dining room. Either way, you really can't lose.

Chez Julien
1 rue du Pont Louis-Philippe, 4th (01.42.78.31.64).
Mº Pont Marie. **Open** noon-3pm, 7.30-11pm Mon-Thur; noon-3pm, 7.30-11.30pm Fri, Sat.
Main courses €22-€38. **Credit** AmEx, MC, V.
Map p409 K6 ② **Bistro**
Thierry Costes discreetly took over this vintage bistro overlooking the Seine in spring 2007. The zebra banquette near the loo upstairs is most reminiscent of the Costes style, but the 1920s dining room is also unmistakably chic with plum walls, a big chandelier and red banquettes, and the terrace outside now stretches across the cobbled pedestrian street. The food is predictable – crab salad, steak with shoestring fries – and pricey, but it's hard not to enjoy this slice of Paris life.

★ € Chez Omar
47 rue de Bretagne, 3rd (01.42.72.36.26).
Mº Arts et Métiers or Temple. **Open** noon-2.30pm, 7-11.30pm Mon-Sat; 7-11.30pm Sun.
Main courses €12-€26. **No credit cards.**
Map p409 L5 ③ **North African**
The once-fashionable Omar doesn't take any reservations, and the queue can often stretch the length of the zinc bar and through the door. Everyone is waiting for the same thing: couscous. Prices range from €11 (vegetarian) to €24 (*royale*); there are no tagines or other traditional Maghreb mains, only a handful of French classics (duck, fish, steak). Overstretched waiters slip through the crowds with mounds of semolina, vats of vegetable-laden broth and steel platters heaving with meat, including the stellar *merguez*. Even on packed nights, there's an offer of seconds – gratis – to encourage you to stay longer. *Photo p154.*

Breizh Café. *See p151.*

Cru
7 rue Charlemagne, 4th (01.40.27.81.84, www.restaurantcru.fr). Mº St-Paul. **Open** 12.30-2.30pm, 7-11pm Tue-Sat; 12.30-3pm Sun. **Main courses** €9-€25. **Prix fixe** *Lunch* €19. **Credit** MC, V. **Map** p409 L7 ④ **Bistro**
Opening a raw-food restaurant is a gamble, so the owners of Cru cheat here and there, offering root vegetable 'chips' and a few *plancha* dishes. Still, the extensive menu has plenty for the crudivore, such as some unusual carpaccios (the veal with preserved lemon is particularly good) and intriguing 'red' and 'green' plates, variations on the tomato and cucumber. The food is perfectly good, but the real reason to come here is the gorgeous courtyard terrace lurking behind this quiet Marais street.

★ Derrière
69 rue des Gravilliers, 3rd (01.44.61.91.95, www.derriere-resto.com). Mº Arts et Métiers. **Open** noon-2.30pm, 8-11.30pm Mon-Sat; noon-4pm, 8-11.30pm Sun. **Main courses** €15-€35. **Prix fixe** *Lunch* €25. **Credit** MC, V. **Map** p409 K5 ⑤ **Bistro**
Mourad Mazouz, the man behind Momo and Sketch in London, has hit on another winning formula with this apartment-restaurant in the same street as his North African restaurant 404 and bar Andy Wahloo. The cluttered-chic look mixes contemporary fixtures and antique furniture, such as the beat-up armchairs in the smoking room hidden behind a wardrobe door upstairs. It attracts a young, hip crowd that appreciates the high-calorie comfort food: roast chicken with buttery mashed potatoes, macaroni gratin with taramasalata, and chocolate mousse.

Le Gaigne

*12 rue Pecquay, 4th (01.44.59.86.72, www.
restaurantlegaigne.fr). M° Rambuteau.* **Open** 12.15-
2pm, 7.30-10.30pm Tue-Sat. **Main courses** €24.
Prix fixe *Lunch* €17, €23, €31. *Dinner* €45, €64.
Credit AmEx, MC, V. **Map** p409 K6 ⑤ **Bistro**
It's a familiar story: young chef with haute cuisine
credentials opens a small bistro in an out-of-the-way
street. Here, the restaurant is even tinier than usual
with only 20 seats and the cooking is unusually
inventive. Chef Mickaël Gaignon has worked with
Pierre Gagnaire, and it shows in dishes such as *l'oeuf
bio* – three open eggshells filled with creamed
spinach, carrot and celeriac.

Le Hangar

*12 impasse Berthaud, 3rd (01.42.74.55.44).
M° Rambuteau.* **Open** noon-2.30pm, 7.30-11pm
Tue-Sat. Closed Aug. **Main courses** €18-€26.
No credit cards. Map p409 K5 ⑤ **Bistro**
It's worth making the effort to find this bistro by
the Centre Pompidou, with its terrace tucked away
in a hidden alley and excellent cooking. A bowl of
tapenade and toast is supplied to keep you going
while choosing from the comprehensive *carte*. It
yields, for starters, tasty and grease-free *rillettes de
lapereau* (rabbit) alongside perfectly balanced
pumpkin and chestnut soup. Main courses include
pan-fried foie gras on a smooth potato purée.

Le Petit Marché

*9 rue de Béarn, 3rd (01.42.72.06.67). M° Chemin
Vert.* **Open** 8am-2am daily. *Food served* noon-
3pm, 7.45pm-midnight daily. **Main courses**
€19. **Prix fixe** *Lunch* €14.50. **Credit** AmEx,
MC, V. **Map** 409 L6 ⑤ **Bistro**

Petit Marché's menu is short and modern with Asian
touches. Raw tuna is flash-fried in sesame seeds and
served with a Thai sauce, making for a refreshing
starter; crispy-coated deep-fried king prawns have
a similar lightness. The main vegetarian risotto is
rich in basil, coriander, cream and al dente green
beans. Pan-fried scallops with lime are precision-
cooked and accompanied by a good purée and more
beans. There's a short wine list. *Photo p155.*

BASTILLE & EASTERN PARIS

★ € A la Biche au Bois

*45 av Ledru-Rollin, 12th (01.43.43.34.38).
M° Gare de Lyon.* **Open** 7-11pm Mon; noon-
2pm, 7-11pm Tue-Fri. Closed 4wks July-Aug
& Christmas wk. **Main courses** €17. **Prix
fixe** €29.50. **Credit** AmEx, DC, MC, V.
Map p407 M8 ⑤ **Bistro**
However crowded it gets here, it doesn't matter
because everyone always seems so happy with the
food and the convivial atmosphere. It's impossible
not to be enthusiastic about the more than generous
portions offered with the prix fixe menu. Mains
might include wild duck in blackcurrant sauce, partridge with cabbage or wild venison stew. If you can
still do dessert, go for one of the home-made tarts
laden with seasonal fruits. The wine list has a reputation as one of the best-value selections in town.

★ Le Bistrot Paul Bert

*18 rue Paul-Bert, 11th (01.43.72.24.01).
M° Charonne or Faidherbe Chaligny.* **Open**
noon-2pm, 7.30-11pm Tue-Sat. Closed Aug.
Prix fixe *Lunch* €18. *Dinner* €36. **Credit**
MC, V. **Map** p407 N7 ⑥ **Bistro**

Chez Hanna

This heart-warming bistro gets it right almost down to the last crumb. A starter salad of *ris de veau* illustrates the point, with lightly browned veal sweetbreads perched on a bed of green beans and baby carrots with a sauce of sherry vinegar. A roast shoulder of suckling pig and a thick steak with a raft of golden, thick-cut *frites* look inviting indeed. Desserts are superb too, including what may well be the best *île flottante* in Paris. *Photos p156.*

Bofinger

5-7 rue de la Bastille, 4th (01.42.72.87.82, www. bofingerparis.com). Mᵒ Bastille. **Open** noon-3pm, 6.30pm-midnight daily. **Main courses** €22. **Prix fixe** €28.90, €34. **Credit** AmEx, DC, MC, V. **Map** p409 L7 ⑳ **Brasserie**

Bofinger draws big crowds for its authentic art nouveau setting and brasserie atmosphere. Downstairs is the prettiest place in which to eat, but the upstairs room is air-conditioned. An à la carte selection might start with plump, garlicky escargots or a well-made langoustine terrine, followed by an intensely seasoned salmon tartare, a generous (if unremarkable) cod steak, or calf's liver accompanied by cooked melon. Alternatively, you could have the foolproof brasserie meal of oysters and fillet steak, washed down with the fine Gigondas. *Photo p157.*

€ L'Encrier

55 rue Traversière, 12th (01.44.68.08.16). Mᵒ Gare de Lyon or Ledru-Rollin. **Open** noon-2.30pm, 7.30-11pm Mon-Fri; 7.30-11pm Sat. Closed Aug &

Chez Omar. *See p152.*

Christmas wk. **Main courses** €10.50-€21. **Prix fixe** *Lunch* €12.50-€24.80. *Dinner* €16.50-€24.80. **Credit** MC, V. **Map** p407 M7 ㉒ **Bistro**

Through the door and past the velvet curtain, you find yourself face to face with the kitchen – and a crowd of locals, many of whom seem to know the charming boss personally. Start with fried rabbit kidneys on a bed of salad dressed with raspberry vinegar, perhaps, an original and wholly successful combination, and follow with goose *magret* with honey – a welcome change from the usual duck version and served with crunchy, thinly sliced sautéed potatoes. To end, share a chocolate cake, or try the popular profiteroles. The Chinon is a classy red.

La Gazzetta

29 rue de Cotte, 12th (01.43.47.47.05, www.la gazzetta.fr). Mᵒ Ledru-Rollin. **Open** noon-3pm, 8-11pm Tue-Sat. Closed Aug. **Main courses** €23. **Prix fixe** *Lunch* €17. *Dinner* €39, €45, €65. **Credit** AmEx, DC, MC, V. **Map** p407 N7 ㉓ **Bistro**

Opened by the team behind bar Le Fumoir, La Gazzetta has a similarly moody feel, with dim lighting, a long zinc bar and retro decor. Chef Petter Nilssen is Swedish, but he made his name in the south of France, and his food shows a strong Scandinavian influence in dishes such as bonito in a sweet-salty marinade with caraway, borage leaves, radish and pomelo, or new potatoes from the island of Noirmoutier off the Atlantic coast with seaweed butter and dill. The €39 menu is a pretty good bet, with five courses and not too many decisions to make.

★ Le Souk

1 rue Keller, 11th (01.49.29.05.08). Mᵒ Bastille or Ledru-Rollin. **Open** 7.30-11.30pm Tue-Fri; 11.30am-2.30pm, 7.30pm-midnight Sat; 11.30am-2.30pm, 7.30-11.30pm Sun. **Main courses** €13-€16. **Prix fixe** €16.50, €22.50. **Credit** DC, MC, V. **Map** p407 N7 ㉔ **North African**

Potted olive trees mark the entrance to this lively den of Moroccan cuisine. Start with savoury *b'stilla*, a pasty stuffed with duck, raisins and nuts, flavoured with orange-blossom water and sprinkled with cinnamon and powdered sugar. Don't fill up, though, as the first-rate tagines and couscous are enormous. The *tagine canette* (duckling stewed with honey, onions, apricots, figs and cinnamon, then showered with toasted almonds) is terrific. For dessert, try the excellent millefeuille with fresh figs, while sweet mint tea is poured in a long stream by a *djellaba*-clad waiter.

Le Train Bleu

Gare de Lyon, pl Louis-Armand, 12th (01.43.43.09.06, www.le-train-bleu.com). Mᵒ Gare de Lyon. **Open** 11.30am-3pm, 7-11pm daily. **Main courses** €40. **Prix fixe** €56, €70, €98. **Credit** AmEx, DC, MC, V. **Map** p407 M8 ㉕ **Brasserie**

Le Petit Marché. *See p153.*

This listed dining room – with vintage frescoes and big oak benches – exudes a pleasant air of expectation. Don't expect cutting-edge cooking, but rather fine renderings of French classics. Lobster served on walnut oil-dressed salad leaves is a generous, beautifully prepared starter, as is the pistachio-studded *saucisson de Lyon* with a warm salad of small *ratte* potatoes. *Photo p158.*

Unico
15 rue Paul-Bert, 11th (01.43.67.68.08, www.resto-unico.com). M° Faidherbe-Chaligny. **Open** 8-10.30pm Mon; 12.15-2.30pm, 8-10.30pm Tue-Thur; 12.15-2.30pm, 8-11pm Fri, Sat. **Main courses** €25-€37. **Prix fixe** *Lunch* €17. **Credit** MC, V. **Map** p407 N7 🚳 **Argentinian**

Architect Marcelo Joulia and photographer Enrique Zanoni were wise enough to retain the vintage 1970s decor of this former butcher's shop when they opened their temple to Argentinian beef. Orange tiles and matching light fixtures provide the backdrop for the fashionable, black-dressed crowd that comes here for thick slabs of meat grilled over charcoal and served with a selection of sauces. If you find yourself hesitating, opt for the *lomo* (fillet) with *chimichurri*, a mild salsa – and don't forget to wash it down with Argentinian wine, a rarity in Paris.

★ Au Vieux Chêne
7 rue du Dahomey, 11th (01.43.71.67.69, www. vieuxchene.fr). M° Faidherbe-Chaligny. **Open** noon-2pm, 8-10.30pm Mon-Fri. Closed 1wk July

& 2wks Aug. **Main courses** €21-€24. **Prix fixe** *Lunch* €15, €19. *Dinner* €28, €33. **Credit** MC, V. **Map** p407 N7 🚳 **Bistro**

Although everyone loves the the zinc-capped bar by the entrance, and the tiled floor, what makes this bistro so special is its desire to please. A starter of langoustines encased in fine crunchy angel hair and garnished with slices of fresh mango is delicious and refreshing, and chilled tomato soup is garnished with mint, a ball of tomato sorbet and a drizzle of olive oil. Stéphane Chevassus is a gifted game cook too, as proved by the tender roast pigeon sautéed with Chinese cabbage.

NORTH-EAST PARIS

Abri
92 rue du Fbg-Poissonnière, 10th (01.83.97.00.00). M° Poissonnière. **Open** 10am-5pm Mon, Sat; noon-2pm, 7-10.30pm Tue-Fri. **Prix fixe** *Lunch* €22. *Dinner* €38.50. **Credit** MC, V. **Map** p402 J3 🚳 **Bistro**

A pocket-sized restaurant next to the Poissonnière métro, Abri ('shelter') serves everything from multi-layered sandwiches (Mondays and Saturdays) to sophisticated French cuisine enhanced with Far Eastern touches: marinated mackerel, for example, with almost transparent sliced vegetables, or a winter squash soup with pumpkin seeds and coffee. The tasting menus are a big draw (four dishes for €22 at lunch, six at dinner for €38.50, including dessert). You'll need to be patient and reserve far in advance to secure a table in the postage stamp-sized room, where the open kitchen takes up half the floor space, but it's definitely worth the effort. Service is charming.

★ € Le Baratin
3 rue Jouye-Rouve, 20th (01.43.49.39.70). M° Pyrénées. **Open** 12.15-2pm, 7.30-11pm Tue-Fri; 7.30-11pm Sat. **Main courses** €18-€30. **Prix fixe** *Lunch* €18. **Credit** MC, V. **Map** p403 N3 🚳 **Bistro**

Star pastry chef Pierre Hermé visits this cheerful little bistro and wine bar high up in Belleville at least every two weeks to fill up on Raquel Carena's homely cooking with the occasional exotic twist. Typical of her style, which draws on her native Argentina, are tuna carpaccio with cherries, roast Basque lamb with new potatoes and spinach, and hazelnut pudding. If the food weren't so fantastic, it would still be worth coming for the mostly organic wines. Le Baratin attracts gourmands from all over Paris – so be sure to book.

Le Cambodge
10 av Richerand, 10th (01.44.84.37.70, www.lecambodge.fr). M° Goncourt or République. **Open** noon-2.30pm, 8-11.30pm Mon-Sat. Closed 1 Aug-8 Sept, 24 Dec-1 Jan. **Main courses** €13. **Credit** MC, V. **Map** p402 L4 🚳 **Cambodian**

CONSUME

Le Bistrot Paul Bert. *See p153.*

The system at Le Cambodge is simple: you write your order on a piece of paper, including any preferences such as 'no coriander', 'no peanuts' or 'extra rice', and after a short wait the dishes appear. Two favourites are the *bobun spécial*, a hot and cold mix of sautéed beef, noodles, salad, bean sprouts and imperial rolls, and *banhoy*, a selection of the same ingredients to be wrapped in lettuce and mint leaves and dipped in a sauce. They also serve soups, salads and curries, including stewed pork in a fragrant coconut sauce.

★ Le Chateaubriand

129 av Parmentier, 11th (01.43.57.45.95, www.lechateaubriand.net). M° Goncourt. **Open** 7.30-11pm Tue-Sat. Closed 2wks Dec. **Prix fixe** *Dinner* €60. **Credit** AmEx, MC, V. **Map** p403 M4 ⓐ **Bistro**
Self-taught Basque chef Iñaki Aizpitarte runs this stylish bistro. Come at dinner to try the cooking at its most adventurous. Dishes have been deconstructed down to their very essence and put back together again. You'll understand if you try starters like chunky steak tartare with a quail's egg, or asparagus with tahini foam and little splinters of sesame-seed brittle. The cooking's not always so cerebral – Aizpitarte's Spanish goat's cheese with stewed apple jam is brilliant. Be sure to book ahead. *Photo p159.*

Au Comptoir de Brice

33 rue du Château-d'Eau, 10th (07.87.36.77.38, www.aucomptoirdebrice.com). M° Château d'Eau. **Open** noon-6pm Tue-Sat; 10.30am-2pm Sun. **Main courses** €15-€20. **Credit** MC, V. **Map** p402 K4 ⓐ **Burgers**
See p162 **Brilliance in a Bun.**

Le Dauphin

131 av Parmentier, 11th (01.55.28.78.88, www.restaurantledauphin.net). M° Goncourt. **Open** noon-2pm, 7-11pm Tue-Fri; 7-11pm Sat. Closed 24 Dec-1 Jan. **Prix fixe** *Lunch* €23-€27. **Tapas** €8-€18 (dinner only). **Credit** MC, V. **Map** p403 N5 ⓐ **Wine bar**
Iñaki Aizpitarte's recently opened Le Dauphin, a Rem Koolhaus-designed tapas-style place a few doors from Le Chateaubriand, offers sub-€15 dishes such as *magret séché, tempura de gambas* and *tarte au citron meringuée*. As at Le Chateaubriand, sourcing is all-important – bread comes from award-winning Du Pain et des Idées.

★ € Dong Huong

14 rue Louis-Bonnet, 11th (01.43.57.42.81). M° Belleville. **Open** noon-11pm Mon, Wed-Sun. Closed 2wks Jan & 3wks Aug. **Main courses** €7. **Credit** MC, V. **Map** p403 N4 ⓐ **Vietnamese**
The excellent food at this Vietnamese noodle joint attracts a buzzy crowd. The delicious *bánh cuôn*, steamed Vietnamese ravioli stuffed with minced meat, mushrooms, bean sprouts, spring onions and

Bofinger. *See p154.*

deep-fried onion, are served piping hot. *Com ga lui*, chicken kebabs with tasty lemongrass, though not as delicate, come with tasty rice. *Bò bùn chà giò* (noodles with beef and small *nem* topped with onion strips, spring onion and crushed peanuts) makes a meal in itself. For dessert, the mandarin, lychee and mango sorbets are tasty and authentic.

★ La Fidélité

12 rue de la Fidélité, 10th (01.47.70.19.34, www.lafidelite.com). M° Gare de L'Est. **Open** 8pm-1am Mon-Sat. **Main courses** €18-€26. **Prix fixe** *Dinner* €55 (groups of 15 or more). **Credit** AmEx, MC, V. **Map** p402 K3 ⓐ **Brasserie**
There was a huge buzz when La Clique took this place over, and so far the brasserie is setting a high standard with its elegant styling. The neighbourhood is arguably one of the least attractive in the capital, but La Fidélité has become a place of pilgrimage not only for A-listers, but also for lovers of good, well-priced food – the *joue de boeuf* is sublime. On Thursdays and Fridays, the basement morphs into Cave de la Fidélité, a jukebox bar. *Photo p160.*

Le Floréal

73 rue du Fbg-du-Temple, 10th (01.40.18.46.79). M° Goncourt. **Open** 8am-2am daily. **Main courses** €12-€35. **Prix fixe** *Lunch* €14, €16. **Credit** MC, V. **Map** p403 M4 ⓐ **Diner**
The proprietors of Chez Jeannette and Chez Justine chose this prime site opposite Le Chateaubriand and Le Dauphin for their new venture, Le Floréal – an

CONSUME

Le Train Bleu. *See p154.*

American-style diner serving hamburgers and cupcakes (and favourite of Matthieu Almeric, Daniel Craig's nemesis in *Quantum of Solace*). *Photo p161.*

Le Galopin

34 rue Sainte-Marthe, 10th (01.42.06.05.03). Mᵒ Belleville or Colonel Fabien. **Open** noon-2.30pm, 7-10.30pm Tue-Sat. **Prix fixe** *Lunch* €25. *Dinner* €44. **Credit** AmEx, MC, V. **Map** p403 M3 ⑰ **Bistro**
Award-winning chef Romain Tischenko serves up a creative, daily-changing menu at this little restaurant on pretty place Sainte-Marthe. The avant-garde Tischenko's USP is taking unfashionable vegetables and turning them into fusion cuisine 2.0 – think parsnips, artichokes, pumpkins and celery combined with cocoa, scallops and caramel. Staff are young, attentive and full of good advice on the wines, all of which are produced by independent winemakers. Make sure you reserve in advance.

€ La Madonnina

10 rue Marie-et-Louise, 10th (01.42.01.25.26). Mᵒ Goncourt or Jacques Bonsergent. **Open** 12.15-2.30pm, 7.30-11pm Mon-Thur; 12.15-2.30pm, 7.30-11.30pm Fri; 7.30-11.30pm Sat. Closed Aug. **Main courses** €13-€18. **Prix fixe** *Lunch* €13. **Credit** MC, V. **Map** p402 L4 ⑱ **Italian**
La Madonnina flirts with kitsch so skilfully that it ends up coming off as cool. With its candles, mustard yellow walls and red-checked tablecloths, it's the perfect place for a romantic night out. La Madonnina describes itself as a *trattoria napoletana*, but most of the dishes are pan-southern Italian. The short menu changes monthly; don't miss the homemade pastas, such as artichoke and ricotta ravioli.

The *cassata*, an extremely sweet Sicilian version of cheesecake, is authentic and unusual to see on menus outside Italy.

THE LATIN QUARTER & THE 13TH

Atelier Maître Albert

1 rue Maître-Albert, 5th (01.56.81.30.01, www.ateliermaitrealbert.com). Mᵒ Maubert Mutualité or St-Michel. **Open** noon-2.30pm, 6.30-11pm Mon-Wed; noon-2.30pm, 6.30pm-1am Thur, Fri; 6.30pm-1am Sat; 6.30-11.30pm Sun. **Main courses** €21.50-€33. **Prix fixe** *Lunch* €25, €30. *Dinner* €35. **Credit** AmEx, DC, MC, V. **Map** p406 K7 ⑲ **Bistro**
This Guy Savoy outpost in the fifth arrondissement has slick decor designed by Jean-Michel Wilmotte. The indigo-painted, grey marble-floored dining room with open kitchen and rôtisseries on view is attractive, but it does mean that the place can get very noisy. The short menu lets you have a Savoy classic or two to start with, including oysters in seawater *gelée*, perhaps, or more inventive dishes such as the ballotine of chicken, foie gras and celeriac in a chicken-liver sauce. Next up could be tuna served with tiny iron casseroles of dauphinois potatoes, accompanied by cauliflower in béchamel sauce.

€ Le Bambou

70 rue Baudricourt, 13th (01.45.70.91.75). Mᵒ Olympiades or Tolbiac. **Open** 11.30am-3.30pm, 7-10.30pm Tue-Sun. **Main courses** €7-€14.50. **Credit** MC, V. **Vietnamese**
The Vietnamese fare here is a notch above what is normally served in Paris. Seating is elbow to elbow and, should you come on your own, the waiter will

draw a line down the middle of the paper tablecloth and seat a stranger on the other side. That stranger might offer pointers on how to eat certain dishes, such as the no.42: grilled marinated pork to be wrapped in lettuce with beansprouts and herbs and eaten by hand, dipped into the accompanying sauce (no.43 is the same thing, but with pre-soaked rice paper wrappers).

Le Buisson Ardent

25 rue Jussieu, 5th (01.43.54.93.02, www. lebuissonardent.fr). M° Jussieu. **Open** noon-2pm, 7.30-10pm Mon-Fri; 7.30-10pm Sat. Closed 2wks Aug. **Main courses** €21-€25. **Prix fixe** *Lunch* €24, €27. *Dinner* €37, €38. **Credit** MC, V. **Map** p406 K8 ㉚ **Bistro**

This bistro's square front dining room with its red banquettes and painted glass panels dating from 1923 has a quintessentially Paris charm, especially when compared to the surrounding kebab shops. There is plenty for adventurous eaters on the menu, such as pan-fried squid with chorizo and quinoa or white bean and pig's ear salad with pan-fried foie gras, but it also does conventional dishes (chestnut velouté with spice bread croûtons) very well. Desserts are less remarkable, but this is one of the area's best finds for the price.

Le Pré Verre

8 rue Thénard, 5th (01.43.54.59.47, www.lepreverre.com). M° Maubert Mutualité. **Open** noon-2pm, 7.30-10.30pm Tue-Sat. Closed 24 Dec-1 Jan. **Main courses** €18.50. **Prix fixe** *Lunch* €13.90, €30.50. *Dinner* €30.50. **Credit** MC, V. **Map** p408 J7 ㉛ **Bistro**

Philippe Delacourcelle knows how to handle spices like few other French chefs. He also trained with the late Bernard Loiseau, and learned the art of French pastry at Fauchon. Salt cod with cassia bark and smoked potato purée is a classic: what the fish lacks in size it makes up for in rich, cinnamon-like flavour and crunchy texture, and smooth potato cooked in a smoker makes a startling accompaniment. Spices have a way of making desserts seem esoteric, but the roast figs with olives are an exception to the rule.

★ Ribouldingue

10 rue St-Julien-le-Pauvre, 5th (01.46.33.98.80, www.restaurant-ribouldingue.com). M° St-Michel. **Open** noon-2pm, 7.30-11pm Mon-Sat. **Prix fixe** *Lunch* €28. *Dinner* €34. **Credit** MC, V. **Map** p408 J7 ㉜ **Bistro**

This bistro facing St-Julien-le-Pauvre church is the creation of Nadège Varigny, who spent ten years working with Yves Camdeborde before opening a restaurant inspired by the food of her childhood in Grenoble. It's usually full of people, including critics and chefs, who love simple, honest bistro fare, such as *daube de boeuf* or seared tuna on a bed of melting aubergine. And if you have an appetite for offal, go for the gently sautéed brains with new potatoes, or the veal kidneys with a perfectly prepared potato gratin. For dessert, try the fresh ewe's cheese with bitter honey.

CONSUME

Le Chateaubriand. *See p157.*

La Fidélité. *See p157.*

CONSUME

La Tour d'Argent

15 quai de la Tournelle, 5th (01.43.54.23.31, www.latourdargent.com). Mº Pont Marie or Cardinal Lemoine. **Open** noon-2pm, 7.30-10pm Tue-Sat. Closed Aug. **Main courses** €85-€140. **Prix fixe** *Lunch* €68. *Dinner* €170, €190. **Credit** AmEx, DC, MC, V. **Map** p409 K7 ⑬ **Haute cuisine**

This Paris institution is regaining its lustre following the death of aged owner Claude Terrail in 2006. In the kitchen, Breton-born Stéphane Haissant has brought a welcome creative touch to the menu, bringing in such creative dishes as a giant langoustine dabbed with kumquat purée and surrounded by lightly scented coffee foam. But he also shows restraint, as in duck (the house speciality) with cherry sauce and a broad-bean flan. Following in his father's footsteps, Terrail's soft-spoken son André now does the rounds. *Photo p163.*

ST-GERMAIN-DES-PRES & ODEON

Le 21

21 rue Mazarine, 6th (01.46.33.76.90). Mº Odéon. **Open** 12.30-2pm, 8-11pm Tue-Sat. **Main courses** €25-€56. **Credit** MC, V. **Map** p408 H6 ⑭ **Bistro**

This clubby restaurant in St-Germain-des-Prés is a big hit with a *beau monde* crowd of antiques dealers, book editors and politicians. Chef Paul Minchelli's original minimalist style has evolved towards more homely preparations, as seen in a delicious sauté of flaked cod, potatoes, onions and green peppers, or squid in a squid ink sauce with black rice. To keep the waistline-watching regulars happy, a few of his old classics, including grilled red mullet, are still

offered. Don't miss the chocolate fondant cake for dessert, and don't be shy about asking for help with the pricey wine list.

★ Bouillon Racine

3 rue Racine, 6th (01.44.32.15.60, www.bouillon-racine.com). Mº Odéon. **Open** noon-11pm daily. **Main courses** €16-€22. **Prix fixe** €29.50, €41. **Credit** MC, V. **Map** p408 H7 ⑮ **Brasserie**

Originally opened as a *bouillon* (soup kitchen) in the early 20th century to feed hungry city workers, this beautifully renovated two-storey brasserie lives on as an art nouveau gem. Food is suitably traditional, with classic dishes such as foie gras, *escargots de Bourgogne* and *confit de canard* dominating the reasonably priced menu. Dishes are served non-stop from noon to 11pm, and you can even drop in for waffles and hot chocolate in the afternoon.

Bread & Roses

7 rue de Fleurus, 6th (01.42.22.06.06, www.bread androses.fr). Mº St-Placide. **Open** 8am-7.15pm Mon-Sat. **Main courses** €18. **Credit** AmEx, MC, V. **Map** p405 G8 ⑯ **Bakery/café**

Come for a morning croissant and you might find yourself staying on for lunch, so tempting are the wares at this Anglo-influenced *boulangerie/épicerie/café*. Giant wedges of cheesecake sit alongside French pastries, and huge savoury puff-pastry tarts are perched on the counter. Attention to detail shows even in the authentically pale taramasalata, which is matched with buckwheat-and-seaweed bread. Prices reflect the quality of the often organic ingredients, but that doesn't seem to deter any of the moneyed locals, who order towering birthday cakes here for their snappily dressed offspring. *Photo p165.*

Le Comptoir

Hôtel Le Relais Saint-Germain, 9 carrefour de l'Odéon, 6th (01.43.29.12.05). Mᵒ Odéon. **Open** noon-6pm, 8.30-11pm (last orders 9pm) Mon-Fri; noon-11pm Sat, Sun. **Main courses** €15. **Prix fixe** *Dinner* (Mon-Fri) €60. **Credit** AmEx, DC, MC, V. **Map** p408 H7 ⑰ **Brasserie**

Yves Camdeborde runs the bijou Hôtel Le Relais Saint-Germain (*see p251*), whose art deco dining room, modestly dubbed Le Comptoir, serves brasserie fare from noon to 6pm and on weekend nights, and a five-course prix fixe feast on weekday evenings. The single dinner sitting lets the chef take real pleasure in his work. On the daily menu, you might find dishes like rolled saddle of lamb with vegetable-stuffed 'Basque ravioli'. The catch? The prix fixe dinner is booked up as much as six months in advance.

★ L'Epigramme

9 rue de l'Eperon, 6th (01.44.41.00.09). Mᵒ Odéon. **Open** noon-2.30pm, 7-10.30pm Tue-Sat. **Prix fixe** *Lunch* €24, €28. *Dinner* €38. **Credit** AmEx, MC, V. **Map** p408 H7 ⑱ **Bistro**

L'Epigramme is a pleasantly bourgeois dining room with terracotta floor tiles, wood beams, a glassed-in kitchen and comfortable chairs. Like the decor, the food doesn't aim to innovate but instead sticks to tried and true classics with the occasional twist. Marinated mackerel in a mustardy dressing on toasted country bread gets things off to a promising start, but the chef's skill really comes through in the main courses, such as perfectly seared lamb with glazed root vegetables and intense jus. Be sure to book well in advance.

La Ferrandaise

8 rue de Vaugirard, 6th (01.43.26.36.36, www.laferrandaise.com). Mᵒ Odéon/RER Luxembourg. **Open** 7-10.30pm Mon; noon-2.30pm, 7-10.30pm Tue-Thur; noon-2.30pm, 7-11pm Fri; 7-11pm Sat. **Main courses** €22. **Prix fixe** *Lunch* €16, €30, €34. *Dinner* €30, €34, €46. **Credit** MC, V. **Map** p408 H7 ⑲ **Bistro**

This bistro has quickly established a following for its solid, classic food with a twist. A platter of excellent ham, sausage and terrine arrives as you study the blackboard menu, and the bread is crisp-crusted, thickly sliced sourdough. Two specialities are the potato stuffed with escargots in a camembert sauce, and a wonderfully flavoured, slightly rosé slice of veal. Desserts might include intense chocolate with rum-soaked bananas and a layered glass of mango and meringue. Wines start at €20.

Germain

25-27 rue de Buci, 6th (01.43.26.02.93). Mᵒ Mabillon or Odéon. **Open** 9am-2am daily. **Main courses** €20. **Credit** AmEx, MC, V. **Map** p408 H7 ⑳ **Brasserie**

Quaint rue de Buci has been shaken up by the extravagance of Germain, a versatile brasserie halfway between *Alice in Wonderland* and London's Sketch. The heated terrace is great for people watching, and the main ground-floor room, which features the lower part of a vast yellow statue piercing through the ceiling above, is perfect for a quick lunch. There's also a cosy salon for cocktails, a more conservative dining room at the back, and a private room on the first floor with a snooker table and the top half of the yellow statue. The food is almost

CONSUME

Le Floréal. *See p157.*

childishly classic, but always with a twist (ham and butter macaroni with truffle) and not as expensive as you might expect. *Photo p167.*

Huîtrerie Régis

3 rue de Montfaucon, 6th (01.44.41.10.07, www.huitrerieregis.com). M° Mabillon. **Open** noon-2.30pm, 6.30-10.30pm Tue-Sun. Closed mid July-mid Sept. **Main courses** €32. **Prix fixe** €18.50-€59. **Credit** MC, V. **Map** p408 H7 ➒ **Oyster bar**
Paris oyster fans are often obliged to use one of the city's big brasseries to get their fix of shellfish, but what if you just want to eat a reasonably priced

platter of oysters? Enter Régis and his cosy 14-seat oyster bar. The tiny room feels pristine and the tables are properly laid. Here you can enjoy the freshest oysters from Marennes for around €25 a dozen. The bread and butter is fresh and wines are well chosen. Hungry souls can supplement their feast with a slice of home-made apple tart or the cheese of the day.

Lapérouse

51 quai des Grands-Augustins, 6th (01.43.26.68.04, www.laperouse.com). M° St-Michel. **Open** noon-2.30pm, 7.30-11pm

Brilliance in a Bun

Where to eat the best burgers in Paris.

Le Camion qui Fume.

Parisians have surprised themselves, as well as the world, by officially going burger bonkers over the past year. This fast-food trend has been most in evidence in the arrival of mobile gourmet burger van **Le Camion qui Fume** (01.84.16.33.75, www.lecamionquifume.com), which began hitting the city's streets in December 2011, garnering top-notch reviews for its real American burgers made with high-quality ingredients (don't miss the tasty blue-cheese version). Run by young Californian chef Kristin Frederick, who previously worked at Spago in LA and later trained at Paris's Ecole Ferrandi, the van brings the Californian food truck trend to all corners of Paris. Visit the website to see where it will be parked, and when. And expect to queue.

Le Camion was followed by **Big Fernand** (*see p149*), an über-trendy takeaway burger joint in the 10th calling itself 'L'atelier du hamburger' – 'the hamburger workshop'. The concept is for customers to build their own burgers, selecting a

tailored combination of meat (beef, chicken, lamb or veal), cheese (goat's cheese, Saint Nectaire, Tomme de Savoie), grilled vegetables, spices and sauces. The bread is top-notch and the fries delicious.

Another popular spot is **Au Comptoir de Brice** (*see p157*), run by TV chef Brice Morvent. Serving gourmet cheeseburgers at the weekend made with sesame-, pistachio- and peanut-sprinkled buns, comté cheese, candied onions and generous helpings of mustard, the friendly green and white space is a popular Saturday go-to.

The latest opening to jump on the American fast-food bandwagon is **Blend** (*see p143*), which has opened its doors in the bobo quarters of Etienne Marcel. And if the queues are anything to go by, this modern 24-seater burger bar is going to be relished for a long time. The secret is in the ingredients: hand-cut veal and beef mince, own-made brioche buns, sweet-potato fries and house tomato sauce. Artisan beers and cool decor round off the experience.

Mon-Fri; 7.30-11pm Sat. Closed 2wks Aug. **Main courses** €35. **Prix fixe** *Lunch* €40, €55. *Dinner* €115, €168. **Credit** AmEx, DC, MC, V. **Map** p408 J6 ② **Brasserie**

One of the most romantic spots in Paris, Lapérouse was formerly a clandestine rendezvous for French politicians and their mistresses; the tiny private dining rooms upstairs used to lock from the inside. Chef Christophe Guibert does a wonderful take on classic French cooking: chateaubriand is glazed with port in a hazelnut crust; tender saddle of rabbit is cooked in a clay crust, flavoured with lavender and rosemary and served with ravioli of onions. The only potential snag is the cost of a meal here, especially the wine.

★ Le Restaurant

L'Hôtel, 13 rue des Beaux-Arts, 6th (01.44.41.99.01, www.l-hotel.com). M° St-Germain-des-Prés. **Open** 12.30-2.30pm, 7.30-10pm Tue-Sat. **Main courses** €39. **Prix fixe** *Lunch* €42, €52. *Dinner* €95, €115, €130 (€160 with wine).* **Credit** AmEx, DC, MC, V. **Map** p408 H6 ③ **Haute cuisine**

L'Hôtel's restaurant is a wonderfully atmospheric spot for lunch or dinner, with a charming terrace during the summer months. You can choose from a short seasonal menu with such dishes as pan-fried tuna, John Dory or suckling pig. But for the same price you can also enjoy the marvellous four-course *menu dégustation* or, even better, the *menu surprise*. Highlights of the autumn menu were the wild Breton crab stuffed with fennel, avocado and *huile d'Argan*, and a main course of pigeon on a bed of beetroot.

La Taverna degli Amici

16 rue du Bac, 6th (01.42.60.37.74). M° Assemblée Nationale or Solférino. **Open** noon-3pm, 7.30-11pm Mon-Sat. Closed Aug & 1wk Dec. **Main courses** €16. **Prix fixe** *Lunch* €18.50. **Credit** MC, V. **Map** p401 G6 ④ **Italian**

La Taverna degli Amici is the ideal spot for a quick business lunch or a big, rumbustious dinner with friends. Spread across two floors, the yellow-walled rooms are well lit and airy. Run by the exceptionally friendly Notaro family, who own, manage and cook, the restaurant is constantly bustling. Don't miss the mixed bruschette, which includes three vegetable toppings, such as grilled courgettes marinated in olive oil, lemon and parsley. Pastas feature fresh, tasty toppings, such as their most popular dish, penne with *caccioricotta* (made with ewe's milk) and rocket. Most of the regulars finish things off with home-made tiramisu.

Le Timbre

3 rue Ste-Beuve, 6th (01.45.49.10.40, www. restaurantletimbre.com). M° Vavin. **Open** noon-2pm, 7-10.30pm Tue-Sat. Closed Aug & 1wk Dec. **Main courses** €17. **Prix fixe** *Lunch* €22, €26. *Dinner* €32 (Sat). **Credit** MC, V. **Map** p405 G8 ⑤ **Bistro**

Chris Wright's restaurant, open kitchen included, might be the size of the average student garret, but this Mancunian aims high. Typical of his cooking is a plate of fresh green asparagus elegantly cut in half lengthwise and served with dabs of anise-spiked sauce and balsamic vinegar, and a little crumbled parmesan. Main courses are also pure in presentation and flavour – a thick slab of pork, pan-fried but not the least bit dry, comes with petals of red onion that retain a light crunch.

MONTPARNASSE & BEYOND

★ La Cerisaie

70 bd Edgar Quinet, 14th (01.43.20.98.98, www.restaurantlacerisaie.com). M° Edgar Quinet or Montparnasse. **Open** noon-2pm, 7-10pm Mon-Fri. Closed Aug & 1wk Dec. **Main courses** €16-€21. **Credit** MC, V. **Map** p405 G9 ⑥ **Bistro**

Nothing about La Cerisaie's unprepossessing red façade hints at the talent that lurks inside. Chef Cyril Lalanne proves his ability to select and prepare the finest produce. On the daily changing blackboard menu you might find *bourride de maquereau*, a thrifty take on the garlicky southern French fish stew, or *cochon noir de Bigorre*, an ancient breed of pig that puts ordinary pork to shame. *Baba à l'armagnac*, a variation on the usual rum cake, comes with stunningly good chantilly.

La Tour d'Argent. *See p160.*

Cobéa

*11 rue Raymond Losserand, 14th
(01.43.20.21.39, www.cobea.fr). Mº Gaîté
or Pernety.* **Open** 12.15-1.45pm, 7.15-9.45pm
Tue-Sat. **Prix fixe** *Lunch* €44. *Dinner* €65,
€75, €95. **Credit** AmEx, DC, MC, V. **Map**
p405 F10 ⑤ **Haute cuisine**

Cobéa is a slick new restaurant launched by friends
Jerome Cobou and Philippe Bellissent, who won
a Michelin star when he was head chef at L'Hôtel.
The ethos here is gastronomy without the snobbery. Set in a renovated 1920s house with big
windows overlooking a green space, it feels wonderfully peaceful and cosy, while touches such as
silverware and Bernardaud porcelain add a luxury
feel. The set menus are a treasure chest of reworked
classics, plus a daily-changing 'chef's surprise'.
Each dish is accompanied by a well-sourced wine
recommendation from Jerome.

La Coupole

*102 bd du Montparnasse, 14th (01.43.20.14.20,
www.flobrasseries.com/coupoleparis). Mº Vavin.*
Open 8.30am-midnight Mon-Wed, Sun; 8.30am-
1am Thur-Sat. **Main courses** €27-€36. **Prix
fixe** €29, €34. **Credit** AmEx, DC, MC, V.
Map p405 G9 ⑨ **Brasserie**

La Coupole still glows with some of the old glamour.
The people-watching remains superb, inside and
out, and the long ranks of linen-covered tables, professional waiters, 32 art deco columns painted by
different artists of the epoch, mosaic floor and sheer
scale of the operation still make coming here an
event. The set menu offers unremarkable steaks, foie
gras, fish and autumn game stews, but the real treat
is the shellfish. Take your pick from the *claires,
spéciales* and *belons*, or go for a platter brimming
with crabs, oysters, prawns, periwinkles and clams.

€ Josselin

*67 rue du Montparnasse, 14th (01.43.20.93.50).
Mº Edgar Quinet.* **Open** 11.15am-3.15pm,
6-11.30pm Tue-Fri; 11.30am-midnight Sat;
11.30am-11pm Sun. Closed 1st wk Jan & Aug.
Main courses €9. **No credit cards**. **Map**
p405 G9 ⑨ **Crêperie**

Josselin is the star *crêperie* of the area, and the one
with the longest queues. The speciality is the Couple
– two layers of galette with the filling in the middle.
Wash it all down with bowls of cider, of which the
brut is best. *Photo p170.*

L'Opportun

*64 bd Edgar Quinet, 14th (01.43.20.26.89).
Mº Edgar Quinet.* **Open** noon-3pm, 7-11.30pm
Mon-Sat. **Main courses** €19. **Prix fixe** *Lunch*
€25. *Dinner* €25, €40. **Credit** AmEx, DC, MC, V.
Map p405 G9 ⑩ **Bistro**

Owner-chef Serge Alzérat is passionate about
Beaujolais, dubbing his convivial cream and yellow
restaurant a centre of 'beaujolaistherapy' and a place
for 'the prevention of thirst'. He's also an advocate
for good, honest Lyonnais food. Thus his menu is
littered with the likes of *sabodet* (thick pork sausage)
with a purée of split peas, duck skin salad, *tête de
veau* (a favourite of ex-president Chirac) and meat –
lots of it. *Fromage* fans should try the st-marcellin
by master cheesemaker Hervé Mons.

CONSUME

Bread & Roses. *See p160.*

Le Plomb du Cantal

3 rue de la Gaîté, 14th (01.43.35.16.92). M° Gaîté.
Open noon-midnight daily. **Main courses** €15.
Credit MC, V. **Map** p405 G9 **101** Bistro
This homage to the Auvergne may suffer from its
1980s decor, but with food like this, who cares? *Aligot*
(potato puréed with fresh tomme cheese) and *truffade*
(potatoes sautéed with tomme) are scraped out of copper pots on to plates at the table, the shoestring fries
arrive by the saucepan-load, and the omelettes are
made with three eggs, 300g of potatoes, and, if you're
really hungry, a supplement of tomme. Wines are
excellent and the service is friendly.

THE 7TH & WESTERN PARIS

Le 144 Petrossian

*144 rue de l'Université, 7th (01.44.11.32.32,
www.petrossian.fr). M° La Tour Maubourg.*
Open 12.15-2.30pm, 7.30-10.30pm Tue-Sat.
Main courses €35. **Prix fixe** *Lunch* €35, €90.
Dinner €35, €90, €250, €425. **Credit** AmEx,
DC, MC, V. **Map** p401 E5 **102** Russian
Young chef Rougui Dia directs the kitchen of this
famed caviar house. You'll find Russian specialities,
such as blinis, salmon and caviar (at €39 an ounce)
from the Petrossian boutique downstairs, but Dia has
added preparations and spices from all over the
world. You might start with a divine risotto made
with carnaroli rice, codfish caviar and parmesan. In
similar Med-meets-Russia vein are such main courses
as roast sea bream with a lemon-vodka sauce.

Afaria

*15 rue Desnouettes, 15th (01.48.42.95.90).
M° Convention.* **Open** noon-2pm, 7-11pm Tue-
Sat. **Main courses** €16-€45. **Prix fixe** *Lunch*
€22, €24. *Dinner* €45. **Credit** MC, V. **Map**
p404 C10 **103** Bistro
Instead of the usual starter, main course and dessert
categories, Basque-born chef Julien Duboué has
divided his menu into such sections as *'les sudistes'*
for southern French-inspired cooking, and *'les petits
appétits'* for lighter dishes. Several dishes are for
sharing, in particular a caveman-sized duck *magret*
with balsamic fig vinegar, served on a terracotta roof
tile with potato gratin perched on a bed of twigs.
Other creations such as oysters with bulgur, hou-
mous and preserved lemon show that Duboué is not
just another Basque bistro chef, but a traveller who
happily borrows ingredients from around the world.

★ L'Ami Jean

*27 rue Malar, 7th (01.47.05.86.89, www.ami
jean.eu). M° Ecole Militaire.* **Open** noon-2pm,
7-10pm Tue-Sat. Closed Aug. **Main courses**
€20. **Prix fixe** *Lunch* €32. *Dinner* €75. **Credit**
MC, V. **Map** p405 D6 **104** Bistro
This long-running Basque address is an ongoing hit
thanks to chef Stéphane Jégo. Excellent bread from
baker Jean-Luc Poujauran is a perfect nibble when

slathered with a tangy, herby *fromage blanc* – as is
a starter of sautéed baby squid on a bed of ratatouille. Tender veal shank comes de-boned with a
lovely side of baby onions and broad beans with
tiny cubes of ham, and house-salted cod is soaked,
sautéed and doused with an elegant vinaigrette.
There's a great wine list, and some lovely Brana *eau
de vie* should you decide to linger.

★ L'Arpège

*84 rue de Varenne, 7th (01.47.05.09.06,
www.alain-passard.com). M° Varenne.* **Open**
noon-2.30pm, 8-10.30pm Mon-Fri. **Main courses**
€96-€140. **Prix fixe** *Lunch* €130. *Dinner* €350.
Credit AmEx, DC, MC, V. **Map** p405 F6 **105**
Haute cuisine
Assuming you can swallow an exceptionally high
bill, chances are you'll have a spectacular time at
chef Alain Passard's Left Bank establishment. His
attempt to plane down and simplify the haute experience – the chrome-armed chairs look like something from the former GDR – seems a misstep; but
then something edible comes to the table, such as
tiny smoked potatoes served with a horseradish
mousseline. A main course of sautéed free-range
chicken with a roasted shallot, an onion, potato
mousseline and pan juices is the apotheosis of comfort food. Desserts are elegant.

€ Le Bistro

*17 rue Pérignon, 15th (01.45.66.84.03).
M° Ségur.* **Open** 8am-10pm Mon-Fri; 8am-3pm
Sat. **Main courses** €12-€15. **Credit** MC, V.
Map p405 E8 **106** Bistro
At first glance there is nothing to distinguish this
corner bistro from hundreds of other cafés in Paris.
In the front room, with its wood-panelled ceiling,
are a plastic-topped bar and a few bare tables with
black banquettes, and in the back is a larger room
with red-and-white checked tablecloths. Then you
see the plates going by, each one – from the goat's
cheese salad to the *pavé de rumsteak* – loaded with
golden fried potato rounds or hand-cut chips. This
is the kind of neighbourhood bistro you had almost
given up hope of finding in Paris.

★ Au Bon Accueil

*14 rue de Monttessuy, 7th (01.47.05.46.11,
www.aubonaccueilparis.com). M° Alma Marceau.*
Open noon-2.30pm, 7-10.30pm Mon-Fri. Closed
3wks Aug. **Main courses** €29-€46. **Prix
fixe** *Lunch* €32-€50. **Credit** MC, V. **Map**
p404 D6 **107** Bistro
Jacques Lacipière runs Au Bon Accueil, and Keita
Kitamura turns out the beautiful food. Perhaps most
impressive is his elegant use of little-known fish, such
as grey mullet and meagre (*maigre*), rather than the
usual endangered species. The €32 lunch menu might
highlight such posh ingredients as *suprême de poulet
noir du Cros de la Géline*, free-range chicken raised
on a farm run by two former cabaret singers. But the

Germain. *See p161.*

CONSUME

biggest surprise comes with desserts, worthy of the finest pastry shops. In summer, book a table on the pavement terrace with its view of the Eiffel Tower.

Les Cocottes

135 rue St-Dominique, 7th (01.45.55.15.05, www.maisonconstant.com). M° Ecole Militaire/RER Pont de l'Alma. **Open** noon-4pm, 7-11pm daily. **Main courses** €15-€29. **Credit** MC, V. **Map** p404 D6 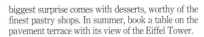 **Bistro**

Christian Constant has found the perfect recipe for pleasing Parisians at his new bistro: a flexible menu of salads, soups, *verrines* (light dishes served in jars) and *cocottes* (served in cast-iron pots), all at bargain prices – for this neighbourhood. Service is swift and the food satisfying, though the *vraie salade César Ritz*, which contains hard-boiled egg, shouldn't be confused with US-style Caesar salad. Soups such as an iced pea velouté are spot-on, and *cocottes* range from sea bream with ratatouille to potatoes stuffed with pig's trotter.

D'Chez Eux

2 av de Lowendal, 7th (01.47.05.52.55, www.chezeux.com). M° Ecole Militaire. **Open** noon-2pm, 7-11pm daily. Closed Aug. **Main courses** €29-€52. **Prix fixe** *Lunch* €29, €34. **Credit** AmEx, MC, V. **Map** p405 E7 **⑩⑨ Bistro**

Arm yourself with stamina for a meal at this jovial south-western *auberge*, which looks touristy with its red-and-white checked tablecloths but attracts *bons vivants* from the neighbourhood. First come the help-yourself lyonnais-style 'salads' (cooked beetroot, lentils, celeriac rémoulade, ratatouille, etc), before hearty main dishes such as cassoulet or calf's liver with sherry vinegar. The heaving dessert cart (think chocolate mousse and rice pudding) will ensure that you waddle out overfed but happy.

Gaya Rive Gauche

44 rue du Bac, 7th (01.45.44.73.73, www.pierre-gagnaire.com). M° Rue du Bac. **Open** noon-2.30pm, 7.30-10.45pm Mon-Fri; noon-3pm,

Time Out Paris 167

Decoding the Menu

From escargots to escabèche.

MEALS (REPAS)

petit déjeuner breakfast. **déjeuner** lunch.
dîner dinner. **souper** late dinner, supper.

PREPARATION (LA PRÉPARATION)

en croûte in a pastry case. **farci** stuffed.
au four baked. **flambé** flamed in alcohol.
forestière with mushrooms. **fricassé** fried
and simmered in stock, usually with creamy
sauce. **fumé** smoked. **garni** garnished.
glacé frozen or iced. **gratiné** topped with
breadcrumbs or cheese and grilled. **à la
grècque** vegetables served cold in the
cooking liquid with oil and lemon juice.
grillé grilled. **haché** minced. **julienne**
(vegetables) cut into matchsticks. **lamelle**
very thin slice. **mariné** marinated. **pané**
breaded. **en papillote** cooked in a packet.
parmentier with potato. **pressé** squeezed.
râpé grated. **salé** salted.

COOKING TYPE (LA CUISSON)

cru raw. **bleu** practically raw. **saignant** rare.
rosé (of lamb, duck, liver, kidneys) pink.
à point medium rare. **bien cuit** well done.

BASICS (ESSENTIELS)

ballotine stuffed, rolled-up piece of meat
or fish. **crème fraîche** thick, slightly soured
cream. **épices** spices. **feuilleté** 'leaves' of
(puff) pastry. **fromage** cheese. **fruits de mer**
shellfish. **galette** round flat cake of flaky
pastry, potato pancake or buckwheat
savoury crêpe. **gelée** aspic. **gibier** game.
gras fat. **légume** vegetable. **maison** of the
house. **marmite** small cooking pot. **miel**
honey. **noisette** hazelnut; small, round
portion of meat. **noix** walnut. **noix de coco**
coconut. **nouilles** noodles. **oeuf** egg; – **en
cocotte** baked egg; – **en meurette** egg
poached in red wine; – **à la neige** *see île
flottante*. **parfait** sweet or savoury mousse-
like mixture. **paupiette** slice of meat or fish,
stuffed and rolled. **timbale** dome-shaped
mould, or food cooked in one. **tisane** herbal
tea. **tourte** covered pie or tart, usually
savoury.

MEAT (VIANDE)

agneau lamb. **aloyau** beef loin. **andouillette**
sausage made from pig's offal. **bavette** beef
flank steak. **biche** venison. **bifteck** steak.
boudin noir/blanc black (blood)/white
pudding. **boeuf** beef; – **bourguignon** beef
cooked Burgundy style, with red wine,

onions and mushrooms; – **gros sel** boiled
beef with vegetables. **carbonnade** beef
stew with onions and stout or beer. **carré
d'agneau** rack of lamb. **cassoulet** stew of
white haricot beans, sausage and preserved
duck. **cervelle** brains. **châteaubriand** thick
fillet steak. **chevreuil** young roe deer. **civet**
game stew. **cochon de lait** suckling pig. –
contre-filet sirloin steak. **côte** chop; – **de
boeuf** beef rib. **croque-madame** sandwich of
toasted cheese and ham topped with an
egg. **croque-monsieur** sandwich of toasted
cheese and ham. **cuisses de grenouille** frogs'
legs. **daube** meat braised in red wine.
entrecôte beef rib steak. **escargot** snail.
estouffade meat that's been marinated,
fried and braised. **faux-filet** sirloin steak.
filet mignon tenderloin. **foie** liver; – **de veau**
calf's liver. **gigot d'agneau** leg of lamb.
hachis parmentier shepherd's pie. **jambon**
ham; – **cru** cured raw ham. **jarret** ham shin
or knuckle. **langue** tongue. **lapin** rabbit. **lard**
bacon. **lardon** small cube of bacon. **lièvre**
hare. **marcassin** wild boar. **merguez** spicy
lamb/beef sausage. **mignon** small meat
fillet. **moelle** bone marrow; **os à la** – marrow-
bone. **navarin** lamb and vegetable stew.
onglet cut of beef, similar to *bavette*. **pavé**
thick steak. **petit salé** salt pork. **pied** foot
(trotter). **porc** pork. **porcelet** suckling pig.
pot-au-feu boiled beef with vegetables.
queue de boeuf oxtail. **ragoût** meat stew.
rillettes potted pork or tuna. **ris de veau**
veal sweetbreads. **rognons** kidneys. **rôti**
roast. **sang** blood. **sanglier** wild boar.
saucisse sausage. **saucisson sec** small
dried sausage. **selle** (*d'agneau*) saddle
(of lamb). **souris d'agneau** lamb knuckle.
tagine slow-cooked North African stew.
tartare raw minced steak (also tuna or
salmon). **tournedos** small slices of beef
fillet, sautéed or grilled. **travers de porc**
pork spare ribs. **veau** veal.

CONSUME

POULTRY (VOLAILLE)

aiguillettes (*de canard*) thin slices (of duck breast). **blanc** breast. **caille** quail. **canard** duck; **confit de** – preserved duck. **coquelet** baby rooster. **dinde** turkey. **faisan** pheasant. **foie gras** fattened goose or duck liver. **gésiers** gizzards. **magret** duck breast. **oie** goose. **perdrix** partridge. **poulet** chicken. **suprême** (*de poulet*) fillets (of chicken) in a cream sauce.

FISH & SEAFOOD (POISSONS & FRUITS DE MER)

anguille eel. **bar** sea bass. **belon** smooth, flat oyster. **bisque** shellfish soup. **bouillabaisse** Mediterranean fish soup. **brochet** pike. **bulot** whelk. **cabillaud** fresh cod. **carrelet** plaice. **colin** hake. **coquille** shell. **coquilles St-Jacques** scallops. **crevettes** prawns (UK), shrimp (US). **crustacé** shellfish. **daurade** sea bream. **eglefin** haddock. **escabèche** sautéed and marinated fish, served cold. **espadon** swordfish. **fines de claire** crinkle-shelled oysters. **flétan** halibut. **hareng** herring. **homard** lobster. **huître** oyster. **langoustine** Dublin Bay prawns, scampi. **limande** lemon sole. **lotte** monkfish. **maquereau** mackerel. **merlan** whiting. **merlu** hake. **meunière** fish floured and sautéed in butter. **moules** mussels; – **à la marinière** cooked with white wine and shallots. **morue** dried, salted cod; **brandade de** – cod puréed with potato. **oursin** sea urchin. **palourde** type of clam. **poulpe** octopus. **raie** skate. **rascasse** scorpion fish. **rouget** red mullet. **St-Pierre** John Dory. **sandre** pike-perch. **saumon** salmon. **seiche** squid. **truite** trout.

VEGETABLES (LEGUMES)

aligot mashed potatoes with melted cheese and garlic. **asperge** asparagus. **céleri** celery. **céleri rave** celeriac. **cèpe** cep mushroom. **champignon** mushroom; – **de Paris** button mushroom. **chanterelle** small, trumpet-like mushroom. **choucroute** sauerkraut; – **garnie** with cured ham and sausages. **ciboulette** chive. **citronelle** lemongrass. **coco** large white bean. **cresson** watercress. **échalote** shallot. **endive** chicory (UK), Belgian endive (US). **épinards** spinach. **frisée** curly endive. **frites** chips (UK), fries (US). **gingembre** ginger. **girolle** small, trumpet-like mushroom. **gratin dauphinois** sliced potatoes baked with milk, cheese and garlic. **haricot** bean;

– **vert** green bean. **mâche** lamb's lettuce. **morille** morel mushroom. **navet** turnip. **oignon** onion. **oseille** sorrel. **persil** parsley. **pignon** pine nut. **poivre** pepper. **poivron** red or green (bell) pepper. **pomme de terre** potato. **pommes lyonnaises** potatoes fried with onions. **riz** rice. **truffes** truffles.

FRUIT (FRUITS)

ananas pineapple. **cassis** blackcurrants; blackcurrant liqueur. **citron** lemon; – **vert** lime. **fraise** strawberry. **framboise** raspberry. **groseille** redcurrant; – **à maquereau** gooseberry. **myrtille** blueberry. **pamplemousse** grapefruit. **pomme** apple. **prune** plum. **pruneau** prune. **quetsche** damson.

DESSERTS & CHEESE (DESSERTS & FROMAGE)

bavarois moulded cream dessert. **beignet** fritter or doughnut. **chèvre** goat; goat's cheese. **clafoutis** baked batter filled with fruit. **crème brûlée** creamy custard dessert with caramel glaze. **crème chantilly** sweetened whipped cream. **fromage blanc** smooth cream cheese. **glace** ice-cream. **île flottante** whipped egg white floating in vanilla custard. **réglisse** liquorice. **tarte aux pommes** apple tart. **tarte tatin** warm, caramelised apple tart cooked upside down.

SOUPS & SAUCES (SOUPES & SAUCES)

aïoli garlic mayonnaise. **anchoïade** spicy anchovy and olive paste. **béarnaise** sauce of butter and egg yolk. **blanquette** 'white' stew made with eggs and cream. **potage** soup. **velouté** stock-based white sauce; creamy soup. **vichyssoise** cold leek and potato soup.

7.30-10.45pm Sat. **Main courses** €18-€42.
Prix fixe *Lunch* €60. **Credit** AmEx, MC, V.
Map p405 G6 ⑩ **Seafood**
Superchef Pierre Gagnaire runs this comparatively affordable fish restaurant. The menu enumerates ingredients without much clue as to how they are put together, though the helpful waiters will explain if you don't like a surprise. The Fats Waller, for instance, turns out to be a soup of grilled red peppers with a bloody mary sorbet in the centre and daubs of quinoa, basmati rice and Chinese spinach. Light desserts complete the formula.

Le Grand Pan
*20 rue Rosenwald, 15th (01.42.50.02.50). M°
Convention.* **Open** noon-2pm, 7.30-11pm Mon-Fri.
Main courses €14-€20. **Prix fixe** *Lunch* €29.
Credit MC, V. **Map** p405 D10 ⑪ **Bistro**
Young chef Benoît Gauthier trained with Christian Etchebest, and he's come up with a clever formula that surfs the current Paris preference for great produce simply cooked. At dinner, a complimentary starter of soup is served – maybe courgette or white bean – and then you choose from the selection of grilled meats and lobster. Everything comes with a delicious mountain of home-made chips and green salad. Desserts run to homely choices like strawberry crumble or rice pudding with caramel sauce.

Josselin. *See p165.*

Jadis
*208 rue de la Croix-Nivert, 15th (01.45.57.73.20,
www.bistrot-jadis.com). M° Convention or Porte de
Versailles.* **Open** 12.15-2pm, 7.15-11pm Mon-Fri.
Main courses €25. **Prix fixe** *Lunch* €29, €36.
Dinner €36, €48, €65. **Credit** AmEx, MC, V.
Map p404 C9 ⑫ **Bistro**
The residential 15th arrondissement has more than its fair share of great bistros, and Jadis confirms the trend. In this grey-painted dining room, young chef Guillaume Delage serves a gently updated take on classic French cuisine. The pared-down presentation of such dishes as snails in puff pastry with oyster mushrooms and romaine lettuce lets each element speak for itself. Don't miss the cheese trolley.

★ Jules Verne
*Pilier Sud, Eiffel Tower, 7th (01.45.55.61.44,
www.lejulesverne-paris.com). M° Bir Hakeim or
RER Tour Eiffel.* **Open** 12.15-1.30pm, 7-9.30pm
daily. **Main courses** €75. **Prix fixe** *Lunch*
€88 (Mon-Fri), €165 (Sat, Sun), €210 (Sat, Sun).
Dinner €210, €310. **Credit** AmEx, DC, MC, V.
Map p404 C6 ⑬ **Haute cuisine**
You have to have courage to take on an icon like the Eiffel Tower, but Alain Ducasse has done just that. He has transformed the cuisine and brought in designer Patrick Jouin. Meanwhile, Ducasse protégé Pascal Féraud updates French classics, combining all the grand ingredients you'd expect with light, modern textures. Try dishes like lamb with artichokes, turbot with champagne zabaglione, and a fabulous ruby grapefruit soufflé. Book ahead.

Les Ombres
*27 quai Branly, 7th (01.47.53.68.00, www.les
ombres-restaurant.com). M° Alma-Marceau.*
Open noon-2.30pm, 7-11pm daily. **Main courses**
€30-€50. **Prix fixe** *Lunch* €38. *Dinner* €82.
Credit AmEx, MC, V. **Map** p404 D5 ⑭ **Bistro**
The view of the Eiffel Tower at night would be reason enough to come to this glass-and-iron restaurant on the top floor of the Musée du Quai Branly, but chef Jean-François Oyon's food also demands that you sit up and take notice. In keeping with its location, the menu is themed by continent, providing the chance to sample everything from tabouleh to duck consommé or NY strip steak.

Il Vino
*13 bd de La Tour-Maubourg, 7th (01.44.11.72.00,
www.ilvinobyenricobernardo.com). M° La Tour-
Maubourg.* **Open** 7pm-midnight Mon-Sat. **Prix
fixe** *Dinner* €98, €150. **Credit** AmEx, DC, MC, V.
Map p401 E5 ⑮ **Italian**
Enrico Bernardo, youngest winner of the World's Best Sommelier award, runs this restaurant where food plays second fiddle to wine. You are presented with nothing more than a wine list. Each of 15 wines by the glass is matched with a surprise dish, or the chef can build a meal around a bottle of your choice.

CONSUME

Cafés & Bars

Drinking in history.

Just as it looked as if the French capital would be totally swamped with trendy New York-style watering holes, in came the credit crunch and out popped the idea of capitalising on the funky period features present in Paris's cafés. Chez Jeannette in the tenth pioneered the idea a few years ago (keeping all of its 1940s gear and picking up a Fooding prize for it); but zinc bars, marble floors and red banquettes across the city are heaving sighs of relief as they too doggedly stay in place, while walls, lighting, sound systems and loos get spruced up around them. And of course, if it's real old-world Paris you're after, there's still a handful of landmark addresses, such as La Palette with its art deco tiles and frescoes. You have to look hard to find them, though.

DRINKING IN PARIS

The traditional boundaries between bar, club, restaurant and dancehall are blurring. Hybrid spaces such as **La Bellevilloise** (a former Paris co-operative) and **Petit Bain** (on board a boat) house restaurant, bar, music venue and exhibition space all under one roof, and **L'Entrepôt** fulfils dual roles as a bastion of culture and coffee south of Montparnasse.

Urban regeneration still seems to be pulling punters northwards, beyond the Canal St-Martin in the tenth (home to fashionable boho bars and satisfying brunch spots) into the now ultra-trendy 19th, along the Canal de l'Ourcq. Those looking for a real 'neighbourhood' feel, meanwhile, should head into the 20th, where hidden gems like the St-Blaise district and the ever-gentrifying eastern edge of Nation are now home to fun, authentic addresses like **Chez Prosper**, **Les Pères Populaires** and the hip **Café Noir** on rue St-Blaise.

Other Right Bank hotspots include the Marais (and its north-west overspill around Etienne Marcel and Arts et Métiers métro stations); the village-like area in and around Abbesses in Montmartre; and Les Batignolles, west of Place de Clichy, where rue des Dames draws the boho overspill from Montmartre into its wealth of cafés and bars. On the Left Bank, St-Germain-des-Prés and Montparnasse continue to trade on a proud literary heritage, and the waterfront by Docks en Seine is now one of the city's hippest hangouts, with party boats galore.

Wine in three colours is ubiquitous, and coffee comes as a strong espresso unless otherwise requested. The sturdy brasserie and noble bistro provide food with formality akin to a restaurant, so if you're just there for a drink, you'll pay more for the social nicety of aproned and waistcoated service. You can usually run a tab, and tipping is optional (service is always included in the bill).

THE LOUVRE & PALAIS-ROYAL

★ Angelina

226 rue de Rivoli, 1st (01.42.60.82.00, www.angelina-paris.fr). M° Tuileries. **Open** 7.30am-7pm Mon-Fri; 8.30am-7pm Sat, Sun. **Credit** MC, V. **Map** p401 G5 ❶
Angelina is home to Paris's most lip-smackingly scrumptious desserts – all served in the faded grandeur of a belle époque salon just steps from the Louvre. The hot chocolate is pure decadence; try the speciality 'African', a velvety potion so thick that you need a spoon to consume it. Epicurean delights include the Mont Blanc dessert, a ball of meringue covered in whipped cream and sweet chestnut, and, for those with a waistline to watch, a sugar- and butter-free *brioche aux fruits rouges*. The place heaves at weekends, so be prepared to queue.

> ❶ Green numbers given in this chapter correspond to the location of each café or bar on the street maps. *See pp400-409.*

Le Café des Initiés

*3 pl des Deux-Ecus, 1st (01.42.33.78.29, www.
lecafedesinities.com). Mº Louvre Rivoli or Les
Halles.* **Open** 7.30am-2am Mon-Fri; 9am-2am
Sat, Sun. **Credit** MC, V. **Map** p402 H5

Friendly staff and a central location have turned this
designer hangout into a top spot for a trendy tipple,
especially after work – cocktails are just €5 between
5pm and 8pm. The main room is lined with aerodynamic red banquettes, a long zinc bar provides character, and sleek, black, articulated lamps peer down
from the ceiling. When hunger strikes, homely
favourites such as shoulder of lamb baked in honey
or tartare of salmon never fail to please.

Café Marly

*93 rue de Rivoli, cour Napoléon, 1st
(01.49.26.06.60). Mº Palais Royal Musée
du Louvre.* **Open** 8am-2am daily. **Credit**
AmEx, DC, MC, V. **Map** p401 H5

In the arcaded terrace overlooking the Louvre's
glass pyramid, this classy, Napoleon III-style hangout (reached through the passage Richelieu, the
entrance for advance Louvre ticket holders) is in an
unrivalled location. One would expect nothing else
from the ubiquitous Costes brothers – it's just a
shame about the beer prices: it's €6 for a Heineken,
so you might as well splash out €12 on a chocolate
martini or a Shark, made of vodka, lemonade and
grenadine. Most wines are under €10 a glass, and
everything is impeccably served by razor-sharp
staff. Brasserie fare and sandwiches are on offer too.

L'Entr'acte

*47 rue de Montpensier, 1st (01.42.97.57.76).
Mº Pyramides or Palais Royal Musée du Louvre.*
Open 10am-1am Mon-Sat; 10am-8pm Sun.
No credit cards. **Map** p402 H5

Take a little detour off avenue de l'Opéra, down an
18th-century staircase, and you'll find an unex-
pected congregation spread across the pavement:
half are here for this little bar near the Comédie
Française, half for the adjoining Sicilian pizzeria.
There's food to be had at L'Entr'acte too – €10
plates of cheese and charcuterie, standard pastas
and so on – but most come to enjoy an early-evening
glass of house Bourgueil. The interior is tiny, with
an equally poky basement, but there's free Wi-Fi
and even laptop loans.

Le Fumoir

*6 rue de l'Amiral-de-Coligny, 1st (01.42.92.00.24,
www.lefumoir.com). Mº Louvre Rivoli.* **Open**
11am-2am daily. **Credit** AmEx, MC, V.
Map p402 H6

There aren't many places around the Louvre that
can compete with this elegant local institution: neo-
colonial fans whirr lazily and oil paintings adorn the
walls. A sleek crowd sips martinis or reads papers
at the long mahogany bar (originally from a Chicago
speakeasy), giving way to young professionals in

Café Marly.

the restaurant and pretty things in the library.
It all feels a wee bit try-hard and resolutely well
behaved, but the cocktails get tongues wagging soon
enough, and food is consistently top notch.

★ La Garde Robe

*41 rue de l'Arbre-Sec, 1st (01.49.26.90.60).
Mº Louvre Rivoli.* **Open** 12.30-2.30pm, 6.30pm-
midnight Mon-Fri; 6.30pm-midnight Sat.
Credit MC, V. **Map** p402 J5

This tiny wine bar (its name means 'wardrobe',
where bottles line the walls like books in a library,
is perfect for an end-of-the-day snifter, preferably
accompanied by one of the platters of delicious
parma ham, cheese or oysters. Organic and biodynamic wines stand their ground next to vintages
from around the world.

OPERA TO LES HALLES

Le Brébant

*32 bd Poissonnière, 9th (01.47.70.01.02).
Mº Grands Boulevards.* **Open** 7.30am-6am
daily. **Credit** MC, V. **Map** p402 J4

The change that continues to sweep the Grands
Boulevards is embodied in this prominent, round-
the-clock bar-bistro. There's a permanently busy
terrace below a colourful, stripy awning, and the cav-
ernous, split-level interior has a cool neo-industrial
feel. Prices are steep, so push the boat out and opt
for an expertly made fruit daiquiri, or a Bonne
Nouvelle of Bombay Sapphire gin and Pisang

Ambon. There are rarer bottled beers too – Monaco, Picon and sundry brews from Brabant. A board advertises a decent range of proper eats: *burger-frites* (€15) and so on.

★ Café de la Paix

12 bd des Capucines, 9th (01.40.07.36.36, www.cafedelapaix.fr). M° Opéra. **Open** 7am-midnight daily. **Credit** AmEx, DC, MC, V. **Map** p401 G4 ⑧

Lap up every detail – this is once-in-a-holiday stuff. Whether you're out on the historic terrace or looking up at the ornate stucco ceiling, you'll be sipping in the footsteps of the likes of Oscar Wilde, Josephine Baker, Emile Zola, and Bartholdi and the Franco-American Union (as they sketched out the Statue of Liberty). Let the immaculate staff bring you a kir (€12) or, for an afternoon treat, the vanilla mille-feuille – possibly the best in Paris.

Christ Inn's Bistro

15 rue Montmartre, 1st (01.42.36.07.56). M° Les Halles. **Open** 11am-2am Mon-Sat. **Credit** MC, V. **Map** p402 J5 ⑨

Some old bistros have the setting, others get the food. This place does a good job with both: the antique public telephone, the imposing zinc counter and the cosy wooden booths are charming reminders of Les Halles' heyday as the city's celebrated food market – note the tiles that depict scenes of the market in all its chaotic splendour. Food-wise, expect hearty, meaty dishes like stuffed pork on a bed of lentils and *confit de canard*, best accompanied by one of the 50 wines on the list. Enjoyed your meal? Write about it in the notebooks tucked away in little nooks.

★ La Conserverie

37bis rue du Sentier, 3rd (01.40.26.14.94, www.laconserveriebar.com). M° Bonne-Nouvelle. **Open** 6pm-midnight Mon, Tue; 6pm-2am Wed-Fri; 8pm-2am Sat. **Credit** AmEx, MC, V. **Map** p402 J4 ⑩

The gorgeous *nuit bleue* interior will win you over as soon as you step inside, and by the time you sit on the velvet sofas and taste the cocktails you'll want to make this your favourite hangout. The staff are incredibly friendly by Parisian standards. There's a quirky selection of nibbles in tin cans – sardines, anyone? – and regular music nights (live gipsy jazz bands on Mondays; electro on Thursdays and Fridays). Highly recommended.

De la Ville Café

34 bd de Bonne-Nouvelle, 10th (01.48.24.48.09, www.delavillecafe.com). M° Bonne Nouvelle. **Open** 11am-2am daily. **Credit** MC, V. **Map** p402 J4 ⑪

De la Ville has brought good news to Bonne-Nouvelle. A major expansion and refurbishment (it used to be a *maison close*) have upped the ante, bringing the in-crowd to this otherwise ignored quarter.

Café de la Paix.

CONSUME

CONSUME

De la Ville Café. *See p173.*

Inside, the distressed walls and industrial-baroque feel remain, but the club section at the back has become very cool. After 10pm on Fridays, Saturdays and some Thursdays, DJs splice into the night.

Dédé la Frite

135 rue Montmartre, 2nd (01.40.41.99.90). *M° Sentier or Bourse.* **Open** 8am-2am daily. **Credit** MC, V. **Map** p402 J4 ⑫

Suits from the nearby Bourse flock here for after-work cocktails (€7) and beers (€4), before giving in to the tempting aromas emanating from the kitchen: Dédé's frites at just €3 a tray are legendary and the rest of the food, reminiscent of an American diner (burgers, fries, ketchup on the bar), is an absolute bargain too. The place looks cool as well, with distressed walls, long bar and bright colours. After hours, when the alcohol flows and the munchies have been satisfied, the music is cranked up and the party really starts.

Le Dernier Bar Avant la Fin du Monde

19 av Victoria, 1st (www.dernierbar.com). *M° Châtelet.* **Open** 10am-midnight Tue-Sun. **Credit** MC, V. **Map** p408 J6 ⑬

The cult of the geek in Paris received a well-oiled boost with the opening of this bar (presumably a reference to Douglas Adams' *Restaurant at the End of the Universe*). Medieval and steampunk dominate the decor, with plenty of other bonkers sci-fi touches: as you walk in, a replica of the Millennium Falcon overlooks a timer counting down to the apocalypse predicted by the Mayans next to a window full of *Star Wars* memorabilia, *World of Warcraft* collectibles and retro video games. Inside, the big, friendly bar is as much about alternative and popular culture as it is about drinking. A library, board games and science fiction books rub shoulders with the holy grail from *Indiana Jones and the Last Crusade* and other philtres, potions and skeletons. The prevailing atmosphere of heroic collaboration keeps prices low, with a pint of Kronenbourg at €5.

★ Harry's New York Bar

5 rue Daunou, 2nd (01.42.61.71.14, www.harrys-bar.fr). *M° Opéra.* **Open** noon-2am Mon-Thur, Sun; noon-3am Fri, Sat. **Credit** AmEx, DC, MC, V. **Map** p401 G4 ⑭

The city's most stylish American bar is an institution beloved of expats, visitors and hard-drinking Parisians (there are over 300 whiskies). The white-coated bartenders mix some of the most sophisticated cocktails in town, from the trademark bloody mary and white lady (both invented here, so they say) to the Pétrifiant, an aptly named elixir of half a dozen spirits splashed into a beer mug. They can also whip up personalised creations that will have you swooning in the downstairs piano bar, where Gershwin composed *An American in Paris*, and where jazz concerts are held most Thursday and Friday nights.

THE BEST TERRACES

For drinking in history
Café de la Paix. *See p173.*

For Left Bank posing
Les Deux Magots. *See p187.*

For Montmartre buzz
Le Sancerre. *See p178.*

O Château

68 rue Jean-Jacques Rousseau, 1st (01.44.73.97.80, www.o-chateau.com). M° Les Halles. **Open** 4pm-midnight daily. **Credit** AmEx, DC, MC, V. **Map** p402 J5 ⑮

The food is great and the vibe convivial, but a night here is all about the wine. There are no less than 500 by the bottle and 40 by the glass, including the chance to taste some very rare and expensive bottles in *soupçon*-sized quantities thanks to high-tech wine-saving devices. Thrice-daily tastings take place in the intimate tasting rooms. *Photos p176.*

Le Tambour

41 rue Montmartre, 2nd (01.42.33.06.90). *M° Sentier.* **Open** 7.30am-3.30am daily. **Credit** MC, V. **Map** p402 J5 ⑯

Decked out with vintage public transport paraphernalia, slatted wooden banquettes and bus stop-sign bar stools, the Tambour has a split personality: there's the daytime Tambour, frequented by pretty much everybody; and then there's the nighttime Tambour, a well-loved nighthawks' bar where the chatty regulars give the 24-hour clock their best shot and post-partygoers pile in for *steak-frites*.

Le Truskel

12 rue Feydeau, 2nd (01.40.26.59.97, www.myspace.com/truskel_paris). M° Bourse. **Open** 8pm-5am Tue-Sat. Closed mid July-mid Aug. **Credit** MC, V. **Map** p402 H4 ⑰

The formula is quite simple at this pub-cum-club: an excellent selection of beers slakes your thirst, while an extensive repertoire of Britpop – sometimes live (ex-Pulp man and Paris resident Jarvis Cocker has been known to splice the night away, as have Pete Doherty and Franz Ferdinand) – assaults your ears. As a cheeky touch, a bar bell rings for no reason whatsoever, causing first-time visitors from the UK to down their drinks in one and dive for the bar.

Zenzoo

13 rue Chabanais, 2nd (01.42.96.27.28, www.zen-zoo.com). M° Quatre-Septembre. **Open** 11.30am-11pm Mon-Sat. **Credit** MC, V. **Map** p402 H4 ⑱

Between 2.30pm and 7pm, this tiny Taiwanese restaurant doubles as a 'tea bar', the only place in Paris that serves China's famous tapioca cocktails – sometimes

CONSUME

known as 'bubble tea', they are served with an extra-wide straw to suck up the little tapioca balls at the bottom. The sensation may seem strange at first, but the tastes are great; among the flavours are mango, coconut and kumquat. Up the road at no.2, a spin-off boutique sells excellent oolong flower teas.

CHAMPS-ELYSEES & WESTERN PARIS

Charlie Birdy

124 rue La Boétie, 8th (01.42.25.18.06, www. charliebirdy.com). M° Franklin D. Roosevelt. **Open** noon-5am daily. **Credit** AmEx, V. **Map** p401 E4 ⑲
Take a New York loft and meld it with a colonial English gentleman's club and you're looking at Charlie Birdy – a large 'pub' with a live music programme of jazz, soul and funk that's worth listening to. If you're in a hurry, stay away – the service can be irritatingly slow. But if you take your time choosing from the 50-strong cocktail menu, sink into a comfy chesterfield and let the evening wash over you, it'll be worth it. Between 4pm and 8pm Monday to Friday, cocktails are half-price.

Le Dada

12 av des Ternes, 17th (01.43.80.60.12). M° Ternes. **Open** 6am-2am Mon-Sat; 7am-10pm Sun. **Credit** AmEx, MC, V. **Map** p400 C3 ⑳
Perhaps the hippest café in this stuffy part of town, Le Dada is best known for its well-placed, sunny terrace. Inside, the wood-block carved tables and red walls provide a warm atmosphere for a crowd that tends towards the well-heeled, well-spoken and, well, loaded. That said, the atmosphere is friendly; if terracing is your thing, you could happily spend a summer's day here – just remember to bring along your Prada shades.

L'Endroit

67 pl du Dr-Félix-Lobligeois, 17th (01.42.29.50.00). M° La Fourche or Rome. **Open** 11am-2am Mon-Tue; 11am-3am Thur; 11am-4am Fri, Sat; 11am-midnight Sun. **Credit** MC, V. **Map** p401 F1 ㉑
L'Endroit is one of the best spots in old Batignolles village, with views over neoclassical Ste-Marie-des-Batignolles church, a cool thirtysomething crowd, decent wines, cocktails a go-go and excellent food that won't break the bank (€12 lunchtime menu).

Flute l'Etoile

19 rue de l'Etoile, 17th (01.45.72.10.14, www.flutebar.com). M° Ternes. **Open** 5pm-2am Tue-Sat. **Credit** AmEx, MC, V. **Map** p400 C3 ㉒
With a menu of some 23 different champagnes and designer decor (slick wooden panelling, blue walls and red velvet), Paris's first champagne lounge may be minuscule, but it certainly looks the part. Indeed the only indication that it's not French (it's American) is the sneaky appearance of a Californian sparkler on the champagne list. For drinkers wishing to sample

different vintages without buying a whole glass (from €9), the small tasting glasses (from €5) are a thoughtful touch. And for anyone bored by plain old bubbly, cocktails such as champagne sangria and Rossini-Tini (champagne, raspberry juice, liqueur and Grey Goose vodka) are sophisticated alternatives.

★ Ladurée

75 av des Champs-Elysées, 8th (01.40.75.08.75, www.laduree.fr). M° George V or Franklin D. Roosevelt. **Open** 7.30am-11pm Mon-Fri; 8.30am-midnight Sat; 8.30am-10pm Sun. **Credit** AmEx, DC, MC, V. **Map** p400 D4 ㉓
Decadence permeates this elegant tearoom, from the 19th century-style interior and service to the labyrinthine corridors that lead to the toilets. While you bask in the warm glow of bygone wealth, indulge in tea, pastries (the pistachio pain au chocolat is heavenly) and, above all, the hot chocolate. It's a rich, bitter, velvety tar that will leave you in the requisite stupor for any lazy afternoon. *Photo p178.*
▶ *The original branch at 16 rue Royale (8th, 01.42.60.21.79) is famed for its macaroons.*
Other location 21 rue Bonaparte, 6th (01.44.07.64.87).

Sir Winston

5 rue de Presbourg, 16th (01.40.67.17.37). M° Charles de Gaulle Etoile. **Open** 9am-2am Mon, Sun; 9am-3am Tue, Wed; 9am-4am Thur-Sat. **Credit** AmEx, V. **Map** p400 C4 ㉔

A bit of an anomaly, this. Grand and imperial, with a bit of Baroque thrown in for good measure, and located within sight of high-end glitz, Sir Winston does a nice line in jazz and gospel brunches on a Sunday. Colonial knick-knacks, chesterfields and chandeliers make up the decor, with Winnie himself framed behind a sturdy bar counter. A battalion of whiskies stands guard beside him, and the wine list is equally *recherché*. Where this place falters is in its somewhat sissy cocktail menu. A Sir Winston Breezer of Bacardi, melon liqueur, pineapple and banana juice? Harrumph!

MONTMARTRE & PIGALLE

Les Caves Populaires
22 rue des Dames, 17th (01.53.04.08.32).
M° Place de Clichy. **Open** 8am-2am Mon-Sat;
11am-2am Sun. **Credit** MC, V. **Map** p401 G2 ㉕
An old soak props up the bar with his *petit rouge*, while others play chess and groups of bobos (bourgeois bohemians) revel in the cheap prices – from €2.50 for a glass of quaffable wine, €3 for a beer and €7 for a cheese or charcuterie platter. It's a charming place and vaguely reminiscent of a wooden chalet, hence its second name, Les Caves du Châlet.

La Fourmi
*74 rue des Martyrs, 18th (01.42.64.70.35). M°
Pigalle.* **Open** 8am-2am Mon-Thur; 8am-4am Fri,
Sat; 10am-2am Sun. **Credit** MC, V. **Map** p402 H2 ㉖

Set on the cusp of the ninth and 18th arrondissements, La Fourmi is an old bistro that has been converted for today's tastes, with picture windows lighting the spacious, roughshod interior, cool staff (and customers) and excellent music. The classic zinc bar counter is crowned by industrial lights, which helps you to see what you're reading as you rifle through the piles of flyers deciding where to go on to next; this is as good a place as any to find out what's happening in town. *Photo p181.*

Le Kremlin
6 rue André Antoine, 18th (06.09.81.93.59).
M° Abbesses or Pigalle. **Open** 6pm-2am daily.
Credit MC, V. **Map** p402 H2 ㉗
This new Russian outpost in the middle of Pigalle has been heaving from the word go – it's difficult to find a path to the bar to order one of the fantastic imported vodkas or original cocktails. Try the Red Star (mezcal, fresh beetroot and Carpano) or the Red Army (Gin Carpano, green Chartreuse and orange bitters). Once you've finally got hold of your drink, pass an eye over the sumptuous communist red decor, punctuated with propaganda posters and quaint Soviet-style furniture. In contrast to the design scheme, the clientele is very Parisian.

Le Poussette Café
*6 rue Pierre Sémard, 9th (01.78.10.49.00, www.le
poussettecafe.com). M° Poissonnière or Cadet.* **Open**
11am-6pm Tue-Sat. **Credit** MC, V. **Map** p402 J3 ㉘

O Château. *See p175.*

Ladurée. See p176.

Fed up with the impracticalities of pushing her pram (*poussette*) into the local café, mother of two Laurence Constant designed her own parent- and child-friendly establishment. This upmarket *salon de thé* caters for the harassed parent (herbal teas, smoothies, quiches and salads) and demanding baby (purées, solids and cuddly toys).

▶ *You can sign up for magic shows and parenting workshops via the café's website.*

Au Rendez-vous des Amis
23 rue Gabrielle, 18th (01.46.06.01.60).
M° Abbesses. **Open** 8am-2am daily. **Credit** AmEx, MC, V. **Map** p402 H1
Considering its proximity to the honeypot that is the Sacré-Coeur, Au Rendez-vous des Amis is still cheap, especially during happy hour (8pm to 10pm), making it popular with locals and foreign students, and the odd tourist. There are some cosy nooks round the back with plenty of upholstered spots to choose from.

★ Rouge Passion
14 rue Jean-Baptiste Pigalle, 9th (01.42.85.07.62, www.rouge-passion.fr). M° St Georges or Pigalle. **Open** noon-3pm, 7pm-midnight Mon-Fri; 7pm-midnight Sat; 11.30am-4pm Sun. Closed 3wks Aug. **Credit** AmEx, MC, V. **Map** p401 G2
Two bright upstarts (Anne and Sébastien) determined to make their mark on Paris's bar scene are behind this venture – and they're going about it the right way. Offering a long list of wines (from just €3), free *assiettes apéros* (peanuts, olives and tapenades on toast) and decor that is perfect vintage chic, the formula is spot on. A small but mouthwatering selection of hot dishes, salads, cheese and *saucisson* platters (set lunch menu €20, mains from €15) help soak up the wine. Look out for the tasting classes, given by a guest sommelier.

Le Sancerre
35 rue des Abbesses, 18th (01.42.58.08.20).
M° Abbesses. **Open** 7am-2am daily. **Credit** MC, V. **Map** p402 H1
This popular Montmartre rock bar is home to a frenzied mix of alcohol-fuelled transvestites, tourists, lovers and bobo locals, who all come for the cheap beer (under €4), trashy music and buzzy terrace. The service is undeniably slow and the food (omelettes, *steak-frites*) nothing special; yet there is something irresistibly refreshing about the no-frills approach that makes this bar stand out from the multitude of try-hard cafés in the area.

BEAUBOURG & THE MARAIS

★ Andy Whaloo
69 rue des Gravilliers, 3rd (01.42.71.20.38).
M° Arts et Métiers. **Open** 6pm-2am Tue-Sat. **Credit** AmEx, MC, V. **Map** p409 K5
Andy Whaloo, created by the people behind its neighbour 404 and London's Momo and Sketch, is Arabic for 'I have nothing'. Bijou? This place brings new meaning to the word. The formidably fashionable crowd fights for coveted 'seats' on upturned paint cans; from head to toe, it's a beautifully designed venue, crammed with Moroccan artefacts and a spice rack of colours. It's quiet early on, with a surge around 9pm, and the atmosphere heats up as the night goes on. *Photos p182.*

L'Apparement Café
18 rue des Coutures St-Gervais, 3rd (01.48.87.12.22). M° St-Sébastien Froissart. **Open** noon-2am Mon-Sat; 12.30pm-midnight Sun. **Credit** MC, V. **Map** p409 L6
The 'Apparently' feels more like a communal living room than a café. The low lighting, cosy nooks and board games (Trivial Pursuit and Taboo, both in

CONSUME

French) make for an excellent place to while away an afternoon. Staff even organise the occasional fortune-telling evening. The location is perfect for shoppers too, being just off the rue Vieille-du-Temple. Lunches consist of simple DIY platters of meats, cheeses and salads, but at €15 for the basic version they're a bit rudimentary for the price. Eating is obligatory during busy periods.

Le Baromètre

17 rue Charlot, 3rd (01.48.87.04.54). M° Arts et Métiers. **Credit** MC, V. **Map** p409 L5 ㉞
This unpretentious wine bar is popular with artisan types. Lunchtimes are heaving, so unless you're after the sit-down *menu du jour* (€13) served at the back, you're better off coming along for a lazy afternoon. Order a plate of cheese or the house speciality, bacon and andouillette gratin, and choose from a 20-strong list of wines by the glass, most under €3.50.

Café Livres

10 rue St-Martin, 4th (01.42.72.18.13). M° Châtelet or Hôtel de Ville. **Open** 8am-11pm Mon-Fri; 9am-11pm Sat; 9am-7pm Sun. **Credit** MC, V. **Map** p406 J6 ㉟

This charming café with a terrace in the shade of the Tour Saint-Jacques has lines and lines of books surrounding patrons inside. Since this is as central as can be, set just around the corner from the Hôtel de Ville, a cappuccino will set you back €6, but the atmosphere is pleasantly relaxing after a shopping marathon on rue de Rivoli. Food is served non-stop from noon to 11pm.

L'Entrée des Artistes

8 rue de Crussol, 11th (09.50.99.67.11). M° Filles du Calvaire or Oberkampf. **Open** 6pm-2am Mon-Sat. **Credit** MC, V. **Map** p409 M5 ㊱
Having mixed drinks at Murano and the Experimental Cocktail Club, two friends decided to open Entrée des Artistes. The relaxed venue offers sophisticated cocktails and a more straightforward wine list, plus smart snacks such as foie gras, Italian cheeses and a classy *plat du jour*. Warm and intimate, the small space has an old-world feel cluttered with beautiful vintage objects, from soda siphons to an old metal cash register. Dandified city slickers and Marais hipsters have quickly appropriated the handful of tables, and the place is packed out from cocktail hour onwards, fuelled by a mix of hip hop, jazz, funk, disco and soul.

Top Tables

Babyfoot is making a high-kicking comeback in the capital's cafés.

Five years ago, Paris's bar scene was virtually devoid of babyfoot options, but now the tables have turned and '*taper un bab*' has become a positively hip way to spend a night on the town.
Saturday night at **Le Mansart** (1 rue Mansart, 9th, 01.48.74.63.30), in the music business district just below Pigalle, and the place is packed. At the babyfoot table right in the window, four thirtysomething guys are involved in a fast-paced game, slamming the defenders, whooping and high-fiving between goals. It turns out they've never met before. 'It's convivial. People who don't know each other can get together and have a laugh. Winning or losing isn't important,' says David, who's come in from the *banlieue* – 'not just to play babyfoot,' he adds. The game is a great mixer – no need for cheesy chat-up lines when you can have so much fun around the table.

Its popularity waned in Paris during the past couple of decades, but babyfoot has remained popular in other parts of France, particularly further south. Fred, playing in a pastis-coloured jumper, is leagues ahead at Le Mansart. 'He's from Marseille, that's why he's so good,' explains his teammate. Fred agrees. 'I played all the time from the age of seven – there was always a café where you could play.'
While Le Mansart is the place to play in the capital, babyfoot has mushroomed all over Paris in recent years. To find a venue, visit the website www.foozball.org, which details the price (€0.50 or €1), location (in a *cave*, near the loos or better) and condition of the table, and the likelihood of meeting good players. For something even more thrilling, try a few shots on the limousine-length tables at the Mama Shelter (*see p248*) or W Hotel (*see p232*).

CONSUME

L'Estaminet

39 rue de Bretagne, 3rd (01.42.72.28.12).
M° Temple. **Open** 9am-8pm Tue-Sat; 9am-
2pm Sun. **Credit** MC, V. **Map** p409 L5 ③

L'Estaminet is tucked away in the Marché des
Enfants-Rouges, a charming neighbourhood market
and one of the city's oldest. The café has a warm interior, with a grandfather clock in the corner and
guests eating €13 *plats du jour* off Limoges porcelain. Wines from around €4 a glass.

★ L'Etoile Manquante

34 rue Vieille-du-Temple, 4th (01.42.72.48.34,
www.cafeine.com). M° Hôtel de Ville or St-Paul.
Open 9am-2am daily. **Credit** V. **Map** p409 K6 ③

L'Etoile Manquante is the hippest of Xavier
Denamur's merry Marais bars. Cocktails are
punchy, traditional tipples just as good, and the
salads and snacks reasonably priced and tasty – but
it's the design and buzz that are the main draws.
The decor is trendy but comfortable, embellished
with interesting art. As in all Denamur's places, no
visit is complete without a trip to the toilets: here,
an electric train shuttles between cubicles, starlight
beams down from the ceiling, and a hidden camera
films you washing your hands. Just watch the small
screen on the wall behind you.

Lizard Lounge

18 rue du Bourg-Tibourg, 4th (01.42.72.81.34,
www.cheapblonde.com). M° Hôtel de Ville.
Open noon-2am daily. **Credit** MC, V.
Map p409 K6 ③

An anglophone favourite located deep in the heart
of the Marais, this loud and lively (hetero) pick-up
joint provides lager in pints (€6), plus cocktails (€7)
and a viewing platform for beer-goggled oglers.
Bare brick and polished woodwork are offset by the
occasional lizard and a housey soundtrack. Bargain
boozing (cocktails €5) kicks off at 5pm; from
8pm to 10pm, there's another happy hour in the
sweaty cellar bar (complete with minuscule dancefloor); on Mondays, it lasts all day. A popular weekend brunch of bacon, sausages and eggs benedict
caters to the homesick.

Le Loir dans la Théière

3 rue des Rosiers, 4th (01.42.72.90.61).
M° St-Paul. **Open** 10am-7.30pm Mon-Fri; 9am-
7.30pm Sat, Sun. **Credit** V. **Map** p409 L6 ④

Le Loir is named after the unfortunate dormouse
that gets dunked in the pot at the Mad Hatter's tea
party in *Alice in Wonderland*. Its squishy sofas
are the perfect complement to its comfort food: it
specialises in baked goods, and the famed lemon
meringue and chocolate fondant are divine. At
weekends, it's packed out with tourists in search of
brunch; long queues of people looking enviously at
your plate, plus occasionally patchy service, can
mar the experience. Come early (before noon) or be
prepared to queue.

La Perle

78 rue Vieille-du-Temple, 3rd (01.42.72.69.93).
M° Chemin Vert or St-Paul. **Open** 6.30am-2am
Mon-Fri; 8am-2am Sat, Sun. **Credit** MC, V.
Map p409 L6 ④

The Pearl achieves a rare balance between all-day
and late-night venue, and has a good hetero/homo
mix. In the morning, it draws early risers; lunchtime
is for a business crowd; the afternoon reels in retired
locals, and in the evening, screenwriters rub elbows
with young dandies, keeping one eye on the mirror
and an ear on the electro-rock. The menu runs from
omelettes to *salade marine*. Expect a DJ later on.

Le Petit Fer à Cheval

30 rue Vieille-du-Temple, 4th (01.42.72.47.47,
www.cafeine.com). M° St-Paul. **Open** 9am-2am
daily. **Credit** MC, V. **Map** p409 K6 ④

Even a miniature Shetland pony would be pushed
to squeeze his hoof into this *fer à cheval* (horseshoe)
– the adorable little café, which has been in business
for more than 100 years, has one of France's smallest bars. Tucked in behind the glassy façade is a
friendly dining room lined with reclaimed métro
benches; if you want scenery, the tables out front
overlook the bustle of rue Vieille-du-Temple. As
with its sister bar L'Etoile Manquante (*see left*), the
loos are worth the detour – they look as if they've
been pummelled out of a defunct Dalek, with metal
panels and strange knobs everywhere.

Stolly's

16 rue Cloche-Perce, 4th (01.42.76.06.76,
www.cheapblonde.com). M° Hôtel de Ville or
St-Paul. **Open** 4pm-2am daily. **Credit** MC, V.
Map p409 K6 ④

This seen-it-all drinking den has been serving a
mainly anglophone crowd for nights immemorial.
The staff make the place what it is, and a summer
terrace eases libation, as do the long happy hours;
but don't expect anyone at Stolly's to faff about
with food. There's football on TV and a plastic
shark to compensate.

BASTILLE & EASTERN PARIS

Le 114

114 rue Oberkampf, 11th (www.durocketduroll.
tumblr.com). M° Ménilmontant or Parmentier.
Open 6pm-3am Tue-Sat. **Credit** MC, V.
Map p403 N5 ④

Just because there are already 36 rock bars in
Oberkampf, it doesn't mean you should restrain your
joy when a new one opens up. Opened in partnership
with Puma Social and in association with the new
magazine Plugged, Le 114 proudly parades its motto
on its front window: 'C'est comme chez toi, mais en
mieux' (It's just like home, but better). Squishy armchairs and huge sofas back up this assertion, even
if the atmosphere isn't quite as warm as the sign
might have you believe. However, the bar's creators

hit on a great concept when they decided to invite groups to play for free on the bar's small stage. The schedule displays decent taste in rock and pop, and the door policy is run according to time-honoured principles: first come, first served.

Le Baron Rouge

1 rue Théophile-Roussel, 12th (01.43.43.14.32). Mº Ledru-Rollin. **Open** 10am-3pm, 5-10pm Tue-Fri; 10am-10pm Sat; 10am-4pm Sun. **Credit** AmEx, MC, V. **Map** p407 N7 ㊺

It sells wine, certainly – great barrels of the stuff are piled high and sold by the glass at very reasonable prices. But the Red Baron is not just a wine bar; it's more like a local chat room, where regulars congregate to yak over their *vin*, or perhaps one of the few draught beers, and maybe a snack of sausages or oysters. Despite its lack of seating (there are only four tables), it's a popular pre-dinner spot, so arrive early and don't expect too much elbow room; drinkers often spill out on to the pavement – joining the smokers.

Café Titon

34 rue Titon, 11th (09.53.17.94.10, www.cafe titon.com). Mº Faidherbe-Chaligny or Rue des Boulets. **Open** 8am-2am Mon-Sat. **Credit** MC, V. **Map** p407 P7 ㊻

The funky Titon is Paris's only Franco-German café – and certainly the only place in town to flog *currywurst* (German sausage in curry sauce) and chips for a bargain €5.50. It even transforms into a giant *biergarten* during Germany's Oktoberfest. Its Parisian side doesn't get forgotten, though, with *croques, tartines*, an unbeatable lunch menu (€9.80 for a main and a *café*) and scrumptious cocktails (€6.90 for a margarita).

Le Calbar

82 rue de Charenton, 12th (01.84.06.18.90, www.lecalbarcocktail.com). Mº Ledru-Rollin. **Open** 3pm-1.30am Mon-Fri; 5pm-1.30am Sat. **Credit** MC, V. **Map** p407 M7 ㊼

The look of this former wine bar recalls a New York loft, with bare bricks, street art, wooden furniture – and waiters decked out in underwear, aprons, braces and bow ties. You have to climb a caged stairway to find the lounge furnished with comfortable chesterfields and post-industrial coffee tables, and hip hop and electro playing in the background. Cocktails feature premium spirits such as Monkey 47 (a German liqueur with 47 ingredients), Nikka Japanese whisky or even Tanqueray Ten (gin made from fresh fruit). There's no happy hour, but instead a monthly *apéro* where underwear as outerwear is a prerequisite for both sexes (free dressing room available) to get hold of the special cocktail, the Dagobear.

★ Chez Prosper

7 av du Trône, 11th (01.43.73.08.51). Mº Nation. **Open** 7am-1am daily. **Credit** AmEx, MC, V. **Map** p407 Q8 ㊽

Chez Prosper welcomes punters all day long with that simplest of gestures: a smile. Yes, even when squeezing past people queuing for a spot on the sun terrace, the waiters are positively beaming. The dining/drinks area – tiled floor, large mirrors, wooden furniture – is run with military precision, and orders

CONSUME

La Fourmi. *See p177.*

arrive promptly. The *steak-frites* and *croques* (served on Poîlane bread) are hearty, and the naughty Nutella tiramisu is worth crossing town for.

China

50 rue de Charenton, 12th (01.43.46.08.09, www.lechina.eu). M° Bastille or Ledru Rollin. **Open** noon-2am Mon-Fri; 5pm-2am Sat. Closed Aug. **Credit** AmEx, MC, V. **Map** p407 M7 ⓸⓹

This sexy take on a 1930s Shanghai gentleman's club, with red walls, leather chesterfields and the longest bar in Paris, serves some of the finest cocktails in town (including its signature singapore sling). The Cantonese cuisine is pricey, so skip dinner and head upstairs to the cigar bar (if you're romantically inclined) or downstairs to the cellar for weekly jazz, pop and world music concerts (website has details).

★ Les Furieux

74 rue de la Roquette, 11th (01.47.00.78.44, www.lesfurieux.fr). M° Bastille or Voltaire. **Open** 4pm-2am Tue-Thur; 4pm-5am Fri, Sat; 7pm-2am Sun. **Credit** MC, V. **Map** p407 M6 ⓹⓪

Just when it looked as if 'lounge attitude' would contaminate every bar on rue de la Roquette, Les Furieux fought back with a healthy dose of rock and metal, padded red walls, faux-leather banquettes, black paint, and rotating photography exhibitions. Locals flock here for the happy hour (6pm to 8pm), when cocktails with rockin' names like Grunge, Scud, and, er, Boris are half price. Diehards can pay tribute to Paris's hedonistic heyday with 12 different absinthes.

Le Houla Oups!

4 rue Basfroi, 11th (01.40.24.18.80, www. myspace.com/lehoulaoups). M° Ledru-Rollin or Voltaire. **Open** 6pm-2am daily. **Credit** MC, V. **Map** p407 N7 ⓹⓵

Just off the main Roquette drag, this hip little den of rock – French rock to be precise – makes up in energy what it lacks in size. There are regular exhibitions, concerts, film nights (usually horror or genre movies), DJs and even auction evenings. During happy hour (6pm to 8pm) beer costs just €3 a pint. To keep in the loop, send an email to houlaoups@gmail.com asking to be put on the mailing list.

Le Motel

8 passage Josset, 11th (01.58.30.88.52). M° Ledru-Rollin. **Open** 6pm-1.45am Tue-Sun. **Credit** MC, V. **Map** p407 M7 ⓹⓶

Le Motel has a simple formula: cheap drinks and excellent music. During happy hour (6pm to 9pm) a pint of *blonde* costs €3.50 and cocktails €3. With DJs almost every night, the music ranges from cutting-edge indie to contemporary neo-folk and rock classics, with the odd Motown hit thrown in for good measure. Friendly twentysomethings cluster around faux Louis XVI armchairs or try their luck in the Sunday pop quiz.

L'Opa

9 rue Biscornet, 12th (01.46.28.12.90, www.opa-paris.com). M° Bastille. **Open** 8pm-2am Wed, Thur; 8pm-6am Fri, Sat. **Credit** V. **Map** p407 M7 ⓹⓷

Andy Whaloo. *See p178.*

Late opening and Eric Perier's diverse range of nightly entertainment – DJs (weekends), videos, live acts and the odd open mic event – are the attractions here, along with free admission and fairly reasonable drinks prices. A couple of comfortable sofas take the edge off the loft-like, institutional interior, with a modest stage in one corner and an upstairs chill-out space and separate bar.

Pause Café

41 rue de Charonne, 11th (01.48.06.80.33). M° Ledru-Rollin. **Open** 8am-2am Mon-Sat; 9am-8pm Sun. **Credit** AmEx, MC, V. **Map** p407 M7 ㉞

Featured in Cedric Klapisch's 1996 film *Chacun Cherche son Chat*, which was shot on location in the neighbourhood, the Pause Café has managed to prolong its moment of glory thanks to its large terrace on the corner of rues Charonne and Keller. Inside, the modern salons benefit from a smattering of primary colours with ornately plastered ceilings and plenty of light. Having been immortalised on celluloid, the friendly staff occasionally let fame go to their heads: service can be excruciatingly slow at times. The food – traditional French café fare with an Asian twist – is not bad, but you might be waiting for a while; best to order a well-mixed cocktail to pass the time.

Les Pères Populaires

46 rue de Buzenval, 20th (01.43.48.49.22, www.myspace.com/perespopulaires). M° Buzenval. **Open** 8am-2am Mon-Fri; 10am-2am Sat, Sun. **Credit** MC, V. **Map** p407 Q7 ㉟

On the far side of Nation, could this funky number be the cheapest bar in Paris? Wine is a mere €2 a glass, beer is €2.40 (€4.50 for a pint) and flavoured rums cost €4. To get an idea of the look of the place, think 1970s canteen-cum-retro classroom and you'll come close. During the day, the local freelance media crowd and a handful of musicians squat the tables for the free Wi-Fi; at night DJs spin electro sounds and a party atmosphere reigns.

Le P'tit Bar

7 rue Richard Lenoir, 11th (no phone). M° Charonne. **Open** 5pm-2am daily. **No credit cards**. **Map** p407 N6 ㊱

You couldn't invent this place if you tried: local soaks, immigrant South Americans, twentysomething students, Brits and retired war veterans all pop in for a taste of the most surreal experience in town, courtesy of the elderly Madame Polo, her fluffy cat and her canaries. Madame P is surely the last living link to a forgotten Paris, and proof that in this age of excessive health and safety concerns, there are still places here that manage to slip through the net. A word of warning, though: don't drink out of the glasses   Madame Polo isn't too keen on cleaning. We recommend you opt instead for a €3 bottle of beer.

Le Temps des Cérises

31 rue de la Cerisaie, 4th (01.42.72.08.63). M° Bastille. **Open** 8.30am-2am daily. **Credit** MC, V. **Map** p409 L7 ㊲

Not to be confused with several other cafés of the same name, this one-room *bistro à vins* has changed very little over the years. Faded net curtains, Duralex tumblers behind the zinc bar and prices that begin at €2.50 for a *vin* or beer are all reminiscent of a bygone age. The blackboard wine list is limited but the selection is always well chosen, and food is old-fashioned and hearty (think beef stew and *blanquette de veau*). The general banter is football-centred, so get ready to rumble with the natives about the goings-on at PSG.

NORTH-EAST PARIS

Le 9b

68 bd de la Villette, 19th (01.40.18.08.10, www. le9b.com). M° Colonel Fabien. **Open** 10am-2am daily. **Credit** MC, V. **Map** p403 M3 ㊳

Does the name remind you of anything? It's our old favourite, Le 9 Billards. This bar – which preceded Les Disquaires on rue Jean-Pierre Timbaud – has just been reborn on boulevard de la Villette, not far from Café Chéri(e). It's already full to bursting each night with a grand blend of electro, hip hop, funk and rock on the crammed dancefloor, and cocktails and couscous on the menu.

L'Alimentation Générale

64 rue Jean-Pierre-Timbaud, 11th (01.43.55.42.50, www.alimentation-generale.net). M° Parmentier. **Open** 7pm-2am Wed, Sun; 7pm-4am Thur-Sat. **Credit** AmEx, MC, V. **Map** p403 M4 ㊴

The 'Grocery Store' is rue Jean-Pierre-Timbaud's answer to La Mercerie (*see p185*): a big old space filled with junk. Cupboards of kitsch china and lampshades made from kitchen sponges are an inspired touch. The beer is well chosen – Flag, Sagres, Picon and Orval by the bottle – and the unusual €8 house cocktail involves basil and figs. DJs rock the joint: expect a €5-€10 cover price for big names or live bands. Oh yes – and it has the most brazen toilet walls this side of town. *Photo p185.*

★ Ave Maria

1 rue Jacquard, 11th (01.47.00.61.73). M° Parmentier. **Open** 6.30pm-2am daily. **No credit cards**. **Map** p403 M5 ㊵

Unlike some places that eschew good food for alcohol and a funky interior, colourful Ave Maria scores highly for all three. The kitsch interior is decked out in a canopy of chinoiserie parasols and a vast collection of Hindu gods. Music, a combination of reggae, funk, soul and dub, is cool but unobtrusive. Strangers sharing wooden benches devour exotic dishes from the Brazilian-inspired menu, which combines meat, spices, lentils, rice and fruit. Cocktails are equally quirky and start at €4.50.

CONSUME

CONSUME

Bar Ourcq

68 quai de la Loire, 19th (01.42.40.12.26, http://barourcq.free.fr). Mº Laumière. **Open** 3pm-midnight Wed, Thur; 3pm-2am Fri, Sat; 3-10pm Sun. **No credit cards. Map** p403 N1 ③

This was one of the first hip joints to hit the Canal de l'Ourcq, with an embankment broad enough to accommodate *pétanque* games (ask at the bar) and a cluster of deckchairs. It's a completely different scene from the crowded bustle along Canal St-Martin – more discerning and less self-satisfied. The cabin-like interior is cosy, and drinks are listed in a hit parade of prices, starting with €2.50 for a *demi* or glass of red. Pastas at €9, exhibitions and a regular DJ spot keep the cool clientele sated. Closed on rainy weekdays in summer.

La Bellevilloise

19 rue Boyer, 20th (01.46.36.07.07, www.labellevilloise.com). Mº Gambetta. **Open** 7pm-1am Wed, Thur; 7pm-2am Fri; 11am-2am Sat; 11.30am-5pm Sun. **Credit** V. **Map** p403 P4 ③

The Bellevilloise is the latest incarnation of a building that once housed the capital's very first workers' co-operative. Now it competently multitasks as a bar, restaurant, club and exhibition space, hosting regular film and music festivals on the top level (where there's a fake lawn with deckchairs and a massage area). Enjoy brunch in the Halle aux Oliviers or decent views of the *quartier* from the charming terrace; downstairs the club-cum-concert venue has launched some of Paris's most exciting new bands, and on '80s nights you can hardly move for the fortysomethings living it up like they were teens again. There's also live jazz music with the Sunday brunch.

Café Charbon

109 rue Oberkampf, 11th (01.43.57.55.13, www.lecafecharbon.com). Mº Parmentier or Ménilmontant. **Open** 9am-2am Mon, Tue, Sun; 9am-3am Thur; 9am-4am Fri, Sat. Closed Aug. **Credit** MC, V. **Map** p403 N5 ③

The bar contained within this beautifully restored belle époque building sparked the Oberkampf nightlife boom. Its booths, mirrors and adventurous music policy put trendy locals at ease, capturing the essence of café culture spanning each end of the 20th century. After more than 15 years, the formula still works – and is copied by nearby bars.

▶ *The management run the popular Nouveau Casino nightclub next door (see p284) and the groovy De la Ville Café (see p173) in the 10th.*

Café Chéri(e)

44 bd de la Villette, 19th (01.42.02.02.05, http://cafecherie.blogspot.com). Mº Belleville. **Open** noon-2am daily. **Credit** MC, V. **Map** p403 M3 ③

This splendid DJ bar is also an all-day café – but it doesn't compromise any of the cool that keeps it well ahead of the pack after dark. Music comes from all

over, and runs from electro, rock, funk, hip hop, indie, dance and jazz to golden oldies and ghetto-inspired grooves. The interior sparkles with wit and invention – note the marvellous mural alluding to the personal sacrifices made for a life of coupledom. There's a front terrace if you need a smoke or con-versational respite from the BPM.

▶ *There's music from Thursdays to Saturdays after 10pm; see p280.*

Le Café Noir

15 rue St-Blaise, 20th (01.40.09.75.80). Mº Alexandre Dumas or Porte de Bagnolet. **Open** noon-2.30pm, 7.30-11pm Mon-Sat. **Credit** MC, V.

In the St-Blaise district (the former village of Charonne annexed to Paris in 1860), with views on to the village church, this gorgeous high-ceilinged café, decorated with old cafetières, draws in artists, workers and an upbeat crowd of local trendies. At mealtimes expect inventive French cuisine, with the likes of foie gras speckled with speculoos biscuits, magret of duck with cardamom and vanilla, and pineapple and mango trifle.

Le Café des Sports

94 rue de Ménilmontant, 20th (01.46.36.48.18, www.myspace.com/lecafedessports). Mº Gambetta. **Open** 10am-2am daily. Closed Aug. **Credit** MC, V. **Map** p403 P4 ③

Le Café des Sports' fine and eclectic music pro-gramme ranges from electro (Saturdays), to pop or *chanson* (Tuesdays and Thursdays) to world dub. Beer and wine are fabulously cheap (just €2 from 6pm to 8pm) and there's even sometimes free cous-cous or tapas with your drink on a Monday evening. Unlike its sprawling neighbours, Le Café des Sports has just one room to call home. DJs play in the space at the back.

★ Chez Jeannette

47 rue du Fbg-St-Denis, 10th (01.47.70.30.89, www.chezjeannette.com). Mº Strasbourg St-Denis or Château d'Eau. **Open** 8am-2am Mon-Sat; 9am-2am Sun. **Map** p402 K3 ③

When she sold her café a few years ago, Jeannette handed over to the young team from Chez Justine because they promised not to change a thing. The monstrous 1940s dust-coated lights, leaky loos, tobacco-stained wallpaper depicting the Moulin Rouge and PVC-covered banquettes have finally been cleaned up, and the café has become one of Paris's hippest spots for an aperitif. There's a *plat du jour* at lunch and plates of cheese and charcuterie at night; at 8pm, the fluorescent lights go off and candlelight takes over, to a cheer.

Chez Prune

36 rue Beaurepaire, 10th (01.42.41.30.47). Mº Jacques Bonsergent. **Open** 8am-2am Mon-Sat; 10am-2am Sun. **Credit** AmEx, MC, V. **Map** p402 L4 ③

L'Alimentation Générale. *See p183.*

Chez Prune is an excellent lunch spot, and still one of the best places in which to spend an evening on the Canal St-Martin. The local bobo HQ, this traditional café, with high ceilings and low lighting, sticks to a simple formula: groups of friends crowd around the cosily ordered banquettes, picking at moderately priced cheese or meat platters. Mostly, though, they come for a few leisurely drinks or an *apéro* before heading off to one of the late-night venues in the area.

Le Cinquante
50 rue de Lancry, 10th (01.42.02.36.83). M° Jacques Bonsergent. **Open** 5.30pm-2am daily. Closed Aug. **Credit** MC, V. **Map** p402 L3 ❸
Just down from the Canal St-Martin, the bare brick, Formica and framed '50s ads of this funky venue attract an inner circle of regulars. These days, it's established enough to produce its own T-shirts and customised bar stools. Reasonable prices – half-litre pitchers of sauvignon, Brouilly and Chablis in the €10 range – attract a mixed bag of tastes and generations. The two rooms behind the main bar are set aside for dining (affordable classics) and music (generally acoustic). Sunday is open-mic night.

La Gouttière
96 av Parmentier, 11th (01.43.55.46.42). M° Parmentier. **Open** 5pm-2am Mon-Sat. **Credit** MC, V. **Map** p403 M4 ❸
Far enough (five minutes) from rue Oberkampf to feel off the beaten track, the Gutter is not out-and-out libertine, but you're on the right lines. Certainly, a come-what-may approach to music, drinking and eye contact abounds in the crowded venue. Decor, assuming you can see it, consists of a few LP covers and the kind of colour scheme often put to good use in adventure playgrounds. Reasonably priced lunches (food is a French and North African mix), the occasional live band, chess and card games complete the picture.

L'Inconnu
17 rue de Mazagran, 10th (01.45.23.95.37, www.inconnu-bar.com). M° Bonne Nouvelle or Strasbourg Saint-Denis. **Open** 11am-2am Mon-Sat. **Credit** MC, V. **Map** p402 K4 ❼⓿
This new bar is in Strasbourg Saint-Denis, an area that's becoming an increasingly attractive nightlife alternative to Pigalle, Oberkampf and Bastille. The friendly welcome, comfy sofas, soft lighting and cheap Paris beer (Gallia) encourage chat, while the DJ sets on Thursdays, Fridays and Saturdays often feature big names such as Teki Latex, Supa Never Smiles or Acid Washed. The downstairs dancefloor keeps going until 2am and is a good place to meet the local crowd of hipsters, artists and musicians.

La Maroquinerie
23 rue Boyer, 20th (01.40.33.35.05, www. lamaroquinerie.fr). M° Gambetta. **Open** 6pm-2am daily. Closed Aug. **Credit** MC, V. **Map** p403 P4 ❼❶
La Maroquinerie's former life as a leather factory is little in evidence these days. It's now a bright café and bar in competition with La Bellevilloise (*see p184*), with a coveted downstairs music venue that hosts the odd literary debate and a wealth of cool acts. The food is excellent – you can eat your way through the menu for around €25 – and wine sourced from across France starts at €3 a glass. The interior, with exposed brick, is cosy, and in summer chirpy locals invade the shaded terrace. *Photo p188.*

La Mercerie
98 rue Oberkampf, 11th (01.56.98.14.10). M° Parmentier. **Open** 5pm-2am Mon-Fri; 3pm-2am Sat, Sun. **Credit** MC, V. **Map** p403 N5 ❼❷
Opposite the landmark Charbon (*see p184*), the spacious Mercerie has cleaned up its act: after years of full-on grunge it has succumbed to the draw of shabby chic – or, to put it another way, a fashionable level of dishevelment. This was probably wise, as the novelty of sticky tables was beginning to wear

thin, and the move has been appreciated by the party freaks who still cross town for its loud, eclectic music, live DJ programme, and cheapo happy hour (7pm to 9pm). The back area, with its tea lights, provides intimacy if that's where your evening's headed.

Au Passage
1bis passage St-Sébastien, 11th (01.43.55.07.52). Mº St-Sébastien Froissart. **Open** 12.30-2pm, 7.30pm-2am Mon-Fri; 7.30pm-2am Sat. **Credit** MC, V. **Map** p409 M5 ⓐ
Tucked down a narrow alleyway off rue Amelot, opposite the back entrance of Pop In, you don't just happen upon Au Passage, you come because you've heard about the cheap lunchtime menus (€12.50) and the colourful local artists and wannabe *marginaux* (all almost as colourful as their teeth, stained with a glass too many of *vin rouge*). There's art on the far wall, some retro cookbooks, and a feeling that entire decades could pass without anyone really noticing.

Le Verre Volé
67 rue de Lancry, 10th (01.48.03.17.34). Mº Jacques Bonsergent. **Open** 9.30am-1am daily. Closed Aug. **Credit** MC, V. **Map** p402 L4 ⓐ
This organic-only *cave à vins* doubles up as a minuscule wine bar and restaurant. Although wine (around €4 per glass) is the focus, you're obliged to eat; a hearty sausage and mash will set you back around €15 (other mains cost up to €20). Purists who would prefer a simple snack to complement their *bon vin* should opt for a plate of charcuterie and cheese at €12. It's good to know that staff will sell you a bottle of wine (and open it) for you to drink by the canal.

THE LATIN QUARTER & THE 13TH

★ Le Crocodile
6 rue Royer-Collard, 5th (01.43.54.32.37). RER Luxembourg. **Credit** MC, V. **Map** p408 J8 ⓐ
Ignore the apparently boarded-up windows at Le Crocodile; if you're here late, then it's open. Friendly young regulars line the sides of this small, narrow bar and try to decide what to drink – not easy, given the length of the cocktail list: at last count there were 317 varieties. The generous €6-per-cocktail happy hour (Monday to Thursday before midnight) will allow you to start with a champagne *accroche-coeur*, followed up with a Goldschläger (served with gold leaf) before moving on to the rest of the list.

Le Merle Moqueur
11 rue de la Butte aux Cailles, 13th (no phone). Mº Place d'Italie. **Open** 5pm-2am daily. **No credit cards.**
Amid semi-faded pseudo-tropical decor and '80s music, the Teasing Blackbird – a Butte-aux-Cailles institution – tantalises students and nostalgists with its splendid selection of rums (over 20) and a long

list of cocktails. The atmosphere gets pretty raucous after 10pm – make sure you get in early to grab one of the three tables.

Le Pantalon
7 rue Royer-Collard, 5th (no phone). RER Luxembourg. **Open** 3pm-2am daily. **No credit cards. Map** p408 J8 ⓐ
A local café that seems familiar yet is utterly surreal. It has the standard fixtures, including the old soaks at the bar – but the regulars and staff are enough to tip the balance firmly into eccentricity. Friendly and funny French grown-ups and foreign students chat in a variety of languages; drinks are cheap enough to make you tipsy without the worry of a cash hangover.

★ Petit Bain
7 port de la Gare, 13th (01.80.48.49.81, www.petitbain.org). Mº Bibliothèque François Mitterrand or Quai de la Gare. **Open** 6pm-2am Wed-Sat; noon-5.30pm Sun (later in summer). **Credit** MC, V. **Map** p407 M10 ⓐ
See p187 **Making Waves.**

Le Requin Chagrin
10 rue Mouffetard, 5th (01.44.07.23.24). Mº Place Monge. **Open** 5pm-2am Mon-Thur, Sun; 11am-5am Fri, Sat. **Credit** MC, V. **Map** p406 J8 ⓐ
The 'depressed shark' hasn't lost its bite. Students and beer guzzlers of all ages still cram in for the ten *bières* on tap and the five-hour happy hour (4-9pm), when drinks are a steal at just €2.50. You'll find the usual Left Bank suspects: groups of friends, blokes trying to get laid and *intellos* from the nearby universities who still stimulate their brains during down time with chess and quoits.

Sputnik
14 rue de la Butte aux Cailles, 13th (01.45.65.19.82, www.sputnik.fr). Mº Place d'Italie. **Open** 2pm-2am Mon-Sat; 4pm-midnight Sun. **Credit** MC, V.
A hip young crowd gathers in this rock-oriented bar, which doubles as a sports bar during important fixtures, and trebles as an internet café at other times. Ever-changing art exhibitions add interest to the walls, and live music once a month draws an indie crowd. Fancy falling in love? Try the €8 love potion cocktail Philtre d'Amour, which is made from gin, Malibu, pine-apple and strawberries.

ST-GERMAIN-DES-PRES & ODEON

★ Le Bar Dix
10 rue de l'Odéon, 6th (01.43.26.66.83, www.lebar10.com). Mº Odéon. **Open** 6pm-2am daily. **No credit cards. Map** p408 H7 ⓐ
Generations of students have glugged back jugs of the celebrated home-made sangria (€3 a glass during happy hour) while squeezed into the cramped upper bar, tattily authentic with its Jacques Brel record

Making Waves

Join Paris's party flotilla for a night of Seine-side fun in the 13th.

The idea of an urban beach went down so well when it was first floated back in 2002 that now Paris-Plages is a victim of its own success: on sweltering summer days, the suncream-slathered crowds descend *en masse* to the banks of the Seine. But it still remains one of the best things to do in Paris during the summer, and has spawned a whole host of bars to soak up the post-beach party crowds. One of the best spots for Seine-side partying is the 13th, in the shadow of the Bibliothèque Nationale de France François Mitterrand, where a veritable flotilla of boat bars are moored up for drinks and dancing. Batofar was the original floating pleasure palace, but **Petit Bain** (*see p186*) has been giving it a run for its money since it first lowered the gangplank in 2010. Designed by the Encore Heureux collective, Petit Bain looks like a fluorescent green barge with a cubist wooden tree house plonked on top, and harbours an excellent line-up of concerts and art exhibitions, plus a coveted terrace that doubles as a bar, restaurant and

octopus's garden, with all manner of aquatic plants housed in white bathtubs repurposed as planters. Below deck, the intimate stage hosts regular gigs with everything from minimalist Norwegian pop and indie folk to rock and jazz making the eclectic playlist.

sleeves, Yves Montand handbills and pre-war light fittings. Spelunkers and hopeless romantics negotiate the hazardous stone staircase to drink in the cellar bar, with its candlelight and century-old advertising murals. Can someone please come and slap a preservation order on the place?

★ Le Bar du Marché
75 rue de Seine, 6th (01.43.26.55.15). M°
Mabillon or Odéon. **Open** 8am-2am daily.
Credit MC, V. **Map** p408 H7 ⑩
The market in question is the Cours des Halles, the bar a convivial corner café opening on to the pleasing bustle of St-Germain-des-Prés. Simple dishes like a ham omelette or a plate of herrings are in the €7 range, and Brouilly or muscadet is €4-€5 a glass – all proffered by waiters dressed in matching dungarees. It couldn't be anywhere else in the world.

Café de Flore
172 bd St-Germain, 6th (01.45.48.55.26,
www.cafedeflore.fr). M° St-Germain-des-Prés.
Open 7am-2am daily. **Credit** AmEx, DC,
MC, V. **Map** p408 H7 ㉛
Bourgeois locals crowd the terrace tables at lunch, eating club sandwiches with knives and forks as anxious waiters frown at couples with pushchairs or single diners occupying tables for four. This historic café, former HQ of the Lost Generation intelligentsia,

attracts tourists and, yes, celebrities from time to time. But a *café crème* is €4.60, and the omelettes and croque-monsieurs are best eschewed in favour of the better dishes on the menu (€15-€25). There are play readings on Mondays and philosophy debates on the first Wednesday of the month, at 8pm, in English.

★ Chez Georges
11 rue des Canettes, 6th (01.43.26.79.15).
M° Mabillon. **Open** noon-2am Tue-Sat. Closed
Aug. **Credit** MC, V. **Map** p408 H7 ㉜
One of a dying breed of *cave-bars* in the Latin Quarter, Chez Georges is beloved of students, professionals and local eccentrics. Regulars pop in during the day to sip wine over a game of chess, and at night the *cave* fills up with people dancing to *chanson*, pop and even the odd bar mitzvah tune. The heat is mascara-melting and it's not for the claustrophobic.

Les Deux Magots
6 pl St-Germain-des-Prés, 6th (01.45.48.55.25,
www.lesdeuxmagots.com). M° St-Germain-des-
Prés. **Open** 7.30am-1am daily. **Credit** AmEx,
DC, MC, V. **Map** p408 H7 ㉝
If you stand outside Les Deux Magots, you have to be prepared to photograph tourists wanting proof of their encounter with French philosophy. The former haunt of Sartre and de Beauvoir now attracts a less pensive crowd that can be all too *m'as-tu vu*,

CONSUME

CONSUME

La Maroquinerie. *See p185.*

particularly at weekends. The hot chocolate is still good, though, and served in generous portions. Visit on a weekday afternoon when the editors return, manuscripts in hand, to the inside tables, leaving enough elbow room for some serious discussion.

Les Editeurs

4 carrefour de l'Odéon, 6th (01.43.26.67.76, www.lesediteurs.fr). Mᵒ Odéon. **Open** 8am-2am daily. **Credit** AmEx, MC, V. **Map** p408 H7 ❹
It's no surprise to see row upon row of books in the bright, modern interior of Les Editeurs. A café with literary leanings, it sits on the lovely carrefour de l'Odéon. Bask in the glory of literary greats as portraits of authors and their editors look down on you. The weekend brunch is good value at €25.50.

★ J'Go

Rue Clément, 6th (01.43.26.19.02, www.lejgo.com). Mᵒ Mabillon or Odéon. **Open** 11am-midnight daily. **Credit** AmEx, MC, V. **Map** p408 H7 ❺
J'Go (pronounced gigot) is all about lamb – well, meat of various kinds, actually: a buzzing Toulouse-style wine bar in the Marché St-Germain by day, it becomes a *rôtisserie* at meal times, serving its speciality spit-roasted lamb from Quercy, black pig from Bigorre, and whole roasted chickens. If you'd rather stick to wine and tapas, sidle up to one of the great wooden barrels, choose your poison and share a plate of charcuterie or foie gras *tartines* (€10).

Moose

16 rue des Quatre Vents, 6th (01.46.33.77.00, www.mooseparis.com). Mᵒ Odeon. **Open** 4pm-2am Mon-Fri; 11am-2am Sat, Sun. **Credit** MC, V. **Map** p408 H7 ❻

This Canadian sports bar serves a vast selection of beers and even some organic Australian wines. A friendly atmosphere and delicious burgers make the Moose a great place to kick off the evening.

★ La Palette

43 rue de Seine, 6th (01.43.26.68.15). Mᵒ Odéon. **Open** 9am-2am Mon-Sat. Closed Aug. **Credit** MC, V. **Map** p408 H6 ❼
La Palette is the café-bar of choice for the very *beaux* Beaux-Arts students who study at the venerable institution around the corner, and young couples who steal kisses in the wonderfully preserved art deco back room decorated with illustrations. It ain't cheap – a glass of Chablis sets you back €6, a demi €4.50 – but you're paying for the prime location once frequented by such luminaries as Jim Morrison, Picasso and Ernest Hemingway.

Prescription Cocktails Club

23 rue Mazarine, 6th (01.46.34.67.73). Mᵒ Odéon. **Open** 7pm-2am Mon-Thur; 7pm-4am Fri, Sat; 8pm-2am Sun. **Credit** MC, V. **Map** p408 H6 ❽
This stylish 1930s-style speakeasy has a retro Prohibition feel but remains severely Left Bank, with crowds of well-dressed people sipping cocktails by candlelight. It's always busy and almost impossible to navigate at weekends.

Le Rostand

6 pl Edmond-Rostand, 6th (01.43.54.61.58). RER Luxembourg. **Open** 8am-midnight daily. **Credit** MC, V. **Map** p408 H8 ❾
Le Rostand has a truly wonderful view of the Jardin du Luxembourg from its classy interior, decked out with oriental paintings, a long mahogany bar and

wall-length mirrors. It's a terribly well-behaved place. Whiskies and cocktails are pricey, as is the brasserie menu, but the snack menu serves delicious omelettes and *croques* for around €8 (salad €4 extra). Perfect for a civilised drink after a stroll round the gardens.

MONTPARNASSE

Le Café Tournesol
9 rue de la Gaîté, 14th (01.43.27.65.72). M° Gaîté.
Open 8.30am-1.30am Mon-Sat; 9.30am-1.30am Sun.
Credit AmEx, MC, V. **Map** p405 G9 ⓾
The Tournesol is young, vibrant and the best of the cafés on rue de la Gaîté. There's outdoor seating in the shadow of the Tour Montparnasse, and an exposed brick interior with a soul, funk and electro soundtrack. A croque-monsieur will set you back €6, a steak €12.50, and a demi of Stella €3.

L'Entrepôt
7-9 rue Francis de Pressensé, 14th (01.45.40.07.50, www.lentrepot.fr). M° Pernéty. **Open** 9am-midnight daily. **Credit** MC, V. **Map** p405 F10 ⓿
L'Entrepôt, housed in a former warehouse, is a wonderful multitasker and has enough to keep you keen all week. There's a café where literary readings are held, a restaurant with a terrace (a godsend in the summer), and a bar on the ground floor with live music most Thursdays, Fridays, Saturdays and Mondays – mainly jazz, rap and *chanson*. There's also an arthouse cinema and exhibition space upstairs.

Le Select
99 bd du Montparnasse, 6th (01.45.48.38.24). M° Vavin. **Open** 7am-2am Mon-Thur, Sun; 7am-4am Fri, Sat. **Credit** MC, V. **Map** p405 G8 ⓿

For a decade between the wars, the junction of boulevards Raspail and du Montparnasse was where Man Ray, Cocteau and Lost Generation Americans hung out in the vast, glass-fronted cafés. Eight decades on, Le Select is the best of what have inevitably become tourist haunts. Sure, its pricey menu is big on historical detail and short on authenticity, but by and large it manages to hold on to its heyday with dignity.

THE 7TH & WESTERN PARIS

Brasserie Thoumieux
79 rue St-Dominique, 7th (01.47.05.79.00, www.thoumieux.fr). M° La Tour Maubourg.
Open noon-midnight daily. Closed 3wks Aug.
Credit AmEx, MC, V. **Map** p405 E6 ⓿
Brasserie Thoumieux is a laid-back destination for cocktails, tapas and big-screen sport. Banquettes snake around the room, and spiky Aztec-pattern lamps light up the faces of the pretty young locals who have made this place their own. The flavoured vodkas are delicious; just watch out for the treacherous, extra-high bar stools.

Le Café du Marché
38 rue Cler, 7th (01.47.05.51.27). M° Ecole Militaire. **Open** 7am-midnight Mon-Sat; 7am-5pm Sun. **Credit** MC, V. **Map** p405 D6 ⓿
This well-loved address is frequented by trendy locals, shoppers hunting down a particular type of cheese and tourists who've managed to make it this far from the Eiffel Tower. Le Café du Marché really is a hub of activity. Its *pichets* of decent house plonk always go down a treat, and mention must be made of the food – such as the huge house salad.

La Palette.

CONSUME

Shops & Services

Get ready for the ultimate spree.

Paris shopping has never been in better shape. Where else in the world can you find so many independent boutiques and specialist shops, right in the middle of some of the most picturesque areas of the city? Whether you're tasting cheeses at Alléosse, trying on clothes behind the velvet curtains of Lanvin or selecting a pair of handmade leather gloves at Maison Fabre, shopping in the French capital is a sensual pleasure based around quality, not quantity. Whereas we have window-shopping, they have window-licking (*lèche-vitrine*). And now, even the chain stores are looking pretty

fly with a slew of mainstream fashion brands – Banana Republic, Levi's, Hugo Boss, Abercrombie & Fitch and even Marks & Spencer – opening exciting new flagship stores on the Champs-Elysées, luring Parisians back to their long-neglected heartland of consumer chic.

HOW TO SHOP

Different areas of the city have different specialities. There are clusters of antiques shops in the seventh arrondissement, and second-hand and rare book outlets in the fifth; crystal and porcelain manufacturers still dot rue de Paradis in the tenth; furniture craftsmen as well as children's clothes shops inhabit rue du Fbg-St-Antoine; bikes and cameras are clustered on boulevard Beaumarchais; and the world's top jewellers can be found on place Vendôme. The historic covered passages in the second and ninth are also fun places to shop, with chic boutiques mixed in with philatelists and booksellers.

Family-run food shops have thankfully not been eroded by supermarket culture, and tend to cluster in 'market streets' such as rue des Martyrs and rue Mouffetard, as well as around the many covered and open-air food markets. Here everything from a vintage bottle of armagnac to a single praline chocolate is lovingly presented, served and wrapped. Informed discussion is still very much part of the purchasing process, and beautiful, old-style shops, unchanged for decades, add to the overall pleasure.

The concept shop trend is a central feature of Paris's shopping scene, crossing boundaries between clothes, music and product design.

The capital's concept kings have decidedly different personalities. There's cosmopolitan, metropolitan, glamorous but down-with-the-kids **Colette**; bobo I-probably-care-more-about-my-home-than-my-wardrobe **Merci**; and sophisticated, avant-garde **L'Eclaireur**. But what all three of these stores have in common is a product range that is both entertainingly diverse and seductively scarce.

General

DEPARTMENT STORES

BHV (Bazar de l'Hôtel de Ville)
52-64 rue de Rivoli, 4th (01.42.74.90.00, www.bhv.fr). M° Hôtel de Ville. **Open** 9.30am-7.30pm Mon, Tue, Thur, Fri; 9.30am-9pm Wed; 9.30am-8pm Sat. **Credit** AmEx, MC, V. **Map** p406 J6.
Homeware heaven: there's even a Bricolage Café with internet access. Upper floors have a good range of men's outdoor wear, upmarket bed linen, toys, books, household appliances – and a large space devoted to every type of storage utility.

★ Le Bon Marché
24 rue de Sèvres, 7th (01.44.39.80.00, www.bonmarche.fr). M° Sèvres Babylone. **Open** 10am-8pm Mon-Wed, Sat; 10am-9pm Thur, Fri. **Credit** AmEx, DC, MC, V. **Map** p405 G7.

The city's oldest department store, which opened in 1848, is also its most swish and user-friendly, thanks to an extensive redesign by LVMH. Luxury boutiques, Dior and Chanel among them, take pride of place on the ground floor; escalators designed by Andrée Putman take you up to the fashion floor, which has an excellent selection of global designer labels, from Lanvin to Claudie Pierlot. Designer names also abound in Balthazar, the prestigious menswear section.

▶ *For top-notch nibbles, try the adjoining Grande Epicerie food hall (01.44.39.81.00, www.lagrandeepicerie.fr, 8.30am-9pm Mon-Sat).*

Galeries Lafayette
40 bd Haussmann, 9th (01.42.82.34.56, fashion shows 01.42.82.30.25, fashion advice 01.42.82.35.50, www.galerieslafayette.com). M° Chaussée d'Antin/RER Auber. **Open** 9.30am-8pm Mon-Wed, Fri, Sat; 9.30am-9pm Thur. **Credit** AmEx, DC, MC, V. **Map** p401 H3.
The store has been undergoing a massive renovation programme of late, with the opening of Espace Luxe on the first floor, featuring luxury prêt-à-porter and accessories, and the unveiling of a vast new shoe department in the basement featuring some 150 brands. The men's fashion space on the third floor, Lafayette Homme, has natty designer corners and a 'Club' area with internet access. On the first floor, Lafayette Gourmet has exotic foods galore, plus a vast wine cellar including its own Bordeauxthèque.
▶ *Lafayette Maison over the road has five floors of home furnishings and interior design products.*
Other locations Centre Commercial Montparnasse, 22 rue du Départ, 14th (01.45.38.52.87).

Marks & Spencer
100 av des Champs-Elysées & 1 rue de Berri, 8th (www.marksandspencer.fr). M° Georges V. **Open** 10am-10pm daily. **Credit** AmEx, DC, MC, V. **Map** p400 D4.
See p198 **Check Out the Champs-Elysées.**

★ Printemps
64 bd Haussmann, 9th (01.42.82.50.00, www.printemps.com). M° Havre Caumartin/RER Auber. **Open** 9.35am-8pm Mon-Wed, Fri, Sat; 9.35am-10pm Thur. **Credit** AmEx, DC, MC, V. **Map** p401 G3.
In the magnificently appointed Printemps you'll find everything you didn't even know you wanted and English-speaking assistants to help you find it. But fashion is where it really excels; an entire floor is devoted to shoes, and the beauty department stocks more than 200 brands. In all, there are six floors of men's and women's fashion. In Printemps de la Mode, French designers sit alongside all the big international designers. The Fashion Loft offers a younger take on current trends. Along with furnishings, Printemps de la Maison stocks everything from tableware to design classics. *Photos p192.*

CONSUME

▶ *For fast refuelling, Printemps has a tearoom, sushi bar and Café Be, an Alain Ducasse bakery. Or head up to Le Déli-cieux, on the ninth floor of Printemps Maison, for a drink on the terrace with wonderful views across Paris.*

Tati
4 bd de Rochechouart, 18th (01.55.29.52.20, www.tati.fr). M° Barbès Rochechouart. **Open** 10am-7pm Mon-Fri; 9.30am-7pm Sat. **Credit** MC, V. **Map** p402 J2.
Expect to find anything from T-shirts to wedding dresses, as well as bargain children's clothes and household goods at this discount heaven. It's unbeatably cheap, but don't expect high quality.
Other locations throughout the city.

MALLS

Bercy Village
Cour St Emilion, 12th (08.25.16.60.75, www.bercyvillage.com). M° Cour St-Emilion. **Open** 11am-9pm daily. **Credit** AmEx, DC, MC, V. **Map** p407 P10.
This retail and leisure development housed in old wine warehouses is a relaxed place in which to shop. Squarely aimed at tourists and out-of-towners, the shops include Agnès b, Nature et Découvertes,

Printemps.
See p191.

The Forum des Halles is Paris's biggest and least pleasant shopping mall, although a massive facelift due to be completed in 2016 should improve matters. Extending three levels underground, it incorporates métro stations, multiplex, gym, swimming pool and numerous restaurants, and is truly labyrinthine. High-street retailers dominate: Mango, Muji, Gap, H&M, Bershka, Sephora, Yves Rocher and a flagship Fnac are all here.

La Galerie du Carrousel du Louvre
99 rue de Rivoli, 1st (01.43.16.47.10, www. carrouseldulouvre.com). M° Palais Royal Musée du Louvre. **Open** 10am-8pm daily. **Credit** AmEx, MC, V. **Map** p406 J6.
This massive underground centre – open every day of the year – is home to more than 35 shops, mostly big-name chains vying for your attention and cash. Options include an Apple Store, Swatch Store and L'Occitane en Provence.

La Vallée Village
3 cours de la Garonne, 77700 Serris (01.60.42.35.00, www.lavalleevillage.com). Eurostar/TGV Marne La Vallée-Chessy-Parc Disneyland/RER Val d'Europe. **Open** 10am-7pm daily. **Credit** AmEx, MC, V.
La Vallée Village, near Disneyland Paris, is discount shopping heaven. Its 90 stores feature all the usual suspects – Armani, Hilfiger and Burberry – as well as Agnès b, Zadig & Voltaire and Antik Batik.

Specialist

BOOKS & MAGAZINES

Gibert Joseph
26 bd St-Michel, 6th (01.44.41.88.88, www. gibertjoseph.com). M° St-Michel. **Open** 10am-8pm Mon-Sat. **Credit** MC, V. **Map** p408 J7.
Formed back in 1929, this string of bookshops is normally packed out with students.
▶ *Further up bd St-Michel (nos.30, 32 & 34) are branches specialising in stationery, CDs, DVDs and art materials.*

★ La Hune
170 bd St-Germain, 6th (01.45.48.35.85). M° St-Germain-des-Prés. **Open** 10am-11.45pm Mon-Sat; 11am-7.45pm Sun. **Credit** AmEx, MC, V. **Map** p405 G7.
This Left Bank institution boasts a global selection of art and design books, and a magnificent collection of French literature and theory. *Photo p194.*

Le Monte-en-l'air
71 rue de Ménilmontant, 20th (01.40.33.04.54). M° Ménilmontant. **Open** 10am-1pm, 2-9pm Mon-Thur, Sun; 10am-1pm, 2-11pm Fri, Sat. **Credit** AmEx, MC, V. **Map** p403 P4.

Pacific Adventure, L'Occitane, Oliviers & Co and Sephora. There are also several cafés and restaurants, a park and a multiplex cinema.

Drugstore Publicis
133 av des Champs-Elysées, 8th (01.44.43.79.00, www.publicisdrugstore.com). M° Charles de Gaulle Etoile. **Open** 8am-2am Mon-Fri; 10am-2am Sat, Sun. **Credit** MC, V. **Map** p400 D4.
A 1960s legend, Drugstore Publicis was clad with neon swirls following a renovation a few years ago; a glass-and-steel café stretches out on to the pavement. On the ground floor there's a newsagent, pharmacy, bookshop and upmarket deli full of quality olive oils and elegant biscuits. The basement is a macho take on Colette, keeping selected design items and lifestyle magazines, and replacing high fashion with fine wines and a cigar cellar.

Forum des Halles
Rue Pierre-Lescot & rue Rambuteau, 1st (01.44.76.96.56, www.forumdeshalles.com). M° Les Halles/RER Châtelet Les Halles. **Open** 10am-8pm Mon-Sat. **Map** p402 J5.

Guillaume Dumora's glorious shop is a literary hybrid, a triple-purpose space with a 'curiosity shop' for atypical and disturbing novels, a 'gallery' where different paintings and photos are hung every three weeks, and the main 'librairie', where you'll find everything from graphic novels to classic literature and modern poetry. Hang around long enough and you might even catch some live music or meet an author on a book signing.

English-language

Abbey Bookshop
29 rue de la Parcheminerie, 5th (01.46.33.16.24). M° St-Michel. **Open** 10am-7pm Mon-Sat. **No credit cards. Map** p408 J7.
Celebrating 20 years in business, the tiny Abbey Bookshop is the domain of Canadian renaissance man Brian Spence, who organises weekend hikes as well as dressing up in doublet and hose for a spot of 17th-century dancing. The tiny, narrow shop stocks old and new works, a specialised Canadian section, and highbrow subjects down the rickety staircase. Several thousand more books are tucked away in storage, and he can normally order titles for collection within two days.

Galignani
224 rue de Rivoli, 1st (01.42.60.76.07, www. galignani.com). M° Palais Royal Musée du Louvre or Tuileries. **Open** 10am-7pm Mon-Sat. **Credit** MC, V. **Map** p401 G5.

Opened in 1802, this was the first English-language bookshop in mainland Europe. Today, it stocks fine art books, French and English literature, philosophical tomes and magazines.

I Love My Blender
36 rue du Temple, 3rd (01.42.77.50.32, www. ilovemyblender.fr). M° Hôtel de Ville. **Open** 10am-7pm Tue-Sat; 10am-5pm Sun. **Credit** AmEx, MC, V. **Map** p409 K6.
Christophe Persouyre left a career in advertising to share his passion for literature: all the books he stocks were originally penned in English and here you can find their mother-tongue and translated versions, along with a delightful mish-mash of board games, postcards and assorted knick-knackery.

★ Shakespeare & Company
37 rue de la Bûcherie, 5th (01.43.25.40.93, www.shakespeareandcompany.com). M° St-Michel. **Open** 10am-11pm Mon-Fri; 11am-11pm Sat, Sun. **Credit** MC, V. **Map** p408 J7.

Bercy Village. *See p191.*

CONSUME

Unequivocably the best bookshop in Paris, the historic and ramshackle Shakespeare & Company is always packed with expat and tourist book-lovers. There is a large second-hand section, antiquarian books next door, and just about anything you could ask for new.

Village Voice

6 rue Princesse, 6th (01.46.33.36.47, www.village voicebookshop.com). Mº Mabillon. **Open** 2-7.30pm Mon; 10am-7.30pm Tue-Sat; noon-6pm Sun. **Credit** AmEx, DC, MC, V. **Map** p405 H7.
New fiction, non-fiction and literary magazines in English, plus literary events and poetry readings.

WH Smith

248 rue de Rivoli, 1st (01.44.77.88.99, www. whsmith.fr). Mº Concorde. **Open** 9am-7pm Mon-Sat; 12.30-7pm Sun. **Credit** AmEx, MC, V. **Map** p401 G5.
With 70,000 English-language titles and extensive magazine shelves, this is a home from home for Brits craving a fix of their native periodicals; the first floor has books, DVDs and audiobooks.

CHILDREN
Fashion

Children's fashion is clustered on rue Bréa (6th), rue Vavin (6th) and rue du Fbg-St-Antoine (12th). **Monoprix** (www.monoprix.fr) is a good source

La Hune. *See p192.*

of inexpensive children's clothes, with some branches stocking Petit Bateau basics. For chic at a snip, try the **Bonpoint** (42 rue de l'Université, 7th, 01.40.20.10.55) stock shop; it may be last season's stuff, but your little five-year-old is never going to know.

Bonton

82 rue de Grenelle, 7th (01.44.39.09.20, www. bonton.fr). Mº Rue du Bac. **Open** 10am-7pm Mon-Sat. Closed 2wks Aug. **Credit** AmEx, MC, V. **Map** p405 F6.
At this concept store for kids and trendy parents, T-shirts and trousers come in rainbow colours, and at pretty steep prices too. Furniture and accessories are also available, as is a children's hairdresser.
Other location 5 bd des Filles du Calvaire, 3rd (01.42.72.34.69).
▶ *The Bonton Bazar store (122 rue du Bac, 7th, 01.42.22.77.69) offers cute kids' homeware for bedroom, bathroom, kitchen and 'library'.*

★ Finger in the Nose

60 rue Saintonge, 3rd (01.42.71.43.40, www.fingerinthenose.com). Mº St-Sébastien Froissart. **Open** 11am-7pm Tue-Sat. **Credit** AmEx, MC, V. **Map** p409 L5.
As the name suggests, there is nothing twee about the kidswear from this Norwegian designer. In this Marais boutique blackboard walls with chalk slogans and drawings set off tough rebel urban wear for six- to 16-year-olds, including bright red Puttas, mod check jumpers, rock'n'roll T-shirts, skinny jeans and shades.

Jacadi

116 rue d'Alésia, 14th (01.40.44.51.87, www. jacadi.fr). Mº Alésia. **Open** 11am-7pm Mon; 10am-7pm Tue-Sat. **Credit** MC, V. **Map** p405 E10.
Jacadi's well-made clothes for babies and children – pleated skirts, smocked dresses, dungarees and Fair Isle knits – are a hit with well-to-do parents. The rue d'Alésia store is the largest.
Other locations throughout the city.

★ Du Pareil au Même

120-122 rue du Fbg-St-Antoine, 12th (01.43.44.67.46, www.dpam.com). Mº Ledru-Rollin. **Open** 10am-7pm Mon-Sat. **Credit** AmEx, MC, V. **Map** p407 N7.
Bright, cleverly designed and well made basics for children aged three months to 14 years, at refreshingly low prices. The Bébé branch, with fashionable accessories and clothing for kids up to two years, is a good source of gifts.
Other locations throughout the city.

Petit Bateau

26 rue Vavin, 6th (01.55.42.02.53, www.petit-bateau.com). Mº Vavin. **Open** 10am-7pm Mon-Sat. **Credit** AmEx, MC, V. **Map** p405 G8.

Shakespeare & Company. *See p193.*

Widely renowned for its comfortable, well-made cotton T-shirts, vests and other separates, Petit Bateau carries an equally coveted teen range.
Other locations throughout the city.

★ Six Pieds Trois Pouces

223 bd St-Germain, 7th (01.45.44.03.72, www.sixpiedstroispouces.com). M° Solférino. **Open** 10.30am-7pm Mon-Fri; 10am-7pm Sat. **Credit** AmEx, DC, MC, V. **Map** p405 F6.
The excellent array of children's and teens' shoes at Six Pieds Trois Pouces runs from Start-rite and Aster to Timberland and New Balance, alongside the shop's own brand.
Other locations 85 rue de Longchamp, 16th (01.45.53.64.21); 78 av de Wagram, 17th (01.46.22.81.64).

Zef

15 rue Debelleyme, 3rd (01.42.76.09.65, www. zef.eu). M° St-Sébastien Froissart. **Open** 10.30am-7pm Mon-Sat; 2-7pm Sun. **Credit** AmEx, DC, MC, V. **Map** p409 L5.
Zef's designer is the daughter of fashion photographer Paolo Roversi. The trendy children's separates have a classic Italian look, in soft muted colours with adorable little details, such as elbow patches on the jackets. Boots, sheepskin gilets and hats are part of the look.
Other locations throughout the city.

Toys & books

Traditional toy shops abound; department stores (*see p190*) go overboard at Christmas. For a selection of children's books in English, try **WH Smith** (*see p194*).

Fnac Junior

19 rue Vavin, 6th (08.92.35.06.66, www.eveil etjeux.com). M° Vavin. **Open** 10am-7.30pm Mon-Sat. **Credit** AmEx, MC, V. **Map** p405 G8.
Fnac Junior stocks a wide range of books, toys, DVDs, CDs and CD-Roms for under-12s. Storytelling and other activities (Wed, Sat) take place for three-year-olds and up.
Other locations throughout the city.

★ Au Nain Bleu

5 bd Malesherbes, 8th (01.42.65.20.00, www. aunainbleu.com). M° Madeleine. **Open** 10am-7pm Mon-Sat. **Credit** AmEx, MC, V. **Map** p401 F4.
The city's best toy shop, decorated like a circus tent, draws gasps of wonder from children. Wooden doll's houses, pirate ships and gorgeous dolls are made to last more than one generation. As this guide went to press, the shop was moving to new premises. Check the website for details.

Village Joué Club

3-5 bd des Italiens, 2nd (01.53.45.41.41, www.joueclub.fr). M° Richelieu Drouot. **Open** 10am-8pm Mon-Sat. **Credit** AmEx, MC, V. **Map** p402 H4.
Village Joué Club, the largest toy store in Paris, is spread out in and around passage des Princes.

FASHION

All the world's big-name designers have their own-label stores in Paris. In addition to international fashion juggernauts Mango, H&M and Zara, the high street has its fair share of Gallic cheapies: think **Etam**, Jennyfer and Pimkie. The highest density is in the

Forum des Halles (*see p192*), on nearby rue de Rivoli, between the métro stations of Châtelet and Louvre Rivoli, and around Galeries Lafayette and Printemps.

Designer

Azzedine Alaïa
7 rue de Moussy, 4th (01.42.72.30.69). M° Hôtel de Ville. **Open** 10am-7pm Mon-Sat. **Credit** AmEx, MC, V. **Map** p409 K6.
Ringing the doorbell gains you entry to the factory-style showroom in the same building as Alaïa's headquarters and apartment, where the Tunisian creator continues to astound with his originality. Stunning haute couture creations are in the back room, and sexy shoes bordering on fetish are scattered among the mannequins and rails.

★ Balenciaga
10 av George V, 8th (01.47.20.21.11, www.balenciaga.com). M° Alma Marceau or George V. **Open** 10am-7pm Mon-Sat. **Credit** AmEx, DC, MC, V. **Map** p400 D5.
With Nicolas Ghesquière at the helm, the Spanish fashion house is ahead of Japanese and Belgian designers in the hip stakes. Floating fabrics contrast with dramatic cuts, producing a sophisticated urban style that the fashion *haut monde* can't wait to slip into. Bags and shoes are also available.

Balmain
44 rue François 1er, 8th (01.47.20.57.58, www.balmain.com). M° George V. **Open** 10.30am-7pm Mon-Sat. **Credit** AmEx, DC, MC, V. **Map** p400 D4.
A large portrait of the late Pierre Balmain surveys the scene at his eponymous shop in the middle of the Triangle d'Or. What would he have made of the clothes around him? Long gone are the afternoon dresses with perfectly positioned waists, full skirts and trapezoidal necklines. While the clothes are still astonishingly expensive and exquisitely finished, the racks are these days lined with bondage trousers, studded jackets and animal print drainpipes. There hasn't been such a good display of grungy, punk glamour since London's Kensington Market closed its doors.

Carlos Miele
380 rue St-Honoré, 1st (01.42.97.53.66, www.carlosmiele.com.br). M° Concorde. **Open** 10am-7pm Mon-Sat. **Credit** AmEx, MC, V. **Map** p402 H5.
The Brazilian designer favoured by the likes of Sandra Bullock, Heidi Klum and J Lo brings luxury with a conscience to the rarefied surroundings of rue St-Honoré. He works with several co-operatives in *favelas* and with Amazonian Indians, honing such traditional techniques as crochet, knotting, embroidery and featherwork.

★ Chanel
31 rue Cambon, 1st (01.42.86.28.00, www.chanel.com). M° Concorde or Madeleine. **Open** 10am-7pm Mon-Sat. **Credit** AmEx, DC, MC, V. **Map** p401 G4.
Fashion legend Chanel has managed to stay relevant, thanks to Karl Lagerfeld. Coco opened her first boutique in this street, at no.21, in 1910, and the tradition continues in this elegant interior. Lagerfeld has been designing for Chanel since 1983, and keeps on revamping the classics – the little black dress and the Chanel suit – with great success.
Other locations 42 av Montaigne, 8th (01.47.23.74.12); 25 rue Royale, 8th (01.44.51.92.93); 21 rue du Fbg-St-Honoré, 8th (01.53.05.98.95).

Comme des Garçons
54 rue du Fbg-St-Honoré, 8th (01.53.30.27.27, www.comme-des-garcons.com). M° Concorde or Madeleine. **Open** 11am-7pm Mon-Sat. **Credit** AmEx, DC, MC, V. **Map** p401 F4.
Rei Kawakubo's design ideas and revolutionary mix of materials have heavily influenced fashions of the past two decades, and are showcased in this fibreglass store.
▶ *Comme des Garçons Parfums (23 pl du Marché-St-Honoré, 1st, 01.47.03.15.03) provides a futuristic setting for the brand's fragrances.*

Dior
26-30 av Montaigne, 8th (01.40.73.73.73, www.dior.com). M° Franklin D. Roosevelt. **Open** 10am-7pm Mon-Sat. **Credit** AmEx, DC, MC, V. **Map** p400 D5.
The Dior universe is here on avenue Montaigne, from the main prêt-à-porter store and jewellery, menswear and eyewear to Baby Dior.
Other locations throughout the city.

Givenchy
28 rue du Fbg-St-Honoré, 8th (01.42.68.31.00, www.givenchy.com). M° Madeleine or Concorde. **Open** 10am-7pm Mon-Sat. **Credit** AmEx, DC, MC, V. **Map** p401 F4.
A few years ago, Givenchy opened this handsome flagship store for men's and women's prêt-à-porter and accessories. It incorporates surreal rooms within rooms – cut-out boxes lined with white, black or mahogany panelling – providing an art gallery setting for Givenchy's cutting-edge, sculptural and monochrome designs.

Hermès
17 rue de Sèvres, 6th (01.42.22.80.83, www.hermes.com). M° Sèvres Babylone. **Open** 10.30am-7pm Mon-Sat. **Credit** AmEx, DC, MC, V. **Map** p405 G7.
If you thought that Hermès was about horsey scarves and little else, a visit to the rue de Sèvres shop should dispel the equestrian rumours forever. Designed by Denis Montel, the concept store is set

CONSUME

Hermès.

in the Hôtel Lutetia's former indoor pool. The renovations have produced one of the best-looking retail spaces on the Left Bank. While the trademark scarves and ties are all present and correct, the three-floor store also focuses strongly on homewares, from wallpaper and carpets to sumptuous reproductions of 1930s-era furniture by renowned designer Jean-Michel Frank.

Hervé Léger
24 rue Cambon, 1st (01.42.60.02.00, www. herveleger.com). M° Concorde. **Open** 10am-7pm Mon-Sat. **Credit** AmEx, DC, MC, V. **Map** p401 G4.
A couple of decades ago, Hervé Léger's silhouette-cinching bandage dresses were as evocative of the era as supermodels Linda, Christy, Naomi and Cindy. But somewhere in the mid-'90s women lost their love of Lycra, longing for the more conventional figure-flattering techniques of bias cut and tailoring. In the past few seasons, however, updated reinterpretations of Léger's style, by the likes of Christopher Kane and Marios Schwab, have been nothing short of a fashion phenomenon. Less modified versions, sold by the Léger label itself (now owned and designed by Max Azria of BCBG fame), have been less critically acclaimed, but celebrities just adore them.

★ Isabel Marant
16 rue de Charonne, 11th (01.49.29.71.55, www.isabelmarant.tm.fr). M° Ledru-Rollin. **Open** 10.30am-7.30pm Mon-Sat. **Credit** AmEx, MC, V. **Map** p407 M7.
Isabel Marant's style is easily recognisable in her ethno-babe brocades, blanket-like coats and decorated sweaters. It's a firm favourite among Paris's young trendies.
Other locations 47 rue Saintonge, 3rd (01.42.78.19.24); 1 rue Jacob, 6th (01.43.26.04.12).

★ Jay Ahr
2-4 rue du 29 Juillet, 1st (01.42.96.95.23, www.jayahr.com). M° Tuileries. **Open** 10am-7pm Mon-Fri; 11am-7pm Sat. **Credit** AmEx, MC, V. **Map** p401 G5.
Former jewellery designer Jonathan Riss opened this shop as a fashion stylist in 2004, and soon struck gold with simple, figure-flaunting, 1960s-inspired dresses. Think plunging necklines and Bianca Jagger in her heyday, with Ali MacGraw and Anita Pallenberg in the mix. There are no price tags on the dresses, so you have to ask; they start at around €500.

Jean-Paul Gaultier
6 rue Vivienne, 2nd (01.42.86.05.05, www.jean paulgaultier.com). M° Bourse. **Open** 11am-7pm daily. **Credit** AmEx, DC, MC, V. **Map** p402 H4.
Having celebrated his 30th year in the fashion business, Gaultier is still going strong. His boudoir boutique with its peach taffeta walls stocks men's and women's ready-to-wear and the reasonably priced JPG Jeans lines.
Other locations 44 av George V, 8th (01.44.43.00.44).
▶ *The haute couture department is strictly by appointment only, and is located above the store.*

Kenzo
60-62 rue de Rennes, 6th (01.45.44.27.88, www.kenzo.com). M° St-Sulpice. **Open** 11am-7.30pm Mon; 11.30am-7.30pm Tue-Sat. **Credit** AmEx, DC, MC, V. **Map** p402 J6.
Kenzo has long been a friend of Paris, having dressed the city itself in its various extravagant publicity campaigns. The flagship store has three floors of men's and women's fashion, and is crowned with the Bulle Kenzo spa and Philippe Starck-designed Kong restaurant on the fifth floor.
Other locations throughout the city.

CONSUME

Check Out the Champs-Elysées

The capital's most famous thoroughfare is undergoing a retail revolution.

Banana Republic.

In 1969, hoary French crooner Joe Dassin released 'Les Champs-Elysées', a perfect piece of cheesy French *chanson* with the lyrics: 'In the sunshine, in the rain, in the dark or in the day, all you need's on the Champs-Elysées'. The song captured the role of the avenue at the time as one of the most fashionable and eclectic streets in Paris. But during the '90s, the 'Champs' lost its magic, becoming smothered in offices, car showrooms, overpriced eateries, run-of-the-mill shops and fume-pumping traffic jams. Novelty megastores Fnac and Virgin failed to overcome its new *déclassé* status, leaving the formerly glamorous avenue to the mercy of tourists and businessmen.

Since 2011, however, things have been looking up. The congestion, the tourists, the showrooms and the daylight robbery restaurants are all still there, of course. But several mainstream fashion brands have chosen to locate exciting new flagship stores on the Champs that promise unique shopping experiences. We've put together a guide to help you stay ahead of the curve.

BANANA REPUBLIC
See p205.
The American megabrand's grown-up preppy style has finally arrived in Paris. Its art deco-style Champs-Elysées flagship features a multitude of mini-boutiques within the larger store. Themed sections include Weekend (casual separates), the eco-friendly Heritage collection and the higher-end Monogram range. One big draw is the free personal shopping service, with no requirement to buy. Reserve in advance, and Magali or Lee (who head the service) will take you round the shop to help tailor your look. This also gives you access to your own rather lovely 1930s-style dressing room away from the throng. For extra sparkle, they'll even serve you champagne.

ABERCROMBIE & FITCH
See p204.
The US brand's flagship store has been causing a stir on the Champs since it opened in 2011, with banging tunes and topless male models standing in the doorway at all times. Like its sister stores in London and New York, the box-hedged garden, dimmed lighting and lingering scent of aftershave make the place feel more like a club than a shop. There are even bouncers ready to tell you off should you dare whip out your camera for a photo op, which is a shame as the decor is stunning, with beautifully painted 1930s-style frescoes depicting male deities in hunting scenes, athletic poses and boxing rings. Things get even sillier with the Barbie-and-Ken shop assistants. Still, whether you're into A&F's preppy ranges or not, the shop is well worth a detour – if only to admire the frescoes.

MARKS & SPENCER
See p191.
People queuing in the rain for M&S? Has the world gone mad? As odd as it may seem to Brits, queuing outside has been the norm since Marks opened its new Paris store in November 2011. Paradoxically, while most French people love nothing more than criticising British food, give them an M&S chicken tikka sarnie or treacle pudding and the superlatives flow like wine from a barrel. They're also secret admirers of British fashion, and M&S offers cuts, colours and fabric not readily available in France. As the queues suggest, this address is perhaps too small. But a vast 7,000sq m store was scheduled to open in Levallois-Perret before the end of 2012.

HUGO BOSS
See p206.
Hugo Boss's new flagship store is all straight lines and steely greys – rather like the signature Boss suits worn by the sales assistants. It feels like businessman territory here, with minimalist decor,

Levi's.

M&S.

wooden sculpture and big screens flashing images of Hugo Boss catwalk shows – inspiration for your shopping as you browse the minimalist rows of the brand's smart designer garb. Boss has other outlets dotted around town, but this is its biggest store and perhaps the most relaxing, thanks to its airy proportions. Personal shoppers are on hand too.

LEVI'S
See p206.
Levi's has always had good marketing strategies, so it's no surprise that the chain is using music and art to draw the crowds into its new flagship store on the Champs-Elysées. The campaign, which goes by the name of 'Vive les Friends', offers shoppers an ever-changing multi-disciplinary in-shop experience, courtesy of different French and American artists and musicians (Ed Banger's Pedro Winter and LCD Soundsystem's James Murphy kick-started the campaign in May 2012). It makes shopping wholly more entertaining and gives folk a reason to keep coming back, not only to discover the new artworks but also to see the limited-edition clothes – each Franco-American duo featured creates a series of funky, limited-edition T-shirts and personalised Levi's 1967 Trucker's jackets. If it's just a plain pair of jeans your after, head downstairs to denim heaven, where the walls are filled with perfectly folded 501s, skinnys and bootleg models.

CONSUME

CONSUME

Lanvin

22 rue du Fbg St-Honoré, 8th (01.44.71.31.73, www.lanvin.com). M° Concorde or Madeleine. **Open** 10.30am-7pm daily. **Credit** AmEx, DC, MC, V. **Map** p401 F4.

The couture house that began in the 1920s with Jeanne Lanvin has been reinvented by the talented and indefatigable Albert Elbaz. In October 2007, he unveiled this, the revamped showroom that set new aesthetic standards for luxury fashion retailing. Lanvin has an exhibition room devoted to her in the Musée des Arts Décoratifs, and this apartment-boutique comes close, incorporating original furniture from the Lanvin archive that has been restored. All this would be nothing, of course, if the clothes themselves were not exquisite.

Lefranc.ferrant

22 rue de l'Echaudé, 6th (01.44.07.37.96, www.lefranc-ferrant.fr). M° St-Germain-des-Prés. **Open** 11am-7pm Tue-Sat and by appointment. **Credit** AmEx, MC, V. **Map** p408 H7.

The opening of this Left Bank boutique was eagerly awaited by keen followers of the talented Paris duo Béatrice Ferrant and Mario Lefranc. Their trademark is a surreal approach to tailoring, as in a strapless yellow evening gown made like a pair of men's trousers – complete with flies. Prices are in the €1,000 range and they love to undertake bespoke commissions.

★ Louis Vuitton

101 av des Champs-Elysées, 8th (01.53.57.52.00, www.vuitton.com). M° George V. **Open** 10am-8pm Mon-Sat; 11am-7pm Sun. **Credit** AmEx, DC, MC, V. **Map** p400 D4.

The 'Promenade' flagship sets the tone for Vuitton's global image, from the 'bag bar', bookstore and jewellery department to the women's and men's ready-to-wear. Contemporary art, including by Tim White Sobieski and a pitch-black elevator by Olafur Eliasson complete the picture. Accessed by lift, the Espace Vuitton hosts temporary art exhibits – but the star of the show is the view over Paris.
Other locations 6 pl St-Germain-des-Prés, 6th (01.45.49.62.32); 22 av Montaigne, 8th (01.45.62.47.00).

Marc Jacobs

34 galerie de Montpensier, 1st (01.55.35.02.60, www.marcjacobs.com). M° Palais Royal Musée du Louvre. **Open** 11am-7pm Mon-Sat. **Credit** AmEx, DC, MC, V. **Map** p402 H5.

By choosing the galleries of the Palais-Royal for his first signature boutique in Europe, Marc Jacobs brought new life – and an influx of fashionistas – to these elegant cloisters. Stocking womenswear, menswear, accessories and shoes, the boutique has become a place of pilgrimage for the designer's legion of admirers, who snap up his downtown New York style.

Sonia Rykiel.

Martin Grant

10 rue Charlot, 3rd (01.42.71.39.49, www.martin grantparis.com). M° Temple. **Open** 10am-6pm Mon-Fri. Closed 3wks Aug. **Credit** MC, V. **Map** p406 K6.

This high-end shop is tucked away in a second-floor Marais apartment. If you're a stickler for steady cuts, pure textiles and unfussy designs, Australian Martin Grant's interpretation of couture is for you.

Martin Margiela

23 & 25bis rue de Montpensier, 1st (womenswear 01.40.15.07.55, menswear 01.40.15.06.44, www.maisonmartinmargiela.com). M° Palais Royal Musée du Louvre. **Open** 11am-7pm Mon-Sat. **Credit** AmEx, DC, MC, V. **Map** p402 H5.

The original Paris outlet for the JD Salinger of fashion is a pristine, white, unlabelled space. His collection for women (Line 1) has a blank label but is recognisable by its external white stitching. You'll also find Line 6 (women's basics) and Line 10 (menswear), plus a range of accessories for men and women and shoes.
Other locations 13 rue de Grenelle, 7th (01.45.49.06.68).

Miu Miu

219 rue St-Honoré, 1st (01.58.62.53.20, www.miumiu.com). M° Tuileries. **Open** 10.30am-7.30pm Mon-Sat. **Credit** AmEx, DC, MC, V. **Map** p401 G5.

Prada's younger sister has this rue St-Honoré store as its main boutique, selling its quirky women's fashions, shoes and bags.

★ Paul & Joe

*64 rue des Sts-Pères, 7th (01.42.22.47.01,
www.paulandjoe.com). Mº Rue du Bac or St-
Germain-des-Prés.* **Open** 10am-7pm Mon-Sat.
Credit AmEx, DC, MC, V. **Map** p405 G6.
International fashionistas have taken a real shine
to Sophie Albou's retro-styled creations. The latest
collection dresses leggy young things in a superb
range of winter shorts, colourful minidresses and
voluminous trousers, and their intellectual para-
mours in slouchy woollens, tailored jackets and
chunky boots.
Other locations *Men* 56 rue Vieille-du-Temple,
3rd (01.42.72.42.06); 62 rue des Sts-Pères, 7th
(01.42.22.98.98). *Women* 2 av Montaigne, 8th
(01.47.20.57.50); 123 rue de la Pompe, 16th
(01.45.53.01.08).

Paule Ka

*223 rue St-Honoré, 1st (01.42.97.57.06, www.
pauleka.com). Mº Tuileries.* **Open** 10.30am-7pm
daily. **Credit** AmEx, DC, MC, V. **Map** p401 G4.
Serge Cajfinger's '60s couture-influenced collections
continue to gather a loyal following. With the opening of his rue St-Honoré boutique, he now has a foot
in each of the city's fashion districts.
Other locations 20 rue Malher, 4th
(01.40.29.96.03); 192 bd St-Germain, 6th
(01.45.44.92.60); 45 rue François 1er, 8th
(01.47.20.76.10).

Paul Smith

*3 rue du Fbg-St-Honoré, 8th (01.42.68.27.10,
www.paulsmith.co.uk). Mº Concorde.* **Open**
10.30am-7pm Mon-Sat. **Credit** AmEx, DC,
MC, V. **Map** p401 F4.
A 'so British' atmosphere is cultivated with '40s
wallpaper, antiques, old books and bric-a-brac, much
of it for sale along with the colourful shirts and
knitwear in which Smith excels. Collections for men,
women and children, along with eyewear and accessories, are all gathered in this elegant apartment.
Other locations 70 rue de Grenelle, 6th
(01.42.22.66.67); 22 bd Raspail, 7th (01.53.63.08.74).

Prada

*10 av Montaigne, 8th (01.53.23.99.40, www.
prada.com). Mº Alma Marceau.* **Open** 10am-7pm
daily. **Credit** AmEx, DC, MC, V. **Map** p400 D5.
Miuccia Prada's elegant stores pull in fashionistas
of all ages. Handbags of choice are complemented
by the coveted ready-to-wear range.
Other locations 5 rue de Grenelle, 6th
(01.45.48.53.14); 6 rue du Fbg-St-Honoré, 8th
(01.58.18.63.30).

Rick Owens

*130 galerie de Valois, 1st (01.40.20.42.52,
www.owenscorp.com). Mº Palais Royal Musée du
Louvre.* **Open** 10.30am-7pm Mon-Fri; 11am-7pm
Sat. **Credit** AmEx, DC, MC, V. **Map** p402 H5.

The Los Angeles designer and rock-star favourite
brings his glamour-meets-grunge style to the Palais-
Royal, with a selection of hoods, zips and asymmet-
rical wrappings for men and women. It's not
the place for animal lovers – the upstairs has a
dedicated mink section.

Rue du Mail

*5 rue du Mail, 2nd (01.42.60.19.20, www.rue
dumail.com). Mº Bourse.* **Open** by appointment
only. **Credit** AmEx, MC, V. **Map** p402 J4.
Martine Sitbon's sexy collection is a hit with Cate
Blanchett, Sofia Coppola, Scarlett Johansson et al.
Swooping V necklines, flirty hemlines, black satin
and fruity chiffons define the look.

★ Sonia Rykiel

*175 bd St-Germain, 6th (01.49.54.60.60,
www.soniarykiel.com). Mº St-Germain-des-Prés
or Sèvres Babylone.* **Open** 10.30am-7pm Mon-
Sat. **Credit** AmEx, DC, MC, V. **Map** p405 G6.
The queen of St-Germain celebrated the 40th birthday of her flagship store with a glamorous black
and smoked glass refit perfect for narcissists: tons
of mirrors reflect the gorgeous flowing gowns.
Menswear is just across the street, and two newer
boutiques stock the younger, more affordable Sonia
by Sonia Rykiel range (61 rue des Sts-Pères,
6th, 01.49.54.61.00) and kids' togs (4 rue de Grenelle,
6th, 01.49.54.61.10).
► *For something on the wild side, the main shop
also stocks a range of designer sex toys.*
Other locations throughout the city.

Stella McCartney

*114-121 galerie du Valois, Jardin du Palais-
Royal, 1st (01.47.03.03.80, www.stellamccartney.
com). Mº Palais Royal Musée du Louvre.* **Open**
10.30am-7pm Mon-Sat. **Credit** AmEx, DC, MC, V.
Map p402 H5.
McCartney is crazy about the 'clash of history, fashion and contemporary art' at the Palais-Royal, where
she opened her sumptuous boutique overlooking
the gardens. Thick carpets, maplewood and metal
sculptures create a rarefied setting for women's prêt-
à-porter, bags, shoes, sunglasses, lingerie, perfume
and skincare.

Yohji Yamamoto

*25 rue du Louvre, 1st (01.42.21.42.93, www.yohji
yamamoto.co.jp). Mº Les Halles or Sentier.* **Open**
10.30am-7pm Mon-Sat. **Credit** AmEx, DC, MC, V.
Map p405 G7.
One of the few true pioneers working in fashion
today, Yamamoto is a master of cut and finish, both
strongly inspired by the kimono and traditional
Tibetan costume. His dexterity with form makes for
unique shapes and styles, largely black. But when
he does colour, it's a blast of brilliance.
Other location 4 rue Cambon, 1st
(01.40.20.00.71).

CONSUME

Yves Saint Laurent

*6 pl St-Sulpice, 6th (01.43.29.43.00, www.ysl.
com). M° St-Sulpice.* **Open** 11am-7pm Mon;
10.30am-7pm Tue-Sat. **Credit** AmEx, DC,
MC, V. **Map** p408 H7.

The memory of the founding designer, who died in
2008, lives on in this elegant boutique, which was
splendidly refitted in red in the same year.

Other locations *Men* 32 rue du Fbg-St-Honoré,
8th (01.53.05.80.80). *Women* 38 rue du Fbg-St-
Honoré, 8th (01.42.65.74.59). *Accessories* 9 rue
de Grenelle, 7th (01.45.44.39.01).

Boutique & concept

★ AB33

*33 rue Charlot, 3rd (01.42.71.02.82). M° Filles du
Calvaire.* **Open** 10.30am-7.30pm Tue-Sat; 11am-
7pm Sun. **Credit** AmEx, MC, V. **Map** p409 L5.

Delicate in summer, cosy in winter, the pretty,
unstructured clothes in AB33 may not make the
wish list of any sultry, groomed Parisienne, but
would be perfect for her up-from-the-country Bardot-
esque cousin. Owner Agathe Buchotte sells Forte,
Forte, Kristina Ti and Philip Lim.

Anikalena Skärström

*16 rue du Pont aux Choux, 3rd (01.44.59.32.85,
www.anikalena.com). M° St-Sébastien Froissart.*
Open 10am-7pm Mon-Fri; noon-7pm Sat. Closed
2wks Aug. **Credit** AmEx, MC, V. **Map** p402 J2.

Clean lines and streamlining are the guiding aesthetic for Anikalena Skärström's collections of
sporty, sexy day and evening dresses and separates,
with the occasional wow piece like the grass-green
suede coat a few seasons ago.

April 77

*49 rue de Saintonge, 3rd (01.40.29.07.30, www.
april77.fr). M° Filles du Calvaire.* **Open** 11am-
7.30pm Mon-Sat. **Credit** MC, V. **Map** p402 J2.

The cult skinny jeans brand has acquired its own
boutique, designed by Steven Thomas, to show off
a collection inspired by the mid-'80s music scene.

★ Colette

*213 rue St-Honoré, 1st (01.55.35.33.90,
www.colette.fr). M° Pyramides or Tuileries.*
Open 11am-7pm Mon-Sat. **Credit** AmEx,
DC, MC, V. **Map** p401 G4.

The renowned and much-imitated one-stop concept
and lifestyle store features a highly eclectic selection
of must-have accessories, fashion, sneakers, books,
media, shiny new gadgets, and hair and beauty
brands själ, Kiehl's and uslu airlines, all in a swanky
space. Expect to find Zippo lighters a few feet away
from Smythson diaries, a few feet away from
Ladurée macaroons, all one flight of stairs away
from Alexander Wang and Valentino.

★ L'Eclaireur

*40 rue de Sévigné, 4th (01.48.87.10.22,
www.leclaireur.com). M° St-Paul.* **Open** 11am-7pm
Mon-Sat. **Credit** AmEx, DC, MC, V. **Map** p409 L6.

Housed in a dandified warehouse, L'Eclaireur
stocks designs by the likes of Comme des Garçons,
Martin Margiela, Dries van Noten, Carpe Diem and
Junya Watanabe. Among its exclusive finds, check
out smocks by Finnish designer Jasmin Santanen.
At the secretive rue Hérold branch you have to
ring the doorbell to enter. A space in rue Boissy
d'Anglas, near Concorde, sells chic fashions for
men and women. *Photos p204.*

Colette.

► *Men are catered for separately at L'Eclaireur Homme (12 rue Malher, 4th, 01.44.54.22.11).* **Other locations** 7 rue Hérold, 1st (01.40.41.09.89); 26 av des Champs-Elysées, 8th (01.45.62.12.32); 10 rue Boissy d'Anglas, 8th (01.53.43.03.70); 39 av Hoche, 8th (no phone).

Galerie Simone

77 rue Charlot, 4th (www.galerie-simone.com). M° Filles du Calvaire or Temple. **Open** noon-7.30pm daily. **Credit** AmEx, DC, MC, V. **Map** p409 L5.
Simone Gaubatz sources and cultivates talented young designers from around the world, displaying their most eye-catching creations on mannequins in this gallery-style space.

Jack Henry

25 rue Charlot, 3rd (www.jackhenry.jp). M° Filles du Calvaire. **Open** 11am-7.30pm Tue-Sun. **Credit** AmEx, MC, V. **Map** p409 L5.
The work of this Paris-trained American designer has real intellectual heft to it, but you only have to touch the silky soft cotton and wool jersey from Japan to want his finely crafted, beautifully conceived tunics, skirts and jackets. Luxurious leather bags and jewellery from designers including Théodora Gabrielli, alias Dorothée, who patiently creates new pieces while serving in the shop, are also on display.

Joseph

147 bd St-Germain, 6th (01.55.42.77.55, www.joseph.co.uk). M° St-Germain-des-Prés. **Open** 10am-7pm Mon-Sat. **Credit** AmEx, DC, MC, V. **Map** p405 G6.
Taking a cue from its London store, Joseph's multibrand shop stocks pieces by the likes of Balmain and Lanvin, as well as accessories by Bijoux de Sophie and handbags by Jérôme Dreyfuss.
Other locations throughout the city.

Kitsuné

52 rue de Richelieu, 1st (01.42.60.34.28, www.kitsune.fr). M° Palais Royal Musée du Louvre or Pyramides. **Open** 11am-7.30pm Mon-Sat. **Credit** AmEx, MC, V. **Map** p402 H4.
The London/Paris style collective now has its own boutique, which offers the entire catalogue of music compilations, as well as branded clothing that takes a back-to-basics approach using quality producers. You'll find Scottish cashmere, Japanese jeans and Italian shirts, together with items made in collaboration with Pierre Hardy, Scheisser underwear and James Heeley.

Kokon To Zai

48 rue Tiquetonne, 2nd (01.42.36.92.41, www.kokontozai.co.uk). M° Etienne Marcel. **Open** 11.30am-7.30pm Mon-Sat. **Credit** AmEx, DC, MC, V. **Map** p402 J5.

Always a spot-on spotter of the latest creations, this tiny style emporium is sister to the Kokon To Zai in London. The neon-lit club feel of the mirrored interior matches the dark glamour of the designs. Unique pieces straight off the catwalk share space with creations by Marjan Pejoski, Noki, Raf Simons, Ziad Ghanem and new Norwegian designers.

LE66

66 av des Champs-Elysées, 8th (01.53.53.33.80, http://le66paris.blogspot.com). M° George V. **Open** 11.30am-8.30pm Mon-Fri; 11.30am-9pm Sat; 1-8pm Sun. **Credit** AmEx, DC, MC, V. **Map** p400 D4.
This fashion concept store is youthful and accessible, with an ever-changing selection of hip brands including Puma Black Label. Assistants, who are also the buyers and designers, make for a motivated team. The Champs-Elysées store takes the form of three transparent modules, the first a book and magazine store run by Black Book of the Palais de Tokyo, and the second two devoted to fashion. It even has its own vintage store, in collaboration with Come On Eline and Kiliwatch. *Photo p205.*

Marc by Marc Jacobs

19 pl du Marché-St-Honoré, 1st (01.40.20.11.30, www.marcjacobs.com). M° Tuileries. **Open** 11am-7pm Mon-Sat. **Credit** AmEx, DC, MC, V. **Map** p401 G4.
The new store for Jacobs' casual, punky line has fashionistas clustering like bees round a honeypot, not least for the fabulously inexpensive accessories that make great gifts. A skateboard table and giant pedalo in the form of a swan are the centrepieces of the store, which stocks men's and women's prêt-à-porter, shoes and special editions.

Margo Milin

4 rue Malher, 4th (06.61.77.14.76, www.margo milin.com). M° St-Paul. **Open** noon-7.30pm Tue-Sat; 2-6.30pm Sun. **No credit cards.** **Map** p409 L6.
Looking like a model herself, St Martin's graduate Marguerite Milin studied theatrical design and produces kimono-influenced wraparound jumpers and party dresses that play with a contrast of textures and pattern versus plain. A fun, girly atmosphere is always found in the boutique.

★ Merci

111 bd Beaumarchais, 3rd (01.42.77.00.33, www.merci-merci.com). M° St-Sébastien Froissart. **Open** 10am-7pm Mon-Sat. **Credit** AmEx, MC, V. **Map** p409 L5.
Merci is housed in an elaborately reconfigured 19th-century fabric factory. Inside, three loft-like floors heave with furniture, jewellery, stationery, fashion, household products, childrenswear and a haberdashery. That's not all. In a move that takes the trend for retailer responsibility to a new level, this most generous of general stores gives all its profits to charity. *Photos p206.*

CONSUME

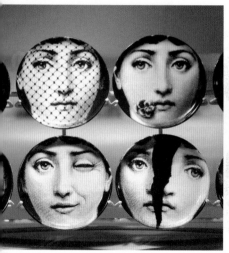

L'Eclaireur. *See p202.*

CONSUME

★ Les Prairies de Paris
23 rue Debelleyme, 3rd (01.40.20.44.12, www.les prairiesdeparis.com). M° St-Sébastien Froissart. **Open** 11am-2pm, 3-7pm Mon-Fri; 11am-7pm Sat. **Credit** AmEx, MC, V. **Map** p409 L5.
The ground floor of Laeticia Ivanez's boutique is given over to art shows, gigs and happenings. Downstairs the 1960s theme continues, with a cocoon-like setting in which to commune with the disco-glam separates and cute children's collection. **Other location** 6 rue du Pré aux Clercs, 7th (same phone number).

Shine
15 rue de Poitou, 3rd (01.48.05.80.10). M° Filles du Calvaire. **Open** 11am-7.30pm Mon-Sat; 1-7pm Sun. **Credit** MC, V. **Map** p407 M7.
See By Chloe, Marc by Marc Jacobs and Acne Jeans, plus Repetto shoes and Véronique Branquino, are among the goodies in this glossy showcase.

Surface 2 Air
108 rue Vieille-du-Temple, 3rd (01.44.61.76.27, www.surface2airparis.com). M° St-Sébastien Froissart. **Open** 11.30am-7.30pm Mon-Sat; 1.30-7.30pm Sun. **Credit** AmEx, MC, V. **Map** p409 L5.
This non-concept concept store also acts as an art gallery. The cult clothing selection takes in Alice McCall's sassy frocks, Fifth Avenue Shoe Repair jeans and printed dresses by Wood Wood. For men, labels include Marios, Wendy & Jim and F-Troupe.

Womenswear

Many brands listed in **Menswear** (*see p206*) also cater for women.

Abercrombie & Fitch
23 av des Champs-Elysées, 8th (08.05.11.15.59, www.abercrombie.com). M° Franklin D Roosevelt. **Open** 10am-8pm Mon-Sat; 11am-7pm Sun. **Credit** AmEx, MC, V. **Map** p401 E4.
See p198 **Check Out the Champs-Elysées.**

★ Agnès b
2, 3, 4 & 6 rue du Jour, 1st (men 01.42.33.04.13, women 01.45.08.56.56, www.agnesb.com). M° Les Halles. **Open** *Oct-Apr* 10am-7pm Mon-Sat. *May-Sept* 10.30am-7.30pm Mon-Sat. **Credit** AmEx, MC, V. **Map** p402 J5.
Agnès b rarely wavers from her design vision: pure lines in fine quality cotton, merino wool and silk. Her mini-empire of men's, women's, children's, travel and sportswear shops is compact.
Other locations throughout the city.

Antoine et Lili
95 quai de Valmy, 10th (01.40.37.41.55, www.antoineetlili.com). M° Jacques Bonsergent. **Open** 11am-7pm Mon, Sun; 11am-8pm Tue-Sat. **Credit** AmEx, DC, MC, V. **Map** p402 L3.
Antoine et Lili's fuchsia-pink, custard-yellow and apple-green shopfronts are a new raver's dream. The bobo designer's clothes, often in wraparound styles, adapt to all sizes and shapes. The Canal St-Martin 'village' comprises womenswear, a kitsch home decoration boutique and childrenswear.
Other locations throughout the city.

ba&sh
22 rue des Francs-Bourgeois, 3rd (01.42.78.55.10, www.ba-sh.com). M° Jacques Bonsergent. **Open** 11am-7.30pm Mon-Sat; 1-7pm Sun. **Credit** AmEx, DC, MC, V. **Map** p402 L3.

This fresh, Paris-based label created by Barbara Boccara and Sharon Krief now has 350 outlets around the world, including eight Paris boutiques. You'll find dresses, skirts and blouses with ethnic touches on one side and drapey jersey on the other. **Other locations** throughout the city.

Banana Republic

22 av des Champs-Elysées, 8th (01.53.89.03.92, www.bananarepublic-france.fr). Mº Franklin D Roosevelt. **Open** 10am-10pm Mon-Sat; 11am-9pm Sun. **Credit** AmEx, MC, V. **Map** p401 E4.
See p198 **Check Out the Champs-Elysées**.

COS

4 rue des Rosiers, 4th (01.44.54.37.70, www. cosstores.com). Mº St-Paul. **Open** 10am-Sat. **Credit** AmEx, MC, V. **Map** p402 J5.
H&M's upmarket brand Collection of Style (COS) now has a Paris outpost, designed by William Russell, in rue des Rosiers, causing some consternation among those who'd rather have kept this a chain-free zone.

Firmaman

200 bd Perèire, 17th (01.44.09.71.32, www. firmaman.com). Mº Porte Maillot. **Open** 11am-1pm, 2-7pm Tue-Sat. **Credit** AmEx, DC, MC, V. **Map** p400 B2.
Realising that pregnant women have long been scouring regular boutiques for a more fashionable maternity look, Marguerite Pineau Valencienne has chosen appropriate clothes from the likes of Isabel Marant, ba&sh and Citizens of Humanity, displayed alongside maternity wear by Blossom, Pietro

Brunelli and Virginie Castaway. The city's first maternity concept store, it also has lingerie, well-being products and gifts.

★ Iro

53 rue Vieille-du-Temple, 4th (01.42.77.25.09, www.iro.fr). Mº St-Paul. **Open** 10.30am-7.30pm Mon-Sat; noon-7pm Sun. **Credit** AmEx, MC, V. **Map** p409 K6.
Fashion editors have tipped designers Laurent and Arik Bitton for stardom with what they call 'basic deluxe': skinny knits, skinny jeans, babydoll dresses and the 'perfecto' mini leather jacket. With a background in music, the brothers know how to hit just the right note for a French silhouette.
Other locations 68 rue des Sts-Pères, 7th (01.45.48.04.06).

Manoush

217 rue St Honoré, 1st (01.40.20.04.44, www. manoush.com). Mº Tuileries. **Open** 10.30am-7.30pm Mon-Sat. **Credit** AmEx, DC, MC, V. **Map** p400 D4.
Manoush, which means 'gypsy' in French slang, has proved more than a flash in the pan from the boho craze of 2005 and now has four boutiques touting designer Frédérique Trou-Roy's kooky vision.
Other locations throughout the city.

Vanessa Bruno

25 rue St-Sulpice, 6th (01.43.54.41.04, www. vanessabruno.com). Mº Odéon. **Open** 10.30am-7.30pm Mon-Sat. **Credit** AmEx, MC, V. **Map** p408 H7.
Mercerised cotton tanks, flattering trousers and feminine tops have a Zen-like quality that stems from Bruno's stay in Japan, and they somehow manage

LE66. *See p203.*

CONSUME

to flatter every figure type. She also makes great bags; the ample Lune was created to mark ten years in the business.

Other locations 12 rue de Castiglione, 1st (01.42.61.44.60); 100 rue Vieille-du-Temple, 3rd (01.42.77.19.41).

Zadig & Voltaire

42 rue des Francs-Bourgeois, 3rd (01.44.54.00.60, www.zadig-et-voltaire.com). M° Hôtel de Ville or St-Paul. **Open** 10.30am-7.30pm Mon-Sat; noon-7.30pm Sun. **Credit** AmEx, DC, MC, V. **Map** p409 K6.

Z&V's relaxed, urban collection is a winner. Popular separates include cotton tops, shirts and faded jeans; its winter range of cashmere jumpers is superb.

▶ *The more upmarket Zadig & Voltaire De Luxe is at 18 rue François 1er (01.40.70.97.89).*
Other locations throughout the city.

Menswear

Shops in **Streetwear & clubwear** (*see p207*) stock more casual clothes; many brands listed in **Designer** (*see p196*) and **Womenswear** (*see p204*) also cater for men.

APC

38 rue Madame, 6th (01.42.22.12.77, www.apc.fr). M° St-Placide. **Open** 11am-7.30pm Mon-Sat; 12.30-6.30pm Sun. **Credit** AmEx, MC, V. **Map** p405 G8.

The look here is simple but stylish: think perfectly cut basics in muted tones. Hip without trying too hard, its jeans are a big hit with denim aficionados – the skinny version nearly caused a stampede when they first came out.

Other locations throughout the city.

★ Christophe Lemaire

28 rue de Poitou, 3rd (01.44.78.00.09, www. christophelemaire.com). M° St-Sébastien Froissart. **Open** 1-7pm Mon; noon-7.30pm Tue-Fri; 11am-7.30pm Sat. **Credit** AmEx, DC, MC, V. **Map** p409 L6.

Creative director for Lacoste for seven years, Lemaire opened his own boutique in an old pharmacy. It's decorated like a fantasy apartment: the salon, in '70s gold and glitz, stocks his own-label menswear and womenswear in high-tech Japanese textiles, and leads into a soundproofed music room with a wall of old speakers where you can buy collectable Lacoste and Lemaire's own fave CDs. Next door the seductive 'Japanese salon' holds the jeans range. You can also buy the vintage lighting on display here.

Eglé Bespoke

26 rue du Mont-Thabor, 1st (01.44.15.98.31, www.eglebespoke.com). M° Concorde. **Open** 11am-7.30pm Mon-Sat & by appointment. **Credit** AmEx, MC, V. **Map** p401 G5.

Merci. *See p203.*

Two young entrepreneurs are reviving bespoke for a new generation in this tiny shop. Custom shirts start from about €120 and can be delivered in a week or so; they will also make or copy shirts for women and produce made-to-order jeans for both sexes. Laser-printed buttons are perfect for stamping your beloved's shirt with a saucy message.

Hugo Boss

115 av des Champs-Elysées, 8th (01.53.57.35.40, www.hugoboss.com). M° George V. **Open** 10.30am-8pm Mon-Sat; 11am-6.30pm Sun. **Credit** AmEx, MC, V. **Map** p400 D4.

See p198 **Check Out the Champs-Elysées**.

Jacenko

38 rue de Poitou, 3rd (01.42.71.80.38). M° St-Sébastien Froissart. **Open** 12.30-8pm Tue-Sat. **Credit** AmEx, MC, V. **Map** p402 J5.

The owner of this tasteful little boutique has a faultless eye for shirts, jackets, woollens and accessories that are dandy but not downright gay. McQ, Viktor & Rolf, Givenchy and John Smedley all appear.

Levi's

76 av des Champs-Elysées, 8th (www.levi.com). M° Franklin D Roosevelt. **Open** 10am-10pm Mon-Sat; 10am-9pm Sun. **Credit** AmEx, MC, V. **Map** p400 D4.

See p198 **Check Out the Champs-Elysées**.

Nodus

22 rue Vieille-du-Temple, 4th (01.42.77.07.96, www.nodus.fr). M° Hôtel de Ville or St-Paul. **Open** 10.45am-2pm, 3-7.30pm Mon-Sat; 1-7.30pm Sun. **Credit** AmEx, DC, MC, V. **Map** p409 K6.

Under the wooden beams of this men's shirt specialist are neat rows of striped, checked and plain dress shirts, silk ties and silver-plated crystal cufflinks. **Other locations** throughout the city.

Pull-In Underwear
8 rue Française, 2nd (01.42.36.91.06, www. pull-in.com). M° Etienne Marcel. **Open** 11am-1.30pm, 2.30-7.30pm daily. **Credit** AmEx, MC, V. **Map** p402 H5.
Hailing from south-west France, Pull-In is the official underwear supplier to the French rugby team. The ultra-trendy brand makes swimwear, but its boxers in wacko patterns have now supplanted Calvin Kleins as *the* visible waistband for Gallic hip hoppers.

Streetwear & clubwear

American Apparel
29 pl du Marché-St-Honoré, 1st (01.44.50.10.65, www.americanapparel.net). M° Opéra, Pyramides or Tuileries. **Open** 10am-8pm Mon-Sat; 2-7pm Sun. **Credit** AmEx, DC, MC, V. **Map** p401 G4.
Paris has acquired a taste for American Apparel's sweatshop-free, unisex cotton basics.
Other locations throughout the city.

Kiliwatch
64 rue Tiquetonne, 2nd (01.42.21.17.37, http://espacekiliwatch.fr). M° Etienne Marcel. **Open** 2-7pm Mon; 11am-7.30pm Tue-Sat. **Credit** AmEx, MC, V. **Map** p402 J5.
The trailblazer of the rue Etienne-Marcel revival is filled with hoodies, casual shirts and washed-out jeans. Brands such as Gas, Edwin and Pepe Jeans accompany pricey, good-condition second-hand garb.

Royal Cheese
24 rue Tiquetonne, 2nd (01.42.21.30.65, www.royalcheese.com). M° Etienne Marcel. **Open** 11am-8pm daily. **Credit** AmEx, DC, MC, V. **Map** p402 J5.
Clubbers hit Royal Cheese to snaffle up hard-to-find imports: Stüssy, Cheap Monday and Lee for the boys; Insight, Sessun, Edwin and Lazy Oaf for the girls. Prices are hefty: Japanese jeans cost €200. **Other locations** 26 rue de Poitou, 3rd (01.78.56.53.56).

Used & vintage

See also p222 **Antiques & flea markets** and *p209* **Vintage Paris**.

Adrenaline
30 rue Racine, 6th (01.44.27.09.05, www. adrenaline-vintage.com). M° Odéon. **Open** 11am-7pm Mon-Sat. **Credit** AmEx, MC, V. **Map** p408 H7.
This *dépot-vente* specialises in vintage luggage and handbags. Iconic Vuitton suitcases and Kelly and Birkin bags command enormous prices, but there are some slightly more affordable pieces and a small collection of '60s couture.

Didier Ludot
24 galerie de Montpensier, 1st (01.42.96.06.56, www.didierludot.fr). M° Palais Royal Musée du Louvre. **Open** 10.30am-7pm Mon-Sat. **Credit** AmEx, DC, MC, V. **Map** p402 H5.
Didier Ludot's temples to vintage haute couture appear in Printemps, Harrods and New York's Barneys. The prices may be steep, but the pieces are stunning: Dior, Molyneux, Balenciaga, Pucci, Féraud and, of course, Chanel, from the 1920s onwards. Ludot also curates exhibitions, using the exclusive shop windows around the Palais-Royal as a gallery.
▶ *Didier Ludot stocks his own line of vintage little black dresses, also available at La Petite Robe Noire (125 galerie de Valois, 1st, 01.40.15.01.04).*

Free 'P' Star
8 rue Ste-Croix-de-la-Bretonnerie, 4th (01.42.76.03.72, www.freepstar.com). M° St-Paul. **Open** 11am-9pm Mon-Sat; noon-9pm Sun. **Credit** MC, V. **Map** p409 K6.
Late-night shopping is fun at this Aladdin's cave of retro glitz, ex-army wear and glad rags that has provided fancy dress for many a Paris party.

★ Gabrielle Geppert
31 & 34 galerie Montpensier, 1st (01.42.61.53.52, www.gabriellegeppert.com). M° Palais Royal Musée du Louvre. **Open** 10am-7.30pm Mon-Sat. **Credit** AmEx, DC, MC, V. **Map** p402 H5.
If Didier Ludot is too intimidating, visit Gabrielle Geppert's shop, where much fun can be had rummaging in the back room or trying on the outrageous

CONSUME

collection of '70s sunglasses (about €380 a pop, but they will get you into any party worth going to). A new exclusive room dedicated to accessories by the likes of Hermès and Manolo Blahnik can be opened on request, and Geppert also carries a range of original costume jewellery by Elisabeth Ramuz.

GoldyMama
14 rue du Surmelin, 20th (01.40.30.08.00, www.goldymama.com). M° Pelleport. **Open** 11am-7.30pm Tue-Sat. **Credit** AmEx, MC, V.
Finding well-presented vintage clothes that have been washed, ironed and don't smell like dirty underpants is possible – GoldyMama is the proof. This small boutique in the heights of the 20th has retro treasures aplenty and makes an original spot for gift hunting. The walls are lined with 1950s skirts, '40s suits, empire dresses, wacky '70s tops and multi-era accessories. Once you've tried on half the shop, free your inner child at GoldyMama's 'Bar à Bonbons' filled with boiled sweets, caramels and all sorts of other naughty treats.

Yukiko
97 rue Vieille-du-Temple, 3rd (01.42.71.13.41, www.yukiko-paris.com). M° St-Sébastien Froissart. **Open** 11am-1pm, 2-7pm Tue-Sat. **Credit** AmEx, MC, V. **Map** p409 L6.
Yukiko's exquisite shop is a world away from the jumble sale vibe of some second-hand clothes dens in Paris. An impressive range of vintage luxury brand accessories, her own line of simple, sexy dresses and the decor of the shop itself are all carefully colour co-ordinated, the result a harmony of burnished gold and milky pearl on salmon pink or chestnut silk against pretty pale green walls.

FASHION ACCESSORIES & SERVICES
Eyewear

★ Alain Mikli
74 rue des Sts-Pères, 7th (01.45.49.40.00, www.mikli.fr). M° Sèvres Babylone or St-Sulpice. **Open** 10am-7pm Mon-Sat. **Credit** AmEx, DC, MC, V. **Map** p405 G7.
Cult French designer Mikli uses cellulose acetate, a blend of wood and cotton sliced from blocks. At his flagship Starck-designed boutique, frames are laid out in a glass counter like designer sweeties. **Other locations** throughout the city.

Anne et Valentin
4 rue Ste-Croix-de-la-Bretonnerie, 4th (01.40.29.93.01, www.anneetvalentin.com). M° Hôtel de Ville or St-Paul. **Open** noon-8pm Mon; 11am-8pm Tue-Sat. Closed 1wk Aug. **Credit** AmEx, DC, MC, V. **Map** p409 K6.
This modish eyewear firm occupies a cosy three-floor Marais boutique. A&V design chic unisex

frames: light titanium models have names like Tarzan and Truman; coloured acetate frames have inventive details and colour combinations.

Hats & gloves

★ Maison Fabre
128 galerie de Valois, 1st (01.42.60.75.88, www.maisonfabre.com). M° Palais Royal Musée du Louvre. **Open** 10.30am-7pm Mon-Sat. **Credit** AmEx, MC, V. **Map** p402 H5.
This Millau glovemaker, which was founded in 1924, has capitalised on its racy designs from the sports-car eras of the 1920s and '60s. Classic gloves made from the softest leather (€100) come in 20 wild colours. Then there are the variations: crocodile, python, coyote, fur-trimmed, fingerless. But the ultimate lust object is the patent leather 'Auto' glove fastened with a massive button – it sits somewhere between the cool of *The Avengers* and the kook of *Austin Powers*.
Other location 60 rue des Sts-Pères, 7th (01.42.22.44.86).

Maison Michel
65 rue Ste-Anne, 2nd (01.42.96.89.77, www.michel-paris.com). M° Pyramides. **Open** by appointment. **Credit** MC, V. **Map** p401 H4.
One of the specialist businesses saved from extinction by Chanel, Maison Michel has been making hats since 1936 and supplies haute couture designers and the Paris opera. They can create the perfect panama or a flamboyant creation for the races, and also launched a prêt-à-porter range in 2006 with a range of sexy, shiny, '60s-inspired cloches and caps.

★ Marie Mercié
23 rue St-Sulpice, 6th (01.43.26.45.83, www.mariemercie.com). M° Odéon. **Open** 11am-7pm Mon-Sat. **Credit** AmEx, DC, MC, V. **Map** p408 H7.
Mercié's creations make you wish you lived in an era when hats were de rigueur. Step out in one shaped like curved fingers (complete with shocking-pink nail varnish and pink diamond ring) or a beret like a face with red lips and turquoise eyes. Ready-to-wear starts at €30; *sur mesure* takes ten days.

Jewellery

Dotted in and around place Vendôme, the key *joailliers* define the luxurious spirit of Paris. The Marais is home to a number of fashion and costume jewellery boutiques.

Boucheron
26 pl Vendôme, 1st (01.42.61.58.16, www.boucheron.com). M° Opéra. **Open** 10.30am-7pm Mon-Sat. **Credit** AmEx, DC, MC, V. **Map** p401 G4.
Boucheron was the first *joaillier* to set up shop on place Vendôme, attracting celebrity custom from the nearby Ritz hotel. Owned by Gucci, the grand

Vintage Paris

Hunt for rare retro finds, from designer dresses to classic scooters.

Vintage shops in London and New York have been adding retro flair to wardrobes for years, but it has taken Paris – the city of 'serious' haute couture – a little longer to jump on the bandwagon. Today, though, the city is dripping in everything your vintage heart could desire, from rare 1920s Chanel accessories and art deco lighting to '60s rock LPs and 1980s kitten boots. And the good news is that many of the best vintage boutiques are condensed on the Right Bank between Palais-Royal and Faidherbe Chaligny (east of Bastille).

Les Années Scooter (23 rue Faidherbe, 01.46.59.47.90) is a tiny den of mid 20th-century scooters, lights, clocks, jukeboxes and street signs. Philippe, the passionate owner, can tell you the story behind every piece on display. A few doors further down, **Restaur'Bronze** (41 rue Faidherbe, 01.43.71. 44.25, www.restaurbronze.com) is one of the last few places in Paris specialising in metal objects from the 1930s and '40s, including some show-stopping art deco lights, all perfectly restored by owner Marc Arguence, who learned the trade from his father.

Bohemian rue Keller is lined with galleries, bars and emerging clothes designers, and **Born Bad** (17 rue Keller, 01.43.38.41.78, www.bornbad.fr) is an Aladdin's cave of second-hand new wave, soul, 1950s rock and '60s surf LPs and CDs that attracts music-savvy Parisians from across town.

A short walk from here is **Adöm** (35 & 56 rue de la Roquette, 01.48.07.15.94), which is split into two small boutiques. Girls head to no.56 for 1970s and '80s jeans and '60s shift dresses, while boys drop into no.35 for 1950s baseball jackets, cowboy boots and a selection of sneakers.

During the last six years, the previously forgotten northern stretch of the Marais has been transformed into one of Paris's hottest shopping areas, with numerous one-off boutiques coveted by fashionistas – including two wonderful vintage finds. The first is **Studio W** (6 rue du Pont-aux-Choux, 3rd, 01.44.78.05.02), a sparsely stocked vintage shop where quality is king. There are clothes – mostly rare designer vintage dresses by YSL and Chanel – but it's the accessories that shine: 1970s boots, '80s stilettos and enough dinky '60s leather clutch bags to make your heart swoon. The second shop, **Matières à Reflexion** (19 rue de Poitou, 3rd, 01.42.72.16.31, www.matieresareflexion.com), is the ultimate vintage bag-maker – a place where old leather jackets and clothes are crafted into one-off bags and satchels.

For punky London retro style, try **Noir Kennedy** (12 & 22 rue du Roi de Sicile, 4th, 01.42.71.15.50; www.noirkennedy.fr), chock full of leather coats, lumberjack shirts, ripped jeans and 1980s T-shirts. If '40s fashion is more your forte, try **Mam'Zelle Swing** (35bis rue du Roi de Sicile, 4th, 01.48.87.04.06).

Finally, take a stroll to Paris's ultimate temple of luxury vintage, **Didier Ludot** (*see p207*). You just have to glimpse the window displays to see that there is something special about Ludot's pieces, many of which look like they could have been cast-offs from Audrey Hepburn. If you're daring enough to go in, you'll discover modern outfits by today's up-and-coming designers too – or the vintage pieces of tomorrow, as the owner likes to call them.

Noir Kennedy.

CONSUME

jeweller produces stunning pieces, using traditional motifs with new accents: take, for example, its fabulous chocolate-coloured gold watch.
Other location 32 rue du Fbg-St-Honoré, 8th (01.44.51.95.20).

★ Cartier
13 rue de la Paix, 2nd (01.58.18.23.00, www. cartier.com). M° Opéra. **Open** 10.30am-7pm Mon-Sat. **Credit** AmEx, DC, MC, V. **Map** p401 G4.
This iconic French jeweller and watchmaker has impressive landmark headquarters. Downstairs, pearls, panthers and the Trinity ring jostle for attention among historic pieces commissioned by crowned heads; the upper salons house perfumer Mathilde Laurent's bespoke scents.
Other locations throughout the city.

Chanel Joaillerie
18 pl Vendôme, 1st (01.40.98.55.55, www.chanel. com). M° Opéra or Tuileries. **Open** 11am-7pm Mon; 10.30am-7pm Tue-Sat. **Credit** AmEx, DC, MC, V. **Map** p401 G4.
Chanel launched its fine jewellery in the 1990s, reissuing the single collection – big on platinum and diamonds – that Coco herself designed some 60 years previously. The current line reinterprets the motifs – camellias, stars and comets – to create a collection of contemporary classics.

Dior Joaillerie
8 pl Vendôme, 1st (01.42.96.30.84, www.dior. com). M° Opéra or Tuileries. **Open** 10.30am-7pm daily. **Credit** AmEx, DC, MC, V. **Map** p401 G4.
The unabashed bling of Victoire de Castellane's designs is responsible for the fad of semi-precious coloured stones and runaway success of the 'Mimi Oui', a ring with a tiny diamond on a slim chain.
Other locations 28 av Montaigne, 8th (01.47.23.52.39).

KarryO'
62 rue des Sts-Pères, 6th (01.45.48.94.67, www.karryo.com). M° St-Germain-des-Prés. **Open** 10.30am-7pm Tue-Sat. **Credit** MC, V. **Map** p405 G7.
Paris socialites come here to source their vintage jewellery, as well as modern gems by owner Karine Berrebi. Her adjacent gallery, Unique, features one-of-a-kind finds, from jewels and decorative objects to Hermès bags and the occasional Schiaparelli fur.

★ Marie-Hélène de Taillac
8 rue de Tournon, 6th (01.44.27.07.07, www. mariehelenedetaillac.com). M° Mabillon. **Open** 11am-7pm Mon-Sat. **Credit** MC, V. **Map** p408 H7.
Marie-Hélène de Taillac is a fine jeweller. But unlike her colleagues across the Seine, her diamonds and emeralds in simple, unpretentious settings work well with jeans and don't make her customers look like ancestral portraits. This combination of precious stones and modern styling has made her popular

with the fashion elite. No doubt they also adore her Left Bank shop – a Tom Dixon-designed space in Marie-Hélène's trademark luminous pale blue and pillar-box red, complete with a technicolour painting of Jaipur (where her studio is based) by Jean-Philippe Delhomme of Barneys New York ad fame.

Viveka Bergström
23 rue de la Grange aux Belles, 10th (01.40.03.04.92, www.viveka-bergstrom.com). M° Colonel Fabien. **Open** noon-7pm Tue-Sat. **Credit** AmEx, MC, V. **Map** p402 L3.
The daughter of Saab's aeroplane designer in the 1950s, Viveka Bergström makes slinky tassel necklaces, oversized beaten gold rings and brooches, and conversation starters like the angel-wing bracelet and a necklace featuring a map of Paris.

Lingerie & swimwear

For swimwear, *see also p225* **Sport & fitness**.

★ Alice Cadolle
4 rue Cambon, 1st (01.42.60.94.22, www. cadolle.com). M° Concorde or Madeleine. **Open** 10.30am-6.30pm Mon, Tue; 10am-7pm Wed-Sat. Closed Aug. **Credit** AmEx, MC, V. **Map** p401 G4.
Five generations of lingerie-makers are behind this boutique, founded by Hermine Cadolle, who claimed to be the original inventor of the bra. Now

Christian Louboutin.

her great-great-granddaughter, Poupie Cadolle, continues the tradition in a cosy space devoted to a luxury ready-to-wear line of bras, panties and corsets.
► *For a special treat, Cadolle Couture (255 rue St-Honoré, 1st, 01.42.60.94.94) will create indulgent bespoke lingerie (by appointment only).*

Erès
2 rue Tronchet, 8th (01.47.42.28.82, www.eres.fr). M° Madeleine. **Open** 10am-7pm Mon-Sat. **Credit** AmEx, DC, MC, V. **Map** p401 G4.
Erès's beautifully cut swimwear has embraced a sexy '60s look complete with buttons on the low-cut briefs. To make life easier, the top and bottom can be purchased in different sizes or you can buy one piece of a bikini.
Other locations 4bis rue du Cherche-Midi, 6th (01.45.44.95.54); 40 av Montaigne, 8th (01.47.23.07.26); 6 rue Guichard, 16th (01.46.47.45.21).

Etam Lingerie
139 rue de Rennes, 6th (01.45.44.16.88, www.etam.com). M° Montparnasse-Bienvenüe. **Open** 10am-8pm Mon-Sat. **Credit** AmEx, DC, MC, V. **Map** p401 G4.
Etam, which started out in lingerie in 1916, has now opened the largest lingerie store in Europe. It may be quantity over quality, but who can resist the 'bar à culottes' or the 'hot and spicy corner'?

★ Fifi Chachnil
231 rue St-Honoré, 1st (01.42.61.21.83, www.fifichachnil.com). M° Tuileries. **Open** 11am-7pm Mon-Sat. **Credit** AmEx, MC, V. **Map** p401 G4.
Chachnil has a new approach to frou-frou underwear in the pin-up tradition. Her chic mixes – deep red silk bras with boudoir-pink bows, and pale turquoise girdles with orange trim – will have ladies and their male admirers purring in delight. The transparent black babydoll negligées with an Empire-line bust are classic saucy retro.
Other locations 68 rue Jean-Jacques-Rousseau, 1st (01.42.21.19.93).

Princesse Tam-Tam
52 bd St-Michel, 6th (01.40.51.72.99, www.princessetamtam.com). M° Cluny La Sorbonne. **Open** 1.30-7pm Mon; 10am-7pm Tue, Thur-Sat; 10am-1.30pm, 2-7pm Wed. **Credit** AmEx, MC, V. **Map** p408 J7.
This inexpensive underwear and swimwear brand, which celebrated its 25th anniversary in 2010, has traffic-stopping promotions. Bright colours and sexily transparent and sporty gear rule.
Other locations throughout the city.

Sabbia Rosa
73 rue des Sts-Pères, 6th (01.45.48.88.37). M° St-Germain-des-Prés. **Open** 10am-7pm Mon-Sat. **Credit** AmEx, MC, V. **Map** p405 G7.

THE BEST SHOE SHOPS

For dancing feet
Repetto. See p212.

For Saint-Tropez style
K Jacques. See p212.

For tiny toes
Six Pieds Trois Pouces. See p195.

Let Moana Moatti tempt you with feather-trimmed satin mules, or satin, silk and chiffon negligées in fine shades of tangerine, lemon, mocha or pistachio. All sizes are medium, others are made *sur mesure*; prices are just the right side of stratospheric.

Yoba
11 rue du Marché-St-Honoré, 1st (01.40.41.04.06, www.yobaparis.com). M° Tuileries. **Open** 11am-8pm Mon-Fri; noon-8pm Sat. **Credit** MC, V. **Map** p401 G5.
Definitely one for the liberated ladies, Yoba is a smart boutique stocking items from wispy lingerie to cheeky sex toys.

Shoes & bags

An entire floor of footwear, including designer labels, can be found at **Printemps** (*see p191*). Rue du Dragon, rue de Grenelle and rue du Cherche-Midi form the backbone of an area that is a must for shoe and accessory addicts.

Christian Louboutin
19 rue Jean-Jacques-Rousseau, 1st (01.42.36.53.66, www.christianlouboutin.com). M° Palais Royal Musée du Louvre. **Open** 10.30am-7pm Mon-Sat. Closed 3wks Aug. **Credit** AmEx, MC, V. **Map** p402 J5.
Every fashionista, WAG and shoe fiend worth her salt owns or hankers after a pair of Louboutin's trademark red-soled creations. Each design is displayed to maximum advantage in an individual frame. There's a made-to-measure service.
Other locations 38 rue de Grenelle, 7th (01.42.22.33.07); 68 rue du Fbg-St-Honoré, 8th (01.42.68.37.65).

★ Hervé Chapelier
1bis rue du Vieux-Colombier, 6th (01.44.07.06.50, www.hervechapelier.fr). M° St-Germain-des-Prés or St-Sulpice. **Open** 10.15am-7pm Mon-Sat. **Credit** AmEx, MC, V. **Map** p407 G7.
Bag yourself a classic, chic, bicoloured tote at Hervé Chapelier. Sizes and prices range from a dinky purse at €22 to a weekend bag at €130. *Photo p212.*
Other location 390 rue Saint-Honoré, 1st (01.42.96.38.04).

CONSUME

Hervé Chapelier. *See p211.*

CONSUME

Iris

28 rue de Grenelle, 7th (01.42.22.89.81, www. irisshoes.com). Mº Rue du Bac or St-Sulpice. **Open** 10.30am-7pm Mon-Sat. **Credit** AmEx, MC, V. **Map** p405 F7.

This white boutique stocks shoes by the likes of Marc Jacobs, John Galliano and Viktor & Rolf.

Jamin Puech

61 rue de Hauteville, 10th (01.40.22.08.32, www.jamin-puech.com). Mº Poissonnière. **Open** 10am-7pm Mon, Wed, Fri; 11am-7pm Tue, Sat. **Credit** AmEx, DC, MC, V. **Map** p402 K3.

The complete collection of Benoît Jamin and Isabelle Puech's dazzling handbags is displayed in a bohemian setting complete with antler-horn chairs. **Other locations** throughout the city.

★ K Jacques

16 rue Pavée, 4th (01.40.27.03.57, www. kjacques.fr). Mº St-Paul. **Open** 10am-7.15pm Mon-Sat; 1-7.15pm Sun. **Credit** MC, V. **Map** p409 L6.

Set up in Saint-Tropez in 1933 by Jacques Keklikian and his wife, the K Jacques workshop started life stitching together basic leather sandals for visitors to the Med resort. The Homère (or Homer) was, and still is, the signature piece – Picasso loved them, and over the years they've counted the likes of Colette and Brigitte Bardot among their fans.

Moss

22 rue de Grenelle, 7th (01.42.22.01.43). Mº Rue du Bac or St-Sulpice. **Open** 11am-7pm Mon; 10.30am-7pm Tue-Sat. **Credit** AmEx, MC, V. **Map** p405 F7.

The three sisters who run this boutique pride themselves on sourcing cutting-edge shoes, that can be hard to find elsewhere, such as creations by former Celine stylist Avril Gau and signature designs by Laurence Dacade, Duccio del Duca and Hartian Bourdin. You'll also find scarves by Octavio Pizzaro and jewellery by Karry O', the fourth sister.

Peggy Huyn Kinh

9-11 rue Coëtlogon, 6th (01.42.84.83.82, www.phk.fr). Mº St-Sulpice. **Open** 11am-7pm Mon-Sat. **Credit** AmEx, MC, V. **Map** p405 G7.

Once creative director at Cartier, Peggy Huyn Kinh now makes bags of boar skin and python, as well as silver jewellery.

★ Pierre Hardy

156 galerie de Valois, 1st (01.42.60.59.75, www.pierrehardy.com). Mº Palais Royal Musée du Louvre. **Open** 11am-7pm Mon-Sat. **Credit** AmEx, DC, MC, V. **Map** p402 H5.

This classy black-and-white shoebox is home to Hardy's range of superbly conceived footwear – with a price tag to match – for men and women. **Other location** 9-11 pl du Palais Bourbon, 7th (01.45.55.00.67).

★ Repetto

22 rue de la Paix, 2nd (01.44.71.83.12, www. repetto.com). Mº Opéra. **Open** 9.30am-7.30pm Mon-Sat. **Credit** AmEx, MC, V. **Map** p401 G4.

This ballet shoe-maker struck gold when it decided to reissue its dance shoes with pavement soles. The prowly *ballerines* and showbiz dance boots in black, metallic and spangly finishes are fun, stylish and

exceptionally comfortable. They are sold alongside the full range of real balletwear; you can try out your *pointes* on a red carpet with a *barre* if you really want to show off.
Other locations 51 rue du Four, 6th (01.45.44.98.65); 51 rue des Francs Bourgeois, 4th (01.70.79.89.37); 36 rue de Passy, 16th (01.70.79.89.41).

Rodolphe Menudier

14 rue de Castiglione, 1st (01.42.60.86.27, www.rodolphemenudier.com). M° Concorde or Tuileries. **Open** 11am-7pm Mon; 10am-7pm Tue-Sat. **Credit** AmEx, MC, V. **Map** p401 G5.
This boutique makes the perfect backdrop for Rodolphe Menudier's racy designs. Silver-handled drawers display his stilettos in profile, as well as outrageous thigh-high boots with Plexiglass soles; more demure customers can opt for a pair of pumps.

Roger Vivier

29 rue du Fbg-St-Honoré, 8th (01.53.43.00.85, www.rogervivier.com). M° Concorde or Madeleine. **Open** 11am-7pm Mon-Sat. **Credit** AmEx, DC, MC, V. **Map** p401 F4.
The fashion editors' shoeman of choice, Vivier is credited with inventing the stiletto.

FOOD & DRINK

You could spend a lifetime sampling the breads, pastries, chocolate and cheeses available in Paris. Open-air markets continue to beckon with their fresh, seasonal produce, and **Galeries Lafayette** (*see p191*) and **Le Bon Marché** (*see p190*) have luxury food halls.

Bakeries

★ Arnaud Delmontel

39 rue des Martyrs, 9th (01.48.78.29.33, www.arnaud-delmontel.com). M° St-Georges. **Open** 7am-8.30pm Mon, Wed-Sun. **No credit cards. Map** p402 H2.
With its crisp crust and chewy crumb shot through with irregular holes, Delmontel's Renaissance bread is one of the finest in Paris.
Other locations 25 rue de Levis, 17th (01.42.27.15.45); 57 rue Damrémont, 18th (01.42.64.59.63).

L'Autre Boulange

43 rue de Montreuil, 11th (01.43.72.86.04, www.lautreboulange.com). M° Faidherbe Chaligny or Nation. **Open** 7.30am-1.30pm, 3-7.30pm Mon-Fri; 7.30am-1pm Sat. Closed Aug. **Credit** MC, V. **Map** p407 P7.
Michel Cousin bakes up to 23 different types of organic loaf in his wood-fired oven – varieties include the *flutiot* (rye bread with raisins, walnuts and hazelnuts) and a spiced cornmeal bread.

K Jacques.

Le Boulanger de Monge

123 rue Monge, 5th (01.43.37.54.20, www. leboulangerdemonge.com). M° Censier Daubenton. **Open** 7am-8.30pm Tue-Sun. **Credit** MC, V. **Map** p406 K9.
Dominique Saibron uses spices to give inimitable flavour to his organic sourdough *boule*. Every day about 2,000 bread-lovers visit this boutique, which also produces one of the city's best baguettes.
Other locations 53 rue Montorgueil, 2nd (01.42.33.31.05); 48 rue de la Clef, 5th (01.47.07.28.19).

Le Grenier à Pain

38 rue des Abbesses, 18th (01.46.06.41.81). M° Abbesses. **Open** 7.30am-8pm Mon, Thur-Sun. **No credit cards. Map** p401 H1.
Expect queues at this bakery, 2010 winner of the Grand Prix de la Baguette de Tradition Française de la Ville de Paris. As well as gaining plenty of new customers, baker Djibril Bodian also picked up a contract to keep Nicolas Sarkozy in bread for a year.
Other locations throughout the city.

THE BEST FOOD SHOPS

For squishy st-marcellin
Alléosse. *See p214.*

For a Grand Prix baguette
Le Grenier à Pain. *See above.*

For Nutella tarts
Bogato. *See p217.*

CONSUME

Moisan

*5 pl d'Aligre, 12th (09.50.27.67.04, www.pain
moisan.fr). M° Ledru-Rollin.* **Open** 7am-8pm Tue-
Sat; 7am-2pm Sun. **Credit** MC, V. **Map** p407 N7.
Moisan's organic bread, *viennoiseries* and rustic
tarts are outstanding. At this branch, situated by the
market, there's always a healthy queue.
Other locations throughout the city.

★ Du Pain et des Idées

*34 rue Yves Toudic, 10th (01.42.40.44.52,
www.dupainetdesidees.com). M° Jacques
Bonsergent.* **Open** 6.45am-8pm Mon-Fri.
Credit (min €15) MC, V. **Map** p402 L4.
Christophe Vasseur is a former winner of the Gault-
Millau prize for Best Bakery. Among his specialities
are Le Rabelais – *pain brioché* with saffron, honey
and nuts; and Le Pagnol aux Pommes, a bread studded with royal gala apple (skin on), raisins and
orange flower water.

★ Poilâne

*8 rue du Cherche-Midi, 6th (01.45.48.42.59,
www.poilane.com). M° Sèvres Babylone or St-
Sulpice.* **Open** 7.15am-8.15pm Mon-Sat. **Credit**
(€20 minimum) AmEx, DC, MC, V. **Map** p405 G7.
Apollonia Poilâne runs the family shop, where locals
queue for fresh country *miches*, flaky-crusted apple
tarts and buttery shortbread biscuits.
▶ *Poilâne finally braved the Right Bank with
the 2011 opening of a new shop in the Marais
(38 rue Debelleyme, 3rd, 01.44.61.83.39).*
Other locations 49 bd de Grenelle, 15th
(01.45.79.11.49).

Cheese

The sign *maître fromager affineur* denotes
merchants who buy young cheeses from farms
and age them on their premises; *fromage fermier*
and *fromage au lait cru* signify farm-produced
and unpasteurised cheeses respectively.

★ Alléosse

*13 rue Poncelet, 17th (01.46.22.50.45, www.
fromage-alleosse.com). M° Ternes.* **Open**
9am-1pm, 4-7pm Tue-Thur; 9am-1pm, 3.30-
7pm Fri, Sat; 9am-1pm Sun. **Credit** MC, V.
Map p400 C2.
People cross town for these cheeses – wonderful
farmhouse camemberts, delicate st-marcellins,
a choice of *chèvres* and several rarities.

Fromagerie Dubois et Fils

*80 rue de Tocqueville, 17th (01.42.27.11.38).
M° Malesherbes or Villiers.* **Open** 8am-1pm,
4-8pm Tue-Fri; 8am-8pm Sat; 9am-1pm Sun.
Closed 1st 3wks Aug. **Credit** AmEx, MC, V.
Map p401 E2.
Superchef darling Dubois stocks 80 types of goat's
cheese, plus prized, aged st-félicien.

★ Fromagerie Quatrehomme

*62 rue de Sèvres, 7th (01.47.34.33.45). M° Duroc
or Vaneau.* **Open** 8.45am-1pm, 4-7.45pm Tue-
Thur; 8.45am-7.45pm Fri, Sat. **Credit** MC, V.
Map p405 F8.
Marie Quatrehomme runs this *fromagerie*. Justly
famous for her beaufort and st-marcellin, she also
sells such specialities as goat's cheese with pesto.
Other locations 9 rue du Poteau, 18th
(01.46.06.26.03).

Marie-Anne Cantin

*12 rue du Champ-de-Mars, 7th (01.45.50.43.94,
www.cantin.fr). M° Ecole Militaire.* **Open** 2-7.30pm
Mon; 8.30am-7.30pm Tue-Sat; 8.30am-1pm Sun.
Credit AmEx, MC, V. **Map** p404 D6.
Cantin, a defender of unpasteurised cheese and supplier to many posh Paris restaurants, offers aged
chèvres and amazing morbier, mont d'or and comté.

Chocolate

Cacao et Chocolat

*29 rue de Buci, 6th (01.46.33.77.63, www.cacao
etchocolat.com). M° Mabillon.* **Open** 10.30am-
7.30pm Mon-Sat; 10am-6.30pm Sun. **Credit**
AmEx, DC, MC, V. **Map** p405 H7.
This shop recalls chocolate's Aztec origins, with its
choice of spicy fillings (honey and chilli, nutmeg,
clove and citrus), chocolate masks and pyramids.
Other locations throughout the city.

Poilâne.

Christian Constant

37 rue d'Assas, 6th (01.53.63.15.15). M° Rennes or St-Placide. **Open** 9.30am-8.30pm Mon-Fri; 9am-8pm Sat, Sun. **Credit** MC, V. **Map** p405 G8.
A master chocolate-maker and *traiteur*, Constant scours the globe for new ideas. His *ganaches* are subtly flavoured with verbena, jasmine or cardamom.

Jacques Génin

133 rue de Turenne, 3rd (01.45.77.29.01). M° Filles de Calvaire. **Open** 11am-7pm Mon-Fri; 11am-8pm Sat. **Credit** MC, V. **Map** p409 L5.
Jacques Génin was voted the 'best *chocolatier* in the world' by critic Mort Rosenblum, but his creations could previously be tasted only in top restaurants. But now his impressive boutique allows you to taste *sur place* or take a bag home. The signature éclairs and tarts glisten in glass cases, and the millefeuilles are made to order for perfect freshness. The chocolate ganaches include Menthe Amante, a two-phase taste sensation that finishes with mint leaves bursting on the tongue. One part of the space is given over to a tearoom, and a spiral staircase leads to the *ateliers*.

★ Jean-Paul Hévin

3 rue Vavin, 6th (01.43.54.09.85, www.jphevin. com). M° Notre-Dame-des-Champs or Vavin. **Open** 10am-7pm Tue-Sat. Closed Aug. **Credit** AmEx, MC, V. **Map** p405 G8.
Hévin specialises in the beguiling combination of chocolate with potent cheese fillings, which loyal customers serve with wine as an aperitif.
Other locations 231 rue St-Honoré, 1st (01.55.35.35.96); 23bis av de La Motte-Picquet, 7th (01.45.51.77.48).

La Maison du Chocolat

120 av Victor-Hugo, 16th (01.40.67.77.83, www.lamaisonduchocolat.com). M° Victor Hugo. **Open** 10am-7.30pm Mon-Sat; 10am-1pm Sun. Closed Mon & Sun in July & Aug. **Credit** AmEx, MC, V. **Map** p400 B4.
Robert Linxe opened his first Paris shop in 1977, and has been inventing new chocolates ever since, using Asian spices, fresh fruits and herbal infusions.
Other locations throughout the city.

Patrick Roger

108 bd St-Germain, 6th (01.43.29.38.42, www. patrickroger.com). M° Odéon. **Open** 10.30am-7.30pm daily. **Credit** MC, V. **Map** p408 H7.
Roger is shaking up the art of chocolate-making. Whereas other *chocolatiers* aim for gloss, Roger may create a brushed effect on hens so realistic you almost expect them to lay (chocolate) eggs.
Other locations throughout the city.

Richart

258 bd St-Germain, 7th (01.45.55.66.00, www.richart.com). M° Solférino. **Open** 10am-7pm Mon-Sat. **Credit** AmEx, MC, V. **Map** p405 F6.

Each of Richart's stunning chocolate *ganaches* has an intricate design, packages look like jewel boxes, and every purchase comes with a tract on how best to savour the stuff.

Drinks

Les Caves Augé

116 bd Haussmann, 8th (01.45.22.16.97, www.cavesauge.com). M° St-Augustin. **Open** 10am-7.30pm Mon-Sat. Closed Mon in Aug. **Credit** AmEx, MC, V. **Map** p401 E3.
Les Caves Augé is the oldest wine shop in Paris – Marcel Proust was a regular customer – and offers a serious and professional service.

Les Caves Taillevent

199 rue du Fbg-St-Honoré, 8th (01.45.61.14.09, www.cavestaillevent.com). M° Charles de Gaulle Etoile or Ternes. **Open** 10am-7.30pm Mon-Sat. Closed 1st 3wks Aug. **Credit** AmEx, DC, MC, V. **Map** p400 D3.
Choose from a vast range of wines at this boutique arm of the smart Taillevent restaurant. Sommeliers are on hand to help you choose and there are bottles for every budget.

★ Lavinia

3 bd de la Madeleine, 1st (01.42.97.20.20, www.lavinia.fr). M° Madeleine. **Open** 10am-8pm Mon-Fri; 9am-8pm Sat. **Credit** AmEx, DC, MC, V. **Map** p401 G4.
Lavinia stocks a wonderfully broad selection of French vintages alongside many non-French wines; its glassed-in *cave* has everything from a 1945 Mouton-Rothschild at €22,000 to trendy and 'fragile' wines for under €10.
▶ *Have fun tasting wine with the dégustation machines on the ground floor, which allow customers to taste a sip of up to ten different wines each week for €10.*

Legrand Filles et Fils

1 rue de la Banque, 2nd (01.42.60.07.12, www.caves-legrand.com). M° Bourse. **Open** 11am-7pm Mon; 10am-7.30pm Tue-Fri; 10am-7pm Sat. Closed Mon in July & Aug. **Credit** AmEx, MC, V. **Map** p402 H4.
Fine wines and brandies, teas and *bonbons,* and a showroom for regular wine tastings.

Ryst Dupeyron

79 rue du Bac, 7th (01.45.48.80.93, www. vintageandco.com). M° Rue du Bac. **Open** 12.30-7.30pm Mon; 10.30am-7.30pm Tue-Sat. Closed 2wks Aug. **Credit** AmEx, MC, V. **Map** p405 F7.
The Dupeyrons have been selling armagnac for four generations, and still have bottles from 1868. Treasures here include 200 fine Bordeaux wines and an extensive range of vintage port.

CONSUME

Saxe-Breteuil.

Global

Les Délices d'Orient
52 av Emile-Zola, 15th (01.45.79.10.00).
Mᵒ Charles Michels. **Open** 8.30am-8.30pm
Tue-Sun. **Credit** MC, V. **Map** p404 B8.
Shelves here groan beneath the weight of stuffed
aubergines, halva, falafel and all manner of Middle
Eastern delicacies.
Other locations 14 rue des Quatre-Frères-
Peignot, 15th (01.45.77.82.93).

Izraël
30 rue François-Miron, 4th (01.42.72.66.23).
Mᵒ Hôtel de Ville. **Open** 11am-1pm, 2-7pm Tue-
Fri; 9.30am-7pm Sat. Closed Aug. **Credit** MC, V.
Map p409 K6.
A Marais fixture, this narrow shop stocks spices and
other delights from Mexico, Turkey and India.

★ Jabugo Ibérico & Co
11 rue Clément-Marot, 8th (01.47.20.03.13).
Mᵒ Alma Marceau or Franklin D. Roosevelt.
Open 10am-9pm Mon-Sat. **Credit** AmEx, DC,
MC, V. **Map** p400 D4.
Spanish hams here have the Bellota-Bellota label,
meaning that the pigs have been allowed to feast on
acorns. Manager Philippe Poulachon compares his
cured hams to the delicacy of truffles.
▶ *Restaurant Bellota-Bellota (18 rue Jean-Nicot,*
7th, 01.53.59.96.96) also sells hams at its
adjoining épicerie.

Markets

The city council has made markets more
accessible to working people by extending
their opening hours. There are now more
than 70 markets in Paris. The city council's
website (www.paris.fr/marches) has full details
of locations and opening hours.

Marché Anvers
Pl d'Anvers, 9th. Mᵒ Anvers. **Open** 3-8.30pm Fri.
Map p402 J2.
An afternoon market that adds to the village atmos-
phere of a peaceful *quartier* down the hill from
Montmartre. Among its highlights are regional veg-
etables, hams from the Auvergne, lovingly aged
cheeses and award-winning honey.

★ Marché Bastille
Bd Richard-Lenoir, 11th. Mᵒ Richard-Lenoir.
Open 7am-3pm Sun. **Map** p403 M5.
One of the biggest markets in Paris. A favourite of
political campaigners, it's also a great source of local
cheeses, farmers' chicken and excellent fish.

Marché Batignolles
Rue Lemercier, 17th. Mᵒ Brochant. **Open** 8.30am-
1pm, 3.30-8pm Tue-Fri; 8.30am-8pm Sat; 8.30am-
3pm Sun. **Map** p401 F1.
Batignolles is more down to earth than the better-
known Raspail organic market, with a quirky selection of stallholders, many of whom produce what
they sell. Prices are higher here than at ordinary
markets, but the goods are worth it.

Marché Beauvau
Pl d'Aligre, 12th. Mᵒ Ledru-Rollin. **Open** 9am-
1pm, 4-7.30pm Tue; 4-7.30pm Wed; 9am-1pm
Thur-Sun. **Map** p407 N7.
This market still remains proudly working class.
Stallholders do their utmost to out-shout each other,
and price-conscious shoppers don't compromise
on quality.

CONSUME

★ Marché Monge

Pl Monge, 5th. M° Place Monge. **Open** 7am-2.30pm Wed, Fri; 7am-3pm Sun. **Map** p406 K8.
This pretty, compact market is set on a leafy square. It has a high proportion of producers and is much less touristy than nearby rue Mouffetard.

Marché Président-Wilson

Av Président-Wilson, 16th. M° Alma-Marceau or Iéna. **Open** 7am-2.30pm Wed; 7am-3pm Sat. **Map** p400 C5.
A classy market attracting the city's top chefs, who snap up ancient vegetable varieties.

Saxe-Breteuil

Av de Saxe, 7th. M° Ségur. **Open** 7am-2.30pm Thur; 7am-3pm Sat. **Map** p405 E8.
Saxe-Breteuil has an unrivalled setting facing the Eiffel Tower, as well as the city's most chic produce. Look for farmer's goat's cheese, rare apple varieties, Armenian specialities, abundant oysters and a handful of dedicated small producers.

Pâtisseries

Arnaud Larher

53 rue Caulaincourt, 18th (01.42.57.68.08, www. arnaud-larher.com). M° Lamarck Caulaincourt. **Open** 10am-7.30pm Tue-Sat; 10am-1pm Sun. **Credit** MC, V. **Map** p401 H1.
Look out for the strawberry-and-lychee flavoured *bonheur* and the chocolate-and-thyme *récif*.

Bogato

7 rue Liancourt, 14th (01.40.47.03.51, www.chez bogato.fr). M° Denfert-Rochereau. **Open** 10am-7pm Tue-Sat. **Credit** MC, V. **Map** p405 G10.
If Hansel and Gretel had a cake shop in Paris it might look like Bogato (a name that sounds like '*beau*

INSIDE TRACK
FOODIE SHOPPING

www.edible-paris.com
Time Out contributor Rosa Jackson leads tours or can prepare you a personalised foodie itinerary.

www.visiterungis.com
How to visit the largest wholesale food market in the world.

gateau' in French, as in 'pretty cake'). Everything here is about temptation, from the quaint wooden furniture to pastry chef Anaïs Olmer's brightly coloured cupcakes, towering under glass bells on the counter like sugary art installations. There are crunchy butter biscuits, smooth Nutella tarts, cherry cheesecakes, chocolate-coated marshmallows, and even Cheshire Cat shortbread biscuits with an edible rice paper smile. Eat in or take out; and if you like what you've scoffed, sign up for a baking class.

Finkelsztajn

27 rue des Rosiers, 4th (01.42.72.78.91, www. laboutiquejaune.com). M° St-Paul. **Open** 10am-7pm Mon, Wed-Sun. Closed 15 July-15 Aug. **Credit** (€20 minimum) AmEx, MC, V. **Map** p409 L6.
This motherly, yellow-fronted shop, in business since 1946, stocks dense Jewish cakes filled with poppy seeds, apples or cream cheese.

Gérard Mulot

76 rue de Seine, 6th (01.43.26.85.77, www. gerard-mulot.com). M° Odéon. **Open** 6.45am-8pm Mon, Tue, Thur-Sun. Closed Easter & Aug. **Credit** V. **Map** p408 H7.

CONSUME

Fauchon. See p218.

Gérard Mulot rustles up stunning pastries. Try the *mabillon*: caramel mousse with apricot marmalade. **Other locations** 6 rue du Pas de la Mule, 3rd (01.42.78.52.17); 93 rue de la Glacière, 13th (01.45.81.39.09).

★ Pierre Hermé

72 rue Bonaparte, 6th (01.43.54.47.77, www. pierreherme.com). M° Mabillon, St-Germain-des-Prés or St-Sulpice. **Open** 10am-7pm Mon-Fri, Sun; 10am-8pm Sat. Closed 1st 3wks Aug. **Credit** AmEx, DC, MC, V. **Map** p405 G7.
Pastry superstar Pierre Hermé attracts connoisseurs from St-Germain and further afield with his wonderful seasonal collections.
Other locations throughout the city.

Treats & traiteurs

★ Berthillon

29-31 rue St-Louis-en-l'Île, 4th (01.43.54.31.61, www.berthillon.fr). M° Pont Marie. **Open** 10am-8pm Wed-Sun. **No credit cards.** **Map** p409 K7.
Founded in 1954, this is the most famous ice-cream shop in Paris – and justly so. Brave the queues to sample flavours such as *caramel au gingembre* or *marron glacé*. There's also an attached *salon de thé* for coffees, teas and pastries.

★ Causses

55 rue Notre-Dame de la Lorette, 9th (01.53.16.10.10, www.causses.org). M° Pigalle or St-Georges. **Open** 10am-9.30pm Mon-Sat. **Credit** AmEx, MC, V. **Map** p401 H2.
Causses, SoPi's (South Pigalle) new *alimentation générale extraordinaire*, feels like an urban farm shop, offering a winning formula of quality seasonal produce (fruit 'n' veg, hams and cheeses), gourmet preserves and take-away breads, sandwiches and salads, plus a fill-your-own-bottle area next to the orange squeezing machine. You'll also find an array of interesting seasonings, including smoked salt and *sel fou* (salt mixed with oriental spices and pink peppercorns). For expats in need of a taste of home, Tyrrell's crisps, Covent Garden soups, HP sauce and quality English biscuits abound. There's also a tempting array of Italian deli pastas and sauces.

Dammann Frères

15 pl des Vosges, 4th (01.44.54.04.88, www. dammann.fr). M° St-Paul. **Open** 11am-7pm daily. **Credit** AmEx, DC, MC, V. **Map** p409 L6.
Dammann Frères, fine tea importers since 1825, have finally opened their own boutique, a wonderful den of a place with a beamed roof and mahogany shelves displaying hundreds of their exquisite black boxes. The *orgue à thés* allows you to sniff the aromas of 160 blends. A small tin of loose tea or 24 tea bags costs €7 and they also sell traditional oriental iron teapots. Everything is attractively giftwrapped, making it perfect gift territory.

Fauchon

26 & 30 pl de la Madeleine, 8th (01.70.39.38.00, www.fauchon.com). M° Madeleine. **Open** *No.26* 8am-8.30pm Mon-Sat. *No.30* 9am-8pm Mon-Sat. **Credit** AmEx, MC, V. **Map** p401 F4.
The city's most famous food shop is worth a visit, particularly for the beautifully packaged gift items and the stunning pastries and cakes – or, as Fauchon likes to call them, '*le snacking chic*'. Photo *p217*.

★ Hédiard

21 pl de la Madeleine, 8th (01.43.12.88.88, www.hediard.fr). M° Madeleine. **Open** 9am-8.30pm Mon-Sat. **Credit** AmEx, DC, MC, V. **Map** p401 F4.
Hédiard's charming shop dates back to 1880, when it introduced exotic foods to Paris, specialising in rare teas and coffees, spices, jams and candied fruits. **Other locations** throughout the city.

Huilerie Artisanale Leblanc

12 rue Jacob, 6th (01.44.07.36.58, www.huile-leblanc.com). M° St-Germain-des-Prés. **Open** 11am-1.30pm, 2.30-7.30pm Tue-Sat. Closed 2wks Aug. **No credit cards.** **Map** p405 H6.
The Leblanc family from Burgundy started making walnut oil before branching out to press pure oils from hazelnuts, almonds, pine nuts, grilled peanuts and olives. There are vinegars and mustards too.

Première Pression Provence

3 rue Antoine Vollon, 12th (01.53.33.03.59, www. premiere-pression-provence.com). M° Ledru Rollin. **Open** 10.30am-2.30pm, 3.30-7.30pm Tue-Sat; 10am-5pm Sun. **Credit** AmEx, MC, V. **Map** p407 N7.
Première Pression Provence is L'Occitan creator Olivier Baussan's project, where you are encouraged to taste spoonfuls of single-producer olive oil to educate your palate about the nuances of *vert*, *mûr* and *noir* (known as the '*fruités*'). Two dozen small producers send their oils direct from their Provençal olive groves to the boutiques, where they are sold in aluminium cans with colour-coded labels.
Other locations 35 rue Charlot, 3rd (01.57.40.69.58); 9 rue des Martyrs, 9th (01.48.78.86.51); 37 rue du Roi de Sicile, 4th (01.49.96.55.40).

Torréfacteur Verlet

256 rue St-Honoré, 1st (01.42.60.67.39, www.cafesverlet.com). M° Palais Royal Musée du Louvre. **Open** 9.30am-6.30pm Mon-Sat. Closed Aug. **Credit** MC, V. **Map** p401 G5.
Eric Duchossoy roasts rare coffee beans to perfection – sip a cup here or take some home to savour.

GALLERIES

Air de Paris

32 rue Louise-Weiss, 13th (01.44.23.02.77, www.airdeparis.com). M° Chevaleret. **Open** 11am-7pm Tue-Sat. **Map** p407 M10.

Deyrolle. *See p220.*

Lambert celebrated 30 years in the business in 2006, and remains a powerhouse of the French scene, with plenty of big-name stuff, a New York offshoot and a personal collection granted museum status in Avignon. The gallery includes a dedicated area for video installations, and the main space shows leading international names – American bigwigs Andres Serrano, Sol LeWitt, Nan Goldin and Jenny Holzer, plus next-generation artists Douglas Gordon and Jonathan Monk. The street-front art bookshop has a window showcase and basement gallery for younger talents.

Polka Galerie
Cour de Venise, 12 rue Saint-Gilles, 3rd (01.71.20.54.97, www.polkagalerie.com). M° Bréguet-Sabin or Chemin Vert. **Open** 11am-7.30pm Tue-Sat. **Map** p409 L6.
'Every photo has a tale to tell': such is the leitmotif at Polka Galerie, where Adélie de Ipanema and Edouard Genestar have entirely devoted their art space to photojournalism. Works on display are signed by photographers such as Ethan Levitas, Marc Riboud, Reza and Diego Morayima. While you're there, pick up a copy of *Polka Magazine*, a fortnightly spread brimming with picture-rich articles, many of which tie in with the exhibitions in the gallery.

GIFTS & SOUVENIRS
Florists

This gallery shows experimental, neo-conceptual and chaotic material. A hip international stable of artists includes Liam Gillick, Carsten Höller, Sarah Morris and Philippe Parreno.

★ Galerie Emmanuel Perrotin
76 rue de Turenne & 10 impasse St-Claude, 3rd (01.42.16.79.79, www.galerieperrotin.com). M° St-Sébastien Froissart. **Open** 11am-7pm Tue-Sat. **Map** p409 L5.
Perrotin is one of the sharpest figures in town: not content with owning a gallery in Miami and a glossy magazine, he has recently jumped on the design bandwagon with shows by Robert Stadler and Eric Benqué. As well as the quirky Japanese set of Takashi Murakami, Mariko Mori et al, and big French names such as Sophie Calle, Xavier Veilhan, Tatiana Trouvé and Bernard Frize, he also features radical Austrian collective Gelatin.

Galerie Fatiha Selam
58 rue Chapon, 3rd (09.83.33.65.69, www.fatiha selam.com). M° Rambuteau or Arts et Métiers. **Open** 11am-7pm Mon-Sat. **Map** p409 K5.
This new addition to a burgeoning gallery street opened in late 2012 with an exhibition of US artist Stephen Schultz's dreamlike canvases. Fatiha Selam brings a fresh eye to the NoMa art scene and promises to explore figurative and abstract contemporary artists both known and emerging.

Galerie Yvon Lambert
108 rue Vieille-du-Temple, 3rd (01.42.71.09.33, www.yvon-lambert.com). M° Filles du Calvaire. **Open** 10am-7pm Tue-Sat. **Map** p409 L5.

★ Culture(s)
46 rue de Lancry, 10th (01.48.03.58.71). M° Jacques Bonsergent or République. **Open** 11am-2pm, 3-7pm Tue-Sat. **Credit** AmEx, MC, V. **Map** p402 L4.
In a loft-style studio, this unusual florist combines exotic flowers, trees and garden-themed items, such as floral printed rain hats. Truly original.

Au Nom de la Rose
87 rue St-Antoine, 4th (01.42.71.34.24, www. aunomdelarose.fr). M° St-Paul. **Open** *Sept-July* 10am-9pm Mon-Sat; 9am-6pm Sun. *Aug* 10am-9pm Mon-Sat. **Credit** AmEx, DC, MC, V. **Map** p409 L7.
Specialising in roses, Au Nom can supply a bouquet, as well as rose-based beauty products and candles. **Other locations** throughout the city.

Gifts & eccentricities

Arty Dandy
1 rue de Furstemberg, 6th (01.43.54.00.36, www.artydandy.com). M° Mabillon. **Open** 10am-7pm Mon-Fri; 11am-8pm Sat. **Credit** AmEx, MC, V. **Map** p408 H7.
'Dandyism is the last spark of heroism amid decadence,' said Baudelaire. Taking this as its motto, Arty Dandy is a concept shop that embraces the

CONSUME

Diptyque.

CONSUME

surreal, the tongue-in-cheek and the poetic – an R.MUTT sticker to create your own Duchampian loo, and the 'Karl who?' bag (which KL himself has carried) are instant pleasers. More sublime offerings include Jaime Hayon's 'Lover' figurines and Sebastien Le Gal watercolours.

Deyrolle
46 rue du Bac, 7th (01.42.22.30.07, www.deyrolle. com). M° Rue du Bac. **Open** 10am-1pm, 2-7pm Mon; 10am-7pm Tue-Sat. **Credit** AmEx, MC, V. **Map** p405 G6.
Opened in 1831 by Jean-Baptiste Deyrolle, a taxidermist and avid traveller, this shop has always been a curiosity, with its bizarre menagerie of lions, giraffes, polar bears, butterflies and bugs. After a fire swept through the shop in 2008, Parisians from all walks of life came together to save the place. At the forefront was a group of 50 artists, who set about raising funds by creating an art collection inspired by the remains of the original Deyrolle collection. The shop reopened in late 2009 and has lost little of its magic – it remains a great place to escape the city, buy a tiger for the living room, or simply to fire your imagination. *Photo p219.*

★ Diptyque
34 bd St-Germain, 5th (01.43.26.77.44, www. diptyqueparis.com). M° Maubert Mutualité. **Open** 10am-7pm Mon-Sat. **Credit** MC, V. **Map** p405 G6.
Diptyque's divinely scented candles are the quintessential gift from Paris. They come in 48 different varieties, from wild fennel to pomander, and are probably the best you'll ever find. Prices are not cheap, but with 50 to 60 hours' burn time, they're worth every euro.

Nature et Découvertes
Carrousel du Louvre, 99 rue de Rivoli, 1st (01.47.03.47.43, www.natureetdecouvertes.com). M° Palais Royal Musée du Louvre. **Open** 10am-8pm daily. **Credit** AmEx, DC, MC, V. **Map** p401 H5.
This store stocks a great range of stuff for junior and grown-up gadgeteers, from infrared parent detectors to high-tech weather stations. It's also worth remembering that ten per cent of all the group's profits go to the Fondation Nature et Découvertes, which supports environmental causes in Europe and Africa. **Other locations** throughout the city.

★ Sennelier
3 quai Voltaire, 7th (01.42.60.72.15, www. magasinsennelier.fr). M° St-Germain-des-Prés. **Open** 2-6.30pm Mon; 10am-12.45pm, 2-6.30pm Tue-Sat. **Credit** AmEx, DC, MC, V. **Map** p405 G6.
Old-fashioned colour merchant Sennelier sells oil paints, watercolours and pastels, rare pigments, primed canvases, varnishes and paper. **Other locations** 4bis rue de la Grande-Chaumière, 6th (01.46.33.72.39).

Studio Harcourt
10 rue Jean Goujon, 8th (01.42.56.67.67, www.studio-harcourt.eu). M° Franklin D Roosevelt. **Open** times vary. Reserve in advance. **Credit** AmEx, DC, MC, V. **Map** p401 E5.
Studio Harcourt is no ordinary photo booth. Founded in 1934, this famous studio celebrated its 75th anniversary in 2009 and past posers have included Alain Delon, Edith Piaf and Jean Reno. For €900 (or €1,900 for a prestige version), you get to pose like a star and come away with a signed portrait. If your star billing doesn't run to €900, you can take a tour of the studio for just €35.

HEALTH & BEAUTY
Cosmetics

★ L'Artisan Parfumeur
24 bd Raspail, 7th (01.42.22.23.32, www.
artisanparfumeur.com). M° Rue du Bac. **Open**
10.30am-7.30pm Mon-Sat. **Credit** AmEx, DC,
MC, V. **Map** p405 G7.
Among the scented candles, potpourri and charms,
you'll find some of the finest perfume Paris can offer
– Mûres et Musc has been a bestseller for more than
two decades.
Other locations throughout the city.

By Terry
21 & 36 passage Véro-Dodat, 1st (01.44.76.00.76,
www.byterry.com). M° Palais Royal Musée du
Louvre. **Open** 10.30am-7pm Mon-Sat. **Credit**
AmEx, MC, V. **Map** p402 H5.
Terry de Gunzburg, who earned her reputation at
Yves Saint Laurent, offers made-to-measure 'haute
couleur' make-up by skilled chemists and colourists
combining high-tech treatments and handmade precision. There's prêt-à-porter, too.
Other locations 30 rue de la Trémoille, 8th
(01.44.43.04.04); 10 av Victor-Hugo, 16th
(01.55.73.00.73).

Détaille 1905
10 rue St-Lazare, 9th (01.48.78.68.50,
www.detaille.com). M° Notre-Dame-de-Lorette.
Open 11am-1pm, 2-7pm Tue-Sat. **Credit**
MC, V. **Map** p401 H3.
Step back in time at this gorgeous shop, opened, as
the name suggests, in 1905 by war artist Edouard
Détaille. There are six fragrances available (three
for men and three for women), all conjured up from
century-old recipes.

Editions de Parfums Frédéric Malle
37 rue de Grenelle, 7th (01.42.22.76.40,
www.editionsdeparfums.com). M° Rue du Bac or
St-Sulpice. **Open** noon-7pm Mon; 11am-7pm Tue-
Sat. **Credit** AmEx, DC, MC, V. **Map** p405 F6.
Choose from a range of eight perfumes by Frédéric
Malle, former consultant to Hermès and Lacroix.
Carnal Flower by Dominique Ropion is seduction
in a bottle.
Other locations 21 rue du Mont-Thabor, 1st
(01.42.22.16.89); 140 av Victor-Hugo, 16th
(01.45.05.39.02).

Guerlain
68 av des Champs-Elysées, 8th (01.45.62.52.57,
www.guerlain.com). M° Franklin D. Roosevelt.
Open 10.30am-8pm Mon-Sat; noon-7pm Sun.
Credit AmEx, DC, MC, V. **Map** p401 E4.
The golden oldie of luxury beauty products and
scents is looking as ravishing than ever. Head to the
first floor to get the full measure of the history

behind the house that created the mythic Samsara,
Mitsouko and L'Heure Bleue.
Other locations 2 pl Vendôme, 1st (01.42.60.68.61);
29 rue de Sèvres, 6th (01.42.22.46.60); 66 bd du
Montparnasse, 15th (01.43.20.95.40).

★ Salons du Palais-Royal Shiseido
Jardins du Palais-Royal, 142 galerie de Valois, 1st
(01.49.27.09.09, www.sergelutens.com). M° Palais
Royal Musée du Louvre. **Open** 10am-7pm Mon-
Sat. **Credit** AmEx, DC, MC, V. **Map** p401 H5.
Under the arcades of the Palais-Royal, Shiseido's
perfumer Serge Lutens practises his aromatic arts.
A former photographer at Paris *Vogue* and artistic
director of make-up at Christian Dior, Lutens is a
maestro of rare taste. Bottles of his concoctions –
Tubéreuse Criminelle, Rahat Loukoum and Ambre
Sultan – can be sampled by visitors. Look out for
Fleurs d'Oranger, which the great man defines as
the smell of happiness. Many of the perfumes are
exclusive to the Salons; prices start at around €100.
Other locations 2 pl Vendôme, 1st
(01.42.60.68.61); 29 rue de Sèvres, 6th
(01.42.22.46.60); 66 bd du Montparnasse, 15th
(01.43.20.95.40).

Sephora
70 av des Champs-Elysées, 8th (01.53.93.22.50,
www.sephora.fr). M° Franklin D. Roosevelt. **Open**
10am-midnight Mon-Thur, Sun; 10am-1am Fri, Sat.
Credit AmEx, DC, MC, V. **Map** p401 E4.
Founded in 1969, the Sephora chain has more than
750 shops around the globe. The Champs-Elysées
flagship houses 12,000 brands of scent and slap.
Other locations throughout the city.

Salons & spas

★ After the Rain
Saint James & Albany Hôtel, 202 rue de Rivoli,
1st (01.44.58.43.77, www.aftertherain.ch).
M° Tuileries. **Open** 7.30am-10pm daily.
Credit AmEx, DC, MC, V. **Map** p405 G5.
This pioneer Swiss urban spa makes a glorious
retreat from the designer shopping stresses of nearby
rue du Faubourg-St-Honoré. Signature massages
include Honey Release and Aroma Stone Therapy,
or enjoy a massage *à deux* – complete with rose petal
bath, strawberries and champagne.

Anne Sémonin
2 rue des Petits Champs, 2nd (01.42.60.94.66,
www.annesemonin.com). M° Bourse. **Open**
10am-7pm Tue-Sat. **Credit** AmEx, DC, MC, V.
Map p402 H5.
Facials involve delicious concoctions of basil, lavender, lemongrass, ginger and plant essences. Also on
offer are reflexology and a selection of massage
styles, from Thai to ayurvedic. Body treatments cost
from €70 to €210. Sémonin's renowned seaweed
skincare products and essential oils are also on sale.

CONSUME

CONSUME

Appartement 217
217 rue St-Honoré, 1st (01.42.96.00.96,
www.lappartement217.com). Mº Tuileries.
Open 10am-7pm Tue-Sat. **Credit** AmEx,
DC, MC, V. **Map** p401 G5.
A beautiful feng-shuied Haussmannian apartment
is the setting for facials using organic beauty guru
Dr Hauschka's products and ayurvedic or deep tis-
sue massages. The water has been decalcified, electrical currents are insulated, and the silky-soft
kimonos are made from organic wood pulp.

Les Bains du Marais
31-33 rue des Blancs-Manteaux, 4th
(01.44.61.02.02, www.lesbainsdumarais.com).
Mº St-Paul. **Open** *Men* 10am-11pm Thur;
10am-8pm Fri. *Women* 11am-8pm Mon; 10am-
11pm Tue; 10am-7pm Wed. *Mixed (swimwear*
required) 7-11pm Wed; 10am-8pm Sat; 10am-
11pm Sun. Closed Aug. **Credit** AmEx, MC, V.
Map p409 K6.
This hammam and spa mixes the modern and traditional (lounging beds and mint tea). Facials, waxing
and essential oil massages (€70) are also available.
The hammam and standard massage are €35 each.

★ Hammam de la Grande Mosquée
39 rue Geoffrey St-Hilaire, 5th (01.43.31.38.20,
www.la-mosquee.com). Mº Censier Daubenton.
Open *Men* 2-9pm Tue; 10am-9pm Sun. *Women*
10am-9pm Mon, Wed, Thur, Sat; 2-9pm Fri.
Credit MC, V. **Map** p406 K9.
The authentic hammam experience in this beautiful
1920s mosque has become popular with parisians,
so avoid the weekends when the volume of traffic
makes it less relaxing. Follow a steam session with
a *gommage* (exfoliation with a rough mitt), then a
massage. The hammam is €15, *gommage* €10 and
massage €10 for 10mins. Swimwear is compulsory.
Towel and gown hire is also available.

★ Hammam Medina Centre
43-45 rue Petit, 19th (01.42.02.31.05,
www.hammammed.com). Mº Ourcq. **Open**
Women 11am-10pm Mon-Fri; 9am-7pm Sun.
Mixed (swimwear required) 10am-9pm Sat.
Credit MC, V. **Map** p403 N5.
This hammam is hard to beat – spotless mosaic-tiled
surroundings, flowered sarongs and a relaxing pool.
The exotic 'Forfait florale' option (€139) will have
you enveloped in rose petals and massaged with
huile d'Argan from Morocco, and the more simple
hammam and *gommage* followed by mint tea and
pastries is €39. Plan to spend a few hours here, as
the soft-voiced staff take things at their own pace.

Spa Nuxe
32 rue Montorgueil, 1st (01.42.36.65.65,
www.nuxe.com). Mº Les Halles. **Open** 10am-9pm
Mon-Fri; 9.30am-7.30pm Sat. **Credit** AmEx,
MC, V. **Map** p402 J4.

This luxurious day spa housed in stone vaults
with wooden cabins and safari-style tents offers
massages and skin treatments using Nuxe's gentle,
plant-based products. The facials, where you
undress completely, begin with a short foot, tummy
and neck message for total relaxation; from €80.

HOUSE & HOME
Antiques & flea markets

No trip to Paris is complete without a visit to
one of the city's flea markets. The enormous
Marché aux Puces de St-Ouen has an
unrivalled abundance of junk and genuine
design classics; in town, traditional antiques
can be found in the **Louvre des Antiquaires**,
and around Carré Rive Gauche (6th), Village
Suisse and rue du Fbg-St-Honoré (1st). You'll
find art deco in St-Germain-des-Prés, and retro
by rue de Charonne (11th). For books, look at
the **bouquinistes** (*see p193* **Inside Track**).

Louvre des Antiquaires
2 pl du Palais-Royal, 1st (01.42.97.27.27,
www.louvre-antiquaires.com). Mº Palais Royal
Musée du Louvre. **Open** 11am-7pm Tue-Sun.
Closed Sun in July & Aug. **Credit** varies.
Map p406 H5.
This upmarket antiques centre houses 250 antiques
dealers: perfect for Louis XV furniture, tapestries,
porcelain, jewellery, model ships and tin soldiers.

Marché aux Puces d'Aligre
Pl d'Aligre, rue d'Aligre, 12th. Mº Ledru-Rollin.
Open 7am-2pm Tue-Sun. **Map** p407 N7.
The only flea market in central Paris, Aligre stays
true to its junk tradition with a handful of *brocan-*
teurs peddling books, phone cards, kitchenware and
oddities at what seem to be optimistic prices.

★ Marché aux Puces de St-Ouen
Av de la Porte de Clignancourt, 18th. Mº Porte
de Clignancourt. **Open** 11am-5pm Mon; 9am-
6pm Sat, Sun.
With 3,000 traders and up to 180,000 visitors each
weekend, this is thought to be the biggest flea market in the world. The fleas left long ago, and since
1885 what started as a rag-and-bone shantytown
outside the city limits has been organised into a
series of enclosed villages, some entirely covered and
others with open-air streets and covered boutiques
for the antiques dealers. South of this sprawls the
canvas-covered part with African tat, joss sticks,
fake Converse trainers and cheap batteries.

Marché aux Puces de Vanves
Av Georges-Lafenestre & av Marc-Sangnier, 14th.
Mº Porte de Vanves. **Open** 7am-2pm Sat, Sun.
Vanves is the smallest of the Paris flea markets,
and the atmosphere is infinitely more tranquil than

Marché aux Puces de St-Ouen.

its much bigger sister at Clingancourt. It's a favourite with serious collectors, so arrive early for the best pick of decent vintage clothes, dolls, costume jewellery and silverware.

Le Village St-Paul
Rue St-Paul, rue Charlemagne & quai des Célestins, 4th (www.levillagesaintpaul.com). M° St-Paul. **Open** 10am-7pm Mon-Sat. **No credit cards**. **Map** p409 L7.
This colony of antiques sellers is a source of retro furniture, kitchenware and wine gadgets.

Design & interiors

The vast **Lafayette Maison** (*see p191*) offers a selection of design and homeware. Also great for modern furniture is the biannual **Les Puces du Design** (www.pucesdudesign.com), which takes place every June and October.

Astier de Villatte
173 rue St-Honoré, 1st (01.42.60.74.13, www.astierdevillatte.com). M° Palais Royal Musée du Louvre. **Open** 11am-7.30pm Mon-Sat. Closed 3wks Aug. **Credit** AmEx, MC, V. **Map** p401 G4.
Once home to Napoleon's silversmith, this ancient warren now houses ceramics inspired by 17th- and 18th-century designs, handmade by the Astier de Villatte siblings in their Bastille workshop.

Byzance Home
129 rue de Turenne, 3rd (01.42.77.89.42). M° Filles du Calvaire. **Open** 11am-1pm, 2-7pm Tue-Sat. **Credit** AmEx, DC, MC, V. **Map** p409 L5.
In a cool loft space, interior designer Soraya Belhadia displays her *coups de coeur* for the home. Italian designers are in the majority, with Zanotta pouffes, Lana leather chaise longues from Palomba and one-off marquetry chests by Camobio.

★ Caravane Chambre 19
19 rue St-Nicolas, 12th (01.53.02.96.96, www. caravane.fr). M° Ledru-Rollin. **Open** 11am-7pm Tue-Sat. Closed 2wks Aug. **Credit** AmEx, MC, V. **Map** p407 M7.
This offshoot of Françoise Dorget's original Marais shop has goodies such as exquisite hand-sewn quilts from west Bengal, crisp cotton and organdie tunics, Berber scarves, lounging sofas and daybeds.
Other locations 6 rue Pavée, 4th (01.44.61.04.20); 22 rue St-Nicolas, 12th (01.53.17.18.55).

Christian Liaigre
42 rue du Bac, 7th (01.53.63.33.66, www. christian-liaigre.fr). M° Rue du Bac. **Open** 10am-7pm Mon-Sat. Closed 3wks Aug. **Credit** AmEx, MC, V. **Map** p405 G6.
This French interior decorator fitted out Marc Jacobs' boutiques. His showroom displays his elegant lighting and furniture designs.
Other location 61 rue de Varenne, 7th (01.47.53.78.76).

Christophe Delcourt
47 rue de Babylone, 7th (01.42.71.34.84, www. christophedelcourt.com). M° Jacques Bonsergent. **Open** 9.30am-6.30pm Mon-Fri. Closed Aug. **Credit** AmEx, DC, MC, V. **Map** p401 G4.
Christophe Delcourt's handsome art deco-influenced, geometrical lights and furniture are given a contemporary spin by their combination of stained wood and black steel.

★ Designpack Gallery
24 rue de Richelieu, 1st (01.44.85.86.00, www. designpackgallery.fr). M° Palais Royal Musée du Louvre. **Open** 11am-7pm Mon-Fri; noon-7.30pm Sat. **Credit** MC, V. **Map** p401 H5.
Too much packaging? Not according to Fabrice Peltier, who is passionate about the art of *emballage*, to the extent of opening his own gallery-boutique not far from the Musée des Arts Décoratifs. Once a Tetrapak designer, he now recycles his own used packaging into desirable objects: red plastic bottles become lighting and clothes hangers, and bottle tops are melted down to become a multicoloured armchair. African tin trinkets, Austrian vases made from cut-down bottles, and other ingenious recycling from around the world is also on sale, along with a library of books about packaging and themed exhibitions on packaging past and present.

CONSUME

★ FR66

*25 rue du Renard, 4th (01.44.54.35.36, www.
fr66.com). M° Hôtel de Ville.* **Open** 10am-7pm
Mon-Sat. Closed 2-3wks Aug. **Credit** AmEx,
MC, V. **Map** p406 K6.

Somewhere between a gallery and a shop, this two-
level experimental space accommodates contemporary artists and designers who produce exciting and
original products for the home.

Galerie Patrick Seguin

*5 rue des Taillandiers, 11th (01.47.00.32.35,
www.patrickseguin.com). M° Bastille or Ledru-
Rollin.* **Open** 10am-7pm Mon-Sat. Closed 2wks
Aug. **Credit** AmEx, MC, V. **Map** p407 M7.

Seguin specialises in French design from the 1950s:
items by Jean Prouvé and Charlotte Perriand are on
display in this handsome showroom designed by
Jean Nouvel. Seguin has also collaborated on some
ground-breaking exhibitions around the world.

★ A La Providence
(Quincaillerie Leclercq)

*151 rue du Fbg-St-Antoine, 11th (01.43.43.06.41).
M° Ledru-Rollin.* **Open** 10am-1pm, 3-6pm Tue-Sat.
Credit MC, V. **Map** p407 N7.

Step into the past at this museum-piece *quincaillerie*
in which 170-year-old wooden cabinets are filled
with knobs, locks and other brass accoutrements for
dolling up or restoring old furniture and doors.
Newly crafted by artisans, the pieces look authentically antique; there is also an expensive range of
glass and crystal doorknobs.

Sentou Galerie

*26 bd Raspail, 7th (01.45.49.00.05, www.sentou.fr).
M° Pont Marie.* **Open** 10am-7pm Tue-Sat. **Credit**
AmEx, MC, V. **Map** p409 K7.

A trend-setting shop for colourful tableware and furniture: painted Chinese flasks, vases and so on.
Other location 29 rue François-Miron, 4th
(01.42.78.50.60).

Silvera

*41 rue du Fbg-St-Antoine, 11th (01.43.43.06.75,
www.silvera.fr). M° Bastille or Ledru-Rollin.*
Open 10am-7pm Mon-Sat. Closed 2wks Aug.
Credit AmEx, MC, V. **Map** p407 M7.

The former Le Bihan was taken over by Silvera in
2005 and is now a three-floor showcase for modern
design. Look out for furniture and lighting from
Perriand, Pesce, Pillet, Morrison, Arad and others.
Other locations throughout the city.

Talents – Création Contemporaine

*1bis rue Scribe, 9th (01.40.17.98.38, www.
ateliersdart.com). M° Opéra.* **Open** 11am-7pm
Mon-Sat. **Credit** AmEx, MC, V. **Map** p401 G4.

This contemporary showroom for 70 creators affil-
iated to the craftworkers' federation Ateliers d'Art
de France is a pure white space in which you'll find

one-off designs in furniture, lighting, glass, ceramics
and jewellery. If you want something made to measure they can put you in touch with the designers.
Other locations 22 & 26 av Niel, 17th
(01.44.40.22.80).

Kitchen & bathroom

★ E Dehillerin

*18 rue Coquillière, 1st (01.42.36.53.13, www.
e-dehillerin.fr). M° Les Halles.* **Open** 9am-12.30pm,
2-6pm Mon; 9am-6pm Tue-Sat. **Credit** MC, V.
Map p402 J5.

This no-nonsense warehouse stocks just about every
kitchen utensil ever invented.

Laguiole Galerie

*1 pl Ste-Opportune, 1st (01.40.06.09.75, www.
forge-de-laguiole.com). M° Châtelet.* **Open** 10.30am-
1pm, 1.40-7pm Mon-Sat. **Credit** AmEx, MC, V.
Map p406 J6.

Philippe Starck designed this chic boutique, a showcase for France's classic knife, the Laguiole.

MUSIC & ENTERTAINMENT

Apple Store

*12 rue Halévy, 9th (01.44.83.42.00, www.apple.
com). M° Opéra.* **Open** 9am-8pm Mon-Wed;
9am-9pm Thur-Sat. **Credit** AmEx, DC, MC, V.
Map p408 J7.

Apple's second Paris store opened in summer 2010
in a stunning belle époque former bank facing the
Opéra Garnier. To fit in with such hallowed surroundings, Apple strayed from its standard store
model, retaining the original carved wooden staircase, wrought-iron railings, marble columns and
mosaic tile floor.
Other locations 99 rue de Rivoli, 1st
(01.43.16.78.00).

Crocodisc

*40-42 rue des Ecoles, 5th (01.43.54.47.95,
www.crocodisc.com). M° Maubert Mutualité.*
Open 11am-7pm Tue-Sat. Closed 2wks Aug.
Credit MC, V. **Map** p408 J7.

The excellent albeit expensive range includes rock,
funk, African, country and classical, in the form of
new and second-hand vinyl and CDs. For jazz and
blues, try sister shop Crocojazz.
Other locations Crocojazz, 64 rue de la
Montagne-Ste-Geneviève, 5th (01.46.34.78.38).

Fargo

*42 rue de la Folie-Méricourt, 11th
(01.48.05.49.52, www.fargostore.com).
M° Parmentier or St-Ambroise.* **Open** 11am-
8pm Mon-Sat. **Credit** MC, V. **Map** p403 M5.

With its handsome wooden façade and neon lights,
Fargo wouldn't look out of place in San Francisco.
It's got a Far West feel inside too (despite being a

CONSUME

stone's throw from the Canal Saint-Martin), with collections that cover country music in all its forms (rock, pop, folk and new wave). The shop has only been around since 2010, but it's got good connections: regular free showcases draw the crowds (Moriarty and Steve Smyth have both played here).

Fnac Forum
Levels -1 to -3, Porte Lescot, Forum des Halles, 1st (08.25.02.00.20, ticket office 08.92.68.36.22, www.fnac.com). M° Les Halles. **Open** 10am-8pm Mon-Sat. **Credit** AmEx, MC, V. **Map** p402 J5.
Fnac is a supermarket of culture: books, DVDs, CDs, audio kit, computers and photographic equipment. Most branches stock everything; others specialise. All branches operate as a concert box office.
▶ *Get discounts on large purchases by signing up for Fnac membership.*
Other locations throughout the city.

Monster Melodies
9 rue des Déchargeurs, 1st (01.40.28.09.39, www.monstermelodies.fr). M° Les Halles. **Open** noon-7pm Mon-Sat. **Credit** MC, V. **Map** p402 J5.
The owners are very willing to help you hunt down your treasured tracks – and with more than 10,000 second-hand CDs of every variety, that's just as well.

Sony Style
39 av George V, 8th (09.69.39.39.39, www.boutiquegeorge5.fr). M° George V. **Open** 11am-7pm Mon-Sat. **Credit** AmEx, DC, MC, V. **Map** p400 D4.
Sony's concept store brings high-tech gadgets and zen decor together in an *hôtel particulier*. Phones, cameras, computers and PlayStations are all here, and the latest innovations from Japan are beamed in on big screens to let you know what the future holds. The store also offers free IT coaching.

Virgin Megastore
52-60 av des Champs-Elysées, 8th (01.49.53.50.00, www.virginmegastore.fr). M° Franklin D. Roosevelt. **Open** 10am-midnight Mon-Sat; noon-midnight Sun. **Credit** AmEx, DC, MC, V. **Map** p401 E4.
The luxury of perusing CDs and DVDs till midnight makes this a choice spot, and the listening posts let you sample any CD by scanning its barcode. Tickets for concerts and sports events are available here too. This main branch has the best selection of books.
Other locations throughout the city.

Musical instruments

Paris Accordéon
80 rue Daguerre, 14th (01.43.22.13.48, www.parisaccordeon.com). M° Denfert Rochereau or Gaîté. **Open** 10.30am-1pm, 2.30-7pm Tue-Sat. **Credit** AmEx, MC, V. **Map** p405 G10.
Accordions, from simple squeezeboxes to beautiful tortoiseshell models, second-hand and new.

SPORT & FITNESS

Unless you're in the market for specialised equipment, you'll find what you want at **Go Sport** (www.go-sport.com) or the excellent **Décathlon** (www.decathlon.fr).

Citadium
50-56 rue de Caumartin, 9th (01.55.31.74.00, www.citadium.com). M° Havre Caumartin. **Open** 10am-8pm Mon-Wed, Fri, Sat; 10am-9pm Thur. **Credit** AmEx, DC, MC, V. **Map** p401 G3.
Cultish emporium of sporting goods, from hip watches to cross-country skis, on four themed floors. Labels include Nike, Burton and North Face.

Nauti Store
18bis rue Brunel, 17th (01.44.09.04.48, www.nautistore.fr). M° Argentine. **Open** 11am-7pm Mon-Sat. **Credit** DC, MC, V. **Map** p400 B3.
This shop stocks a vast range of sailing clothes and shoes from labels such as Helly Hansen, Musto, Aigle and Sebago.

René Pierre
35 rue de Maubeuge, 9th (01.44.91.91.21, www.rene-pierre.fr). M° Poissonnière. **Open** 10am-1pm, 2-6.30pm Mon-Fri; 10am-6.30pm Sat. **Credit** MC, V. **Map** p402 H3.
France's finest table-football tables, ready for free delivery as far as Calais for UK buyers.

TICKETS

The easiest way to reserve and buy tickets for concerts, plays and matches is from a **Fnac** store (*see left*). You can also reserve on www.fnac.com or by phone (08.92.68.36.22). **Virgin** (*see left*) has now teamed up with Ticketnet to create an online ticket office (www.virginmega.fr). Tickets can also be purchased by phone (08.25.12.91.39) and sent to your home for a €6.45 fee.

TRAVEL AGENTS

Nouvelles Frontières
13 av de l'Opéra, 1st (01.42.61.02.62, www.nouvelles-frontieres.fr). M° Pyramides. **Open** 9am-7pm Mon-Sat. **Credit** V. Map p401 H5.
Agent with 16 branches in Paris.
Other locations throughout the city.

Thomas Cook
38 av de Wagram, 8th (08.26.82.67.77, www.thomascook.fr). M° Ternes. **Open** 10am-7pm Mon-Fri; 10am-1pm, 2-6.30pm Sat. **Credit** AmEx, DC, MC, V. **Map** p400 C3.
Travel agent with more than 30 branches in and around Paris.
Other locations throughout the city.

CONSUME

Inspiration wherever you are

Hotels

Sleep tight in the city of light.

After a slew of new hotel openings in the last couple of years, the big news during 2012 was all about closures, with two of the city's most famous palace hotels shutting their doors for major renovations. The Ritz and the Crillon will both be shut for business until 2014, as they freshen themselves up to try to contend with the influx of Asian super-luxury from the likes of Shangri-La, Raffles and Mandarin Oriental. In the meantime, these new five-star arrivals have taken service and design to a new level, although rack rates can be eye-watering. For something a little less *luxe*, the city's burgeoning boutique hotel selection means you can still afford good design, as long as you can make do without the uniformed doormen.

STAYING IN PARIS

Paris's luxury palaces continue to offer the ultimate dream hotel experience: at the **Bristol**, the **George V** and the **Plaza Athénée** uniformed flunkeys whisk you through the revolving doors to an otherworldly domain of tinkling china, thick carpets and concierges for whom your wish is their desire, for a generous tip. And the last few years have brought even more competition to the luxury sector with the completion of a new **Shangri-La** in the 16th, the complete makeover of the **Royal Monceau** on avenue Hoche by Philippe Starck, plus the arrival of the **W Paris-Opéra** and **Mandarin Oriental** – one can only wonder why it took quite so long for Mandarin Oriental to set up in a city seemingly made for its brand of high-end, low-key chic.

If palaces are beyond your pocket, then opt for one of Paris's increasingly luxurious boutique hotels. You can be soothed by fine linen, marble baths and a dreamy pool and hammam at **Le Metropolitan**, walk through silk taffeta curtains to your own terrace at **Le Petit Paris**, fall into a deep sleep at the pure white technological marvel that is the **Hôtel Gabriel**, gaze across the Marais rooftops from the cool new **Jules et Jim**, and fraternise at the trendy cava bar of the Spanish-owned **Banke**. For those who like a bit more glitz, the sparkly **Opéra Diamond** and unabashedly sexy **Sublim Eiffel** use fibre optics to create your own starry galaxy. All of these hotels have made

the smooth move of abandoning petty pay-per-hour Wi-Fi in favour of providing it free, and Nespresso machines and iPod docks are making an appearance in bedrooms too.

Further down the scale, there is now a wide choice of moderately priced and even budget design hotels, especially in the trendy east and north-east of the city, such as the Starck-designed **Mama Shelter, Standard Design Hotel, Le Quartier Bastille, 20 Prieuré** and **Hôtel Crayon**. And shoestring travellers should consider **St Christopher's Inn** on the Canal d'Ourcq, whose façade is lit up like an art installation at night. But if Paris wouldn't be Paris for you without chintzy wallpaper, springy beds and a bathroom on the landing never fear: faithful stalwart the **Henri IV** is still going strong.

Hotels are graded according to an official star rating system designed to sort the deluxe from the dumps – but we haven't followed it in this guide, as the ratings merely reflect room size and amenities such as lifts or bars, rather than other important factors such as decor, staff or atmosphere. Instead, we've divided the hotels by area, then listed them in four categories, according to the standard prices (not including seasonal offers or discounts) for one night in a

❶ Red numbers given in this chapter correspond to the location of each hotel as marked on the street maps. *See pp400-409.*

CONSUME

double room with en suite shower/bath. For **Deluxe** hotels, you can expect to pay more than €350; for properties in the **Expensive** bracket, €250-€350; for **Moderate** properties, allow €150-€250; while **Budget** rooms go for less than €150. For **gay hotels**, *see p279*.

Note that all hotels in France charge a room tax (*taxe de séjour*) of around €1 per person per night, although this is sometimes included in the rate. Children under 12 often stay for free when sharing a room with parents (check when booking), and small pets usually cost between €10 and €20 extra per night. Hotels are often booked solid and cost more during the major trade fairs (January, May, September), and it's hard to find a good room during Fashion Weeks (January, March, July and October). At quieter times, hotels can often offer special deals at short notice; phone ahead or check their websites.

THE ISLANDS
Expensive

★ Hôtel du Jeu de Paume
54 rue St-Louis-en-l'Ile, 4th (01.43.26.14.18, www.jeudepaumehotel.com). M° Pont Marie. **Rates** €285-€360 double. **Credit** AmEx, DC, MC, V. **Map** p409 K7 **❶**
With a discreet courtyard entrance, 17th-century beams, a private garden and a unique timbered breakfast room that was once a real tennis court built under Louis XIII, this is a charming and romantic hotel. These days, it is filled with an attractive array of modern and classical art, and has a coveted billiards table. A dramatic glass lift and catwalks lead to the guestrooms as well as two self-catering

apartments, which are simple and tasteful, the walls hung with Pierre Frey fabric.
Bar. Gym. Internet (free, wireless). Room service. TV.

Moderate

Hôtel des Deux-Iles
59 rue St-Louis-en-l'Ile, 4th (01.43.26.13.35, www.deuxiles-paris-hotel.com). M° Pont Marie. **Rates** €215 double. **Credit** AmEx, MC, V. **Map** p409 K7 **❷**
This peaceful 17th-century townhouse offers 17 rooms kitted out in toned-down stripes, *toile de Jouy* fabrics and neo-colonial style furniture. Its star features are a tiny courtyard off the lobby and a vaulted stone breakfast area. All the bedrooms and bathrooms were freshened up in 2007 (fortunately saving the lovely tiles on the bathroom walls).
Concierge. Internet (free, wireless). Room service. TV.
▶ *The equally pleasant Hôtel le Lutèce (65 rue St-Louis-en-l'Ile, 01.43.26.23.52, www.paris-hotel-lutece.com) is run by the same team.*

Budget

Hospitel Hôtel Dieu
1 pl du Parvis-Notre-Dame, 4th (01.44.32.01.00, www.hotel-hospitel.com). M° Cité or Saint-Michel. **Rates** €145 double. **Credit** MC, V. **Map** p408 J7 **❸**
If the thought of sleeping in a working hospital doesn't put you off (half the rooms here are used by families of the Hôtel Dieu hospital's in-patients and staff), you can stay in one of 14 recently renovated, spotless rooms with colourful contemporary decor, right in the middle of Ile de la Cité. A medical smell is present but not strong, bathrooms are quite large, and you couldn't ask for a better sightseeing base.
Disabled-adapted rooms. Internet (free, wireless). No smoking throughout. Room service. TV.

Hôtel du Jeu de Paume.

CONSUME

W Factor

The luxury hotel chain's new Paris outpost is wacky, wild and wonderful.

'Wacky, 'wild' and 'wonderful' – the 'W' in the upmarket **Hotel W Paris-Opéra** (*see p232*) could stand for any of the above. This new hotel, overlooking the Opéra Garnier, is the Starwood group's latest venture. It took two and a half years to finish, but it was worth the wait, with 91 rooms designed by American architect Rockwell that ooze NYC style from every nook and cranny; a clubbing theme that is taken to the extreme with a stream of DJ nights by La Clique (aka André and Lionel from Le Baron); a DJ booth; and black corridors with sparkling lights that make you feel as though you're walking through the reverse side of a disco ball. David Guetta eat your heart out.

In the guest rooms, nightclub touches prevail in the light fittings (which replicate the corridor walls), but otherwise the vibe is relaxing, with thick velvet and satin fabrics, super-soft pillows and dreamy views over the Opéra Garnier. For an all-out treat, the 'Extreme Wow' suite will set you back a whopping €2,300 (don't worry, standard doubles start at a more affordable €340), but you'll get 88sq m of smart modern design all to yourself, and the feeling that you've walked on to the set of a James Bond movie, with a hidden shower, a circular bed and proper belle époque mouldings (a nod to the building's Haussmannian past) – the perfect space for organising your own party.

Back on the ground floor, the bar is an airy space for a cocktail, with a giant mirror decorated in black cartoon characters and a list of tempting drinks that include the house special, Spark (champagne, orange juice and raspberries). The hotel brought in a barmaid from Washington DC to create the menu. But it's in the restaurant that things get really interesting: once you've been shown to your seat by a beautiful team, who look as if they've stepped out of a *Vogue* shoot, you tuck into cuisine such as white asparagus on a bed of almonds and olives, and Barcelona-style *canellones* (braised chicken, veal, pork, béchamel sauce and crispy toasted parmesan cheese) – all concocted by Michelin-starred chef Sergi Arola, considered to be one of Spain's most creative food maestros.

CONSUME

LE MARCEAU BASTILLE ★★★★

Hôtel-Gallery
13 rue Jules César
75012 Paris
Tél: 00.33(0)1 43 43 11 65
Fax: 00.33(0)1 43 41 67 70
infos@hotelmarceaubastille.com
Géneral Manager: Christophe Diallo

Le Marceau Bastille – Hotel gallery is a charming and contemporary 4 stars hotel, located nearly a few steps away from the Bastille square, as well as the "Gare de Lyon" train station and the historic Marais neighbourhood. The hotel interiors denote a characteristically contemporary style.

Le Marceau Bastille Hotel offers 55 rooms of two kinds: First, the "urban" option guarantees a cozy and resolutely avant-garde type atmosphere swathed in vibrant color, still seeped in elegance. The "ecological" option provides calm and sunny rooms set off by bright yet soft tones, natural materials, organic forms and sleek lines. The furnishings are contemporary and combine delicacy with modern technology. The living room and the restaurant walls are dedicated to the Art with the permanent collections of contemporary artists.

Hotel Facilities

General

Bar, 24-Hour Front Desk, Newspapers, Non-Smoking Rooms, Rooms/Facilities for Disabled Guests, Elevator, free Safety Deposit Box, Heating, Design Hotel, Luggage Storage, Air-conditioning, Fitness room.

Services

Massage Room Service, Laundry, Dry Cleaning, Breakfast in the Room, Fax/Photocopying.
Free! All children under 2 years stay free of charge for cots.
Free! Wi-Fi is available in the entire hotel and is free of charge.
Free! Pets are allowed on request. No extra charges.
Extra beds are available on request only. Any type of extra bed or baby cot is upon request and needs to be confirmed by the hotel. Public parking is possible at a location nearby with preferential rates for clients of the hotel.

Hotel Policies

Check-in 13:00 & Check-out 12:00

Accepted credit cards

American Express, Visa, Euro/MasterCard, Carte Bleue, Diners Club, JCB

Area Information

Architect, Historic and Art Area.

Place de la Bastille - L'Opéra Bastille - L'Hôtel Sully - L'Hôtel Carnavalet - L'Institut du Monde Arabe et la Mosquée de Paris - Le Pavillon de l'Arsenal. Le Quartier du Marais - La Place des Vosges - Cour Saint - Emilion

Stroll and Walk Area

La Promenade Plantée - Le Port de Plaisance de Paris Arsenal - Le Jardin des Plantes and Muséum National d'Histoire Naturelle - L'Ile Saint Louis

Hôtel Henri IV

*25 pl Dauphine, 1st (01.43.54.44.53, www.henri
4hotel.fr). M° Pont Neuf.* **Rates** *€60-€83 double
(incl breakfast).* **Credit** MC, V. **Map** p408 J6 ❹
On tree-lined, triangular Place Dauphine, surrounded
by some of Paris's most expensive real estate on Ile
de la Cité and a stone's throw from Notre-Dame, the
Henri IV remains Paris's best value budget hotel. You
therefore need to book well ahead to get a room. The
rooms are simple and unadorned, but clean, and the
three paupers' penthouses with balconies and rooftop
views go first. Eleven of the 15 room have en suite
bathrooms; the others offer very, very cheap rates.
No smoking throughout.

THE LOUVRE & PALAIS-ROYAL

Deluxe

Hôtel Costes

*239 rue St-Honoré, 1st (01.42.44.50.00, www.
hotelcostes.com). M° Concorde or Tuileries.* **Rates**
€600-€800 double. **Credit** AmEx, DC, MC, V.
Map p401 G5 ❺
Attitude definitely counts in this temple of notoriety
– a place so trendy its website contains an online
boutique of its own *ultra-branché* products, and
where innumerable A-listers still gravitate to the
low-lit bar after all these years. The Costes boasts
one of the best pools in Paris, a sybaritic, Eastern-
inspired affair with an underwater music system.
Rooms are a modern take on Napoleon III, designed
by Jacques Garcia.
*Bars (2). Business centre. Concierge. Disabled-
adapted rooms. Gym. Internet (free, wireless).
No-smoking rooms. Parking. Pool (indoor).
Restaurant. Room service. Spa. TV.*

Hôtel de Crillon

*10 pl de la Concorde, 8th (01.44.71.15.00,
www.crillon.com). M° Concorde.* **Rates** *€680-€860
double.* **Credit** AmEx, DC, MC, V. **Map** p401 F4 ❻
The Crillon lives up to its *palais* reputation with
decor strong on marble, mirrors and gold leaf.
Les Ambassadeurs restaurant has an acclaimed
chef and a kitchen with a glassed-in private dining
area for groups of no more than six who wish to
dine amid the bustle of the 80-strong kitchen staff.
If you have euros to spare, opt for the Presidential
Suite. The Winter Garden tearoom is a must. The
hotel is scheduled to close for major renovations on
31 March 2013.
*Bar. Business centre. Concierge. Gym. Internet
(free, wireless). No-smoking rooms. Parking.
Restaurants (2). Room service. TV.*

Hôtel Sofitel le Faubourg

*15 rue Boissy-d'Anglas, 8th (01.44.94.14.14,
www.sofitel.com). M° Concorde or Madeleine.*
Rates *€355-€600 double.* **Credit** AmEx, DC,
MC, V. **Map** p401 F4 ❼

This hotel is close to all the major couture boutiques,
which is no surprise, as it used to house the *Marie
Claire* offices. The rooms have Louis XVI armchairs,
large balconies, walk-in wardrobes and Roger &
Gallet goodies in the bathrooms; for shopping wid-
owers, there's a small gym and a hammam. It's quiet
too: the street has been closed to traffic since 2001
because the American embassy is on the corner.
*Bar. Business centre. Concierge. Disabled-
adapted rooms. Gym. Internet (charge, wireless).
No-smoking rooms. Parking. Restaurant.
Room service. TV.*
Other locations Sofitel Arc de Triomphe,
14 rue Beaujon, 8th (01.53.89.50.50); Hôtel Scribe,
1 rue Scribe, 9th (01.44.71.24.24).

★ Le Meurice

*228 rue de Rivoli, 1st (01.44.58.10.10, www.
lemeurice.com). M° Tuileries.* **Rates** *€920-€1,170
double.* **Credit** AmEx, DC, MC, V. **Map** p401 G5 ❽
With its extravagant Louis XVI decor, mosaic-tiled
floors and modish restyling by Philippe Starck, Le
Meurice is looking grander than ever. All 160 rooms
are done up in distinct historical styles; the Belle
Etoile suite on the seventh floor provides panoramic
views of Paris from its terrace. You can relax in the
Winter Garden to the strains of regular jazz performances; for more intensive intervention, head over to
the lavish spa with treatments by Valmont.
*Bar. Business centre. Concierge. Disabled-adapted
rooms. Gym. Internet (charge, wireless).
No-smoking rooms. Restaurants (2). Room
service. Spa. TV: DVD.*
▶ *Don't miss dinner at the hotel's three Michelin-
starred restaurant; see p140.*

Le Westin

*3 rue de Castiglione, 1st (01.44.77.11.11, www.
thewestinparis.com). M° Tuileries.* **Rates** *(incl
breakfast) €425-€720 double (incl breakfast).*
Credit AmEx, DC, MC, V. **Map** p401 G5 ❾
In the heart of shopping HQ, the Westin mixes belle
époque features with pale limestone walls, beautiful
vintage-style furniture (inspired by the 1930s and
'40s), a neoclassical fountain and a patio. Its sleek
modern bedrooms, decked out with top-end gadgets
and the award-winning Heavenly Bed, sport balcony
views over the Tuileries gardens. The bathrooms
are sumptuous, and some have their own balconies.
There's an excellent restaurant, Le First, with a
sleek, boudoir-like interior by Jacques Garcia.
*Bar. Business centre. Concierge. Disabled-adapted
rooms. Gym. Internet (charge, wireless). No-smoking
rooms. Restaurant. Room service. Spa. TV.*

Moderate

★ Hôtel Brighton

*218 rue de Rivoli, 1st (01.47.03.61.61, www.esprit-
de-france.com). M° Tuileries.* **Rates** *€180-€320
double.* **Credit** AmEx, DC, MC, V. **Map** p401 G5 ❿

CONSUME

CONSUME

With several rooms overlooking the Tuileries gardens, the Brighton is great value, so book well ahead for a room with a view. Recently restored, it has a classical atmosphere, from the high ceilings in the rooms to the faux-marble and mosaic downstairs.
Bar. Concierge. Disabled-adapted rooms. Internet (free, wireless). No-smoking rooms. Room service. TV.

Hôtel Mansart
5 rue des Capucines, 1st (01.42.61.50.28, www.esprit-de-france.com). M° Madeleine or Opéra. **Rates** €190-€250 double. **Credit** AmEx, DC, MC, V. **Map** p401 G4 ⑪
This spacious hotel has real style, with a light, roomy lobby decorated with murals inspired by formal gardens. The 57 bedrooms feature pleasant fabrics, antiques and paintings; five of the rooms have an excellent view of place Vendôme.
Bar. Concierge. Internet (free, wireless). Room service. TV.

Hôtel des Tuileries
10 rue St-Hyacinthe, 1st (01.42.61.04.17, www.hotel-des-tuileries.com). M° Tuileries. **Rates** €200-€270 double. **Credit** AmEx, DC, MC, V. **Map** p401 G5 ⑫
The fashion pack adores this 18th-century hotel (the staircase is listed), located in prime shopping territory. Done out with ethnic rugs, a smattering of animal prints, bright art and antique furniture, the 26 comfy bedrooms feel like they belong more in an eccentric family home than a central Paris hotel.
Concierge. Internet (charge, shared terminal or wireless). TV.

Hôtel Westminster.

Le Relais du Louvre
19 rue des Prêtres St-Germain-l'Auxerrois, 1st (01.40.41.96.42, www.relaisdulouvre.com). M° Pont Neuf or Louvre-Rivoli. **Rates** €175-€230 double. **Credit** AmEx, MC, V. **Map** p402 H6 ⑬
The cellar of this characterful hotel, with its antiques and wooden beams, was once used by revolutionaries to print anti-royalist literature. It also inspired Puccini's Café Momus in *La Bohème*. The rooms are decorated in floral fabrics, and the front ones look out on to St-Germain-l'Auxerrois church. There's also a top-floor apartment for up to five people.
Concierge. Internet (free). No-smoking rooms. TV.

Budget

Hotel du Lion d'Or
5 rue de la Sourdière, 1st (01.42.60.79.04, www.hotel-louvre-paris.com). M° Tuileries. **Rates** €120-€165 double. **Credit** MC, V. **Map** p401 G5 ⑭
Simple, brightly coloured rooms and fully furnished studios (with kitchenettes) that can sleep up to five make the Golden Lion a popular choice for families and groups of friends.
Internet (free, wireless). TV (some rooms).

OPERA TO LES HALLES
Deluxe

Hotel W Paris-Opéra
4 rue Meyerbeer, 9th (01.77.48.94.94, www.wparis opera.fr). M° Opéra/RER Auber. **Rates** from €340 double. **Credit** AmEx, DC, MC, V. **Map** p401 H4 ⑮
See p229 **W Factor.**
Bar. Business centre. Concierge. Gym. Internet (charge, wireless). No-smoking rooms. Restaurant. Room service. TV.

Hôtel Westminster
13 rue de la Paix, 2nd (01.42.61.57.46, www.warwickwestminsteropera.com). M° Opéra/RER Auber. **Rates** €350-€630 double. **Credit** AmEx, DC, MC, V. **Map** p401 G4 ⑯
This luxury hotel near place Vendôme has more than a touch of British warmth about it, no doubt owing to the influence of its favourite 19th-century guest, the Duke of Westminster (after whom the hotel was named). The hotel fitness centre has a top-floor location, with a tiled steam room and views over the city, and the cosy bar features deep leather chairs, a fireplace and live jazz at weekends.
Bar. Concierge. Gym. Internet (free, wireless). No-smoking rooms. Parking. Restaurant. Room service. Spa. TV.

★ InterContinental Paris Le Grand
2 rue Scribe, 9th (01.40.07.32.32, www.paris.intercontinental.com). M° Opéra. **Rates** €355-€450 double. **Credit** AmEx, DC, MC, V. **Map** p401 G4 ⑰

Mandarin Oriental

This 1862 hotel is the chain's European flagship – but, given its size, perhaps 'mother ship' would be more appropriate: this landmark establishment occupies the entire block (three wings, almost 500 rooms) next to the opera house; some 80 of the honey-coloured rooms overlook the Palais Garnier. The space under the vast *verrière* is one of the best oases in town, and the hotel's restaurant and coffeehouse, the Café de la Paix, poached its chef, Laurent Delarbre, from the Ritz. For a relaxing daytime break, head to the I-Spa for one of its seawater treatments.

Bar. Business centre. Concierge. Gym. Internet (charge, high speed; free, wireless). No-smoking rooms. Parking. Restaurants (2). Room service. Spa. TV.

Mandarin Oriental

251 rue St-Honoré, 1st (01.70.98.78.88, www.mandarinoriental.com). M° Tuileries. **Rates** from €920 double. **Credit** AmEx, DC, MC, V. **Map** p401 G4 ⓱

Set in a 1930s building on rue St-Honoré, the Mandarin Oriental has a wonderfully indulgent location – and the interior doesn't disappoint either, with 138 luxurious rooms, fusion restaurants, a vast interior garden, and smart spa with pool and seven spa suites with private hammams. Decor-wise, think art deco meets oriental boudoir with chic, kitschy touches throughout. In the lobby, fake diamonds decorate the curtain holders and the imposing grey walls are encrusted with stripes of jewels. The boudoir theme continues into the bedrooms, where steely grey, gold or white walls are contrasted with plum-pink cushions and trimmings. Back on the ground floor, the main draw is the choice of eateries, all managed by top chef Thierry Marx. Marx's gastronomic offering is the Sur Mesure restaurant, an all-white affair where the chef creates Asian-influenced delights. Next door sits Bar 8, replete with a theatrical marble bar, walls inlaid with raindrop

Lalique crystals, and resolutely snazzy cocktails. It's a top spot for a sophisticated slurp, especially in summer when tables spill out into the gardens.
Bar. Business centre. Concierge. Internet (charge, wireless). No-smoking rooms. Parking. Pool (indoor). Restaurants. Room service. Spa. TV.

Expensive

Hôtel Ambassador

16 bd Haussmann, 9th (01.44.83.40.40, www.radissonblu.com). M° Chaussée d'Antin or Richelieu Drouot. **Rates** €350-€380 double. **Credit** AmEx, DC, MC, V. **Map** p401 H4 ⓳

If you're looking for some vintage style but can't face another gilded Louis XIV interior, check into this historic, Haussmann-era hotel, which sets traditional furniture against contemporary decor in each of the 294 bedrooms. The low-lit Lindbergh Bar is named after the pilot, who dropped in for a celebratory drink and cigar after his solo transatlantic flight in 1927. The hotel is ideally situated for shopping at the *grands magasins*.
Bar. Business centre. Concierge. Disabled-adapted rooms. Gym. Internet (charge, shared terminal; free, wireless). No-smoking rooms. Restaurant. Room service. TV.

Hôtel Concorde Opéra Paris

108 rue St-Lazare, 8th (01.40.08.44.44, www.concorde-hotels.com). M° St-Lazare. **Rates** €270-€300 double. **Credit** AmEx, DC, MC, V. **Map** p401 G3 ⓴

Guests here are cocooned in soundproofed luxury. The 19th-century Eiffel-inspired lobby with jewel-encrusted pink granite columns is a historic landmark: the high ceilings, walls and sculptures look much as they have for over a century. Rooms are spacious, with double entrance doors and exclusive Annick Goutal toiletries; the belle époque brasserie,

Café Terminus, and sexy Golden Black Bar were designed by Sonia Rykiel. Guests have access to a nearby fitness centre.

Bar. Business centre. Concierge. Internet (charge, shared terminal; free, wireless). No-smoking rooms. Parking. Restaurant. Room service. TV.

Moderate

Hôtel Amour

8 rue Navarin, 9th (01.48.78.31.80, www.hotel amourparis.fr). M° St-Georges. **Rates** €155-€285 double. **Credit** AmEx, MC, V. **Map** p402 H2 ㉑
Opened back in 2006, this boutique hotel is a real hit with the in crowd. Each of the 20 rooms is unique, decorated on the theme of love or eroticism by a coterie of contemporary artists and designers, such as Marc Newson, M&M, Stak, Pierre Le Tan and Sophie Calle. Seven of the rooms contain artists' installations, and two others have their own private bar and a large terrace on which to hold your own party. The late-night brasserie has a coveted outdoor garden, and the crowd is young and beautiful and loves to entertain.
Bar. Internet (charge, wireless). No-smoking rooms only. Restaurant.

Hôtel Arvor Saint Georges

8 rue Laferrière, 9th (01.48.78.60.92, www. arvor-hotel-paris.com). M° St-Georges. **Rates** €150-€180 double. **Credit** AmEx, DC, MC, V. **Map** p402 H2 ㉒
Don't be put off by the slightly austere façade; the owner intended it this way to contrast with the homely atmosphere that reigns inside. Although you're right in the middle of the city, the hotel has the feel of a quiet country house. The decor is delicate and uncluttered, and most of the 30 spacious rooms, including six suites, overlook the rooftops (no.503 has the best view of the Eiffel Tower). The small terrace is the ideal spot to take a break from the Paris buzz.
Internet (free, wireless). No-smoking rooms. TV.

Hôtel Britannique

20 av Victoria, 1st (01.42.33.74.59, www.hotel-britannique.fr). M° Châtelet/RER Châtelet les Halles. **Rates** €208-€241 double. **Credit** AmEx, MC, V. **Map** p408 J6 ㉓
Smiling staff in stripy waistcoats welcome you to this adorable hotel, where guest areas and rooms are cocooned in thick drapes, luscious carpets and a mishmash of British colonial-style furniture that make you feel like you've stepped into an English country cottage. Enjoy deeply delicious pastries in the warm, rustic breakfast room, or book a top-floor *chambre* and eat them on your plant-filled balcony – a rare oasis of greenery for such a central and reasonably priced hotel.
Bar. Concierge. Internet (free, wireless). No-smoking rooms. TV.

★ Hôtel Crayon

25 rue du Bouloi, 1st (01.42.36.54.19, www. hotelcrayon.com). M° Les Halles. **Rates** €129-€239. **Credit** AmEx, DC, MC, V. **Map** p402 H5 ㉔
Brilliantly situated near the Louvre in a neighbourhood full of great restaurants, Hôtel Crayon offers colour therapy with rooms painted top to toe in a choice of 16 hues. Each also features a life-size hand-drawn nude pencilled on the wall in a Matisse style, a white bathroom with colour accents where vintage furniture has been adapted to support contemporary sinks, silky smooth cotton bedlinen and random vintage holiday snaps collected from flea markets and mounted in frames. You can order a selection of meals via room service, and a copious breakfast is served in the vaulted breakfast room. The ground floor also has an honesty bar decked out with 1950s furniture and a selection of newspapers and magazines. For the same price as a run-of-the-mill three-star, this boutique hotel offers a wonderful experience in a great location. *Photo p236.*
Bar. Concierge. Internet (free, wireless). No-smoking rooms. TV.

Hôtel Langlois

63 rue St-Lazare, 9th (01.48.74.78.24, www. hotel-langlois.com). M° Trinité. **Rates** €170-€180 double. **Credit** MC, V. **Map** p401 H3 ㉕
Built as a bank in 1870, this belle époque building became the Hôtel des Croisés in 1896. In 2001, after featuring in the Jonathan Demme film *Charade*, it changed its name to Hôtel Langlois in honour of the founder of the Cinémathèque Française. Its 27 spacious, air-conditioned bedrooms are decorated in art nouveau style; the larger ones have delightful hidden bathrooms.
Internet (free, wireless). Room service. TV.

Hotel O

19 rue Hérold, 1st (01.42.36.04.02, www.hotel-o-paris.com). M° Palais Royal-Musée du Louvre or Les Halles. **Rates** from €200 double. **Credit** AmEx, MC, V. **Map** p402 J5 ㉖
See p245 **Sleep in Style**.
Bar. Concierge. Internet (free, wireless). No-smoking rooms. Room service (5pm-1.30am). TV.

Budget

Hôtel Chopin

10 bd Montmartre or 46 passage Jouffroy, 9th (01.47.70.58.10, www.hotel-chopin.com). M° Grands Boulevards. **Rates** €98-€118 double. **Credit** MC, V. **Map** p402 J4 ㉗
Handsomely set in a historic, glass-roofed arcade next door to the Grévin museum, the Chopin's original 1846 façade adds to its old-fashioned appeal. The 36 rooms are quiet and functional, done out in either salmon and green or blue.
TV.

CONSUME

Hôtel Crayon. *See p235.*

Hôtel du Cygne

3 rue du Cygne, 1st (01.42.60.14.16, www.hotel ducygne.fr). M° Etienne Marcel/RER Châtelet Les Halles. **Rates** €90-€132 double. **Credit** MC, V. **Map** p402 J5 ㉘

This traditional hotel located in a handsome 17th-century building has 20 compact, cosy and simple rooms embellished with touches such as antiques and home-made furnishings. It's on a pedestrianised street in the bustling Les Halles district, so light sleepers might prefer to book one of the rooms overlooking the courtyard.

Internet (free, wireless). TV.

Résidence Hôtel des Trois Poussins

15 rue Clauzel, 9th (01.53.32.81.81, www. les3poussins.com). M° St-Georges. **Rates** €110-€220 double. **Credit** AmEx, DC, MC, V. **Map** p402 H2 ㉙

Just off the beaten track in a pleasant *quartier*, and within walking distance (uphill) of Montmartre, the Résidence Hôtel des Trois Poussins offers hotel accommodation in the traditional manner, and also has some rare self-catering studios for people who'd rather cook than eat out. Now completely redone, the decor is pleasantly traditional, with a preference for yellow.

Concierge. Disabled-adapted room. Internet (charge, wireless). Room service (nighttime only). TV.

CHAMPS-ELYSEES & WESTERN PARIS

Deluxe

★ Four Seasons George V

31 av George V, 8th (01.49.52.70.00, www. fourseasons.com/paris). M° Alma Marceau or George V. **Rates** €925-€1,375 double. **Credit** AmEx, DC, MC, V. **Map** p400 D4 ㉚

There's no denying that the George V is serious about luxury: chandeliers, marble and tapestries; glorious flower arrangements; divine bathrooms; and ludicrously comfortable beds in some of the largest rooms in all of Paris. The Versailles-inspired spa includes whirlpools, saunas and a menu of treatments for an unabashedly metrosexual clientele; non-guests can now reserve appointments. If you can afford it, it's worth every euro.

Bar. Business centre. Concierge. Disabled-adapted rooms. Gym. Internet (charge, high speed). No-smoking rooms. Parking. Pool (indoor). Restaurants (2). Room service. Spa. TV.

Hôtel le A

4 rue d'Artois, 8th (01.42.56.99.99, www.paris-hotel-a.com). M° Franklin D. Roosevelt or St-Philippe-du-Roule. **Rates** €369-€449 double. **Credit** AmEx, DC, MC, V. **Map** p401 E4 ㉛

The black-and-white decor of this designer boutique hotel provides a fine backdrop for the models, artists and media types hanging out in the lounge bar area; the only splashes of colour come from the graffiti-like artworks by conceptual artist Fabrice Hybert. The 26 rooms all have granite bathrooms, and the starched white furniture slip covers, changed after each guest, make the smallish spaces seem larger than they are. The dimmer switches are a nice touch – as are the lift lights changing colour at each floor.

Bar. Concierge. Disabled-adapted rooms. Internet (charge, wireless). No-smoking rooms. Room service. TV.

Hôtel le Bristol

112 rue du Fbg-St-Honoré, 8th (01.53.43.43.00, www.hotel-bristol.com). M° Champs-Elysées Clémenceau. **Rates** €800-€1,020 double. **Credit** AmEx, DC, MC, V. **Map** p401 E4 ㉜

Set on the exclusive rue du Faubourg St-Honoré, near luxury boutiques such as Christian Lacroix, Azzaro, Salvatore Ferragamo, Givenchy and Dolce & Gabbana, the Bristol is a luxurious 'palace' hotel with a loyal following of fashionistas and millionaires drawn by the location, impeccable service, larger than average rooms and a three Michelin-starred restaurant with Eric Fréchon at the helm. The Bristol's impressive new seven-storey wing opened in late 2009. *Photo p239.*
Bar. Business centre. Concierge. Disabled-adapted rooms. Gym. Internet (charge, high speed & wireless). No-smoking rooms. Parking. Pool (indoor). Restaurant. Room service. Spa. TV.

Hôtel Daniel

8 rue Frédéric-Bastiat, 8th (01.42.56.17.00, www.hoteldanielparis.com). M° Franklin D. Roosevelt or St-Philippe-du-Roule. **Rates** €420-€490 double. **Credit** AmEx, DC, MC, V. **Map** p401 E4 ③③

A romantic hideaway close to the monoliths of the Champs-Elysées, this Relais & Châteaux property is decorated in chinoiserie and a palette of rich colours, with 26 rooms cosily appointed in *toile de Jouy* and an intricately hand-painted restaurant that feels like a courtyard. With meals at around €50 a head, the gastronomic restaurant Le Lounge is a good deal for this neighbourhood; the bar menu is served at all hours.
Bar. Concierge. Disabled-adapted rooms. Internet (free, wireless). No-smoking rooms. Parking. Restaurant. Room service. TV.

Hôtel le A.

Hôtel Fouquet's Barrière

46 av George V, 8th (01.40.69.60.00, www.fouquets-barriere.com). M° George V. **Rates** €750-€990 double. **Credit** AmEx, DC, MC, V. **Map** p400 D4 ③④

This grandiose five-star hotel is built around the famous *fin-de-siècle* brasserie Le Fouquet's. Five buildings form the hotel complex, housing 107 rooms (including 40 suites), upmarket restaurant Le Diane, the Sparis spa, an indoor swimming pool and a rooftop terrace for hire. Jacques Garcia, of Hôtel Costes and Westin fame, was responsible for the interior design, which retains the Empire style of the exterior while incorporating luxurious modern touches inside – flatscreen TVs and mist-free mirrors as standard in the marble bathrooms. And, of course, it's unbeatable in terms of location: right at the junction of avenue George V and the Champs-Elysées.
Bar. Business centre. Concierge. Disabled-adapted rooms. Gym. Internet (free, high speed & wireless). No-smoking rooms. Parking. Pool (indoor). Restaurants (2). Room service. Spa. TV.

Hôtel Plaza Athénée

25 av Montaigne, 8th (01.53.67.66.65, www.plaza-athenee-paris.com). M° Alma Marceau. **Rates** €1,025-€1,150 double. **Credit** AmEx, DC, MC, V. **Map** p400 D5 ③⑤

This palace is ideally placed for power shopping at Chanel, Louis Vuitton, Dior and other avenue Montaigne boutiques. Material girls and boys will enjoy the high-tech room amenities, such as remote-controlled air con, internet and video-game access on the TV via infrared keyboard, and mini hi-fi.
Bar. Business centre. Concierge. Disabled-adapted rooms. Gym. Internet (charge, high speed & wireless). No-smoking rooms. Parking. Restaurants (2; 4 in summer). Room service. TV.
► *Make sure you factor in time for a drink in the Bar du Plaza, a cocktail bunny's most outré fantasy, with flattering lighting, high chairs for maximum leg-crossing opportunities and ridiculous drinks.*

Hôtel de Sers

41 av Pierre-1er-de-Serbie, 8th (01.53.23.75.75, www.hoteldesers.com). M° Alma Marceau or George V. **Rates** €460-€690 double. **Credit** AmEx, DC, MC, V. **Map** p400 D4 ③⑥

Behind its stately 19th-century façade, the Hôtel de Sers calls itself a baby palace, displaying an ambitious mix of minimalist contemporary furnishings, with a few pop art touches. Original architectural details, such as the grand staircase and reception, complete the picture. The large top-floor apartment affords dreamy views over Paris's rooftops.
Bar. Concierge. Disabled-adapted rooms. Gym. Internet (free, wireless). No-smoking rooms. Parking. Restaurant. Room service. TV.

CONSUME

★ Hôtel de la Trémoille

*14 rue de la Trémoille, 8th (01.56.52.14.00,
www.hotel-tremoille.com). M° Alma-Marceau.*
Rates €365-€610 double. **Credit** AmEx, DC,
MC, V. **Map** p400 D4 ⑰
The recent opening of a new restaurant-bar-lounge
and improved spa and fitness facilities have made the
Trémoille a serious competitor to the other palaces
nearby. The 93 rooms are decorated to evoke no fewer
than 31 different 'atmospheres', and the bathrooms
are filled with Molton Brown products. A unique feature is the 'hatch', which enables room service to
deliver your meal without disturbing you.
*Bar. Business centre. Concierge. Disabled-adapted
rooms. Gym. Internet (charge, high speed). No-
smoking rooms. Restaurant. Room service. Spa. TV.*

Hôtel de Vigny

*9-11 rue Balzac, 8th (01.42.99.80.80, www.hotel
devigny.com). M° George V.* **Rates** €440-€520
double. **Credit** AmEx, DC, MC, V. **Map** p400 D3 ㉞
This hotel has the feel of a private, plush townhouse. Although it's just off the Champs-Elysées,
the Vigny pulls in a discerning, low-key clientele.
Its 37 bedrooms and suites are decorated in tasteful
stripes or florals, with marble bathrooms. Enjoy
dinner in the art deco Baretto restaurant.
*Bar. Concierge. Internet (charge, high speed).
No-smoking rooms. Parking. Restaurant.
Room service. TV.*

★ Jays Paris

*6 rue Copernic, 16th (01.47.04.16.16, www.
jays-paris.com). M° Kléber or Victor Hugo.*
Rates €450-€750 suite. **Credit** MC, V.
Map p400 C4 ㊳
Introducing a new concept on the Paris hotel scene,
Jays is a luxurious *boutique-apart* hotel that trades
on a clever blend of antique furniture, modern design
and high-tech equipment. The marble staircase, lit
entirely by natural light filtered through the glass
atrium overhead, gives an instant feeling of
grandeur, and leads to five suites, each with a fully
equipped kitchenette. A cosy salon is available to
welcome in-house guests and their visitors.
*Bar. Concierge. Internet (free, high speed &
wireless). No smoking throughout. Parking.
Room service. TV.*

Opéra Diamond

*4 rue de la Pépinière, 8th (01.44.70.02.00,
www.bestwestern.com). M° St-Lazare.* **Rates**
€450-€510 double. **Credit** AmEx, DC, MC, V.
Map p401 F3 ㊵
This sparkling Best Western Premier hotel in the
Opéra/St-Lazare district lives up to its name with a
night-sky decor made up of black granite resin punctuated with crystals and LEDs. The 30 rooms are
equally splendid, with Swarovski crystal touches to
the furniture, black bathrooms and satin curtains
that close to become a huge photomontage of a

Hôtel le Bristol. *See p236.*

CONSUME

female nude crossed with architectural imagery. The
Executive rooms on the fifth floor have iPod stations,
Nespresso machines, and speakers in the bathrooms.
A grassy courtyard with a fountain adds to the
appeal. Unashamedly bling, but rather magical
when night falls. Check the website as rates are often
heavily discounted.
*Bar. Concierge. Internet (free, wireless).
No-smoking rooms. Room service. TV.*

Pershing Hall

*49 rue Pierre-Charron, 8th (01.58.36.58.00,
www.pershinghall.com). M° George V.* **Rates**
€540-€640 double. **Credit** AmEx, DC, MC, V.
Map p400 D4 ㊶
The refreshing mix of 19th-century grandeur and
contemporary comfort makes Pershing Hall feel
quite large, but this luxury establishment is really a
cleverly disguised boutique hotel with just 26 rooms.
Fashionable locals frequent the stylish bar and
restaurant terrace. Designed by Andrée Putman, the
neat bedrooms emphasise natural materials, with
stained grey oak floors and fine mosaic-tiled bathrooms with geometric styling and copious towels.
*Bar. Concierge. Gym. Internet (free, high speed;
pay as you go, wireless). No-smoking rooms.
Restaurant. Room service. Spa. TV.*

Renaissance Paris Arc de Triomphe

*39 av de Wagram, 17th (01.55.37.55.37,
www.marriott.com). M° Ternes.* **Rates** €400-
€509 double. **Credit** AmEx, DC, MC, V.
Map p400 C3 ㊷

You can't miss it. This six-storey undulating glass façade on avenue de Wagram is like no other part of the neighbourhood. All rooms are stylishly done out in pale greys, charcoals and dark wood, with Eames-style furniture. Nice high-tech touches include an iPod dock on the bedside radio and a large flat-screen TV with Wi-Fi keyboard. Bathrooms are a glory of polished metal, tasteful tiles and gleaming glass. The Makassar restaurant serves delicate and delicious Franco-Asian fusion food.

Bar. Business centre. Concierge. Disabled-adapted rooms. Gym. Internet (charge, high speed). No-smoking rooms. Parking. Restaurant. Room service. Spa. TV.

Royal Monceau

37 Avenue Hoche, 8th (01.42.99.88.00, www. leroyalmonceau.com). M° Charles de Gaulle Etoile. **Rates** €680-€850 double. **Credit** AmEx, DC, MC, V. **Map** p400 D3 ⓸

This new Starck-designed incarnation of the legendary old grande dame opened to the public (or at least those who could afford it) in October 2010, offering everything from cosy studio rooms to the 190sq m Royal Monceau suite, a snip at €10,000 a night. With no fewer than three restaurants, desserts from star pastry chef Pierre Hermé and an indoor pool and spa, the Royal Monceau is firmly back in the big league.

Bar. Business centre. Concierge. Disabled-adapted rooms. Gym. Internet (free, wireless). No-smoking rooms. Parking. Pool (indoor). Restaurant. Room service. Spa. TV.

THE BEST SUITES

For romantic assignations
Sublim Eiffel. *See p255.*

For a view from your pillow
Le Metropolitan. *See p242.*

For Montmartre magic
Hôtel Particulier Montmartre. *See p242.*

Le Sezz

6 av Frémiet, 16th (01.56.75.26.26, www.hotel sezz.com). M° Passy. **Rates** €335-€470 double. **Credit** AmEx, DC, MC, V. **Map** p404 B6 ⓸

Le Sezz opened its doors in 2005 with 27 deluxe rooms and suites – the work of acclaimed French furniture designer Christophe Pillet. The understated decor represents a refreshingly modern take on luxury, with black parquet flooring, rough-hewn stone walls and bathrooms partitioned off with sweeping glass façades. The bar and public areas are equally chic.

Bar. Concierge. Internet (free, wireless). No-smoking rooms. Parking. Room service. Spa. TV.

Shangri-La Paris

10 av d'Iéna, 16th (01.53.67.19.98, www. shangri-la.com). M° Iéna. **Rates** €750-€1,265 double. **Credit** AmEx, DC, MC, V. **Map** p404 C5 ⓸

Les Jardins de la Villa. *See p242.*

Pierre-Yves Rochon's design at the Shangri-La is an ode to French imperialism, with lavish colonial-style paintings, knick-knacks and light fittings, artfully mixed with century-old marble floors, stained-glass windows and thick velveteen fabrics. Half of the 81 rooms and suites look out on to Eiffel's filigree tower, and the top-floor Suite Panoramique provides what could easily be Paris's best panorama over the Left Bank. Shangri-La may be a Chinese company, but it has gone out of its way to ensure that the building's 'French' architectural heritage remains intact: the mansion, built in 1896 by botanist Roland Bonaparte (Napoleon Bonaparte's great-nephew), drips in Napoleonic carvings and gilding; and there's a Louis XIV-style salon, the splendour of which rivals Versailles. Dining-wise, expect the best of France and Asia, including Shang Palace, Paris's first gourmet Cantonese restaurant.

Bar. Business centre. Concierge. Disabled-adapted rooms. Gym. Internet (free, wireless). No-smoking rooms. Parking. Pool (indoor). Restaurant. Room service. Spa. TV.

Hôtel Particulier Montmartre.
See p242.

Expensive

Hôtel Keppler

10 rue Keppler, 16th (01.47.20.65.05, www.keppler.fr). M° George V or Charles de Gaulle Etoile. **Rates** €300-€500 double. **Credit** AmEx, DC, MC, V. **Map** p400 C4 **46**

This newly renovated boutique hotel is a family-run treasure, decorated with striped wallpaper, funky mirrors, animal prints and various knick-knacks. None of the 39 rooms is huge, but all are cleverly thought through, so that lack of space is never an issue and the whole experience is pleasantly cosy. The top-floor suites have their own (large) balcony – perfect for an alfresco breakfast – and views over Paris's rooftops towards the Eiffel Tower.

Bar. Concierge. Internet (free, wireless). Gym. No-smoking rooms. Room service. Sauna. TV.

Hôtel Pergolèse

3 rue Pergolèse, 16th (01.53.64.04.04, www.pergolese.com). M° Argentine. **Rates** €270-€300 double. **Credit** AmEx, DC, MC, V. **Map** p400 B3 **47**

The Pergolèse was one of the first designer boutique hotels in town, but still looks contemporary a decade or so after being kitted out by Rena Dumas-Hermès with art deco-style furniture by Philippe Starck and rugs by Hilton McConnico. Rooms feature pale wood details and cool, white-tiled bathrooms.

Bar. Concierge. Internet (free, wireless). No-smoking rooms. Room service. TV.

★ Hôtel Regent's Garden

6 rue Pierre-Demours, 17th (01.45.74.07.30, www.hotel-regents-paris.com). M° Charles de Gaulle Etoile or Ternes. **Rates** €290-€440 double. **Credit** AmEx, DC, MC, V. **Map** p400 C2 **48**

This elegant hotel – built for Napoleon III's physician – features appropriately Second Empire high ceilings and plush upholstery, and a lounge overlooking a lovely walled patio. There are 39 large bedrooms, some with gilt mirrors and fireplaces. It's an oasis of calm just ten minutes from the Champs-Elysées, and the first hotel in Paris to receive an Ecolabel, for its recycling and energy- and water-saving efforts.

Concierge. Internet (charge, shared terminal; free, wireless). No-smoking rooms. Parking. Room service (daytime only). TV.

Hôtel Square

3 rue de Boulainvilliers, 16th (01.44.14.91.90, www.hotelsquare.com). M° Passy/RER Avenue du Pdt Kennedy. **Rates** €270-€380 double. **Credit** AmEx, DC, MC, V. **Map** p404 A7 **49**

Located in the upmarket 16th, this courageously modern hotel has a dramatic yet welcoming interior, and attentive service that comes from having to look after only 22 rooms. They're decorated in amber, brick or slate colours, with exotic woods, quality fabrics and bathrooms seemingly cut from one huge chunk of Carrara marble. View the exhibitions in the atrium gallery or mingle with the media types at the hip Zebra Square restaurant and DJ bar.
Bar. Concierge. Disabled-adapted rooms. Internet (free, wireless). No-smoking rooms. Parking. Restaurant. Room service. TV.

Les Jardins de la Villa
5 rue Bélidor, 17th (01.53.81.01.10, www.jardins delavilla.com). M° Porte Maillot. **Rates** €300-€450 double. **Credit** AmEx, MC, V. **Map** p400 B2 **⑩**
Behind a sober frontage, this 33-room boutique hotel is an unexpectedly playful affair, with a couture theme and a penchant for fuchsia pink. It's dotted with surreal touches – not least the high heel-shaped couch in reception. Beautifully appointed rooms pair modern luxuries (Nespresso machines, free Wi-Fi, sleek flatscreen TVs) with old-fashioned attention to detail (proper soundproofing and thick, light-blocking curtains), while suites come with extra floor space and flourishes. The location is off the tourist trail, though close to the métro. *Photo p240.*
Bar. Business centre. Concierge. Disabled-adapted rooms. Gym. Internet (free, wireless). No-smoking rooms. Parking. Room service. TV.

★ Le Metropolitan
10 pl de Mexico, 16th (01.56.90.40.04, www. radissonblu.com). M° Trocadero. **Rates** €300-€420 double. **Credit** AmEx, DC, MC, V. **Map** p400 B5 **⑪**
This new 40-room offering from Radisson Blu is supremely sleek. The discreet entrance is only a few metres wide, but once inside the triangular structure opens out into surprising volumes, with a monumental art deco-style fireplace, and cream leather and black granite reminiscent of New York in the 1930s. The first floor contains a swank insiders' cocktail bar, but the biggest surprise of all is the breathtaking view of the Eiffel Tower from the front façade, best enjoyed through the huge oval window while lying on the four-poster bed of the sixth-floor suite. All rooms exude *luxe, calme et volonté* with solid oak floors, linen curtains and baths or showers carved from black or cream marble. And below ground is a sublime swimming pool and hammam reserved for guests.
Bar. Concierge. Internet (free, wireless). No-smoking rooms. Parking. Pool (indoor). Restaurant. Room service. TV.

Moderate

Hôtel Elysées Ceramic
34 av de Wagram, 8th (01.42.27.20.30, www.elysees-ceramic.com). M° Charles de

Hôtel Banke.

Gaulle Etoile. **Rates** €230 double. **Credit** AmEx, DC, MC, V. **Map** p400 D3 **⑫**
Situated between the Arc de Triomphe and place des Ternes, this comfortable hotel has one of Paris's finest art nouveau ceramic façades, dating from 1904; inside, the theme continues with a ceramic cornice around the reception. All 57 rooms have been renovated in sophisticated chocolate or pewter tones with modern, art nouveau-inspired wallpaper and light fixtures. Outside is a terrace garden perfect for taking afternoon tea or evening cocktails.
Bar. Concierge. Internet (charge, wireless). Room service (breakfast only). TV.

MONTMARTRE & PIGALLE
Deluxe

★ Hôtel Particulier Montmartre
23 av Junot, 18th (01.53.41.81.40, www.hotel-particulier-montmartre.com). M° Lamarck Caulaincourt. **Rates** €390-€590 suite. **Credit** AmEx, MC, V. **Map** p401 H1 **⑬**
Visitors lucky (and wealthy) enough to manage to book a suite at the Hôtel Particulier Montmartre will find themselves in one of the city's hidden gems. Nestled in a quiet passage off rue Lepic, in the heart of Montmartre and opposite a mysterious rock known as the Rocher de la Sorcière (witch's rock), this sumptuous Directoire-style house is dedicated to art, with each of the five luxurious suites personalised by an avant-garde artist. The private garden conceived by Louis Bénech (famous for the Tuileries renovation) adds the finishing touch. *Photos p241.*
Concierge. Internet (free, wireless). No-smoking rooms. Restaurant. Room service. TV.

Expensive

Hôtel Banke

*20 rue La Fayette, 9th (01.55.33.22.22, www.
derbyhotels.com). M° Le Peletier.* **Rates** €315-€395
double. **Credit** AmEx, MC, V. **Map** p401 H3
The Banke may well have the most eye-popping
lobby in the city, a huge two-storey space done in
outrageous belle époque style, all crimson, black pillars and gold leaf beneath a whopping glass roof.
After such opulence, the rooms are perhaps something of a let-down; but they are stylish and comfort-
ably equipped. The mezzanine bar partakes of the
lobby's luxe, and the Josefin restaurant serves nouvelle Med cuisine.
*Bars (2). Concierge. Gym. Internet (free, wireless).
Restaurants (2). Room service. Spa. TV.*

Kube Hotel

*1-5 passage Ruelle, 18th (01.42.05.20.00, www.
kubehotel.com). M° La Chapelle.* **Rates** €318-€424
double. **Credit** AmEx, DC, MC, V. **Map** p402 K1
The younger sister of the Murano Urban Resort (*see
p244*), Kube is an edgier and more affordable hotel.
Like the Murano, it sits behind an unremarkable
façade in an unlikely neighbourhood – in this case,
the ethnically diverse Goutte d'Or. The Ice Kube bar
by Grey Goose serves up vodka glasses that, like the
bar itself, are carved from ice; drinkers pay €38 to
down four vodka cocktails in 30 minutes. Also on the
menu, 'aperifood' and 'snackubes' by culinary
designer Nicolas Guillard. The art brunch on Sundays
introduces a different artist each month, with DJs and
a buffet. To top off the futuristic style, access to the
41 rooms is by fingerprint technology.
*Bars (2). Concierge. Disabled-adapted rooms.
Gym. Internet (free, wireless). No-smoking rooms.
Parking. Restaurant. Room service. TV.*

Moderate

Hôtel des Arts

*5 rue Tholozé, 18th (01.46.06.30.52, www.arts-
hotel-paris.com). M° Abbesses or Blanche.* **Rates**
€140-€160 double. **Credit** MC, V. **Map** p401 H1
This Montmartre gem is pleasantly decorated with
oriental rugs, wooden bookcases and Provençal-style
furniture. The rooms here are simple but inviting,
some affording pleasant views of the hidden roof gardens and windmills of the Butte. Art by local artists
is displayed in the basement breakfast room.
Bar. Concierge. Internet (wireless).

Hôtel Royal Fromentin

*11 rue Fromentin, 9th (01.48.74.85.93, www.
hotelroyalfromentin.com). M° Blanche or Pigalle.*
Rates €159 double. **Credit** AmEx, DC, MC, V.
Map p401 H2
Wood panelling, art deco windows and a vintage
glass lift echo the hotel's origins as a 1930s cabaret
hall; its theatrical feel attracted Blondie and Nirvana.
It's just down the road from the Moulin Rouge, and
many of its 47 rooms overlook Sacré-Coeur. Rooms
have been renovated in French style, with bright fabrics and an old-fashioned feel.
*Bar. Concierge. Internet (free, shared terminal
& wireless). No-smoking rooms. TV.*

Terrass Hotel

*12-14 rue Joseph-de-Maistre, 18th (01.46.06.72.85,
www.terrass-hotel.com). M° Place de Clichy.* **Rates**
€200-€270 double. **Credit** AmEx, DC, MC, V.
Map p401 H1
There's nothing spectacular about this classic hotel,
but for people willing to pay top euro for the best
views in town, it fits the bill. Ask for room 704 and
you can lie in the bath and look at the Eiffel Tower.

CONSUME

Kube Hotel.

Julien Rocheteau, trained by Ducasse, is at the helm of gastronomic restaurant Diapason; in decent weather, opt for a table on the seventh-floor terrace, open from June to September.

Bar. Concierge. Disabled-adapted rooms. Internet (free, wireless). No-smoking rooms. Restaurant. Room service. TV.

Timhotel Montmartre
11 rue Ravignan, 18th (01.42.55.74.79, www.timhotel.fr). M° Abbesses or Pigalle. **Rates** €150-€180 double. **Credit** AmEx, DC, MC, V. **Map** p401 H1 ❺❾
The location adjacent to picturesque place Emile-Goudeau makes this one of the most popular hotels in the Timhotel chain. It has 59 rooms, comfortable without being plush; try to bag one on the fourth or fifth floor for stunning views. Special offers are often available at quieter times of the year; ring for details.
Concierge. Internet (free, wireless). No-smoking rooms. TV.

Budget

Hôtel Eldorado
18 rue des Dames, 17th (01.45.22.13.42, www.eldoradohotel.fr). M° Place de Clichy. **Rates** €79-€89 double. **Credit** AmEx, DC, MC, V. **Map** p401 G1 ❻⓪
This eccentric hotel is decorated with flea market finds. The Eldorado's winning features include a wine bar, one of the best garden patios in town and a loyal fashionista following. The cheapest rooms have shared bathrooms and toilets.
Bar. Internet (free, wireless). Restaurant.

Hôtel Ermitage
24 rue Lamarck, 18th (01.42.64.79.22, www. ermitagesacrecoeur.fr). M° Lamarck Caulaincourt. **Rates** (incl breakfast) €110 double. **No credit cards. Map** p402 J1 ❻❶
This 12-room townhouse hotel stands on the calm, non-touristy north side of Montmartre, only five minutes from Sacré-Coeur. The bedrooms are large and endearingly overdecorated, with bold floral wallpaper; those higher up have fine views.
No-smoking rooms. Parking. Room service (morning only).

BEAUBOURG & THE MARAIS
Deluxe

★ Murano Urban Resort
13 bd du Temple, 3rd (01.42.71.20.00, www. muranoresort.com). M° Filles du Calvaire or Oberkampf. **Rates** €440-€499 double. **Credit** AmEx, DC, MC, V. **Map** p409 L5 ❻❷
Behind this unremarkable façade is a super cool and supremely luxurious hotel, popular with the fashion set for its lounge-style design, excellent restaurant

and high-tech flourishes – including coloured light co-ordinators that enable you to change the mood of your room at the touch of a button. The handsome bar has a mind-boggling 140 varieties of vodka to sample, which can bring the op art fabrics in the lift to life and make the fingerprint access to the hotel's 43 rooms and nine suites (two of which feature private pools) a late-night godsend.
Bar. Concierge. Gym. Internet (free, wireless). No-smoking rooms. Parking. Restaurant. Room service. TV.

Expensive

Hôtel Bourg Tibourg
19 rue du Bourg-Tibourg, 4th (01.42.78.47.39, www.hotelbourgtibourg.com). M° Hôtel de Ville. **Rates** €270-€300 double. **Credit** AmEx, DC, MC, V. **Map** p409 K6 ❻❸
The Bourg Tibourg has the same owners as Hôtel Costes (*see p231*) and the same interior decorator – but don't expect this jewellery box of a boutique hotel to be a miniature replica. Aside from its enviable location in the heart of the Marais and its fashion-pack fans, here it's all about Jacques Garcia's neo-Gothic-cum-Byzantine decor – impressive and imaginative. Scented candles, mosaic-tiled bathrooms and luxurious fabrics in rich colours create the perfect escape. There's no restaurant or lounge – posing is done in the neighbourhood bars.
Concierge. Disabled-adapted rooms. Internet (free, wireless). Room service. TV.

Moderate

★ Hôtel de la Bretonnerie
22 rue Ste-Croix-de-la-Bretonnerie, 4th (01.48.87.77.63, www.bretonnerie.com). M° Hôtel de Ville. **Rates** €145-€175 double. **Credit** MC, V. **Map** p409 K6 ❻❹
With wrought ironwork, exposed stone and wooden beams, the labyrinth of corridors in this 17th-century *hôtel particulier* is full of atmosphere. Tapestries, rich colours and the occasional four-poster bed give the 29 rooms individuality. Location is convenient too.
Concierge. Disabled-adapted room. Internet (free, wireless). TV.

Hôtel Duo
11 rue du Temple, 4th (01.42.72.72.22, www.duoparis.com). M° Hôtel de Ville. **Rates** €200-€380 double. **Credit** AmEx, MC, V. **Map** p406 K6 ❻❺
An unbeatable location, designer decor, a gym with sauna and a convivial cocktail bar make this a popular choice for laptop-wielding young professionals. Its Jean-Philippe Nuel decor is so striking that passers-by sometimes enquire about the price of the outsize lampshades and mustard-coloured armchairs in the huge lounge lobby, which also has a bamboo courtyard garden. Based on a palette of

CONSUME

brown with contrasting turquoise, mustard, lime green, pink or blue, each room is different and you can request a balcony, beams, wallpaper, a bath, separate loo, and road or courtyard preference.
Bar. Concierge. Disabled-adapted rooms. Gym. Internet (free, wireless). Sauna. TV.

Hôtel Jules & Jim
11 rue des Gravilliers, 4th (01.44.54.13.13, www.hoteljulesetjim.com). M° Arts et Métiers. **Rates** €200-€310 double. **Credit** AmEx, DC, MC, V. **Map** p409 K5 ⑥⑥
Located in the heart of the Marais, this modern hotel is surrounded by two paved courtyards and has lovely rooftop views. Guest rooms are comfortable,

with all mod cons (iPod dock, flatscreen TV), while a continental buffet breakfast is served in the chic dining area. Guests can enjoy cocktails at the bar or on the terrace.
Bar. Concierge. Disabled-adapted rooms. Internet (free, wireless). No-smoking rooms. TV.

★ Hôtel du Petit Moulin
29-31 rue de Poitou, 3rd (01.42.74.10.10, www.hoteldupetitmoulin.com). M° St-Sébastien Froissart. **Rates** €195-€390 suite. **Credit** AmEx, DC, MC, V. **Map** p409 L5 ⑥⑦
Within striking distance of the hip shops around rue Charlot, this turn-of-the-century façade masks what was once the oldest *boulangerie* in Paris, lovingly

Sleep in Style

Get back to the future at the oh-so-cool O.

CONSUME

Sandwiched between bustling Les Halles and chocolate-box place des Victoires, with its smart designer shops and stately Louis XIV statue, the brand new **Hotel O** (*see p235*) is a sleek, 29-room venture that adds some welcome hip to the arrondissement accommodation options.

Rooms (styled by cool young design company Ora-Ito, hence the 'O' in the hotel's name) are small but exquisite, with retro-futuristic features that make you feel like you're on board a 1970s spaceship, with clean lines, gracious curves and blocks of pink, grey, purple and dark turquoise. The centrepiece of each room is anchored by a curvilinear wooden headboard that melds into the ceiling and gives a cocoon-like feel – until you throw open the window and gaze out across the

rooftops. Another fun touch and clever space-saving element is a glass bathroom wall separating the bed from the shower. Don't worry, though, you won't have to gaze at your partner in the tub as there's a slight mirror effect on the bedroom side.

While the bedrooms feel resolutely urban, with free Wi-Fi and flatscreen TVs, the communal areas have been designed with a more back-to-nature vibe: the lobby is dominated by a lone pale wood layered 'tree' that rises to the ceiling, while the bar is decked out with giant honeycomb-shaped features on its all-green walls.

Head outside and *le tout Paris* is laid out before you, with the smart shops of the Palais-Royal a five-minute walk west and the Louvre and Jardin des Tuileries a ten-minute stroll to the south-west.

restored as a boutique hotel by Nadia Murano and Denis Nourry. The couple recruited no lesser figure than Christian Lacroix for the decor, and the result is a riot of colour, trompe l'oeil effects and a savvy mix of old and new. Each of its 17 exquisitely appointed rooms is unique, and the walls in rooms 202, 204 and 205 feature drawings and scribbles taken from Lacroix's sketchbook.
Bar. Concierge. Internet (free, wireless). Parking. Room service. TV.

Hôtel St-Louis Marais
1 rue Charles V, 4th (01.48.87.87.04, www.saintlouismarais.com). M° Bastille or Sully Morland. **Rates** €149-€219 double. **Credit** AmEx, DC, MC, V. **Map** p409 L7 ⓺⓼
Built as part of a 17th-century Célestin convent, this peaceful hotel had its bathrooms redone and Wi-Fi access installed in 2005. Rooms are compact and cosy, with wooden beams, tiled floors and simple, traditional decor.
Concierge. Internet (free, wireless). No-smoking rooms. Parking. Room service (breakfast). TV.
Other locations Hôtel St-Louis Bastille, 114 bd Richard Lenoir, 11th (01.43.38.29.29).

Les Jardins du Marais
74 rue Amelot, 11th (01.40.21.20.00, www. lesjardinsdumarais.com). M° Bastille. **Rates** €212-€455 double. **Credit** AmEx, DC, MC, V. **Map** p409 L5 ⓺⓽
The centrepiece of this ultra-swish hotel is a vast courtyard, filled with tables, potted plants and lampposts that wouldn't look out of place in Narnia. Inside, it's smart and modern; the lobby looks tastefully trendy in its steely black and white marble, with purple furnishings and Philippe Starck chairs.
Bar. Concierge. Disabled-adapted facilities. Gym. Internet (free, wireless). No-smoking rooms. Restaurant. Room service. TV.

Budget

Grand Hôtel Jeanne d'Arc
3 rue de Jarente, 4th (01.48.87.62.11, www. hoteljeannedarc.com). M° Chemin Vert or St-Paul. **Rates** €96-€119 double. **Credit** MC, V. **Map** p409 L6 ⓻⓿
The Jeanne d'Arc's strong point is its location on a quiet road close to pretty place du Marché-Ste-Catherine. A recent refurbishment has made the reception area striking, with a huge mirror adding the illusion of space. The bedrooms are colourful and comfortable.
Internet (free, wireless). No-smoking rooms. TV.

Hôtel Paris France
72 rue de Turbigo, 3rd (01.42.78.00.04, www. paris-france-hotel.com). M° Temple. **Rates** €120-€140 double. **Credit** AmEx, MC, V. **Map** p402 L5 ⓻⓵

A great central location, sweet lift, spruce staff and clean, pleasant rooms are on offer here. The attic has views of Montmartre and (if you lean out far enough) the Eiffel Tower.
Bar. Internet (free, wireless). No-smoking rooms. TV.

Hôtel du Septième Art
20 rue St-Paul, 4th (01.44.54.85.00, www.paris-hotel-7art.com). M° Pont Marie or St-Paul. **Rates** €100-€160 double. **Credit** AmEx, MC, V. **Map** p409 L7 ⓻⓶
Ideally located in a lively part of the Marais, the quaint façade hides a treasure trove of movie memorabilia, which takes up most of the reception space. Exposed brick walls and devoted staff make for a friendly, cosy atmosphere. The decor in the bedrooms isn't exactly groundbreaking, but everything is clean and well equipped. There's no lift.
Bar. Gym. Internet (charge, shared terminal; free, wireless). TV.

BASTILLE & EASTERN PARIS
Deluxe

Hôtel Marceau Bastille
13 rue Jules César, 12th (01.43.43.11.65, www. hotelmarceaubastille.com). M° Bastille. **Rates** €350-€450 double. **Credit** AmEx, DC, MC, V. **Map** p409 M7 ⓻⓷
This slick boutique hotel has 55 rooms divided into two different styles: urban or *écolo* (eco-friendly), some with a balcony. The bar-lounge, overlooking a pleasant, bamboo-planted patio, is surrounded by a gallery that exhibits works of contemporary artists.
Bar. Concierge. Disabled-adapted rooms. Gym. Internet (free, wireless). No-smoking rooms. Room service (2-10.15pm). TV.

Moderate

Hi Matic
71 rue de Charonne, 11th (01.43.67.56.56, www. hi-matic.net). M° Charonne. **Rates** from €130 double. **Credit** AmEx, DC, MC, V. **Map** p407 N7 ⓻⓸

INSIDE TRACK NO VACANCIES

Perhaps as a result of the spate of five-star openings in the last couple of years, with everyone from Shangri-La to Mandarin Oriental setting up shop in the city, two of Paris's most famous palace hotels, the Ritz (www.ritzparis.com) and the Crillon (*see p231*), are closing their doors for major upgrades. With the opening of a Peninsula Paris in 2013, expect a battle royal when the two old-timers rip off the dust sheets in 2014.

CONSUME

Mama Shelter.

CONSUME

The decor at the eco-friendly Hi Matic hotel near Bastille is positively multicoloured: every inch of wall space is either blue, lime, purple or yellow. The rooms are titchy but multi-task, so you can whip out your duvet at night and roll it back up in the day. Breakfast is organic, and a masseur will come to your room if you fancy a well-being massage (€85). *Bar. Disabled-adapted room. Internet (free, wireless). No-smoking rooms. TV.*

Le Pavillon Bastille

65 rue de Lyon, 12th (01.43.43.65.65, www. pavillonbastille.com). M° Bastille. **Rates** €155-€215 double. **Credit** AmEx, DC, MC, V. **Map** p407 M7 ⓴
The best thing about this hotel is its location between the Bastille opera and the Gare de Lyon. The 25 rooms may be small, but you're a stone's throw from the Viaduc des Arts (*see p91*).
Bar. Disabled-adapted room. Internet (free, wireless). No-smoking rooms. TV.

Standard Design Hotel

29 rue Taillandiers, 11th (01.48.05.30.97, www.standard-hotel.com). M° Ledru Rollin. **Rates** €185-€250 double. **Credit** AmEx, MC, V. **Map** p407 M6 ⓴
The Standard's black and white interior, with the occasional splash of colour, is a winner with visitors looking for a break from the sometimes heavy atmosphere of more traditional hotels. The rooms have all mod cons, the breakfast room awakens the senses with bold stripes, and you can roll into bed after a night out in Bastille's cool bars and restaurants.
Bar. Internet (free, wireless). No-smoking rooms. TV.

Budget

★ Mama Shelter

109 rue de Bagnolet, 20th (01.43.48.48.48, www.mamashelter.com). M° Alexandre Dumas,

Maraîchers or Porte de Bagnolet. **Rates** €89-€229 double. **Credit** AmEx, DC, MC, V.
Philippe Starck's latest design commission is set a stone's throw east of Père Lachaise, and its decor appeals to the young-at-heart with Batman and Incredible Hulk light fittings, dark walls, polished wood and splashes of bright fabrics. Every room comes equipped with an iMac computer, TV, free internet access and a CD and DVD player; and when hunger strikes, there's a brasserie with a romantic terrace. If you're sure of your dates, book online and take advantage of the saver's rate.
Bar. Internet (free, wireless). No-smoking rooms. Restaurant. TV.

★ Le Quartier Bercy Square

33 rue de Reuilly, 12th (01.44.87.09.09, www.lequartierhotelbs.com). M° Daumesnil or Dugommier. **Rates** €125-€165 double. **Credit** AmEx, DC, MC, V. **Map** p407 P9 ⓱
You'd never think that lime green and brown stripes would match bold silver and white replica 19th-century wallpaper, but it does at the boutique Quartier Bercy Square in the trendy 12th arrondissement. Rooms are small but inviting, often using coloured light to create atmosphere.
Bar. Internet (free, wireless). No-smoking rooms. TV.

NORTH-EAST PARIS

Moderate

Le 20 Prieuré Hôtel

20 rue du Grand Prieuré, 11th (01.47.00.74.14, www.hotel20prieure.com). M° République. **Rates** €199 double. **Credit** AmEx, MC, V. **Map** p402 M5 ⓲
In a road where budget sleeps are fast metamorphosing into hip hotels, this young, funky place benefits from particularly welcoming staff. Each bedroom features an enormous blow-up of a Paris

landmark covering the entire wall behind the bed, giving you the illusion that you are sleeping halfway up the Eiffel Tower, or on Bir-Hakeim bridge as the métro speeds by (great for *Last Tango in Paris* fans). Bathrooms are mundane in comparison, but things brighten up again in the light-flooded breakfast room, with pop art portraits and a reworked 1970s look.

Concierge. Internet (free, wireless). No-smoking rooms. TV.

Hôtel Gabriel

25 rue du Grand Prieuré, 11th (01.47.00.13.38, www.gabrielparismarais.com). M° République. **Rates** €168-€280 double. **Credit** AmEx, DC, MC, V. **Map** p402 M5 ⑲

Paris's first 'detox hotel' is a shrine to quality kip and healthy living. The air-conditioned, pure white rooms are not short on techno wizardry: there's an iPod station for which you can borrow an iPod pre-programmed with anything from Goldfrapp to Shirley Bassey; free Wi-Fi, of course; and the *sine qua non* of sleep aids, the NightCove device. This white box is easily programmed to emit sounds and light that stimulate melatonin: choose between sleep, nap or wake-up programmes. If you're still feeling run-down, head downstairs for a detox massage courtesy of Franco-Japanese masseuse Mitchiko and her colleagues. A partner gym, suggested jogging routes and green taxis complete the healthy vibe.

Bar. Concierge. Internet (free, wireless). No smoking throughout. Room service. TV.

Hôtel Le Général

5-7 rue Rampon, 11th (01.47.00.41.57, www. legeneralhotel.com). M° République. **Rates** €192-€252 double. **Credit** AmEx, DC, MC, V. **Map** p402 L5 ⑳

A fashionable find near the nightlife action of the 11th, Le Général was one of Paris's first boutique bargains when it opened back in 2003. It is still notable for its remarkably moderate rates and sleek, neutral-toned interior.

Bar. Business centre. Concierge. Disabled-adapted rooms. Gym. Internet (free, wired). No-smoking rooms. Sauna. TV.

Budget

Hôtel Beaumarchais

3 rue Oberkampf, 11th (01.53.36.86.86, www.hotelbeaumarchais.com). M° Filles du Calvaire or Oberkampf. **Rates** from €80 double. **Credit** AmEx, MC, V. **Map** p409 L5 ㉑

This contemporary hotel is located in the heart of the Oberkampf area. Its 31 rooms are brightly decorated with colourful walls, bathroom mosaics and wavy headboards; breakfast is served on the tiny garden patio or in your room.

Concierge. Internet (free, high speed & wireless). Room service. TV.

Hôtel Garden Saint-Martin

35 rue Yves Toudic, 10th (01.42.40.17.72, www.hotel-gardensaintmartin-paris.com). M° Jacques Bonsergent. **Rates** €98-€105 double. **Credit** MC, V. **Map** p402 L4 ㉒

The shops, cafés and bars along the Canal St-Martin draw visitors to this hotel, where creature comforts are guaranteed at an excellent rate. No prizes will be won for the ordinary decor, but there is a very pleasant patio garden, and the staff are helpful.

Internet (free, wireless). No-smoking rooms. TV.

THE LATIN QUARTER & THE 13TH

Expensive

Hôtel Résidence Henri IV

50 rue des Bernardins, 5th (01.44.41.31.81, www.residencehenri4.com). M° Cardinal Lemoine. **Rates** €260-€350 double. **Credit** AmEx, DC, MC, V. **Map** p406 K7 ㉝

This belle-époque-style hotel has a mere eight rooms and five apartments, so guests are assured of the staff's full attention. Peacefully situated next to leafy square Paul-Langevin, it's just a few minutes' walk away from Notre-Dame. The four-person apartments come with a handy mini-kitchen featuring a hob, fridge and microwave – although you may be reduced to eating on the beds in the smaller ones.

Concierge. Internet (free, wireless). No-smoking rooms. TV.

★ Le Petit Paris

214 rue St-Jacques, 5th (01.53.10.29.29, www. hotelpetitparis.com). M° Maubert Mutualité/RER Luxembourg. **Rates** €240-€320 double. **Credit** AmEx, MC, V. **Map** p408 J8 ㉔

This Latin Quarter venture is a dynamic exercise in taste and colour. The 20 rooms, designed by Sybille de Margerie, are arranged by era, running from the puce and purple of the medieval rooms to the wildly decadent orange, yellow and pink of the swinging '60s rooms, replete with specially commissioned sensual photographs of Paris monuments. Luxury abounds with finest silks, velvets and taffetas. Some of the rooms have small terraces, and those with baths have a TV you can watch while soaking. An honesty bar in the lounge and ultra-modern jukebox encourage conviviality.

Bar. Concierge. Disabled-adapted room. Internet (free, wireless). No-smoking rooms. TV.

Moderate

★ Five Hôtel

3 rue Flatters, 5th (01.43.31.74.21, www. thefivehotel.com). M° Les Gobelins or Port Royal. **Rates** €202-€342 double. **Credit** AmEx, MC, V. **Map** p406 J9 ㉟

The rooms in this stunning boutique hotel may be small, but they're all exquisitely designed. Fibre optics built into the walls create the illusion of sleeping under a starry sky, and you can choose from four different fragrances to subtly perfume your room (the hotel is entirely non-smoking). Guests staying in the suite have access to a private garden with a jacuzzi.
Concierge. Internet (free, wireless). No smoking throughout. TV.

Hôtel la Demeure
51 bd St-Marcel, 13th (01.43.37.81.25, www.hotel-paris-lademeure.com). M° Les Gobelins. **Rates** €170-€230 double. **Credit** AmEx, DC, MC, V. **Map** p406 K9 ⓴
This comfortable, modern hotel on the edge of the Latin Quarter has 43 air-conditioned rooms, plus suites with sliding doors to separate sleeping and living space. The wraparound balconies of the corner rooms offer lovely views of the city, and bathrooms feature either luxurious tubs or shower heads with elaborate massage possibilities.
Internet (free, wireless). No-smoking rooms. Parking. TV.

Select Hôtel
1 pl de la Sorbonne, 5th (01.46.34.14.80, www.selecthotel.fr). M° Cluny La Sorbonne. **Rates** (incl breakfast) €195-€309 double. **Credit** AmEx, DC, MC, V. **Map** p408 J8 ⓱
Located at the foot of the Sorbonne, this 68-room hotel delivers pure, understated chic with its clever blend of modern art deco features, traditional stone walls and wooden beams. The winter garden and airy common areas have recently been redone in a sleek, contemporary style.
Bar. Concierge. Internet (free, wireless). No-smoking rooms. Room service (until 10pm). TV.

Budget

Familia Hôtel
11 rue des Ecoles, 5th (01.43.54.55.27, www.hotel-paris-familia.com). M° Cardinal Lemoine or Jussieu. **Rates** (incl breakfast) €114-€135 double. **Credit** AmEx, DC, MC, V. **Map** p406 K8 ⓲
This old-fashioned Latin Quarter hotel has balconies hung with tumbling plants and walls draped with replica French tapestries. Owner Eric Gaucheron extends a warm welcome, and the 30 rooms have personalised touches such as sepia murals, cherry-wood furniture and stone walls. The Gaucherons also own the Hôtel Minerve next door.
Concierge. Internet (free, wireless). Parking. TV.

★ Hôtel les Degrés de Notre-Dame
10 rue des Grands-Degrés, 5th (01.55.42.88.88, www.lesdegreshotel.com). M° Maubert-Mutualité or St-Michel. **Rates** (incl breakfast) €115-€170 double. **Credit** MC, V. **Map** p406 J7 ⓳

On a tiny street across the river from Notre-Dame, this vintage hotel is an absolute gem. Its ten rooms are full of character, with original paintings, antique furniture and exposed wooden beams (nos.47 and 501 have views of the cathedral). It has an adorable restaurant and, a few streets away, two studio apartments that the owner rents out to preferred customers only.
Bar. Internet (free, wireless). No-smoking rooms. Restaurant. Room service (noon-midnight). TV.

Hôtel du Panthéon
19 pl du Panthéon, 5th (01.43.54.32.95, www.hoteldupantheon.com). M° Cluny La Sorbonne or Maubert Mutualité/RER Luxembourg. **Rates** €100-€310 double. **Credit** AmEx, DC, MC, V. **Map** p408 J8 ⓵
The 36 rooms of this elegant hotel are beautifully decorated with classic French *toile de Jouy* fabrics, antique furniture and painted woodwork. Some enjoy impressive views of the Panthéon; others squint out on to a hardly less romantic courtyard, complete with chestnut tree.
Internet (free, wireless). No-smoking rooms. TV.

Hôtel Résidence Gobelins
9 rue des Gobelins, 13th (01.47.07.26.90, www.hotelgobelins.com). M° Les Gobelins. **Rates** €98-€108 double. **Credit** AmEx, MC, V. **Map** p406 K10 ⓷
A tiny lift leads to colourful rooms, all equipped with satellite TV and telephone. The breakfast room overlooks a private garden, and there's free internet use available at the reception. The hotel is entirely non-smoking.
Internet (free, shared terminal). No smoking throughout. TV.

★ Hôtel de la Sorbonne
6 rue Victor-Cousin, 5th (01.43.54.58.08, www.hotelsorbonne.com). M° Cluny La Sorbonne/RER Luxembourg. **Rates** €100-€350 double. **Credit** AmEx, DC, MC, V. **Map** p408 J8 ⓶
It's out with the old at this charming, freshly renovated hotel, with bold, designer wallpapers, floral prints, lush fabrics and quotes from French literature woven into the carpets. Rooms are all equipped with iMac computers.
Concierge. Internet (free, wireless). No-smoking rooms. TV.

ST-GERMAIN-DES-PRES & ODEON

Deluxe

Villa d'Estrées
17 rue Gît-le-Coeur, 6th (01.55.42.71.11, www.villadestrees.com). M° St-Michel. **Rates** €365-€405 double. **Credit** AmEx, DC, MC, V. **Map** p408 J7 ⓼

Hôtel de l'Abbaye Saint-Germain.

Jewel colours, sumptuous fabrics, stripes and patterns are the hallmarks of this polished boutique hotel; there's nothing at all minimalist about Villa d'Estrées, which was designed by Jacques Garcia. Each of the ten rooms and suites is individually decorated, all with a nod to Empire style and a crisp, slightly masculine feel.
Bar. Concierge. Internet (free, wireless). No-smoking rooms. Restaurant. Room service (until 11pm). TV.

Expensive

Artus Hotel

34 rue de Buci, 6th (01.43.29.07.20, www.artus hotel.com). M° Mabillon. **Rates** €250-€310 double (incl breakfast). **Credit** AmEx, DC, MC, V. **Map** p408 H7 ⓭
The recently renovated Artus Hotel is the ideal spot for a classic taste of Paris – you couldn't be any closer to the heart of the Left Bank action if you tried. Inside, the look is chic boutique, with 27 individually designed rooms and suites, ranging from cosy to capacious. Staff are eager to help and full of local tips.
Bar. Concierge. Internet (free, wireless). TV.

★ L'Hôtel

13 rue des Beaux-Arts, 6th (01.44.41.99.00, www.l-hotel.com). M° Mabillon or St-Germain-des-Prés. **Rates** €285-€660 double. **Credit** AmEx, DC, MC, V. **Map** p408 H6 ⓭
Guests at the sumptuously decorated L'Hôtel these days are more likely to be models and film stars than the starving writers who frequented the place during Oscar Wilde's last days (the playwright died here in November 1900). Under Jacques

Garcia's careful restoration, each room has its own special theme: Mistinguett's *chambre* retains its art deco mirror bed, while Oscar's tribute room is appropriately clad in green peacock murals.
Bar. Concierge. Internet (shared terminal; free, wireless). Pool (indoor). Restaurant. Room service (until 11pm). Sauna. TV.
► *Don't miss out on dinner in the fabulously decadent restaurant, run by chef Julien Montbabut (see p163).*

Hôtel de l'Abbaye Saint-Germain

10 rue Cassette, 6th (01.45.44.38.11, www. hotelabbayeparis.com). M° Rennes or St-Sulpice. **Rates** (incl breakfast) €266-€415 double. **Credit** AmEx, MC, V. **Map** p405 G7 ⓭
A monumental entrance opens the way through a courtyard into this tranquil hotel, originally part of a convent. Wood panelling, well-stuffed sofas and an open fireplace in the drawing room make for a relaxed atmosphere, but, best of all, there's a surprisingly large garden. The 43 rooms and duplex apartments are tasteful and luxurious.
Bar. Concierge. Internet (free, shared terminal). Room service. TV.

Hôtel Lutetia

45 bd Raspail, 6th (01.49.54.46.46, www.lutetia-paris.com). M° Sèvres Babylone. **Rates** €310-€380 double. **Credit** AmEx, DC, MC, V. **Map** p405 G7 ⓭
This historic Left Bank hotel is a masterpiece of art nouveau and early art deco architecture that dates from 1910. It has a plush jazz bar and lively brasserie. Its 250 rooms, revamped in purple, gold and pearl grey, maintain a 1930s feel. Big-name guests in years gone by have included Picasso, Josephine Baker and de Gaulle. It was also the Abwehr (German military intelligence) HQ during the Nazi occupation.
Bar. Business centre. Concierge. Gym. Internet (free, wireless). No-smoking rooms. Restaurants (2). Room service. TV.

★ Relais Saint-Germain

9 carrefour de l'Odéon, 6th (01.44.27.07.97, www.hotel-paris-relais-saint-germain.com). M° Odéon. **Rates** (incl breakfast) €285-€370 double. **Credit** AmEx, DC, MC, V. **Map** p408 H7 ⓭
The rustic, wood-beamed ceilings remain intact at the Relais Saint-Germain, a 17th-century hotel bought and renovated by much-acclaimed chef Yves Camdeborde (originator of the *bistronomique* dining trend) and his wife Claudine. Each of the 22 rooms has a different take on eclectic Provençal charm, and the marble bathrooms are positively huge by Paris standards.
Bar. Concierge. Internet (free, high speed & wireless). No-smoking rooms. Restaurant. Room service (until 10pm). TV.
► *Guests get first dibs on a sought-after seat in Le Comptoir restaurant next door; see p161.*

CONSUME

La Villa
29 rue Jacob, 6th (01.43.26.60.00, www.villa-saint-germain.com). M° St-Germain-des-Prés. **Rates** €260-€370 double. **Credit** AmEx, DC, MC, V. **Map** p408 H6 **99**
The charismatic La Villa features cool faux crocodile skin on the bedheads and crinkly taffeta over the taupe-coloured walls. Wonderfully, your room number is projected on to the floor outside your door; very useful for any drunken homecomings.
Bar. Concierge. Internet (free, wireless). No-smoking rooms. Room service (until 10.30pm). TV.

Moderate

Le Clos Médicis
56 rue Monsieur-le-Prince, 6th (01.43.29.10.80, www.closmedicis.com). M° Odéon/RER Luxembourg. **Rates** €215-€270 double. **Credit** AmEx, DC, MC, V. **Map** p408 H8 **100**
More like a stylish, private townhouse than a hotel, Le Clos Médicis is located by the Luxembourg gardens. Decor is refreshingly modern, with rooms done out with taffeta curtains and chenille bedcovers, and antique floor tiles in the bathrooms. The cosy lounge has a working fireplace.
Bar. Concierge. Internet (free, high speed & wireless). No-smoking rooms. TV.

Grand Hôtel de l'Univers
6 rue Grégoire-de-Tours, 6th (01.43.29.37.00, www.hotel-paris-univers.com). M° Odéon. **Rates** €185-€280 double. **Credit** AmEx, DC, MC, V. **Map** p408 H7 **101**
Making the most of its 15th-century origins, this hotel features exposed wooden beams, high ceilings, antique furnishings and toile-covered walls. Manuel Canovas fabrics lend a posh touch, but there are also useful services such as a laptop for hire.
Bar. Concierge. Internet (charge, shared terminal; free, wireless). No-smoking rooms. TV.

Hôtel du Globe
15 rue des Quatre-Vents, 6th (01.43.26.35.50, www.hotel-du-globe.fr). M° Odéon. **Rates** €170 double. **Credit** MC, V. **Map** p408 H7 **102**
The Hôtel du Globe has managed to retain much of its 17th-century character – and very pleasant it is too. Gothic wrought-iron doors open into the florid corridors, and an unexplained suit of armour supervises guests from the tiny salon. The rooms with baths are somewhat larger than those with showers, and if you're an early booker you might even get the room with the four-poster bed (ask when reserving).
Internet (free, wireless). TV.

Hôtel des Saints-Pères
65 rue des Sts-Pères, 6th (01.45.44.50.00, www.espritfrance.com). M° St-Germain-des-Prés. **Rates** €180-€235 double. **Credit** AmEx, MC, V. **Map** p405 G7 **103**

Built in 1658 by one of Louis XIV's architects, this hotel has an enviable location near St-Germain-des-Prés' designer boutiques. It boasts a charming garden and a sophisticated, if small, bar. The most coveted room is no.100, with its fine 17th-century ceiling by painters from the Versailles School; it also has an open bathroom, so you can gaze at scenes from the myth of Leda and the Swan while you scrub.
Bar. Concierge. Internet (free, wireless). TV.

Hôtel Villa Madame
44 rue Madame, 6th (01.45.48.02.81, www.hotelvillamadameparis.com). M° St-Sulpice. **Rates** €189-€300 double. **Credit** AmEx, MC, V. **Map** p408 G7 **104**
This revamped hotel (formerly the Regents) located in a quiet street is a lovely surprise, its courtyard garden used for breakfast in the summer months. Honey- and chocolate-coloured woods mix with warm-toned velvets to make the rooms (all with plasma screens) feel cosy and inviting; some even have small balconies with loungers.
Concierge. Disabled-adapted rooms. Internet (free, wireless). Room service (breakfast only). TV.

Le Placide
6 rue St-Placide, 6th (01.42.84.34.60, www.leplacidehotel.com). M° Sèvres-Babylone, St-Placide or Vanneau. **Rates** €171-€530 double. **Credit** AmEx, DC, MC, V. **Map** p405 G7 **105**
With only ten rooms, the Placide is just about as bijou as it gets. White, chrome and neutral tones reign throughout (as does bark- or bamboo-inspired wallpaper), broken only by the occasional funky cushion. Rooms are spacious: all have large bathrooms as well as their own sitting area. The stylish ground-floor duplex has been designed for disabled guests.
Bar. Concierge. Disabled-adapted rooms. Internet (free, wireless). Room service. TV.

Budget

Hôtel de Nesle
7 rue de Nesle, 6th (01.43.54.62.41, www.hotel denesleparis.com). M° Odéon. **Rates** €85-€100 double. **Credit** MC, V. **Map** p408 H6 **106**
Only nine of the 20 rooms are en suite, but all are decorated with colourful murals, and many overlook a charming garden courtyard.
Internet (free, wireless). Parking.

MONTPARNASSE
Expensive

★ Hôtel Aviatic
105 rue de Vaugirard, 6th (01.53.63.25.50, www.aviatic.fr). M° Duroc, Montparnasse Bienvenüe or St-Placide. **Rates** €245-€295 double. **Credit** AmEx, DC, MC, V. **Map** p405 F8 **107**

CONSUME

This historic hotel has masses of character, from the Empire-style lounge and garden atrium to the bistro-style breakfast room and polished marble floor in the lobby. New decoration throughout, in beautiful steely greys, warm reds, elegant, striped velvets and *toile de Jouy* fabrics, lends an impressive touch of glamour, and the service is consistently with a smile.

Concierge. Internet (free, wireless). Parking. TV.

Moderate

Hôtel des Académies et des Arts

15 rue de la Grande Chaumière, 6th (01.43.26.66.44, www.hotel-des-academies.com). Mº Notre-Dame des Champs, Raspail or Vavin. **Rates** €189-€314 double. **Credit** AmEx, DC, MC, V. **Map** p405 G8 ⑩⑧

This small boutique hotel scores highly on style. There are cosy salons, fireplaces and an extensive collection of art books. The 20 immaculate rooms are individually designed around four themes (Paris, Actor, Man Ray or Rulhmann), and offer wonderful views over the rooftops or down on to the spectacular Jérôme Mesnager mural in the courtyard.

Concierge. Disabled-adapted room. Internet (free, shared terminal & wireless). TV.

Hôtel Delambre

35 rue Delambre, 14th (01.43.20.66.31, www.delambre-paris-hotel.com). Mº Edgar Quinet or Vavin. **Rates** €140-€160 double. **Credit** AmEx, MC, V. **Map** p405 G9 ⑩⑨

Occupying a narrow slot in a small street between Montparnasse and St-Germain, this hotel was home to surrealist André Breton in the 1920s. Today it's modern and friendly, with cast-iron details in the 13 rooms and newly installed air-conditioning. The mini suite in the attic, comprising two separate rooms, is particularly pleasant and sleeps up to four.

Concierge. Disabled-adapted room. Internet (charge, wireless). No-smoking rooms. TV.

Budget

Hôtel Istria Saint-Germain

29 rue Campagne-Première, 14th (01.43.20.91.82, www.hotel-istria-paris.com). Mº Raspail. **Rates** €85-€130 double. **Credit** AmEx, DC, MC, V. **Map** p405 G9 ⑩⑩

Behind this unassuming façade is the place where the artistic royalty of Montparnasse's heyday – the likes of Man Ray, Marcel Duchamp and Louis Aragon – once lived. The Istria Saint-Germain has been modernised since then, but it still has plenty of charm, with 26 bright, simply furnished rooms.

Concierge. Disabled-adapted room. Internet (free, wireless). No-smoking rooms. Parking. Room service. TV.

▶ *Film fans take note: the artists' studios next door featured in Godard's A Bout de Souffle.*

Solarhôtel

22 rue Boulard, 14th (01.43.21.08.20, www.solarhotel.fr). Mº Denfert Rochereau. **Rates** €69 double. **Credit** AmEx, DC, MC, V. **Map** p405 G10 ⑪⑪

This hotel has managed to strike a great balance between price and sustainability. The simple ensuite bedrooms are all equipped with low-energy lamps, and corridors are fitted with sensor-operated lights. Clients and staff are encouraged to recycle, with separate bins for plastics, paper, glass and batteries, and biodegradable waste from the organic breakfast gets turned into compost in a barrel in the garden.

Internet (shared terminal). TV.

THE 7TH & WESTERN PARIS

Deluxe

★ Le Bellechasse

8 rue de Bellechasse, 7th (01.45.50.22.31, www.lebellechasse.com). Mº Assemblée Nationale or Solférino/RER Musée d'Orsay. **Rates** (incl breakfast) €340-€390 double. **Credit** AmEx, DC, MC, V. **Map** p405 F6 ⑫⑫

A former *hôtel particulier*, the Bellechasse fell into the hands of Christian Lacroix, already responsible for the makeover of the Hôtel du Petit Moulin (*see p245*). It reopened in July 2007, duly transformed into a trendy boutique hotel. Only a few steps away from the Musée d'Orsay, it offers 34 splendid – though rather small – rooms.

Bar. Internet (free, shared terminal & wireless). No-smoking rooms. TV.

★ Le Montalembert

3 rue Montalembert, 7th (01.45.49.68.68, www.montalembert.com). Mº Rue du Bac. **Rates** €414 double. **Credit** AmEx, DC, MC, V. **Map** p405 G6 ⑬⑬

Grace Leo-Andrieu's impeccable boutique hotel is a benchmark of quality. It has everything that *mode* maniacs (who flock here for Fashion Week) could want: bathrooms stuffed with Molton Brown toiletries, a set of digital scales and plenty of mirrors with which to keep an eye on their figure. Clattery stairwell lifts are a nice nod to old-fashioned ways in a hotel that is otherwise *tout moderne*.

Bar. Concierge. Internet (free, wireless). No-smoking rooms. Restaurant. Room service. TV: DVD.

Expensive

Hôtel Duc de Saint-Simon

14 rue de St-Simon, 7th (01.44.39.20.20, www.hotelducdesaintsimon.com). Mº Rue du Bac. **Rates** €265-€295 double. **Credit** AmEx, DC, MC, V. **Map** p405 G6 ⑭⑭

A lovely courtyard leads the way into this popular hotel situated on the edge of St-Germain-des-Prés.

Of the 34 romantic bedrooms, four have terraces over a closed-off, leafy garden. It's perfect for lovers, though if you can do without a four-poster bed there are more spacious rooms than the Honeymoon Suite. *Bar. Concierge. Internet (free, shared terminal & wireless). No-smoking rooms. Room service. TV.*

Moderate

Hôtel La Bourdonnais

111-113 av de La Bourdonnais, 7th (01.47.05.45.42, www.hotellabourdonnais.com). M° Ecole Militaire. **Rates** €180-€250 double. **Credit** AmEx, DC, MC, V. **Map** p404 D7 ⑮
The Bourdonnais feels more like a traditional French bourgeois townhouse than a hotel, with 56 bedrooms decorated in rich colours, antiques and Persian rugs. The lobby opens on to a winter garden. *Concierge. Internet (free, wireless). Parking. TV.*

Hôtel Lenox

9 rue de l'Université, 7th (01.42.96.10.95, www.lenoxsaintgermain.com). M° St-Germain-des-Prés. **Rates** €180-€260 double. **Credit** AmEx, DC, MC, V. **Map** p405 G6 ⑯
This venerable literary and artistic haunt is unmistakably part of St-Germain-des-Prés. The art deco-style Lenox Club Bar, open to the public, features comfortable leather club chairs and jazz instruments on the walls. Bedrooms, reached by an astonishing glass lift, have more traditional decor and city views. *Bar. Concierge. Internet (free, wireless). No-smoking rooms. Room service. TV.*

Le Bellechasse.

Sublim Eiffel

94 bd Garibaldi, 15th (01.40.65.95.95, www. sublimeiffel.com). M° Sèvres-Lecourbe. **Rates** €159-€229 double. **Credit** AmEx, MC, V. **Map** p405 E8 ⑰
Some Barry White on your iPod is essential for this luuurve hotel not far from the Eiffel Tower. Carpets printed with paving stones and manhole covers lead to the rooms, where everything has been put in place for steamy nights. It's all to do with the lighting effects, which include a starry Eiffel Tower or street-scene lights above the bed and sparkling LEDs in the showers, filtered by coloured glass doors. Lovers should head for the suite, with its jacuzzi, huge shower, bathrobes and DVDs, and book the Romance package (rose petals on the bed and champagne). All guests get the use of the mini-gym and hammam, and there is a massage room too. The bar adds a bit of jazz to a neighbourhood in need of some action. *Concierge. Bar. Gym. Hammam. Internet (free, wireless). Room service. TV.*

Budget

Hôtel Eiffel Rive Gauche

6 rue du Gros-Caillou, 7th (01.45.51.51.51, www.hotel-eiffel.com). M° Ecole Militaire. **Rates** €105-€180 double. **Credit** AmEx, MC, V. **Map** p404 D6 ⑱
The Provençal decor and warm welcome make this a pleasant retreat. For the quintessential Paris view at a bargain price, ask to stay on one of the upper floors: you can see the Eiffel Tower from nine of the 29 rooms. All of them feature Empire-style headboards and modern bathrooms. Outside, there's a tiny, tiled courtyard. *Concierge. Internet (free, wireless). TV.*
► *If this is fully booked, try sister hotel Eiffel Villa Garibaldi (48 bd Garibaldi, 15th, 01.56.58.56.58), which has equally reasonable rates.*

YOUTH ACCOMMODATION

Auberge Internationale des Jeunes

10 rue Trousseau, 11th (01.47.00.62.00, www.aijparis.com). M° Ledru-Rollin. **Rates** (incl breakfast, per person) €18-€20. **Credit** AmEx, MC, V. **Map** p407 N7 ⑲
Cleanliness is a high priority at this large, 120-bed hostel close to Bastille and within easy distance of the Marais. Rooms accommodate between two and four people, and the larger ones have their own shower and toilet. With the lowest hostel rates in central Paris, the place does tend to fill up fast during the summer months, but advance reservations can be made. Although the hostel is open all hours without any late-night curfew, the rooms are closed for cleaning every day between 10am and 3pm. Under-35s only. *Internet (free, wireless). Microwave.*

CONSUME

Dear Mary,

I followed your advice and checked the ParisAddress website to look for an apartment. This place we booked is just amazing, it has everything we were expecting and even more !

> Instant availabil
> Instant booking
> Easy process
> Prices all include no hidden fees !
> Personal greetin
> Assistance 7/7

WWW.PARISADDRESS.COM

You wish to live like a true Parisian ?
Saint-Germain-Des-Prés, the Latin Quarter, St Louis Island, the Marais, Eiffel Tower and so man other great areas for you to discover !
To make your next trip in Paris an unique and unforgettable experience, rent an apartment and discover Paris from 'within'.
ParisAddress invites you to discover picturesque and fully furnished apartments !

www.parisaddress.com - booking@parisaddress.com - +33 1 43 20 91 57 Parisaddres

Auberge Jules-Ferry

8 bd Jules-Ferry, 11th (01.43.57.55.60,
www.hihostels.com). M° République. **Rates**
(incl breakfast & linens, per person) €25.
Credit MC, V. **Map** p402 M4 ❿
This friendly IYHF hostel has 100 beds in rooms for
two to six. There's no curfew, though rooms are
closed between 10am and 2pm.
Internet (charge, shared terminal).

BVJ Paris/Quartier Latin

44 rue des Bernardins, 5th (01.43.29.34.80,
www.bvjhotel.com). M° Maubert Mutualité.
Rates (incl breakfast, per person) €30 dorm;
€35 double. **No credit cards. Map** p406 J7 ❿
The BVJ hostel has 121 beds with homely tartan
quilts in clean but bare modern dorms (accommo-
dating up to ten), and rooms with showers. There's
also a TV lounge and a work room.
Internet (charge, shared terminal).
Other locations BVJ Paris/Louvre, 20 rue Jean-
Jacques-Rousseau, 1st (01.53.00.90.90).

★ MIJE

6 rue de Fourcy, 4th (01.42.74.23.45, www.
mije.com). M° St-Paul. **Rates** (incl breakfast,
per person; €2.50 obligatory membership) €31
dorm (18-30s); €38 double. **No credit cards.**
Map p409 L6 ❿
MIJE runs three 17th-century Marais residences –
one is a former convent – that provide the most
attractive hostel sleeps in Paris. Its plain, clean
rooms have snow-white sheets and sleep up to eight
people; all have a shower and basin. The Fourcy
address has its own restaurant (evenings only).
Internet (charge, shared terminal).
Other locations (same phone) 12 rue des Barres,
4th; 11 rue du Fauconnier, 4th.

St Christopher's Inn

159 rue de Crimée, 19th (01.40.34.34.40, www.
st-christophers.co.uk/paris-hostels). M° Crimée,
Jaurès, Laumière or Stanlingrad. **Rates** per
person €28-€40 dorm; €70-€110 double. **Credit**
MC, V. **Map** p403 N1 ❿
If you don't mind bunking up with others, you could
try this branch of the youth hostel chain on the Canal
de l'Ourcq. The decor in the bedrooms has a sailor's
cabin feel, with round mirrors, bubble-pattern wallpaper and 1950s-inspired cabin furniture. The hostel
really comes into its own in its bar Belushi's, where
the usual backpack brigade are joined by Parisians
bent on taking advantage of the canal setting.
Bar. Internet (free, wireless). No-smoking rooms.
Restaurant.

BED & BREAKFAST

Alcove & Agapes

(01.44.85.06.05, www.bed-and-breakfast-
in-paris.com).

This B&B booking service offers over 100 *chambres
d'hôtes* (€80-€320 for a double, including breakfast;
three-, four- and five-bed rooms available too) with
hosts who range from artists to grannies. Extras can
include anything from dinner to cooking classes.

Good Morning Paris

43 rue Lacépède, 5th (01.47.07.28.29,
www.goodmorningparis.fr).
This company has 100 rooms in the city. Prices
range from €79 to €119 for doubles, and €116 for an
apartment that sleeps two to four people. There's a
minimum stay of two nights.

APART-HOTELS
& FLAT RENTAL

A deposit is usually payable on arrival. Small
ads for private short-term lets run in the
fortnightly anglophone mag *FUSAC* (www.
fusac.fr); or check out www.frenchconnections.
co.uk, which has a selection of furnished
apartments for four or more people, and
www.apartmentservice.com.

Citadines Apart'hotel

Central reservations 01.41.05.79.05, www.
citadines.com. **Rates** €110-€615. **Credit**
AmEx, DC, MC, V.
The 16 modern Citadines complexes across Paris
tend to attract a mainly business clientele. Room
sizes vary from slightly cramped studios to quite
spacious two-bedroom apartments.

Paris Address

Central reservations 01.43.20.91.57, www.paris
address.com. **Rates** €80-€400. **Credit** AmEx,
DC, MC, V.
Paris Address has over 280 apartments for rent in
the heart of Paris and offers a friendly reception
service – a great alternative to staying in a hotel.

Paris Appartements Services

20 rue Bachaumont, 2nd (01.40.28.01.28,
www.paris-apts.com). M° Sentier. **Open** 9am-6pm
Mon-Fri. *Key pick-up* 24hrs. **Rates** (min 5 nights)
€100-€214. **Credit** AmEx, MC, V.
This organisation specialises in short-term rentals,
offering furnished studios and one-bedroom flats in
the first to fourth arrondissements.

Swell Apartments

11 rue Duhesme, 18th (+44 (0)7725 056 421,
www.swell-apartments.co.uk). M° Lamarck
Caulincourt. **Rates** €113-€131 (min 3 nights).
Credit MC, V. **Map** p401 H1.
Don't be put off by the tatty entrance; this one-bedroom flat on the north side of Montmartre (sleeping
two) is lovely inside. The bedroom, with blue and
white walls, has a crystal chandelier and marble fireplace. The cosy lounge has elegant furniture.

CONSUME

Arts & Entertainment

Children

We love Paris in the playtime.

For all its commotion and traffic-clogged boulevards, the French capital is actually a very child-friendly place to visit. Most Parisians have to raise their children in gardenless apartments, so the city powers ensure that there is plenty of provision for youngsters to expend their energy outside the home: every *arrondissement* has spaces with playgrounds, and in big parks such as the Jardin du Luxembourg and Buttes-Chaumont, pony rides, sandpits, swings, puppet shows and boating ponds spice up the childhood of many a young Parisian. Museums and other attractions don't ignore younger visitors either, with events, workshops and child-focused exhibits.

Paris's museums and other attractions cater to children as well as adults, and also offer blissful opportunities to offload your kids on to someone else with children's workshops, held on Saturdays and Wednesdays during the school year, and daily during school holidays. If your children don't speak French, you can usually request an English speaker in advance. To find out what's coming up, contact the individual museums or check out www.paris.fr. Listings magazines *Pariscope*, *L'Officiel des Spectacles*, *Figaroscope* (with Wednesday's *Le Figaro*) and Télérama's *Sortir* all have kids' sections; and the free bi-monthly magazine *Paris-Mômes* is distributed with daily newspaper *Libération* in the city's toy shops and public libraries.

Sightseeing with children can be made easier with planning. Queues at prime spots such as the **Eiffel Tower** (*see p129*), **Louvre** (*see p41*) and the towers at **Notre-Dame** (*see p39*) are less disheartening in the morning.

GETTING AROUND

One word of advice: walk whenever possible. The métro is difficult to negotiate with babies and toddlers. Two of you might manage a pushchair, but lone travellers won't and passers-by are notoriously selfish about helping out. If your babe is small enough for a baby carrier, it will save you a lot of hassle when navigating the tight turnstiles and never-ending staircases. Also try to travel between 10.30am and 5pm to avoid the rush-hour crowds. The driverless line 14 (St-Lazare to Olympiades) is a big hit with kids, who can sit at the front and peer down the tunnel as the train advances; the mostly overground lines six (Nation to Charles de Gaulle Étoile) and two (Nation to Porte Dauphine) offer attractive city views; a number of RER stations have lifts, although they are frequently broken.

Buses, on the other hand, are easier thanks to priority seats near the front for passengers with young children; many, such as nos.24, 63 and 95 (www.ratp.fr), pass numerous sights. Three- to 11-year-olds qualify for a half-price *carnet* (a book of ten tickets) for all transport, including the Montmartrobus minibus and Montmartre funicular. Taxi drivers will usually take a family of four (charging €1 to carry a pushchair and a little extra for the fourth person). If you're stuck, try **G7 taxis** (36.07, www.taxisg7.fr), which has an English-speaking booking line.

For older kids, the recent addition of extra cycle paths across the centre (especially along the Seine, up the Canal St-Martin and along the Canal de l'Ourcq) makes a spin *en famille* an enjoyable way to get around the city while seeing the sights. Short distances are easily covered using the city's **Vélib** self-service scheme (www.velib.fr; *see p369*). For day-long fun try **Paris à Vélo c'est Sympa** (22 rue Alphonse Baudin, 11th, 01.48.87.60.01, www.parisvelosympa.com). For a day out in beautiful surroundings, the Bois de Vincennes in the east and the Bois de Boulogne in the west provide woodlands, picnic areas, boating lakes and lawns.

EATING OUT

Affordable **Chartier** (7 rue du Fbg-Montmartre, 9th, 01.47.70.86.29, www.restaurant-chartier. com) is always a fun place to take the kids, with its belle époque dining room and waiters clad in black and white. **Tokyo Eat** at the Palais de Tokyo (13 av du Président-Wilson, 16th, 01.47.20.00.29, www.palaisdetokyo.com) is good too, with wacky decor and round, family-sized tables. If you fancy browsing for baby clothes while slurping on a hot coffee, the **Poussette Café** (6 rue Pierre Sémard, 9th, 01.78.10.49.00, www.lepoussettecafe.com) is a haven, with parking for buggies and milk-warming facilities.

BABIES & TODDLERS

Always pack a portable changing mat. A facility worth remembering is the WC chalet in the Jardin du Luxembourg, where €0.60 gives you access to loos with a padded changing table; the **Galeries Lafayette** and **Printemps** (for both, see p191) department stores have clean, well-equipped nappy-changing facilities, as does the **Poussette Café** (see above). Breastfeeding in public is more common than ever, but still often frowned upon, so take a scarf for places where modesty is essential, or choose a quiet corner.

A city break with tots in tow doesn't have to mean missing out on the city's galleries and museums. Almost all of the main attractions have child-friendly activities or green spaces nearby – handy as a reward for good behaviour. There's a carefully tended garden by Notre-Dame, and the dignified **Musée Rodin** (see p129) has outdoor distractions such as a sandpit to dig in, a sculpture-filled garden to explore (free entry to parents with a pushchair) and a tempting ice-cream stand. And if the heady heights of the Eiffel Tower prove too daunting, more down-to-earth amusements can be found at the adjacent Champ de Mars, with its play areas and seasonal donkey rides; or there are old-style merry-go-rounds by the river.

BABYSITTING

Many hotels can organise babysitting (ask when you reserve). The **American Church in Paris** (65 quai d'Orsay, 7th, 01.40.62.05.00,

www.acparis.org) has a noticeboard displaying ads from English-speaking babysitters and au pairs; **Baby Sitting Services** (01.46.21.33.16, www.babysittingservices.com) can organise babysitting at short notice.

MUSEUMS & SIGHTSEEING

Most museums offer children's workshops (in French) on Wednesday afternoons, at weekends and in the holidays. At the **Louvre** (see p41) the programme for kids varies from learning about facial expressions in paintings to Egyptian sculpture. Next door, the **Museé des Arts Décoratifs** (see p55) offers hands-on art workshops for ages four to 14 and special tours (tailored to different age groups). The **Palais de Tokyo** (see p71) has inventive 'Tok Tok' story-reading for three- to five-year-olds, workshops for five- to seven-year-olds and family visits (4.30pm Sun), often led by notable contemporary artists. The **Musée Rodin** (see p129) runs children's clay workshops.

★ Centre Pompidou – Galerie des Enfants

Rue St-Martin, 4th (01.44.78.12.33, www. centrepompidou.fr/enfants). Mº Hôtel de Ville or Rambuteau/RER Châtelet Les Halles. **Open** Museum 11am-9pm Mon, Wed-Sun. Workshops most Wed, Sat & Sun afternoons & school holidays. **Admission** Museum €11-€13; €9-€10 reductions; free under-18s, under-26s (EU citizens). Workshops €10 (1 child & 1 adult). **Credit** MC, V. **Map** p402 K5.

In this ground-floor gallery, wonderfully thought-out exhibitions introduce children to interesting aspects of modern art, design and architecture. Kids are kept enthralled with interactive elements and the opportunity to touch. There are also hands-on workshops for three- to 12-year-olds, and family workshops. Audio guides for six- to 12-year-olds can also be hired for €4. If you just fancy a gawp over the rooftops from the sixth floor, it's €4 (free under-26s). Outside, look for the colourful Stravinsky fountain on the south side, designed by Niki de Saint Phalle and Jean Tinguely.

Cité de l'Architecture

Palais de Chaillot, 1 pl du Trocadéro, 16th (01.58.51.52.00, www.citechaillot.fr). Mº Trocadéro. **Open** 11am-7pm Mon, Wed, Fri-Sun; 11am-9pm Thur. **Admission** €8; €5 reductions; free under-18s, under-26s (EU citizens). **Credit** MC, V. **Map** p400 B5.

More than 850 life-size copies of France's architectural treasures (including portions of great cathedrals such as Chartres) make for a fascinating visit for children of all ages. To help them understand the exhibits, colourful interactive games are dotted around the permanent displays, so they can try their hand at architecture and learn the concepts of

ARTS & ENTERTAINMENT

Musée de la Musique.

This wonderfully kitsch version of Madame Tussauds is a hit with kids, who can have their photo taken alongside waxworks of showbiz stars and personalities such as Zinédine Zidane, Brigitte Bardot, the Queen and Barack Obama, plus new arrivals such as Nicolas Cage, Penélope Cruz and Scrat from *Ice Age*. Landmark historical moments, such as Neil Armstrong walking on the moon, are re-enacted in the 'snapshots of the 20th century' area; a small gallery at the top of a spiral staircase near the end shows how waxworks are made; and an impressive hall of mirrors (designed by France's fetish illusionist Arturo Brachetti and with music by Manu Katche) plunges you into scenes such as an Aztec temple.

▶ *On Saturday and Sunday afternoons during termtime there are special children's guided tours (French only) for seven- to 12-year-olds (€19).*

Musée des Arts et Métiers

60 rue Réamur, 3rd (01.53.01.82.00, www.arts-et-metiers.net). M° Arts et Métiers. **Open** 10am-6pm Tue, Wed, Fri-Sun; 10am-9.30pm Thur. **Admission** €6.50; €4.50 reductions; free under-18s, under-26s (EU citizens), all 1st Sun of mth & after 6pm Thur. *Audio guides* €5. **Credit** V. **Map** p402 K5.

Abbot Grégoire founded the fascinating 'arts and trades' museum in the late 18th century as 'a store for useful, new inventions'. Today, it thrills budding scientists, mechanics, astronomers, pilots or kids simply curious about the world around them with highlights that include Foucault's original pendulum, used by physician Léon Foucault in 1851 to make the rotation of the earth visible to the human eye; Clément Ader's steam-powered Avion III, officially the world's first working plane (1897); and Henry Ford's Model T car.

Romanesque and Gothic as they create fantastical animal heads, design stained-glass windows or build a Romanesque arch. On Wednesday and Saturday afternoons, three- to seven-year-olds can have a go at doing some building themselves with wooden blocks. Entry is €8 and you don't need to reserve (just turn up about 30 minutes beforehand).

Etoiles du Rex

1 bd Poissonnière, 2nd (01.45.08.93.58, www.legrandrex.com). M° Bonne Nouvelle. **Open** 10am-7pm Wed-Sun (tours leave every 5mins); daily during school holidays. **Admission** €10; €8.50 under-12s. **Credit** AmEx, MC, V. **Map** p402 J4.

The slick but cheesy 50-minute backstage tour of the glorious art deco Grand Rex cinema is a treat for any kids with acting aspirations. Be prepared to ham your heart out when, propelled by automatic doors, lifts and mystery voices, you visit the projection room, climb behind the giant screen and are thrust into a whirlwind of sound dubbing, special effects and an audition for *King Kong*.

Grévin

10 bd Montmartre, 9th (01.47.70.85.05, www.grevin.com). M° Grands Boulevards. **Open** 10am-6.30pm (last admission 5.30pm) Mon-Fri; 10am-7pm (last admission 6pm) Sat, Sun. **Admission** €22; €15-€19 reductions; free under-6s. **Credit** AmEx, DC, MC, V. **Map** p402 H4.

Musée des Egouts

Entrance opposite 93 quai d'Orsay, by Pont de l'Alma, 7th (01.53.68.27.81). M° Alma-Marceau/ RER Pont de l'Alma. **Open** *May-Sept* 11am-5pm Mon-Wed, Sat, Sun. *Oct-Apr* 11am-4pm Mon-Wed, Sat, Sun. **Admission** €4.30; €3.50 reductions; free under-6s. **Credit** MC, V. **Map** p400 D5.

The sewer museum retraces the pungent history of all 2,100km (1,305 miles) of Paris's underworld through a genuinely fascinating series of films, exhibits and a trip through the tunnels. During bad weather, visiting times may change or the museum may close as sudden surges in water can make the sewers dangerous.

Musée de la Magie

11 rue St-Paul, 4th (01.42.72.13.26, www.musee delamagie.com). M° St-Paul or Sully-Morland. **Open** 2-7pm Wed, Sat, Sun (open extra hours & days during school holidays, check website for details). **Admission** €9; €7 reductions. **No credit cards. Map** p409 L7.

Small kids love the distorting mirrors and putting their hands in the lion's mouth at this museum of magic and curiosities, which is housed in vaulted cellars. A short magic show is included in the visit – it's in French, but rabbits out of hats translate well into any language. There's a great automated museum too (extra charge), where 100 mechanical toys move into action before your kids' eyes.

Musée de la Musique

Parc de la Villette, 221 av Jean-Jaurès, 19th (01.44.84.45.00, www.cite-musique.fr). Mº Porte de Pantin. **Open** noon-6pm Tue-Sat; 10am-6pm Sun. **Admission** €6.40; free under-26s. **Credit** MC, V. **Map** p403 inset.

This innovative music museum houses a gleamingly restored collection of instruments from the old Conservatoire, interactive computers and scale models of opera houses and concert halls. Visitors are supplied with an audio guide in a choice of languages, and the musical commentary is a joy, playing the appropriate instrument as you approach each exhibit. There are also regular free interactive workshops and concerts for children over seven.

★ Musée National de la Marine

Palais de Chaillot, 17 pl du Trocadéro, 16th (01.53.65.69.69, www.musee-marine.fr). Mº Trocadéro. **Open** 11am-6pm Mon, Wed, Thur; 11am-9.30pm Fri; 11am-7pm Sat, Sun. **Admission** €7; €5 reductions; free under-18s, under-26s EU citizens). **Credit** *Shop* MC, V. **Map** p400 B5.

Musée National de la Marine.

Sail your family back in time through 400 years of French naval history. Highlights include the *Océan*, a 19th-century sailing vessel equipped with an impressive 120 cannon; a gilded barge built for Napoleon; and some extravagant, larger-than-life figureheads, from serene-faced angels to leaping seahorses. There are also dozens of model boats, dating from the 18th to the 20th century, and several old-fashioned divers' suits. Guided tours for children run during the school holidays.

Musée de la Poupée

Impasse Berthaud, 3rd (01.42.72.73.11, www.musee delapoupeeparis.com). Mº Rambuteau. **Open** 10am-6pm Tue-Sun. **Admission** €8; €4-€6 reductions; free under-3s. **No credit cards. Map** p406 L7.

This small, private museum and doll hospital enchants little girls with its collection of some 500 dolls (mostly of French origin) and their accompanying accessories and pets, which are arranged in thematic tableaux. A few teddies and quacking ducks are thrown in for young boys, and storytelling sessions and workshops (along the lines of making doll's clothes or miniature food for dolls' houses) are held on Wednesday afternoons (in French, reserve in advance; €10-€14). There's even a *clinique pour poupées* if your doll is falling apart at the seams.

★ Muséum National d'Histoire Naturelle

36 rue Geoffroy-St-Hilaire, 2 rue Bouffon, 57 rue Cuvier, 5th (01.40.79.30.00, www.mnhn.fr). Mº Gare d'Austerlitz or Jussieu. **Open** 10am-6pm Mon, Wed-Sun. **Admission** *Grande Galerie de l'Evolution* €7; €5 reductions. *Galeries de Paléontologie et d'Anatomie Comparée* €7; €5 reductions; free under-26s. *Galerie des Enfants* €7; €5 reductions; free under-4s. *Combined 2-day ticket for all sites* €25; €20 reductions. **Credit** MC, V. **Map** p406 K9.

At the Natural History Museum's impressive Grande Galerie de l'Evolution, stuffed creatures parade majestically through their various habitats. Animals of all kinds teach children about the diversity of nature and, in the endangered and vanished section (where a dodo takes pride of place), about the importance of protecting them. Also in the Jardin des Plantes complex are the small Ménagerie zoo (*see p264*); the bony remains of fish, birds, monkeys, dinosaurs and humans in the Galerie de Paléontologie et d'Anatomie Comparée; and the excellent Galerie des Enfants. This 600sq m space is specially designed to help children increase their awareness of the planet's future through three different environments – the city (Paris), the river (La Bassée), and the tropical forest (Kayapo native land in Brazil). Finally, scaling things up to planetary level, they can get to grips with a brief history of life and major ecological issues such as global warming, before finding out what action they can take now and in the future.

★ Stade de France

Guided visits via entrance Porte G, Stade de France, Seine St-Denis (01.55.93.00.00, tours 08.92.70.09.00, www.stadefrance.com). M° St-Denis Porte de Paris/RER Stade de France St-Denis. **Tours** *French* every 2hrs 11am-5pm daily (every hr from 10am Apr-Aug). *English* 10.30am, 2.30pm daily. **Admission** €15; €10-€12 reductions; free under-5s. **Credit** AmEx, DC, MC, V.

Football- and rugby-crazy kids will absolutely love the behind-the-scenes tours of France's handsome national sports stadium. After a quick scan of the newly renovated museum (featuring photos, football shirts and electric guitars from the rock stars who also play here), the tour begins by sitting in the stands and ends with a runout through the tunnel to the sound of applause. On the way, you can visit the changing and shower rooms and learn about the on-site hospital and prison cells. On match or concert days, tours are not available.

AQUARIUMS & ZOOS

Cinéaqua

2 av des Nations Unies, 16th (01.40.69.23.23, www.cineaqua.com). M° Trocadéro. **Open** 10am-7pm daily. **Admission** €19.50; €12.90-€15.50 reductions; free under-3s. **Credit** MC, V. **Map** p400 B5.

Paris's first 'ocean entertainment centre' is a hybrid aquarium-cinema complex containing more tham 500 species of fish, invertebrates, sharks and coral,

Ménagerie du Jardin des Plantes.

along with several film screens. There are kids' clubs, with face-painting and games, from 2pm to 5pm daily, plus a touch pool offering the chance to stroke carp and sturgeon.

Ménagerie du Jardin des Plantes

57 rue Cuvier, 5th (01.40.79.37.94, www.mnhn.fr). M° Gare d'Austerlitz, Jussieu or Place Monge. **Open** 9am-6pm Mon-Sat; 9am-6.30pm Sun. **Admission** €10; €8 reductions; free under-4s. **Credit** AmEx, MC, V. **Map** p406 K8.

Heads rolled during the Terror, leaving many an aristocratic collection of exotic animals without a home. This *ménagerie* became the solution in 1794. Nowadays, its inhabitants include vultures, monkeys, orang-utans, ostriches, flamingos, a century-old turtle, plus another one rescued from the sewers, a lovely red panda and lots of satisfyingly scary spiders and snakes. There's a petting zoo with farm animals for small kids, and older ones can zoom in on microscopic species in the Microzoo.

Palais de la Porte Dorée Aquarium Tropical

293 av Daumesnil, 12th (01.53.59.58.60, www.aquarium-portedoree.fr). M° Porte Dorée. **Open** 10am-5.30pm Tue-Fri; 10am-7pm Sat, Sun. **Admission** €4.50; €3 reductions; free under-4s. **No credit cards.**

The basement of this art deco palace, built for the Colonial Exhibition in 1931, contains the small but much-loved city aquarium. Four alligators were introduced recently when the last of the aquarium's original crocodiles, brought from Senegal in 1948, died; other watery residents include cuttlefish, sharks and luminous deep-water species.

▶ *Palais de la Porte Dorée is also home to the Cité Nationale de l'Histoire de l'Immigration (see p91).*

Parc de Thoiry

78770 Thoiry-en-Yvelines (01.34.87.53.76, www.thoiry.net). 45km (28 miles) west of Paris; by car A13, A12, then N12 towards Dreux until Thoiry. **Open** times vary, see website for details. **Admission** *Safari park, park & château* €27.50; €21-€25 reductions; free under-3s. **Credit** MC, V.

As well as a beautiful château, the Parc de Thoiry houses one of Europe's first animal reserves. Follow the long safari park trail, accessible only by car, and see zebras rub their noses over your windscreen and bears amble down tracks. In the adjoining zoo, rarities include Siberian lynx and Tonkean macaques.

PERFORMING ARTS

When school's out on Wednesday afternoons, at weekends and during holidays, fairytales, fables and folk stories keep children entertained at the city's theatres and *café-théâtres*. The varied programme at the **Théâtre Dunois** (7 rue Louise-Weiss, 13th, 01.45.84.72.00,

Sweet Success

Keep them happy with a baking masterclass at Bogato.

If Hansel and Gretel owned a cake shop in Paris, it might look something like **Bogato** (7 rue Liancourt, 14th, 01.40.47.03.51, www.chezbogato.fr) – a name that sounds like *beau gateau* in French, as in 'pretty cake'. Everything here is designed around temptation, from the quaint wooden furniture to pastry chef Anaïs Olmer's brightly coloured cupcakes, towering under glass bells on the counter like sugary art installations. Kids will be in sweet heaven as they sample crunchy butter biscuits, smooth Nutella tarts, cherry cheesecakes, chocolate-coated marshmallows, and even Cheshire Cat shortbread biscuits with an edible rice paper smile. Once the sugar rush has settled down, you can sign the kids up for a baking class where they can learn how to make Bogato's gooey macaroons, cream-filled choux buns and cupcakes. Lessons cost €58 for adults and €26 for children, or you can book a two-hour workshop for up to ten children (€300, over-sevens) either *chez* Bogato or *chez vous*.

If you have older children, the **Ecole Lenôtre** (Pavillon Elysée, 10 av des Champs-Elysées, 8th, 01.42.65.97.60, www.lenotre.fr) cooking school on the Champs-Elysées runs special cooking classes most Wednesdays for eight- to 17-year-olds. Younger kids' recipes stay simple (think cookies, fruit crumble and guacamole), but teenagers can test their skills on more complicated creations such as herb-crusted cod with vegetable confit or tiramisu. Prices begin at €40, which is nothing compared to the priceless meals they'll be preparing for you when you get back home.

Bogato.

www.theatredunois.org) is almost entirely geared towards children. For children's theatre in an unusual setting, the **Abricadabra Péniche Antipode** (opposite 55 quai de Seine, 19th, 01.42.03.39.07, www.penicheantipode.fr) is a riverboat on the Canal de l'Ourcq.

In general, children's films are dubbed into French, but you can see VO (*version originale*) screenings of the latest Hollywood hits at most venues across town. Keep a lookout for kids' showings on Wednesdays and Saturday afternoons at the Cinémathèque Française and L'Ecran des Enfants at the **Centre Pompidou** (*see p269*). The IMAX in La Villette's **Géode** (*see p268*) will keep kids enthralled too.

Circus

★ Cirque d'Hiver Bouglione

110 rue Amelot, 11th (01.47.00.28.81, www.cirquedhiver.com). M° Filles du Calvaire.
Shows *Late Oct-mid Mar* days vary. **Admission** €27-€62. **Credit** AmEx, MC, V. **Map** p409 L5.
This famous circus has been in the same family for decades. Crowds flock for its twice-yearly seasons, which include tigers, horses and very silly clowns.

Cirque Pinder

Pelouse de Reuilly, Bois de Vincennes, 12th (01.45.90.21.25, www.cirquepinder.com). M° Porte de Charenton or Porte Dorée. **Shows** *Mid Nov-mid Jan.* **Admission** prices vary.
Credit AmEx, DC, MC, V.
Big cats are the stars of the show, but horses, elephants and monkeys also make Pinder the most traditional travelling circus in France.

Espace Chapiteaux

Parc de La Villette, 19th (01.40.03.75.75, www.villette.com). M° Porte de la Villette. **Shows** vary.
Admission varies. **Credit** MC, V. **Map** p403 inset.
This big top hosts high-flying companies such as Cirque Plume, Centre National des Arts du Cirque and aerialists Les Arts Saut.

SPORTS

Waterbabies can choose between 38 public pools (www.paris.fr), including the floating **Piscine Josephine-Baker** (*see p319*), moored on the Seine; the art nouveau **Piscine Butte-aux-Cailles** (*see p319*), with indoor and outdoor pools fed by artesian wells; and the

ARTS & ENTERTAINMENT

recently restored **Espace Sportif Pailleron** (32 rue Edouard Pailleron, 19th, 01.40.40.27.70, www.pailleron19.com), near Buttes-Chaumont, which has two pools and an ice rink. At the indoor **Aquaboulevard** (*see p317*), over-threes can splash down slides and ride the waves. Bathing caps are obligatory everywhere.

Patinoire Sonja Henie
Palais Omnisports de Paris-Bercy (01.40.02.60.67, www.bercy.fr). Mº Bercy. **Open** *Sept-mid June* 3-6pm Wed; 9.30pm-12.30am Fri; 3-6pm, 9.30pm-12.30am Sat; 10am-noon, 3-6pm Sun. **Admission** €3-€6. **No credit cards. Map** p407 N9.
Bercy's Omnisports arena contains an ice rink, open on Wednesdays and weekends for skaters of all levels. Teenagers can also skate until late on Fridays and Saturdays, when disco lights colour the ice.

PARKS & THEME PARKS

Disneyland Paris/Walt Disney Studios Park
Marne-la-Vallée (www.disneylandparis.com). 32km E of Paris. RER A or TGV Marne-la-Vallée-Chessy. By car, A4 exit 14. **Open** Times vary, see website for details. **Admission** Prices vary, see website for details. **Credit** AmEx, MC, V.
Young ones will get a real kick out of Fantasyland, with its Alice maze, Sleeping Beauty's castle and teacup rides. Walt Disney Studios focuses on special effects and the tricks of the animation trade. The Twilight Zone Tower of Terror sends daredevils plummeting down a 13-storey lift shaft and the Rock 'n' Roller Coaster in the Back Lot takes off at mega speed, before hurtling round hairpin turns and loops to the funky rhythm of Aerosmith.

Jardin d'Acclimatation
Bois de Boulogne, 16th (01.40.67.90.85, www.jardindacclimatation.fr). Mº Les Sablons. **Open** *Apr-Sept* 10am-7pm daily. *Oct-Mar* 10am-6pm daily. **Admission** €3; €1.50 reductions; free under-3s. **Credit** (€15 minimum) MC, V.
Founded in 1860, this amusement park and garden has animals, a Normandy-style farm and an aviary, plus boat rides, a funfair with mini rollercoasters, flying chairs, the Enchanted House for children aged two to four and two playgrounds. There's also a place to steer radio-controlled boats and mini golf. Many of the attractions cost €2.70 a go; others are free. A miniature train runs from Porte Maillot through the Bois de Boulogne to the park entrance, and has space for pushchairs (€2.70 return; €4.20-€5.70 with entry included).

Jardin du Luxembourg
Main access 2 rue Auguste Compte, 6th. Mº Odéon/RER Luxembourg. **Open** *Summer* 7.30am-dusk daily. *Winter* 8am-dusk daily. **Map** p408 H8.
The 25-hectare park is a prized family attraction. Kids come from across the city for its pony rides, ice-cream stands, puppet shows, pedal karts, sandpits, metal swingboats and merry-go-round. The playground has an entrance fee.

★ Parc Astérix
60128 Plailly (08.26.30.10.40, www.parcasterix.fr). 36km N of Paris. By coach from the Louvre, the Eiffel Tower or RER Roissy-Charles de Gaulle 1 (check website for times). By car, A1 exit Parc Astérix. **Open** Times vary, see website for details. **Admission** €44; €33 reductions; free under-3s. **Parking** €8. **Credit** MC, V.
The park is split into Ancient Greece, the Roman Empire, the Land of the Vikings, the indomitable Gaulish Village and the all-new Egypt zone. Thrill-seekers can defy gravity on Goudurix, Europe's largest rollercoaster, while younger kids get wet on the Grand Splatch log flume. For a real rush of blood to the head, though, climb aboard the brand-new Oziris inverted rollercoaster. For some serious hand-shaking, Astérix, Obélix and friends wander around and a jamboree of live acts pumps up the pace.

Parc des Buttes-Chaumont
Rue Botzaris, rue Manin, rue de Crimée, 19th. Mº Buttes Chaumont. **Open** *Winter* 7am-8pm daily. *Summer* 7am-10pm daily. **Map** p407 N2.
This area, which was formerly mined for gypsum, was turned into a sumptuous park under Napoleon III. Spectacular in every way (including the views over Paris), it is a family magnet with Punch and Judy stands, pony rides, sandpits, waterfalls, picnic and games areas and drinks stands.

★ Parc de la Villette
Av Corentin-Cariou, 19th (01.40.03.75.75, www.villette.com). Mº Porte de la Villette. Av Jean-Jaurès, 19th. Mº Porte de Pantin. **Map** p403 inset.
Aside from being home to Europe's largest science museum (which also contains the brilliant Cité des Enfants, *see p94*), a music museum, an IMAX cinema, theatres, and concert and exhibition venues, the city's former abattoir district is now made up of a succession of gardens and playgrounds. Jardin des Voltiges has climbing ropes and balancing games, and the modern Jardin des Dunes et Vents has pedal windmills, waves of bouncy tubes and giant hamster wheels. A wonderful family day out.

Film

Box-office bonanza in the birthplace of cinema.

Filmgoing has long been a central part of Paris life, with more tickets per head bought here than anywhere else in Europe; in any given week, the choice of films to watch exceeds 350, and the range of screening venues is a rich mix of multiplexes and doughty historic *art et essai* cinemas. And during the last 18 months, two French films have set tongues wagging across the globe. Michel Hazanavicius's 2011 silent, black-and-white romcom *The Artist* became the most successful French film in history, winning three Golden Globes, seven BAFTAs, six Césars and five Oscars, including best actor for Jean Dujardin, making him the first French actor to win the award. Then, also in 2011, Olivier Nakache and Eric Toledano's *Intouchables*, a moving comedy about a quadriplegic millionaire and his petty-criminal carer, raked in $391 million worldwide. Omar Sy became the first black actor to win a César and the Weinstein Company acquired the rights for a US remake.

MOVIEGOING IN PARIS

Happily, the rapid rise of the multiplex hasn't meant a reduction in the variety of films on offer in Paris. Multiplexes regularly show films from Eastern Europe, Asia and South America, and countless independent cinemas continue to screen a hugely eclectic assortment of cult, classic and just plain obscure films. As well as retrospectives and cut-price promotions, there are often visits from directors and stars.

Local interest is strong enough to sustain several monthly movie magazines and there's a decent selection of specialist film bookshops, such as **Contacts**, in the city. Finally, French DVD labels produce some of the most expertly curated discs in the world. At **Fnac** and **Virgin Megastore** (for both, *see p225*), you're more than likely to find American and British titles otherwise unavailable in the US or UK.

INFORMATION AND TICKETS

New releases hit the screens on Wednesdays. Hollywood is well represented, of course, but Paris audiences have a balanced cinematic diet that satisfies their appetite for international films as well as shorts and documentaries. On top of this there are the 150-plus annual releases funded or part-funded with French money (the French film industry is still the world's third largest, after the US and India).

For venues, times and prices, consult one of the city's two main weekly listings magazines: *L'Officiel des Spectacles* and *Pariscope*. Films *nouveaux* are new releases, *Exclusivités* are the also-showing titles, and *Reprises* means rep. For non-francophone flicks, look out for two letters somewhere near the title: VO (*version originale*) means a screening in the original language with French subtitles; VF (*version française*) means that it has been dubbed into French.

Buy tickets in the usual way at the cinema – for new blockbusters, it pays to buy in advance. Online booking may entail a fee. Seats are often discounted by 20 to 30 per cent at Monday or Wednesday screenings, and the Mairie sponsors cut-price promotions throughout the year. If you're in town for a while, it might be a good

INSIDE TRACK NEW RELEASES

The first few months of 2013 will see the launch of several new film venues around town, including the **Fondation Jérôme Seydoux-Pathé** (www.fondation-jerome seydoux-pathe.com), the renovation of the grand old **Louxor** cinema (www.paris-louxor.fr) and a new arthouse multiplex, **Ciné-Lilas** (www.etoile-cinemas.com).

Cinémathèque Française.

idea to pick up a *carte illimitée*, a season ticket that allows unlimited viewing: every multiplex chain offers a version.

CINEMAS
Giant screens & multiplexes

La Géode
26 av Corentin-Cariou, 19th (01.40.05.79.99, www.lageode.fr). M° Porte de la Villette.
Admission €10.50-€12.50; €9-€11 reductions.
Credit MC, V. **Map** p403 inset.
The IMAX cinema at the Cité des Sciences occupies a shiny geodesic dome. The vast screen lets you experience 3D plunges through natural scenery, and adventures in which figures zoom out to grab you.

★ Le Grand Rex
1 bd Poissonnière, 2nd (08.92.68.05.96, www.legrandrex.com). M° Bonne Nouvelle.
Admission €7.50-€13; €6-€11 reductions.
Les Etoiles du Rex tour €9.80; €8 reductions.
Credit MC, V. **Map** p402 J4.
With its wedding-cake exterior and the largest auditorium in Europe (2,650 seats), this listed historical monument is one of the few cinemas to upstage whatever it screens. Its blockbuster programming (usually in French) is suited to its vast screen. There are six smaller screens too.
► *The Etoiles du Rex tour is a 50-minute, SFX-laden taste of movie magic.*

Max Linder Panorama
24 bd Poissonnière, 9th (01.48.24.00.47, www.maxlinder.com). M° Grands Boulevards.

Admission €9.20; €7.20 reductions. **Credit** MC, V. **Map** p402 J4.
This state-of-the-art cinema, with THX surround sound and an 18m (60ft) screen, is named after the dapper French silent comedian who owned it between 1914 and 1925. The walls and 700 seats are all black to prevent even the tiniest twinkle of reflected light distracting the audience from what's happening on the screen. Look for all-nighters and one-off showings of rare vintage films.

★ MK2 Bibliothèque
128-162 av de France, 13th (08.92.69.84.84, www.mk2.com). M° Bibliothèque François Mitterrand or Quai de la Gare. **Admission** €10.70; €4.90-€7.90 reductions; €20.08 monthly pass. **Credit** MC, V. **Map** p407 M10.
The MK2 chain's flagship offers an all-in-one night out: 14 screens, four restaurants, a bar open until 5am at weekends and two-person 'love seats'. A paragon of imaginative programming, MK2 is growing all the time; it has added ten more venues in town. See the website for full details of the Illimitée season ticket.

UGC Ciné Cité Bercy
2 cour St-Emilion, 12th (08.92.70.00.00, www.ugc.fr). M° Cour St-Emilion. **Admission** €10.90; €4.90-€7.50 reductions; €20.08 monthly pass. **Credit** MC, V. **Map** p407 P10.
This ambitious 18-screen development screens art movies as well as mainstream fodder, and hosts regular meet-the-director events. The 19-screen UGC Ciné Cité Les Halles branch (7 place de la Rotonde, Nouveau Forum des Halles, 1st, 08.92.70.00.00), serves the same mix of cinema and events.

Showcases

Auditorium du Louvre

Musée du Louvre, 99 rue de Rivoli, 1st (01.40.20.55.00, www.louvre.fr). M° Palais Royal Musée du Louvre. **Admission** prices vary. **Credit** MC, V. **Map** p402 H5.

The 420-seat Auditorium du Louvre was designed by IM Pei, as part of the Mitterrand-inspired renovation of the Louvre. Film screenings are often related to current exhibitions at the museum; silent movies with accompanying live music are regulars.

Centre Pompidou

Rue St-Martin, 4th (01.44.78.12.33, www.centre pompidou.fr). M° Hôtel de Ville or Rambuteau. **Admission** €6; €4 reductions. **Credit** MC, V. **Map** p406 K6.

The varied programme at the Centre Pompidou features themed series, experimental and artists' films, and a weekly documentary session. This is also the venue for the Cinéma du Réel festival in March (www.cinereel.org).

Le Cinéma des Cinéastes

7 av de Clichy, 17th (08.92.68.97.17, www.cinema-des-cineastes.fr). M° Place de Clichy. **Admission** €9; €7 reductions. **Credit** MC, V. **Map** p401 G2.

Done out to evoke the studios of old, this three-screen showcase of world cinema holds meet-the-director sessions and festivals of classic, foreign, gay and documentary films. The cinema is also big on film for kids, and is one of the hosts of the annual Mon Premier Festival (www.monpremierfestival.org) for three- to 15-year-olds.

★ Cinémathèque Française

51 rue de Bercy, 12th (01.71.19.33.33, www.cinematheque.fr). M° Bercy. **Admission** *Films* €6.50; €3.50-€5.50 reductions. *Museum* €5; €2.50-€4 reductions; free under-6s. **Credit** MC, V. **Map** p407 N9.

Relocated to Frank Gehry's striking, spacious cubist building, the Cinémathèque Française boasts four screens, a bookshop, a restaurant, exhibition space and the Musée du Cinéma, where it displays a fraction of its huge collection of memorabilia. In the spirit of founder Henri Langlois, the Cinémathèque hosts retrospectives, cult movies, classics, experimental cinema and Q&A sessions.

Forum des Images

2 rue du Cinéma, Forum des Halles, 1st (01.44.76.63.00, www.forumdesimages.net). M° Les Halles. **Admission** (per day) €5; €4 under-12s. Membership available (€96-€132 per year). **Credit** AmEx, MC, V. **Map** p402 J5.

Partly a screening venue for old and little-known movies, and partly an archive for every kind of film featuring Paris. Today, the Forum's collection numbers over 6,500 documentaries, adverts, newsreels and films, from the work of the Lumière brothers to 21st-century reportage. They have all been digitised.

Arthouses

Accattone

20 rue Cujas, 5th (01.46.33.86.86). M° Cluny La Sorbonne/RER Luxembourg. **Admission** €7; €6 Wed, students, under-20s (except Fri nights and weekends). **No credit cards. Map** p408 J8.

Le Balzac. *See p270.*

Named after Pasolini's first film, this tiny Latin Quarter cinema has a clear preference for old Italian arthouse. That said, there's still plenty of room on the rolling weekly programme for the likes of Buñuel, Oshima, Roeg and Ken Russell.

Action

Action Christine *4 rue Christine, 6th* *(01.43.25.85.78, www.actioncinemas.com).* *M° Odéon or St-Michel.* **Admission** €8; €6 reductions. **No credit cards. Map** p408 J7.
Grand Action *5 rue des Ecoles, 5th* *(01.43.54.47.62, www.legrandaction.com).* *M° Cardinal Lemoine.* **Admission** €9; €6.50 reductions. **No credit cards. Map** p406 K8.
A Left Bank stalwart, the Action group is renowned for screening new prints of old movies. It's heaven for anyone who's nostalgic for Tinseltown classics and quality US independents.

★ Le Balzac

1 rue Balzac, 8th (01.45.61.10.60, www.cinema balzac.com). M° George V. **Admission** €10; €6.50-€8 reductions. **No credit cards. Map** p400 D4.
Built in 1935 and boasting a mock ocean-liner foyer, Le Balzac scores highly for design and programming. Jean-Jacques Schpoliansky, whose grandfather opened the cinema in 1935, has been the manager for the last 35 years and is often found welcoming punters in person. The Balzac awards prizes according to audience votes. *Photo p269.*

Le Champo

51 rue des Ecoles, 5th (01.43.54.51.60, www. lechampo.com). M° Cluny La Sorbonne or Odéon. **Admission** €8; €5-€6 reductions. **No credit cards. Map** p408 J7.
The two-screen Champo has been in operation for nearly seven decades, a venerable past recognised in 2000 when it was given historic monument status. In the 1960s, it was a favourite haunt of *nouvelle vague* directors such as Claude Chabrol. Novel programming includes the occasional Nuits du Champo, a trio of films beginning at midnight and ending with breakfast (€15).

★ Le Chaplin Denfert

24 pl Denfert-Rochereau, 14th (www.cinema denfert.fr). M° Denfert Rochereau/RER Denfert Rochereau. **Admission** €8; €6-€7 reductions. **No credit cards. Map** p405 H10.
This charming little cinema offers a nicely eclectic repertory selection that ranges from François Ozon and Hayao Miyazaki to shorts and animation, as well as new-release foreign films.

Le Cinéma du Panthéon

13 rue Victor-Cousin, 5th (01.40.46.01.21, www.whynotproductions.fr/pantheon). RER Luxembourg. **Admission** prices vary. **Credit** MC, V. **Map** p408 J8.

To celebrate its centenary in 2007, the city's oldest surviving movie house opened a tearoom with interior design by Catherine Deneuve. The Cinéma du Panthéon continues to screen new, often obscure international films, and hosts meet-the-director nights and discussions.

L'Entrepôt

7-9 rue Francis-de-Pressensé, 14th (01.45.40.07.50, www.lentrepot.fr). M° Pernety or Plaisance. **Admission** €7.80; €4-€6.50 reductions. **No credit cards. Map** p405 F10.
Located off the beaten tourist track, this multi-disciplinary arts centre and cinema is known for its leftfield documentaries, shorts, gay repertoire and productions from developing nations. Regular debates, poetry nights and concerts complete the programme. There's also a restaurant with a coveted garden terrace.

Le Mac Mahon

5 av Mac-Mahon, 17th (01.43.80.24.81, www.cinemamacmahon.com). M° Charles de Gaulle Etoile. **Admission** €7; €5 reductions. **No credit cards. Map** p400 C3.
This single-screen, 1930s-era cinema has changed little since its 1960s heyday (tickets are still of the tear-off variety), when its all-American programming fostered the label '*mac-mahonisme*' among the buffs who haunted the place. Americana still makes up the bulk of what's on the screen.

Le Nouveau Latina

20 rue du Temple, 4th (01.42.78.47.86, www.lenouveaulatina.com). M° Hôtel de Ville. **Admission** €8.50; €7 reductions. **No credit cards. Map** p406 K6.
The exciting programming at this flag-bearer for Latin cultures runs the gamut from Argentinian to Romanian films.

★ La Pagode

57bis rue de Babylone, 7th (01.45.55.48.48, www.etoile-cinema.com). M° St-François-Xavier. **Admission** €9; €7.50 reductions. **No credit cards. Map** p405 F7.
This glorious Left Bank edifice is not, as local legend might have it, a block-by-block import, but a 19th-century replica of a pagoda. Renovated in the 1990s, this is one of the loveliest cinemas in the world. *Photo p272.*

Studio 28

10 rue Tholozé, 18th (01.42.54.18.11, www. cinemastudio28.com). M° Abbesses or Blanche. **Admission** €7.50; €6.30 reductions. **No credit cards. Map** p401 H1.
Studio 28 was the venue for the first screening of Buñuel's scandalous *L'Age d'Or*. It offers a decent mixture of classics and recent movies, complete with Dolby sound and a civilised bar.

Essential Paris Films

You're in film-set Paris the second you get off the train.

HOTEL DU NORD
MARCEL CARNE (1938)
The Hôtel du Nord is, thanks to Carné's film, a national monument: it, and the adjacent iron footbridge and chunk of Canal St-Martin, were re-created in the studio by Alexandre Trauner. On the bridge, Arletty gives suitor Louis Jouvet the brush-off with the immortal '*Atmosphère! Est-ce que j'ai une gueule d'atmosphère?*'

INTOUCHABLES
OLIVIER NAKACHE &
ERIC TOLEDANO (2011)
François Cluzet is Philippe, a wealthy man left paralysed by an accident. Interviewing for the job of carer, he's struck by Driss (Omar Sy), a street-smart criminal who's merely applying to receive benefits. He hires Driss and moves him into his Paris mansion. Bonding ensues, amid many raised eyebrows.

LA HAINE
MATTHIEU
KASSOVITZ (1995)
Twenty-four hours in the Paris projects: an Arab boy is critically wounded in hospital, gut-shot, and a police revolver has found its way into the hands of a young Jewish skinhead, Vinz (Cassel), who vows to even the score if his pal dies. A vital, scalding piece of work.

LES 400 COUPS
FRANCOIS TRUFFAUT
(1959)
Tearaway 13-year-old kid Antoine Doisnel (Jean-Pierre Léaud in his first role) gets around large parts of Paris, helping to launch the *nouvelle vague* on the way. His troubles start when he catches his mum in an adulterous clinch on place de Clichy. Still one of the cinema's most perceptive forays into childhood.

SUBWAY
LUC BESSON (1985)
Safecracker Christophe Lambert hides out with a bunch of eccentric social misfits in the netherworld of the Paris métro as he attempts to escape from a wealthy businessman's wife (Isabelle Adjani) with whom he has fallen in love, from her husband's thugs and from the métro police in this electrically charged 1980s punk-chic fantasy.

LE FABULEUX DESTIN
D'AMELIE POULAIN
JEAN-PIERRE JEUNET
(2001)
Jeunet's rose-tinted Parisian romance stars the wonderful Audrey Tautou as Amélie, who works in a Montmartre café (Café des Deux Moulins, 15 rue Lépic) and has a revelation that her life's work should be to bring good to others. A charming love poem to *la vie Parisienne.*

Studio Galande

42 rue Galande, 5th (01.43.54.72.71, www. studiogalande.fr). M° Cluny La Sorbonne or St-Michel. **Admission** €8; €6 reductions. **No credit cards. Map** p408 J7.

Some 20 different films are screened in subtitled versions at this venerable Latin Quarter venue every week: it's mostly international arthouse fare, combined with the occasional instalment from a blockbuster series.

▶ *On Fridays and Saturdays, fans of The Rocky Horror Picture Show turn up in drag, equipped with rice and water pistols (€9).*

Festivals & events

The city plays host to a range of film festivals, including **Printemps du Cinéma** and **Côté Court**. *See also pp26-31* **Diary**.

Festival International de Films de Femmes

Maison des Arts, pl Salvador-Allende, 94040 Créteil (01.49.80.38.98, www.filmsdefemmes. com). M° Créteil-Préfecture. **Date** Mar.

Now in its 34th year, this highly regarded festival features a selection of retrospectives and new international films by female directors.

La Pagode. *See p270.*

Printemps du Cinéma

Various venues (www.printempsducinema.com). **Date** Mar.

Three days of bargain €3.50 entry films at cinemas all across Paris.

Côté Court

Ciné 104, 104 av Jean-Lolive, 93500 Pantin (01.48.91.24.91, www.cotecourt.org). M° Eglise de Pantin. **Date** June.

Côté Court puts on a great selection of new and old short films shown at Ciné 104 and a handful of neighbouring venues.

Paris Cinéma

Various venues (01.55.25.55.25, www.paris cinema.org). **Date** June-July.

The 11th edition of the capital's flagship festival is taking place in 2013, complete with official competitions and attendant stars.

★ Cinéma au Clair de Lune

Various venues (01.44.76.63.00, www.forum desimages.net). **Date** Aug.

Night-time films on giant open-air screens in squares and public gardens around town.

★ L'Etrange Festival

Forum des Images, for listing see p269 (01.44.76.63.00, www.etrangefestival.com). **Date** Sept. **Map** p404 J5.

Explicit sex, gore and weirdness in the screenings and 'happenings' at this annual feast of all things unconventional draw large crowds.

La Master Class

Forum des Images (see p269). **Date** monthly throughout the year. **Map** p404 J5.

Each month film critic Pascal Mérigeau interviews a well-known figure. Recent interviewees have included Hanif Kureishi and Denis Podalydès.

BOOKSHOPS

Ciné Reflet

14 rue Monsieur le Prince, 6th (01.40.46.02.72, www.cinereflet.com). M° Odéon. **Open** 1-8pm Mon-Sat; 3-7pm Sun. **Credit** MC, V. **Map** p408 H7.

This sprawling shop is well stocked with old photos, posters, and new and second-hand books. The strong English-language selection includes magazines such as *Sight & Sound*.

★ Contacts

14 rue St-Sulpice, 6th (01.43.59.17.71, www.la-chambre-claire.fr). M° Odéon. **Open** 2-7pm Mon; 11am-7pm Tue-Sat. **Credit** MC, V. **Map** p408 H7.

Truffaut's favourite *librairie* has been selling books on film for over 40 years. The stock is well organised, with a large and up-to-date selection of English-language titles, plus a few DVDs.

Gay & Lesbian

Good times abound in Gay Paree.

Paris is home to a thriving LGBT community that is visibly involved in every walk of life – and right at the top of the tree sits mayor Bertrand Delanoë, who came out two years before running for office. Local gays and lesbians say that they encounter very little, if any, discrimination during their day-to-day lives, and feel integrated into mainstream society. However, the annual Marche des Fiertés (Gay Pride), held on the last Sunday in June, is a powerful reminder of what the gay rights movement has accomplished over the last 30 years, and of what is yet to be achieved.

GETTING OUT AND ABOUT

Beaubourg and the '**gay Marais**' are particularly gay-friendly. Most of the dedicated venues are to be found in the area bounded by rue des Archives, rue Vieille-du-Temple and rue Ste-Croix-de-la-Bretonnerie. A light lunch, coffee or cocktail at a neighbourhood café will provide ample opportunity to check out the talent, and a casual stroll through the nearby streets will introduce you to a seductive selection of shops. Fetishists, funky fashionistas, bohemians and bibliophiles will each find a boutique to suit their fancy. A good place to start is **Les Mots à la Bouche**, where you can peruse the gay and lesbian press or pick up a few of the free monthly magazines listing the hottest events.

In the evening, kick off the action at a café or a restaurant before moving on to the bars and clubs, which don't really get going until after midnight. Start by mixing it up at the **Open Café** or the nearby red-hot **Raidd Bar**. The **Queen** on the Champs-Elysées remains a clubbing institution, as does the smaller and more intimate **Le Tango**. The popular

La Scène Bastille (*see p285*) is a relatively new trendsetter; on the other side of the coin is the oldest gay club in Paris, **Le Club 18**, which is always fun and still draws a great crowd, and the always surprising **Le Tango**. Lesbians can find a few nice bars of their own on rue du Roi de Sicile, or relax at the popular and friendly **Chez Moune** near Pigalle.

Information and resources

Magazines *Têtu* (www.tetu.com) and *Préf* (www.prefmag.com) report on goings-on in gay life and have text in English; *La Dixième Muse* (www.ladixiememuse.com) provides similar information for lesbians. There are also several free bi-weekly publications, distributed in gay bookshops, bars and clubs, including *Tribumove* (www.tribumove.com). And for the girls, there's *Barbi(e)turix* (www.barbieturix.com). Two excellent and informative websites provide regularly updated listings (in English) of all things gay and lesbian in the city: www.paris-gay.com and www.gayvox.com.

Centre Gai et Lesbien

63 rue Beaubourg, 3rd (01.43.57.21.47, www.centrelgbtparis.org). M° Arts et Métiers or Rambuteau. **Open** 6-8pm Mon; 3.30-8pm Tue, Wed, Thur; 1-8pm Fri; 1-7pm Sat. *Library* 6-8pm Mon-Wed; 3-5pm Fri; 5-7pm Sat. **Map** p402 K6.
After many years on rue Keller, the Centre Gai et Lesbien has moved into more centrally located digs in the Marais. In addition to providing information on topics ranging from the sociopolitical (if you don't know what rights gays and lesbians have or

---

INSIDE TRACK TAKE PRIDE

Don't miss out on the action in June as a stream of outrageous floats and flamboyant costumes parade towards Bastille for **Gay Pride** (www.gaypride.fr); then there's an official *fête* and various club events.

Café Cox.

The Bears' Den is a friendly local for bears, muscle bears, chubbies and their admirers. Visit the website for details on comically named theme nights such as 'Charcuterie'.

▶ *Bears, wolves and men who love hairy men also gather at the nearby Wolf; see p275.*

★ Le Café Arena
29 rue St-Denis, 1st (01.45.08.15.16). M° Châtelet. **Open** 9am-6am daily. **Credit** MC, V. **Map** p406 J5.
This bar-restaurant has a great terrace for people-watching and friendly staff; it's still one of the hottest rendezvous in Les Halles.

Café Cox
15 rue des Archives, 4th (01.42.72.08.00, www.cox.fr). M° Hôtel de Ville. **Open** 5.30pm-2am Mon-Thur; 4.30pm-2am Fri-Sun. **No credit cards. Map** p409 K6.
Beefy, hairy, shaven-headed men congregate on the pavement in front of Café Cox for post-work drinks, before moving on to more intimate surroundings.

Le Duplex
25 rue Michel-le-Comte, 3rd (01.42.72.80.86, www.duplex-bar.com). M° Hôtel de Ville or Rambuteau. **Open** 8pm-2am Mon-Thur, Sun; 8pm-4am Fri, Sat. **Credit** V. **Map** p409 K5.
This small bar just round the corner from the Centre Pompidou caters to a thirtysomething crowd. It's a popular meeting place for various gay associations, with friendly staff and local art on the walls.

Eagle
33bis rue des Lombards, 1st (01.42.33.41.45, www.eagleparis.com). M° Les Halles. **Open** 6pm-4am Tue-Thur, Sun; 6pm-6am Fri, Sat. **No credit cards. Map** p402 J6.
Formerly called the London, this old bar has found new life, becoming a real hit with bears, daddies, leathermen and the men who admire them. Indulge in tea and cake on the patio early on, a shot of Jack at the bar later, or penetrate deeper and enjoy the disco backroom.

Etamine Café
13 rue des Ecouffes, 4th (01.44.78.09.62, www.etamine-cafe.com). M° St-Paul. **Open**

don't have in France, you can find out all you need to know here) to the biomedical (the latest developments in the treatment of HIV, where to get tested for free), this multifunctional centre and library also hosts meetings for a variety of support groups and associations.

Inter-LGBT
c/o Maison des Associations du 3ème, boîte 8, 5 rue Perrée, 75003 Paris (01.72.70.39.22, www.inter-lgbt.org). **Map** p409 L5.
The Interassociative Lesbienne, Gaie, Bi & Trans is an umbrella group of 50 LGBT associations. It organises the Printemps des Assoces every April and the annual Gay Pride March in June.

SOS Homophobie
08.10.10.81.35, www.sos-homophobie.org. **Open** 6-10pm Mon-Fri; 2-4pm Sat; 6-8pm Sun (2pm-midnight 1st Mon of mth).
Victims of and witnesses to homophobic crimes and discrimination can report them to this confidential service, which offers support and publishes an annual report on homophobia.

GAY PARIS
Bars & cafés

Le Bears' Den
6 rue des Lombards, 4th (01.42.71.08.20, www.bearsden.fr). M° Châtelet or Hôtel de Ville. **Open** 4pm-2am Mon-Fri; 4pm-6am Sat, Sun. **Credit** MC, V. **Map** p406 J6.

THE BEST HANGOUTS

For big wigs and ballgowns
Crazyvores. *See p276.*

For bears and muscle bears
Le Bear's Den. *See left.*

For backroom action
Next. *See p277.*

ARTS & ENTERTAINMENT

Open Café.

noon-midnight Tue-Sun. **Credit** AmEx, MC, V. **Map** p409 K6.
This simple café is located very close to the lesbian bars of the Marais, and offers a contemporary and inventive twist on old classics. Excellent food, affordable prices, good atmosphere.

★ Open Café
17 rue des Archives, 4th (01.42.72.26.18, www.opencafe.fr). M° Hôtel de Ville or Rambuteau. **Open** 11am-2am Mon-Thur, Sun; 11am-4am Fri, Sat. **Credit** MC, V. **Map** p409 K6.
Cruise and be cruised in the café everybody visits at some point in the evening. Pop out on to the terrace, and enjoy the people-watching. *Photos p276.*

★ Le Quetzal
10 rue de la Verrerie, 4th (01.48.87.99.07). M° Hôtel de Ville. **Open** 5pm-5am daily. **Credit** MC, V. **Map** p409 K6.
This bar is considered to be one of the 'musts' on the Marais circuit, as it's often filled with hot men and a few drag queens to keep things lively. You might be able to find some action in the small dark space upstairs. *Photos p276.*

Raidd Bar
23 rue du Temple, 4th (01.42.77.04.88, www.raiddbar.com). M° Hôtel de Ville. **Open** 5pm-4am Mon-Thur; 5pm-5am Fri, Sat, Sun. **Credit** (min €10) MC, V. **Map** p406 K6.
The Raidd is a Marais LGBT venue to be reckoned with. Famous for its bare-chested barmen straight of a modelling agency, the major draw is surely the soap sud-covered, brief-sporting, body-building go-go dancers who flaunt their wares under the front window's built-in showers (summer only). It gets pretty wild, sometimes bordering on a riot. The red velvet rooms downstairs are cosier and more relaxed. With free entry, a warm welcome and reasonably priced drinks, this humming club is always busy and closes late all week. Tuesday night is nostalgia night, Wednesdays are Latino, and weekends electro, giving everyone plenty of opportunities to dress up while wearing as little as possible.

★ Wolf
37 rue des Lombards, 1st (01.40.28.02.52, www.wolfparis.com). M° Les Halles. **Open** 5pm-2am daily. **No credit cards**. **Map** p402 J6.
Popular with bears, wolves, otters and a variety of other species, mostly on the hairy side. Everyone is welcome, though, and the ambience is laid-back.

Restaurants

Le Bar à Manger (BAM)
13 rue des Lavandières-Ste-Opportune, 1st (01.42.21.01.72). M° Les Halles. **Open** noon-3pm, 7-11pm Mon-Sat. **Credit** MC, V. **Map** p408 J6.
Excellent, creative cuisine in a pleasant, relaxed setting. There are *prix fixe* menus available at lunch (€19.50) and dinner (€34).

Le Gai Moulin
10 rue St-Merri, 4th (01.48.87.06.00, www.le-gai-moulin.com). M° Hôtel de Ville. **Open** noon-midnight daily. **Credit** MC, V. **Map** p406 K6.

One of the oldest gay-run restaurants in Paris, the Gai Moulin recently moved a few doors down from its original location. The owner is famously convivial, creating a lovely, friendly atmosphere. On Tuesdays, a pianist belts out French songs, and it's not uncommon for the whole room to sing along.

Le Kofi du Marais
54 rue Ste-Croix-de-la-Bretonnerie, 4th (01.48.87.48.71). M° Hôtel de Ville. **Open** 6pm-2am daily. **Credit** AmEx, MC, V. **Map** p406 K6.
Modern, simple cooking with an American twist is the speciality here. Club sandwiches, burgers and salads are menu staples. Prices are reasonable and the service is good too.

Ze Restoo
41 rue des Blancs-Manteaux, 3rd (01.42.74.10.29). M° Rambuteau. **Open** 7.30pm-1am Mon-Sat. **Credit** AmEx, MC, V. **Map** p409 K6.
This restaurant has become a popular place in which to eat with friends before heading out for a fun-filled evening. There's a very relaxed atmosphere, with good service and imaginative dishes.

Clubs

As well as the venues listed below, a mixed but increasingly gay crowd mingles at **Nouveau Casino** (*see p284*) and **La Scène Bastille** (*see p285*). Most of the gay clubs are very hetero-friendly.

★ Le Club 18
18 rue de Beaujolais, 1st (01.42.97.52.13, www.club18.fr). M° Palais-Royal or Pyramides. **Open** midnight-dawn Fri-Sun. **Admission** (incl 1 drink) €10. **Credit** *Bar* MC, V. **Map** p402 H5.
The oldest gay club in Paris attracts a young and beautiful clientele. It is not very big, and the decor isn't all that great, but the music is fun and there's a very laid-back vibe. Everyone is here to dance and have a good time.

Le CUD Bar
12 rue des Haudriettes, 3rd (01.42.77.44.12, www.cud-paris.com). M° Rambuteau. **Open** 11.30pm-7am daily. **Credit** MC, V. **Map** p409 K5.
Upstairs is a laid-back bar, but downstairs in the old cellar is a dancefloor that can get very crowded, especially after 2am. The crowd is a mixed bunch, and it's popular with the bears.

Les Follivores & les Crazyvores
Bataclan, 50 bd Voltaire, 11th (www.follivores.com). M° Oberkampf. **Open** times vary. **Admission** (incl 1 drink) €18. **Credit** V. **Map** p407 M5.
Twice a month, the Bataclan concert hall transforms itself into a club to host these two parties. Crazyvores features music from the 1970s and '80s, and at Follivores the DJs spin gay classics from all eras mixed up with cutting-edge techno. These are big events with exuberant crowds; the drag queens put on their best ball-gowns and biggest wigs, and the men sport their tightest tops. Great fun.

Le Quetzal. See p275.

Queen
102 av des Champs-Elysées, 8th (01.53.89.08.90, www.queen.fr). M° George V. **Open** midnight-7am Mon-Thur, Sun; midnight-8am Fri, Sat. **Admission** €15 Mon-Thur, Sun; €20 Fri, Sat. **Credit** *Bar* AmEx, MC, V. **Map** p400 D4.
One of the oldest and largest clubs, Queen's main gay night is Overkitsch on Sundays, but every night is a little gay. Big-name DJs often spin here to a crowd peppered with VIPs.

★ Le Tango (La Boîte à Frissons)
13 rue au Maire, 3rd (01.42.72.17.78, www.boite-a-frissons.fr). M° Arts et Métiers. **Open** 8pm-2am Thur; 10.30pm-5am Fri, Sat; 6-11pm Sun. **Admission** €8; free Thur. **Credit** V. **Map** p409 K5.
Wacky crowd, Madonna songs and accordion tunes. At the Friday and Saturday Bal de la Boîte à Frissons, couples dance the foxtrot, tango, madison or *guinguette* in the early part of the evening, followed after midnight by music of every variety except techno.

Sex clubs & saunas

Le Bunker
150 rue St-Maur, 11th (01.53.36.78.87, www.bunker-cruising.com). M° Goncourt. **Open** 4pm-2am Mon-Fri; 4pm-3.30am Sat; 4pm-midnight Sun. **Admission** €8.50. **Map** p403 M4.
This cruising club is the hottest in Paris. It features all-naked and underwear-only nights during the week, and hardcore themes at the weekend. Friday

is a very popular night, as is the first Saturday of the month, when Le Bunker hosts its S&M 'Red and Black Night' – not for the faint-hearted.

Le Dépot
10 rue aux Ours, 3rd (01.44.54.96.96, www.ledepot.com). M° Etienne Marcel. **Open** 2pm-8am daily. **Admission** €8.50 before 9pm Mon-Sat; €10 before 2am Mon-Thur; €13 (incl 1 drink) 2-8am Mon-Thur, Sun & after 11pm Sat; €8.50 before 5pm Sun. **Credit** MC, V. **Map** p402 K5.
A very busy dance club upstairs with a labyrinthine maze of cubicles, glory holes and darkrooms downstairs. The Dépot's glory days are gone now, but it still draws a crowd, particularly at weekends. Pickpockets work the darkrooms, so be careful.

★ IDM
4 rue du Fbg-Montmartre, 9th (01.45.23.10.03, www.idm-sauna.com). M° Grands Boulevards. **Open** noon-1am daily. **Admission** €21; €15 before 9.30pm & under-35s. **Credit** MC, V. **Map** p402 J4.
The city's best gay sauna has three levels and plenty of cabins and corridors to prowl. The wet sauna is on two levels, and the small relaxation pool and showers are always at the perfect temperature. A few times a month, there are also performances by drag queens and other singers.

Next
87 rue St-Honoré, 1st (www.lenext.fr). M° Les Halles. **Open** noon-3am Mon-Thur; 24hrs Fri-Sun. **Admission** €7 before 7pm; €10-€13 (incl 1 drink) after 7pm; €6 (incl 1 drink) under-26s. **Credit** MC, V. **Map** p402 J5.
This hot sex club is located in one of the chicest parts of the capital. It doesn't really get going until after many clubs have closed, and at 6am on a Sunday morning it's probably the hottest, hardest place in town. The bar upstairs is a nice place in which to mingle before heading down to the sexy labyrinth.

Sun City
62 bd de Sébastopol, 3rd (01.42.74.31.41, www.suncity-paris.fr). M° Etienne Marcel. **Open** noon-6am daily. **Admission** €19.50 Mon-Thur; €20 Fri-Sun; €15 after 3am; €12 under-26s. **Credit** MC, V. **Map** p402 J5.
Owned and operated by the Dépot team (*see above*), this Bollywood-themed venue is the largest gay sauna in Europe, with a pool, large steam room, gym and bar. The clientele is very good-looking and knows it, so there's a lot of attitude.

Shops & services

Boy'z Bazaar
5 rue Ste-Croix-de-la-Bretonnerie, 4th (01.42.71.67.00, www.boyzbazaar.com). M° Hôtel de Ville or St-Paul. **Open** noon-8pm Mon-Sat; 1-8pm Sun. **Credit** AmEx, MC, V. **Map** p409 K6.

ARTS & ENTERTAINMENT

IEM.

Stocks some of the city's trendiest clothes for night-clubbers, fashionistas and urban hipsters. **Other locations** 5 rue des Guillemites, 4th (01.42.71.63.86).

Les Dessous d'Apollon
15 rue du Bourg-Tibourg, 4th (01.42.71.87.37, www.lesdessousdapollon.com). M° Hôtel de Ville or St-Paul. **Open** 11am-8pm Mon-Sat; 2-8pm Sun. **Credit** AmEx, DC, MC, V. **Map** p409 K6.
Probably the most extensive selection of underwear – from the functional to the downright eccentric – that you'll ever see, plus T-shirts and accessories.

IEM
16 rue Ste-Croix-de-la-Bretonnerie, 4th (01.42.74.01.61, www.iem.fr). M° Hôtel de Ville. **Open** noon-8pm Mon-Thur; noon-9pm Fri, Sat; 2-8pm Sun. **Credit** AmEx, MC, V. **Map** p403 M4.
This sex hypermarket caters for those keen on the harder side of gay life. Videos, clothes and gadgets can all be found, and there are leather and rubber goods upstairs.

★ Legay Choc
45 rue Ste-Croix-de-la-Bretonnerie, 4th (01.48.87.56.88, www.legaychoc.fr). M° Hôtel de Ville. **Open** 7.30am-8pm Mon, Wed-Sun. **No credit cards. Map** p409 K6.
Run by two brothers (one gay, one straight) whose surname just happens to be Legay, this Marais *boulangerie* and *pâtisserie* is very popular. The pastries are delightful, and the lunch-hour sandwiches are generous, so expect queues. A satellite store, serving only sandwiches, is at 17 rue des Archives.

★ Les Mots à la Bouche
6 rue Ste-Croix-de-la-Bretonnerie, 4th (01.42.78.88.30, www.motsbouche.com). M° Hôtel de Ville or St-Paul. **Open** 11am-11pm Mon-Sat; 1-9pm Sun. **Credit** AmEx, MC, V. **Map** p409 K6.
An institution in the Marais, this bookshop has a large selection of gay fiction, non-fiction, magazines, and English-language books.

Nickel
48 rue des Francs-Bourgeois, 3rd (01.42.77.41.10, www.nickel.fr). M° Hôtel de Ville or Rambuteau. **Open** 11am-7.30pm Mon, Tue, Fri, Sat; 11am-9pm Wed, Thur. **Credit** AmEx, MC, V. **Map** p406 L6.
Body and skincare treatments, strictly for men. A one-hour facial is €74-€82, a manicure €25 and a 50-minute massage €69-€79. Staff are adept, friendly and knowledgeable.

Plus Que Parfait
23 rue des Blancs-Manteaux, 4th (01.42.71.09.05). M° Hôtel de Ville or St-Paul. **Open** 3-8pm Mon; noon-8pm Tue-Sat; 3-7pm Sun. *Clothes deposit* Mon-Fri. **Credit** MC, V. **Map** p409 K6.
This *dépôt vente*, where pristine, second-hand designer clothing is sold on commission, is a great place for men's fashion finds.

Space Hair
10 rue Rambuteau, 3rd (01.48.87.28.51, www.space-hair.com). M° Rambuteau. **Open** noon-10pm Mon; 10am-10pm Tue-Sat; 11.30am-8pm Sun (summer only). **Credit** MC, V. **Map** p409 K6.

Space Hair is divided into two salons, Cosmic and Classic, with a 1980s kitsch feel, late opening hours and cute stylists; it's best to book ahead.

Where to stay

Hôtel Duo
11 rue du Temple, 4th (01.42.72.72.22, www.duoparis.com). M° Hôtel de Ville. **Rates** €200-€380 double. **Credit** AmEx, DC, MC, V. **Map** p406 K6.
The mixed but very gay-friendly Hôtel Duo is a stylish place in which to rest your head. What's more, it has helpful staff at the reception – something of a rarity in this trendy area.

LESBIAN PARIS

Famous club Pulp is much missed, but the girlie scene continues to flourish, especially near the corner of rue du Roi de Sicile and rue des Ecouffes in the Marais. Most of the bars welcome men accompanied by women, but a few are women only. Some girl-only parties are staged at clubs such as **Le Tango** (*see p277*); see the free monthly magazine *Barbi(e)turix* for listings.

★ La Champmeslé
4 rue Chabanais, 2nd (01.42.96.85.20, www.la champmesle.com). M° Bourse or Pyramides. **Open** 4pm-4am daily. **Credit** MC, V. **Map** p402 H4.
This veteran girlie bar remains a popular venue for lesbian locals and visitors. Beer is the drink of choice; pull up a seat and enjoy the regular cabaret nights.

Chez Moune
54 rue Pigalle, 9th (01.45.26.64.64). M° Pigalle. **Open** 11pm-late Wed-Sat. **Credit** MC, V. **Map** p401 H2.
Probably the oldest lesbian cabaret in Paris, Chez Moune opened in 1936 and still has nightly shows. Saturdays are traditionally women only, but in the last year other phallo-friendly dance parties and cabaret shows have been held occasionally.

Le Day Off
10 rue de l'Isly, 8th (01.45.22.87.90). M° Gare St-Lazare. **Open** 11.30am-3am Mon-Fri. **Credit** MC, V. **Map** p401 G3.
An apt name for this weekday-only pub-restaurant – heavy drinking enjoyed by work-weary lesbians. It gets crowded in the early evening.

Dollhouse
24 rue du Roi de Sicile, 4th (01.40.27.09.21, www.dollhouse.fr). M° St-Paul. **Open** 2-8pm Mon, Sun; 1-8pm Tue-Sat. **Credit** MC, V. **Map** p409 L6.
This store specialises in lingerie and gadgets for the girls. Upstairs you'll find a selection of sophisticated underwear; head downstairs for the sexcessories.

Legay Choc.

Les Jacasses
5 rue des Ecouffes, 4th (01.42.71.15.51). M° St-Paul. **Open** 5pm-2am Tue-Sun. **Credit** MC, V. **Map** p409 K6.
This relaxed bar for women, which is located just around the corner from all the girlie bars on rue du Roi de Sicile in the Marais, makes a welcome addition to the neighbourhood.

★ Le Rive Gauche
1 rue du Sabot, 6th (01.40.20.43.23, www.lerive gauche.com). M° St-Germain-des-Prés. **Open** 11pm-dawn Sat. **Admission** €15 (incl 1 drink). **No credit cards. Map** p405 G7.
This weekend women-only nightclub is one of the hottest places on the lesbian scene. The decor is '70s and the music eclectic.

Le So What!
30 rue du Roi de Sicile, 4th (no phone). M° St-Paul. **Open** 9.30pm-2am Wed-Thur; 10pm-4am Fri, Sat. **Credit** MC, V. **Map** p409 L6.
The So What! is primarily a girlie bar, but everyone's welcome. Recent theme nights have included live rock and drag queens.

Le Troisième Lieu
62 rue Quincampoix, 4th (01.48.04.85.64, www. myspace.com/letroisiemelieu). M° Rambuteau. **Open** 6pm-2am Mon-Fri; 6pm-5am Sat. **Credit** MC, V. **Map** p406 K5.
Elaborate *tartines*, delicious desserts and strong drinks are the fare at this lesbian-run bar and restaurant. Despite its militant subtitle ('Cantine des Ginettes Armées'), the vibe is jovial.

ARTS & ENTERTAINMENT

Nightlife

From alt rock to art du nu, Paris shines brightly after dark.

Serious nighthawks may have migrated long ago to more happening cities such as London, New York and Berlin, but the French capital is fighting back with a string of great new leftfield Left Bank venues pumping out everything from gypsy jazz to electro-tropical candomblé to the Seine-side party crowds. Go early if you want to avoid the queues, but bear in mind that Parisians tend to go out clubbing late and most venues will be pretty empty if you turn up before midnight. Also look out for flyers, join the MySpace and Facebook groups of your favourite venues, and most importantly, make friends with people in the places you go to: it's the best way to hear about cool underground parties coming up. Many of these new nightlife stars double up as gig venues too, giving much-needed stage space to the city's up-and-coming bands.

Back on the heritage trail, Paris's traditional cabarets still cater (surprisingly well) to the throngs of tourists and businessmen who drop in for an eyeful of boob-bouncing, posh nosh and champers. Alternatively, if the get-your-glitz-out-for-the-boys genre isn't your cup of tea, then a Gallic giggle can still be had old-fashioned *café-théâtres*, where songs and sketches accompany dinner and a bottle of plonk. Check out the new Time Out Paris website (www.timeout.fr) for comprehensive nightlife listings.

ARTS & ENTERTAINMENT

Clubs

Ritzy places such as the **VIP Room** and **Le Baron** are still the talk of the Right Bank, but a string of new Seine-side clubs in the 13th arrondissement are now drawing hip locals south of the river for late-night fun (*see p287* **River Dance**). Batofar was the original trail-blazer, but it's now been joined by the likes of **La Dame de Canton** and club venue *du jour* **Wanderlust**, with an outpost of Le Baron about to join the party. With everything from ping pong games to documentary screenings and free fashion workshops on offer, the emphasis on the Left Bank is more about having fun than posing (*see also p187* **Making Waves**).

For listings, check www.parisbouge.com, www.novaplanet.com, www.radiofg.com and www.lemonsound.com. Radio stations FG (98.2FM) and Nova (101.5FM) also provide details on what's happening.

RIGHT BANK

Club bars

★ Andy Whaloo

69 rue des Gravilliers, 3rd (01.42.71.20.38, www.andywhaloo-bar.com). M° Arts et Métiers. **Open** 6pm-2am Tue-Sat. **Admission** free. **Credit** AmEx, MC, V. **Map** p409 K5.

Owned by the people behind the hugely successful Momo and Sketch in London, Andy Whaloo serves sumptuous snack food and is tastefully decorated with Moroccan artefacts and a spice rack of colours. The seating is made from upturned paint cans, and the DJs play an eclectic mix, featuring everything from hip hop to techno and stepping up the volume as the night progresses.

Café Chéri(e)

44 bd de la Villette, 19th (01.42.02.02.05). M° Belleville. **Open** noon-2am daily. **Admission** free. **Credit** MC, V. **Map** p403 M3.

Chacha Club.

A popular DJ bar, especially during the summer months, when fashionistas flock to the terrace. Live music is played from Thursdays to Saturdays after 10pm. Expect anything from electro punk to rock, funk, hip hop, rare groove, indie, dance, jazz and '80s classics.

★ Chacha Club
47 rue Berger, 1st (01.40.13.12.12, www. chachaclub.fr). Mº Châtelet. **Open** 8pm-6am Tue-Sat. **Admission** varies. **Credit** MC, V. **Map** p402 J5.

Paris's fetishistic obsession with the cigarette has produced a new nightlife phenomenon: the fumoir. The Chacha Club was the first high-profile establishment to open one, and it forms just one of the sexy attributes of this hot haunt near Les Halles that is attracting a spectacularly good-looking clientele through its doors. In the style of a private club, but with no membership requirement (only a trio of exacting 'physionomists' stand at the door), it combines restaurant, bar and club in a suite of intimate rooms with subdued lighting and seductive, 1930s-inspired decor.

★ La Fourmi
74 rue des Martyrs, 18th (01.42.64.70.35). Mº Pigalle. **Open** 8.30am-2am Mon-Thur, Sun; 8am-4am Fri, Sat. **Admission** free. **Credit** MC, V. **Map** p402 H2.

La Fourmi was a precursor to the industrial-design, informal, music-led bars that have sprung up around Paris – and it's still very much a style leader, attracting everyone from in-the-know tourists to fashionable Parisians. Great throughout the day for coffees or a beer, it has a small seating area outside and an

always busy bar with DJ decks. You can stay into the early hours at weekends, but it's also a handy pre-club rendezvous and flyer supplier.

Lizard Lounge
18 rue du Bourg-Tibourg, 4th (01.42.72.81.34, www.cheapblonde.com). Mº Hôtel de Ville or St-Paul. **Open** noon-2am daily. **Admission** free. **Credit** MC, V. **Map** p409 K6.

This three-level, trendy Marais hangout has a boozer upstairs serving beer in pint glasses, a mezzanine for crowd voyeurs, and a more full-on DJ bar in the booth-filled basement – often full, due to its rather modest proportions. Local DJs play a variety of contemporary styles.

★ Panic Room
101 rue Amelot, 11th (01.58.30.93.43, www. panicroomparis.com). Mº St-Sébastien Froissart. **Open** 6.30pm-2am Mon-Sat. Closed 2wks Aug. **Admission** free. **Credit** MC, V. **Map** p409 L5.

This newcomer has quickly carved out a niche on the rock scene, and it's not nearly as daunting as its name suggests. The excellent Goldrush collective has live acts and DJs blasting the sound system in the basement, while upstairs friendly barmen serve affordable cocktails behind a concrete counter. The indie crowd and occasional media celebs are loving it.

Le Troisième Lieu
62 rue Quincampoix, 4th (01.48.04.85.64). Mº Rambuteau. **Open** 6pm-2am Mon-Fri; 6pm-5am Sat. **Admission** free. **Credit** MC, V. **Map** p402 K5.

Opened by Les Ginettes Armées, organisers of renowned Sunday lesbian and mixed events, the Troisième Lieu tends towards electro and house. The

MOULIN ROUGE

Féerie

THE SHOW OF THE MOST
FAMOUS CABARET IN THE WORLD !
DINNER & SHOW AT 7PM FROM 180€
SHOW AT 9PM & 11PM : 109€

MONTMARTRE
82, BLD DE CLICHY - 75018 PARIS
TEL : 33(0)1 53 09 82 82

WWW.MOULIN-ROUGE.C
FACEBOOK.COM/LEMOULINROUGEOFFIC

ground floor hosts DJs mixing eclectic sounds for chatting and relaxing to, whereas the basement is more dancefloor-oriented.

Le Zèbre de Belleville
63 bd de Belleville, 20th (01.43.55.55.55, www.lezebre.com). M° Belleville. **Open** times vary. **Admission** €6-€15. **No credit cards.** **Map** p403 N4.

This stylish cabaret/theatre bar is used by Dan Ghenacia and the Freak 'n' Chic posse for buzzy after-parties on Sundays. It's usually a more traditional circus and cabaret venue; check flyers for event information.

Clubs

Le Baron
6 av Marceau, 8th (01.47.20.04.01, www.club lebaron.com). M° Alma Marceau. **Open** 11pm-6am daily. **Admission** free. **Credit** MC, V. **Map** p400 D5.

This small but supremely exclusive hangout for the international jet set used to be an upmarket brothel, and has the decor to prove it. It only holds 150, most of whom are regulars you'll need to befriend in order to get past the door. But if you do manage to get in, you'll be rubbing shoulders with celebrities and super-glossy people.

Le Cab
2 pl du Palais-Royal, 1st (01.58.62.56.25, www.cabaret.fr). M° Palais Royal-Musée du Louvre. **Open** 11.30pm-5am Thur-Sat. *Restaurant* 8-11.30pm Tue-Sat. **Admission** free Tue, Wed; €20 Thur-Sat. **Credit** AmEx, MC, V. **Map** p402 H5.

Le Cab is owned by the management behind Club Mix and Queen, and R&B and commercial house dominate the playlist. The doormen are tough, and if they don't like you, you won't get in (unless you've booked for dinner).

Le Cabaret Sauvage
59 bd Macdonald, 19th (01.42.09.03.09, www.cabaretsauvage.com). M° Porte de la Villette. **Open** 9pm-dawn, days vary. **Admission** €10-€20. **Credit** AmEx, MC, V. **Map** p403 inset.

A stylish venue that's taken over by outside promoters for occasional club nights. There often used to be a world music element, but recently electronic and drum 'n' bass nights have begun to be held here, and, since the demise of Pulp, techno label Kill the DJ has started using the venue. Check the website for full details.

La Chapelle des Lombards
19 rue de Lappe, 11th (01.43.57.24.24, www.la-chapelle-des-lombards.com). M° Bastille. **Open** 11.30pm-6am Tue-Sun. **Admission**

free Mon-Thur, Sun; €20 Fri, Sat (incl 1 drink and free for women before midnight Fri). **Credit** MC, V. **Map** p407 M7.

With Afrojazz and Latino bands and DJs providing the music, Latinos and Africans lead the dancefloor in this popular world music venue. Smart dress only.

Le Divan du Monde
75 rue des Martyrs, 18th (01.40.05.06.99, www.divandumonde.com). M° Abbesses or Pigalle. **Open** times vary. **Admission** €5-€30. **Credit** AmEx, MC, V. **Map** p402 H2.

After a drink at the cool Fourmi opposite, pop over to the Divan for one-off parties and regular events. The upstairs specialises in VJ events, and downstairs holds dub, reggae, funk and world music nights.

★ Favela Chic
18 rue du Fbg-du-Temple, 11th (01.40.21.38.14, www.favelachic.com). M° République. **Open** 8pm-2am Tue-Thur; 8pm-4am Fri, Sat. **Admission** free Tue-Thur; €10 (incl 1 drink) Fri, Sat. **Credit** MC, V. **Map** p402 L4.

Past the usually steely-faced door attendants, the Brazilian-themed Favela Chic attracts an up-for-it, international crowd for some serious samba and other Latin dancing. There are decent DJs, live acts, and Brazilian food and drinks. *Photo p284.*

Le Gibus
18 rue du Fbg-du-Temple, 11th (01.47.00.78.88, www.gibus.fr). M° République or Temple. **Open** midnight-6am Fri, Sat. **Concerts** 8-11.30pm Fri. **Admission** €5-€20. **Credit** *Bar* MC, V. **Map** p402 L4.

A famous 1980s punk venue, Le Gibus has gone through plenty of style changes during its life. Today, it takes in R&B, reggae, '80s pop and hip hop, plus the occasional *striptease mixte*.

Le Glaz'art
7-15 av de la Porte de la Villette, 19th (01.40.36.55.65, www.glazart.com). M° Porte de la Villette. **Open** 8.30pm-5am (sometimes 7am) on concert nights (check website). **Admission** €5-€15. **Credit** MC, V. **Map** p403 inset.

This converted coach station is way out to the north-east, but its strong DJ nights and live acts pull punters in from central Paris. Dub step, break-beat, electro and drum 'n' bass nights have made the venue a magnet for breaks fans.

La Java
105 rue du Fbg-du-Temple, 10th (01.42.02.20.52, www.la-java.fr). M° Belleville or Goncourt. **Open** 8.30pm-late Mon-Thur; midnight-dawn Fri, Sat; 2pm-2am Sun. **Admission** €5-€10. **Credit** MC, V. **Map** p403 M4.

Tucked inside the crumbling, disused Belleville market, La Java plays rock, salsa and world music, with live bands every weekend.

Favela Chic. See p283.

La Machine du Moulin Rouge

90 bd de Clichy, 18th (01.53.41.88.89, www. lamachinedumoulinrouge.com). M° Blanche. **Open** times vary. *Terrace* 7-10pm Fri-Sun. **Admission** prices vary. **Credit** MC, V. **Map** p401 G2.

So long La Loco, enter La Machine. This three-floor bar/club/live venue has had a substantial makeover and is now reborn with a dash of decadence. The main dancefloor, La Chaufferie, used to be the Moulin Rouge's boiler room and the old pipes remain, but the new *Alice in Wonderland*-style decor is a breath of fresh air. If you can't take the heat, head for the new terrace or switch to the bouncing Central, a concert hall showcasing a selection of new and established talent.

MadaM

128 rue de la Boétie, 8th (01.53.76.02.11). M° Franklin D. Roosevelt or George V. **Open** 7pm-2am Thur; midnight-6am Fri, Sat; 10.30pm-4am Sun. **Admission** free. **Credit** AmEx, DC, MC, V. **Map** p401 E4.

MadaM's late-night sessions (kicking in at 4am at weekends) are renowned for the young, moneyed crowd they attract. The music on offer is mainly electro and house (French), with several up-to-date international tunes thrown into the mix.

★ Le Magnifique

25 rue de Richelieu, 1st (01.42.60.70.80, www.lemagnifique.fr). M° Palais Royal-Musée du Louvre. **Open** 11pm-5am daily. **Admission** free. **Credit** AmEx, DC, MC, V. **Map** p401 H5.

Named after a 1970s film starring Jean-Paul Belmondo, this snazzy cocktail bar is a real retro treat. The decor, dominated by wood, dark leather and animal furs, is elegant, with a hint of porno chic that leaves you picturing Warhol and his posse partying in a corner. The place really comes to life after midnight, when the bar turns into a club with a soundtrack of dancefloor-fillers from the past

three decades. The fantastic cocktail menu, a selection of sushi (€8-€30) and the separate *fumoir* add to the overall appeal.

Mains d'Oeuvres

1 rue Charles-Garnier, 93400 St-Ouen (01.40.11.25.25, www.mainsdoeuvres.org). M° Garibaldi. **Open** times vary. **Admission** €5-€15. **Credit** *Bar* MC, V.

This rehearsal space and live venue for new bands (*see p292*) occasionally turns into a club venue, with rooms devoted to different music styles.

★ New Morning

7-9 rue des Petites-Ecuries, 10th (01.45.23.51.41, www.newmorning.com). M° Château d'Eau. **Open** times vary. **Admission** approx €20. **Credit** MC, V. **Map** p402 K3.

Jazz fans crowd into this hip, no-frills joint to natter, drink and boogie to the excellent live music. Low key it may be, but it's still worth looking out for the occasional A-lister.

Nouveau Casino

109 rue Oberkampf, 11th (01.43.57.57.40, www.nouveaucasino.net). M° Parmentier. **Open** 7pm-5am Wed-Sat. **Admission** prices vary. **Credit** *Bar* MC, V. **Map** p403 M5.

Conveniently surrounded by the numerous bars of rue Oberkampf and tucked behind the legendary Café Charbon, Nouveau Casino is a concert venue that also hosts some of the city's liveliest club nights. Local collectives, international names and record labels, such as Versatile, host nights here; it's worth checking the website for one-offs and after-parties.

★ Point Ephémère

200 quai de Valmy, 10th (01.40.34.02.48, www.pointephemere.org). M° Jaurès or Louis Blanc. **Open** noon-2am Mon-Sat; noon-9pm Sun. **Admission** varies. **Credit** AmEx, DC, MC, V. **Map** 402 L2.

This hunk of Berlin in Paris was only ever meant to be temporary, but thankfully it's still around. An uncompromising programming policy delivers some of the best electronic music in town; there's also a restaurant and bar with decks and a gallery, and terrace space by the canal in summer. *See also p293.*

Queen
102 av des Champs-Elysées, 8th (01.53.89.08.90, www.queen.fr). M° George V. **Open** midnight-7am Mon-Thur, Sun; midnight-8am Fri, Sat. **Admission** €15 Mon-Thur, Sun; €20 Fri, Sat. **Credit** *Bar* AmEx, MC, V. **Map** p400 D4.
Once the city's most fêted gay club and the only venue that could hold a torch to the Rex, with a roster of top local DJs holding court, Queen's star faded a little in the early noughties but is now starting to shine more brightly again. Last year, it introduced more themed nights, and still packs 'em in seven nights a week.
▶ *For more on Queen's gay nights, see p277.*

★ Le Régine
49 rue de Ponthieu, 8th (01.40.39.07.07) M° St-Philippe-du-Roule. **Open** 7pm-5am Thur; midnight-6am Fri, Sat. **Admission** €10-€20. **Credit** MC, V. **Map** p401 D4.
Régine was once a key figure on the Paris nightlife scene, and the club she created is experiencing a rejuvenation. Her portrait still sits by the entrance for a touch of '70s nostalgia, but the revamped venue has shifted from disco to sophisticated electro, inviting the cream of international DJs to the decks. The afterwork La French, followed by the insane Pan-Pan Cul-Cul night (where guys get in for free if they're dressed as girls), makes a safe bet for a wild Thursday.

★ Rex
5 bd Poissonnière, 2nd (01.42.36.10.96, www.rexclub.com). M° Bonne Nouvelle. **Open** 11.30pm-6am Wed-Sat. **Admission** free-€15. **Credit** *Bar* MC, V. **Map** p402 J4.
The Rex's new sound system puts over 40 different sound configurations at the DJ's fingertips, and has proved to be a magnet for top turntable stars. Once associated with iconic techno pioneer Laurent Garnier, the Rex has stayed at the top of the Paris techno scene, and occupies an unassailable position as the city's serious club music venue.

River's King
Opposite Maison de la Radio, av du Président Kennedy, 16th (01.40.56.02.82, www.rivers king.fr). M° Assemblée Nationale/RER Musée d'Orsay. **Open** 8pm-6am Fri, Sat. **Admission** €20 (incl 3 drinks). **Credit** MC, V. **Map** p404 B7.
With its terrace and voluminous dancefloor, this two-level boat is a clubbing paradise in the summer. The celebrated Respect crew held a popular, fondly remembered Wednesday night here, and are still involved in putting on parties at the venue. Location sometimes varies; check the programme.

La Scène Bastille
2bis rue des Taillandiers, 11th (01.48.06.50.70, www.la-scene.com). M° Bastille. **Open** 7.30pm-midnight Mon-Thur; midnight-6am Fri-Sun. Closed Aug. **Admission** €10-€12. **Credit** *Bar* MC, V. **Map** p407 M7.
This tastefully decorated club-bar-restaurant holds rock concerts, as well as club events most weekends. The programming here changes constantly, so check what's on. Popular gay nights too.

Showcase. *See p286.*

Batofar.

Le Scop'Club

5 av de l'Opéra, 8th (01.42.60.64.45, www.
lescopclub.com). Mº Pyramides. **Open** 8-11pm
Tue-Thur; 11pm-5am Fri, Sat. **Admission**
€10-€15. **Map** p401 H5.

Don't let the picture of Beethoven fool you: this small
club is all about electro-rock, with black-painted
walls and live acts taking to the stage at weekends.
Gigs aren't free, but DJ sets by the likes of MGMT
and 'music label battles' are interesting alternatives
on other nights. The crowd is young and dressed to
impress, but the Scop'Club is easier to get into than
it ever was when it was Paris Paris.

Showcase

Below Pont Alexandre III, 8th (01.45.61.25.43,
www.showcase.fr). Mº Champs-Elysées Clemenceau.
Open 11.30pm-dawn Fri, Sat. **Admission** free-
€15. **Credit** MC, V. **Map** p401 E5.

This vast venue, in converted boat hangars below
Pont Alexandre III, is where music-crazed insomni-
acs come at weekends to discover up-and-coming
bands and dance until daybreak. The club has lost
some of its hype over the last couple of years, but
high-profile guest DJs have been setting the bar
higher lately: Carol Cox, will.i.am and Calvin Harris
have all made appearances. *Photo p285.*

Silencio

142 rue de Montmartre, 2nd (www.silencio-
club.com). Mº Bourse or Grands Boulevards.
Open 6pm-6am Tue-Sun. **Admission** varies.
Credit AmEx, MC, V. **Map** p402 J4.

If there's one thing Paris has been missing for years
it's a decent private club – one that encourages artistic networking, before letting the public in for a night
of soulful partying. Cue Silencio, David Lynch's joint
named after the cult venue in his 2001 movie
Mulholland Drive. The director has designed every
aspect of the decor, from the gold-leaf walls to the
1950s-style furniture. There are concerts by up-and-
coming bands, film premieres, eclectic club nights

and a stream of prestigious guests. If you're not up
for full-blown membership (€780 plus proof of your
artistic credentials), access is after midnight; but
you'll have to look right to get in.

★ Le Social Club

142 rue Montmartre, 2nd (01.40.28.05.55,
www.parissocialclub.com). Mº Bourse or Grands
Boulevards. **Open** 11pm-3am Tue, Wed; 11pm-
6am Thur-Sat. **Admission** free-€12. **Credit**
AmEx, MC, V. **Map** p402 J4.

Set right in the hub of the city's club activity around
Grands Boulevards, this electro venue has some of
the hippest acts from the French and international
scene, thanks to its owner's multidisciplinary career
as a producer and founder of the record label
Uncivilized World.

Toro

74 rue Jean-Jacques-Rousseau, 1st (01.44.76.00.03,
www.toroparis.com). Mº Les Halles. **Open** *Live*
performances 9pm-midnight Thur-Sat. *DJ sets*
times vary. **Admission** free. **Credit** AmEx,
MC, V. **Map** p402 J5.

This no-frills tapas bar hides a small but wonderfully wacky dancefloor in the basement where DJs
mix up house music with flamenco tunes.

VIP Room

188 rue de Rivoli, 1st (01.58.36.46.00,
www.viproom.fr). Mº Palais Royal-Musée du
Louvre or Tuileries. **Open** midnight-5am Thur-
Sat. **Admission** free. **Credit** AmEx, DC, MC, V.
Map p401 H1.

The VIP has moved from its Champs-Elysées
address into the former Scala nightclub, but other
than that, nothing has changed. It's still a hit with
the people who also enjoy the VIP's sister venues
in Cannes and Saint-Tropez during the summer, and
the music is still dance-oriented. The opening of
smart Italian restaurant Gioia, serving food until
5am at weekends, is a welcome addition.

LEFT BANK

Club bars

La Mezzanine de l'Alcazar

62 rue Mazarine, 6th (01.53.10.19.99, www.alcazar.fr). M° Odéon. **Open** 7pm-2am daily. **Admission** free. **Credit** AmEx, DC, MC, V. **Map** p406 H7.

The super-stylish, Conran-owned Mezzanine is the upstairs posher sister of the Wagg (*see p288*). Both are well-heeled hangouts, but the Mezzanine remains the venue of choice for the suited and booted.

Clubs

★ Batofar

Opposite 11 quai François-Mauriac, 13th (09.71.25.50.61, www.batofar.org). M° Quai de la Gare. **Open** 11pm-6am Mon-Sat; 6am-noon 1st Sun of mth. **Admission** free-€12. **Credit** MC, V. **Map** p407 N10.

In recent years, the Batofar has gone through a rapid succession of management teams, with varying levels of success. The current managers have helped to revive the venue's tradition of playing cutting-edge music, including electro, dub step, techno and dancehall nights featuring international acts.

La Dame de Canton

Port de la Gare, 13th (01.53.61.08.49, www.damedecanton.com). M° Quai de la Gare. **Open** 7.30pm-2am Tue-Thur; 7.30pm-6am Fri, Sat. **Admission** free-€8. **No credit cards**. **Map** p407 N10.

The Dame de Canton, housed in a superb Chinese junk, features a concert space, a striking wooden dancefloor, a romantic restaurant in the hold and a

---

River Dance

The 13th is Paris's new nightlife central.

The long-delayed Cité de la Mode et du Design on the quai d'Austerlitz has finally opened its doors, and its first on-site club is setting tongues wagging. **Wanderlust** (*see p288*) has joined the likes of Batofar and La Dame de Canton along the banks of the Seine, making the 13th arrondissement the new undisputed clubbing capital. Spread across a vast space, it includes a wooden terrace perfect for sunset drinks (although you'll need deep pockets – a beer costs €8 and a bottle of rosé €35), an open-air cinema, art installations and a restaurant run by TV chef Benjamin Darnaud with dishes such as *steak-frites*, poached cod with lemongrass and runny chocolate tart.

Running the venue is the ultra-hip Savoir Faire team (the brains behind Le Social Club, Le Baron and Silencio), so it should come as no surprise that the dress code is designer, the bouncers are unforgiving and the queues are long (come very early or late). On the plus side, though, entry is free and there are fashion-themed nights on Fridays that might include documentary screenings, catwalk shows and installations run in association with the Musée Galliera, plus free fashion workshops for children and adults. You'll also find ping pong tables, weekend yoga lessons and chill-out areas dotted with chaises longues. Music is minimal techno and house on a top-notch sound system, getting the crowd going to the point where, if you're outside, you can watch a sea of well-dressed backsides gyrating together in the club's huge street-level bay windows. In late 2012, the hip factor was set to be turned up yet another notch with the opening of a Le Baron outpost on the roof.

Wagg.

sun-drenched bridge for *apéros*. The music is eclectic: breakbeats, electro-swing gypsy jazz, electrotropical candomblé DJs, Thai-funk electro disco, ragga, kompa and plenty more alternative world music you've never heard of.

★ Mix Club
24 rue de l'Arrivée, 15th (01.56.80.37.37, www.mixclub.fr). Mᵒ Montparnasse Bienvenüe. **Open** 11pm-6am Thur-Sat. **Admission** free-€20. **Credit** MC, V. **Map** p405 F8.
The Mix Club has one of the city's biggest dancefloors. Regular international visitors include Erick Morillo's Subliminal and Ministry of Sound parties, and in-house events include David Guetta's 'Fuck Me I'm Famous', 'Hipnotic' and 'One Night With Paulette', plus just about everyone else who's big in France – or anywhere in the world, for that matter.

Le Montana
28 rue St-Benoît, 6th (no phone). Mᵒ St-Germain-des-Prés. **Open** 11pm-5am daily. **Admission** free. **Credit** AmEx, DC, MC, V. **Map** p408 H7.
It's hard to believe that any place could out-hype Le Baron (*see p283*), and yet this exclusive St-Germain club manages it. Revamped by über-cool graphic artist André, Le Montana is a VIP magnet – Lenny Kravitz, Vanessa Bruno and Kate Moss have all hit the floor here.

Wagg
62 rue Mazarine, 6th (01.55.42.22.01, www.wagg.fr). Mᵒ Odéon. **Open** 11pm-6.45am Fri, Sat; 3.30pm-midnight Sun. **Admission** €12 Fri, Sat; €12 Sun (incl drink). **Credit** AmEx, DC, MC, V. **Map** p406 H7.
Refurbished as part of the Conran makeover of the Mezzanine (*see p287*) upstairs, Wagg went through a period of big-name DJs, but has settled down as home to a well-to-do crowd. Expect funk, house and disco, plus salsa lessons on Sundays.

Wanderlust
32 quai d'Austerlitz, 13th (www.wanderlust paris.com). Mᵒ Quai de la Gare. **Open** 6pm-6am Wed-Sun. **Admission** free. **Credit** AmEx, DC, MC, V. **Map** p407 M9.
See p287 **River Dance**.

Cabaret, comedy & café-théâtre

The year the Eiffel Tower raised its final girders (1889), the Moulin Rouge was raising something of its own: skirts. The risqué *quadrille réaliste* (later dubbed the cancan) became such a trademark that more than 120 years later, busty babes are still slinking across the stages of Paris. These days, cabaret

Le Lido.

is an all-evening affair, traditionally served with champers and a meal. Male dancers and magicians complement the foxy foxtrots, the dancing is perfectly synchronised and the whole caboodle is now perfectly respectable.

RIGHT BANK

Cabaret

Crazy Horse Saloon

12 av George V, 8th (01.47.23.32.32, www.lecrazy horseparis.com). M° Alma Marceau or George V. **Shows** 8.15pm, 10.45pm Mon-Fri, Sun; 7pm, 9.30pm, 11.45pm Sat. **Admission** *Show only* €105. *Show* (incl champagne) €125. **Credit** AmEx, DC, MC, V. **Map** p400 D4.

More risqué than the other cabarets, the Horse, whose *art du nu* was invented in 1951 by Alain Bernadin, is an ode to feminine beauty: lookalike dancers with provocative names like Daisy Blu and Zula Zazou, and identical body statistics (when standing, the girls' nipples and hips are all at the same height), move around the stage, clad only in rainbow light and strategic strips of black tape. In their latest show, Désirs, the girls put on some tantalising numbers, with titles such as 'God Save Our Bare Skin' (a sexy take on the Changing of the Guards) and the sensual 'Vestel's Desire'.

Le Lido

116bis av des Champs-Elysées, 8th (01.40.76.56.10, www.lido.fr). M° Franklin D. Roosevelt or George V. **Lunch** 1pm. **Matinée** 3pm Tue, Sun (dates vary). **Dinner** 7pm. **Shows** 9.30pm, 11.30pm daily. **Admission**

Lunch & matinée show (incl champagne) €140. *9.30pm show* €80. *11.30pm show* €80. *9.30pm show* (incl champagne) €105. *11.30pm show* (incl champagne) €145. *Dinner & show* €160-€300. *Show & backstage tour* price varies. **Credit** AmEx, DC, MC, V. **Map** p400 D4.

This is the largest cabaret of all: high-tech touches optimise visibility, and chef Philippe Lacroix provides fabulous gourmet nosh. On stage, 60 Bluebell Girls and a set of hunky dancers slink around, shaking their bodies with sequinned panache in breathtaking scenes. For a special treat, opt for the 'behind the scenes' Coulisses tour which, before the show, takes you into the heart of the action.

Moulin Rouge

82 bd de Clichy, 18th (01.53.09.82.82, www. moulin-rouge.com). M° Blanche. **Dinner** 7pm. **Shows** 9pm, 11pm daily. **Admission** *Show* (incl champagne) €105. *Dinner & show* €175-€200. *Show only* €95. **Credit** AmEx, DC, MC, V. **Map** p401 G2.

Toulouse-Lautrec posters, glittery lamp-posts and fake trees lend tacky charm to this revue. On stage, 60 Doriss dancers cavort with faultless synchronisation. Costumes are flamboyant and the *entr'acte* acts funny. The downer is the space, with tables packed in like sardines. There are also occasional matinée performances. A new brasserie and luxury rooftop suite are planned for 2013.

Café-théâtre

Les Blancs Manteaux

15 rue des Blancs-Manteaux, 4th (01.48.87.15.84, www.blancsmanteaux.fr). M° Hôtel de Ville. **Shows** from 7pm daily (phone for details). **Admission**

Show €20; €17 students, under-25s; *2 shows* €34 (except Sat). *Dinner & 1 show* €40. **No credit cards. Map** p409 K6.
For the past 40 years, this Marais institution has been launching new talent with weekly comedy platforms. With a dinner-and-show ticket, you can dine on Thai cuisine at nearby Suan Thai.

Chez Michou
80 rue des Martyrs, 18th (01.46.06.16.04, www.michou.com). M° Pigalle. **Dinner** 8.30pm daily. **Shows** 10.30pm approx. **Admission** *Show* €55-€65. *Dinner & show* €110-€140. **Credit** MC, V. **Map** p402 H2.
Drag, sparkling costumes, good food and wine: Michou's show is not quite as 'blue' as his azure attire suggests. Book ahead if you want to dine.

Le Grenier
3 rue Rennequin, 17th (01.43.80.68.01, www.legrenier-dinerspectacle.com). M° Ternes. **Shows** from 7.30pm daily. **Admission** *Show* €18-€20. *Dinner & show* €30-€60. **Credit** MC, V. **Map** p400 D2.
If you fancy being entertained while you eat, consider a night at the Grenier, which still retains the allure of an old *café-théâtre* with an eclectic line-up of stand-up, *chansonniers* and magic acts all on the same bill.

★ Au Lapin Agile
22 rue des Saules, 18th (01.46.06.85.87, www.au-lapin-agile.com). M° Lamarck Caulaincourt. **Shows** 9pm-1am Tue-Sun. **Admission** *Show* (incl 1 drink) €24. **No credit cards. Map** p402 H1.

The prices have gone up and they sell their own compilation CDs, but that's all that seems to have changed since this quaint, pink bar first opened in 1860. Tourists now outnumber the locals, but the Lapin harbours an echo of old Montmartre.

Comedy

Café de la Gare
41 rue du Temple, 4th (01.42.78.52.51, www.cdlg.org). M° Hôtel de Ville. **Shows** times vary. **Admission** €22-€24. **Credit** MC, V. **Map** p406 K6.
Running since 1968, the most famous fringe theatre in Paris has 300 stage-hugging seats and hosts quality French stand-up and raucous comedies.

Caveau de la République
1 bd St-Martin, 3rd (01.42.78.44.45, www.caveau.fr). M° République. **Shows** 8.30pm Thur-Sat; 3.30pm Sun. Closed Aug. **Admission** €24. **Credit** MC, V. **Map** p402 L4.
This traditional *chanson* venue has been churning out political-satirical songs and sketches for more than a century. Nowadays, stand-up comedy is the main draw. Five artists perform each night.

Le Comedy Club
42 bd de Bonne Nouvelle, 10th (01.73.54.17.00, www.lecomedyclub.fr). M° Bonne Nouvelle. **Shows** days vary. **Admission** €15-€25. **Credit** MC, V. **Map** p402 J4.
Jamel Debbouze, the comic known for his one-man shows and his roles in films such as *Le Fabuleux Destin d'Amélie Poulain*, gives the comedy trade a helping hand with this theatre. Tuesdays and Wednesdays (7.30pm) are open mic nights.

Paradis Latin.

★ Le Point Virgule

7 rue Ste-Croix-de-la-Bretonnerie, 4th (01.42.78.67.03, www.lepointvirgule.com). M° Hôtel de Ville. **Shows** times vary, see website for details. **Admission** €19. *2 shows* €29, *3 shows* €36. *Children's show* €12; €10 children. **No credit cards. Map** p409 K6.

This small Marais theatre has become the ultimate launch pad for up-and-coming comedians, with shows, a *café-théâtre* school and an annual comedy festival in September. The theatre launched a new venue in Montparnasse in late 2012, the Grand Point Virgule (8bis rue de l'Arrivée, 15th, 01.42.78.67.03, www.legrandpointvirgule.com), to provide some Left Bank laughs.

LEFT BANK

Cabaret

★ Paradis Latin

28 rue Cardinal Lemoine, 5th (01.43.25.28.28, www.paradislatin.com). M° Cardinal Lemoine. **Dinner** 8pm. **Show** 9.30pm daily. **Admission** *Show* (incl champagne) €88. *Dinner & show* €127-€185. *Show only* €60. **Credit** AmEx, DC, MC, V. **Map** p406 K8.

This is the most authentic of the cabarets, not only because it's family-run (the men run the cabaret, the daughter does the costumes), but also because the clientele is mostly French, something that has a direct effect on the prices (this is the cheapest revue) and the cuisine, which tends to be high quality. Show-wise you can expect the usual fare: generous doses of glitter, live singing and cheesy *entr'acte* acts performed in a stunning belle époque room. There's also a twice-monthly matinée.

Music

Paris's music scene is bubbling with talent, and the recent emergence of some great new bands speaks volumes about the creativity of today's up-and-coming artists. The capital is overflowing with authentic concert venues, from monster stadiums to intimate bars and jazz clubs, and venues like Nouveau Casino and L'International give precious stage space to those on the way up the musical ladder.

Chanson française is still going strong, helped by the success of Les Trois Baudets, a government-subsidised *chanson* hall in the heart of Pigalle – French law dictates that 40 per cent of music broadcast in France must be in the French language.

Jazz is having a mini revival too: after the disappearance of old flames like Le Slow Club (once one of the most famous jazz joints in Europe), Le Bilboquet and Les 7 Lézards, a handful of new joints have opened up, while flagship clubs Au Duc des Lombards, New Morning and Le Sunset/Le Sunside continue to book a range of top-notch acts from around the globe. Paris is also a European leader for world music, particularly African and Arab acts. And don't forget that every 21 June, the whole city turns into one giant music venue for the **Fête de la Musique** (*see p29*), when a party in the street is guaranteed.

INFORMATION AND RESOURCES

The weekly magazine *Les Inrockuptibles* is a valuable resource. Alternatively, try bi-monthly gig bible *Lylo*, free in bars and branches of Fnac. The **Fnac** and **Virgin Megastore** ticket offices (for both, *see p225*) also display details of up-and-coming concerts. For reduced-price tickets try www.billetreduc.com. Depending on your tastes (and your French) radio can be useful for tip-offs: Nova (101.5FM) does electro, lounge and world; TSF (89.9FM) and FIP (105.1FM) cover jazz; and Le Mouv' (92.1FM) and OuiFM (102.3FM) are for rock fans.

Box offices are usually closed in the daytime, and most venues take a break in August. Several excellent venues, like La Bellevilloise, host regular free nights – ideal if you're feeling adventurous and/or are on a budget. For concerts, it's best to turn up at the time stated on the ticket: strict noise curfews mean that start times are adhered to pretty closely.

RIGHT BANK

Rock & pop

Le Bataclan

50 bd Voltaire, 11th (01.43.14.00.30, www.le-bataclan.com). M° Oberkampf. **Open** times vary. **Credit** MC, V. **Map** p403 M5.

This distinctive venue, fashioned like a Chinese pagoda with a distinctive multi-coloured façade, first opened in 1864 and remains admirably discerning in its booking of rock, world, jazz and hip hop acts.

Le Bus Palladium

6 rue Fontaine, 9th (01.45.26.80.35, www.lebuspalladium.com). M° St-Georges, Pigalle or Blanche. **Open** *Concerts* 9pm-midnight. *Club* midnight-5am Thur-Sat. **Credit** MC, V. **Map** p401 H2.

This legendary rock venue, graced by the likes of Mick Jagger and The Beatles in its heyday, is back on the map after a 20-year spell out of the limelight with a vintage house vibe somewhere between retro rockabilly and punk psychedelia. While the new generation gets wild in the pit, former regulars are trying to catch their breath at the restaurant upstairs (8pm-5am Tue-Sat). Check the programme for concerts. Club nights on Tuesdays, Fridays and Saturdays are a guaranteed riot.

ARTS & ENTERTAINMENT

ARTS & ENTERTAINMENT

★ La Cigale/La Boule Noire
120 bd de Rochechouart,18th (01.49.25.89.99, www.lacigale.fr; 01.49.25.81.75, www.laboule-noire.fr). Mº Anvers or Pigalle. **Open** times vary. **Credit** MC, V. **Map** p402 J2.
This is easily one of Paris's finest concert venues. The lovely, horseshoe-shaped theatre La Cigale is linked to more cosy venue La Boule Noire, which is good for catching cult-ish visiting indie and rock acts.

Les Disquaires
4-6 rue des Taillandiers, 11th (01.40.21.94.60, www.lesdisquaires.com). Mº Bastille. **Open** 7pm-late daily. **Credit** MC, V. **Map** p407 M6.
This party bar provides live pop, rock, DJs and electro to a hip crowd of thirtysomethings. It's a fine spot for discovering underground Paris sounds.

La Flèche d'Or
102bis rue de Bagnolet, 20th (01.44.64.01.02, www.flechedor.fr). Mº Alexandre Dumas. **Open** 8pm-2am Wed-Sat. *Concerts* times vary. **Credit** MC, V.
This much-loved indie and electro venue, which reopened a couple of years ago after a six-month shutdown, is a great place to check out the capital's live music scene, with three or four bands playing a night. It also gives monthly residencies to local groups and DJs.

★ L'International
5-7 rue Moret, 11th (01.49.29.76.45, www.linternational.fr). Mº Ménilmontant. **Open** 6pm-2am daily. **Concerts** times vary. **Credit** MC, V. **Map** p403 N4.
This concert-bar is a breath of fresh air, with free entry and a string of on-the-up bands playing to hip indie crowds every night of the week. Once a month there's an after-party until 4am.

Mains d'Oeuvres
1 rue Charles-Garnier, 93400 St-Ouen (01.40.11.25.25, www.mainsdoeuvres.org). Mº Garibaldi or Porte de Clignancourt. **Open** *Bar* 9.30am-midnight Mon-Fri; 11am-midnight Sat; noon-9pm Sun. *Concerts* times vary. **Credit** *Bar* MC, V.
A veritable hub for fringe musical and performance activity just outside Paris, the Mains d'Oeuvres is a huge former leisure centre for car factory workers that specialises in leftfield electro, rock mavericks and multimedia artists. It frequently hosts the Festival des Attitudes Indé (Sept-Oct) for up-and-coming bands.

La Flèche d'Or.

L'International.

La Maroquinerie
23 rue Boyer, 20th (01.40.33.35.05,
www.lamaroquinerie.fr). M° Gambetta. **Open**
Box office (in person only) 2.30-7pm Mon-Fri.
Concerts times vary. Closed Aug. **Credit**
MC, V. **Map** p403 P4.
Literary discussion and rock 'n' roll coexist happily
at this happening locale. It's home to the Inrocks
Indie Club nights, featuring up-and-coming rock
acts, but there are still plenty of traces of its world
music roots.

★ La Mécanique Ondulatoire
8 passage Thiéré, 11th (www.myspace.com/
lamecanique). M° Bastille or Ledru Rollin.
Open 6pm-2am Mon-Sat. **Concerts** times
vary. **Credit** MC, V. **Map** p407 M7.
Cementing Bastille's status as Paris's prime hangout
for rockers, this exciting venue has three levels and
alternates eclectic DJs with live acts in the cellar, plus
there's jazz on Tuesday nights. It was forced to close
in September 2012 after complaints from the neighbours, but reopened the following month.

Le Motel
8 passage Josset, 11th (01.58.30.88.52, www.
myspace.com/lemotel). M° Ledru Rollin. **Open** 6pm-
1.45am Tue-Sun. **Credit** MC, V. **Map** p407 M7.
This most Anglophile of Paris bars, with Stone
Roses and Smiths posters adorning the walls, manages to fit plenty of live bands, including some of the
best new local talent, on to its tiny stage.

Nouveau Casino
109 rue Oberkampf, 11th (01.43.57.57.40,
www.nouveaucasino.net). M° Ménilmontant,
Parmentier or St-Maur. **Open** *Concerts* times
vary. **Credit** *Bar* MC, V. **Map** p403 N5.
A bankable and loveable, albeit rather commercial,
venue run by the adjacent Café Charbon, with fab
gigs and club nights featuring rock, dub and garage,
plus reasonable drinks prices.

Olympia
28 bd des Capucines, 9th (08.92.68.33.68, www.
olympiahall.com). M° Opéra. **Open** *Box office* noon-
7pm daily. *Concerts* times vary. **Credit** AmEx,
DC, MC, V. **Map** p401 G4.
The Beatles, Frank Sinatra, Jimi Hendrix and Edith
Piaf have all performed here. Now it's mainly home
to nostalgia and *variété*, although big names still
drop by – Crystal Castles are performing in 2013.

O'Sullivans by the Mill
92 bd de Clichy, 18th (01.53.09.08.49, www.
osullivans-pubs.com). M° Blanche. **Open** noon-5am
Mon-Thur, Sun; noon-6am Fri, Sat. **Concerts**
times vary. **Credit** MC, V. **Map** p401 G2.
This Irish chain bar is all about late, late nights,
with grizzly weekend rock gigs that last until sun-
rise, DJs and open mic nights the first Wednesday
of the month. Thursday nights are always wild.

Palais des Congrès
2 pl de la Porte Maillot, 17th (01.40.68.22.22,
www.viparis.com). M° Porte Maillot. **Open** times
vary. **Credit** MC, V. **Map** p400 B2.
The sound and the views are good wherever you sit
in this state-of-the-art amphitheatre. Diana Krall and
Paolo Conte have recently graced the stage.

Palais Omnisports de Paris-Bercy
8 bd de Bercy, 12th (08.92.39.04.90, www.bercy.fr).
M° Bercy. **Box office** 11am-6pm Mon-Sat. **Credit**
AmEx, DC, MC, V. **Map** p407 N9.
The traditional venue for rock and pop behemoths:
Justin Bieber, Pink and Iron Maiden are among the
big draws in 2013.

★ Point Ephémère
200 quai de Valmy, 10th (01.40.34.02.48,
www.pointephemere.org). M° Jaurès or Louis
Blanc. **Open** noon-2am Mon-Sat; noon-9pm Sun.
Concerts times vary. **Credit** AmEx, DC, MC, V.
Map p402 L2.

ARTS & ENTERTAINMENT

This converted warehouse is a classy affair, bringing together up-and-coming local rock, jazz and world gigs with a decent restaurant, dance and recording studios and exhibitions.

Le Reservoir
16 rue de la Forge-Royale, 11th (01.43.56.39.60, www.reservoirclub.com). M° Faidherbe Chaligny or Ledru-Rollin. **Open** 8pm-late Tue-Sat. **Credit** AmEx, DC, MC, V. **Map** p407 N7.
This classy, Anglo-inspired venue hosts regular club nights and live indie acts, as well as low-key performances from larger acts.

La Scène Bastille
2bis rue des Taillandiers, 11th (01.48.06.50.70, www.la-scene.com). M° Bastille. **Open** 7.30-10.30pm Mon-Wed, Sun; 7.30pm-6am Fri, Sat. *Concerts* 7.30pm. Closed Aug. **Credit** MC, V. **Map** p407 M7.
This beautifully designed bar offers you the option of chilling out in alcoves or joining the kids to groove to hip hop, funk and jazz.

Zénith
211 av Jean-Jaurès, 19th (www.zenith-paris.com). M° Porte de Pantin. **Open** times vary. **Credit** MC, V. **Map** p403 inset.
State-of-the-art sound and credible bands make this the large venue of choice. Florence and the Machine and Lionel Richie played here in 2012.

Chanson

★ La Bellevilloise
19-21 rue Boyer, 20th (01.46.36.07.07, www. labellevilloise.com). M° Gambetta or Ménilmontant. **Open** 7pm-1am Wed, Thur; 7pm-2am Fri; 11am-2am Sat; 11.30am-midnight Sun. **Credit** MC, V. **Map** p403 P4.
Is there anything that Paris's former co-operative doesn't do? There's food, drinks, DJs and live music – lashings of it, not only in the downstairs concert hall but in the Oliviers restaurant and upstairs bar too. The music selection is eclectic. *Photo p296.*

Chez Adel
10 rue de la Grange-aux-Belles, 10th (01.42.08.24.61). M° Jacques Bonsergent. **Open** noon-midnight Tue-Sun. *Concerts* 6pm Tue-Sun. **Credit** MC, V. **Map** p402 L3.
Patron Adel is probably the most renowned *chanson* café owner in Paris, and this fine den of kitsch attracts countless devotees with its repertoire of *chanson* and Eastern European sounds.

Le Limonaire
18 Cité Bergère, 9th (01.45.23.33.33, http:// limonaire.free.fr). M° Grands Boulevards. **Open** 6pm-2am daily. *Concerts* 9pm Mon; 10pm Tue-Sat; 7pm & 9.30pm Sun. **Credit** MC, V. **Map** p402 J4.

Serious *chanson* takes the limelight and performances vary from piano-led *chansonniers* to cabaret. Arrive at 8pm if you want to eat (Tue-Sun).

Sentier des Halles
50 rue d'Aboukir, 2nd (01.42.61.89.90, www.lesentierdeshalles.fr). M° Sentier. **Open** times vary. *Concerts* 7.45pm & 9.45pm Mon-Sat; 3.15pm Sun. Closed Aug. **Credit** MC, V. **Map** p402 J4.
Le Sentier has developed beyond its traditional *chanson* base to embrace a variety of modern styles plus the occasional stand-up act.

Les Trois Baudets
64 bd de Clichy, 18th (01.42.62.33.33, www. lestroisbaudets.com). M° Pigalle. **Open** times vary. **Credit** MC, V. **Map** p401 H2.
All dolled up in black and red, with a 250-seater theatre, an enviable sound system, two bars and a restaurant, this concert hall encourages *chanson française* and other musical genres (rock, electro, folk and slam) – as long as they're in French.

★ Le Vieux Belleville
12 rue des Envierges, 20th (01.44.62.92.66, www. le-vieux-belleville.com). M° Pyrénées. **Open** 11am-3pm, 7pm-2am Thur-Sat. *Concerts* 9pm Thur-Sat. Closed mid Aug. **Credit** V. **Map** p403 N4.
If you're looking for an authentic Belleville rendezvous, there's no better location than this old-style café with terrace, where the traditions of accordion music and croaky-voiced *chanson* endure.

World & traditional

Cité de la Musique
221 av Jean-Jaurès, 19th (01.44.84.44.84, www.cite-musique.fr). M° Porte de Pantin. **Box office** noon-6pm Tue-Sat; 10am-6pm Sun. *By phone* 11am-7pm Mon-Fri. *Concerts* times vary. **Credit** MC, V. **Map** p403 inset.
This excellent museum/concert complex welcomes plenty of big names, and also does a fine line in contemporary classical, avant-jazz and electronica.

Le Kibélé
12 rue de l'Echiquier, 10th (01.48.24.57.74, www.kibele.fr). M° Bonne Nouvelle. **Open** noon-2.30pm, 7pm-midnight Mon-Sat. *Concerts* 8pm & 9.30pm Mon-Sat. **Credit** AmEx, MC, V. **Map** p402 K4.
Music from across the Mediterranean and beyond in an intimate vaulted cellar, with a decent Turkish restaurant overhead. Before the concerts, other acts such as one-man shows take to the stage from 7.30pm.

Musée Guimet
6 pl d'Iéna, 16th (01.56.52.53.00, auditorium 01.40.73.88.18, www.guimet.fr). M° Iéna. **Open** 10am-6pm Mon, Wed-Sun. *Concerts* 8.30pm some Thur, Fri & Sat. **Credit** MC, V. **Map** p404 C5.

Essential Paris Albums

Sounds of the city.

AUX ARMES ET CÆTERA
SERGE GAINSBOURG
(1979)
Recorded in Kingston, Jamaica, and featuring vocals from the I-Threes, this era-defining classic shifted more than a million copies. The title track (a variation of *La Marseillaise*) was one of the first reggae songs to hit France and so polemical that the Parisian megastar received death threats.

SUPREME NTM
NTM (1998)
Essential listening from *banlieue* tough boys Nique Ta Mère (Mother Fuckers), made up of rappers Joey Starr (Didier Morville) and Kool Shen (Bruno Lopès). This controversial hip hop album influenced a generation with songs such as 'Seine Saint Denis Style', 'Back dans les Bacs' and the erotic dancehall-style 'Ma Benz'.

HYMNE A LA MOME
EDITH PIAF (2012)
Edith Piaf, who was born in Belleville, is still hailed by many as the greatest singer France has ever known. This newly released, digitally remastered box set of 45 of her most famous songs, including 'La Vie en Rose', 'L'Hymne à l'Amour' and 'Non, Je ne Regrette Rien', serves as a wonderful reminder of her raw talent.

THE NO COMPRENDO
LES RITA MITSOUKO
(1986)
Les Rita Mitsouko (guitarist Fred Chichin and singer Catherine Ringer) produced wacky electro pop with real musical substance and quirky text. Three tracks from the *No Comprendo* album – 'Andy', 'C'est Comme Ca' and 'Les Histoires d'a' – are still dancefloor staples today.

MY GOD IS BLUE
SEBASTIEN TELLIER
(2012)
Tellier's fourth album plies his trademark brand of cool, transgressive, electro-sexy pop. The bearded guru (who, bizarrely, sang for France in the 2008 Eurovision Song Contest), is the only Parisian who doles out serious electro music without taking himself too seriously.

MIDNIGHT IN PARIS
VARIOUS ARTISTS
(2011)
Woody Allen's *Midnight in Paris* is a love letter to a city and, like *Manhattan*, opens with an adoring montage, set to jazz, of the city by day and night. Cue this soundtrack, featuring the likes of Sidney Bechet and Josephine Baker, that added real soul to Allen's romantic ode to the capital.

ARTS & ENTERTAINMENT

La Bellevilloise. *See p294.*

Indian and Asian music by visiting troupes, as well as dance and theatre, takes pride of place in the auditorium of the Musée Guimet.

Satellit' Café
44 rue de la Folie-Méricourt, 11th (01.47.00.48.87, www.satellit-cafe.com). Mº Oberkampf, Parmentier or St-Ambroise. **Open** *Bar* 7pm-1am Tue-Thur; 7pm-6am Fri, Sat; 6pm-2am Sun. *Club* 11pm-6am Fri, Sat; 6pm-2am Sun. *Concerts* 8-11pm Wed-Sat. **Credit** *Bar* MC, V. **Map** p403 M5.
This bar lends its sound system to all things global, but the focus is on traditional African music mixed in with the occasional bit of Bollywood.

★ Théâtre de la Ville
2 pl du Châtelet, 4th (01.42.74.22.77, www. theatredelaville-paris.com). Mº Châtelet. **Open** *Box office* 11am-7pm Mon; 11am-8pm Tue-Sat. *By phone* 11am-7pm Mon-Sat. *Concerts* times vary. **Credit** MC, V. **Map** p408 J6.
Music and dance of the highest order can be found here, with jazz and music from just about anywhere you can think of (Iraq, Japan, Thailand, Brittany) amid the classical recitals.

Jazz & blues

Ateliers de Charonne
21 rue de Charonne, 11th (01.40.21.83.35, www.ateliercharonne.com). Mº Charonne or Ledru-Rollin. **Open** 8pm-1am daily. Concerts 9pm Mon-Sat; 7pm Sun. **Credit** MC, V. **Map** p407 M7.
This jazz club is the place in which to see the rising stars of gypsy jazz (*jazz manouche*). If you want to grab a good spot, reserve for dinner and the show.

Autour de Midi-Minuit
11 rue Lepic, 18th (01.55.79.16.48, www.autour demidi.fr). Mº Blanche. **Open** noon-2.30pm, 7pm-late Tue-Sat. *Concerts* 9.30pm Tue-Thur; 10pm Fri, Sat. **Credit** MC, V. **Map** p401 H2.
The Tuesday night *boeuf* (jam session) is always free, as are many other concerts – some by big names such as Laurent Epstein and Bruno Casties.

Le Baiser Salé
58 rue des Lombards, 1st (01.42.33.37.71, www.lebaisersale.com). Mº Châtelet. **Open** 5pm-6am daily. *Concerts* daily (times vary). **Credit** AmEx, DC, MC, V. **Map** p406 J6.
The 'Salty Kiss' divides its time between passing *chanson* merchants, world artists and jazzmen of every stripe, from trad to fusion.

★ Au Duc des Lombards
42 rue des Lombards, 1st (01.42.33.22.88, www.ducdeslombards.com). Mº Châtelet. **Open** 7pm-midnight Mon-Thur; 7pm-4am Fri, Sat. *Concerts* 8pm, 10pm Mon-Sat. **Credit** AmEx, MC, V. **Map** p406 J6.
This venerable jazz spot goes from strength to strength, attracting a high class of performer and a savvy crowd. Check out the '*bon plans*' section of the website, which offers reduced price tickets.

Lionel Hampton Jazz Club
Hôtel Méridien Etoile, 81 bd Gouvion-St-Cyr, 17th (01.40.68.30.42, www.jazzclub-paris.com). Mº Porte Maillot. **Open** 7am-1am Mon, Tue, Sun; 7am-1.30am Wed-Sat. *Concerts* 9.30pm-1.30am Wed-Sat; 12.30-3pm Sun. **Credit** AmEx, DC, MC, V. **Map** p400 B2.

This hotel venue has a strong US bias, with lots of R&B and gospel, but native acts get a look in as well.

★ New Morning
7-9 rue des Petites-Ecuries, 10th (01.45.23.51.41, www.newmorning.com). **Open** 8pm daily. *Concerts* times vary. **Credit** MC, V. **Map** p402 K3.
One of the best places in which to see the latest jazz exponents, with a policy that also embraces *chanson*, blues, world music and sophisticated pop.

Le Sunset/Le Sunside
60 rue des Lombards, 1st (01.40.26.46.60, www. sunset-sunside.com). Mᵒ Châtelet. **Open** 5pm-2am daily. *Concerts* times vary. **Credit** MC, V. **Map** p406 J6.
A split-personality venue, with Sunset dealing in electric groups and Sunside hosting acoustic performances. Their renown pulls in big jazz names from both sides of the Atlantic.

Théâtre du Châtelet
1 pl du Châtelet, 4th (01.40.28.28.40, www. chatelet-theatre.com). Mᵒ Châtelet. **Open** times vary. **Credit** AmEx, DC, MC, V. **Map** p406 J6.
This venerable theatre and classic music hall has another life as a jazz and *chanson* venue, with performances by top-notch international musicians.

LEFT BANK
Rock & pop

Batofar
Opposite 11 quai François-Mauriac, 13th (09.71.25.50.61, www.batofar.org). Mᵒ Bibliothèque François-Mitterrand or Quai de la Gare. **Open** times vary. **Credit** MC, V. **Map** p407 N10.
This enduringly hip party boat lays on DJs, rappers and assorted underground noise-merchants for the benefit of an up-for-it crowd. It comes into its own in the summer, when the terrace opens at 7pm.
▶ *For more on Batofar's club nights, see p287.*

Le Who's Bar
13 rue du Petit Pont, 5th (01.43.54.80.71, www.myspace.com/whosbar). Mᵒ St-Michel. **Open** 5pm-5am Mon-Thur; 5pm-6am Fri-Sun. *Concerts* 10.30pm-5am Fri, Sat. **Credit** MC, V. **Map** p408 J7.
With Picasso-style frescoes lining the walls and a nightly programme of live pop and rock, Le Who's is St-Michel's hippest music bar. Expect to hear live acoustics on weekdays and rock at weekends.

Chanson

Au Magique
42 rue de Gergovie, 14th (01.45.42.26.10, www.aumagique.com). Mᵒ Pernety. **Open** 8pm-2am Wed-Sun. *Concerts* 9pm. **No credit cards.** **Map** p405 F10.

Artiste-in-residence Marc Havet serenades punters with politically incorrect *chanson* at weekends; you can also expect poetry events and exhibitions of photos and paintings.

World & traditional

Institut du Monde Arabe (Auditorium Rafik Hariri)
1 rue des Fossés-St-Bernard, 5th (01.40.51.38.38, www.imarabe.org). Mᵒ Jussieu. **Open** 10am-6pm (8.30pm performance days) Tue-Sun. *Tickets* 10am-5pm Tue-Sun; 90mins before show. *Concerts* usually 8.30pm Fri, Sat. **Credit** MC, V. **Map** p409 K7.
This huge, plush auditorium attracts some of the biggest names in the world of Arab music.

Jazz & blues

Caveau de la Huchette
5 rue de la Huchette, 5th (01.43.26.65.05, www. caveaudelahuchette.fr). Mᵒ St-Michel. **Open** 9.30pm-2.30am Mon-Wed, Sun; 9.30pm-6am Thur-Sat. *Concerts* 10.15pm. **Credit** MC, V. **Map** p408 J7.
This medieval cellar has been a Paris mainstay for more than 60 years. Jazz shows are followed by early-hours performances in a swing, rock, soul or disco vein.

Caveau des Oubliettes
52 rue Galande, 5th (01.46.34.23.09, www.caveau desoubliettes.fr). Mᵒ St-Michel. **Open** 5pm-2am Mon, Tue, Sun; 5pm-4am Wed-Sat. *Concerts* 10pm Wed-Sun. **Credit** MC, V. **Map** p408 J7.
A foot-tapping frenzy echoes in this medieval dungeon, complete with instruments of torture, a guillotine and underground passages. Mondays are Pop Rock Jam nights with the JB Manis Trio, Tuesdays are Jazz Jam Boogaloo nights with Jeff Hoffman, and there are various other jam sessions during the rest of the week.

Le Petit Journal Montparnasse
113 rue du Commandant René-Mouchotte, 14th (01.43.21.56.70, www.petitjournalmontparnasse. com). Mᵒ Gaîté or Montparnasse-Bienvenüe. **Open** 7am-2am Mon-Sat. *Concerts* 9.30pm Mon-Thur; 10pm Fri, Sat. **Credit** MC, V. **Map** p405 F9.
A two-level jazz brasserie with New Orleans sound, big bands, Latin and soul-gospel.

Le Swan Bar
165 bd de Montparnasse, 6th (01.44.27.05.84, www.swanbar.fr). Mᵒ Raspail or Vavin. **Open** 7pm-1am Tue-Sat. *Concerts* 7.30pm & 9.30pm Tue-Sat. **Credit** MC, V. **Map** p405 H9.
The Swan Bar is a modern, American-style jazz bar for traditional jazz, torch songs and jamming. Occasional classical and tango concerts are thrown in for good measure.

ARTS & ENTERTAINMENT

Performing Arts

It's a full house, from big-name ballet to the banlieue fringe.

The big news in the world of classical music is the construction of Jean Nouvel's dramatic Philharmonie. The much-vaunted 2,400-seat concert hall is set to open in 2015 in Parc de la Villette and will finally give the city a world-class venue for the symphonic repertoire. In the meantime, historic venues such as Salle Pleyel and Palais Garnier provide a stunning setting for the city's rich calendar of opera and classical music performances, and with tickets starting at just €10 accessibility isn't restricted to the *haut monde*.

Accessibility issues of a different sort come into play with Paris's theatre scene. French-speaking drama buffs can choose from some 450 productions every week, from offbeat indie shows to highbrow classics at the grandiose Comédie Française, whereas Anglophones have to make do with a handful of international companies performing in their mother tongue.

Paris is home to a thriving dance scene, a rich programme of major international companies and plenty of home-grown talent. There's no shortage of ballet productions at the Théâtre du Châtelet and Palais Garnier, and the annual Festival d'Automne features an impressive line-up of innovative dance.

Check out the new Time Out Paris website (www.timeout.fr) for comprehensive cultural listings throughout the year.

Classical Music & Opera

The Théâtre des Champs-Elysées celebrates 100 years in the limelight with a host of big-name soloists and conductors appearing in 2013. The Opéra de Paris, meanwhile, splits its major productions between the bunker-like Bastille (*Falstaff*, *Carmen*) and the glorious Palais Garnier (*Hänsel und Gretel*). The main musical provider in summer is **Paris Quartier d'Eté** (01.44.94.98.00, www.quartierdete.com), with concerts in gardens across the city. The **Festival de Saint-Denis** (01.48.13.06.07, www.festival-saint-denis.com) offers top names in a spectacular setting, while the candlelit **Chopin Piano Festival** takes place in the Jardin de Bagatelle (www.frederic-chopin.com).

INFORMATION AND TICKETS

For comprehensive listings, see *L'Officiel des Spectacles* or *Pariscope*. Monthly *Diapason* also lists classical concerts, while *Opéra* magazine provides good coverage of all things vocal. Look out too for *Cadences* and *La Terrasse*, two free monthlies distributed outside concerts.

ORCHESTRAS & ENSEMBLES

★ Les Arts Florissants
01.43.87.98.88, www.arts-florissants.com.
William Christie's 'Arts Flo' remains France's leading Early Music group, and his conducting has become a benchmark of authentic performance. The group has not neglected passing on the secrets of Baroque ornamentation to the next generation, with the Jardin des Voix busy cultivating exciting young talent.

Ensemble Intercontemporain
01.44.84.44.50, www.ensembleinter.com.
Glamorous Finnish conductor Susanna Mälkki is the musical director of this bastion of contemporary music founded by, and still often conducted by, Pierre Boulez. The exacting standard of the 31 soloists is beyond reproach, and the ensemble has an enviable international reputation, making it one of the most popular on the Paris music scene.

Night at the Opera

Now the Palais Garnier has it all.

Under Gérard Mortier, ex-director of the Opéra de Paris, the opera split its activities between its two flagship monuments: Opéra Bastille for opera (see p302) for ballet. While it was (and still is) wonderful to see opera at Bastille, it did seem a shame that works by greats such as Wagner, Rossini and Mozart were only rarely performed in the Garnier's beautiful Italianate, belle époque theatre. From its ornate stage curtain and gilded statues to Chagall's ceiling and the vast crystal chandelier, the auditorium is one of the most beautiful in the world, and its red velvet boxes cry out for opera.

Since Nicolas Joël succeeded Mortier, and Swiss conductor Philippe Jordan arrived in 2009, opera has increasingly crept back into the Garnier's programme, with at least one major performance most months – highlights for 2013 include Handel's *Giulio Cesare*, which was first performed in 1724.

And now there's even more reason to make a night of it at the Garnier, since the building's first-ever restaurant opened in 2011. Set in the east wing, beneath the arcades that were once used for horse-drawn carriages, the Restaurant de l'Opéra serves food from 6pm to midnight, so you can dine in style before or after the show. The setting, designed by architect Odile Decq, is resolutely futuristic, with an organic, curvaceous structure that glides between the walls and ceiling without touching any of the original structure; even the windows undulate freely between the opera's pillars. The menu – think smoked salmon with sorbet mustard, pata negra pork served with courgette gratin and Opéra honey, and the classic Opéra *pâtisserie* for around €60 a head – is designed by Michelin-starred chef Christophe Aribert but overseen in the kitchen by Yann Tanneau, who previously worked at Mama Shelter.

Fans of the Garnier might also like to know that the building is set above an underground lake that inspired Gaston Leroux to write the *Phantom of the Opera* (now used by Paris's fire brigade for diving practice), and beehives on the roof supply the restaurant and boutique with honey.

ARTS & ENTERTAINMENT

Orchestre de Chambre de Paris

08.00.42.67.57, www.ensemble-orchestral-paris.com.
The orchestra has often struggled in recent years to find its specificity in a competitive field, but that is all hopefully set to improve after a change of name (Orchestre de Chambre de Paris) and leadership in 2012, which should help to give the group focus.

Orchestre Colonne

01.42.33.72.89, www.orchestrecolonne.fr.
Sometimes to be found at the Salle Gaveau (*see p303*), this orchestra – led by composer Laurent Petitgirard – has intelligent programming, with every concert teaming a contemporary work with more popular repertoire. The excellent series of *concerts éveil* continues to provide bargain tickets for parents and children, making an ideal introduction to classical music.

Orchestre Lamoureux

01.58.39.30.30, www.orchestrelamoureux.com.
This worthy orchestra, which made the first recording of Ravel's *Boléro*, remains woefully underfunded, and its concert appearances in the capital are sparse. But musical director Yutaka Sado is a fine conductor, and his programming is uncompromising and prepared to take on the challenge of new and unusual repertoire.

Orchestre National de France

01.56.40.15.16, www.radiofrance.fr.
Daniele Gatti is now firmly in charge of France's leading orchestra, bringing along his own brand of warm Italianate theatricality, in sharp contrast to his predecessor, veteran Kurt Masur, and his more structured Germanic approach.

★ Orchestre de Paris

01.42.56.13.13, www.orchestredeparis.com.
Many consider this orchestra to be the finest in France, and the arrival of Estonian-born Paavo Järvi as musical director in 2010 has done even more to boost its lofty reputation. Highlights for early 2013 include a performance of Chopin's *Piano Concerto No.2* by Nikolai Lugansky, and Leonidas Kavakos playing Sibelius in April.

Orchestre Pasdeloup

01.42.78.10.00, www.concertspasdeloup.com.
The Pasdeloup is the oldest orchestra in Paris, and the 2012/13 season features a great collection of concerts under the watchful eye of artistic director Patrice Fontanarosa.

Orchestre Philharmonique de Radio France

01.56.40.15.16, www.radiofrance.fr.
Myung-Whun Chung has been the musical director here for more than a decade. The standard of the orchestra is traditionally considered to lag behind that of the Orchestre National de France, but it has a dynamic programme and does plenty to try to attract younger audiences.

VENUES
Right Bank

Auditorium du Louvre

Entrance through Pyramid, Cour Napoléon, Musée du Louvre, rue de Rivoli, 1st (01.40.20.55.55, reservations 01.40.20.55.00, www.louvre.fr). M° Palais Royal Musée du Louvre. **Box office** 9am-5.30pm Mon, Wed-Fri. Closed July, Aug. **Admission** €5-€30. **Credit** MC, V. **Map** p401 H5.
The Auditorium du Louvre packs in a full season with chamber music, lunchtime concerts and music on film. The season is divided into themed groups, presenting artists performing a wide range of music, including a series of performances to coincide with the opening of the new Islamic Arts Galleries (*see p45* **Unseen Treasures**).

Châtelet – Théâtre Musical de Paris

1 pl du Châtelet, 1st (01.40.28.28.40, www. chatelet-theatre.com). M° Châtelet. **Box office** (17 av Victoria) 11am-7pm Mon-Sat; 1hr before performance Sun. *By phone* 10am-7pm Mon-Sat. Closed July, Aug. **Admission** €10-€118. **Credit** AmEx, DC, MC, V. **Map** p408 J6.
Jean-Luc Choplin has radically changed the programming of this bastion of Paris music-making. An attempt to rediscover the theatre's popular roots has seemingly been achieved at the expense of traditional fine music subscribers. However, the 2013 season has plenty of appeal, with performances by artists as diverse as pianist Julien Clerc and Israeli songstress Noa.

★ Cité de la Musique

221 av Jean-Jaurès, 19th (01.44.84.44.84, www. cite-musique.fr). M° Porte de Pantin. **Box office** noon-6pm Tue-Sat; 10am-6pm Sun. *By phone* 11am-7pm Mon-Fri. **Admission** €8-€41. **Credit** MC, V. **Map** p403 inset.
The energetic programming here features a vast non-classical repertoire that includes world music

---

INSIDE TRACK
CLASSICAL CUTS

Many venues and orchestras offer cut-rate tickets to students under 26 an hour before curtain-up. For the Fête de la Musique (21 June) all events are free, and year-round freebies crop up at the Maison de Radio France and the Conservatoire de Paris, as well as in certain churches.

ARTS & ENTERTAINMENT

Cité de la Musique. *See p301.*

and jazz. Concerts are frequently grouped into series with a pedagogic aim, tending to concentrate on the Baroque and the contemporary.
▶ *The Conservatoire (209 av Jean-Jaurès, 19th, 01.40.40.45.45) hosts world-class performers, and features many free concerts.*

IRCAM

1 pl Igor-Stravinsky, 4th (01.44.78.48.43, www.ircam.fr). M° Hôtel de Ville. **Map** p406 K6.
The underground bunker next to the Centre Pompidou, set up in 1969 by the avant-garde composer Pierre Boulez to create electronic microtonal music, is looking less redundant nowadays with a full programme of courses and conferences. Not many concerts take place in the building itself, but IRCAM sponsors concerts with a modernist theme across the city. See the website for concert venues, and details of courses.

Maison de Radio France

116 av du Président-Kennedy, 16th (01.56.40.15.16, www.radiofrance.fr). M° Passy/ RER Avenue du Pdt Kennedy. **Box office** 11am-6pm Mon-Sat. *By phone* 10am-6pm Mon-Sat. **Admission** €10-€85. **Credit** AmEx, DC, MC, V. **Map** p404 A7.
State-owned radio station France Musique broadcasts a broad range of classical concerts. The quality of music-making from the Orchestre National de France and the Orchestre Philharmonique de Radio France is impressive. *Photo p304.*

Opéra National de Paris, Bastille

Pl de la Bastille, 12th (08.92.89.90.90, from abroad 01.71.25.24.23, www.operadeparis.fr). M° Bastille. **Box office** (130 rue de Lyon, 12th) 2.30-6.30pm Mon-Sat. *By phone* 9am-6pm Mon-Fri; 9am-1pm Sat. **Admission** €5-€180. **Credit** AmEx, MC, V. **Map** p409 M7.
The Bastille is never going to be a beautiful building, and the unflattering acoustics and miles of corridors combine to create an atmosphere more akin to an airport than an opera house. But the standard of performance is what matters and the Bastille has some exciting evenings planned under director Nicolas Joel. The 2013 season brings to the stage great classics such as Verdi's *Falstaff*, Wagner's *Siegfried* and Bizet's *Carmen*.

★ Opéra National de Paris, Palais Garnier

Pl de l'Opéra, 9th (08.92.89.90.90, from abroad 01.71.25.24.23, www.operadeparis.fr). M° Opéra. **Box office** 11.30am-6.30pm Mon-Sat. *By phone* 9am-6pm Mon-Fri; 9am-1pm Sat. **Admission** €10-€180. **Credit** AmEx, MC, V. **Map** p401 G4.
The Palais Garnier, with its extravagant decor and ceiling by Marc Chagall, is the jewel in the crown of Paris music-making, as well as a glistening focal

ARTS & ENTERTAINMENT

point for the Right Bank. The Opéra National often favours the high-tech Bastille (*see p302*) for new productions, but the matchless acoustics of the Palais Garnier are superior to the newer Bastille's, and they will surely be shaken by a stunning production of Engelbert Humperdinck's *Hänsel und Gretel* in April 2013.

Péniche Opéra
Facing 46 quai de la Loire, 19th (01.53.35.07.77, www.penicheopera.com). M° Jaurès or Laumière. **Box office** *By phone* 10.30am-6pm Mon-Fri; 2-6pm Sat. **Admission** €12-€20. **Credit** MC, V. **Map** p401 M1.
The Péniche Opéra is an enterprising, barge-based company that produces chamber-scale shows and concerts, directed by the indefatigable Mireille Larroche. Programming ranges from Baroque rarities to contemporary creations via charming revue-style shows. This is one Paris institution that deserves to be kept afloat.

Salle Cortot
78 rue Cardinet, 17th (01.47.63.47.48, www.ecolenormalecortot.com). M° Malesherbes. **No box office. Admission** free-€30 (phone for details). **Map** 401 E2.
This intimate concert hall in the Ecole Normale de Musique has excellent acoustics for chamber music and master classes, which are often free of charge.

Salle Gaveau
45-47 rue de la Boétie, 8th (01.49.53.05.07, www.sallegaveau.com). M° Miromesnil. **Box office** 10am-6pm Mon-Fri & 30mins before performance. **Admission** €15-€75. **Credit** MC, V. **Map** p401 E3.
An ideal venue for chamber music, the Salle Gaveau seems to be passing through one of the least productive stages of its history. The top-quality chamber music that used to be the hall's core repertoire is a rarity. Too many variety shows and dark evenings make for sorry reading.

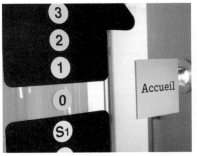

IRCAM.

ARTS & ENTERTAINMENT

Salle Pleyel

252 rue du Fbg-St-Honoré, 8th (01.42.56.13.13, www.sallepleyel.fr). M° Ternes. **Box office** noon-7pm Mon-Sat; 2hrs before show Sun. *By phone* 11am-7pm Mon-Sat; 11am-5pm Sun & 1hr before performance. **Admission** €10-€190. **Credit** MC, V. **Map** p400 D3.

Home to the Orchestre de Paris, the restored concert hall looks splendid. If the improved acoustics are only partially successful, the venue has nevertheless regained its status as the capital's leading concert hall for large-scale symphonic concerts, and should keep it until the completion of the city's new concert hall in 2015. The 2013 season includes appearances by the likes of Boris Berezovsky and Radu Lupu.

★ Théâtre des Bouffes du Nord

37bis bd de la Chapelle, 10th (01.46.07.34.50, www.bouffesdunord.com). M° La Chapelle. **Box office** 1-6pm Mon-Sat. **Admission** €5-€24. **Credit** MC, V. **Map** p402 K1.

This elegant theatre boasts one of the most imaginative programmes of chamber music in the capital. Adventurous programming for 2013 includes a concert by violinist Viktoria Mullova.

Théâtre des Champs-Elysées

15 av Montaigne, 8th (01.49.52.50.50, www.theatrechampselysees.fr). M° Alma Marceau. **Box office** noon-7pm Mon-Sat; 2hrs before show Sun. *By phone* 11am-6pm Mon-Fri; 2-6pm Sat. **Admission** €5-€160. **Credit** AmEx, MC, V. **Map** p400 D5.

This beautiful art nouveau theatre, with bas-reliefs by Bourdelle, celebrates its centenary in 2013, having hosted the scandalous première of Stravinsky's *Le Sacre du Printemps* in 1913. It remains the favourite venue for visiting foreign orchestras, and the prestigious line-up of visiting maestros includes Zubin Mehta and Esa-Pekka Salonen, as well as performances by Hélène Grimaud and Johan Bohta. Staged performances include a production of Mozart's *Don Giovanni* and Donizetti's *La Favorite.*

Théâtre National de l'Opéra Comique

Pl Boieldieu, 2nd (01.42.44.45.40, tickets 08.25.01.01.23, www.opera-comique.com). M° Richelieu Drouot. **Box office** 11am-7pm Mon-Sat; 11am-5pm Sun. **Admission** €5-€120. **Credit** MC, V. **Map** p402 H4.

Its promotion to national theatre status has brought this jewel box of a theatre back to life and the opening seasons, exploring a specifically French repertoire often ignored by the larger houses, have been welcomed with enthusiasm by press and public alike. The 2013 season includes Viardot's *Cendrillon* and Reynaldo Hahn's *Ciboulette.*

Théâtre de la Ville

2 pl du Châtelet, 4th (01.42.74.22.77, www.theatre-delaville-paris.com). M° Châtelet. **Box office** 11am-7pm Mon; 11am-8pm Tue-Sat. *By phone* 11am-7pm Mon-Sat. **Admission** €15-€30. **Credit** MC, V. **Map** p408 J6.

The programming in this concrete amphitheatre, hidden behind a classical façade, features hip chamber music outfits such as the Kronos and Takács Quartets and Early Music pioneer Fabio Biondi.

▶ *The season here spills over to performances at Les Abbesses (31 rue des Abbesses, 18th), which shares the same phone number and box office hours, but is closed on Mondays.*

Maison de Radio France. *See p302.*

Salle Pleyel.

Left Bank

Musée National du Moyen Age

6 pl Paul-Painlevé, 5th (01.53.73.78.16, www. musee-moyenage.fr). M° Cluny La Sorbonne.
Admission €12-€16; €10-€13 reductions.
Credit MC, V. **Map** p408 J7.
The museum presents a worthy programme of medieval concerts in which troubadours reflect the museum's collection. There are also occasional 45- minute *heures musicales* in a similar style.

Musée d'Orsay

62 rue de Lille, 7th (01.40.49.47.57, www.musee-orsay.fr). M° Solférino/RER Musée d'Orsay.
Admission €8-€35. **Credit** MC, V. **Map** p405 G6.
The museum runs a full series of lunchtime and evening concerts. The lunchtime concerts at 12.30pm concentrate on promising young artists. Evening concerts are more prestigious.

Dance

In 2013, the Théâtre de la Ville and Théâtre National de Chaillot will see new pieces by Ballet Lausanne and Rosas. There's no shortage of ballet productions at the Théâtre du Châtelet and Palais Garnier either, including *La Sylphide* choreographed by Pierre Lacotte, and the Festival d'Automne will again feature an impressive line-up of innovative dance. As the HQ for over 600 regional companies, the Centre National de la Danse in Pantin reaches out to its audience with well-devised performances, and smaller dance 'laboratories' such as Ménagerie de Verre and Regard du Cygne showcase new work by smaller companies.

INFORMATION AND RESOURCES

For listings, *see Pariscope* and *L'Officiel des Spectacles*. For events coverage, look out for two monthlies: *La Terrasse* (distributed free at major dance venues) and the glossy *Danser*. For shoes and equipment, **Sansha** (52 rue de Clichy, 9th, 01.45.26.01.38, www.sansha.com) has a good reputation, and **Repetto** (22 rue de la Paix, 2nd, 01.44.71.83.12, www.repetto.com) supplies the Opéra with pointes and slippers; **Menkes** (12 rue Rambuteau, 3rd, 01.40.27.91.81, www.menkes.es) sells serious flamenco gear as well as outsize glam-rock boots.

MAJOR VENUES

Centre National de la Danse

1 rue Victor-Hugo, 93507 Pantin (01.41.83.27.27, box office 01.41.83.98.98, www.cnd.fr). M° Hoche/RER Pantin.
Open *Box office* 10am-7pm Mon-Fri & performance days. **Admission** €10-€18.
Credit AmEx, MC, V.
This centre first opened its doors in 2004, with the mission to bridge the divide between stage and spectator. It invites audiences to its quarterly *'Grandes leçons de danse'*, contemporary dance master classes. It also offers an expertly curated selection of performances presented in the studios, exhibitions, and a phenomenal archive of films and choreographic material. *Photo p307.*

INSIDE TRACK RIVER DANCE

From May to September, the amphitheatres of the **Jardin Tino Rossi** (5th), a thin strip of green by the Seine, fill up with salsa, rock, tango, Irish, hip hop, traditional dance from Brittany and just about any other dance form you can think of. Informal classes are held from 7pm, then the *bal* begins, keeping everyone swaying until midnight.

Maison des Arts de Créteil

*Pl Salvador-Allende, 94000 Créteil (01.45.13.19.19,
www.maccreteil.com). M° Créteil-Préfecture.* **Open**
Box office 1-7pm Tue-Sat & show days. Closed mid
July-Aug. **Admission** €23-€35. **Credit** MC, V.
This suburban arts centre is a vibrant hub of artistic
creation, featuring an eclectic programme of theatre,
dance, music and digital art. Don't miss the
International Exit Festival of contemporary dance
(4-14 Apr 2013), which will feature Chris Haring's
Liquid Loft company.

★ Palais Garnier

*Pl de l'Opéra, 9th (08.92.89.90.90, from abroad
01.71.25.24.23, www.operadeparis.fr). M° Opéra.*
Open *Box office* 11.30am-6.30pm Mon-Sat.
Phone bookings 9am-6pm Mon-Fri; 9am-1pm Sat.
Closed 15 July-end Aug. **Admission** €10-€92
(ballet). **Credit** AmEx, MC, V. **Map** p401 G4.
The Ballet de l'Opéra National de Paris manages to
tread successfully between classics and new productions, at the Bastille and Palais Garnier. Highlights
in 2013 include Jiri Kylian's *Kaguyahimé* and Pierre
Lacotte's adaptation of *La Sylphide*.

Théâtre du Châtelet

*1 pl du Châtelet, 1st (01.40.28.28.40, www.
chatelet-theatre.com). M° Châtelet.* **Open**

Festivals Dance

What to see, when.

Faits d'Hiver (Jan, www.faitsdhiver.com)
and hip hop festival **Suresnes Cités
Danse** (Jan, www.theatre-suresnes.fr)
start the year off with a kick, followed
by **Rencontres Chorégraphiques de
Seine-St-Denis** (May, www.rencontres
choregraphiques.com) and **Onze Bouge**
(June, www.festivalonze.org). Founded
in 2005, **Les Etés de la Danse** (July,
www.lesetesdeladanse.com) puts the
spotlight on one or two companies or
choreographers, with three weeks of
performances. Shows are accompanied
by workshops. The ever-popular **Paris
Quartier d'Eté** festival (July-Aug, www.
quartierdete.com) features eclectic
programmes and plenty of free outdoor
performances in Paris and the suburbs.
For more than 40 years, the **Festival
d'Automne** (Sept-Dec, www.festival-
automne.com) has shown the way
forward in the performing arts. With a
focus on leading French experimental
companies, the festival also invites
big-name choreographers from around
the world to perform.

Box office 11am-7pm Mon-Sat & 1hr before show
Sun. **Admission** €16.50-€80.50. **Credit** AmEx,
MC, V. **Map** p402 J6.
This classical music institution is strengthening its
reputation in other live artistic disciplines. Merce
Cunningham's LA Dance Project will perform in May
2013. The theatre also plays host to the esteemed Etés
de la Danse festival.

Théâtre National de Chaillot

*1 pl du Trocadéro, 16th (01.53.65.30.00, www.
theatre-chaillot.fr). M° Trocadéro.* **Open** *Box office*
11am-7pm Mon-Sat. *Phone bookings* 11am-7pm
Mon-Sat. Closed 2wks Aug. **Admission** €15-€33.
Credit MC, V. **Map** p400 C5.
Chaillot's three auditoriums range from cosy and
experimental to a vast 2,800-seater amphitheatre.
The 2013 programme sees the long-awaited return
of Béjart Ballet Lausanne with *Light*.

★ Théâtre de la Ville

*2 pl du Châtelet, 4th (01.42.74.22.77, www.
theatredelaville-paris.com). M° Châtelet.* **Box
office** 11am-7pm Mon; 11am-8pm Tue-Sat.
By phone 11am-7pm Mon-Sat. **Admission**
€20-€35. **Credit** MC, V. **Map** p406 J6.
This leading venue has nurtured collaborations with
international choreographers. The 2013 programme
includes Anne Teresa de Keersmaeker's Rosas company performing *Drumming Live*.
▶ *Some performances take place at sister venue
Théâtre des Abbesses (31 rue des Abbesses, 18th).*

FRINGE VENUES

L'Etoile du Nord

*16 rue Georgette-Agutte, 18th (01.42.26.47.47,
www.etoiledunord-theatre.com). M° Guy Môquet.*
Open *Box office* 1hr before performance. Closed
July, Aug. **Admission** €14. **Credit** V.
This smaller venue splits its programme between
theatre and contemporary multimedia dance. The
Avis de Turbulences festival (Sept-Oct) features a
decent selection of mixed bills.

Ménagerie de Verre

*12-14 rue Léchevin, 11th (01.43.38.33.44, www.
menagerie-de-verre.org). M° Parmentier.* **Open** *Box
office* 1hr before performance. *Phone bookings*
10am-6pm Mon-Fri. Closed July, Aug. **Admission**
€15. **No credit cards**. **Map** p403 N5.
This multidisciplinary hothouse is rooted in the
avant-garde, with contemporary dance and classes
given by a succession of guest teachers.

★ Le Regard du Cygne

*210 rue de Belleville, 20th (01.43.58.55.93,
bookings 09.71.34.23.50, www.leregarducygne.
com). M° Télégraphe.* **Open** *Box office* 1hr before
show. Closed Aug. **Admission** free-€15.
No credit cards. **Map** p403 Q3.

Centre National de la Danse. *See p305.*

This pared-down studio in Belleville is a great place to get a taste of the alternative dance scene.
▶ *The Spectacles Sauvages nights allow unknowns to show a ten-minute piece to the public, while the Rencontres focus on the work of a particular artist and are open to all, free of charge.*

Théâtre de la Bastille
76 rue de la Roquette, 11th (01.43.57.42.14, www.theatre-bastille.com). M° Bastille or Voltaire. **Open** *Box office* 10am-6pm Mon-Fri; 2-6pm Sat. Closed July, Aug. **Admission** €24-€27. **Credit** MC, V. **Map** p407 M6.
This small theatre showcases innovative contemporary dance and drama pieces. Worth checking out in April 2013 is *Bal en Chine* by Caterina Sagna.

DANCE CLASSES

Centre de Danse du Marais
41 rue du Temple, 4th (01.42.77.58.19, www. parisdanse.com). M° Hôtel de Ville or Rambuteau. **Open** 9am-9pm Mon-Fri; 9am-8pm Sat; 9am-7pm Sun. **Classes** €18. **Map** p402 K5.
There's a huge choice of classes here, with big-name teachers such as belly dance star Leila Haddad and ballet's Casati-Lazzarelli team.
▶ *The five-class 'sampler' pass is a good deal at €74.*

★ Studio Harmonic
5 passage des Taillandiers, 11th (01.48.07.13.30, www.studioharmonic.fr). M° Bastille. **Open** *Office* 10am-5pm Mon-Fri. *Classes* 9.30am-10pm Mon-Fri; 9am-7.30pm Sat. Closed 3wks Aug. **Classes** €16. **Map** p407 M7.
The rising star among Paris's top dance schools. Studio Harmonic's claim to fame is the trademark Ragga Jam class – created by Laure Courtellemont – which combines ragga, dancehall, African dance and hip hop.

Theatre

The last year has been a tumultuous one for some of Paris's most prestigious theatres, with a strike over pay and the temporary closure of the main auditorium at the Comédie Française, and riot police called in to protect the Théâtre du Rond Point after a wave of Catholic protests against its staging of Rodrigo Garcia's play *Golgota Picnic*. Fortunately, though, 2013 looks set to be calmer, with a season marked by trusty old regulars such as Molière and Feydeau, major big-name foreign musical productions, plus a flood of innovative international and home-grown performances.

TICKETS AND INFORMATION
For weekly listings check out *L'Officiel des Spectacles* and *Pariscope* (available from news kiosks). Tickets can be bought at the theatres, from **Fnac** or **Virgin Megastore** (for both, *see p225*) or online at www.theatreonline.com. Check out www.theatresprives.com for half-price tickets to performances during the first week of a new show.

VENUES
Right Bank

Cartoucherie de Vincennes
Route du Champ de Manoeuvre, Bois de Vincennes, 12th. M° Château de Vincennes, then shuttle bus.
Théâtre de l'Aquarium *(01.43.74.72.74, www.theatredelaquarium.com).*
Théâtre du Chaudron *(01.43.28.97.04, www.theatreduchaudron.fr).*
Théâtre de l'Epée de Bois *(01.48.08.39.74, www.epeedebois.com).*

Théâtre du Soleil *(01.43.74.24.08,*
www.theatre-du-soleil.fr).
Théâtre de la Tempête *(01.43.28.36.36,*
www.la-tempete.fr).
Past the Château de Vincennes in the middle of the
woods, five independent theatres offer up a first-
class selection of politically committed fare. The
most famous outfit is Ariane Mnouchkine's avant-
garde Théâtre du Soleil, which first transformed
these ex-army munitions warehouses into perfo-
mance spaces back in 1970.

★ Comédie Française
All *www.comedie-francaise.fr.*
Salle Richelieu *2 rue Richelieu, 1st*
(08.25.10.16.80). M° Palais Royal Musée du
Louvre. **Box office** 11am-6pm daily. **Admission**
€12-€39. *1hr before show* €5 for cheapest seats
only. **Credit** AmEx, MC, V. **Map** p401 H5.
Studio-Théâtre *Galerie du Carrousel du Louvre,*
99 rue de Rivoli, 1st (01.44.58.98.58). M° Palais
Royal Musée du Louvre. **Box office** 2-5pm
Wed-Sun. **Admission** €18. **Credit** MC, V.
Map p401 H5.
Théâtre du Vieux Colombier *21 rue du Vieux*
Colombier, 6th (01.44.39.87.00). M° St-Sulpice.
Box office 11am-6pm Mon-Sat. **Admission** €29.
Credit MC, V. **Map** p405 G7.
The gilded mother of French theatres, the Comédie
Française turns out season after season of classics,
as well as lofty new productions. The red velvet and
gold-flecked Salle Richelieu is located right by the

ARTS & ENTERTAINMENT

Behind the Lines

Who's who in French theatre.

From dark medieval plays to 17th-century
tragicomedies and 20th-century absurdist
theatre, the French have always known
how to pack a punch with new acting styles
and popular dramatic movements. Titles
such as *Tartuffe*, *Le Cid* and *La Cantatrice
Chauve* are well known; here we round up
the creative talents behind them.

MOLIERE (1622-1673)
As the Sun King's official playwright
and founder of the Comédie Française,
Jean-Baptiste Poquelin (Molière) created
powerful stories able to veer between farce
and dark drama. He is associated with
alexandrine, the 12-syllable-per-line metre
that characterised much of 17th-century
French theatre. Among Molière's best-
known works are his comedies *L'Ecole
des Femmes*, *Le Misanthrope*, *Tartuffe*
and *Le Malade Imaginaire*.

PIERRE CORNEILLE (1606-1684)
Along with Molière and Racine, Corneille
was one of France's great dramatists.
Hailed as the 'founder of French tragedy',
he turned out plays for over 40 years,
including the world-famous *Le Cid* (based
on Guillén de Castro's *Las Mocedades del
Cid*) – a tale of love, loss and war.

JEAN RACINE (1639-1699)
Racine was educated by Jansenist monks,
and his works are heavily influenced by
Greek and Latin classics. Molière produced
his second play, *La Thébaïde*, and his
third, *Andromaque*, but Racine didn't enjoy
the latter production and gave the text to

the rival company at the Hôtel de
Bourgogne. There he produced a string of
successful tragedies, such as *Britannicus*,
which chronicles the story of Agrippina
and her son Nero, and *Phèdre*, based on
Euripides' *Hippolytus*, an exploration of
a woman's passion for her stepson.

PIERRE DE MARIVAUX (1688-1763)
Marivaux's contribution to 18th-century
French theatre was so great that the deft
and witty bantering of his dialogues were
given their own term, *marivaudage* (verbal
preciousness). He wrote numerous
comedies for the Comédie Française,
including *La Surprise de l'Amour* and
Les Fausses Confidences.

GEORGES FEYDEAU (1862-1921)
During his lifetime, Feydeau was frequently
dismissed as a light entertainer. Now, he is
considered to be one of the belle époque's
greatest playwrights, and a precursor of
surrealist and Dadaist theatre. His legacy
of lively farces includes *La Dame de chez
Maxim*, *L'Hôtel du Libre Echange* and
Hortense a dit: 'Je m'en fous!'.

EUGENE IONESCO (1909-1994)
French-Romanian Ionesco is known for
his absurdist pieces, his most famous
being *La Cantatrice Chauve* (still played
in the Théâtre de la Huchette; *see p310*).
Ionesco's plays are famed for their
characters caught in hopeless situations
and forced to do repetitive or meaningless
actions, with plenty of clichéd play on
words and nonsense dialogue.

Palais-Royal. It's closed for renovations until early 2013 and a temporary theatre (Théâtre Ephémère) has been constructed in wood in a courtyard of the Palais-Royal. Under the same management are the Studio-Théâtre, a black box inside the Carrousel du Louvre, and the Théâtre du Vieux Colombier. The line-up for 2013 includes plenty of Molière, plus productions of *Phèdre* and *Cyrano de Bergerac*.

★ Théâtre des Bouffes du Nord

37bis bd de la Chapelle, 10th (01.46.07.34.50, www.bouffesdunord.com). M° La Chapelle. **Box office** 1-6pm Mon-Sat. **Admission** €18-€35; €14-€28 reductions. **Credit** MC, V. **Map** p402 K2.
Peter Brook's former playground treats us to an adaptation of Michael Ondaatje's *The Collected Works of Billy the Kid* in 2013.
▶ *The Bouffes du Nord also has one of the best chamber music programmes in the capital.*

Théâtre du Châtelet

1 pl du Châtelet, 1st (01.40.28.28.40, www.chatelet-theatre.com). M° Châtelet. **Box office** 11am-7pm Mon-Sat; 1hr before show Sun. **Admission** €28.50-€100.50. **Credit** AmEx, DC, MC, V. **Map** p408 J6.
The Châtelet is fast becoming Paris's main venue for musicals hailing from Broadway and the West End – such as *West Side Story* and *Carousel* – which are usually performed in the original language by visiting companies. It's the only venue in Paris to offer such quality musical theatre.

Théâtre de la Madeleine

19 rue de Surène, 8th (01.42.65.07.09, www. theatremadeleine.com). M° Madeleine. **Box office**

11am-7pm Mon-Sat. **Admission** €17-€54. **Credit** MC, V. **Map** p401 F4.
The theatre where Sacha Guitry composed 24 of his plays, between 1932 and 1940, continues to contribute to France's repertoire with top-notch creations by emerging and established artists. After Samuel Beckett's *Oh Les Beaux Jours* (*Happy Days*), Ben Jonson's *Volpone* took to the stage in late 2012.

Théâtre Marigny

Av de Marigny, 8th (08.92.22.23.33, www.theatre marigny.fr). M° Champs-Elysées Clemenceau or Franklin D. Roosevelt. **Box office** 11am-6.30pm Mon-Sat. **Admission** €25-€79. **Credit** MC, V. **Map** p401 E4.
Théâtre Marigny is one of the most expensive nights out for theatregoers in Paris. But then not many other theatres can boast so much: a location off the Champs-Elysées; a deluxe interior conceived by Charles Garnier (of Opéra fame); high-profile casts and an illustrious pedigree stretching back more than 150 years. Productions in 2012 included *Le Bonheur* starring Marie-Anne Chazel.

ARTS & ENTERTAINMENT

Théâtre des Bouffes du Nord.

Théâtre National de Chaillot

*1 pl du Trocadéro, 16th (01.53.65.30.00,
www.theatre-chaillot.fr). M° Trocadéro.* **Box
office** 11am-7pm Mon-Sat. **Admission** €20-€33;
€15-€25 reductions. **Credit** MC, V. **Map** p400 B4.
Get here early, grab a cocktail and gaze in awe at the
Eiffel Tower through the lobby window. Chaillot's
three auditoriums range from cosy and experimental
to a 2,800-seater amphitheatre. Highlights in 2012
included David Bobee's exciting adaptation of
Romeo and Juliet, complete with acrobats.

Théâtre du Rond Point

*2bis av Franklin D. Roosevelt, 8th (01.44.95.98.21,
www.theatredurondpoint.fr). M° Champs-Elysées
Clemenceau or Franklin D. Roosevelt.* **Box office**
noon-7pm Tue-Sat; noon-4pm Sun (performance
days). **Admission** €28-€36; €15 under-30s; €26
over-60s. **Credit** MC, V. **Map** p401 E4.
More than just a theatre, this historic venue multitasks as a bookshop, tearoom and restaurant. So
once you've fed your mind on contemporary, avant-
garde and sometimes politically slanted theatre,
make a night of it and opt for dinner as well.

★ Théâtre de la Ville & Théâtre des Abbesses

*01.42.74.22.77, www.theatredelaville-paris.
com.* **Admission** €16-€35; €8-€26 reductions.
Credit MC, V.
Théâtre de la Ville *2 pl du Châtelet, 4th.
M° Châtelet.* **Box office** 11am-7pm Mon;
11am-8pm Tue-Sat. **Map** p406 J6.

Théâtre National de Chaillot.

Théâtre des Abbesses

*31 rue des Abbesses,
18th. M° Abbesses.* **Box office** 5-8pm Tue-Sat.
Map p402 H1.
At its two sites, the 'City Theatre' turns out the
most consistently innovative programming in Paris.
Instead of running a standard rep company, the
house imports music, dance and theatre productions.
Highlights for 2013 include Compagnie 1927's *The
Animals and Children Took to the Streets* at Théâtre
des Abbesses.

Left Bank

Le Lucernaire

*53 rue Notre-Dame-des-Champs, 6th
(01.42.22.26.50, www.lucernaire.fr). M° Notre-
Dame-des-Champs or Vavin.* **Box office** 11am-
12.30pm, 1.30-10pm Mon-Thur; 11am-12.30pm,
1.30-11pm Fri; 1.30-11pm Sat; 1.30-10pm Sun.
Admission €25-€30; €15-€25 reductions.
Credit MC, V. **Map** p401 F4.
Three theatres, three cinemas, a restaurant and a bar
make up this versatile cultural centre. Theatre-wise,
Molière and other classic playwrights get a good
thrashing, but so do up-and-coming authors.

★ Odéon, Théâtre de L'Europe

*Pl de l'Odéon, 6th (01.44.85.40.00, bookings
01.44.85.40.40, www.theatre-odeon.fr). M° Odéon.*
Box office 11am-6pm Mon-Sat. **Admission**
€12-€34; €6-€20 reductions. **Credit** MC, V.
Map p408 H7.
Highlights for 2013 include Samuel Beckett's *Fin
de Partie (Endgame)* and Molière's *Misanthrope*.
The theatre also plays host to the Impatience festival
for young theatre companies in May.

Théâtre de la Cité Internationale

*17 bd Jourdan, 14th (01.43.13.50.50,
www.theatredelacite.com). RER Cité Universitaire.*
Box office 1hr before show. *By phone* 1-7pm
Mon-Fri; 2-7pm Sat. **Admission** €22; €7-€16
reductions. **Credit** MC, V.
A polished, professional theatre based on the
campus of the Cité Universitaire, the Théâtre de la
Cité displays an international flair worthy of its
setting. In addition to the main theatre and dance
season, the prestigious Ecole du Théâtre National
de Strasbourg occupies the stage for a short stint
each summer.

Théâtre de la Huchette

*23 rue de la Huchette, 5th (01.43.26.38.99, www.
theatre-huchette.com). M° Cluny La Sorbonne
or St-Michel.* **Box office** 5-10.30pm Mon-Fri;
3.30-9pm Sat. **Admission** €23; €16 reductions.
Double bill ticket €35; €25 reductions. **Credit**
MC, V. **Map** p408 J7.
Ionesco's absurdist classic *La Cantatrice Chauve*
(The Bald Soprano) has been playing here since
1957, running on a double bill with his *La Leçon*.

Théâtre de la Huchette.

Beyond the Périphérique

Culture doesn't end at the city ring road. A combination of measures designed to bring theatre to the masses and extortionate rental rates for productions inside Paris has led to the creation of several excellent out-of-town venues.

In the north-east, **MC93 Bobigny** (1 bd Lénine, 93000 Bobigny, 01.41.60.72.72, www.mc93.com) is a slick institution dedicated to promoting global cross-cultural exchange with visiting companies from across France and abroad – Howard Barker's *Judith* is getting an airing in 2013. The **Théâtre Gérard-Philipe** (59 bd Jules-Guesde, 93200 St-Denis, 01.48.13.70.00, www.theatregerardphilipe.com), run by Christophe Rauck, offers consistently good fare of an experimental nature, including the Et Moi Alors? festival for youngsters.

Just beyond La Défense's towers, the **Théâtre Nanterre Amandiers** (7 av Pablo Picasso, 92022 Nanterre, 01.46.14.70.00, www.nanterre-amandiers.com, shuttle bus from RER Nanterre-Préfécture 1hr before show) provides an eclectic mix of probing modern theatre (often of a sticky political nature), as well as the great classics and occasional opera. And the **Théâtre d'Ivry Antoine Vitez** (1 rue Simon Dereure, 94200 Ivry, 01.43.90.11.11, www.theatre-quartiers-ivry.com) has a theatre, dance studio and auditorium, where an interesting mix of classics and contemporary works are performed.

ALTERNATIVE THEATRE

The bastion of alternative theatre in the north is the **Lavoir Moderne Parisien** (35 rue Léon, 18th, 01.42.52.09.14, www.rueleon.net), a converted washhouse where shows often tackle themes of immigration and identity. The **Point Ephémère** and its gargantuan older brother **Mains d'Oeuvres** (for both, *see p284*) are cool urban arts centres (in former warehouses) that stage multidisciplinary performances. **Confluences** (190 bd de Charonne, 20th, 01.40.24.16.46, http://confluences.jimdo.com) is an all-in-one cultural centre – also housed in an old warehouse – equipped with an art gallery, theatre and projection room; and **Les Laboratoires d'Aubervilliers** (41 rue Lécuyer, 93300 Aubervilliers, 01.53.56.15.90, www.leslaboratoires.org) churns out some wonderful, conceptualist productions that frequently mix and match acting with the various disciplines of other resident artists (video, sound, dance). **Le Tarmac** (159 av Gambetta, 20th, http://letarmac.fr) houses the TILF (Théâtre International de Langue Française), the only theatre in France dedicated to the Francophone world, welcoming texts and visiting troupes from as far afield as Martinique, Burkina Faso and Réunion.

Sport & Fitness

Soak up the Six Nations or swim in a Seine-side pool.

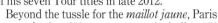

While the focus of 2012's calendar may have been all about what was taking place on the other side of La Manche, the eyes of the sporting world will be back on France in 2013 as the world's biggest bike race sets off on its centennial slog around France. Novelties abound, with a Brit defending the title for the first time, a new start in Corsica and an evening finish on the Champs-Elysées, but the murky past will inevitably overshadow the whole event, with Lance Armstrong stripped of his seven Tour titles in late 2012.

Beyond the tussle for the *maillot jaune*, Paris hosts a further 600 sports events, including 170 at national or international level. Its 366 sports complexes include 32 stadiums, 38 swimming pools and 43 tennis centres. These municipal facilities offer generously subsidised tariffs, while world-class professional venues enjoy heavy investment. Current projects include a planned revamp for Stade Roland Garros, home to the French tennis open, a major expansion of rugby's Stade Jean-Bouin, and the reopening of the legendary art deco swimming pool, the Piscine Molitor.

SPECTATOR SPORTS

The national stadium is the 80,000-capacity **Stade de France** (*see p264*), served by stations on the RER B (La Plaine Stade de France) and RER D (Stade de France St-Denis) lines just one stop from the Gare du Nord. It was built for the 1998 football World Cup and staged the final, in which France beat Brazil 3-0 to claim the title for the first time. As well as hosting top football matches, it hosts home legs for rugby's Six Nations and athletics meetings.

Indoor events, including judo, basketball, handball and tennis, take place at the **Palais Omnisports de Paris-Bercy** (8 bd de Bercy, 12th, 08.92.39.01.00, www.popb.fr, Mº Bercy). The **Stade Roland Garros** (Porte des Mousquetaires, 2 av Gordon-Bennett, 16th, 01.47.43.48.00, www.fft.fr/rolandgarros, Mº Porte d'Auteuil) stages the French tennis open; the **Parc des Princes**, home of Paris St-Germain football club, also hosts rugby and other sporting events.

The three-week **Tour de France** (www. letour.fr) is still a national obsession, and huge crowds flock to the Champs-Elysées every July to welcome the riders home. The 2012 race was won by Bradley Wiggins, the first British winner, with fellow Brit and Sky team-mate Chris Froome in second place. For details of the Tour de France and all the country's other major sporting events, *see pp26-31* **Diary**.

Tickets for many sports are sold online at www.ticketnet.fr, and at branches of **Fnac** and **Virgin Megastore** (for both, *see p225*). For football and rugby internationals held at the Stade de France, contact the respective national associations (www.fff.fr, www.ffr.fr). The influential daily newspaper *L'Equipe* offers excellent press coverage (in French) of all major sports events.

Basketball

Paris-Levallois Basket

Stade Coubertin, 82 av Georges-Lafont, 16th (01.45.27.79.12, www.parislevallois.com). Mº Porte de St-Cloud. **Tickets** from €8. **Credit** MC, V. *Palais des Sports Marcel-Cerdan, 141 rue Danton, 92300 Levallois (01.46.17.06.30, www.parislevallois.com). Mº Pont de Levallois.* **Tickets** from €8. **Credit** MC, V.

PL was born in 2007 following the merger of the region's two biggest clubs, Paris Basket Racing and Levallois Sporting Club Basket. The plan to create a superpower fell flat when the club was relegated to the Pro B league (second division) in its first season, but it has since climbed back into Pro A. Games are played at the Paris and Levallois sites.

Football

Paris St-Germain

Stadium *Parc des Princes, 24 rue du Commandant-Guilbaud, 16th (01.47.43.71.71, tickets & information 32.75, www.psg.fr). M° Porte de St-Cloud.* **Tickets** €25-€100. **Credit** MC, V.
Shops *27 av des Champs-Elysées, 8th (01.56.69.22.22). M° Franklin D. Roosevelt.* **Open** 10am-10pm Mon-Sat; 10am-8pm Sun. **Credit** AmEx, MC, V. *Parc des Princes (01.47.43.72.91).* **Open** 10am-7pm Mon-Sat & 2hrs after game on match days. **Credit** AmEx, MC, V.
A group of donors set up PSG by amalgamating local clubs in 1970. During the 1980s and '90s, the club won silverware aplenty, but its star faded after that. However, things are looking up again, and the team managed a second place finish behind Montpellier in Ligue 1 in 2012.
▶ *For tickets, book online and pick them up from any branch of Fnac (see p225).*

Horse racing

The full racing schedule, the *Calendrier des Courses*, is published by *France Galop* (www.france-galop.com). For information on trotting, France's most popular form of racing, consult www.cheval-francais.com. Tickets are €1.50-€8 (free for under-18s).

Hippodrome d'Auteuil

Route des Lacs, 16th (01.40.71.47.47).
M° Porte d'Auteuil.
See p318 **Day at the Races**.

THE BIGGEST
SPORTING EVENTS IN 2013

16 March Six Nations France vs Scotland at Stade de France. *See p26.*
9 June Men's final day at the French Tennis Open at Roland Garros. *See p28.*
21 July Tour de France final stage. *See p29.*

★ Hippodrome de Chantilly

16 av du Général-Leclerc, 60500 Chantilly (03.44.62.44.00). Train from Gare du Nord.
See p318 **Day at the Races**.

Hippodrome d'Enghien

Pl André-Foulon, 95230 Soissy-sous-Montmorency (01.34.17.87.00). Train from Gare du Nord.
Steeplechasing and floodlit trotting at this course 18km (11 miles) north of Paris.

★ Hippodrome de Longchamp

Rte des Tribunes, 16th (01.44.30.75.00).
M° Porte d'Auteuil then free bus.
See p318 **Day at the Races**.

Hippodrome de Maisons-Laffitte

1 av de la Pelouse, 78602 Maisons-Laffitte (01.39.12.81.70). RER Maisons-Laffitte then bus.
Flat racing.

Hippodrome de Paris-Vincennes

2 route de la Ferme, 12th (01.49.77.14.70).
M° Château de Vincennes/RER Joinville-le-Pont then free bus.
See p318 **Day at the Races**.

ARTS & ENTERTAINMENT

Stade de France.

Sport & Fitness

Hippodrome de St-Cloud
*1 rue du Camp Canadien, 92210 St-Cloud
(01.47.71.69.26). RER Rueil-Malmaison.*
Flat racing.

Rugby

★ Stade Français Paris
*Stade Jean-Bouin, 26 av du Général-Sarrail,
16th (01.46.51.55.40, www.stade.fr). M° Porte
d'Auteuil.* **Tickets** €5-€65. **Credit** AmEx, MC, V.
Stade Français are one of the top teams in France.
Note that the stadium was undergoing major work
in 2012, and home matches were being played at
Stade Charléty.

ACTIVITIES & TEAM SPORTS

The Mairie manages many of the facilities
across the capital, ensuring very reasonable
entry prices. For details, consult its free annual
Parisports: Guide du Sport à Paris or view the
online version at www.sport.paris.fr. If you're
looking for sportswear and equipment, head for
the excellent **Décathlon** (www.decathlon.fr)
or **Go Sport** (www.go-sport.com) chain stores.
   Some venues require proof of health
insurance, ID and passport-sized photos for
membership. Note that joining a club or taking
part in a competitive event (even a fun run)
usually requires a medical certificate.

All-round sports clubs

The **Standard Athletic Club** (rte Forestière
du Pavé de Meudon, 92360 Meudon-la-Forêt,
01.46.26.16.09, www.saclub.org) is a private
sports club. Full membership costs €985 per
year. There are tennis and squash courts, a
heated outdoor pool and workout facilities.
   Local multi-sports clubs include **Lagardère
Paris Racing** (01.45.67.55.86, www.lagardere
parisracing.com), **ASPTT de Paris**
(01.58.14.21,80, www.aspttparis.com),
Paris Université Club (01.44.16.62.62,
www.puc.asso.fr) and **Stade Français**
(01.40.71.33.45, www.stadefrancais.com).

American football

There are about 15 teams in the suburbs, plus
'no-tackle' flag football teams for men and
women, and cheerleader squads. Contact the
**Fédération Française de Football
Américain** (01.43.11.14.70, www.fffa.org).

Athletics & running

Paris has plenty of municipal tracks; for details
pick up the *Guide du Sport (see above)*. Joggers
use the banks of the Seine and the parks (Jardin

MurMur

du Luxembourg, Tuileries and Parc de la
Villette), as well as the Bois de Boulogne and
Bois de Vincennes. The Paris Marathon takes
place in April (*see pp26-31* **Diary**). The **Hash
House Harriers** organise weekly runs. Log
on to http://parishhh.free.fr for details.

Baseball, softball & cricket

Most teams practise in the Bois de Vincennes.
The **Fédération Française de Baseball,
Softball et Cricket** (01.44.68.89.30, www.ffbsc.
org) has details. An expat runs the **Château de
Thoiry Cricket Club** (78770 Thoiry, www.
thoirycricket.fr), 40km (25 miles) from Paris.
Paris University Club (01.44.16.62.62, www.
pucbaseball.com) has baseball teams for all ages.

Basketball

Free practice courts are dotted around the city's
parks and gardens, while almost every municipal
sports centre has a club. Contact the **Fédération
Française de Basketball** (01.53.94.25.00,
www.basketfrance.com) for details.

Boules, pool & bowling

Boules or *pétanque* pitches are scattered all over
Paris. Contact the **Fédération Française de
Pétanque** (04.91.14.05.80, www.ffpjp.info).
Some pool venues require ID or a passport.

Bowling Mouffetard
*73 rue Mouffetard, 5th (01.43.31.09.35,
www.bowlingmouffetard.fr). M° Place Monge.*
Open 3pm-2am Mon-Fri; 10am-2am Sat, Sun.
Admission €3.50-€6.70 per set. *Shoe hire* €2.
Credit MC, V. **Map** p406 K9.
Central venue with eight lanes and pool tables.

ARTS & ENTERTAINMENT

Cercle Clichy Montmartre

84 rue de Clichy, 9th (01.48.78.32.85, www. cerclecm.com). M° Place de Clichy. **Open** 1pm-6am daily. **Admission** *Pool* from €12/hr. *Billiards* from €12/hr. **Credit** (€25 min) MC, V. **Map** p401 G2.
Historic venue with pool tables aplenty. No under-18s are allowed.

Climbing

To use any municipal climbing wall, you will need to obtain a personal ID card. Take a photo, your passport, proof of valid insurance and the fee (€4 per month) to the centre you want to use. For the real thing, try the superb boulder formations in the Forêt de Fontainebleau; **Grimporama** (www.grimporama.com) has full details, including maps, on its website. The **Club Alpin du pays de Fontainebleau** (01.64.22.67.18, http://caf77.free.fr) organises group climbs and weekend outings.

Centre Sportif Poissonnier

2 rue Jean-Cocteau, 18th (01.42.51.24.68). M° Porte de Clignancourt. **Open** 6am-8pm Mon-Fri; 8am-9.30pm Sat; 8am-5pm Sun. **Admission** free. **No credit cards**.
This sports centre is home to the largest of the six municipal walls in Paris.

★ MurMur

55 rue Cartier-Bresson, 93500 Pantin (01.48.46.11.00, www.murmur.fr). M° Aubervilliers–Pantin Quatre Chemins. **Open** 9.30am-11pm Mon-Fri; 9.30am-6.30pm Sat, Sun. **Admission** €9-€20; €4-€7.50 reductions. *Joining fee* €20. **Credit** AmEx, MC, V.
One of Europe's best climbing walls, with 1,550sq m (16,000sq ft) of wall.

Cycling

City cycling is growing in popularity, thanks to Mayor Delanoë's expansion of bike lanes and the Vélib initiative. The **Fédération Française de Cyclisme** (01.49.35.69.00, www.ffc.fr) has details of the many local cycle clubs. The **Stade Vélodrome Jacques-Anquetil** (Bois de Vincennes, 12th, 01.43.68.01.27) is regularly open to amateur cyclists, and the circuits by the Hippodromes at **Vincennes** and **Longchamp** (for both, *see p313*) attract large groups of road cyclists. **Mieux se Déplacer à Bicyclette** (01.43.20.26.02, www.mdb-idf.org) organises free rides for members (€30 per year).

Mountain biking (VTT, or *vélo tout terrain*) is popular in the many forests on the outskirts of Paris, including the Forêt de Montmorency in the north and the Fôret de Meudon in the south.

Buzibi

67 rue de Croulebarbe, 13th (01.47.07.16.75, www.buzibi.fr). M° Corvisart. **Open** 10am-7.30pm daily. **Credit** MC, V. **Map** p406 K10.
A specialist electric bike shop. Buy, rent or get repairs.

★ Gepetto & Vélos

59 rue du Cardinal-Lemoine, 5th (01.43.54.19.95, www.gepetto-velos.com). M° Cardinal Lemoine. **Open** 9am-7pm Tue-Sun. **Credit** MC, V. **Map** p406 K8.
Rents, sells and repairs all types of bicycles.

Paris à Vélo c'est Sympa

22 rue Alphonse Baudin, 11th (01.48.87.60.01, www.parisvelosympa.com). M° Richard Lenoir. **Open** 9.30am-1pm, 2-6pm Mon, Wed-Fri; 9.30am-1pm Tue; 9am-7pm Sat, Sun. **No credit cards**. **Map** p406 L7.
Repairs, rentals and guided cycling tours of the city.

Diving

Courses for the French diving licence are offered at the **Club de Plongée du 5ème** (www.clubdeplongeedu5.org), which makes use of a nearby swimming pool and runs trips to the Med. **Bleu Passion** (94 bd Poniatowski, 12th, 01.43.45.26.12, www.bleu-passion.fr) runs a diving school and sells equipment.

Fencing

For a list of clubs, consult www.escrime-ffe.fr. The fencing section at the **Lagardère Paris Racing** (5 rue Eblé, 7th, 01.40.61.60.94, www.lagardereparisracing.com) is suitable for leisure or competition, with 12 fencing masters and 18 pistes. All levels and ages are welcome.

Fitness clubs

Club Med (www.clubmedgym.fr) dominates the health club scene, with 22 branches in Paris and the western suburbs, including five Waou Clubs with spa facilities. Single visits cost €26, and annual memberships start at €840. Other leading fitness centres include **Vit'Halles** (*see p316*) and **Forest Hill** (www.forest-hill.com).

The non-profit **La Gym Suédoise** (01.45.00.18.22, www.gymsuedoise.com) holds one-hour gym sessions in ten locations across Paris. Membership is €75-€125 per term, or €10 per session. Unlike most gyms, it runs free trials at specified locations.

There are free weekly 'Sport Nature' sessions of outdoor stretching, aerobics and running, set up by the Mairie at 13 locations around town. Check the annual *Guide du Sport* or visit www.sport.paris.fr.

★ Espace Vit'Halles

48 rue Rambuteau, 3rd (01.42.77.21.71, www.
vithalles.fr). M° Rambuteau. **Open** 8am-10.30pm
Mon-Fri; 9am-7pm Sat; 10am-7pm Sun. **Admission**
€25/day. **Credit** AmEx, MC, V. **Map** p406 K5.
This health club has Technogym fitness machines,
a sauna and some of the best classes in the city, particularly for step and spinning; the classes cost extra.

Football

For information on the local amateur leagues,
contact the **Ligue Ile-de-France de**
Football (01.42.44.12.12, paris-idf.fff.fr).
To join a weekend kickabout, try the Bois
de Boulogne near Bagatelle, the Bois de
Vincennes or the Champ de Mars.

Golf

The suburbs are full of courses suitable for all
levels and budgets. Contact the **Fédération**
Française de Golf (01.41.49.77.00, www.ff
golf.org) for more information.

Golf du Bois de Boulogne

Hippodrome d'Auteuil, 16th (01.44.30.70.00,
www.golfduboisdeboulogne.fr). M° Porte d'Auteuil.
Open *Aug-Apr* 8am-9pm daily. **Admission**
€2.50-€4. **Credit** AmEx, MC, V.
This municipal site has putting greens and a practice
area complete with bunkers and water obstacles. It's
closed on horse-racing days, so check beforehand.

Golf National

2 av du Golf, 78280 Guyancourt (01.30.43.36.00,
www.golf-national.com). RER St-Quentin-en-Yvelines
then taxi. **Open** *May-Oct* 7.30am-7pm Mon-Fri; 7am-
8pm Sat, Sun. *Nov, Feb* 8am-6pm daily. *Dec, Jan*
8.30am-5.30pm daily. *Mar, Apr* 8am-7pm Mon-Fri;
7.30am-7pm Sat, Sun. **Admission** €11-€130;
annual membership from €800. **Credit** MC, V.
This is the home of the French Open. There are two
18-hole courses and one nine-hole course.

Horse riding

To enjoy the trails in the Bois de Boulogne or
the Bois de Vincennes, you need to join a riding
club such as **La Société d'Equitation de**
Paris (Centre Hippique du Bois de Boulogne,
16th, 01.45.01.20.06, www.equitation-paris.com),
the **Centre Hippique du Touring** (Bois
de Boulogne, 16th, 01.45.01.20.88, www.tcf-
equitation.com) or the **Cercle Hippique**
du Bois de Vincennes (8 rue de Fontenay,
94130 Nogent-sur-Marne, 01.48.73.01.28,
www.chbv.fr). Beginners can learn at the
Club Bayard Equitation in the Bois de
Vincennes (Centre Bayard, UCPA Vincennes,
12th, 01.43.65.46.87, www.clubbayard.com).

During July and August, you can have one-off
lessons (€24) or take a special five-day course
for €308. Out near Versailles, the **Haras de**
Jardy (boulevard de Jardy, 92430 Marnes-
la-Coquette, 01.47.01.35.30, www.haras-de-
jardy.com) is open every day and offers
lessons by the hour for all ages, with no
membership fee. Leisurely rides in the forests
of Fontainebleau are run by **La Bleausière**
(06.82.01.21.18, http://la.bleausiere.free.fr).

Ice skating

The most popular open-air skating rink is the
free one set up in front of the Hôtel de Ville
(Dec-Feb). Smaller wintertime rinks are also
erected at other venues around the capital.
See also pp26-31 **Diary**.

Patinoire de Boulogne

1 rue Victor-Griffuelhes, 92100 Boulogne-
Billancourt (01.46.08.00.88, www.patinoire
boulogne.com). M° Marcel Sembat. **Open** 3-6pm
Wed; 10.30am-1pm, 3-6pm, 9pm-midnight Sat;
10am-1pm, 3-6pm Sun (open daily during school
hols). **Admission** €5.60; €4.70 reductions.
No credit cards.
Year-round indoor rink with free skate rental.

Patinoire Pailleron

32 rue Edouard-Pailleron, 19th (01.40.40.27.70,
www.pailleron19.com). M° Bolivar. **Open** times
vary; see website for details. **Admission** €4-€6;
€3-€4 reductions. **No credit cards**. **Map** p403 N2.
Reopened in 2006, this rink is part of a renovated
art deco sports complex. Skaters can sign up for
hockey and dance lessons on the ice.

Patinoire Sonja Henie

Palais Omnisports de Paris-Bercy (01.40.02.60.60,
www.bercy.fr). M° Bercy. **Open** *Sept-mid June*
3-6pm Wed; 9.30pm-12.30am Fri; 3-6pm, 9.30pm-
12.30am Sat; 10am-noon, 3-6pm Sun. **Admission**
€3-€6. **No credit cards**. **Map** p407 N9.
Protection, helmets and skates for hire (€3).

In-line skating

You can hire skates from **Nomades** (37 bd
Bourdin, 4th, 01.44.54.07.44, www.nomade
shop.com). For lessons for all ages, try the
Roller Squad Institute (01.56.61.99.61,
www.rsi.asso.fr). And for impressive in-line
skating and skateboard acrobatics, head for
the **Espace Glisse de Paris** (*see p317*).

Rowing & watersports

Paris residents can row, canoe and kayak for
free on Saturdays at the **Base Nautique de**
la Villette (41bis quai de la Loire, 19th,

Piscine Josephine-Baker See p319.

01.42.40.29.90). Reserve a week in advance and bring along proof of residence, two photos and a swimming certificate (obtainable at any pool). You can go waterskiing and wakeboarding at the **Club Nautique du 19ème** (Bassin de Vitesse de St-Cloud, 92100 Boulogne-Billancourt, 01.42.03.25.24, www.cn19.fr). Serious rowers can join the annual Traversée de Paris. Contact the **Ligue Ile-de-France d'Aviron** (94736 Nogent-sur-Marne, 01.48.75.79.10). For a leisurely paddle, hire a boat at Lac Daumesnil or Lac des Minimes in the Bois de Vincennes, or at Lac Supérieur in the Bois de Boulogne.

Rugby

For a good standard of play, try the **Athletic Club de Boulogne** (Stade du Saut du Loup, av de la Butte-Mortemart, 16th, 01.41.10.25.30, www.acbb.fr), which fields two teams. The **British Rugby Club of Paris** (58-60 av de la Grande Armée, 17th, www.brfcparis.com) fields two teams in the corporate league.

Skateboarding

In 2008, the Mairie inaugurated the **Espace Glisse de Paris** (*see right*), doubtless hoping to reduce skateboarding in public places. Nonetheless, the most popular skateboarding spots remain the riverfront courtyard at the **Palais de Tokyo**, known as 'Le Dôme', and the ledges and steps at **Trocadéro**. The **Palais Omnisports de Paris-Bercy** (*see p312*) has vast ledges and some almighty gaps. A more relaxed scene is to be found at the **place des Innocents** (by the Forum des Halles, 1st), which has low ledges and smooth ground, and at the **Opéra Bastille** (11th).

Cosanostra Skatepark
18 rue du Tir, 77500 Chelles (01.64.72.14.04, www.cosanostraskatepark.net). RER Chelles-Gournay. **Open** times vary; see website for

details. **Admission** €6. *Season ticket €274; €258 under-13s.* **No credit cards.**
A huge indoor street course and micro-ramp, which hosts international competitions.

★ Espace Glisse de Paris
Stade des Fillettes, 54bis bd Ney, 18th (01.40.05.62.00). Mº Porte de la Chapelle. **Open** daily. **Admission** free.
This covered complex provides urban sports fans with a vast space. There are bowls and street furniture, plus a funbox and beginners area. Different time slots are allocated for skaters, bladers and BMXers, so check ahead. Equipment can be hired.

Squash

The **Standard Athletic Club** (*see p314*) rents squash courts to members or on payment of a €280 seasonal fee.

Squash Montmartre
14 rue Achille-Martinet, 18th (01.42.55.38.30, www.squash-montmartre.fr). Mº Lamarck Caulaincourt. **Open** 10am-11pm Mon-Fri; 10am-8pm Sat, Sun. **Admission** from €16. **Credit** MC, V.
Period memberships are available at this club, as well as equipment hire.

Swimming

Pools are plentiful and cheap. Most require a swimming cap and ban bermudas, and many are open late. Times given below may change during holidays.

Aquaboulevard
4 rue Louis-Armand, 15th (01.40.60.10.00, www.aquaboulevard.com). Mº Balard. **Open** 9am-midnight Mon-Fri; 8am-midnight Sat; 8am-11pm Sun. **Admission** *6hrs* €22-€28; €15 reductions. **Credit** AmEx, MC, V. **Map** p404 A10.
With year-round summer temperatures, this water park under a giant atrium is great fun for kids. An extra charge gets you a steam bath and three saunas.

Day at the Races

Paris's best bets for a trackside treat.

The Paris region is home to some of France's most prestigious racecourses. Just east of the centre, the **Hippodrome de Paris-Vincennes** (*see p313*) is the temple of French trotting, and hosts the prestigious Prix d'Amérique Marionnaud, also dubbed the 'world harness racing championship'. Founded in 1920, the race brings together 18 of the world's best trotters to compete for a €1m purse. Drivers sit behind the horse in two-wheeled carts called sulkies, occasionally using a long whip to direct their steed. With pom-pom girls and acrobats also on the bill, this January fixture is known for its festive vibe.

The classier end of the racing scene is showcased at the world-famous Prix de l'Arc de Triomphe, held on the first Sunday of October at **Longchamp** (*see p313*) in the Bois de Boulogne. With a prize fund of €4m, the 'Arc' is Europe's richest race, and attracts the world's best thoroughbreds for its flagship flat race. In the reserved enclosures elegant dress is de rigueur, but many spectators in the main grandstand also choose to dress up. Given the entry fee of just €8, there's certainly room to budget for a posh hat. Choose the right one and you may even win a prize. Since 2001, the 'Chapeaux de l'Arc' has been awarded to women sporting the most spectacular headwear, with prizes given for both professionally designed hats and DIY creations. Expect tough competition,

though. Longchamp also hosts the Grand Prix de Paris on 14 July, France's big national holiday. As a flat race, it's an important rendezvous for three-year-old thoroughbreds before the season's big autumn meetings. Entry is free and the evening ends with Bastille Day fireworks.

The region's other major flat race venue is **Chantilly** (*see p313*), 25 miles north of Paris. In June, the Prix du Jockey Club attracts leading colts, while the Prix de Diane is for fillies. Steeplechasing, meanwhile, is showcased at **Auteuil** (*see p313*), also in the Bois de Boulogne. The prestigious Grand Steeple-Chase de Paris in May features a course with some 23 obstacles over its 5.8km (3.5-mile) length.

Betting for all races is done via the state-owned PMU. Odds (*la côte*) can be consulted on monitors, while tips should be garnished from the *Paris Turf* newspaper (www.paris-turf.com). To place a bet at the counters, announce the number of your horse, the amount you're betting and the type of bet. The simplest bets on a single horse are *gagnant* (to win) or *placé* (in the first three, or first two if there are fewer than eight starters). If you're confident of picking the top two or three horses (without stating the order), ask for *couplé gagnant* or *trio gagnant* respectively. For major gains, though, try your luck at predicting the finishing order of the top three (*tiercé*), four (*quarté*) or even five (*quinté*).

Piscine Butte-aux-Cailles

*5 pl Paul-Verlaine, 13th (01.45.89.60.05). M°
Place d'Italie.* **Open** 7-8.30am, 11.30am-1.30pm,
4.30-9pm Tue; 7am-7pm Wed; 7-8.30am, 11.30am-
6.30pm Thur, Fri; 7-8.30am, 10am-6.30pm Sat;
8am-6pm Sun. **Admission** €3; €1.70 reductions.
Credit AmEx, MC, V.
This listed complex, built in the 1920s, has one main
indoor pool and two outdoor pools (open in the summer). The water is a temptingly warm 28°C, thanks
to the natural sulphurous spring.

Piscine Georges-Vallerey

*148 av Gambetta, 20th (01.40.31.15.20). M° Porte
des Lilas.* **Open** 11.45am-1.30pm Mon; 11.45am-
1.30pm, 5.15-10pm Tue, Thur; 10am-1pm, 2-7pm
Wed; 9am-5pm Sat, Sun. **Admission** €3; €1.70
reductions. **Credit** (€15 minimum) MC, V.
Built for the 1924 Olympics, this complex features a
retractable Plexiglas roof, a 50m pool (often split into
two 25m pools) and one for kids.

★ Piscine Josephine-Baker

*Quai François-Mauriac, 13th (01.56.61.96.50).
M° Quai de la Gare.* **Open** 7-8.30am, 1-9pm
Mon, Wed, Fri; 1-11pm Tue, Thur; 11am-8pm
Sat; 10am-8pm Sun. **Admission** €3; €1.70
reductions. **Credit** MC, V. **Map** p407 M10.
Moored on the Seine by the Bibliothèque Nationale,
the pool boasts a 25m main pool (with sliding glass
roof), a paddling pool and café, and a busy schedule
of exercise classes. *Photo p317.*

Piscine Keller

*14 rue de l'Ingénieur Keller, 15th (01.45.71.81.00).
M° Charles Michels.* **Open** noon-10pm Mon;
7-8.30am, noon-10pm Tue, Thur; 7am-2pm Wed;
noon-10pm Fri; 9am-9pm Sat; 9am-7pm Sun.
Admission €3; €1.70 reductions. **Credit** V.
Map p404 B8.
This 50m pool features a retractable roof and uses a
chlorine-free water treatment method. Lane-swim-
ming is prioritised, and there's a 15m pool for kids.

Piscine Nakache

*4-12 rue Desnoyez, 20th (01.58.53.57.80). M°
Belleville.* **Open** 7-8.30am, 11.30am-1.30pm, 4.30-
6pm Tue, Fri; 7am-6pm Wed; 7-8.30am, 11.30am-
1.30pm, 4.30-10pm Thur; 7-8am, 10am-6pm Sat;
8am-6pm Sun. **Admission** €3; €1.70 reductions.
No credit cards. Map p403 N4.
The city's newest swimming complex boasts two
pools (25m and 12.5m) and a children's paddling pool,
all treated with ozone rather than chlorine. There's
also a gym and sauna.

★ Piscine Pontoise Quartier Latin

*18 rue de Pontoise, 5th (01.55.42.77.88). M°
Maubert Mutualité.* **Open** 7-8.30am, 12.15-1.30pm,
4.30-8pm Mon, Fri; 7-8.30am, 12.15-1.30pm, 4.30-
7pm Tue, Thur; 7-8.30am, 11.30am-7.30pm Wed;

10am-7pm Sat; 8am-7pm Sun. *Night swimming*
8.15-11.45pm Mon-Fri. **Admission** €4.50; €2.70
reductions; €10 for all 8.15-11.45pm. **No credit
cards. Map** p406 K7.
A beautiful art deco pool with two mezzanine levels.
It has private locker rooms, plus night swimming to
underwater music. Small fee for lockers.

Piscine Suzanne-Berlioux

*Forum des Halles, 10 pl de la Rotonde, 1st
(01.42.36.98.44). M° Les Halles.* **Open** 11.30am-
11pm Mon; 11.30am-10pm Tue, Thur, Fri;
7-8.15am, 10am-11pm Wed; 9am-7pm Sat,
Sun. **Admission** €4; €3 reductions. **Credit**
(€8 minimum) MC, V. **Map** p402 J5.
Although usually pretty busy, this 50m pool with
its own tropical greenhouse is good for lane swimming. There are no lockers, so you need to check in
belongings with the attendants. It reopened in 2010
after renovation.

Tennis & table tennis

The six tennis courts at the **Jardin du
Luxembourg** (01.43.25.79.18) are convenient,
but there's a better selection on offer at the
Centre Sportif La Faluère (113 route de
la Pyramide, 12th, 01.43.74.40.93) in the Bois
de Vincennes.

To find public table tennis in parks around
town, consult the *Guide du Sport* (*see p314*).

Centre Sportif Suzanne-Lenglen

*2 rue Louis-Armand, 15th (01.44.26.26.50).
M° Balard.* **Open** 8am-10pm Mon-Sat; 8am-6pm
Sun. **Admission** from €4.50. **No credit cards.**
Map p404 A10.
Fourteen courts, two of which are covered.

Club Forest Hill

*4 rue Louis-Armand, 15th (01.40.60.10.00,
www.forest-hill.fr). M° Balard/RER Bd Victor.*
Open 7am-midnight daily. **Admission** prices
vary. **No credit cards. Map** p404 A10.
Tennis, table tennis and other racquet sports at most
of the dozen branches in and around Paris.

Triathlon

The multi-discipline effort of triathlon (swim,
bike, run) is one of Europe's fastest growing
sports, and the Paris area hosts some of the
biggest clubs. The **Paris Triathlon** (www.
triathlondeparis.fr) offers a short-distance
event for beginners, with the main race
comprising a 1.5km swim in the Seine, plus
a 40km bike leg around the Bois de Boulogne
and a 10km run in the Hippodrome de
Longchamp. For full details of local clubs,
contact the **Ligue Ile de France de
Triathlon** (www.idftriathlon.com).

Escapes & Excursions

Escapes & Excursions

Head out of town for châteaux and champagne by the bucketload.

The forests surrounding Paris were once the playground of royalty and aristocracy, and their extravagant legacy is plain to see in sumptuous châteaux such as Fontainebleau and Versailles. Further afield, the vineyards of Champagne are less than an hour from the capital, and even the Med is only a few hours away by TGV.

In this chapter, divided into **Excursions** (day trips) and **Escapes** (destinations further afield), we've listed local tourist information centres, which have details about specific areas. For the main entries – cathedrals, châteaux and other big attractions – we've included details of opening times, admission and transport; but be aware that these can change without notice. Always phone in advance. For a list of mainline stations in Paris and their destinations, *see p368.*

For a list of mainline stations in Paris and their destinations, *see p368.*

Excursions

AUVERS-SUR-OISE

This rural retreat is where Vincent van Gogh spent his last weeks. His tiny attic room at the **Auberge Ravoux** is open to the public. Other Auvers residents included fellow artists Camille Pissarro, Paul Cézanne and Charles-François Daubigny. Today, you can explore the **Musée Daubigny** (Manoir des Colombières, rue de la Sansonne, 01.30.36.80.20, www.musee-daubigny. com) and his studio (61 rue Daubigny, 01.30.36.60.60, www.atelier-daubigny.com), which is still decorated with his murals.

Another attraction is the **Musée de l'Absinthe** (44 rue Callé, 01.30.36.83.26, www.musee-absinthe.com), a rather modest collection of art and artefacts related to the notorious drink. Banned in France from 1915, the green concoction is once again legal.

The local artistic legacy has not been overlooked by Auvers' main historical attraction, either. The 17th-century **Château d'Auvers** (rue de Léry, 01.34.48.48.48, www.chateau-auvers.fr) features a walk-through tour with an Impressionist theme.

Auberge Ravoux
1 pl de la Mairie, 95430 Auvers-sur-Oise (01.30.36.60.60, www.maisondevangogh.fr).

Open *Mar-Oct* 10am-6pm Wed-Sun. **Admission** €6; €4 reductions; free under-12s. **Credit** *Shop & restaurant* AmEx, MC, V.

Where to eat & stay

You can always do as Van Gogh might have done, and dine at the **Auberge Ravoux** (*see above*). Otherwise, try **L'Impressionist' Café** (Château d'Auvers, rue de Léry, 01.34.48.48.48), which does cheap lunches. The **Hostellerie du Nord** (6 rue Général-de-Gaulle, 01.30.36.70.74, www.hostelleriedunord.fr) has chef Joël Boilleaut running the kitchen; upstairs there are eight double rooms (€99-€189).

Getting there

By car
35km (22 miles) north of Paris by A15, exit 7, then N184, exit Méry-sur-Oise for Auvers.

By train
From Gare du Nord, changing at St-Ouen L'Aumone (whole journey takes about 1hr).

Tourist information

Office de Tourisme
Manoir des Colombières, rue de la Sansonne, 95430 Auvers-sur-Oise (01.30.36.10.06, www.auvers-sur-oise.com). **Open** *Apr-Oct* 9.30am-12.30pm, 2-6pm Tue-Sun. *Nov-Mar* 9.30am-12.30pm, 2-5pm Tue-Sun.

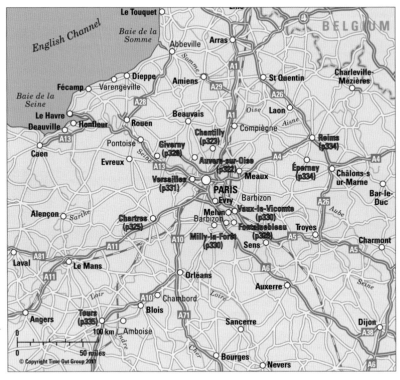

CHANTILLY & SENLIS

From the 14th century until 1897, the town of **Chantilly** was the domain of the Princes of Condé, the cousins of the French kings. As well as its impressive **château**, Chantilly, with its hunting forests and prestigious horse-racing centres, has a rich equestrian history.

Much of the cream-coloured château was destroyed during the Revolution, leaving the main wing to be reconstructed in the 19th century by Henri d'Orléans, Duc d'Aumale. When the duke died in 1897, he bequeathed the Domaine de Chantilly – including the Grand Stables, the Hippodrome and the 61-square-kilometre (23-square-mile) forest – to the Institut de France on the condition that the château be opened to the public as the **Musée Condé**, and that none of the artworks would be moved or loaned to other museums. His remarkable collection is complemented by the surrounding **park**, beautifully landscaped by André Le Nôtre (of Versailles fame).

The Grandes Ecuries ('great stables') at the château were commissioned in 1719 by Prince Louis-Henri de Bourbon (who believed he would be reincarnated as a horse). Later, they became one of Napoleon's equestrian training grounds, having suffered only light damage during the Revolution. In 1982, the great horseman Yves Bienaimé restored the stables and turned them into the **Musée Vivant du Cheval**. The Bienaimé family has also restored the **Potager des Princes**.

The **Forêt de Chantilly** is full of hiking and cycling trails. A pleasant walk of around seven kilometres (four miles) circles four small lakes, the Etangs de Commelles, and passes the Château de la Reine Blanche, a mill that was converted in the 1820s into a pseudo-medieval hunting lodge. For trail details, ask at the Office National des Forêts (1 av de Sylvie, 03.44.57.03.88, www.onf.fr).

Senlis, not far east of Chantilly, is known as the birthplace of the French monarchy.

Château de Chantilly/Musée Condé

Chantilly (03.44.27.31.80, www.chateaudechantilly. com). **Open** *Apr-Oct* 10am-6pm Mon, Wed-Sun (daily July, Aug). *Nov-Mar* 10.30am-5pm Mon, Wed-Sun. **Admission** *Château & park* €14; €5.50 reductions; free under-4s. **Credit** MC, V.

Château de Chantilly. *See p323.*

The major attraction on show here is the collection of paintings and drawings at the Musée Condé. The hugely impressive collection includes three paintings by Raphael, and the *Très Riches Heures du Duc de Berry*, a medieval book of hours, containing the most exquisite colours imaginable. If you thought the Middle Ages were dull, think again. The joint Passeport Chantilly ticket gives access to the park, château and Musée Vivant du Cheval (€18; €7.50 reductions).

★ Château park

Chantilly (03.44.27.31.80, www.chateaude chantilly.com). **Open** *Apr-Oct* 10am-8pm (last admission 6pm) Mon, Wed-Sun (daily July, Aug). *Nov-Mar* 10.30am-6pm (last admission 5pm) Mon, Wed-Sun. **Admission** *Park only* €7; €3 reductions; free under-4s. **Credit** MC, V.

The main section of the château's sprawling park, designed by royal landscape architect Le Nôtre, features traditional French formal parterres and an extensive canal system, which allows visitors to see the park from electric-powered boats. Get off the beaten path to explore the English Garden, the Island of Love, the kangaroo zoo and the original hamlet that inspired Marie-Antoinette to build her own version at Versailles.

Musée Vivant du Cheval

Les Grandes Ecuries, Chantilly (03.44.27.31.80, www.museevivantducheval.fr). **Open** *Mar-Oct* 10am-5pm Mon, Wed-Sun. *Dec* 1.30-5pm Mon, Wed-Sun. **Admission** €11; €4.50 reductions; free under-4s. **Credit** MC, V.

This museum is an interactive affair, where kids can pet the ponies and everyone gets to learn how the horses are trained to perform in the ring.

Potager des Princes

Parc de la Faisanderie, 17 rue de la Faisanderie, Chantilly (03.44.57.39.66, www.potager desprinces.com). **Open** *Apr-Oct* 2-7pm daily. **Admission** €8.50; €7.50 reductions. **Credit** MC, V.

The restored princes' kitchen garden is a 19th-century English garden with vegetable plots, trained fruit trees, a small farmyard and an open-air theatre next to the lake.

Where to eat & stay

Try the home-style cooking at **Le Goutillon** (61 rue du Connétable, 03.44.58.01.00). **La Capitainerie** (03.44.57.15.89, www.chateau dechantilly.com) offers good French food in what were originally the château kitchens. To sample Chantilly whipped cream, stop for tea at the **Restaurant du Hameau** (03.44.57.46.21, closed mid Nov-mid Mar) in the *hameau* at the château.

To live like a prince, book a bed at the brand new **Auberge du Jeu de Paume** (4 rue du Connétable, 03.44.65.50.00, www.aubergedujeu depaumechantilly.fr) in the heart of town, with luxurious rooms, two restaurants and a spa. For something a little less regal, the **Hôtel du Parc Best Western** (36 av du Maréchal-Joffre, 03.44.58.20.00, www.hotel-parc-chantilly.com, doubles €130-€150) is a decent central option.

Getting there

By car
40km (25 miles) north of Paris by N16 (direct)
or A1 (Chantilly exit).

By train
SNCF Chantilly-Gouvieux from Gare du Nord
(30mins), then 5min walk to town, 20mins to
château. Some trains stop at Creil, then loop
back to Chantilly.

Tourist information

Office de Tourisme (Chantilly)
*60 av Maréchal-Joffre, 60500 Chantilly
(03.44.67.37.37, www.chantilly-tourisme.com).*
Open *Oct-Apr* 9.30am-12.30pm, 1.30-5.30pm
Mon-Sat. *May-Sept* 9.30am-12.30pm, 1.30-5.30pm
Mon-Sat; 10am-1.30pm Sun.

Office de Tourisme (Senlis)
*Pl du parvis Notre-Dame, 60302 Senlis
(03.44.53.06.40, www.senlis-tourisme.fr).*
Open *Mar-Oct* 10am-12.30pm, 2-6.15pm Mon-
Sat; 10.30am-1pm, 2-6.15pm Sun. *Nov-Feb*
10am-12.30pm, 2-5pm Mon-Sat; 10.30am-
12.30pm, 2-5pm Sun.

CHARTRES

Seen from a distance, the mismatched
spires and dazzling silhouette of **Chartres
cathedral** burst out of the Beauce cornfields
and dominate the skyline of this modest town
some 90 kilometres (56 miles) south-west of
Paris. Chartres was a pilgrimage site long
before the cathedral was built, ever since the
Sacra Camisia (said to be the Virgin Mary's
birthing garment) was donated in 876 by
the king. The cathedral is one of the finest
examples of Gothic architecture in the world:
its doorways bristling with sculpture, along
with its stained glass, embody a complete
medieval world view.

The town of Chartres is an attractive tangle
of narrow, medieval streets on the banks of the
river Eure. Two sights merit a special mention:
the **Musée des Beaux-Arts** (29 cloître Notre-
Dame, 02.37.90.45.80), which houses a collection
of 18th-century French paintings by Watteau
and others; and the **memorial to Jean
Moulin**, the legendary figure of the Resistance.
A wartime prefect of Chartres until he was
dismissed by the Vichy government after his
refusal to co-operate with the Nazis, Moulin
became de Gaulle's man in France, and died
under torture in Lyon in 1943. His memorial is
a ten-minute walk west of the cathedral, at the
corner of rue Collin d'Arleville and boulevard
de la Résistance.

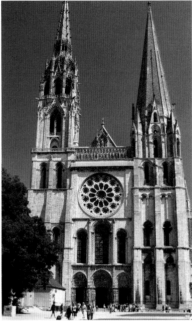

Cathédrale Notre-Dame,
Chartres. *See p326.*

ESCAPES & EXCURSIONS

★ FREE Cathédrale Notre-Dame

Pl de la Cathédrale (02.37.21.75.02). **Open**
Cathedral 8.30am-7.30pm daily. *Tower* May-Aug
9.30am-12.30pm, 2-6pm Mon-Sat; 2-6pm Sun.
Sept-Apr 9.30am-12.30pm, 2-5pm Mon-Sat;
2-5pm Sun. **Admission** *Cathedral* free. *Tower*
€7; €4.50 reductions; free under-18s, under-26s
(EU citizens). **No credit cards**.

The west front, or 'Royal Portal', of this High Gothic
cathedral – which was modelled in part on St-Denis
– has three sculpted doorways. Inside, there's
another era of sculpture, represented in the 16th-
century scenes of the life of Christ that surround the
choir. In particular, note the circular labyrinth of
black and white stones in the floor. The cathedral
is famed, above all, for its stained-glass windows
depicting biblical scenes, saints and medieval trades
in brilliant 'Chartres blue', punctuated by rich
reds. During World War II, the windows were
removed and stored nearby for safety, only being
reinstalled once the war was over. Climb the tower
for a fantastic view over the surrounding town
and country. English-language tours by lecturer
Malcolm Miller – one of the world's most knowledgeable and entertaining experts on the cathedral
– take place twice daily for most of the year (noon
& 2.45pm Mon-Sat, €10, €5 reductions). Audio
guides can also be hired. *Photo p325.*
▶ *Malcolm Miller is also available for private
tours of the cathedral (02.37.28.15.58,
millerchartres@aol.com).*

Where to eat & stay

Tourists flock to the **Café Serpente**
(2 cloître Notre-Dame, 02.37.21.68.81,
www.leserpente.com), in the shadow of the
cathedral, but if it's full, there are plenty
of easy and worthwhile options nearby. For
restaurant cuisine with a riverside view, try
L'Estocade (1 rue de la Porte Guillaume,
02.37.34.27.17, closed all day Mon & Sun eve).
For fireside treats, **La Vieille Maison** (5 rue
au Lait, 02.37.34.10.67, www.lavieillemaison.fr,
closed Mon & Sun) has a cosy 14th-century
dining room. For a local speciality, order
some Chartres pâté at **Le Saint-Hilaire**
(11 rue Pont St-Hilaire, 02.37.30.97.57).

Two perfectly serviceable chain hotels
on the ring road, not far from the centre, are
the **Grand Monarque** (22 pl des Epars,
02.37.18.15.15, www.bw-grand-monarque.com,
doubles €130-€190) and the **Ibis Centre**
(14 pl Drouaise, 02.37.36.06.36, www.ibishotel.
com, doubles from €82).

Getting there

By car
90km (56 miles) south-west of Paris by A10,
then A11.

By train
Direct from Gare Montparnasse (1hr).

Tourist information

Office de Tourisme
*Pl de la Cathédrale, 28000 Chartres
(02.37.18.26.26, www.chartres-tourisme.com).*
Open *Apr-Sept* 9am-7pm Mon-Sat; 9.30am-5.30pm
Sun. *Oct-Mar* 10am-6pm Mon-Sat; 10am-1pm,
2.30-4.30pm Sun.

FONTAINEBLEAU

Home to 14 French kings since François I,
Fontainebleau was once a sort of aristocratic
club where gentlemen of the day came to hunt
and learn the art of chivalry. The town grew
up around the **château** in the 19th century,
and is a pleasant place to visit.

The château is bite-sized compared to the
sprawling grandeur of Versailles. The style
adopted by the Italian artists brought in by
François I is still visible, as are the additions
by later rulers. The extensive château gardens,
park and grand canal, all free for visitors to
enter, are also worth exploring.

The 170-square-kilometre (66-square-mile)
Forêt de Fontainebleau has bizarre
geological formations and diverse wildlife. It's
the wildest slice of nature to be found near Paris.
There are a number of well-marked trails, such
as the GR1 from Bois-le-Roi train station, but
more serious yompers would be better off with
an official map such as the TOP25 IGN series
2417-OT, which covers the entire forest.

Château de Fontainebleau.

Trail maps are on sale at the **Fontainebleau tourist office**, which hires out bicycles and has information on the villages of Barbizon and Moret-sur-Loing. Bikes can also be hired from **A la Petite Reine** (14 rue de la Paroisse, 01.60.74.57.57, www.alapetitereine.com).

★ Château de Fontainebleau

Pl du Général-de-Gaulle (01.60.71.50.70, www.musee-chateau-fontainebleau.fr). **Open** *Château* Apr-Sept 9.30am-6pm Mon, Wed-Sun. Oct-Mar 9.30am-5pm Mon, Wed-Sun. *Park & gardens* Mar, Apr, Oct 9am-6pm daily. May-Sept 9am-7pm daily. Nov-Feb 9am-5pm daily. **Admission** *Château* €10; €8 reductions; free under-18s, under-26s (EU citizens). *Park & gardens* free. PMP. **Credit** AmEx, MC, V.

The Château de Fontainebleau, a former hunting lodge, is a real mix of styles. In 1528, François I brought in Italian artists and craftsmen to help architect Gilles le Breton transform a neglected lodge into the finest Italian Mannerist palace in France. This style, noted for its grotesqueries, contorted figures and crazy fireplaces, is still visible in the ballroom and Long Gallery. Henri IV added a tennis court, Louis XIII built a double-horseshoe entrance staircase, and Louis XIV and XV added classical trimmings. Napoleon and Louis-Philippe also spent a fortune on redecoration. The château gardens include Le Nôtre's Grand Parterre. There is also a park.

Where to eat & stay

Rue Grande is lined with restaurants such as **Au Délice Impérial** (no.1, 01.64.22.20.70) and **Au Bureau** (no.12, 01.60.39.00.01,

www.au-bureau.fr), with Tex-Mex specialities. At no.92, picnickers can find an array of cheeses at **Fromagerie Barthélémy** (01.64.22.21.64). For a blow-out meal, try **Le Caveau des Ducs** (24 rue Ferrare, 01.64.22.05.05).

Some of the dozen rooms at the charming, central **Hôtel de Londres** (1 pl du Général-de-Gaulle, 01.64.22.20.21, www.hoteldelondres.com, doubles €130-€180) have balconies overlooking the château. The elegant **Hôtel Napoléon** (9 rue Grande, 01.60.39.50.50, www.hotelnapoleon-fontainebleau.com, doubles €165-€260) provides appropriately grand meals at its restaurant.

Getting there

By car

60km (37 miles) south of Paris by A6, then N7 (about 75mins). Be prepared for traffic jams when heading back to Paris on Sundays.

By train

Gare de Lyon to Fontainebleau-Avon (35mins), then bus AB (marked 'Château'). Ask for a 'Forfait Château de Fontainebleau' at the Gare de Lyon; it includes train, bus connection, château entrance and audio guide.

Tourist information

Office de Tourisme

4 rue Royale, 77300 Fontainebleau (01.60.74.99.99, www.fontainebleau-tourisme.com). **Open** *May-Oct* 10am-6pm Mon-Sat; 10am-1pm, 2-5.30pm Sun. *Nov-Apr* 10am-6pm Mon-Sat; 10am-1pm Sun.

Fondation Claude Monet.

GIVERNY

In 1883, Claude Monet moved his mistress and their eight children into a quaint pink-brick house he had rented in bucolic Giverny, and spent as much time cultivating a beautiful garden here as painting the water lilies in it.

The leader of the Impressionist movement thrived on outdoor scenes, whether along the Seine near Argenteuil or by the Thames in London. Having once seen the tiny village of Giverny from the window of a train, he was smitten. By 1890, he had bought his dream home and soon had a pond dug, bridges built and a tableau of greenery created. As Monet's eyesight began to fail, he produced endless impressions of his man-made paradise, each trying to capture how the leaves and water reflected light. He died here in 1926.

Of the hundreds of tourists who visit here every day, not all are art-lovers; there are none of his original paintings actually on display here (though you will see the 32 Japanese woodblock prints collected by the artist). Most visitors are simply here for the lilies, and a good photo opportunity.

The garden is as much a masterpiece as any of Monet's paintings, its famous water-lily pond, weeping willows and Japanese bridge still remarkably intact from the master's day; and the charming house, the **Fondation Claude Monet**, is dotted with touching mementos. But once you're back in the village, be prepared for some difficulty finding a table at one of the scarce eating places, and long queues of impatient tourists almost everywhere you turn. Get here early, or book ahead for dinner at the famous **Hôtel Baudy** museum-restaurant (81 rue Claude Monet, 02.32.21.10.03, www.restaurantbaudy.com, closed Nov-Mar), where Monet's American disciples (such as Willard Metcalf and Dawson-Watson) set up their easels for several decadent years, expanding the old hotel into an *art-atelier extraordinaire*, complete with ballroom, rose garden and tennis courts – Cézanne stayed for a month. Today, it's essential to book ahead for accommodation in Giverny, but do so and you'll be first to the Monet museum in the morning. Up the road, the **Musée des Impressionnismes Giverny** (99 rue Claude-Monet, 02.32.51.94.65, www.museedesimpressionnismesgiverny.com) houses works by the American Impressionist colony.

★ Fondation Claude Monet
84 rue Claude-Monet, 27620 Giverny (02.32.51.28.21, www.fondation-monet.com). **Open** 9.30am-6pm daily. Closed Nov-Mar. **Admission** *House & garden* €9; €4-€5 reductions; free under-7s. **Credit** AmEx, MC, V.

Where to stay

For hotels and B&Bs in the area, visit www.giverny.org. Pretty **Le Clos Fleuri** (5 rue de la Dîme, 02.32.21.36.51, www.giverny-leclosfleuri.fr, doubles €95, closed Nov-Mar) is in Giverny, close to the Musée des Impressionnismes.

Celebrating Cocteau

The Maison de Jean Cocteau is a fitting tribute to one of France's finest artists.

As a revered poet, painter, playwright and filmmaker, Jean Cocteau has left an artistic legacy that pervades many aspects of French culture. Yet the man was always an elusive figure. But now, thanks to the hefty financial input of Pierre Bergé (partner of the late Yves Saint Laurent and a close friend of Cocteau's), his old country house in Milly-la-Forêt, less than an hour from Paris, is open as the **Maison de Jean Cocteau** (*see p330*).

Cocteau moved to Milly-la-Fôret in 1947 to escape the glitz of the capital. Following his death from a heart attack at the age of 74, in 1963, his long-term partner Edouard Dhermite (who starred in Jean-Pierre Melville's 1950 film of Cocteau's 1929 novel *Les Enfants Terribles*) locked up the study, bedroom and living room, leaving more than 500 oil paintings, drawings, sculptures and photographs untouched for decades.

The three rooms have been faithfully restored, leaving one with the impression that Cocteau left only a few minutes earlier. The living room is wonderfully flamboyant, with antique furniture and gold palm trees framing a Bérard painting of Oedipus. The bedroom, meanwhile, with its four-poster bed and a mural of a castle, boasts a fairytale quality reminiscent of Cocteau's masterful 1946 romantic fantasy film *La Belle et la Bête*. Finally the study, with its leopard-print walls and erotic memorabilia, offers the most intimate glimpse into the artist's creative process, by turns both inspiring and provocative.

The rest of the house has been converted into exhibition space with two galleries: one houses a collection of portraits of Cocteau by such artists as Picasso, Warhol and Modigliani; the other is dedicated to temporary exhibitions. A projection room showing documentaries and Cocteau's films concludes the visit, but the adventure continues in the gardens surrounding the house, dotted with sculptures, where he used to enjoy strolling and writing.

Cocteau's body rests nearby, in the Chapelle Saint-Blaise-des-Simples (rue de l'Amiral de Graville, Milly-la-Forêt, 01.64.98. 84.94, open 10am-12.30pm, 2-6pm Wed-Sun). The interior, like a scaled-down Sistine Chapel, is covered in murals painted by Cocteau in 1960. His epitaph, 'Je reste avec vous' (I remain with you), seems to have as much resonance today as ever.

ESCAPES & EXCURSIONS

Getting there

By car

80km (50 miles) west of Paris by A13 to Bonnières, then D201.

By train

Gare St-Lazare to Vernon (45mins), then 5km taxi ride or bus from the station.

Tourist information

Office de Tourisme des Portes de l'Eure

36 rue Carnot, 27200 Vernon (02.32.51.39.60, www.cape-tourisme.fr). **Open** *May-Sept* 9am-12.30pm, 2-6pm Mon-Sat; 10am-noon, 2-4pm Sun. *Oct-Apr* 9am-12.30pm, 2-5.30pm Mon-Sat.

MILLY-LA-FORET

★ Maison de Jean Cocteau

15 rue du Lau (01.64.98.11.50, www.jean cocteau.net). **Open** *Mar-Oct* 10am-7pm Wed-Sun. *Early Jan, Nov-Dec* 2-6pm Sat, Sun (Wed-Sun 19 Dec-1 Jan). Closed mid Jan-Feb. **Admission** €7; €4.50 reductions; free under-10s. *See p329* **Celebrating Cocteau**.

Getting there

By car

64km (40 miles) south of Paris by A6, exit 13 for Milly-la-Forêt.

By train

RER D (direction Malesherbes) to Maisse, then 7km taxi ride. Maisse is a tiny place, so it's essential to reserve a taxi in advance (01.64.98.88.51 or 01.64.22.00.06) to get to and from the station.

VAUX-LE-VICOMTE

This lavish country château has a valuable lesson to teach: never, ever out-do your king. When Nicolas Fouquet (1615-80), Louis XIV's finance minister (and protégé of Cardinal Mazarin), decided to build an abode fit for his position, he had several hamlets moved away, called on three of France's most talented men (architect Louis Le Vau, painter Charles Lebrun and landscape gardener André Le Nôtre) and hired star sculptors such as Giradon, Lespagnandel and Nicolas Poussin to chip in with the decor. Its completion was celebrated in 1661 with a huge party for which Molière wrote a play.

All would have gone swimmingly had it not been for one minor detail: Fouquet invited the king. Louis was disgusted at his minister's display of grandeur; soon after, Fouquet was given a show trial for the embezzlement of state funds. His personal effects were seized by the crown and he was sent into exile, dying 19 years later in prison. But Fouquet's legacy did live on, as Louis later hired Le Vau, Lebrun and Le Nôtre to work some of their magic on Versailles.

Vaux-le-Vicomte.

Château de Versailles. See p332.

A self-guided tour of the interior includes Fouquet's personal suite, the servants' dining room, the huge basement and wine cellar, and the copper-filled kitchen. The dome, with its unfinished ceiling – Lebrun only had time to paint the sky and one eagle before Fouquet was arrested – and the roof are optional extras.

On the south side, a staircase descends to the handsomely ordered gardens, where boxed hedges and flowerbeds sweep into a vast expanse of lawns, grottoes, canals, lakes and fountains. Electric cars can be hired to help you cover the site. Entrance to the château includes the Musée des Equipages.

Vaux-le-Vicomte

77950 Maincy (01.64.14.41.90, www.vaux-le-vicomte.com). **Open** *Château* Late Mar-early Nov 10am-6pm daily. *Candlelight evenings* Early May-early Oct 8pm-midnight Sat. Closed early Nov-late Mar. **Admission** €14; €11 reductions; free under-6s. *Candlelight evenings* €17; €15 reductions; free under-6s. **Credit** AmEx, MC, V.

Getting there

By car

55km (35 miles) south-east of Paris by A5 (direction Troyes). Exit at first toll and then follow signs.

By train

Gare de Lyon to Melun (25mins) or RER D to Melun, then 6km taxi ride.

VERSAILLES

Centuries of makeovers have made **Château de Versailles** the most sumptuously clad château in the world – a brilliant, unmissable cocktail of extravagance. Architect Louis Le Vau first embellished the original building – a hunting lodge built during Louis XIII's reign – after Louis XIV saw Vaux-le-Vicomte, the impressive residence of his finance minister, Nicolas Fouquet. André Le Nôtre turned the boggy marshland into terraces, parterres, fountains and lush groves.

After Le Vau's death in 1670, Jules Hardouin-Mansart took over as principal architect, transforming Versailles into the château we know today. He dedicated the last 30 years of his life to adding the two main wings, the Cour des Ministres and the Chapelle Royale. In 1682, Louis moved in, accompanied by his court; thereafter, he rarely set foot in Paris. In the 1770s, Louis XV commissioned Jacques-Ange Gabriel to add the sumptuous Opéra Royal, now used for concerts by the Centre de Musique Baroque (01.39.20.78.10). The expense of building and running Versailles

INSIDE TRACK HEAD SOUTH

Thanks to the TGV, you can now reach the Med city of **Marseille** from Paris in just three hours. France's second city will be European Capital of Culture in 2013 and boasts steep streets, tranquil squares and bustling 19th-century thoroughfares that provide a patchwork of backdrops for souk-like markets, chic shops, and the colourful Vieux Port, where fishmongers sell their wares along the boat-lined quayside. For breathtaking views, climb up to the Notre-Dame de la Garde basilica, or stay grounded over a plate of bouillabaisse and go shopping around the vintage shops on Cours Julien.

cost France dear. With the fall of the monarchy in 1792, most of the furniture was lost – but the château was saved from demolition by Louis-Philippe.

The **gardens** of Versailles are really works of art in themselves, their ponds and statues once again embellished by a fully working fountain system. On summer weekends, the spectacular jets of water are set to music, a prelude to the occasional fireworks displays of the Fêtes de Nuit.

Beyond the gardens are the Grand Canal and the wooded land and sheep-filled pastures of the estate's park. Outside the château gates are the **Potager du Roi** (the Sun King's vegetable garden), and stables that now house the **Académie du Spectacle Equestre**. The **Hall of Mirrors** – a 73-metre (240-foot) gallery overlooking the garden, hung with chandeliers – was commissioned in 1678 by Louis XIV and then decorated by Le Brun. It holds 357 mirrors.

In the town of Versailles, grab a *Historical Places* brochure free from the tourist office and explore. The Quartier St-Louis opposite the Potager was developed by Louis XV around the Cathédrale St-Louis. Just off rue d'Anjou are the Carrés St-Louis, four market squares surrounded by 18th-century boutiques. Northeast of the château is the Quartier Notre-Dame, part of the 'new town' designed by the Sun King himself. Eglise Notre-Dame is where members of the royal family were baptised and married. Around the corner is the Marché Notre-Dame, a market square dating back to 1671 and surrounded by restaurants and cafés. The covered market is closed on Mondays.

Académie du Spectacle Equestre

Grandes Ecuries, Château de Versailles (01.39.02.07.14, bookings 08.92.68.18.91, www.acadequestre.fr).

Les Matinales des Ecuyers (*to watch riding practice & visit*) **Viewings** Times vary. **Admission** €12; €6.50-€10 reductions. **Credit** MC, V.
La Voie de l'Ecuyer (*performance & visit*) **Performances** *Feb-Apr, mid Sept-Dec* 6pm Sat; 3pm Sun. *May-mid July* 8pm Sat; 3pm Sun. **Admission** €25; €16-€22 reductions. **Credit** MC, V.

Across from the château entrance are the Sun King's magnificent stables, restored in 2003. They house the Académie du Spectacle Equestre, which is responsible for the elaborate shows of tightly choreographed theatrics on horseback, run by famous horse trainer Bartabas.

★ Château de Versailles

78000 Versailles (01.30.83.78.00, advance tickets 08.92.68.46.94, www.chateauversailles.fr).
Open *Apr-Oct* 9am-6.30pm Tue-Sun. *Nov-Mar* 9am-5.30pm Tue-Sun. *Gardens* Apr-Oct 7am-dusk daily. Nov-Mar 8am-dusk daily.
Admission €15; €13 reductions; free under-18s, under-26s (EU citizens), all 1st Sun of mth (Nov-Mar). PMP. **Credit** AmEx, DC, MC, V.
Grandes-Eaux Musicales (*01.30.83.78.88*).
Open *Apr-Oct* Sat, Sun. **Admission** €8.50; €6.50 reductions; free under-6s. **Credit** AmEx, DC, MC, V.

Versailles is a masterpiece – and usually packed with visitors. Allow yourself a whole day to appreciate the sumptuous State Apartments and the Hall of Mirrors, the highlights of any visit, and mostly accessible with a day ticket. The Grand Appartement, where Louis XIV held court, consists of six gilded salons, all opulent examples of Baroque craftsmanship. No less luxurious, the Queen's Apartment includes her bedroom, where royal births took place in view of the court. Hardouin-Mansart's showpiece, the Hall of Mirrors, where a united Germany was proclaimed in 1871 and the Treaty of Versailles signed in 1919, is flooded with natural light from its 17 vast windows. Designed to catch the last of the day's rays, it was here that the Sun King would hold extravagant receptions. Other apartments can be seen only as part of a guided tour. The château is undergoing a full-scale restoration, so it's worth checking the website to see which rooms are closed before you visit. The Passeport Versailles (€18) gives access to the château, plus the Grand Trianon, Petit Trianon and Domaine de Marie-Antoinette (*see p333*).

Sprawling across some eight square kilometres (three square miles), the carefully planned gardens consist of formal parterres, ponds, elaborate statues – many commissioned by Colbert in 1674 – and a spectacular series of fountains, served by an ingenious hydraulic system only recently restored to working order. On weekend afternoons from spring to autumn, the fountains are set to music for the Grandes-Eaux Musicales – and they also serve as a backdrop, seven times a year, for the extravagant Fêtes de Nuit, capturing the regal splendour of the Sun King's celebrations with a mixture of fireworks, music and theatre. *Photo p331.*

Grand Trianon/Petit Trianon/ Domaine de Marie-Antoinette

01.30.83.78.00. **Open** *Apr-Oct* noon-6.30pm Tue-Sun. *Nov-Mar* noon-5.30pm Tue-Sun. **Admission** €10; €6 reductions; free under-18s, under-26s (EU citizens), all 1st Sun of mth (Nov-Mar). PMP. **Credit** AmEx, DC, MC, V.

In 1687, Hardouin-Mansart built the pink marble Grand Trianon in the north of the park, away from the protocol of the court. Here Louis XIV and his children's governess and secret second wife, Madame de Maintenon, could admire the intimate gardens from the colonnaded portico. It retains the Empire decor of Napoleon, who stayed here with his second Empress, Marie-Louise.

The Petit Trianon, built for Louis XV's mistress Madame de Pompadour, is a wonderful example of neoclassicism. It later became part of the Domaine de Marie-Antoinette, an exclusive hideaway in the wooded parkland. Given to Marie-Antoinette as a wedding gift by her husband Louis XVI in 1774, the domain also includes the chapel adjoining the Petit Trianon, plus a theatre, a neoclassical 'Temple d'Amour', and Marie-Antoinette's fairy-tale farm and dairy, the Hameau de la Reine. Here, the queen escaped from the discontent of her subjects and the revolutionary fervour of Paris.

Cathédrale Notre-Dame, Reims. See p334.

Potager du Roi

10 rue Maréchal-Joffre (01.39.24.62.62, www. potager-du-roi.fr). **Open** *Nov, Dec* 10am-6pm Tue, Thur; 10am-1pm Sat. *Jan-Mar* 10am-1pm Tue, Thur. *Apr-Oct* 10am-6pm Tue-Sun. **Admission** *Tue-Fri* €4.50; €3 reductions; free under-11s. *Sat, Sun* €6.50; €3 reductions; free under-11s. **Credit** AmEx, DC, MC, V.

The Potager du Roi, the king's vegetable garden, features 16 small squares surrounded by 5,000 fruit trees espaliered into fabulous shapes.

Where to eat & stay

Set in a building dating back to the construction of the château, **Au Chapeau Gris** (7 rue Hoche, 01.39.50.10.81, www.auchapeaugris. com, closed dinner Tue, all day Wed) is the oldest restaurant in Versailles, and serves French country cuisine under wooden beams. **Boeuf à la Mode** (4 rue au Pain, Marché Notre-Dame, 01.39.50.31.99, www.leboeufala mode-versailles.com) is an authentic 1930s brasserie serving steak and seafood. Another long-established restaurant is the traditional **Brasserie du Théâtre** (15 rue des Réservoirs, 01.39.50.03.21, www.brasserietheatre.com), which stays open until 11.30pm for the after-show crowd from the Montansier theatre next door. You'll also find plenty of late-night bars around the Marché Notre-Dame.

The town centre has several reasonably priced hotels. One of the more historic is the **Hôtel du Cheval Rouge** (18 rue André-Chénier, 01.39.50.03.03, www.chevalrouge.fr.st, doubles €82-€96), built in Louis XIV's former stable overlooking the Marché Notre-Dame. Across from the château, the **Hôtel de France** (5 rue Colbert, 01.30.83.92.23, www.hotelfrance-versailles.com, doubles from €119) is set in an 18th-century townhouse and has period decor.

Getting there

By car

20km (12.5 miles) west of Paris by A13 or D10.

By train

For the station nearest the château, take the RER C5 (VICK or VERO trains) to Versailles-Rive Gauche; or take a Transilien SNCF train from Gare St-Lazare to Versailles-Rive Droite (10mins on foot to the château).

Tourist information

Office de Tourisme

2bis av de Paris, 78000 Versailles (01.39.24.88.88, www.versailles-tourisme.com). **Open** *Apr-Oct* 10am-6pm Mon; 9am-7pm Tue-Sun. *Nov-Mar* 11am-5pm Mon, Sun; 9am-6pm Tue-Sat.

Champagne.

ESCAPES & EXCURSIONS

Escapes

CHAMPAGNE COUNTRY

Named after the region in which it's produced, champagne – nearly all 300 million bottles a year of it – comes from the towns of **Reims** (nasally pronounced 'Ranse') and **Epernay**, some 25 kilometres (16 miles) apart. At less than an hour by train from Paris, both are ideal destinations for a weekend break. A tour of a champagne cellar is a big part of most visits. Most cellars give detailed explanations of how the drink is produced – from the grape varieties used to the strict name and quality controls – and guided tours finish with a sample.

Epernay developed in the 19th century as expanding champagne houses moved out from Reims to acquire more space. Today, the aptly named avenue de Champagne is home to most major brands – but the best tours are at **Moët & Chandon** and **Mercier**.

In Reims, most of the major champagne houses are open by appointment only: Krug (03.26.84.44.20, www.krug.com); Lanson (03.26.78.50.50, www.lanson.fr); Louis Roederer (by appointment *and* recommendation only, 03.26.40.42.11, www.champagne-roederer.com) and Veuve Clicquot (03.26.89.53.90, www.veuve-clicquot.com). **Champagne Pommery** is set in an intriguing Elizabethan building.

Home of the coronation church of most French monarchs since Clovis in 496, Reims was an important city even in Roman times. Begun in 1211, the current **Cathédrale Notre-Dame**

(03.26.47.55.34, www.cathedrale-reims.com) has rich Gothic decoration that includes thousands of well-preserved figures on the portals. Look out, too, for the splendid stained-glass windows in the axial chapel, designed by Chagall. The statues damaged during shelling in World War I can be seen next door in the former archbishop's palace, the Palais de Tau (2 pl du Cardinal-Luçon, 03.26.47.81.79).

L'Ancien Collège des Jésuites (1 pl Museux, 03.26.35.34.70) is a classic example of 17th-century Baroque architecture, housing a library decorated with religious carvings.

Champagne Pommery
5 pl du Général-Gouraud, 51100 Reims (03.26.61.62.56, www.pommery.com). **Open** *Apr-Oct* 10am-6pm daily. *Nov-Mar* 10am-5pm daily. **Admission** (incl 1 glass) from €12; free under-10s. **Credit** MC, V.
Built in 1868, this unusual château was modelled on Elizabethan architecture. The visit takes place some 30m (98ft) underground, in 18km (11 miles) of tunnels linking 120 Gallo-Roman chalk quarries.

★ Mercier
68 av de Champagne, 51200 Epernay (03.26.51.22.22, www.champagnemercier.fr). **Open** *Apr-mid Nov* 9.30-11am, 2-4pm daily. *Mid Nov-mid Dec, mid Feb-Mar* 9.30-11am, 2-4pm Mon, Thur-Sun. **Admission** (incl 1 glass) from €11; €5 reductions; free under-10s. **Credit** MC, V.
Some 7,000 tonnes of chalk were extracted to create the 18km (11 miles) of cellars at Mercier, opened in 1858. Note the 20-tonne champagne barrel at the

entrance: it took 24 bulls and 18 horses to drag it from Epernay to Paris for the 1889 Exposition Universelle. The interesting 45-minute underground tour takes place on a little train.

★ Moët & Chandon

20 av de Champagne, 51200 Epernay (03.26.51.20.20, www.moet.com). **Open** *Apr-mid Nov* 9.30-11.30am, 2-4.30pm daily. *Mid Nov-Mar* 9.30-11.30am, 2-4.30pm Mon-Fri. Closed Jan. **Admission** (incl 1 glass) from €16.50; €9.50 reductions; free under-10s. **Credit** AmEx, DC, MC, V.

Moët & Chandon started life in 1743 as champagne supplier to Madame de Pompadour, mistress of Louis XV. It later supplied Napoleon and Alexander I of Russia. Since then it has kept pole position, with the largest domaine and more than 250 global outlets. In the hour-long tour, visitors are led through a section of the 28km (17 miles) of tunnels.

Where to eat & stay

In Reims, countless cafés and brasseries line lively **place Drouet d'Erlon**, as do many hotels. If you fancy staying at a working champagne domaine, contact **Ariston Fils Champagne** (4-8 Grande-Rue, 51170 Brouillet, 03.26.97.43.46, www.champagneaspasie.com, doubles €55-€60), which has three rooms and pampers its guests. To sleep like a king, book one of the luxuriously extravagant rooms at the **Château les Crayères** (64 bd Henry Vasnier, 03.26.24.90.00, www.chateaules crayeres.com, doubles €345-€700), a grand country-house hotel set in lush grounds.

In Epernay, **La Cave à Champagne** (16 rue Léon Gambetta, 03.26.55.50.70, www.la-cave-a-champagne.com) does good traditional French food, as does **Théâtre** (8 pl Pierre-Mendès-France, 03.26.58.88.19, www.epernay-rest-letheatre.com, closed dinner Tue & Sun, all Wed). Known for its champagnes, **Les Cépages** (16 rue Fauvette, 03.26.55.16.93, closed Wed & Sun) serves homely food. Set in a 19th-century red-brick mansion, **Le Clos Raymi** (3 rue Joseph-de-Venoge, 03.26.51.00.58, www.closraymi-hotel.com, doubles €155-€175) is a cosy mix of traditional and modern. Part of the Best Western chain, the **Hôtel de Champagne** (30 rue Eugène-Mercier, 03.26.53.10.60, www.bw-hotel-champagne.com, doubles €95-€120) is comfy, and the **Hôtel Kyriad** (3bis rue de Lorraine, www.kyriad-epernay.fr, doubles from €60) has basic rooms.

Getting there

By car

150km (93 miles) north-east of Paris by A4. For Epernay, exit at Château Thierry and take the N3.

By train

From Gare de l'Est, trains take about 45mins for Reims and Epernay.

Tourist information

Office de Tourisme (Epernay)

7 av de Champagne, 51200 Epernay (03.26.53.33.00, www.ot-epernay.fr). **Open** *Mid Apr-mid Oct* 9.30am-12.30pm, 1.30-7pm Mon-Sat; 11am-4pm Sun. *Mid Oct-mid Apr* 9.30am-12.30pm, 1.30-5.30pm Mon-Sat.

Office de Tourisme (Reims)

2 rue Guillaume-de-Machault, 51100 Reims (08.21.61.01.60, www.reims-tourisme.com). **Open** *Apr-Sept* 9am-7pm Mon-Sat; 10am-6pm Sun. *Oct-Mar* 9am-6pm Mon-Sat; 10am-4pm Sun.

TOURS

Novelist Honoré de Balzac (1799-1850) once described his beloved birthplace as being 'more fresh, flowery and perfumed than any other town in the world', and Tours has a lot going for it today. In fact, it's a positively pleasant city, bursting with history, medieval quarters, a lively student population, colourful flower markets (Wednesday and Saturday on boulevard Béranger) and enticing bars and restaurants. Only an hour from Paris by TGV, it is the official gateway to the Loire Valley, and a choice place in which to refuel before overdosing on sumptuous Renaissance castles.

Sandwiched between the Loire (north) and the Cher (south) rivers, it began life as a fertile floodplain, prized by the Turones – a Celtic tribe that gave modern Tours its name. In 57 BC, Julius Caesar conquered the city, modestly changing its name to Caesarodunum (Caesar's hill). Traces of the third-century Gallo-Roman city wall and amphitheatre can still be seen in the Musée des Beaux-Arts gardens.

INSIDE TRACK AMBOISE

A leisurely 20-minute drive east from Tours (*see above*), Amboise is a small town of narrow streets and quaint residences overlooking the Loire river. It is also home to two star sites: the imposing **Château Royal d'Amboise** (www.chateau-amboise.com), set on a rocky spur and one of the most historically important buildings in the region; and Leonardo da Vinci's former home, the **Clos Lucé** (www.vinci-closluce.com), an exquisitely restored manor house with landscaped gardens and a museum of da Vinci's inventions.

When Christianity arrived, St Martin, the founder of France's first monastery, became bishop of Tours. After his death in 397, his relics, laid to rest in the **Basilique St-Martin**, were believed to have healing powers, drawing in thousands of pilgrims en route to Santiago de Compostela in Spain, and prompting the construction of Tours' medieval quarters.

Throughout the 15th and 16th centuries, the city vied with Paris as the seat of power: Charles VII, Louis XI (who established Tours' silk industry), Charles VIII and François I all cherished Tours; Henry IV preferred Paris.

The city was bombarded by the Prussians in 1870 and suffered widespread damage in World War II, especially in the historic centre, which by the 1960s was a no-go zone of crumbling masonry. Nowadays, after 40 years of regeneration, the medieval quarters contain some of Tours' most charming streets. Pedestrianised **place Plumereau**, with its half-timbered façades housing cafés, galleries and boutiques, is the hub of the town. Wander down lanes like rue Briçonnet to find concealed courtyards, more half-timbered houses and the occasional crooked tower. In **place de Châteauneuf**, a lone Romanesque tower is the only intact segment of the original Basilique-St-Martin, which was sacked by the Huguenots in 1562. The neo-Byzantine **Basilique St-Martin** (02.47.05.63.87, www.basiliquesaintmartin.com) houses St-Martin's shrine further up the road, opposite the ruined vestiges.

The east of Tours is dominated by the **Cathédrale St-Gatien** (02.47.70.21.00). Work began on this splendid building in the 13th century and ended in the 16th century, demonstrating the French Gothic style in its entirety. The stained-glass windows inside are often compared to those of Sainte-Chapelle in Paris. Next door, the archbishop's palace and **Musée des Beaux-Arts** (18 pl François-Sicard, 02.47.05.68.73, www.mba.tours.fr) has a rich collection of paintings by Degas, Rembrandt and Delacroix, plus sculptures by Rodin and Bourdelle. Check out the enormous 200-year-old cedar of Lebanon in the garden.

North of here, Tours' **Château Royal** (25 av André Malraux) looks over the Loire with dishevelled majesty. You can best take in its assorted architecture by following the river: the **Tour de Guise** (look out for machicolations and a pepper-pot roof) was a 13th-century fortress, and the 15th-century **Logis des Gouverneurs** on the quay has gable dormers and a chunk of Gallo-Roman wall at its base.

Further west, the **Eglise St-Julien** has managed to insinuate a wine museum, the **Musée des vins de Touraine** (16 rue Nationale, 02.47.21.62.20, open 9am-noon, 2-6pm Fri-Sun), into its Gothic, monastic cells.

Next door, the **Musée du Compagnonnage** (8 rue Nationale, 02.47.21.62.20, www.musee compagnonnage.fr, open 9am-12.30pm, 2-6pm Mon, Wed-Sun, daily mid June-mid Sept) is a dinky museum, showcasing the handiwork of master craftsmen of the guilds.

Sadly, the only place still keeping the local silk industry alive is the **Manufacture Le Manach** (35 quai Paul Bert), on the right bank of the Loire. The weaving methods here have remained unchanged since the early 19th century, and it is one of the few manufacturers in France capable of reproducing authentic fabrics using patterns from the 17th century. Enquire at the tourist office if you fancy a visit.

Where to eat & stay

For dreamy regional dishes such as *crépine de dinde* (a giant turkey meatball cooked in red wine) and *poire tappée* (poached pear), head to **Le Petit Patrimoine** (58 rue Colbert, 02.47.66.05.81). If *moules-frites* is more your thing, the **Taverne de l'Homme Tranquille** (22 rue du grand Marché, near pl Plumereau, 02.47.61.46.04) has a large selection.

For a few sneaky glasses of Touraine wine before you head back, **Au Chien Jaune** (74 rue Bernard Palissy, 02.47.05.10.17), a former brothel, is in a handy spot by the tourist office.

If you're on a budget, a good, cheap option in a central location is **Hôtel Mondial** (3 pl de la Résistance, 02.47.05.62.68, www.hotelmondial tours.com, doubles €58-€89). For a touch more luxury, follow in the footsteps of Winston Churchill and try Tours' only four-star hotel, **L'Hôtel de l'Univers** (5 bd Heurteloup, 02.47.05.37.12, www.hotel-univers.fr, doubles €201-€295); or for somewhere a little more modest, with decent rooms and a pretty garden, the **Best Western Central Hôtel** (21 rue Berthelot, 02.47.05.46.44, www.bestwestern centralhoteltours.com, doubles €104-€160), is more charming than other chain hotels in Tours.

Getting there

By car

235km (146 miles) west from Paris by A10.

By train

From Gare Montparnasse to Tours centre (1hr).

Tourist information

Office de Tourisme

78 rue Bernard Palissy, 37042 Tours (02.47.70.37.37, www.tours-tourisme.fr). **Open** *Apr-Sept* 8.30am-7pm Mon-Sat; 10am-12.30pm, 2.30-5pm Sun & bank hols. *Oct-Mar* 9am-12.30pm, 1.30-6pm Mon-Sat; 10am-1pm Sun & bank hols.

Moving Masterpieces

Paris's most visited museums make for the provinces.

Paris's twin cultural giants, the **Louvre** and the **Centre Pompidou**, are the capital's two most visited museums, bringing in more than eight million visitors each year to gawp at the artistic treasures within. But while the galleries are stacked full of masterpieces ancient and modern, the problem has always been that their vaults are heaving with acres of unseen treasures. So the Pompidou decided to follow in the footsteps of Tate Liverpool and the Guggenheim Bilbao, and open an outpost in the eastern city of Metz (www.centrepompidou-metz.fr) in 2010 with the same *raison d'être* as the original – namely to 'present and help discover all forms of artistic expression, raise public awareness of the major works of the 20th and 21st centuries, and take part in Europe's cultural landscape'. And, presumably, to shift some of the stock sitting in the basement in Paris. The experiment has been a great success so far, with some 550,000 visitors checking out the Shigeru Ban-designed multi-disciplinary space.

Not to be outdone, the Louvre is now playing its own regeneration game with an outpost in the gritty northern industrial town of Lens (www.louvrelens.fr). Far from the grandiose surroundings of the 1st arrondissement, the museum sprawls across the site of an old mine works and opened in December 2012. Metz lies just 80 minutes from Paris by TGV and Lens is even closer (70 minutes), which puts it firmly in day-trip distance, as well as tapping into the Lille catchment area.

At Lens, the main display space, the 2,000sq m Galerie du Temps, will display some 300 artworks taken from every department in the Louvre. There's also a 300-seat auditorium, La Scène, which will aim to bring the Louvre's collection to life through live performance.

Centre Pompidou Metz.

In Context

History

Gauls, guillotines and grands projets.

The earliest settlers seem to have arrived in Paris around 120,000 years ago. One of them lost a flint spear-tip on the hill now called Montmartre, and the dangerous-looking weapon is to be seen today in the Stone Age collection at the Musée des Antiquités Nationales. There was a Stone Age weapons factory under present-day Châtelet, and the redevelopment of Bercy in the 1990s unearthed ten neolithic canoes, five of which are now sitting high and dry in the Musée Carnavalet.

By 250 BC, a Celtic tribe known as the Parisii had put the place firmly on the map. The Parisii were river traders, wealthy enough to mint gold coins; the Musée de la Monnaie de Paris has an extensive collection of their small change. Their most important *oppidum*, a primitive fortified town, was located on an island in the Seine river, which is generally thought to have been what is today's Ile de la Cité. A superb strategic location and the capacity to generate hard cash were guaranteed to attract the attention of the Romans.

ROMAN PARIS

Julius Caesar arrived in southern Gaul as proconsul in 58 BC, and soon used the pretext of dealing with invading barbarians to stick his Roman nose into the affairs of northern Gaul. Caesar had a battle on his hands, but eventually the Paris region and the rest of Gaul were in Roman hands. Roman Lutetia (as Paris was known) was a prosperous town of around 8,000 inhabitants. As well as centrally heated villas and a temple to Jupiter on the main island (the remains of both are visible in the Crypte Archéologique), there were the sumptuous baths (now the Musée National du Moyen Age) and the 15,000-seater Arènes de Lutèce.

CHRISTIANITY

Christianity arrived in around 250 AD in the shape of Denis of Athens, who became the first bishop of Paris. Legend has it that when he was decapitated by Valerian on Mons Martis, the mount of the martyrs (today better known as Montmartre), Denis picked up his head and walked with it to what is now St-Denis, to be buried there. The event is depicted in Henri Bellechose's *Retable de Saint-Denis*, now exhibited in the Louvre.

Gaul was still a tempting prize. Waves of barbarian invaders began crossing the Rhine from 275 onwards. They sacked more than 60 cities in Gaul, including Lutetia, where the people were massacred and the buildings on the Montagne Ste-Geneviève were pillaged and burned. The bedraggled survivors used the rubble to build a rampart around the Ile de la Cité and to fortify the forum.

It was at this time that the city was renamed Paris. Protected by the Seine and the new fortifications, its main role was as a rear base for the Roman armies defending Gaul, and it was here in 360 that Julian was proclaimed emperor by his troops. Around 450, with the arrival of the Huns in the region, the people of Paris prepared once again to flee. They were dissuaded by the feisty Geneviève, famed for her piety. Seeing the walls of the city defended against him, no less a pillager than Attila the Hun was forced to turn back; he was defeated soon afterwards.

'Legend has it that when Denis of Athens was decapitated by Valerian on Mons Martis (Montmartre), he picked up his head and walked to what is now St-Denis, to be buried there.'

CLOVIS

In 464, Paris managed to resist another siege, this time by the Francs under Childeric. However, by 486, after a further blockade lasting ten years, Geneviève had no option but to surrender the city to Childeric's successor, Clovis, who went on to conquer most of Gaul and founded the Merovingian dynasty. He chose Paris as capital of his new kingdom, and it stayed that way until the seventh century, in spite of conflicts among his successors. Under the influence of his wife, Clotilde, Clovis converted to Christianity. He founded, and was buried in, the basilica of the Saints-Apôtres, later rededicated to Ste Geneviève when the saviour and future patron saint of Paris was interred there in 512. All that remains of the basilica today is a pillar in the grounds of the Lycée Henri IV; but there's a shrine dedicated to St Geneviève and some relics in the fine Gothic church of St-Etienne-du-Mont next door. Geneviève and Clovis had set a trend. The Ile de la Cité was still the heart of the city, but, under the Merovingians, the Left Bank was the up-and-coming area for fashion-conscious Christians, with 11 churches built here in the period (whereas there were only four on the Right Bank and one on Ile de la Cité). Not everyone was sold on the joys of city living, though. From 614 onwards, the Merovingian kings preferred the *banlieue* at Clichy, or

IN CONTEXT

wandered the kingdom trying to keep rebellious nobles in check. When one of the rebels, Pippin 'the Short', decided to do away with the last Merovingian in 751, Paris was starting to look passé.

Pippin's son, Charlemagne, built his capital at Aix-la-Chapelle (now Aachen in Germany), and his successors, the Carolingian dynasty, moved from palace to palace, consuming the local produce. Paris, meanwhile, was doing nicely as a centre for Christian learning, and had grown to a population of 20,000 by the beginning of the ninth century. This was the high point in the political power of the great abbeys like St-Germain-des-Prés, where transcription of the Latin classics was helping to preserve much of Europe's Roman cultural heritage. Power in the Paris area was exercised by the counts of Paris.

PARIS FINDS ITS FEET

From 845, Paris had to fight off another threat – the Vikings. But after various sackings and seiges, the Carolingians were finally able to secure the city. The dynasty gave way to the Capetian dynasty in 987, when Hugues Capet was elected king of France. Under the Capetians, although Paris was now at the heart of the royal domains, the city did not yet dominate the kingdom. Robert 'the Pious', king from 996 to 1031, stayed more often in Paris than his father had done, restoring the royal palace on the Ile de la Cité, and Henri I (1031-60) issued more of his charters in Paris than in Orléans. In 1112, the abbey of St-Denis replaced St-Benoît-sur-Loire as principal monastery.

Paris itself still consisted of little more than Ile de la Cité and small settlements under the protection of the abbeys on each bank. On the Left Bank, royal largesse helped to rebuild the abbeys of St-Germain-des-Prés, St-Marcel and Ste-Geneviève, although it took more than 150 years for the destruction wrought there by the Vikings to be repaired. The Right Bank, where mooring was easier, prospered from river commerce, and three boroughs grew up around the abbeys of St-Germain-l'Auxerrois, St-Martin-des-Champs and St-Gervais. Bishop Sully

of Paris began building the cathedral of Notre-Dame in 1163. The reign of Philippe-Auguste (1180-1223) was a turning point in the history of Paris. Before, the city was a confused patchwork of royal, ecclesiastical and feudal authorities. Keen to raise revenues, Philippe favoured the growth of the guilds, especially the butchers, drapers, furriers, haberdashers and merchants; so began the rise of the bourgeoisie.

He also ordered the building of the first permanent market buildings at Les Halles, and a new city wall, first on the Right Bank to protect the commercial heart of Paris, and later on the Left Bank. At the western end of the wall, Philippe built a castle, the Louvre, to defend the road from the ever-menacing Normandy, whose duke was also King of England.

A GOLDEN AGE

Paris was now the principal residence of the king and the uncontested capital of France. To accommodate the growing royal administration, the Palais de la Cité, site and symbol of power for the previous thousand years, was remodelled and enlarged. Work was begun by Louis IX (later St Louis) in the 1240s, and continued under Philippe IV ('le Bel'). This architectural complex, of which the Sainte-Chapelle and nearby Conciergerie can still be seen, was inaugurated with great pomp at Pentecost 1313.

The palace was quickly filled with functionaries, so the king spent as much of his time as he could outside Paris at the royal castles of Fontainebleau and, especially, Vincennes. The needs of the plenipotentiaries left behind to run the kingdom were met by a rapidly growing city population, piled into less chic buildings.

Paris was also reinforcing its identity as a major religious centre: as well as the local clergy and dozens of religious orders, the city was home to the masters and students of the university of the Sorbonne (established in 1253), who were already gaining a reputation for rowdiness. An influx of scholars from all over Europe gave the city a cultural and intellectual cachet it was never to lose.

IN CONTEXT

By 1328, Paris was home to 200,000 inhabitants, making it the most populous city in Europe. However, that year was also notable for being the last of the medieval golden age: the dynasty of Capetian kings spluttered to an inglorious halt when Charles IV died without an heir. The English quickly claimed the throne for Edward III, the son of Philippe IV's daughter. Refusing to recognise his descent through the female line, the late king's cousin, Philippe de Valois, claimed the French crown as Philippe VI. So began the Hundred Years War between France and England – a war that in fact would go on for 116 years.

'In 1431, Henry VI of England was crowned King of France in Notre-Dame. He didn't last. Five years later, Henry was driven back to Calais by the Valois king, Charles VII.'

TROUBLES AND STRIFE

To make matters worse, the Black Death (bubonic plague) ravaged Europe from the 1340s onwards. Citizens not finished by the plague had to contend with food shortages, increasing taxes, riots, repression, currency devaluations and marauding mercenaries. Meanwhile, in Paris, the honeymoon period for the king and the bourgeoisie was coming to an end. Rich and populous, Paris was expected to bear the brunt of the war burden; and as defeat followed defeat (notably the disaster at Crécy in August 1346), the bourgeoisie and people of the city were increasingly exasperated by the futility of the sacrifices they were making for the hideously expensive war. To fund the conflict, King Jean II tried to introduce

new tax laws – without success. When the king was captured by the English at Poitiers in 1356, his problems passed to his 18-year-old son, Charles.

The Etats Généraux, consultant body to the throne, was summoned to the royal palace on the Ile de la Cité to discuss the country's woes. The teenage king was besieged with angry demands for reform from the bourgeoisie, particularly from Etienne Marcel, then provost of the local merchants. Marcel seized control of Paris and began a bitter power struggle with the crown; in 1357, fearing widespread revolt, Charles fled to Compiègne. But as he ran, he had Paris blockaded. Marcel called on the peasants, who were raging against taxes, but they were crushed. He then called on Charles 'the Bad' of Navarre, ally to the English, but his arrival in Paris made many of Marcel's supporters nervous. On 31 July 1358, Marcel was murdered, and the revolution was over. As a safeguard, the returning Charles built a stronghold to protect Paris: the Bastille.

By 1420, following the French defeat at Agincourt, Paris was in English hands; in 1431, Henry VI of England was crowned King of France in Notre-Dame. He didn't last. Five years later, Henry and his army were driven back to Calais by the Valois king, Charles VII. Charles owed his power to Jeanne d'Arc, who led the victorious French in the Battle of Orléans, only to be betrayed by her compatriots, who decided she was getting too big for her boots. She was captured and sold to the English, who had her burned as a witch.

By 1436, Paris was once again the capital of France. But the nation had been bled nearly dry by war and was still divided politically, with powerful regional rulers across France continuing to threaten the monarchy. Outside the French borders, the ambitions of the Austrian Habsburg dynasty represented a serious threat. In this general atmosphere of instability, disputes over trade, religion and taxation were all simmering dangerously.

RENAISSANCE AND REFORMATION

In the closing decades of the 15th century, the restored Valois monarchs sought to reassert their position. A wave of building projects was the public sign of this effort, producing such masterpieces as St-Etienne-du-Mont, St-Eustache and private homes like Hôtel de Cluny (which today houses the Musée National du Moyen Age) and the Hôtel de Sens, which now accommodates the Bibliothèque de Forney. The Renaissance in France had its peak under François I. As well as being involved in the construction of the magnificent châteaux at Fontainebleau, Blois and Chambord, François was responsible for transforming the Louvre from a fortress into a royal palace.

Despite burning heretics by the dozen, François was unable to stop the spread of Protestantism, launched in Germany by Martin Luther in 1517. Resolutely Catholic, Paris was the scene of some horrific violence against the Huguenots, as supporters of the new faith were called. By the 1560s, the situation had degenerated into open warfare. Catherine de Médicis, the scheming Italian widow of Henri II, was the real force in court politics. It was she who connived to murder prominent Protestants gathered in Paris for the marriage of the king's sister on St Bartholomew's Day (23 August 1572). Catherine's main aim was to dispose of her powerful rival, Gaspard de Coligny, but the situation got out of hand, and as many as 3,000 people were butchered. Henri III attempted to reconcile the religious factions and eradicate the powerful families directing the conflict, but the people of Paris turned against him and he was forced to flee. His assassination in 1589 brought the Valois line to an end.

THE BOURBONS

The throne of France being up for grabs, Henri of Navarre declared himself King Henri IV, launching the Bourbon dynasty. Paris was not impressed. The city closed its gates against the Huguenot king, and the inhabitants endured a four-year siege by supporters of the new ruler. Henri managed to break the impasse by having himself converted to Catholicism (and is supposed to have said, '*Paris vaut bien une messe*' – Paris is well worth a mass).

Henri set about rebuilding his ravaged capital. He completed the Pont Neuf, the first bridge to span the whole Seine. He commissioned place Dauphine and the city's first enclosed residential square – the place Royale, now place des Vosges.

Henri also tried to reconcile his Catholic and Protestant subjects, issuing the Edict of Nantes in 1598, effectively giving each religion equal status. The Catholics hated the deal, and the Huguenots were suspicious. Henri was the subject of at least 23 attempted assassinations by fanatics of both persuasions. Finally, in 1610, a Catholic by the name of François Ravaillac fatally stabbed the king while he was in traffic on rue de la Ferronnerie.

TWO CARDINALS

Since Henri's son, Louis XIII, was only eight at the time of his father's death, his mother, Marie de Médicis, took up the reins of power. We can thank her for the Palais du Luxembourg and the 24 paintings she commissioned from Rubens, now part of the Louvre collection. Louis took up his royal duties in 1617, but Cardinal Richelieu, chief minister from 1624, was the man who ran France. Something of a schemer, he outwitted the king's mother, his wife (Anne of Austria) and a host of others. Richelieu helped to strengthen the power of the monarch, and he did much to limit the independence of the aristocracy.

The Counter-Reformation was at its height, and lavish churches such as the Baroque Val-de-Grâce were an important reassertion of Catholic supremacy. The 17th century was 'le Grand Siècle', a time of patronage of art and artists, even if censorship forced the brilliant mathematician and philosopher René Descartes into exile. The first national newspaper, *La Gazette*, hit the streets in 1631; Richelieu used it as a propaganda tool. The cardinal founded the Académie Française, which is still working, slowly, on the dictionary of the French language that Richelieu commissioned from them in 1634. Richelieu died in 1642; Louis XIII followed suit a few months later. The new king, Louis XIV, was five years old. Anne of Austria became regent, with the Italian Cardinal Mazarin, a Richelieu protégé, as chief minister. Rumour has it that Anne and Mazarin may have been married. Mazarin's townhouse is now home to the Bibliothèque Nationale de France – Richelieu.

Endless wars against Austria and Spain had depleted the royal coffers and left the nation drained by exorbitant taxation. In 1648, the royal family was chased out of Paris by a popular uprising, 'la Fronde', named after the catapults used by some of the rioters. Parisians soon tired of the anarchy that followed. When Mazarin's army retook the city in 1653, the boy-king was warmly welcomed. Mazarin died in 1661 and Louis XIV, now 24 years old, decided he would rule France without the assistance of any chief minister.

SHINE ON, SUN KING

The '*Roi Soleil*', or Sun King, was an absolute monarch. '*L'état, c'est moi*' (I am the State) was his vision of power. To prove his grandeur, the king embarked on wars against England, Holland and Austria. He also refurbished and extended the Louvre, commissioned place Vendôme and place des Victoires, constructed the Observatory and laid out the *grands boulevards* along the line of the old city walls. His major project was the palace at Versailles. Louis moved his court there in 1682.

Louis XIV owed much of his brilliant success to the work of Jean-Baptiste Colbert, who was nominally in charge of state finances, but eventually took control of all the important levers of the state machine. Colbert was the force behind the Sun King's redevelopment of Paris. The Hôtel des Invalides was built to accommodate the crippled survivors of Louis' wars, the Salpêtrière to shelter fallen women. In 1702, Paris was divided into 20 quartiers (not until the Revolution was it re-mapped into arrondissements). Colbert died in 1683, and Louis' luck on the battlefield ran out. Hopelessly embroiled in the War of the Spanish Succession, the country was devastated by famine in 1692. The Sun King died in 1715, leaving no direct heir. His five-year-old great-grandson, Louis XV, was named king, with Philippe d'Orléans as regent.

The court moved back to Paris. Installed in the Palais-Royal, the regent set about enjoying his few years of power, hosting lavish dinners that degenerated into orgies. The state, meanwhile, remained chronically in debt.

THE ENLIGHTENMENT

Some of the city's more sober residents were making Paris the intellectual capital of Europe. Enlightenment thinkers such as Diderot, Montesquieu, Voltaire and Rousseau were active during the reign of Louis XV. Literacy rates were increasing – 50 per cent of French men could read, 25 per cent of women – and the publishing industry was booming.

The king's mistress, Madame de Pompadour, encouraged him to finance the building of the Ecole Militaire and the laying out of place Louis XV, known to us as place de la Concorde. The church of St-Sulpice was completed in 1776. Many of the great houses in the area bounded by rue de Lille, rue de Varenne and rue de Grenelle date from the first half of the 18th century. The private homes of aristocrats and wealthy bourgeois, these would become the venues for numerous salons, the informal discussion sessions often devoted to topics raised by Enlightenment questioning.

The Enlightenment spirit of rational humanism finally took the venom out of the Catholic–Protestant power struggle, and the increase in public debate helped to change views about the nature of the state and the place and authority of the monarchy. As Jacques Necker, Louis XVI's finance minister on the eve of the Revolution, put it, popular opinion was 'an invisible power that, without treasury, guard or army, gives its laws to the city, the court and even the palaces of kings'. Thanks to the Enlightenment, and a growing burden of taxation on the poorest strata of society to prop up the wealthiest, that power would eventually overturn the status quo.

THE FRENCH REVOLUTION

The great beneficiary of the French Revolution, Napoleon Bonaparte, once remarked that lucky generals were to be

Louis IX. *See p343.*

preferred over good generals. The same applies to kings, and the gods of fortune certainly deserted Louis XVI in 1789, when bad weather and worse debts brought France to its knees. But few would have predicted the next five years would see the execution of the king and most of the royal family, terror stalking the streets in the name of revolution, and the steady rise of a young Corsican soldier. For an account of the Revolution, *see p348* **The French Revolution**.

NAPOLEON

Amid the post-Revolutionary chaos, power was divided between a two-housed Assembly and a Directory of five men. The French public reacted badly to hearing of England's attempts to promote more popular rebellion; when a royalist rising in Paris needed to be put down, a young officer from Corsica was the man to do it – Napoleon Bonaparte.

Napoleon quickly became the Directory's right-hand man. When they needed someone to lead a campaign against Austria, he was the man. Victory saw France – and Napoleon – glorified. After an aborted campaign to Egypt in 1799, Napoleon returned home to put down another royalist plot, made himself the chief of the newly governing three-man Consul – and by 1804 was emperor.

After failing to squeeze out the English by setting up the Continental System to block trade across the Channel, Napoleon waged massive wars against Britain, Russia and Austria. On his way to the disaster of Moscow, Napoleon gave France the *lycée* educational system, the Napoleonic Code of civil law, the Legion of Honour, the Banque de France, the Pont des Arts, the Arc de Triomphe, the Madeleine church (he re-established Catholicism as the state religion), La Bourse and rue de Rivoli.

The French Revolution

From conception to bloody execution.

In the winter of 1788-89, Louis XVI was losing grip on his country's problems. Wars had left the state practically bankrupt; harvests had failed and food prices soared. Distress and discontent reigned, and with it came demands for an end to absolute monarchy and wider participation in government. Under pressure, Louis allowed the formation of an Assemblée Nationale, which began work on a national constitution. But behind the scenes, he began gathering troops to force it to disband; and on 12 July, he dismissed the commoner's ally, finance minister Jacques Necker. On 14 July, a crowd stormed the Bastille prison in response. Only seven prisoners were inside but the symbolic victory was huge.

The establishment of the constitution forged ahead. Tax breaks for the nobility and clergy were abolished; Church property was seized. But the price of bread remained high. In October, a mob of starving women marched the 12 miles to Versailles and demanded that the king come to Paris. He promised to send them grain, an offer they rejected by decapitating some of his guards.

Louis transferred to the Tuileries. In the months that followed, the Jacobins roused powerful Republican feeling. The king and his family tried to flee Paris on 20 June 1791, but were apprehended.

On 14 September, Louis accepted the constitution. But other monarchies were plotting to reinstate him. In 1792, Austrian and Prussian troops invaded France. The Republicans, correctly, suspected Louis of conspiracy, and raised an army to capture him. He and his family were incarcerated by the radical Commune de Paris, headed by Danton, Marat and Robespierre.

Then came a massacre. Republicans invaded the prisons and murdered 2,000 so-called traitors. The monarchy was abolished on 22 September; the king was executed on 21 January 1793. Headed by Robespierre, the Jacobins vowed to wage terror against all dissidents. The Great Terror of 1794 saw the guillotine slice through 1,300 necks in six weeks. Eventually there was no more stomach for killing. On 28 July 1794, Robespierre was executed and the bloodiest of revolutions was over.

He was also responsible for the centralised bureaucracy that still drives the French public mad.

As Russian troops – who had chased Napoleon's once-mighty army all the way from Moscow and Leipzig – invaded France, Paris itself came under threat. Montmartre, then named Montnapoléon, had a telegraph machine at its summit, one that had given so many of the emperor's orders and transmitted news of so many victories. The hill fell to Russian troops. Napoleon gave the order to blow up the city's main powder stores, and thus Paris itself. His officer refused. Paris accommodated carousing Russian, Prussian and English soldiers while Napoleon was sent to exile in Elba. A hundred days later, he was back, leading an army against Wellington and Blücher's troops in the mud of Waterloo, near Brussels. A further defeat saw the end of him. Paris survived further foreign occupation. The diminutive Corsican died on the South Atlantic prison island of St Helena in 1821.

ANOTHER ROUND OF BOURBONS

Having sampled revolution and military dictatorship, the French were now ready to give monarchy a second chance. The Bourbons got back in business in 1815, in the person of Louis XVIII, Louis XVI's elderly brother. Several efforts were made to adapt the monarchy to the new political realities, though the new king's Charter of Liberties was not a wholly sincere expression of how he meant to rule.

When another brother of Louis XVI, Charles X, became king in 1824, he decided that enough royal energy had been wasted trying to reconcile the nation's myriad factions. It was time for a spot of old-fashioned absolutism. But the forces unleashed during the Revolution, and the social divisions that had opened as a result, were not to be ignored – and the people were happy to respond with some old-fashioned rebellion.

In the 1830 elections, the liberals won a hefty majority in the Chamber of Deputies, the legislative body. Charles's unpopular minister Prince Polignac, a returned émigré, promptly dissolved the Chamber, announced a date for new elections and curtailed the number of voters. Polishing off this collection of bad decisions was the 26 July decree abolishing the freedom of the press. The day after its issue, 5,000 print workers and journalists filled the streets and three newspapers went to press. When police tried to confiscate copies, they sparked a three-day riot, 'les Trois Glorieuses', with members of the disbanded National Guard manning the barricades. On 30 July, Charles dismissed Polignac, but it was too late. He had little choice but to abdicate, and fled to England. As French revolutions go, it was a neat, brief affair.

Another leftover from the *ancien régime* was now winched on to the throne – Louis-Philippe, Duc d'Orléans, who had some Bourbon blood in his veins. A father of eight who never went out without his umbrella, he was eminently acceptable to the newly powerful bourgeoisie. But the poor, who had risked their lives in two attempts to change French society, were unimpressed by the new king's promise to embrace a moderate and liberal version of the Revolutionary heritage.

THE NINETEENTH CENTURY

Philosopher Walter Benjamin declared Paris 'the capital of the 19th century', and he had a point. Though it was smaller than its global rival, London, in intellectual and cultural spheres it reigned supreme. On the demographic front, its population doubled to one million between 1800 and 1850. Most of the new arrivals were rural labourers, who had come to find work on the city's expanding building sites. Meanwhile, the middle classes were doing well, thanks to the relatively late arrival of the industrial revolution in France, and the solid administrative structures inherited from Napoleon. The poor were as badly off as ever, only now there were more of them. The back-breaking hours worked in the factories would not be curbed by legislation: 'Whatever the lot of the workers is, it is not the manufacturer's responsibility to improve it,' said one trade minister. In Left Bank cafés, a new bohemian tribe of students derided the materialistic government. Workers'

IN CONTEXT

pamphlets and newspapers, such as *La Ruche Populaire*, gave voice to the starving, crippled poor. A wave of ill feeling was gradually building up against Louis-Philippe.

On 23 February 1848, hundreds of Parisians – men, women and students – moved along the boulevards towards a public banquet at La Madeleine. The king's minister, François Guizot, had forbidden any direct campaigning by opposition parties in the forthcoming election, so the parties held banquets instead of meetings.

One diarist of the time noted that some of the crowd had stuffed swords and daggers underneath their shirts, but the demonstration was largely peaceful – until the troops stationed on the boulevard des Capucines opened fire, igniting a riot.

As barricades sprang up all over the city, a trembling Louis-Philippe abdicated and a liberal provisional government declared a republic. The virtual epidemic of poverty and unemployment was stemmed by creating national *ateliers*, but such 'radical' reforms made the right extremely nervous. A conservative government took power in May 1848, and shut down the *ateliers*. A month later, the poor were back in the streets. Some 50,000 took part in the 'June Days' protests, which were quite comprehensively crushed by General Cavaignac's troops. In total, about 1,500 Parisians died and some 5,000 were deported. As the pamphleteer Alphonse Karr said of the revolution's aftermath, '*plus ça change, plus c'est la même chose*' (the more things change, the more they stay the same). In December 1848, Louis Bonaparte – nephew of Napoleon – was elected president. By 1852, he had moved into the Tuileries palace and declared himself Emperor Napoleon III.

THE SECOND EMPIRE

The emperor appointed a lawyer as *préfet* to mastermind the reconstruction of Paris. In less than two decades, prefect Georges-Eugène Haussmann had created the most magnificent city in Europe. His goals included better access to railway stations, better water supplies, and a long list of new hospitals, barracks, theatres and *mairies*. It was a colossal project, and it transformed the capital with a network of wide avenues that were more hygienic than the narrow streets they replaced.

Not everyone was happy. Haussmann's works destroyed thousands of buildings, including beautiful Middle Ages monuments; on the whole of Ile de la Cité only Notre-Dame and a handful of houses survived. Entire residential areas were wiped off the map, and only the owners of the buildings themselves were compensated; tenants were merely booted out. Writers and artists lamented the loss of the more quirky Paris they used to know, and criticised the unfriendly grandeur of the new city. But there was no going back.

At home, the rapid industrialisation of the city saw the rise of Socialism and Communism among the disgruntled working classes, and Napoleon III gave limited rights to trade unions. Abroad, though, the now constitutional monarch was a disaster. After the relatively successful Crimean War of the mid 1850s, he tried in vain to impose the Catholic Maximilian as ruler of Mexico. The Franco-Prussian war was his next misadventure. France was soon defeated. At Sedan, in September 1870, 100,000 French troops were forced to surrender to Bismarck's Prussians; Napoleon III himself was captured, never to return.

The war continued, and back in Paris, a provisional government hastily took power. Elections gave conservative monarchists the majority, though the Paris vote was firmly Republican. Former prime minister Adolphe Thiers assumed executive power. Meanwhile, Prussian forces marched on Paris and laid siege to the city. Paris held out, starving, for four brave months, its citizens picking rats from the gutter for food. Léon Gambetta, a young politician, escaped in style (by hot-air balloon) but failed to raise an army in the south. In January 1871, the provisional government signed a bitter armistice that relinquished the industrial heartlands of Alsace and Lorraine and agreed to pay a five-million-franc indemnity. German troops would stay on French soil until the bill was paid.

But with occupying army camps stationed around their city, Parisians considered the treaty a dishonour and remained defiant. Thiers ordered his soldiers to enter the city and strip it of its cannons, but the insurgents cut them short. The new government scuttled off to the haven of Versailles, and on 26 March Paris elected its own municipal body, the Commune, so called in memory of the spirit of 1792. The 92 members of the Commune hailed from the left and working classes; their agenda was liberal (schools would be secularised, debts suspended) but war-like (Germany must be defeated). Paris itself was given a little makeover: the column extolling Napoleonic glory on place Vendôme was pulled down, and statues of the great emperor were smashed all over town.

Thiers would not stand by and watch. Artillery fire picked at the Communards' sandbag barricades on the edges of Paris, and the suburbs fell by 11 April. In the sixth week of fighting, troops broke in through the Porte de St-Cloud and covered the springtime city in blood. The ill-equipped Communards faced a massacre: some 25,000 were killed in a matter of days. In revenge, around 50 hostages were taken and shot, including the Archbishop of Paris. The infamous *pétroleuses*, women wielding petrol bombs, burned off their anger, torching the Tuileries and the Hôtel de Ville. On the last day of *la semaine sanglante*, 28 May, 147 Communards were trapped and shot in Père-Lachaise cemetery, against the 'Mur des Fédérés', still an icon of the Commune struggle. The dead were buried in the streets, the prisons crammed with 40,000 Communards; thousands were deported, many to penal colonies in New Caledonia.

THE THIRD REPUBLIC

Thanks mainly to the huge economic boost provided by colonial expansion in Africa and Indo-China, the horrors of the Commune were soon forgotten in the self-indulgent materialism of the turn of the century and the Third Republic. The Eiffel Tower was built as the centrepiece of the 1889 Exposition Universelle. For the next

Exposition Universelle, in 1900, the Grand Palais and Petit Palais, the Pont Alexandre III and the Gare d'Orsay (now the Musée d'Orsay) were built to affirm France's position as a world power, and the first line of the métro opened. The first film screening had been held (1895), and clubs like the Moulin Rouge were buzzing. The lurid life of Montmartre – and its cheap rents – would attract the world's artistic community.

THE GREAT WAR

On 3 August 1914, Germany declared war on France. Although the Germans never made it to Paris in World War I – German troops were stopped 20 kilometres (12 miles) short of the city thanks to the French victory in the Battle of the Marne – the artillery was audible. Paris, and French society as a whole, suffered terribly, despite ultimate victory.

The nations gathered at Versailles to make the peace, and established new European states. The League of Nations was formed. Artists responded to the horrors and absurdity of the conflict with Surrealism, a movement founded in Paris by André Breton, a doctor who had treated troops in the trenches and embraced Freud's theories of the unconscious. In 1924, Surrealism had a manifesto, a year later its first exhibition. Again, artists (and photographers) flocked to Paris. Montmartre was now too expensive, and Montparnasse became the hub of artistic life. The interwar years were a whirl of activity in artistic and political circles. Paris became the avant-garde capital of the world, recorded by Hemingway, F Scott Fitzgerald and Gertrude Stein.

Meanwhile, the Depression unleashed a wave of political violence, Fascists fighting Socialists and Communists for control. At the same time, many writers were leaving Paris for Spain to cover – and, indeed, to take part in – the Civil War. Across the German border, the contentious territories of Alsace-Lorraine – and the burden of the World War I peace agreements signed in Paris – became one of many bugbears held by the new chancellor, Adolf Hitler. As war broke out,

IN CONTEXT

France believed its Maginot line would hold against the German threat. When the Nazis attacked France in May 1940, they simply bypassed the fortifications and came through the Ardennes.

WORLD WAR II

Paris was in German hands by June. The city fell without a fight. A pro-German government was set up in Vichy, headed by Marshall Pétain, and a young army officer, Charles de Gaulle, went to London to organise the Free French opposition. For Frenchmen happy to get along with the German army, the period of the Occupation presented few hardships and, indeed, some good business opportunities. Food was rationed, and tobacco and coffee went out of circulation, but the black market thrived. For people who resisted, there were the Gestapo torture chambers at avenue Foch or rue Lauriston. The Germans further discouraged uncooperative behaviour with executions: one victim, whose name now adorns a métro station, was Jacques Bonsergent, a student caught fly-posting and shot because he refused to reveal the names of his friends who escaped.

The Vichy government was so eager to please the Germans, it organised anti-Semitic measures without prompting. From the spring of 1941, the French authorities deported Jews to the death camps, frequently via the internment camp at Drancy. Prime Minister Pierre Laval argued that it was a necessary concession to his Third Reich masters. In July 1942, 12,000 Jewish French citizens were rounded up in the Vélodrome d'Hiver, a sports complex on the quai de Grenelle, and then dispatched to Auschwitz.

THE LIBERATION

Paris survived the war practically unscathed, ultimately thanks to the bravery of one of its captors. On 23 August 1944, as the Allied armies of liberation approached the city, Hitler ordered his commander, Dietrich von Choltitz, to detonate the explosives that had been set all over town in anticipation of a retreat. Von Choltitz refused. On 25 August, French troops, tactfully placed at the head of the US forces, entered the city, and General de Gaulle led the parade down the Champs-Elysées. Writers and artists swept back into Paris to celebrate. Hemingway held court at the Ritz and Scribe hotels with the great journalists of the day, clinking glasses with veterans of the Spanish Civil War such as photographer Robert Capa and George Orwell. Picasso's studio was besieged by well-wishers.

However, the Liberation was by no means the end of France's troubles. De Gaulle was the hero of the hour, but relations between the interim government he commanded and the Resistance – largely Communist – were still tricky. Orders issued to maquis leaders in the provinces were often ignored. The Communists wanted a revolution, and de Gaulle suspected them of hatching plans to seize Paris prior to August 1944. Meanwhile, de Gaulle knew that he had to commit every available French soldier to the march on Germany, or risk being sidelined by the other Allies after the war. He had to leave homeland security to the very people – the 'patriotic militias' – who were most likely to be at least sympathetic to the Communist cause; or, even more dubiously, gendarmes who had previously worked with the occupying power.

Recovery was slow. There were shortages of everything; indeed, many complained they had been better off under the Germans. Even in the ministries, paper was so scarce that correspondence had to be sent out on Vichy letterhead with the sender crossing out 'Etat Français' at the top and writing 'République Française' instead.

THE FOURTH REPUBLIC

On 8 May 1945, de Gaulle made a broadcast to the nation to announce Germany's surrender. Paris went wild, but the euphoria didn't last. There were strikes. And more strikes. Liberation had proved to be a restoration, not the revolution the Communists, now the most powerful political force in the land, had hoped for. The Communist Party was, in at least one respect, as pragmatic as everyone else: it did its utmost to turn parliamentary democracy to its advantage, to wit, getting as many of the top jobs as it could.

A general election was held on 21 October 1945. The Communists secured 159 seats, the Socialists got 146 and the Catholic Mouvement Républicain Populaire got 152. A fortnight later, at the Assemblée Nationale's first session, a unanimous vote was passed maintaining de Gaulle in his position as head of state – but he remained an antagonistic leader. His reluctance to take a firm grip on the disastrous economic situation alienated many intellectuals and industrialists who had once been loyal to him, and his characteristic aloofness only made the misgivings of the general populace worse. He, on the other hand, was disgusted by all the political chicanery. On 20 January 1946, de Gaulle resigned.

France, meanwhile, looked to swift industrial modernisation under an ambitious plan put forward by internationalist politician Jean Monnet. Although the economy and daily life remained grim, brash new fashion designer Christian Dior put together a stunning collection of strikingly simple yet luxurious clothes: the New Look. Such extravagance horrified many locals, but the fashion industry boomed. Meanwhile, the divisions in Paris between its fashionable and run-down working-class areas became more pronounced. The northern and eastern edges – areas revived only in the late 20th century by a taste for retro, industrial decor and cheap rent – were forgotten about. Félix Gouin, the new Socialist premier, quickly nationalised the bigger banks and the coal industry. But the right wing was growing, and there was even a rise of royalist hopes. A referendum was held in May 1946 to determine the crucial tenet of the Fourth Republic's constitution: should the Assemblée Nationale have absolute or restricted power? The results were a narrow victory for people who, like de Gaulle, had insisted the Assemblée's

IN CONTEXT

The Liberation of Paris in 1944.

power should be qualified. De Gaulle's prestige increased, but it was another 12 years, and a whole new constitution – the Fifth Republic – before he came back to power. He spent much of his '*passage du désert*' writing his memoirs.

THE ALGERIAN WAR AND MAY 1968

The post-war years were marked by the rapid disintegration of France's overseas interests and her rapprochement with Germany to create what would become the European Community. When revolt broke out in Algeria in 1956, almost 500,000 troops were sent in to protect national interests. A protest by Algerians in Paris on 17 October 1961 led to the deaths of hundreds of people at the hands of the city's police force. The extent of the violence was officially concealed for decades, as was the use of torture against Algerians by French troops. Algeria became independent in 1962.

Meanwhile, the slow, painful discoveries of collaboration in World War II, often overlooked in the rush to put the country back on its feet, were also being faced. The younger generation began to question the motives of the older one. De Gaulle's Fifth Republic was felt by many to be grimly authoritarian. In the spring of 1968, students unhappy with overcrowded university conditions took to the streets of Paris at the same time as striking Renault workers. These *soixante-huitards* sprang the greatest public revolt in French living memory. Many students were crammed into universities that had been cheaply expanded to accommodate them. Political discourse grew across the campuses, turning against the government's stranglehold on the media and President de Gaulle's poor grasp of the economy. Ministers did indeed at the time have a sinister habit of leaning on the leading newspaper editors of the day, and television was dubbed 'the government in your dining room'. Inflation was high, and the gap between the working classes and the bourgeoisie was becoming a chasm. Still, de Gaulle echoed many when he said the events of May 1968 were '*incompréhensible*'. The touchpaper was lit at overcrowded Nanterre university, on

the outskirts of Paris, where students had been protesting against the war in Vietnam and the tatty state of the campus.

On 2 May, exhausted by the protests, the authorities closed the university down and threatened to expel some of the students. The next day, a sit-in was held in sympathy at the Sorbonne. Police were called to intervene, but made things worse, charging into the crowd with truncheons and tear gas. The city's streets were soon flooded with thousands of student demonstrators, now officially on strike. The trade unions followed, as did the *lycées*. By mid May, nine million people were on strike. On 24 May, de Gaulle intervened. His speech warned of civil war and pleaded for people's support. It didn't go down well: riots broke out, with students storming the Bourse.

Five days later, as street violence peaked, de Gaulle fled briefly to Germany and Prime Minister Pompidou sent tanks to the edges of Paris. But the crisis didn't materialise. Pompidou conceded pay rises of between seven and ten per cent and increased the minimum wage; France went back to work. An election was called for 23 June, by which time the right had gathered enough momentum to gain a safe majority.

MITTERRAND

Following the presidencies of right-wingers Georges Pompidou and Valéry Giscard d'Estaing, the Socialist François Mitterrand took up the task in 1981. His *grands projets* had a big impact on Paris. Mitterrand commissioned IM Pei's Louvre pyramid, the Grande Arche de la Défense, the Opéra Bastille and the more recent Bibliothèque Nationale de France – François Mitterrand.

CHIRAC, BUSH AND IRAQ

France may still boast the world's fourth-largest economy, the nuclear deterrent and a permanent seat on the UN Security Council, but her influence on the world stage had been waning for years until President Chirac, flushed from re-election and well aware he was on to a PR winner, stood up in early 2003 to oppose the US-led invasion of Iraq. France's official

Aiming for the Top

French politics can be a deadly business.

Paris is notorious for its revolutions; much less familiar is the city's equally distinguished record of assassination. Its annals of political violence tell of the day in 1610 when Catholic fanatic François Ravaillac ran into a traffic jam near Les Halles to stab Henri IV, and of the rifle bullets fired at Jacques Chirac by a lone far-right supporter on Bastille Day in 2002. One of the city's most famous killings produced one of its most famous paintings, David's portrait of Marat, knifed in his bath in 1793; other political murders have been largely forgotten, including the shooting of President Paul Doumer in 1932.

The victim of the most resonant Paris assassination was neither king nor president, but the charismatic leader of the Socialist party, Jean Jaurès. At 9.40pm on 31 July 1914, the aptly named Raoul Villain leaned in through a window of the Café du Croissant, on the corner of rue du Croissant and rue Montmartre, and aimed his revolver at the bearded Jaurès, sitting with friends on the other side of the room. One shot went wide, but the other hit Jaurès in the head, and he died within minutes. The shooting was remarkable in many ways, not least for an almost unparalleled stroke of reporter's luck. A correspondent for the *Manchester Guardian* happened to be dining in the café, and saw the whole event. The next day, he described the aftermath as 'heartrending – men and women were in tears'. The loss of Jaurès, a prominent anti-war campaigner, deepened the gloom as the great powers geared up for World War I.

Villain was locked up for the duration of the conflict, only to be acquitted at a new trial in 1919 on the ludicrous grounds that he had done France a patriotic favour; more ludicrous still, Jaurès' widow was ordered to pay costs. Villain moved to Spain, but met a sticky end of his own in 1936, when he was executed as a spy by opponents of Franco. Seven decades later, nearly every town in France has a thoroughfare named after Jaurès – and the Café du Croissant is still in business, its awning and plaque reminding passers-by of that bloody night in 1914.

Estates of Emergency

When rioting ripped through the suburbs.

In November 2005, violent suburban riots in Paris sent shockwaves through the country and abroad. The rundown estates around the capital became the scene for explosive confrontations with the police, as warehouses, restaurants and thousands of cars were set ablaze. Before long, the violence spread to other French cities. The government called a state of emergency, imposing curfews and banning public meetings at the weekends. Nevertheless, it was almost three weeks before the worst of the rioting was over.

The trigger for this unprecedented outbreak of violence was the accidental death on 27 October of two North African teenagers, in the north-east Paris suburb of Clichy-sous-Bois. According to locals, Bouna Traore, 15, and Zyed Benna, 17, panicked when they saw other black youths being chased by the police, and sought shelter in an electrical sub-station. As they entered the site, they were electrocuted, plunging the town into a blackout. To make matters worse, the incident came just two days after then Interior Minister Nicolas Sarkozy had made inflammatory remarks about the need to rid the *banlieue* of the '*racaille*', a highly pejorative term that can be translated as 'rabble' or 'scum'.

If this chain of events formed an explosive catalyst for the riots, the root cause went much deeper. When the economy plummeted in the 1970s, the populations of these high-rise estates found themselves struggling with factory closures and unemployment. While the wealthier moved to more desirable areas, the remaining residents – mainly North African families – were effectively left stranded in a suburban desert.

Over the three weeks of violence, nearly 3,000 arrests were made, more than 10,000 cars were set ablaze, and 300 buildings were firebombed. Initially, the government seemed to take a liberal view of its immigrant population, voting in a number of equal opportunities measures. Yet just two months later, Sarkozy's immigration bill reintroduced a hard line, laying down much stricter terms for immigrants seeking residency.

disapproval of George Bush culminated in the threat to use her Security Council veto against any resolution authorising the use of force without UN say-so. Chirac's stance brought him popularity at home and abroad. But his domestic popularity couldn't last.

His prime minister, Jean-Pierre Raffarin, and the centre-right government began attacking some of France's more prized national institutions with a programme of reforms, starting with the state pension system. This led to some of the largest nationwide protests France has seen since 1995, with striking métro staff, hospital and postal workers, teachers and rubbish collectors creating havoc and bringing the capital to a virtual standstill. Planned restrictions on the uniquely Gallic, exceptionally generous system of unemployment benefit for out-of-work performing-arts professionals led to a further round of protests, as well as the cancellation of France's equivalents of Edinburgh and Glyndebourne, the Avignon and Aix summer cultural festivals. Then came the official mismanagement and aloofness that characterised the two-week heatwave of August 2003, during which as many as 14,000 elderly people died. The national mood stayed gloomy through 2004, and the clouds darkened further in 2005, as Paris lost its Olympic bid.

Then, in October 2005, the accidental deaths of two North African teenagers in Clichy-sous-Bois sparked riots that spread through the *banlieue* like wildfire (*see p356* **Estates of Emergency**). Eventually Chirac declared a state of emergency that was lifted only in January 2006. Then, in March, trouble flared once again, this time provoked by an unpopular new employment bill, the CPE – which, after three months of strikes and protests, the government was forced to withdraw.

PRESIDENT BLING-BLING

Despite his provocations during the riots, Sarkozy was elected president in May 2007, beating the Socialist candidate Segolène Royal. Aside from a few desultory Molotov cocktails hurled in place de la Bastille on the night of the election, the response on the Left to

Sarkozy's victory was characterised more by bemusement than anger. For a few months, bemusement held sway in the population at large, especially when Sarkozy embarked on a very public whirlwind romance with *chanteuse* and ex-model Carla Bruni. But voters soon sickened of the spectacle, and of Sarkozy's parallel courtship of several tycoons; by the time 'Président Bling-Bling' married Bruni in February 2008, his popularity had plummeted to less than 35 per cent.

During the next couple of years, Sarkozy's popularity continued to decline, but 2011 brought about something of a reversal of fortune as the country geared up for the presidential elections in 2012. Pictures of himself and a pregnant Carla on the beach during the summer contrasted strongly with the coverage of his main rival on the left, Dominique Strauss-Kahn, who was fighting sexual assault charges in New York. This wholesome image, coupled with a boost from his high-profile role in the Libya crisis, saw his approval rating jump to 37 per cent by September 2011.

HOLLANDE TO THE FORE

With the scandal engulfing Strauss-Kahn, François Hollande came to the fore as the leading Socialist candidate, defeating rival Martine Aubry in a run-off for the party candidacy in October 2011 with 56 per cent of the vote. The first round of the presidential election took place on 22 April 2012. Hollande came in first place and faced Sarkozy in the second round run-off on 6 May 2012, when he was duly elected 24th President of the French Republic and the first Socialist president in almost two decades. But Hollande's post-election elation was short-lived and after his first 100 days in charge, a flagging economy, sliding opinion polls and close media scrutiny of his love life – his current partner is Valérie Trierweiler, but his former partner was Ségolène Royal, the mother of his four children and herself a former Socialist party presidential candidate – meant Hollande's honeymoon period was most definitely over.

IN CONTEXT

Architecture

Something old, something new.

TEXT: NATASHA EDWARDS

Paris's rulers have always understood the key role of architecture in the exercise of power. Long before François Mitterrand made his presidential mark on the capital in the 1980s with his *grands projets* – including the Opéra Bastille, Grande Arche de la Défense, Louvre Pyramid and Ministry of Finance – Colbert had glorified Louis XIV with the place Vendôme, place des Victoires and a series of triumphal arches. Yet the city is also one of Europe's most densely inhabited and lived-in capitals. For all its apparent uniformity, caused in large part by the prevalence of golden stone, Paris has never ceased to evolve and experiment, with aristocratic mansions, Baroque churches and Haussmannian apartments existing happily alongside concrete avant-garde houses, industrial premises, the cast iron of the Eiffel Tower, the high-tech Centre Pompidou, and Rudy Ricciotti and Mario Bellini's dramatic new Islamic Arts department set beneath the Louvre's Cour Visconti.

ROMANESQUE TO GOTHIC

Medieval Paris congregated on the Ile de la Cité and the Latin Quarter, following the broad lines of the Roman city. Although the clusters of medieval housing around Notre-Dame were razed by Haussmann in the 19th century, much of the medieval street plan remains. A few churches still survive as examples of simple Romanesque architecture, including the tower of **St-Germain-des-Prés** (*see p110*) and the well-preserved interior of **St-Julien-le-Pauvre** (*see p98*).

The Gothic trademarks of pointed arches, ogival vaulting and flying buttresses had their beginning at the **Basilique St-Denis** (*see p132*), started in the 12th century and completed in the 13th by master mason Pierre de Montreuil. **Notre-Dame** (*see p39*) continued the style with its sculpted façade, rich, delicate rose windows and fine, tendon-like buttresses (not to mention its menagerie of gargoyles). Montreuil's **Sainte-Chapelle** (*see p40*), built 1246-48, represents the peak of Gothic design, reducing stonework to a minimum between the expanses of stained glass. The Flamboyant Gothic style that followed unleashed an orgy of decoration. **Eglise St-Séverin** (*see p98*), with its twisting spiral column, is particularly original. Civil architecture can be seen in the impressive vaulted halls of the **Conciergerie** (*see p39*). The **Tour Jean Sans Peur** (*see p64*) is a rare fragment of an early 15th-century mansion. The city's two finest medieval mansions are the Hôtel de Cluny (now the **Musée National du Moyen-Age**; *see p99*) and the **Hôtel de Sens** (*see p86*).

RENAISSANCE

Italianate town planning, with its ordered avenues, neat squares and public spaces, came late to Paris. It was instigated by François I, who installed Leonardo da Vinci at Amboise, brought over Primaticcio and Rosso to work on his palace at **Fontainebleau** (*see p326*), and began transforming the **Louvre** (*see p41*) with the Cour Carrée. The **Eglise St-Etienne du Mont** (*see p101*) and the massive **Eglise St-Eustache** (*see p64*) display

a transitional style, adding the classical motifs of the Renaissance over an essentially Gothic structure. Aristocratic quarters were established in St-Germain-des-Prés and the developing Marais; the latter has the **Hôtel Carnavalet** (*see p84*) and the **Hôtel de Lamoignon** (24 rue Pavée, 4th), the finest examples of Renaissance mansions in Paris.

THE ANCIEN REGIME

Henri IV took control of Paris in 1594 after a long siege. He found a city knee-deep in bodies and rubble, and promptly organised public building projects. Half-timbering was banned for façades, to be replaced by brick and stone, and bridges over the Seine were cleared of houses and shops. **Place Dauphine** (1st) and **place des Vosges** (*see p85*) reflected Henri's taste for classicism; the latter is irresistibly elegant, with symmetrical design, red-brick vaulted galleries and steeply pitched roofs, reflecting the influence of northern Renaissance style as well as Italy.

The nouveaux riches flocked to build mansions in the Marais and on the Ile St-Louis. Those in the Marais follow a symmetrical U-shaped plan, with the main residence at the rear of an elegant *cour d'honneur*; look through the entrance archways of the **Hôtel de Sully** (*see p83*) or the **Hôtel Salé** (*see p83*), where façades are richly decorated, in contrast with the face they present to the street.

The **Palais du Luxembourg** (*see p115*), built in the 1620s by Salomon de Brosse in Italianate style for Marie de Médicis, combines classic French château design with the more dramatic rustication of the Pitti Palace in Marie's native Florence. The 17th century was a high point in French power, and the monarchy desired buildings that reflected its grandeur. Great architects emerged under court patronage: de Brosse, François Mansart, Libéral Bruand and landscape architect André le Nôtre, who redesigned the Tuileries gardens, created the park and fountains at Versailles and planned the Champs-Elysées. The **Eglise du Val-de-Grâce** (*see p102*), designed by Mansart and finished by Jacques Lemercier, is a grand Baroque statement designed to promote the

IN CONTEXT

Catholic Counter-Reformation, with its painted dome and barley sugar columns. Hospitals got the royal treatment: Libéral Bruand created the grand classical façades and polygonal chapel at the **Salpêtrière** (13th) and **Les Invalides** (see p127), with its grandiose galleried courtyard and domed double church. But even at **Versailles** (see p331), ultimate architectural symbol of royal absolutism in the scale and glittery reflections of the Hall of Mirrors, Baroque never reached the decorative excesses of Italy or Austria.

Under Colbert, Louis XIV's chief minister, the creation of stage sets to magnify the Sun King's power proceeded apace. The Louvre grew as Claude Perrault created the sweeping west wing, triumphal arches at **Porte St-Denis** and **Porte St-Martin** (see p61) commemorated military victories, while Hardouin-Mansart's circular **place des Victoires** (see p57) and **place Vendôme** (see p55), an elegant octagon, were designed to show off equestrian statues of the king.

ROCOCO AND NEO-CLASSICISM

In the early 18th century, the Faubourg St-Germain overtook the Marais as the city's most fashionable quarter, as the nobility built smart mansions with tall windows and elegant wrought ironwork, such as the **Hôtel Matignon**, today home of the French prime minister. However, the finest example of frivolous rococo decoration is the **Hôtel de Soubise** (60 rue des Francs-Bourgeois, 3rd), with panelling, plasterwork and paintings by celebrated decorators of the day, including Boucher, Restout and van Loo. In furniture-makers' **Faubourg St-Antoine**, a different sort of accommodation grew up, with workshops around long, narrow courtyards and lodgings up above.

Under Louis XV, several sumptuous buildings were commissioned, among them La Monnaie (now the **Musée de la Monnaie de Paris**; see p109), the **Panthéon** (see p102), the **Ecole de Droit** (place du Panthéon, 5th) and many new theatres. Soufflot's Panthéon, like Jacques-Ange Gabriel's neo-classical **place de la Concorde** (see p55), was inspired by ancient Rome, as were the

toll gates put up in 1785 by Nicolas Ledoux, famed for his almost minimalist geometrical style (still visible at Nation, Denfert-Rochereau and Parc Monceau) for the Mur des Fermiers Généraux.

THE 19TH CENTURY

The street fighting of the Revolution left Paris in a dilapidated state. Napoleon redressed this situation with a suitably grandiose vision to make Paris the most beautiful city in the world. He confiscated land from the aristocracy and the Church, and ordered a massive building spree. As well as five new bridges and 56 ornamental fountains, he built the **Eglise de la Madeleine** (see p59), a mock Greek temple in honour of the Grande Armée, plus a rash of statues and arches, most notably the **Arc de Triomphe** (see p66) and the **Arc du Carrousel** (see p51).

In 1853, Bonaparte's nephew Louis Napoleon appointed Baron Haussmann as the préfet of Paris, with a brief to remake the city. A fearsome administrator rather than an architect, Haussmann faced problems of sanitation, sewage and traffic-clogged streets. He set about bringing order, cutting broad, long boulevards through the urban fabric. An estimated 27,000 houses were razed in the process. The Haussmannian apartment block has endured, setting an adaptable format that endured well into the 20th century, its utilitarian lines set off by mansarded roofs and rows of wrought-iron balconies. Haussmann also introduced English-style public parks, such as the **Buttes-Chaumont** (see p96), along with prisons, hospitals, train stations and sewers. Amid the upheaval, one building epitomised the grand style of the Second Empire: Charles Garnier's sumptuous **Palais Garnier** opera house (1862-75; see p59).

Haussmann could also be an innovator, persuading Baltard to build new market pavilions at Les Halles in lacy iron rather than stone. Iron frames had already been used by Henri Labrouste in his lovely reading room at the Bibliothèque Ste-Geneviève (1844-50; 10 place du Panthéon, 5th), and they became increasingly common: stations such as Hittorff's **Gare du Nord** (1861-65;

see p93) and Laloux's Gare d'Orsay (now **Musée d'Orsay**; see p129) are simply shells around an iron frame, producing spacious, light-filled interiors. The most daring iron construction of them all was, of course, the **Eiffel Tower** (see p129). When it was built in 1889, it was the tallest structure in the world. Stylistically, eclecticism ruled, from the neo-Renaissance **Hôtel de Ville** (see p82) to neo-Byzantine **Sacré-Coeur** (see p77).

EARLY 20TH CENTURY

An outburst of extravagance for the 1900 Exposition Universelle marked the beginning of the 20th century, notably the **Grand Palais** (see p68), with its massive glass and steel nave, and the **Petit Palais**, awash in sculptures, mosaics, marble and wrought iron, with design inspired by the Grand Trianon at Versailles. The **Train Bleu** brasserie in the Gare de Lyon (see p154) is an ornate example of the heavy, florid Beaux Arts style of this period. Art nouveau at its most fluid and flamboyant can be seen in Hector Guimard's instantly recognisable métro stations and his 1901 **Castel Béranger** (see p73).

All this was a long way from the roughly contemporary work of Henri Sauvage, who created a large social housing project in rue des Amiraux (18th), tiled artists' studio flats in **rue La Fontaine** (16th), and the overtly art deco 1920s extension of **La Samaritaine** (19 rue de la Monnaie, 1st). Funded by philanthropists, social housing began to appear in the city.

THE MODERN MOVEMENT

After World War I, two people stand out by virtue of their innovation and influence: Auguste Perret, architect of the **Théâtre des Champs-Elysées** (see p304), and Le Corbusier. A third architect, Robert Mallet-Stevens, is unrivalled for his elegance, best seen in his villas on rue Mallet-Stevens. Paris is one of the best cities in the world for Modern Movement houses and studios (many situated in the 16th and Montparnasse), but also in a more diluted form for town halls and schools built in the socially minded 1930s.

Perret stayed largely within a classical aesthetic, but was a pioneer in the use of reinforced concrete. Le Corbusier tried out his ideas in private houses, such as the Villa La Roche in the 16th (now **Fondation le Corbusier**). His **Pavillon Suisse** at the **Cité Universitaire** (see p122) and **Armée du Salut** hostel (12 rue Cantagrel, 13th) can be seen as a mid point between these villas and his Villes Radieuses mass housing schemes, which became so influential across Europe after 1945.

IN CONTEXT

Rives de Seine project. See p363.

Meanwhile, the new love of chrome, steel and glass found its way into art deco cafés such as **La Coupole** (*see p165*). As in the 19th century, world fairs provided an excuse for grandiose state architecture, with a return to monumental classicism in the **Palais de la Porte Dorée**, built for the 1931 Exposition Coloniale, and the Palais de Chaillot and **Palais de Tokyo** (*see p70*), built for the 1937 Exposition Internationale.

POST-WAR PARIS

The aerodynamic aesthetic of the post-war era yielded the 1958 **UNESCO building** (*see p130*) by Bernard Zehrfuss, Pier Luigi Nervi and Marcel Breuer, and the beginnings of **La Défense** (*see p131*) with the same architects' **CNIT** building, then the largest concrete span in the world. In the 1960s and '70s, tower blocks sprouted in the suburbs and new towns to replace the *bidonvilles* (shanty towns) that had served as immigrant housing. Inside the city, redevelopment was limited, although new regulations allowed taller buildings; in 1960, the 67-metre-high, 23-storey **33 rue Croulebarbe** in the

13th arrondissement, the tubular steel structure of which allowed a large degree of prefabrication, marked Paris's first high-rise residential block, designed by Edouard Albert, setting the way for high-rise clusters at Les Olympiades (13th), Fronts de Seine (15th) and in the 19th.

President Georges Pompidou embraced modernity too, disastrously in the case of the expressways along the Seine, and more benignly in the form of the **Centre Pompidou** (*see p81*), which opened in 1977. But after the construction of the controversial **Tour Montparnasse** (*see p121*), Pompidou's successor, Valéry Giscard d'Estaing, prevented the Paris horizon from rising any higher.

THE 1980S AND '90S

President François Mitterrand's *grands projets* dominated the 1980s and '90s, with Jean Nouvel's **Institut du Monde Arabe** (*see p104*), IM Pei's **Louvre Pyramid** (*see p41*) and Johan Otto Von Sprecklesen's **Grande Arche de la Défense** (*see p131*), as well as Carlos Ott's more dubious **Opéra Bastille** (*see p302*), Dominique Perrault's **Bibliothèque**

Grande Arche de la Défense.

Fondation Cartier.

Nationale (*see p107*) and Chemetov & Huidobro's **Bercy** finance ministry. The buzzword was 'transparency', from Pei's pyramid to Nouvel's **Fondation Cartier** (*see p118*), with its clever slices of glass. Christian de Portzamparc pursued a more eclectic postmodern style with his **Cité de la Musique** (*see p95*), a series of geometrical blocks set around a colourful internal street.

THE 21ST CENTURY

Jacques Chirac managed to squeeze one last legacy project into his reign with the completion of Nouvel's **Musée du Quai Branly** (*see p130*) in 2006, a highly colourful baroque structure. Younger architects are making their mark too: Manuelle Gautrand's **Citroën** showcase on the Champs-Elysées, for example, plays on the firm's chevrons logo in a fine example of architecture as branding, and she was also behind the revamp of the **Théâtre de la Gaîté Lyrique** (*see p83*) as a new multimedia arts centre.

Other areas have also come up for a makeover: the much-maligned 1970s **Forum des Halles** (*see p64*) complex is set for a new green canopy and re-landscaped gardens, while plans to pedestrianise a 2.5km stretch along the banks of the Seine between the Musée d'Orsay and the Pont de l'Alma were finally approved in 2012, with a riverside park, pedestrian promenades, floating gardens, restaurants and even perhaps an archipelago of artificial islands. But the biggest project of all will soon start to take shape at La Défense with the construction of Hermitage Plaza, a pair of skyscrapers courtesy of Norman Foster, topping London's Shard by a few metres.

Meanwhile, the city also continues to benefit from exciting new cultural buildings. After the appearance of **104** (*see p94*) in the former municipal undertakers in 2008, Frank Gehry's cloudlike glass Fondation Louis Vuitton in the Bois de Boulogne (due to open 2013), Renzo Piano's egg-like Fondation Pathé (due to open 2013) on avenue des Gobelins, and Jean Nouvel's new Philharmonic concert hall at La Villette (due to open 2015) are all well under way. And one long-awaited cultural creation that has finally come to fruition is the opening of the new Islamic Arts department in the **Cour Visconti** (*see p41*) at the Louvre. Led by Rudy Ricciotti and Mario Bellini, the project is the museum's greatest architectural work since the Grand Louvre. Skyscrapers may be all the rage beyond the Périphérique, but it seems that for now, at least, reinvention is the key for the heart of the French capital.

IN CONTEXT

Getting Around

ESSENTIAL INFORMATION

ARRIVING & LEAVING

By air

Roissy-Charles-de-Gaulle airport
01.70.36.39.50, www.adp.fr.
Most international flights use Roissy-Charles-de-Gaulle airport, which is situated 30km (19 miles) north-east of Paris. Its three main terminals are some way apart, so check which one you need for your return flight. The terminals are linked by the free CDGVAL driverless train.

The **RER B** (RATP helpline, 36.58, www.transilien.com) is the quickest way to central Paris (about 40mins to Gare du Nord; 45mins to RER Châtelet-Les Halles; €9.10 single). RER trains run every 10-15mins, 4.58am-11.58pm daily from the airport to Paris.

Air France buses (08.92.35.08.20, www.cars-airfrance.com; €15 single, €24 return, €7.50 under-11s, free under-2s) leave every 20-30mins, 6am-11pm daily, from both terminals, and stop at porte Maillot and place Charles-de-Gaulle (35-50min trip). Air France buses also run to Gare Montparnasse and Gare de Lyon (€16.50 single, €27 return, €8 under-11s, free under-2s) every 30mins (45-60min trip), 6am-10pm daily; there's a shuttle bus between Roissy and Orly (€19 no return), €9.50 under-11s, free under-2s) every 30mins, 5.55am-10.30pm daily from Roissy; 6.30am-10.30pm Mon-Fri, 7am-10.30pm Sat, Sun from Orly.

The **RATP Roissybus** (32.46, www.ratp.fr; €10) runs every 15-20mins, 5.45am-11pm daily, between the airport and the corner of rue Scribe/rue Auber (at least 45mins); buy tickets on the bus. **Paris Airports Service** is a door-to-to-door minibus service between airports and hotels, 24/7. The more passengers on board, the less each one pays. Roissy prices go from €26 for one person to €99 for eight people, 6am-8pm (minimum €42, 4-6am, 8-10pm); book on 01.55.98.10.80, www.parisairport service.com. A **taxi** to central Paris takes 30-60mins depending on traffic. Expect to pay approx €40-€50, plus €1 per item of luggage.

Orly airport
01.70.36.39.50, www.adp.fr.
Domestic and international flights use Orly, 18km (11 miles) south of the city. It has two terminals: Orly-Sud (mainly international) and Orly-Ouest (mainly domestic).

Air France buses (08.92.35.08.20, www.cars-airfrance.com; €11.50 single, €18.50 return, €5.50 under-11s, free under-2s) leave both terminals every 20-30mins, 6am-11.30pm daily, and stop at Invalides and Montparnasse (30-45mins). The **RATP Orlybus** (32.46, www.ratp.fr; €7) runs between the airport and Denfert-Rochereau every 15mins, 5.35am-11.30pm daily (30min trip); buy tickets on the bus. The high-speed **Orlyval** (www.orlyval.fr) shuttle train runs every 4-7mins (6am-11pm daily) to RER B station Antony (€10.75 to Châtelet-les-Halles); getting into central Paris takes about 35mins.

You could also catch the **Paris par le train bus** (€6.45) to Pont de Rungis, where you can take the RER C into central Paris. Buses run every 20mins, 4.34am-11.14pm daily from Orly-Sud; 35min trip. Orly prices for the **Paris Airports Service** door-to-door facility (*see left*) are the same as for Roissy-Charles-de-Gaulle. A **taxi** into town takes 20-40mins and costs €16-€26, plus €1 per piece of luggage.

Paris Beauvais airport
08.92.68.20.66, www.aeroport beauvais.com. Beauvais, 70km (44 miles) from Paris, is served by budget airlines such as **Ryanair** (08.92.78.02.10, www.ryanair.com). Buses (€15) leave for Porte Maillot 15-30mins after each arrival; buses the other way leave 3hrs 15mins before each departure. Get tickets from the arrivals lounge (information: 08.92.68.20.64) or buy tickets on the bus.

Major airlines

Aer Lingus
08.21.23.02.67, www.aerlingus.com.
Air France
36.54, www.airfrance.fr.
American Airlines
08.26.46.09.50, www.americanairlines.fr.

British Airways
08.25.82.54.00, www.britishairways.fr.
Continental
01.71.23.03.35, www.continental.com.
Easyjet
08.20.42.03.15, www.easyjet.com.
KLM & NorthWest
08.92.70.26.08, www.klm.com.
United
08.10.72.72.72, www.united.fr.

By car

Options for crossing the Channel with a car include: **Eurotunnel** (08.10.63.03.04, www.eurotunnel.com); **Brittany Ferries** (08.25.82.88.28, www.brittanyferries.com); **P&O Ferries** (08.25.12.01.56, www.poferries.com); and **My Ferry Link** (0044.8442.482.100).

Shared journeys

Allô-Stop
30 rue Pierre Sémard, 9th (01.53.20.42.42, www.allostop.net). M° Poissonnière. **Open** 10am-1pm, 2-6pm Mon-Fri; 10am-1pm, 2-4pm Sat. **Credit** MC, V.
Call several days ahead to be put in touch with drivers. There's a fee (€5 under 250km, 155 miles; €8 over 250km), plus a contribution towards the petrol expenses, paid to the driver (from €5 under 100km, 62 miles, up to €95 for over 2,000km, 1,243 miles).

By coach

International coach services arrive at the Gare Routière Internationale Paris-Gallieni at Porte de Bagnolet, 20th. For reservations (in English), call **Eurolines** on 08.92.89.90.91 (€0.34 per min) or 01.41.86.24.21 from abroad, or visit www.eurolines.fr. Fares start from £25 for a single from London to Paris.

By rail

From London, **Eurostar** services (UK: 0044.8432.186186, www.eurostar.com) to Paris depart from the dedicated terminal at St Pancras International. Thanks to the new high-speed track, the journey from London to Paris now takes 2hrs

15mins direct, slightly longer for trains stopping at Ashford and Lille. Eurostar services from the new terminal at Ebbsfleet International, near junction 2 of the M25, take 2hrs 5mins direct. Fares start at £69/€88 for a London-Paris return ticket. Passengers must check in at least 30mins before departure time. Trains arrive at Gare du Nord (08.92.35.35.35, www.sncf.fr), with easy access to public transport and taxi ranks.

Cycles can be taken as hand luggage if they are dismantled and carried in a bike bag. You can also check them in at the EuroDespatch depot at St Pancras (Esprit Parcel Service, 0844 822 5822) or Sernam depot at Gare du Nord (01.48.74.14.80). Check-in should be done at least 24 hours ahead; a Eurostar ticket must be shown. The service costs £20/€25.

MAPS

Free maps of the métro, bus and RER systems are available at airports and métro stations. Other brochures from métro stations are *Paris Visite – Le Guide*, with details of transport tickets and a small map, and *Plan de Paris*, a fold-out one showing *Noctambus* night bus lines. A Paris street map (*Plan de Paris*) can be bought from newsagents. The blue *Paris Pratique* is clear and compact.

PUBLIC TRANSPORT

Almost all of the Paris public transport system is run by the **RATP** (Régie Autonome des Transports Parisiens; 32.46, www.ratp.fr): the bus, métro (underground) and suburban tram routes, as well as lines A and B of the RER (Réseau Express Régional) suburban express railway, which connects with the métro within the city centre. National rail operator **SNCF** (36.35, www.sncf.com) runs RER lines C, D and E, and serves the Paris suburbs (*Banlieue*), as well as French regions and international destinations (*Grandes Lignes*).

Fares & tickets

Paris and suburbs are divided into six travel zones; zones 1 and 2 cover the centre. RATP tickets and passes are valid on the métro, bus and RER. Tickets and *carnets* can be bought at métro stations, tourist offices and *tabacs* (tobacconists); single tickets can also be bought

on buses. Hold on to your ticket in case of spot checks; you'll also need it to exit RER stations.

● A single ticket *T+* costs €1.70, but it's more economical to buy a *carnet* of ten for €12.50.
● A one-day *Mobilis* pass costs from €6.40 for zones 1 and 2 to €15.20 for zones 1-5.
● A one-day *Paris Visite* pass for zones 1-3 is €9.75; a five-day pass is €31.15, with discounts on some attractions.
● One-week or one-month passes (passport photo needed) offer unlimited travel in the relevant zones; if bought in zones 1 or 2, each is delivered as a Navigo swipe card. A *forfait mensuel* (monthly pass valid from the first day of the month) for zones 1 and 2 costs €62.90; a weekly *forfait hebdomadaire* (weekly pass valid Mon-Sun inclusive) for zones 1 and 2 costs €19.15 and is better value than *Paris Visite* passes.

Métro & RER

The Paris **métro** is the fastest and cheapest way of getting around the city. Trains run 5.30am-12.40am Mon-Thur, 5.30am-1.30am Fri-Sun. Individual lines are numbered, with each direction named after the last stop. Follow the orange *Correspondance* to change lines. Be prepared for the fact that some interchanges, such as Châtelet-Les-Halles, Montparnasse-Bienvenüe and République, involve long walks. The exit (*Sortie*) is indicated in blue. The driverless line 14 runs from Gare St-Lazare to Olympiades. Pickpockets and bag-snatchers are rife on the network – pay special attention as the doors are closing.

The five **RER** lines (A, B, C, D and E) run 5.30am-1am daily through Paris and out into the suburbs. Within Paris, the RER is useful for faster journeys – Châtelet-Les-Halles to Gare du Nord is one stop on the RER, and six on the métro. Métro tickets are valid for RER journeys within zones 1 and 2.

Buses

Buses run 6.30am-8.30pm, with some routes continuing until 12.30am, Mon-Sat; limited services operate on selected lines on Sunday and public holidays. You can use a métro ticket, a ticket bought from the driver (€1.90) or a travel pass to travel on the bus.

Tickets should be punched in the machine next to the driver; passes should be shown to the driver. When you want to get off, press the red request button.

Night buses
After the métro and normal buses stop running, the only public transport – apart from taxis – are the 47 **Noctilien** lines, running between place du Châtelet and the suburbs (hourly 12.30am-5.30am Mon-Thur; half-hourly 1am-5.35am Fri, Sat); look out for the Noctilien logo on bus stops or the N in front of the route number. A ticket costs €1.70 (€1.90 from the driver); travel passes are valid.

River transport

Batobus
(08.25.05.01.01, www.batobus.com). River buses stop every 17-35mins at: Eiffel Tower, Musée d'Orsay, St-Germain-des-Prés (quai Malaquais), Notre-Dame, Jardin des Plantes, Hôtel de Ville, Louvre, Champs-Elysées (Pont Alexandre III). They run Sept-Mar 10am-7pm; Apr-Aug 10am-9.30pm. A one-day pass is €14 (€7, €9 reductions); two-day pass €18 (€9, €12 reductions); five-day pass €21 (€10, €14 reductions); season-ticket €60 (€38 reductions). Tickets can be bought at Batobus stops, online at www.batobus.com, RATP ticket offices and the Office de Tourisme (*see p381*).

Trams

Two modern tram lines operate in the suburbs, running from La Défense to Issy-Val de Seine and from Bobigny Pablo Picasso to St-Denis; a third runs between the Garigliano Bridge in the west of the city to Porte d'Ivry in the south-east. They connect with the métro and RER; fares are the same as for buses.

RAIL TRAVEL

Suburban destinations are served by the RER. Other locations farther from the city are served by the SNCF railway; the TGV high-speed train has slashed journey times and is being extended to all the main regions. There are few long-distance bus services. Tickets can be bought at any SNCF station (not just the one from which you'll travel), SNCF shops and travel agents. If you reserve online or by phone, you can pay and pick up your tickets from the station or have them sent to your home. SNCF automatic machines (*billeterie automatique*) only work with French credit/debit cards. Regular trains have full-rate White (peak) and cheaper Blue (off-peak) periods. You can save on TGV fares by buying special cards. The *Carte 12/25* gives under-26s a 25-50 per cent reduction; even without it, under-26s are entitled to 25 per cent off. Buy tickets in advance to secure the cheaper fare. Before you board any train, stamp your ticket in the orange *composteur* machines located on the platforms, or you might have to pay a hefty fine. *See also p375* **Lost Property**.

SNCF reservations & tickets

National reservations & information 36.35 (€0.34 per min), www.sncf.com. **Open** 7am-10pm daily.

Mainline stations

Gare d'Austerlitz
Central and south-west France and Spain.
Gare de l'Est
Alsace, Champagne and southern Germany.
Gare de Lyon
Burgundy, the Alps, Provence and Italy.
Gare Montparnasse
West France, Brittany, Bordeaux, the south-west.
Gare du Nord
Eurostar, Channel ports, north-east France, Belgium and the Netherlands.
Gare St-Lazare
Normandy.

TAXIS

Paris taxi drivers are not known for their flawless knowledge of the Paris street map; if you have a preferred route, say so. Taxis can also be hard to find, especially at rush hour or early in the morning. Your best bet is to find a taxi rank (*station de taxis*, marked with a blue sign) on major roads, crossroads and at stations. A white light on a taxi's roof indicates the car is free; an orange light means the cab is busy. There is a service charge of €2.20. The rates are then based on zone and time of day: **A** (10am-5pm Mon-Sat central Paris, €0.89 per km); **B** (5pm-10am Mon-Sat, 7am-midnight Sun central Paris; 7am-7pm Mon-Sat inner suburbs and airports, €1.14 per

km); **C** (midnight-7am Sun central Paris; 7pm-7am Mon-Sat, all day Sun inner suburbs and airports; all times outer suburbs, €1.38 per km). Most journeys in central Paris cost €6-€12; there's a minimum charge of €6, plus €1 for each piece of luggage over 5kg or bulky objects, and a €0.70 surcharge from mainline stations. Most drivers will not take more than three people, but they should take a couple and two children. There is a charge of €2.95 for a fourth adult passenger.

Don't feel obliged to tip, although rounding up to the nearest euro is polite. Taxis are not allowed to refuse rides if they deem them too short and can only refuse to take you in a certain direction during their last half-hour of service (both rules are often ignored). If you want a receipt, ask for *un reçu* or *la note*. Complaints should be made to the **Bureau des Taxis et des Transports Publics**, 36 rue des Morillons, 75732 Paris Cedex 15 (01.55.76.20.05). *See also p375* **Lost Property**.

Phone cabs

These firms take phone bookings 24/7; you also pay for the time it takes your taxi to reach you. If you wish to pay by credit card, mention this when you order.

Alpha
01.45.85.85.85, www.alphataxis.fr.
G7
36.07, www.taxis-g7.fr.
Taxis Bleus
08.91.70.10.10, www.taxis-bleus.com.

DRIVING

If you bring your car to France, you must bring its registration and insurance documents.

As you come into Paris, you will meet the Périphérique, the giant ring road that carries traffic into, out of and around the city. Intersections, leading on to other main roads, are called *portes* (gates). Driving on the Périphérique is not as hair-raising as it might look, though it's often congested. Some hotels have parking spaces that can be paid for by the hour, day or by types of season tickets.

In peak holiday periods, the organisation Bison Futé hands out brochures at motorway *péages* (toll gates), suggesting less crowded routes. French roads are categorised as *Autoroutes*

(motorways, with an 'A' in front of the number), *Routes Nationales* (national 'N' roads), *Routes Départementales* (local, 'D' roads) and rural *Routes Communales* ('C' roads). *Autoroutes* are toll roads; some sections, including most of the area around Paris, are free.

Infotrafic *08.92.70.77.66 (€0.34 per minute), www.infotrafic.fr.*
Bison Futé
08.00.10.02.00, www.bison-fute.equipement.gouv.fr.

Breakdown services

Beaking down in France can be an expensive business, so it's advisable to take out additional breakdown insurance cover before you travel, for example with a company such as the **AA** (www.theaa.com) or **Green Flag** (www.greenflag.com). **Dan Dépann Auto** (08.00.25.10.00, www.dandepann.fr) operates a 24-hour breakdown services in the Paris area.

Driving tips

● At junctions where no signposts indicate right of way, the car coming from the right has priority. Many roundabouts now give priority to those on the roundabout. If this is not indicated (by road markings or a sign with the message *Vous n'avez pas la priorité*), priority is for those coming from the right.
● Drivers and all passengers must wear seat belts.
● Under-tens are not allowed to travel in the front of a car, except in baby seats facing backwards.
● You should not stop on an open road; you must pull off to the side.
● When drivers are flashing their lights at you, this often means they will not slow down and are warning you to keep out of the way.

Parking

There are still a few free on-street parking areas in Paris, but they're often full. If you park illegally, you risk getting your car clamped or towed away). It's forbidden to park in zones marked for deliveries (*livraisons*) or taxis. Parking meters have now been replaced by *horodateurs*, pay-and-display machines, which take a special card (*carte de stationnement* at €15 or €40, available from *tabacs*). Parking is often free at weekends, after 7pm and in August.

Car hire

To hire a car, you must be 25 or over and have held a licence for at least a year. Some agencies accept drivers aged 21-24, but a supplement of €20-€25 per day is usual. Take your licence and passport with you. Bargain firms may have an extremely high charge for damage: make sure you read the small print.

Hire companies

Ada
www.ada.fr.
Avis
08.21.23.07.60, www.avis.fr.
Budget
08.25.00.35.64, www.budget.fr.
EasyCar
www.easycar.com.
Europcar
08.25.35.83.58, www.europcar.fr.
Hertz
01.55.31.93.21, www.hertz.fr.
Rent-a-Car
08.91.70.02.00, www.rentacar.fr.

Chauffeur-driven cars

Chauffeur Services Paris
(01.80.40.00.86, www.csparis. com). **Open** 24hrs daily. **Prices** from €105 airport transfer; €240 for 4 hours. **Credit** AmEx, DC, MC, V.

CYCLING

In 2007, the mayor launched a municipal bike hire scheme, **Vélib** (www.velib.paris.fr), which has become a model for similiar projects around the world. There are now more than 20,000 bicycles available 24 hours a day, at nearly 1,800 'stations' across the city. Just swipe your travel card to release the bikes from their stands. The *mairie* actively promotes cycling in the city and the Vélib scheme is complemented by the 400km (250 miles) of bike lanes snaking their way around Paris.

The Itinéraires Paris-Piétons-Vélos-Rollers – scenic strips of the city that are closed to cars on Sundays and holidays – continue to multiply; www.paris.fr can provide an up-to-date list of routes and a downloadable map of cycle lanes. A free *Paris à Vélo* map can be picked up at any mairie or from bike shops. Cycle lanes (*pistes cyclables*) run mostly N–S and E–W. N–S routes include rue de Rennes, av d'Italie, bd Sébastopol and av Marceau. E–W routes take in the

rue de Rivoli, bd St-Germain, bd St-Jacques and av Daumesnil. You could be fined if you don't use them. Cyclists are also entitled to use certain bus lanes (especially the new ones, set off by a strip of kerb stones); look out for traffic signs with a bike symbol. Don't let the locals' blasé attitude to helmets and lights convince you it's not worth using them.

Cycles & scooters for hire

Bike insurance may not cover theft; check when you book.

Freescoot
63 quai de la Tournelle, 5th (01.44.07.06.72, www.freescoot.fr). M° Maubert Mutualité or St-Michel. **Open** 9am-1pm, 2-7pm daily; closed Sun Oct-mid Apr. **Credit** AmEx, MC, V. Hires out bicycles (from €15 per day) and scooters (from €45 per day).
Left Bank Scooters
(06.82.70.13.82, www.leftbankscooters.com). This company hires out vintage-style Vespas (from €55 per day), with delivery and collection from your apartment or hotel. Various tours also available.

WALKING

Walking is easily the best way to explore Paris; just remember to remain vigilant at all times. Brits should be aware that traffic will be coming from the 'wrong' direction and that zebra crossings mean very little. By law, drivers are only obliged to stop at a red traffic light – even then, many will take a calculated risk.

TOURS

Bus tours

The following companies offer hop-on, hop-off bus tours of the city with commentary available in a variety of languages.

Les Cars Rouges
01.53.95.39.53, www.carsrouges. com. **Tickets** €29; €13 4-11s. Tours leave every 7-15mins and the round trip takes 2hrs 15mins. You can hop on and off along the way and tickets are valid for two consecutive days.
Paris City Vision
www.pariscityvision.com. **Tickets** €31; €15 4-11s. Choose beetween four different Open Tour routes around Paris.

Bike tours

Fat Tire Bike Tours
01.56.58.10.54, http://fattirebiketours.com/paris. **Tickets** €30; €26 reductions. Bike tours of the city, with the main tour starting at the south leg of the Eiffel Tower. Tours run daily at 11am, with a 3pm tour added in summer. Check online for full details.

Boat tours

Cruising along the River Seine is a delightful way to see Paris. The companies below all run a variety of tours on the river. Most boats depart from the quays in the 7th and 8th, and proceed to go on a circuit around the islands. Check online for full tour details and times: many companies operate more than one type of tour, though the basic tour usually runs every 20-60mins in summer. Rates are for one day only, though other tickets may be available.

Bateaux-Mouches
Pont de l'Alma, 8th (01.42.25.96.10, www.bateaux-mouches.fr). M° Alma-Marceau. **Tickets** €11.50; €5.50 reductions; free under-4s.
Bateaux Parisiens
Port de la Boudonnais, 7th (01.76.64.14.45, www.bateaux parisiens.com). RER Champ de Mars. **Tickets** €12; €5 reductions; free under-3s.
Batobus Tour Eiffel
Various stops (08.25.05.01.01, www.batobus.com). **Tickets** €14; €7 reductions.
Vedettes de Paris
Port de Suffren, 7th (01.44.18.19.50, www.vedettes deparis.com). M° Bir-Hakeim. Tickets €11; €5 reductions; free under-4s.
Vedettes du Pont-Neuf
Sq du Vert-Galant, 1st (01.46.33.98.38, www.vedettes dupontneuf.com). M° Pont-Neuf. **Tickets** €13; €7 under-12s; free under-4s.

Walking tours

Paris Walking Tours
01.48.09.21.40, www.paris-walks.com. **Tickets** €12; €8-€10 reductions. Led by long-term resident expats, these daily two-hour walking tours (times vary by season) explore various city locales (€12 adults, €8-€10 reductions).

ESSENTIAL INFORMATION

Resources A-Z

ESSENTIAL INFORMATION

ADDRESSES

Paris arrondissements are indicated by the last two digits of the postal code: 75002 denotes the second, 75015 the 15th, and so on. The 16th arrondissement is divided into two sectors, 75016 and 75116. Some business addresses have a more detailed postcode, followed by a Cedex number, which indicates the arrondissement; *bis* or *ter* is the equivalent of 'b' or 'c' after a building number.

AGE RESTRICTIONS

For heterosexuals and homosexuals, the age of consent is 15. You must be 18 years old to drive, and to consume alcohol in a public place. You must be 16 to buy cigarettes.

ATTITUDE & ETIQUETTE

Parisians take manners seriously and are generally more courteous than their reputation may have led you to believe. If someone brushes you accidentally when passing, they will more often than not say '*pardon*'; you can do likewise, or say '*c'est pas grave*' (don't worry). In shops it is normal to greet the assistant with a '*bonjour madame*' or '*bonjour monsieur*' when you enter, and say '*au revoir*' when you leave. The business of '*tu*' and '*vous*' can be tricky for English speakers. Strangers, people significantly older than you and professional contacts should be addressed with the respectful '*vous*'; friends, relatives, children and pets as '*tu*'. When among themselves, young people will often launch straight in with '*tu*'.

BUSINESS

The best first stop for initiating business is the CCIP (Chambre de Commerce et d'Industrie de Paris; *see p371*). Banks can refer you to lawyers, accountants and tax consultants.

Conventions & conferences

CNIT *2 pl de la Défense, BP 321, 92053 Paris La Défense (01.40.68.22.22, www.viparis.com). Mº/RER Grande Arche de La Défense.* Mainly computer fairs.
Palais des Congrès *2 pl de la Porte-Maillot, 17th (01.40.68.22.22, www.viparis.com). Mº Porte-Maillot.*
Parc des Expositions de Paris-Nord Villepinte *Zac Paris Nord 2, 93420 Villepinte (01.40.68.22.22, www.viparis.com). RER Parc des Expositions.*
Trade fair centre near Roissy.
Paris-Expo *1 pl de la Porte de Versailles, 15th (01.40.68.22.22, www.viparis.com). Mº Porte de Versailles.*
The city's biggest expo centre.

Courier services

ATV *08.11.65.56.05, www.coursiers.com.* **Open** 24hrs daily. **Credit** MC, V.
Bike or van messengers 24/7. Rates rise after 8pm and at weekends.
Chronopost *08.25.80.18.01, www.chronopost.com.* **Open** 9am-8pm Mon-Fri; 9am-1pm Sat (in post offices). **Credit** MC, V.
This overnight delivery offshoot of the state-run post office is the most widely used service for parcels.
UPS *08.21.23.38.77, www.ups.com.* **Open** 8am-7pm Mon-Fri; 8am-1pm Sat. **Credit** AmEx, MC, V.
International courier services.

Secretarial services

ADECCO Experts *57-59 bd Malesherbes, 8th (01.77.69.12.12, www.adecco.fr). Mº St-Augustin.* **Open** 8.30am-12.30pm, 2-6.30pm Mon-Fri.
Employment agency specialising in bilingual secretaries and staff. **Other locations** throughout the city.

Translators & interpreters

Documents such as birth certificates, loan applications and so on must be translated by certified legal translators, listed at the CCIP (*see p371*) or embassies. For business translations there are dozens of reliable independents.

Association des Anciens Elèves de l'Esit *01.44.05.41.46, www.aaeesit.com.* **Phone enquiries** 8am-8pm Mon-Fri; 8am-6pm Sat. **Booking** (via email only) at mdttraducteurs@aaeesit.com.
A translation and interpreting co-operative whose 900 members are graduates of the Ecole Supérieure d'Interprètes et de Traducteurs.
International Corporate Communication *3 rue des Batignolles, 17th (01.43.87.29.29, www.iccparis.com). Mº Place de Clichy.* **Open** 9am-1pm, 2-6pm Mon-Fri.
Translators of financial and corporate documents, plus simultaneous translation.

Useful organisations

American Chamber of Commerce *77 rue de Miromesnil, 8th (01.56.43.45.67, www.amchamfrance.org). Mº Miromesnil.*
Closed to the public, calls only.

British Embassy Commercial Library *35 rue du Fbg-St-Honoré, 8th (01.44.51.31.00, www. ukinfrance.fco.gov.uk). M°* *Concorde.* **Open** by appointment. Stocks trade directories, and assists British companies that wish to develop or set up in France.

CCIP (Chambre de Commerce et d'Industrie de Paris) *27 av de Friedland, 8th (08.20.01.21.12, www.ccip.fr). M° Charles de Gaulle Etoile.* **Open** 8.30am-6.30pm Mon-Fri.

A variety of services for people doing business in France, and very useful for small businesses. Pick up the free booklet *Discovering the Chamber of Commerce* from its head office. There's also a legal advice line (08.92.70.51.00, 9am-4.30pm Mon-Thur, 9am-1pm Fri). **Other locations**: Bourse du Commerce, 2 rue de Viarmes, 1st (has a free library and bookshop); 2 rue Adolphe-Jullien, 1st (support for businesses wishing to export goods and services to France).

US Commercial Service *Postal address: US Embassy, 2 av Gabriel, 8th. Visit: US Commercial Service, NEO Building, 14 bd Haussmann, 9th (01.43.12.71.28, www.buyusa.gov/france).* *M° Richelieu Drouot.* **Open** by appointment 9am-6pm Mon-Fri. Helps American companies looking to trade in France.

CONSUMER

In the event of a serious problem, try one of the following:

Direction Départementale de la Concurrence, de la Consommation et de la Répression des Fraudes *8 rue Froissart, 3rd (01.40.27.16.00). M° St-Sébastien Froissart.* **Open** 9am-noon, 2-5pm Mon-Fri. Come here to file a consumer complaint concerning problems with Paris-based businesses.

Institut National de la Consommation *80 rue Lecourbe, 15th (08.92.70.75.92, www.conso.net). M° Sèvres Lecourbe.* **Open** *by phone* 9am-12.30pm Mon-Fri; recorded information at other times. Deals with questions on housing, consumer, regulatory and administrative issues.

CUSTOMS

Custom declarations are not usually necessary if you arrive from another EU country and are carrying legal goods for personal use. The amounts given below are a guide only: if you come close to the maximums in several categories, you may still have to explain your personal habits to customs.

● 1,000 cigarettes, 400 small cigars, 200 cigars or 1kg loose tobacco.
● 10 litres of spirits (more than 22% alcohol), 90 litres of wine (of which 60 litres sparkling wine) or 110 litres of beer.

Coming from a non-EU country, you can bring:
● 200 cigarettes, 100 small cigars, 50 cigars or 250g tobacco.
● 1 litre of spirits (more than 22% alcohol; 2 litres if less than 22% alcohol), 4 litres of wine or 16 litres of beer.
● 50g (1.76oz) of perfume.

Tax refunds

Non-EU residents can claim a refund or *détaxe* (around 12 per cent) on VAT if they spend over €175 in any one day in one shop and if they live outside the EU for more than six months in the year. At the shop concerned ask for a *bordereau de vente à l'exportation*, and when you leave France have it stamped by customs. Then send the stamped form back to the shop. *Détaxe* does not cover food, drink, antiques, services or works of art.
Customs Information Centre *(08.11.20.44.44).*

DISABLED

It's always wise to check up on a site's accessibility and provision for disabled access before you visit. There is information (in French) available on the **Secrétaire d'Etat aux Personnes Handicapées** website: www.handicap.gouv.fr, telephone 08.20.03.33.33.

Association des Paralysés de France *13 pl de Rungis, 13th (01.53.80.92.97, www.apf.asso.fr). M° Place d'Italie.* **Open** 9am-12.30pm, 1.30-5.30pm Mon-Thur; 9am-12.30pm, 1.30-5pm Fri. Publishes *Guide 98 Musées, Cinémas* (€3.81) listing accessible museums and cinemas, and also has a guide to monuments and sights.
Fédération APAJH (Association pour Adultes et Jeunes Handicapés) *29th Floor, Tour Montparnasse, 33 av du Maine, 15th (01.44.10.23.40, www.apajh.org). M° Montparnasse Bienvenüe.*

Advice for disabled people living in France.
Maison Départementale des Personnes Handicapées de Paris *69 rue de la Victoire, 9th (08.05.80.09.09, www.mdph.fr).* **Open** 9am-4pm Mon, Tue, Thur, Fri; 9am-5pm Wed.
Advice available in French to disabled persons living in or visiting Paris. The Office de Tourisme website (www.parisinfo. com) also provides plenty of useful information for disabled visitors.

Getting around

The métro and buses are not wheelchair-accessible, with the exception of métro line 14 (Méteor), stations Barbès-Rochechouard (line 2) and Esplanade de la Défense (line 1), and bus lines 20, 21, 22, 24, 26, 27, 28, 29, 30, 31, 32, 38, 39, 42, 43, 46, 47, 48, 52, 53, 54, 56, 57, 58, 60, 61, 62, 63, 64, 65, 66, 67, 68, 69, 70, 72, 73, 74, 75, 76, 80, 81, 82, 83, 84, 85, 86, 87, 88, 89, 91, 92, 93, 94, 95, 96 and PC (Petite Ceinture) 1, 2 and 3. Forward seats on buses are intended for people with poor mobility. RER lines A, B, C, D and some SNCF trains are wheelchair-accessible in parts. For a full list of wheelchair-accessible stations: 08.10.64.64.64, www.infomobi.com. All Paris taxis are obliged by law to take passengers in wheelchairs.

DRUGS

French police have the power to stop and search anyone. It's wise to keep prescription drugs in their original containers and, if possible, to carry copies of the original prescriptions. If you're caught in possession of illegal drugs, you can expect a prison sentence and/or a fine. *See also p372* **Health**.

ELECTRICITY

Electricity in France runs on 220V. Visitors with British 240V appliances can change the plug or use an adaptor (*adaptateur*). For US 110V appliances, you'll need to use a transformer (*transformateur*), available at BHV, Fnac and Darty.

EMBASSIES & CONSULATES

For a full list of embassies and consulates, see the *Pages Jaunes* (www.pagesjaunes.fr) under 'Ambassades et Consulats'. Consular services (passports, etc) are for citizens of that country only.

ESSENTIAL INFORMATION

Australian Embassy *4 rue Jean-Rey, 15th (01.40.59.33.00, www.france.embassy.gov.au). M° Bir-Hakeim.* **Open** *Consular services* 9am-noon, 2-4pm Mon-Fri.

British Embassy *35 rue du Fbg-St-Honoré, 8th (01.44.51.31.00, www.ukinfrance.fco.gov.uk). M° Concorde. Consular services: 18bis rue d'Anjou, 8th. M° Concorde.* **Open** 9.30am-1pm, 2.30-6pm Mon-Fri.

British citizens wanting consular services (new passports, etc) should ignore the long queue stretching along rue d'Anjou for the visa department, and instead walk straight in at no.18bis.

Canadian Embassy *35 av Montaigne, 8th (01.44.43.29.00, www.amb-canada.fr). M° Franklin D. Roosevelt.* **Open** 9am-noon, 2-5pm Mon-Fri.
Consular services: 01.44.43.29.02.
Open 9am-noon Mon-Fri.
Visas: 37 av Montaigne, 8th (01.44.43.29.16). **Open** 8.30-10.30am Mon-Fri.

Irish Embassy *12 av Foch, 16th. (01.44.17.67.00, www.embassy ofireland.fr). M° Charles de Gaulle Etoile.* **Open** *Consular/visas* 9.30am-noon Mon-Fri; by phone 9.30am-1pm, 2.30-5.30pm Mon-Fri.

New Zealand Embassy *7ter rue Léonard-de-Vinci, 16th (01.45.01.43.43, www.nz embassy.com/france). M° Victor Hugo.* **Open** 9am-1pm Mon-Fri. *Visas* 9am-12.30pm Mon-Fri.
Visas for travel to New Zealand can be applied for on the website www.immigration.govt.nz.

South African Embassy *59 quai d'Orsay, 7th (01.53.59.23.23, www.afriquesud.net). M° Invalides.* **Open** 8.30am-5.15pm Mon-Fri.
Consulate & visas: 01.47.53.99.70.
Open 9am-noon Mon-Fri.

US Embassy *2 av Gabriel, 8th (01.43.12.22.22, http://france. usembassy.gov). M° Concorde. Consulate & visas: 4 av Gabriel, 8th (08.10.26.46.26). M° Concorde.* **Open** *Consular services* 9am-12.30pm, 1-3pm Mon-Fri. *Visas* 08.92.23.84.72 or check website for non-immigration visas.

EMERGENCIES

Most of the following services operate 24 hours a day. In a medical emergency, such as a road accident, phone the Sapeurs-Pompiers, who have trained paramedics.
See also **Health: Accident & Emergency; Doctors; Helplines;** and **Police.**

Ambulance (SAMU) 15
Police 17
Fire (Sapeurs-Pompiers) 18
Emergency (from a mobile phone) 112
Centre anti-poison 01.40.05.48.48

GAY & LESBIAN

For information on HIV and AIDS, *see below* **Health.** *See also pp273-279* **Gay & Lesbian.**

HEALTH

Nationals of non-EU countries should take out insurance before leaving home. EU nationals staying in France can use the French Social Security system, which refunds up to 70 per cent of medical expenses. UK residents travelling in Europe require a European National Health Insurance Card (EHIC). This allows them to benefit from free or reduced-cost medical care when travelling in a country belonging to the European Economic Area (EEA) or Switzerland. The EHIC is free of charge. For further information, refer to www.dh.gov.uk/travellers.

If you're staying for longer than three months, or working in France but still making National Insurance contributions in Britain, you will need form E128 filled in by your employer and stamped by the NI contributions office in order to get a French medical number. Consultations and prescriptions have to be paid for in full on the spot, and are reimbursed on receipt of a completed *fiche*. If you undergo treatment, the doctor will give you a prescription and a *feuille de soins* (bill of treatment). Stick the small stickers from the medication boxes on to the *feuille de soins*. Send this, together with the prescription and details of your EHIC card, to the local **Caisse Primaire d'Assurance Maladie** for a refund. For those resident in France, more and more doctors now accept the **Carte Vitale**, which lets them produce a digital *feuille de soins* and allows you to pay only the non-reimbursable part of the bill. Information on health insurance can be found at www.ameli.fr, where you can also track refunds online. See also the Ministry of Health's website at www.sante.gouv.fr.

Accident & emergency

Hospitals specialise in one type of emergency or illness – refer to the Assistance Publique's website (www.aphp.fr). In a medical emergency, call the Sapeurs-Pompiers or SAMU (*see left* **Emergencies**). The following (arranged in order of district) have 24-hour accident and emergency services:

ADULTS
Hôpital Hôtel-Dieu *1 pl du Parvis Notre-Dame, 4th (01.42.34.82.34).*
Hôpital St-Louis *1 av Claude-Vellefaux, 10th (01.42.49.49.49).*
Hôpital St-Antoine *184 rue du Fbg-St-Antoine, 12th (01.49.28.20.00).*
Hôpital de la Pitié-Salpêtrière *47-83 bd de l'Hôpital, 13th (01.42.16.00.00).*
Hôpital Cochin *27 rue du Fbg-St-Jacques, 14th (01.58.41.41.41).*
Hôpital Européen Georges Pompidou *20 rue Leblanc, 15th (01.56.09.20.00).*
Hôpital Bichat-Claude Bernard *46 rue Henri-Huchard, 18th (01.40.25.80.80).*
Hôpital Tenon *4 rue de la Chine, 20th (01.56.01.70.00).*

CHILDREN
Hôpital Armand Trousseau *26 av du Dr Arnold-Netter, 12th (01.44.73.74.75).*
Hôpital St-Vincent de Paul *74-82 av Denfert-Rochereau, 14th (01.58.41.41.41).*
Hôpital Necker *149 rue de Sèvres, 15th (01.44.49.40.00).*
Hôpital Robert Debré *48 bd Sérurier, 19th (01.40.03.20.00).*

PRIVATE HOSPITALS
American Hospital in Paris *63 bd Victor-Hugo, 92200 Neuilly (01.46.41.25.25, www.american-hospital.org). M° Porte Maillot, then bus 82.* **Open** 24hrs daily.
English-speaking hospital. French Social Security refunds only a small percentage of the total treatment costs.
Hertford British Hospital (Hôpital Franco-Britannique) *3 rue Barbès, 92300 Levallois-Perret (01.46.39.22.22, www.british-hospital.org). M° Anatole-France.* **Open** 24hrs daily.
Most staff here speak English.

Contraception & abortion

To get the pill (*la pilule*) or coil (*stérilet*), you need a prescription, available on appointment from the two places listed below, from a *médecin généraliste* (GP) or from a gynaecologist. The morning-after pill (*la pilule du lendemain*) can be had from pharmacies without

ESSENTIAL INFORMATION

prescription but is not reimbursed. Condoms (*préservatifs*) and spermicides are sold in pharmacies and supermarkets, and there are condom machines in most métro stations, club lavatories and on some street corners.

Centre de Planification et d'Education Familiales
27 rue Curnonsky, 17th (01.48.88.07.28). M° Porte de Champerret. **Open** 9am-5pm Mon-Fri.
Free consultations on family planning and abortion.

MFPF (Mouvement Français pour le Planning Familial)
10 rue Vivienne, 2nd (01.42.60.93.20, www.planning-familial.org). M° Bourse. **Open** 2-7pm Mon; 11am-1pm Tue; 1.30-4.30pm Wed; noon-3pm Thur.
Phone for an appointment for prescriptions and contraception advice. For abortion advice, turn up at the centre at one of the designated time slots.

Dentists

Dentists are found in the *Pages Jaunes* under *Dentistes*. For emergencies, contact:

Hôpital de la Pitié-Salpêtrière
(*see p372*) also offers 24hr emergency dental care.

SOS Dentaire
87 bd Port-Royal, 13th (01.43.37.51.00). M° Les Gobelins/RER Port-Royal. **Open** by phone for appointment after 6pm.
A telephone service for emergency dental care.

Doctors

You'll find a list of GPs in the *Pages Jaunes* under *Médecins: Médecine générale*. For a social security refund, choose a doctor or dentist who is *conventionné* (state registered). Consultations cost €22 or more, of which a proportion can be reimbursed. Seeing a specialist costs more still.

Centre Médical Europe
44 rue d'Amsterdam, 9th (01.42.81.93.33, www.centre-medical-europe.com). M° St-Lazare. **Open** With appointment 8am-7pm Mon-Fri; 8am-6pm Sat.
Practitioners in all fields; modest consultation fees.

SOS Médecins
36.24, www.sosmedecins.com. House calls cost approx €35 before 7pm; from €50 after and on holidays; prices are higher if you don't have French social security.

Urgences Médicales de Paris
01.53.94.94.94, www.ump.fr. Doctors make house calls for approx €35 during the day (€60 if you don't have French social security); €50/€80 until midnight; €65/€90 after midnight. Some speak English.

Opticians

Branches of **Alain Afflelou** (www.alainafflelou.com) and **Lissac** (www.lissac.fr) stock hundreds of frames and can make up prescription glasses within the hour. For an eye test, you'll need to go to an *ophtalmologiste* – ask the optician for a list. Contact lenses can be bought over the counter if you have your prescription details with you.

Hôpital des Quinze-Vingts
28 rue de Charenton, 12th (01.40.02.15.20). Specialist eye hospital offers on-the-spot consultations for eye problems.
SOS Optique
01.48.07.22.00, www.sosoptique.com.
Offers 24hr repair service for glasses.

Pharmacies

French *pharmacies* sport a green neon cross. A rota of *pharmacies de garde* operate at night and on Sundays; see below for a list of these night pharmacies. If closed, a pharmacy will have a sign indicating the nearest one open. Staff can provide basic medical services such as bandaging wounds (for a small fee) and will indicate the nearest doctor on duty. *Parapharmacies* sell almost everything pharmacies do but cannot dispense prescription medication. Toiletries and sanitary products are often less expensive in supermarkets.

Grande Pharmacie de la Nation
13 pl de la Nation, 11th (01.43.73.24.03). M° Nation. **Open** 8am-midnight daily.
Matignon 1 av Matignon, 8th (01.43.59.86.55). M° Franklin D. Roosevelt. **Open** 8.30am-2am daily.
Pharmacie des Champs-Elysées 84 av des Champs-Elysées, 8th (01.45.62.02.41). M° George V. **Open** until 2am daily.
Pharmacie Européene de la Place de Clichy 6 pl de Clichy, 9th (01.48.74.65.18). M° Place de Clichy. **Open** 24hrs daily.
Pharmacie des Halles 10 bd de Sébastopol, 4th (01.42.72.03.23). M° Châtelet. **Open** 9am-midnight Mon-Sat; 9am-10pm Sun.

Pharmacie d'Italie
61 av d'Italie, 13th (01.44.24.19.72). M° Tolbiac. **Open** 8am-midnight daily.
Pharma Presto 01.61.04.04.04, www.pharma-presto.com. **Open** for emergencies 24hrs daily. Delivery (€45 8am-6pm; €55 6pm-8am & weekends) of medication.

STDs, HIV & AIDS

Cabinet Médico-Social Municipal Figuier
2 rue Figuier, 4th (01.49.96.62.70). M° Pont-Marie. **Open** HIV test walk-in 1.30-6.30pm Mon-Fri. With appointment 9am-1pm Thur; 9.15am-noon Sat. STD tests walk-in 9am-noon Mon-Fri.
Free, anonymous tests (*dépistages*) for HIV, hepatitis B and C and syphilis (wait one week for results). Good counselling service, too.

Le Kiosque Infos Sida-Toxicomanie
48 rue François Miron, 4th (01.44.78.00.00, www.lekiosque.org). M° St-Paul. **Open** Walk-in 11am-7pm Mon; 10am-7pm Tue-Fri; 10am-2pm, 3-6pm Sat.
Youth association offering information and counselling on AIDS, sexuality and drugs, and fast AIDS tests for gay men. Also works with Checkpoint (36 rue Geoffroy l'Asnier, 4th, 01.44.78.24.44).

SIDA Info Service
08.00.84.08.00, www.sida-info-service.org. **Open** 24hrs daily.
Confidential AIDS information in French.

HELPLINES

Alcoholics Anonymous in English
01.46.34.59.65, www.aaparis.org. A 24hr recorded message gives details of Alcoholics Anonymous meetings at the American Cathedral or American Church (*see p378*).

Allô Service Public
39.39, www.service-public.fr. **Open** 8am-8pm Mon-Fri; 8.30am-6pm Sat.
A source of information and contacts for all aspects of tax, work and administration matters. They even claim to be able to help if you have problems with neighbours. The catch: operators speak only French. Foreigners can call Info Migrants on 01.53.26.52.82.

Counseling Center
01.47.23.61.13, www.american cathedral.org. Walk-in clinic 11am-1pm 1st & 3rd Thur of mth.
English-language counselling, based at the American Cathedral.

Drogues Info Service
08.00.23.13.13, Ecoute Alcool 08.11.91.30.30, Ecoute Cannabis

ESSENTIAL INFORMATION

08.11.91.20.20, *Tabac Info Service 39.89, www.drogues.gouv.fr*.
Phone service, in French, for help with drug, alcohol and tobacco problems.

Narcotics Anonymous
01.43.72.12.72, www. narcotiquesanonymes.org.
The helpline is open daily 8-10pm. Meetings in English are held every week.

SOS Dépression *01.40.47.95.95, http://sos.depression.free.fr*. **Open** 24hrs daily.
People listen and/or give advice to those suffering from depression. SOS Dépression can send round a counsellor or psychiatrist in case of a crisis.

SOS Help *01.46.21.46.46, www.soshelpline.org*. **Open** 3-11pm daily.
English-language helpline.

ID

French law requires that some form of identification be carried at all times. You should be prepared to produce your passport or **EHIC** card (*see p372*).

INSURANCE

See p372 **Health**.

INTERNET

ISPs

Free *10.44, www.free.fr*.
Open 24hrs daily.
SFR *10.23, www.sfr.fr*.
Open 8am-10pm daily.
Orange *39.00, www.orange.fr*.
Open 24hrs daily.
Bouygues *10.34, www.bouyguestelecom.fr*.
Open 8am-8pm Mon-Sat.

Internet access

An increasing number of public spaces now offer Wi-Fi hotspots.

Milk *31 bd de Sébastopol, 1st (01.40.13.06.51, www.milklub.com). Mº Châtelet/RER Châtelet Les Halles*. **Open** 24hrs daily.
The biggest internet café in Paris.
Other locations 28 rue du 4 Septembre, 2nd (01.40.06.00.70); 5 rue d'Odessa (01.43.20.10.37).

LANGUAGE

See p383 **Vocabulary**; for a glossary of food terms, *see p168* **Decoding the Menu**.

LEFT LUGGAGE

Gare du Nord

There are self-locking luggage lockers (6.15am-11.15pm daily) situated on Level -1 under the main station concourse.

Roissy-Charles-de-Gaulle airport

Bagages du Monde
(01.34.38.58.90, www.bagages dumonde.com). **Terminal 1**
Niveau Départ, Porte 14 (01.34.38.58.82). Open 9.15am-1.30pm, 3.30-7pm daily. **Between Terminal 2C & 2E** *Gare TGV Niveau 4 (01.48.16.02.15).*
Open 6am-9.30pm daily.
Company with counters in Roissy-Charles-de-Gaulle and an office in Paris (102 rue de Chemin-Vert, 11th, 01.34.38.58.97, open 10am-1pm, 3.30-7.30pm Mon-Fri). Can ship baggage worldwide or store it.

LEGAL HELP

Mairies can answer some legal enquiries; ask for times of their free *consultations juridiques*.
See also p371 **Embassies**.

Direction Départementale de la Concurrence, de la Consommation et de la Répression des Fraudes *8 rue Froissart, 3rd (01.40.27.16.00). Mº St-Sébastien Froissart*. **Open** 9am-noon, 2-5pm Mon-Fri.
Part of the Ministry of Finance; deals with consumer complaints.
Palais de Justice Galerie de Harlay *Escalier S, 4 bd du Palais, 4th (01.44.32.49.01). Mº Cité*.
Open 9.30am-noon Mon-Fri.
Free legal consultation. Arrive early and obtain a ticket for the queue.
SOS Avocats *08.25.39.33.00*.
Open 7-11.30pm Mon-Fri.
Free legal advice by phone.

LIBRARIES

Every arrondissement has a free public library. To get a library card, you need to provide ID and evidence of a fixed address in Paris.

American Library *10 rue du Général-Camou, 7th (01.53.59.12.60, www.american libraryinparis.org). Mº Ecole-Militaire/RER Pont de l'Alma*.
Open 10am-7pm Tue-Sat; 1-7pm Sun (shorter hours in Aug).
Admission day pass €14; €10 reductions; annual €110.

A useful resource: this is the largest English-language lending library on the Continent. It receives 400 periodicals, as well as popular magazines and newspapers.
Bibliothèque Historique de la Ville de Paris *Hôtel Lamoignon, 24 rue Pavée, 4th (01.44.59.29.40). Mº St-Paul*. **Open** 10am-6pm Mon-Sat. **Admission** free (bring passport photo and ID).
A decent range of books and documents on Paris history.
Bibliothèque Marguerite Durand *79 rue Nationale, 13th (01.53.82.76.77). Mº Tolbiac*. **Open** 2-6pm Tue-Sat. **Admission** free.
This library holds some 40,000 books and 120 periodicals on women's history. The feminism collection includes letters of Colette and Louise Michel.
Bibliothèque Nationale de France François Mitterrand *quai François-Mauriac, 13th (01.53.79.59.59, www.bnf.fr). Mº Bibliothèque*. **Open** 2-7pm Mon; 9am-7pm Tue-Sat; 1-7pm Sun. Closed 2wks Sept & bank holidays. **Admission** day pass €3.50; annual €38; €20 reductions.
Books, papers and periodicals, plus titles in English. An audio-visual room lets you browse photo, film and sound archives.
Bibliothèque Publique d'Information (BPI) *Centre Pompidou, 4th (01.44.78.12.75, www.bpi.fr). Mº Hôtel de Ville/ RER Châtelet Les Halles*. **Open** noon-10pm Mon, Wed-Fri; 11am-10pm Sat, Sun. Closed 1 May. **Admission** free.
Now on three levels, the Centre Pompidou's vast library has a huge global press section, reference books and language-learning facilities.
BIFI (Bibliothèque du Film) *51 rue de Bercy, 12th (01.71.19.32.32, www.bifi.fr). Mº Bercy*. **Open** 10am-7pm Mon, Wed-Fri; 1-6.30pm Sat. Closed 2wks Aug. **Admission** €3.50 day pass; €34 annual; €15 reductions.
Housed in the same building as the Cinémathèque Française, this world-class researchers' and film buffs' library offers books, magazines, film stills and posters, as well as films on video and DVD.
Documentation Française *29-31 quai Voltaire, 7th (01.40.15.71.10, www.ladocumentationfrancaise.fr). Mº Rue du Bac*. **Open** 10am-6pm Mon-Fri. Closed Aug & 1st wk Sept.
The official government archive and central reference library has information on French politics and economy since 1945.

LOCKSMITHS

There are numerous round-the-clock repair services handling locks, plumbing and, sometimes, car repairs. Most of them charge a minimum €18-€20 call-out (*déplacement*) and €30 per hour, plus parts. Charges are higher on Sunday and at night.

Allô Serrurerie *01.40.29.44.68, www.alloserrurerie.com.*
SOS Dépannage *08.20.22.23.33, www.okservice.fr.*
SOS Dépannage is double the price of most services, but claims to be twice as reliable.

LOST PROPERTY

Bureau des Objets Trouvés
36 rue des Morillons, 15th (08.21.00.25.25, www.prefecture depolice.interieur.gouv.fr). M° Convention. **Open** 8.30am-5pm Mon-Thur; 8.30am-4.30pm Fri.
Visit in person to fill in a form specifying details of the loss. This may have been the first lost property office in the world, but it is far from the most efficient. Huge delays in processing claims mean that if your trip to Paris is short, you may need to nominate a proxy to collect found objects after you leave, although small items can be posted. If your passport was among the items lost, you'll need to go to your consulate to get a single-entry temporary passport in order to leave the country.

SNCF lost property
Some mainline SNCF stations have their own lost property offices. *See also p368.*

MEDIA

See also p384 **Websites**.

Magazines

Arts & listings Two modest local publications compete for consumers of basic Wednesday-to-Tuesday listings: the handbag-sized **L'Officiel des Spectacles** (€0.35, www.offi.fr) and **Pariscope** (€0.40). Look out also for **Lylo**, a free bi-monthly booklet distributed around bars and clubs, for information on gigs and DJ nights. **Technikart** tries – not entirely successfully – to mix clubbing with the arts. Highbrow TV guide **Télérama** has superb arts coverage and comes with **Sortir**, a Paris listings insert. **Les Inrockuptibles** (fondly

known as *Les Inrocks*) deals with contemporary music scenes at home and abroad; it has strong coverage of film and books too.

There are specialist magazines for every interest. The choice of film-related titles, in particular, is wide, and includes intellectual heavyweights **Les Cahiers du Cinéma** and **Positif**, fluffy **Studio** and celebrity-heavy **Première**.

Business **Capital**, its sister magazine **Management** and weightier **L'Expansion** are the notable monthlies. **Défis** has tips for the entrepreneur; **Initiatives** is for the self-employed.

English **Time Out Essential Paris for Visitors** is on sale in newsagents across the city. **FUSAC** (France-USA Contacts) is a small-ads magazine that lists flat rentals, job ads and appliances for sale.

Gossip The French love gossip. **Public** gives weekly celebrity updates; **Voici** is the juiciest scandal sheet; **Gala** tells much the same stories without the sleaze. **Paris Match** is a French institution founded in 1948, packed with society gossip, celebrity interviews and regular photo scoops. **Point de Vue** specialises in royalty (no showbiz fluff). Monthly **Entrevue** aims to titillate and tends towards features on nonconformist sex.

News Weekly news magazines are an important sector in France, offering news and cultural sections as well as in-depth reports; they range from such respected organs as **L'Express**, **Le Point** and **Le Nouvel Observateur** to the sardonic, chaotically arranged **Marianne**. Weekly **Courrier International** publishes an interesting selection of articles, translated into French, from newspapers all over the world.

Women, men & fashion **Elle** was a pioneer among women's magazines and has editions around the globe. In France it's a weekly, and spot-on for interviews and fashion. Monthly **Marie-Claire** takes a more feminist, campaigning line. Both have design spin-offs (**Elle Décoration**, **Marie-Claire Maison**), and *Elle* has also spawned foodie **Elle à Table**. **DS** has lots to read and coverage of social issues. **Vogue**, bought for its fashion coverage and big-name

guests, is rivalled during fashion week by **L'Officiel de la Mode**.

Meanwhile the underground prefers to more radical publications such as **Crash** and the new wave of fashion/lifestyle mags: **WAD** (stands for We Are Different), **Citizen K**, **Jalouse** and **Numéro**. Men's mags include the naughty-bizarre **Echo des Savanes** and French versions of lad bibles **FHM**, **GQ** and **Men's Health**.

Newspapers

French national dailies, with relatively high prices and low print runs, are in dire straits. Only 20 per cent of France read a national paper; regional dailies dominate outside Paris. Serious, centre-left **Le Monde** is must-read material for business types, politicians and intellectuals, and despite its lofty reputation, subject matter is eclectic.

The conservative upper and middle classes go for daily broadsheet **Le Figaro**, which has a devotion to politics, shopping, food and sport. Taken over in 2004 by the head of the Dassault defence and media group, it steers clear of controversial industrial issues. Its sales are aided by pages of property and job ads and Wednesday's **Figaroscope** Paris listings.

Founded in the aftershocks of 1968 by a group that included Sartre and de Beauvoir, **Libération**, once affectionately known as *Libé*, is shedding readers and has yet to find a modern identity. It is still the preferred read of the *gauche caviar* (champagne socialists) and worth buying for news and arts coverage.

For business and financial news, the French dailies **La Tribune**, **Les Echos** and the weekly **Investir** are the tried and trusted sources. The easy-read tabloid **Le Parisien** is strong on consumer affairs, social issues, local news, events and vox pops. Downmarket **France Soir** has gone tabloid. **La Croix** is a Catholic, right-wing daily. Sunday broadsheet **Le Journal du Dimanche** comes with **Fémina** magazine.

L'Equipe is the doyen of European sports dailies – Saturday's edition comes with a magazine. Its sister bi-weekly **France Football** is the bible of world soccer. Each was instrumental in setting up the game's top competitions during the golden age of French sports journalism after the war. **Paris-Turf** is for horse fans.

English-language papers

Paris-based **International Herald Tribune** is on sale throughout the city; British dailies, Sundays and **USA Today** are widely available on the day of issue at larger kiosks in the centre, though often without their supplements. The most popular (and many esoteric) English and US newspapers and magazines can be found in central bookshops (*see pp192-194*).

Satirical papers

Wednesday institution **Le Canard Enchaîné** is the Gallic *Private Eye* – in fact it was the inspiration for the *Eye*. It's a broadly left-wing satirical weekly that's full of in-jokes and breaks political scandals.

Radio

For a list of Paris radio frequencies, go to www.bric-a-brac.org/radio. A mandatory state-defined minimum of 40 per cent French music has led to overplay of Gallic pop oldies and to the creation of dubious hybrids by local groups that mix words in French with a refrain in English. Trashy phone-in shows proliferate.

English You can receive the **BBC World Service** (648 KHz AM), with English-language news, current events, pop and drama; also on 198KHz LW, from midnight to 5.30am daily. At other times 198KHz LW carries **BBC Radio 4**, with British news, talk and *The Archers*. **RFI** (738 KHz AM; www.rfi.fr) has an English-language programme of news and music 7-8am, 2.30-3.30pm and 4.30-5pm daily. There's also the French capital's first all-English station, Paris Live (www.paris-live.com).

Television

In 2005, the choice of free TV channels in France more than doubled. Under the acronym TNT (Télévision Numérique Terrestre, or terrestrial digital television), seven new channels – available via the traditional rooftop aerial with a decoder or automatically to cable and satellite customers – began broadcasting. For listings, pick up a copy of weekly mag *Télérama*.

TF1 *(www.tf1.fr)*. The country's biggest channel. Reality shows, soaps and football are staples.
France 2 *(www.france2.fr)*. This state-owned station mixes game shows, chat, documentaries and the usual cop series and films.

France 3 *(www.france3.fr)*. This, the more heavyweight of the two state channels, offers wildlife and sports coverage, debates and *Cinéma de Minuit* – classic films in VO (original language).
Canal+ *(www.canalplus.fr)*. Subscription channel shows recent films, exclusive sport and late-night porn. A week's worth of satirical puppets show *Les Guignols* is broadcast unscrambled on Sundays at 1.55pm.
France 5 *(www.france5.fr)*. France 5 principally features educational programming.
M6 *(www.m6.fr)*. Dubbed US sci-fi series and made for TV movies, plus investigative reportage, popular science and kids' shows.
Arte *(www.arte-tv.com)*. Intellectual Franco-German hybrid.
Cable TV & satellite France offers a decent range of cable and satellite channels but content in English is still limited. CNN and BBC World offer round-the-clock news coverage. BBC Prime keeps you up to date on *EastEnders* (omnibus Sun 2pm), while Teva supplies comedy shows.
Numericable *(10.55, www.numericable.fr)*. The first cable provider to offer an interactive video service via the internet.
TNT (www.tvnt.net). Offers 18 free channels.

MONEY

The amount of currency visitors may carry is not limited. However, sums worth over €10,000 must be declared to customs when entering or leaving the country.

The euro

Non-French debit and credit cards can be used to withdraw and pay in euros, and currency withdrawn in France can be used subsequently all over the euro zone. Daylight robbery occurs, however, if you try to deposit a euro cheque from any country other than France in a French bank: they are currently charging around €15 for this service, and the European parliament has backed down on its original decision that cross-border payments should be in line with domestic ones across the euro zone. This is good news for the British, though: if you transfer money from the UK to France in euros, you will pay the same charges as if Britain were within the euro zone (but it pays to watch the exchange rate carefully).

ATMs

Withdrawals in euros can be made from bank and post office automatic cash machines. The specific cards accepted are marked on each machine, and most can give instructions in English. Credit card companies charge a fee for cash advances, but rates are often better than banks.

Banks

French banks usually open 9am-5pm Mon-Fri (some close at lunch); some banks also open on Sat. All are closed on public holidays, and from noon on the previous day. Note that not all banks have foreign exchange counters. The commission rates vary between banks; the state-owned Banque de France usually offers good rates. Most banks accept travellers' cheques, but may be reluctant to accept personal cheques even with the Eurocheque guarantee card, which is not widely used in France.

Bank accounts

To open an account (*ouvrir un compte*), French banks require proof of identity, address and your income (if any). You'll probably be required to show your passport, an electricity, gas or phone bill in your name and a payslip/letter from your employer. Students need a student card and may need a letter from their parents. Of the major national banks (BNP, Crédit Lyonnais, Société Générale, Banque Populaire, Crédit Agricole), Société Générale tends to be the most foreigner-friendly. Most banks don't hand out a Carte Bleue/Visa card until several weeks after you've opened an account. A chequebook (*chéquier*) is usually issued in about a week. Payments made with a Carte Bleue are debited directly from your current account, but you can arrange for purchases to be debited at the end of every month. French banks are tough on overdrafts, so try to anticipate any cash crisis in advance and work out a deal for an authorised overdraft (*découvert autorisé*) or you risk being blacklisted as '*interdit bancaire*' – forbidden from having a current account – for anything up to ten years. Depositing foreign currency cheques can be slow, so try to use wire transfer or a bank draft in euros to receive funds from abroad.

Bureaux de change

If you happen to be arriving in Paris early in the morning or late at night, you will be able to change money at the **Travelex** bureaux de change in terminals 1 (6.30am-10.30pm), 2A (7am-5pm & 6am-10.30pm), 2B (6am-10.30pm), 2C (7.30am-7pm & 6am-10.30pm), 2D (6.30am-10.30pm), 2F (6am-10.30pm & 6.30am-10.30pm), and 3 (6.30am-10;30pm) at Roissy, and at Orly Sud. Travelex also has bureaux de change at the following stations:

Gare Montparnasse
01.42.79.03.88. **Open** 9am-7pm Mon-Sat; 10am-5pm Sun.
Gare du Nord *01.40.82.96.59.* **Open** 6.45am-10.30pm Mon-Sat; 6.45am-9.30pm Sun.
Gare St-Lazare *01.42.93.74.58.* **Open** 8am-7pm Mon-Sat; 10.30am-5pm Sun.

Credit cards

Major international credit cards are widely used in France; Visa (more commonly known in France as *Carte Bleue*) is the most readily accepted. French-issued credit cards have a security microchip (*puce*) in each card. The card is slotted into a reader, and the holder keys in a PIN to authorise the transaction. Non-French cards work, but generate a credit slip to sign. In case of credit card loss or theft, call one of the following 24hr services with English-speaking staff:

American Express
01.44.77.72.00.
Diners Club *08.20.82.01.43.*
MasterCard *08.00.90.13.87.*
Visa *08.92.70.57.05.*

Foreign affairs

American Express *11 rue Scribe, 9th (01.47.77.70.00, www. americanexpress.com). M° Opéra.* **Open** 9am-6.30pm Mon-Sat.
Travel agency, bureau de change, *poste restante* (you can leave messages for other card holders), card replacement, travellers' cheque refund service, money transfers and cash machine for AmEx cardholders.
Barclays *6 rond-point des Champs-Elysées, 8th (01.44.95.13.80, www.barclays.fr). M° Franklin D. Roosevelt.* **Open** 9.15am-4.30pm Mon-Fri.
Barclays' international Expat Service handles direct debits, international transfer of funds, and so on.

Citibank *1-5 rue Paul Cézanne, 8th (01.70.75.50.00, www. citibank.fr). M° St-Philippe-du-Roule.* **Open** 10am-5.30pm Mon-Fri.
Bank clients get good rates for international money transfers, preferential exchange rates and commission-free travellers' cheques.
Travelex *52 av des Champs-Elysées, 8th (01.42.89.80.33, www.travelex.com/fr). M° Franklin D. Roosevelt.* **Open** 9am-10.30pm Mon-Sat; 10am-9pm Sun.
Travelex issues travellers' cheques and insurance and also deals with bank transfers.
Western Union Money Transfer
www.westernunion.com. Many post offices in the city (*see right*) provide Western Union services. Transfers from abroad should arrive within 15 minutes; charges paid by sender.

Tax

French VAT (*taxe sur la valeur ajoutée* or TVA) is arranged in three bands: 2.1 per cent for items of medication and newspapers; 5.5 per cent for food, books, CDs and DVDs; and 19.6 per cent for all other types of goods and services (the TVA for restaurants has been lowered from 19.6 per cent to 5.5 per cent).

NATURAL HAZARDS

Paris has no natural hazards as such, though in recent years the town hall has produced evacuation plans to cover flooding.

OPENING HOURS

Standard opening hours for shops are 9 or 10am to 7 or 8pm Monday to Saturday. Some shops are closed on Monday. Shops and businesses often close at lunchtime, usually 12.30-2pm; many shops close in August. Sunday opening is found in the Marais, on the Champs-Elysées, at Bercy Village and in the Carrousel du Louvre. Most areas have a local grocer that stays open into the night and will often open on Sundays and public holidays too.

24hr florist Elyfleur *82 av de Wagram, 17th (01.47.66.87.19, www.elyfleurs.com). M° Wagram.* **Credit** MC, V.
24hr garage Shell *6 bd Raspail, 7th (01.45.48.43.12). M° Rue du Bac.*
This garage has an extensive array of everyday supermarket products on sale from the Casino chain. No alcohol is sold 10pm-8am.

24hr newsagents include: *33 av des Champs-Elysées, 8th, M° Franklin D. Roosevelt. 2 bd Montmartre, 9th, M° Grands Boulevards.*
Late-night tabacs Le Brazza *86 bd du Montparnasse, 14th (01.43.35.42.65). M° Montparnasse-Bienvenüe.* **Open** 6am-2am daily. **La Favorite** *3 bd St-Michel, 5th (01.43.54.08.02). M° St-Michel.* **Open** 7am-2am daily.

POLICE

The French equivalent of 999 or 911 is **17** (**112** from a mobile), but don't expect a speedy response. That said, the Préfecture de Police has no fewer than 94 outposts in the city. If you're assaulted or robbed, report the incident as soon as possible. You'll need to make a statement (*procès verbal*) at the *point d'accueil* closest to the site of the crime. To find the nearest, call the Préfecture Centrale (08.91.01.22.22) or go to www. prefecturedepolice.interieur. gouv.fr. Stolen goods are unlikely to be recovered, but you'll need a police statement for insurance. *See also p372* **Emergencies**.

POSTAL SERVICES

Post offices (*bureaux de poste*) are open 8am-7.30pm Mon-Fri; 8am-1pm Sat, apart from the 24-hour post office listed below. Details of all branches are included in the phone book: under 'Administration des PTT' in the *Pages Jaunes*; under 'Poste' in the *Pages Blanches*. Most post offices contain automatic machines (in French and English) that weigh your letter, print out a stamp and give change, saving you from wasting time in an enormous queue. You can also usually buy stamps and sometimes envelopes at a tobacconist (*tabac*). For more information refer to www.laposte.fr.

Main Post Office *52 rue du Louvre, 75001 Paris, 1st (36.31). M° Les Halles or Louvre Rivoli.* **Open** 24hrs daily for poste restante, telephones, stamps, faxes, photocopying and a modest amount of banking operations. This is the best place to arrange to have your mail sent to if you haven't got a fixed address in Paris. Mail should be addressed to you in block capitals, followed by Poste Restante, then the post office's address. There will be a charge of €0.50 for each letter received.

RECYCLING & RUBBISH

The city has a recently established system of colour-coded domestic recycling bins. A yellow-lidded bin can take paper, cardboard cartons, tins and small electrical items; a white-lidded bin takes glass. All other rubbish goes in the green-lidded bins, except for used batteries (shops that sell batteries should accept them), medication (take it back to a pharmacy), toxic products (call 01.43.61.57.36 to have them picked up) or car batteries (take them to an official tip or return to garages exhibiting the '*Relais Verts Auto*' sign). Green, hive-shaped bottle banks can be found on many street corners. More information is available at www.environnement.paris.fr.

RELIGION

Churches and religious centres are listed in the *Pages Jaunes* under 'Eglises' and 'Cultes'. Paris has several English-speaking churches. The *International Herald Tribune*'s Saturday edition lists Sunday church services in English.

American Cathedral *23 av George V, 8th (01.53.23.84.00, www.americancathedral.org). M° George V.*
American Church in Paris *65 quai d'Orsay, 7th (01.40.62.05.00, www.acparis.org). M° Invalides.*
Emmanuel International Church of Paris *56 rue des Bons Raisins, Rueil-Malmaison (01.47.51.29.63, www.eicparis.org). RER Reuil-Malmaison, then bus 244.*
Kehilat Gesher *10 rue de Pologne, 78100 St-Germain-en-Laye (01.39.21.97.19, www.kehilat gesher.org). RER St-Germain-en-Laye.*
The Liberal English-speaking Jewish community has services in Paris and the western suburbs.
La Mosquée de Paris *2bis pl du Puits de l'Ermite, 5th (01.45.35.97.33, www.mosquee-de-paris.org). M° Place Monge.*
St George's Anglican Church *7 rue Auguste-Vacquerie, 16th (01.47.20.22.51, www.stgeorges paris.com). M° Charles de Gaulle Etoile.*
St Joseph's Roman Catholic Church *50 av Hoche, 8th (01.42.27.28.56, www.stjoeparis.org). M° Charles de Gaulle Etoile.*
St Michael's Church of England *5 rue d'Aguesseau, 8th (01.47.42.70.88, www.saintmichaels paris.org). M° Madeleine.*

RENTING A FLAT

Rental apartments are generally cheapest in northern, eastern and south-eastern Paris. You can expect to pay approximately €20 per square metre per month (which works out as, for example, €700 per month for a modest 35sq m apartment). Studios and one bedroom flats fetch the highest prices proportionally; the provision of lifts and cellars will also boost the rent.

Flat-hunting Given the scarcity of housing in Paris, it's a landlord's world; you'll need to search actively, or even frenetically, in order to find an apartment. The internet is a decent place to start: www.explorimmo.fr lists rental ads from *Le Figaro* and specialist real estate magazines; you can place a classified ad or check lettings on www.avendrealouer.fr. Thursday morning's *De Particulier à Particulier* (www.pap.fr) is a must for those who want to rent directly from the owner, but be warned – most flats go within hours. Fortnightly *Se Loger* (www.seloger.com) is also worth getting, though most of its ads are placed by agencies.

Landlords keen to let to foreigners advertise in the *International Herald Tribune* and English-language *FUSAC* (www.fusac.fr); rents tend to be higher than in the French press. There are also assorted free ad brochures that can be picked up from agencies. Private landlords often set a visiting time; prepare to meet hordes of other flat-seekers and have your documents and cheque book to hand.

There's also the option of flat-sharing – one that's been growing in popularity in recent years. To look for housemates, pick up a copy of *FUSAC* or browse the 3,000-odd weekly announcements found at www.colocation.fr, which also organises monthly soirée Le Jeudi de la Colocation, a chance to meet potential flatmates in the flesh.
Rental laws The minimum lease (*bail de location*) on an unfurnished flat is three years (though the tenant can give notice and leave before this period is up); furnished flats are generally let on one-year leases. During this period the landlord can raise the rent only by the official construction inflation index. At the end of the lease, the rent can be adjusted, but tenants can object before a rent board.

Tenants can be evicted for non-payment, or if the landlord wishes to sell the property or use it as his own residence. It is illegal to throw people out in winter.

Landlords will probably insist you present a dossier with pay slips (*fiches de paie/bulletins de salaire*) showing income equivalent to three to four times the monthly rent, and for foreigners in particular, provide a financial guarantor (someone who will sign a document promising to pay the rent if you abscond). When taking out a lease, payments usually include the first month's rent, a deposit (*caution*) of the equivalent of two months' rent, and an agency fee, if applicable.

It's customary to have an inspection of the premises (*état des lieux*) at the start and end of the rental, the cost of which (around €150) is shared by landlord and tenant. Landlords may try to rent their flats *non-declaré* – without a written lease – and get rent in cash. This can make it difficult for tenants to establish their rights – which is one reason why landlords do it.

Centre d'information et de défense des locataires *9 rue Severo, 14th. M° Pernety.* **Open** by appointment 10am-12.30pm, 2.30-3.30pm Mon-Thur.
Helps sort out problems with landlords, rent hikes, etc.

SAFETY & SECURITY

Beware of pickpockets, especially around the city's crowded tourist hotspots and métro stations. *See also p367* **Métro & RER** and *p377* **Police**.

SHIPPING SERVICES

Hedley's Humpers *6 bd de la Libération, 93284 St-Denis (01.48.13.01.02, www.hedleys humpers.com). M° Carrefour Pleyel.* **Open** 9am-1pm, 2-6pm Mon-Fri. Closed 2wks Aug.
Specialist in transport of furniture and antiques. **In UK:** 3 St Leonards Road, London NW10 6SX (020 8965 8733). **In USA:** 271 Scholes Street, Brooklyn, New York NY 11101 (1-718 433 4005).

SMOKING

Although smoking seems to be an essential part of French life (and death), the French state and public health groups have recently waged war against the cigarette on several fronts. Smoking is now banned in all enclosed public spaces, including bars, cafés, clubs, restaurants, hotel foyers and shops, as well as on public transport. Many bars, cafés and clubs offer smoking gardens or terraces. There are also increasingly strident anti-smoking campaigns in France. Prices have soared.

For information about stopping smoking, contact the Tabac Info Service (39.89, www.tabac-info-service.fr). If you're a dedicated smoker, you'll soon learn that most *tabacs* close at 8pm (for a few that don't, *see p376* **Opening hours**). Some bars sell cigarettes behind the counter, generally only to customers who have a drink.

STUDY

Language

Most of the large multinational language schools, such as **Berlitz** (01.40.74.00.17, www.berlitz.com), have at least one branch in Paris. **Alliance Française** *101 bd Raspail, 6th (01.42.84.90.00, www.alliancefr.org). M° St-Placide.* The Alliance Française is a non-profit French-language school. Beginner and specialist courses start every month. **Institut Catholique de Paris** *21 rue d'Assas, 6th (01.44.39.52.68, www.icp.fr/ilcf). M° St-Sulpice.* Courses in French culture and language. You must hold a *baccalauréat*-level qualification and be 18 or over (but you don't have to be Catholic). **La Sorbonne – Cours de Langue et Civilisation** *47 rue des Ecoles, 5th (01.44.10.77.00, www.ccfs-sorbonne.fr). M° Cluny-La Sorbonne/RER Luxembourg.* Classes for foreigners ride on the name of this eminent institution. Teaching is grammar-based. **University of London Institute in Paris** *9-11 rue Constantine, 7th (01.44.11.73.83, www.ulip.lon. ac.uk). M° Invalides.* Linked to the University of London, this 4,000-student institute offers English courses for Parisians, and French courses at university level.

Specialised

Many of the prestigious Ecoles Nationales Supérieures (including film schools La FEMIS and ENS Louis Lumière) offer summer courses in addition to their full-time degree courses – ask for *formation continue.*

Adult education courses

www.paris.fr or your local mairie. A huge range of inexpensive adult education classes is run by the city of Paris, including French as a foreign language, computer skills and applied arts. **American University of Paris** *6 rue du Colonel Combes, 7th (01.40.62.07.20, www.aup.edu). M° Ecole-Militaire/RER Pont de l'Alma.* International college awarding four-year American liberal arts degrees (BA/BSc). **Cordon Bleu** *8 rue Léon-Delhomme, 15th (01.53.68.22.50, www.cordonbleu.edu). M° Vaugirard.* Courses range from three-hour sessions on classical and regional cuisine to a nine-month diploma for those starting a culinary career. Bon appétit! **Ecole du Louvre** *Palais du Louvre, porte Jaujard, place du Carrousel, 1st (01.55.35.18.00, www.ecole dulouvre.fr). M° Palais Royal Musée du Louvre.* Art history and archaeology courses. Foreign students not wanting to take a degree can attend lectures. **INSEAD** *bd de Constance, 77305 Fontainebleau (01.60.72.40.00, www.insead.edu).* Highly regarded international business school offering a ten-month MBA course in English as well as PhDs in a range of business subjects. **Parsons School of Design** *14 rue Letellier, 15th (01.45.77.39.66, www.parsons-paris.com). M° La Motte-Picquet-Grenelle.* Subsidiary of the New York art college offering BFA programmes in fine art, photography, fashion, marketing and interior design. **Ritz-Escoffier Ecole de Gastronomie Française** *38 rue Cambon, 1st (01.43.16.30.50, www.ritzparis.com). M° Madeleine.* Everything from afternoon demonstrations in the Ritz kitchens to diplomas. Courses in French with English translation.

Student life

Student & youth discounts

To claim a *tarif étudiant* (around €1.50 off cinema seats, up to 50 per cent off museums and standby theatre tickets), you must have a French student card or International Student Identity Card (ISIC), available from **CROUS** (*see right*), student travel agents and the **Cité Universitaire** (*see right*). ISIC cards are valid in France only

if you are under 26. Under-26s can get up to 50 per cent off rail travel on some trains with the SNCF's Carte 12/25 and the same reduction on the RATP network with the Imagine R card.

Long-term visas & housing benefit

UK and other students from the EU may stay in France for as long as their passport is valid. To work legally during their course in Paris, they can find out more information about their rights at www.jcomjeune.com.

Foreign students from outside the EU wishing to study in Paris for longer than three months must apply for a long-term visa through the French embassy in their particular country.

Student accommodation

The simplest budget lodgings for medium-to-long stays can be found at the **Cité Universitaire** or *foyers* (student hostels). There are some 37 halls of residence set in landscaped gardens, with sports facilities and a theatre (*see p310*). Another option is a *chambre contre travail* – free board in exchange for childcare, housework or English lessons; for this, look out for ads at language schools and the American Church. For cheap hotels and youth hostels, *see pp227-257*. As students often cannot provide proof of income, a *porte-garant* (guarantor) who will guarantee the payment of rent and bills is required.

Cité Universitaire *17 bd Jourdan, 14th (01.44.16.64.00, www.ciup.fr). RER Cité Universitaire.* **Open** *Offices* 9am-5pm Mon-Wed, Fri; 2-5pm Thur. Foreign students enrolled on a university course, or interns who are also studying, can apply for a place at this campus of halls of residence (but be forewarned: only about ten per cent of the students who apply are actually successful). Rooms can be booked for a week, a month or for an entire academic year. Rents are approximately €300-€400 per month for a single room and €200-€300 per person for a double. UK citizens must apply to the Collège Franco-Britannique, and Americans to the Fondation des Etats-Unis.

CROUS (Centre Régional des Oeuvres Universitaires et Scolaires) *39 av Georges-Bernanos, 5th (01.40.51.36.00,*

ESSENTIAL INFORMATION

08.92.25.75.75, www.crous-paris.fr). Service du Logement: (01.40.51.36.12). RER Port-Royal. **Open** 9am-5pm Mon-Fri. Manages all University of Paris student residences, posts ads for rooms and has a list of hostels. Requests for rooms must be made by 1 April for the next academic year. CROUS also runs cheap canteens (listed on website) and is the clearing house for all *bourses* (grants) issued to foreign students. Call the Service des Bourses on 01.40.51.36.12.

Ethic Etapes *27 rue de Turbigo, 2nd (01.40.26.57.64, www.ethic-etapes.fr). M° Etienne Marcel.* **Open** 9.30am-6pm Mon-Fri. Operates cheap, short-stay hostels from two help centres: 5th (01.43.29.34.80); 14th (01.43.13.17.00).

Working as a student

Foreign students can legally work up to 20 hours per week. Non-EU members studying in Paris must apply for an *autorisation provisoire de travail* from the DDTEFT (www.travail.gouv.fr). The job service at CROUS (01.40.51.37.53) finds part-time jobs for students.

Useful organisations

CIDJ (Centre d'Information et de Documentation Jeunesse) *101 quai Branly, 15th (01.44.49.12.00, www.cidj.com). M° Bir-Hakeim/ RER Champ de Mars.* **Open** 1-6pm Tue-Fri; 1-5pm Sat.
The library here can give students advice on choices of courses and careers; the youth bureau of Pôle Emploi (formerly Agence Nationale pour l'Emploi; www.pole-emploi.fr) can assist with job applications.
Maison des Initiatives Etudiantes (MIE) *50 rue des Tournelles, 3rd (01.49.96.65.30, www.paris.fr).* **Open** 10am-10pm Mon-Fri; 10am-7pm Sat.
Provides student associations with logistical assistance and Paris-based resources like meeting rooms, grants and computers. Radio Campus Paris, a radio station for students, has been broadcasting since September 2004.
Socrates-Erasmus Programme **Britain**: *UK Socrates-Erasmus Council, British Council, 1 Kingsway, Cardiff CF10 3AQ (02920 924311, www.erasmus.ac.uk).* **France**: *Agence Socrates-Leonardo Da Vinci, 25 quai des Chartrons,*

33080 Bordeaux Cedex (05.56.00.94.00, www.socrates-leonardo.fr).
The international Socrates-Erasmus scheme lets EU students with reasonable written and spoken French spend a year of their degree in the French university system. Applications must be made via the Erasmus co-ordinator at your home university. Non-EU students should find out from their university whether it has an agreement with the French university system.

American students can find out more from the following organisations:
MICEFA *26 rue du Fbg-St-Jacques, 14th (01.40.51.76.96, www.micefa.org).*
Relais d'accueil (Foreign students helpdesk) *Cité Universitaire, 17 bd Jourdan, 14th. RER Cité Universitaire. CROUS de Paris, 39 av Georges-Bernanos, 5th (01.40.51.37.65). RER Port-Royal.* **Open** *Sept-Nov* 9.15am-12.30pm, 1.15-4.30pm Mon-Fri (Cité); 9am-4.30pm Mon-Fri (CROUS).
Provides advice on housing, banking, visas, social security and university registration (by appointment) to foreign students at addresses above.

TELEPHONES
Mobile phones

A subscription (*abonnement*) will normally get you a free phone if you sign up for at least one year. Two hours' calling time a month costs about €35 per month. International calls are normally charged extra – a lot extra.
Remember that using your UK mobile phone in France can cost considerably more than at home, especially if you use data roaming.
The three companies that rule the mobile phone market in France are:

Bouygues Télécom *10.64, www.bouyguestelecom.fr.*
France Télécom/Orange *39.70, www.orange.fr.*
SFR *10.23, www.sfr.fr.*

Dialling & codes

All French phone numbers have ten digits. Paris and Ile-de-France numbers begin with 01; the rest of France is divided into four zones (02-05). Mobile phone numbers start with 06. 08 indicates a special rate; numbers beginning with 08 can only be reached from inside France.

If you are calling France from abroad, leave off the 0 at the start of the ten-digit number. The country code is 33. To call abroad from France dial 00, then the country code, then the number.

Operator services

Operator assistance, French directory enquiries (*renseignements*) *12.* To make a reverse-charge call within France, ask to make a call *en PCV*.
Airparif *01.44.59.47.64, www.airparif.asso.fr.*
Information about pollution levels and air quality in Paris and Ile-de-France: invaluable for asthmatics.
International directory enquiries *32.12,* then country code. €3 per call.
International news (France Inter recorded message, in French), *08.92.68.10.33* (€0.34 per min).
Telegram *all languages, international 08.00.33.44.11; within France 36.55.*
Telephone engineer *10.13.*
Time *36.99.*
Traffic news *08.26.02.20.22.*
Weather *08.99.70.12.34* (€1.39 then €0.34 per min) for enquiries on weather in France and abroad, in French or English; you can also dial 08.92.68.02.75 (€0.34 per min) for a recorded weather announcement for Paris and the region.

Public phones

Most public phones in Paris, almost all of which are maintained by France Télécom, use *télécartes* (phonecards), which are sold at post offices, *tabacs*, airports and train and métro stations. For cheap international calls, you can also buy a *télécarte à puce* (card with a microchip) or a *télécarte pré-payée*, which features a numerical code you dial before making a call; these can be used on domestic phones too. Travelex's International Telephone Card can be used in more than 80 countries (available from **Travelex** agencies, *see p377*). Cafés have coin phones, while post offices usually have card phones. In a phone box, the display screen will read '*Décrochez*'. Pick up the phone. When '*Introduisez votre carte*' appears, put your card into the slot; the screen should read '*Patientez SVP*'. '*Numérotez*' is your signal to dial. '*Crédit épuisé*' means you have no more units left. Hang up ('*Raccrochez*') – and don't forget your card. Some public phones take credit cards. If you're using a credit

SIZE CHARTS

WOMEN'S CLOTHES

British	French	US
4	32	2
6	34	4
8	36	6
10	38	8
12	40	10
14	42	12
16	44	14
18	46	16
20	48	18

WOMEN'S SHOES

British	French	US
3	36	5
4	37	6
5	38	7
6	39	8
7	40	9
8	41	10
9	42	11

MEN'S CLOTHES

British	French	US
34	44	34
36	46	36
38	48	38
40	50	40
42	52	42
44	54	44
46	56	46
48	58	48

MEN'S SHOES

British	French	US
6	39	7
7.5	40	7.5
8	41	8
8	42	8.5
9	43	9.5
10	44	10.5
11	45	11
12	46	11.5

card, insert the card, enter your PIN number and *Patientez SVP'* will appear.

Telephone directories

Telephone books can be found in all post offices and most cafés. The *Pages Blanches* (White Pages) list people and businesses alphabetically; the *Pages Jaunes* (Yellow Pages) list businesses and services by category order. Online versions can be found at www.pagesjaunes.fr.

Telephone charges

All local calls in Paris and Ile-de-France (to numbers beginning with 01) cost €0.11 for three minutes, standard rate and €0.04/min thereafter. This applies only to calls to other landlines. Calls beyond a 100km radius (*province*) are charged at €0.11 for the first 39 seconds, then €0.24 per minute.

International destinations are divided into 16 zones. Reduced-rate periods for calls within France and Europe are 7pm-8am during the week and all day Saturday and Sunday. Reduced-rate periods for the US and Canada are 7pm to 1pm Monday to Friday and all day Saturday and Sunday.

Cheap providers

Getting wise to the market demand, the smaller telephone providers are becoming increasingly popular, as rates from France Télécom are not at exactly bargain-basement. levels. The following can offer alternative rates – although you will still need to rent your telephone line from France Télécom:

AT&T Direct (local access) *08.00.99.00.11.*
Free *10.44, www.free.fr.*
With the Freebox (Free's modem for ADSL connection), €29.99 per month gets you ten hours of free calls to landlines (additional calls cost €0.01 per minute), €0.19 per minute to mobiles and €0.03 per minute for most international calls.
IC Télécom *08.05.13.26.26, www.ictelecom.fr.*
Onetel *08.92.13.50.50, www.onetel.fr.*

Special-rate numbers

0800 Numéro Vert
Freephone.
0810 Numéro Azur
€0.11 under three minutes, then €0.04/min.
0820 Numéro Indigo
€0.118/min.
0825 Numéro Indigo II
€0.15/min.
0836.64/0890.64/0890.70
€0.112/min.
0890.71 €0.15/min.
0891.67/0891.70 €0.225/min.
0836/0892 €0.337/min. This line is for the likes of ticket agencies, cinema and transport information.

10.14 France Télécom information; free (except from mobile phones).

TIME

France is one hour ahead of Greenwich Mean Time (GMT). France uses the 24hr system (for example, 18h means 6pm).

TIPPING

A service charge of ten to 15 per cent is legally included in your bill at all restaurants, cafés and bars. However, it is polite either to round up the final amount for drinks, or to leave a cash tip of €1-€2 or more for a meal, depending on the restaurant and, of course, the quality of the service.

TOILETS

The city's automatic street toilets are not really as terrifying as they first appear. Each loo is completely washed down and disinfected after use.

If a space age-style lavatory experience doesn't appeal, you can nip into the toilets of a café; although theoretically reserved for customers' use, a polite request should win sympathy with the waiter – and you may find you have to put a €0.20 coin into a slot in the door-handle mechanism, customer or not. Fast-food chain toilets often have a code on their toilet doors that is made known to paying customers only.

TOURIST INFORMATION

Office de Tourisme et des Congrès de Paris *25 rue des Pyramides, 1st (08.92.68.30.00 recorded information available in English & French, www.paris info.com). M° Pyramides.* **Open** *Summer* 9am-7pm daily. *Winter* 10am-7pm daily.
Information on Paris and the suburbs, shop, bureau de change, hotel reservations, phonecards, museum cards, travel passes and tickets. Multilingual staff.
Other locations: *Gare de Lyon* 20 bd Diderot, 12th. M° Gare de Lyon. **Open** 8am-6pm Mon-Sat. *Gare du Nord* 18 rue de Dunkerque, 10th. M° Gare du Nord. **Open** 8am-6pm daily. *Anvers* 72 bd Rochechouart, 18th. M° Anvers. **Open** 10am-6pm daily. *Porte de Versailles* 1 pl de la Porte de Versailles, 15th. **Open** 11am-7pm during trade fairs.

ESSENTIAL INFORMATION

VISAS & IMMIGRATION

EU nationals don't need a visa to enter France, nor do US, Canadian, Australian, New Zealand or South African citizens for stays of up to three months. Nationals of other countries should enquire at the nearest French embassy or consulate before leaving home. If they are travelling to France from one of the countries in the Schengen agreement (most of the EU, but not Britain or Ireland), the visa from that country should be sufficient.

EU citizens may stay in France for as long as their passport is valid. Non-EU citizens who wish to stay for longer than three months must apply to the French embassy or consulate in their own country for a long-term visa. For more information, contact:

CIRA (Centre Interministeriel de Renseignements Administratifs) *39.39, www.service-public.fr.* **Open** 8am-7pm Mon-Fri; 8am-noon Sat. CIRA gives advice on most French administrative procedures via its local-rate phone line.
Préfecture de Police de Paris Service Etrangers *7-9 bd du Palais, 4th (01.53.73.53.73, www. prefecturedepolice.interieur.gouv.fr).* *Mº Cité.* **Open** 9am-4pm Mon-Fri. This office can provide information on residency, along with work permits for foreigners.

WEIGHTS & MEASURES

France uses only the metric system; remember that all speed limits are in kilometres per hour. One kilometre is equivalent to 0.62 miles (1 mile = 1.6km). Petrol, like other liquids, is measured in litres (one UK gallon = 4.54 litres; 1 US gallon = 3.79 litres).

WHAT TO TAKE

Binoculars for studying high-altitude details of monuments, a pocket knife with corkscrew (for improvised picnics) and – vital for getting around the city on foot – comfortable shoes.

WHEN TO GO

In July and August, during the long school holidays, there are often great deals to be had on hotels and a good range of free events laid on by the city (such as Paris-Plages), but many family-run restaurants and shops close as the locals go off *en vacances*. Avoid October, with its fashion weeks and trade shows.

WOMEN

Although Paris is not an especially threatening city for women, the precautions you would apply in any major metropolis apply here: be careful at night in certain areas, including Pigalle, the rue St-Denis, Stalingrad, La Chapelle, Château Rouge, Gare de l'Est, Gare du Nord, the Bois de Boulogne and Bois de Vincennes. If you receive unwanted attention, a politely scathing *N'insistez pas!* (Don't push it!) will make your feelings abundantly clear. If things get too heavy, go into the nearest shop or café.

CIDFF (Centre d'Information sur les Droits des Femmes et des Familles) *17 rue Jean Poulmarch, 10th (01.44.52.19.20, www.info femmes.com).* *Mº Porte de Pantin.* **Open** 10am-12.30pm, 1.30-5.30pm Mon-Thur; 10am-12.30pm Fri. The CIDFF offers plenty of health, legal and professional advice for women.

Violence Conjugale: Femmes Info Service *39.19.* **Open** 8am-10pm Mon-Sat. A hotline for the victims of domestic violence, directing them towards medical aid, shelters and other services.
Viols Femmes Informations *08.00.05.95.95.* **Open** 10am-7pm Mon-Fri. Freephone service. Help and advice available, in French, to rape victims.

WORK

Most EU nationals – including Irish and UK citizens – are legally entitled to work in France, but should apply for a French social security number. Some job advertisements can be found at branches of the French national employment bureau, **Pôle Emploi** (formerly ANPE), or on its website (www.pole-emploi.fr). Branches of ANPE are also the place to sign up as a *demandeur d'emploi*, to be placed on file as available for work and possibly to qualify for French unemployment benefits.

Britons can claim French unemployment benefit only if they were already signed on before leaving the UK. Non-EU nationals need a work permit and cannot use the ANPE network without having valid work papers.

Club des Quatre Vents *01.43.29.60.20, www.cei4vents.fr.* Provides three-month work permits for US students at university or recent graduates.
Espace Emploi International (OMI et Pôle Emploi) *48 bd de la Bastille, 12th (01.53.02.25.50, www.pole-emploi-international.fr).* *Mº Bastille.* **Open** 9am-5pm Mon-Thur; 9am-noon Fri. This organisation provides work permits of up to 18 months for Americans aged 18-35.
Language Network *01.43.08.35.19, www.thelanguage network.fr.* Helps native English speakers who wish to find work teaching.

Job ads

Help wanted ads sometimes appear in the *International Herald Tribune*, in *FUSAC* and on noticeboards at language schools.

If you're looking for professional work, make sure you have your CV translated, including French equivalents for any qualifications. Most job applications require a photo and a handwritten letter.

THE LOCAL CLIMATE

Average temperatures and monthly rainfall in Paris.

	High (°C/°F)	Low (°C/°F)	Rainfall (mm/in)
Jan	7 / 45	2 / 36	53 / 2.1
Feb	10 / 50	2 / 36	43 / 1.7
Mar	13 / 55	4 / 39	49 / 1.9
Apr	17 / 63	6 / 43	53 / 2.1
May	20 / 68	9 / 48	65 / 2.6
June	23 / 73	12 / 54	54 / 2.1
July	25 / 77	15 / 59	62 / 2.4
Aug	26 / 79	16 / 61	42 / 1.7
Sept	23 / 73	12 / 54	54 / 2.1
Oct	20 / 68	8 / 46	60 / 2.4
Nov	14 / 57	4 / 39	51 / 2.0
Dec	7 / 45	3 / 37	59 / 2.3

Vocabulary

In French, the second person singular (you) has two forms. Phrases here are given in the more polite *vous* form. The *tu* form is used with family, friends, children and pets; you should be careful not to use it with people you do not know sufficiently well. Courtesies such as *monsieur*, *madame* and *mademoiselle* are used more than their English equivalents.

GENERAL

Good morning/afternoon, hello bonjour; **good evening** bonsoir; **goodbye** au revoir; **OK** d'accord; **yes** oui; **no** non; **how are you?** comment allez vous?/vous allez bien?; **how's it going?** comment ça va?/ça va? (familiar)

Sir/Mr monsieur (M.); **madam/Mrs** madame (Mme); **miss** mademoiselle (Mlle); **please** s'il vous plaît; **thank you** merci; **sorry** pardon; **excuse me** excusez-moi; **I am going to pay** je vais payer

Do you speak English? parlez-vous anglais?; **I don't speak French** je ne parle pas français; **I don't understand** je ne comprends pas; **speak more slowly, please** parlez plus lentement, s'il vous plaît

It is c'est; **it isn't** ce n'est pas; **good** bon/bonne; **bad** mauvais/mauvaise; **small** petit/petite; **big** grand/grande; **beautiful** beau/belle; **well** bien; **badly** mal; **a bit** un peu; **a lot** beaucoup; **very** très

With avec; **without** sans; **and** et; **or** ou; **because** parce que; **who?** qui?; **when?** quand?; **what?** quoi?; **which?** quel?; **where?** où?; **why?** pourquoi?; **how?** comment?; **at what time/when?** à quelle heure?

Forbidden interdit/défendu; **out of order** hors service (HS)/en panne; **daily** tous les jours (tlj)

ON THE PHONE

Hello allô; **who's calling?** c'est de la part de qui?/qui est à l'appareil?; **this is...** speaking c'est... à l'appareil; **I'd like to speak to...**

j'aurais voulu parler à…; **hold the line** ne quittez pas; **please call back later** rappelez plus tard s'il vous plaît; **you must have the wrong number** vous avez dû composer un mauvais numéro

GETTING AROUND

Where is the (nearest) métro? où est le métro (le plus proche)?; **when is the next train for?** c'est quand le prochain train pour… ?; **ticket** un billet; **station** la gare; **platform** le quai; **entrance** entrée; **exit** sortie; **left** gauche; **right** droite; **straight on** tout droit; **far** loin; **near** pas loin/près d'ici

SIGHTSEEING

Museum un musée; **church** une église; **exhibition** une exposition; **ticket** (*museum*) un billet; (*theatre, concert*) une place; **open** ouvert; **closed** fermé; **free** gratuit; **reduced price** un tarif réduit

ACCOMMODATION

Do you have a room (for this evening/for two people)? avez-vous une chambre (pour ce soir/pour deux personnes)?; **full** complet; **room** une chambre; **bed** un lit; **double bed** un grand lit; **(a room with) twin beds** (une chambre à) deux lits; **with bath(room)/shower** avec (salle de) bain/douche; **breakfast** le petit déjeuner; **included** compris

EATING OUT

I'd like to book a table (for three/at 8pm) je voudrais réserver une table (pour trois personnes/à vingt heures); **lunch** le déjeuner; **dinner** le dîner; **coffee** (*espresso*) un café; **tea** un thé; **wine** le vin; **beer** une bière; **mineral water** eau minérale; **tap water** une carafe d'eau; **the bill, please** l'addition, s'il vous plaît

SHOPPING

Cheap pas cher; **expensive** cher; **how much?/how many?** combien?; **have you got change?** avez-vous de la monnaie?; **I'll take**

it je le prends; **I would like…** je voudrais…; **may I try this on?** est-ce que je pourrais essayer cet article?; **do you have a smaller/larger size?** auriez-vous la taille en-dessous/au dessus?; **I'm a size 38** je fais du 38

STAYING ALIVE

Be cool restez calme; **I don't want any trouble** je ne veux pas d'ennuis; **I only do safe sex** je ne pratique que le safe sex

NUMBERS

0 zéro; **1** un, une; **2** deux; **3** trois; **4** quatre; **5** cinq; **6** six; **7** sept; **8** huit; **9** neuf; **10** dix; **11** onze; **12** douze; **13** treize; **14** quatorze; **15** quinze; **16** seize; **17** dix-sept; **18** dix-huit; **19** dix-neuf; **20** vingt; **21** vingt-et-un; **22** vingt-deux

30 trente; **40** quarante; **50** cinquante; **60** soixante; **70** soixante-dix; **80** quatre-vingts; **90** quatre-vingt-dix; **100** cent

1,000 mille; **10,000** dix mille; **1,000,000** un million

DAYS, MONTHS & SEASONS

Monday lundi
Tuesday mardi
Wednesday mercredi
Thursday jeudi
Friday vendredi
Saturday samedi
Sunday dimanche

January janvier
February février
March mars
April avril
May mai
June juin
July juillet
August août
September septembre
October octobre
November novembre
December décembre

Spring le printemps
Summer l'été
Autumn l'automne
Winter l'hiver

Further Reference

ESSENTIAL INFORMATION

BOOKS

Non-fiction

Robert Baldick *The Siege of Paris* A gripping account of the Paris Commune of 1871.
Antony Beevor & Artemis Cooper *Paris after the Liberation* Rationing, freedom, Existentialism.
NT Binh *Paris au cinéma* Attractively illustrated hardback round-up of Paris sights on film.
Henri Cartier-Bresson *A propos de Paris* Classic black-and-white shots by a giant among snappers.
Vincent Cronin *Napoleon* A fine biography of the emperor.
Léon-Paul Fargue *Le Piéton de Paris* The city anatomised, just before World War II.
Jean-Marie Gourio *Brèves de comptoir* An anthology of wisdom and weirdness overheard at café counters. A French classic.
Alastair Horne *The Fall of Paris* Detailed chronicle of the Siege and Commune 1870-71.
J-K Huysmans *Croquis Parisiens* The world that Toulouse-Lautrec painted.
Ian Littlewood *Paris: Architecture, History, Art* Paris's history and its treasures.
Henri Michel *Paris Allemand; Paris Résistant* Detailed, two-volume account of life in Paris during the Occupation.
Noel Riley Fitch *Literary Cafés of Paris* Who drank what, where.
Virginia Rounding *Les Grandes Horizontales* Entertaining lives of four 19th-century courtesans.
Simon Schama *Citizens* Epic, readable account of the Revolution.
Thibaut Vandorselaer *Paris BD* A lovely series of walking trails around the city, illustrated entirely with 'BD' (cartoon) frames.

Fiction & poetry

Honoré de Balzac *Illusions perdues; La Peau de chagrin; Le Père Goriot; Splendeurs et misères des courtisanes* Much of the 'Comédie Humaine' cycle of novels is set in Paris.
Charles Baudelaire *Le Spleen de Paris* Prose poems, Paris settings.
Louis-Ferdinand Céline *Mort à crédit* Vivid, splenetic account of an impoverished Paris childhood.

Victor Hugo *Notre Dame de Paris* Romantic vision of medieval Paris. Quasimodo! Esmeralda! The bells!
W Somerset Maugham *Christmas Holiday* Young, middle-class Brit spends Christmas with a prostitute in Paris.
Gérard de Nerval *Les Nuits d'octobre* Late-night Les Halles and environs, mid 19th century.
Georges Perec *La Vie, mode d'emploi* Cheek-by-jowl life in a Haussmannian apartment building.
Raymond Queneau *Zazie dans le Métro* Paris in the 1950s: bright and very *nouvelle vague*.
Nicolas Restif de la Bretonne *Les Nuits de Paris* The sexual underworld of Louis XV's Paris.
Georges Simenon *Rue Pigalle; Maigret et les braves gens*, etc. Many of the famous Maigret books are set in Paris.
Emile Zola *L'Assommoir; Nana; Le Ventre de Paris* Accounts of the underside of the Second Empire from the master Realist.

The ex-pat angle

Janet Flanner *Paris Journal* Three volumes of reports on postwar Paris arts and politics, written for the *New Yorker*.
Henry Miller *Tropic of Cancer* Love and low life: lusty and funny.
George Orwell *Down and Out in Paris and London* Work in a Paris restaurant, hunger in a Paris hovel, suffering in a Paris hospital.

FILM

Luc Besson *Subway* Christophe Lambert goes underground.
Marcel Carné *Hôtel du Nord* Arletty stars in this poetic slice of life by the Canal St-Martin.
René Clair *Paris qui dort* Clair's surrealist silent comedy is one of the best Paris films ever made.
Louis Feuillade *Fantômas* Supervillain Fantomas repeatedly outwits Paris law enforcers in Feuillade's masterful silent serials.
Jean-Luc Godard *A Bout de Souffle* Belmondo, Seberg, Godard, the Champs-Elysées, the attitude, the famous ending. Essential.
Michel Hazanavicius *The Artist* Silent black-and-white blockbuster that won five Oscars, including best actor for Jean Dujardin.

Edouard Molinaro *Un Témoin dans la ville* Lino Ventura on the run in 1950s nocturnal Paris. Superb *noir*.
François Truffaut *Les 400 Coups* The first of the Antoine Doinel cycle.
Agnès Varda *Cléo de 5 à 7* The *nouvelle vague* heroine spends an anxious afternoon in the city.

MUSIC

Miles Davis *Ascenseur pour l'échafaud* The soundtrack to Louis Malle's film is superb after-dark jazz.
Baptiste Trotignon *Song Song Song* Jazz-chanson from this supremely talented pianist.
Fréhel *1930-1939* The immortal Fréhel sings of love, drugs and debauchery in true *chanson réaliste* style.
Naive New Beaters *Wallace* Great pop from a hot Paris band.
Sebastien Tellier *My God is Blue* Transgressive electro pop.
Serge Gainsbourg *Le Poinçonneur des Lilas* Classic early Gainsbourg.

WEBSITES

www.pagesjaunes.fr The Paris yellow pages, with maps and photos of every address in the city.
www.parisinfo.com Official site of the Office de Tourisme et des Congrès de Paris.
www.ratp.fr Everything you'll need to know about using the buses, métro, RER and trams.
www.timeout.fr Your critical guide to arts, culture and going out in Paris (English and French).
www.velib.paris.fr All you need to know about using Velib'.
www.autolib.eu All you need to know about using Autolib'.

IPHONE APPS

Patrimap (free) Pinpoints nearby monuments along with potted descriptions, and also features a series of itineraries.
RATP (free) Access a wide range of Paris transport maps.
Vélib' (free) Tells you where bikes are available around the city.
Louvre (free) All you need to know before you visit the Louvre.

Index

INDEX

Index

INDEX

INDEX

INDEX

INDEX

Bags packed, milk cancelled, house raised on stilts.

You've packed the suntan lotion, the snorkel set, the stay-pressed shirts. Just one more thing left to do – your bit for climate change. In some of the world's poorest countries, changing weather patterns are destroying lives.

You can help people to deal with the extreme effects of climate change. Raising houses in flood-prone regions is just one life-saving solution.

Climate change costs lives.
Give £5 and let's sort it *Here & Now*

www.oxfam.org.uk/climate-change

Oxfam is a registered charity in England and Wales (No.202918) and Scotland (SCO039042). Oxfam GB is a member of Oxfam International.

Be Humankind Oxfam

Advertisers' Index

Please refer to the relevant pages for contact details.

Maps

Paris Arrondissements

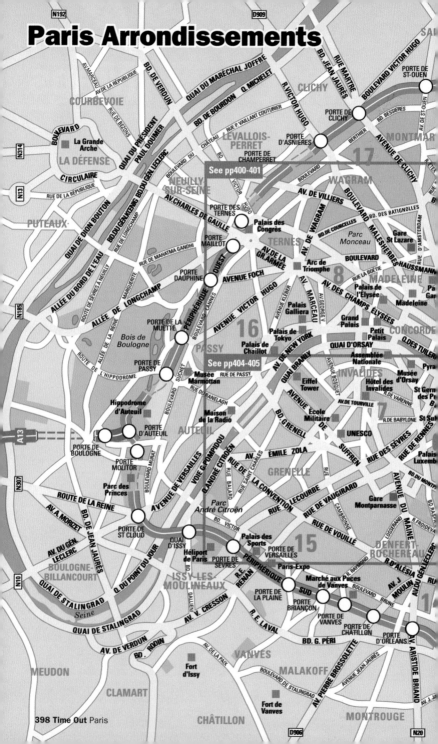

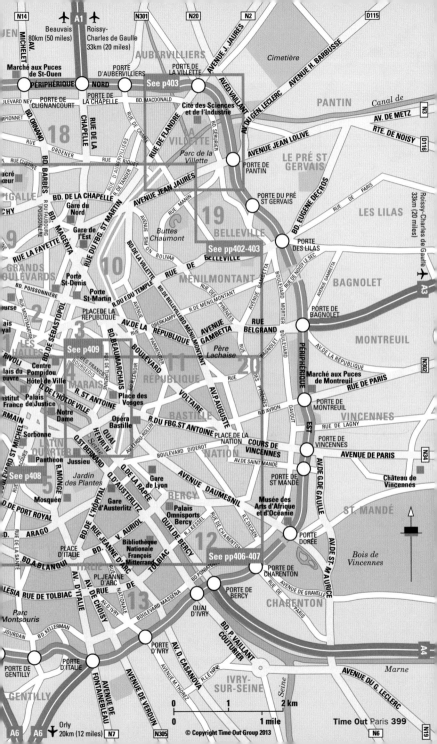

© Copyright Time Out Group 2013

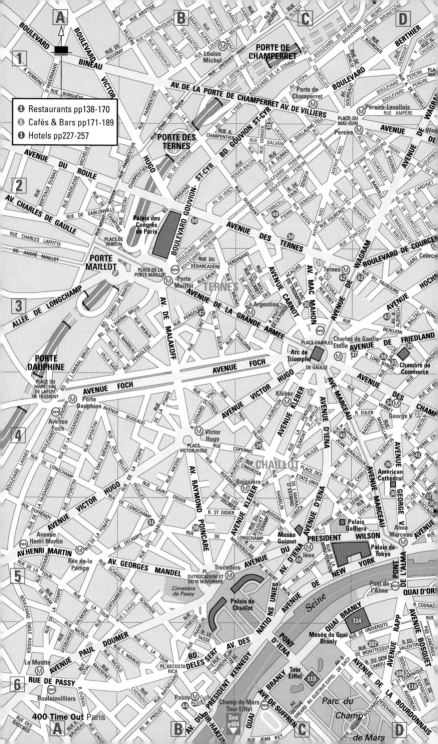

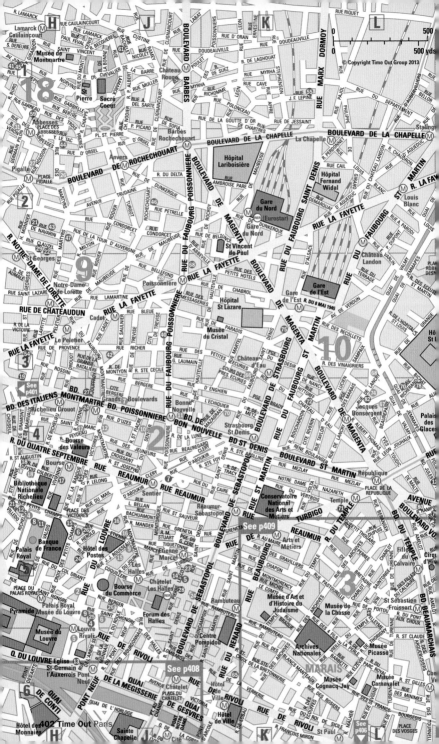

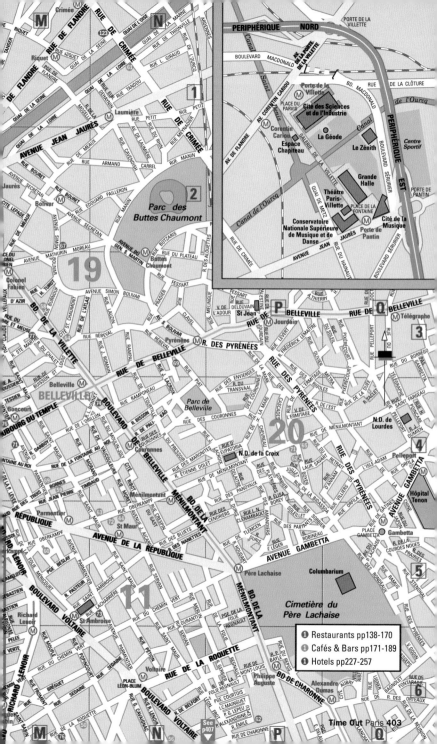

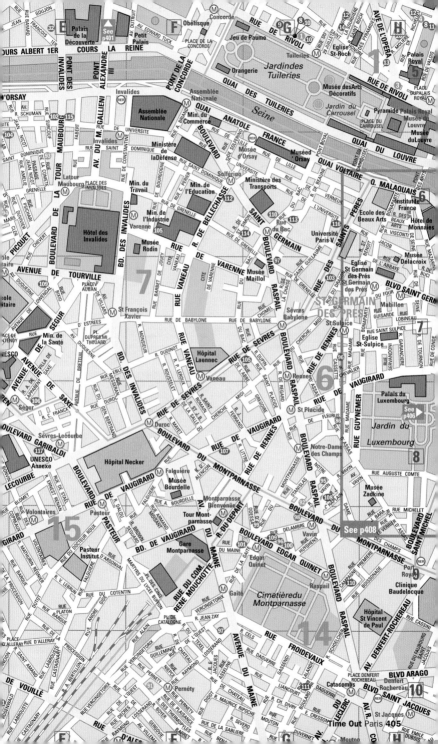

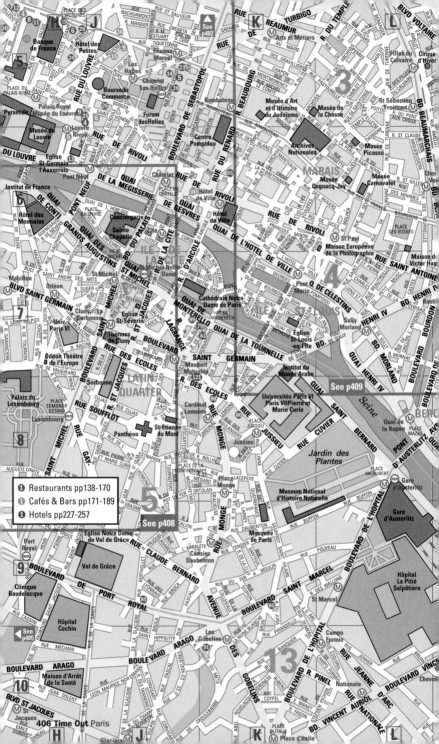

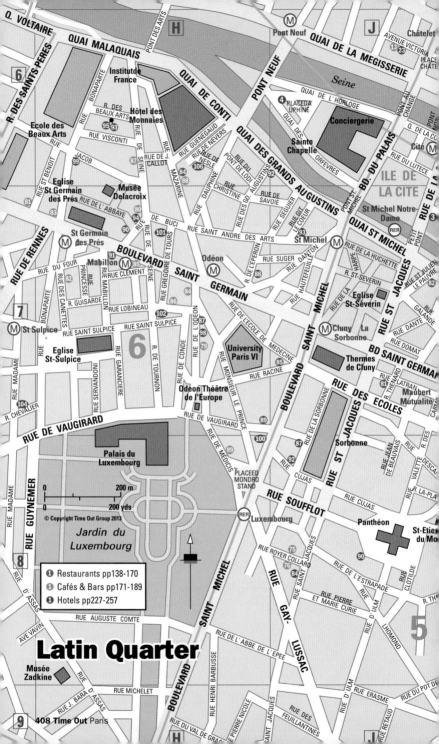

Latin Quarter

❶ Restaurants pp138-170
❶ Cafés & Bars pp171-189
❶ Hotels pp227-257

© Copyright Time Out Group 2013

0   200 m
0   200 yds

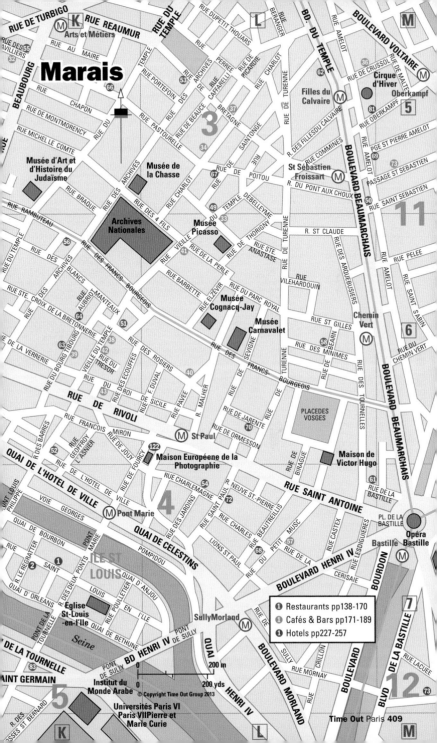

Marais

Musée d'Art et d'Histoire du Judaïsme

Musée de la Chasse

Archives Nationales

Musée Picasso

Musée Cognacq-Jay

Musée Carnavalet

Cirque d'Hiver

Oberkampf

Filles du Calvaire

St Sébastien Froissart

Chemin Vert

Maison Européene de la Photographie

St Paul

Maison de Victor Hugo

PLACE DES VOSGES

Pont Marie

Opéra Bastille

ILE ST LOUIS

Eglise St-Louis-en-l'Ile

Sully Morland

Institut du Monde Arabe

Universités Paris VI Paris VII Pierre et Marie Curie

Seine

❶ Restaurants pp138-170
❶ Cafés & Bars pp171-189
❶ Hotels pp227-257

0   200 m
0   200 yds

© Copyright Time Out Group 2013

Street Index

STREET INDEX

STREET INDEX

STREET INDEX

STREET INDEX

Paris Métro

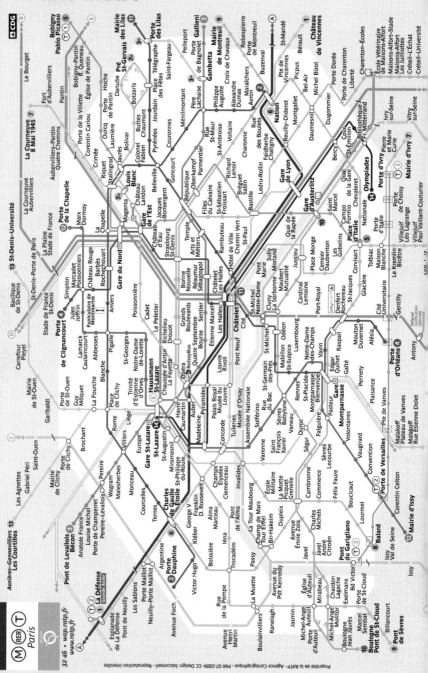